D1104190

MACHINE LEARNING

A Multistrategy Approach
Volume IV

MACHINE LEARNING

A Multistrategy Approach
Volume IV

Contributors:

Jerzy W. Bala
Cristina Baroglio
Marco Botta
Maurice Bruynooghe
Jaime Carbonell
Michael Cox
Andrea P. Danyluk
Hugo de Garis
Kenneth De Jong
Luc De Raedt
Jeffrey Gould
Michael Hieb
Lawrence Hunter
Yves Kodratoff
Robert Levinson
Stephen C-Y. Lu
Stan Matwin
Douglas L. Medin
Ryszard S. Michalski
Raymond J. Mooney

Katharina Morik
Dirk Ourston
Peter W. Pachowicz
Michael Pazzani
Boris Plante
Ashwin Ram
Yoram Reich
Lorenza Saitta
Jakub Segen
Jude W. Shavlik
Gheorghe Tecuci
Geoffrey G. Towell
Manuela Veloso
Haleh Vafaie
Bradley L. Whitehall
Gerhard Widmer
Edward J. Wisniewski
Janusz Wnek
Jianping Zhang

Editors:

Ryszard S. Michalski
George Mason University

Gheorghe Tecuci
*George Mason University and
Romanian Academy*

MORGAN KAUFMANN PUBLISHERS
SAN FRANCISCO, CALIFORNIA

Editor and Publisher   *Michael B. Morgan*
Project Management   *Professional Book Center*
Electronic Composition   *Professional Book Center*
Cover Design   *Andrea Hendricks*

Library of Congress Cataloging-in-Publication Data

(Revised for volume 4)

Machine learning.
   Vol. [1] previously published: Palo Alto, Calif. :
Tioga Pub. Co., c1983.
   Vols. 1 and 2 edited by Ryszard Michalski, Jaime G.
Carbonell, Tom M. Mitchel ; contributing authors, John
Anderson . . . [et al.].
   Vol. 3 edited by Yves Kodratoff and Ryszard S.
Michalski.
   Vol. 4 edited by Ryszard S. Michalski and
Gheorghe Tecuci.
   Includes bibliographies and indexes.
   1. Machine learning. 2. Artificial intelligence.
I. Anderson, John R. (John Robert), 1947–   .
II. Michalski, Ryszard Stanislaw, 1937–   .
III. Carbonell, Jaime G. (Jaime Guillermo) IV. Mitchell,
Tom M. (Tom Michael), 1951–   .
Q325.M32 1983b   006.3'1   86-2953
ISBN 0-934613-09-5 (v. 1)

Q325
.M32
1983b
Vol. 4

Printed in the United States of America

10 9 8 7 6 5 4 3 2 1

MORGAN KAUFMANN PUBLISHERS, INC.
Editorial Offices
340 Pine Street, Sixth Floor
San Francisco, CA 94104
415-392-2665

CONTENTS

PREFACE

Ryszard S. Michalski
(George Mason University)

Gheorghe Tecuci
(George Mason University and
(Romanian Academy)

This is the fourth volume in a series of books on Machine Learning that aim at contributing to a global prospective on the progress of this field. Individual volumes contain selected contributions made by leading researchers during a given period of time. The first volume (Michalski, Carbonell, and Mitchell, 1983) contained specially prepared chapters and significantly revised and updated versions of the presentations from the First Workshop on Machine Learning, held in 1980 at Carnegie Mellon University in Pittsburgh, Pennsylvania. Subsequent volumes, Volume II (Michalski, Carbonell, and Mitchell, 1986) and Volume III (Kodratoff and Michalski, 1990), contain reviews and research contributions representative of major research areas in machine learning for the covered period. All volumes also contain extensive indexed bibliographies of this field.

Volume IV continues this tradition, except for one major change. In view of the extraordinary expansion and diversification of research in machine learning that has occurred in recent years, it is no longer possible to provide in a single volume a representative coverage of all major research directions and paradigms of this field. Therefore, we decided to focus the book on the area of *multistrategy learning* that constitutes a major long-term challenge for this field. Multistrategy learning represents an effort to unify the entire field of machine learning and is likely to become a central research theme for the field in the future.

In the past, most research in machine learning was concerned with methods that employ a single learning strategy, that is, with *monostrategy* methods. Such methods implement one primary type of inference, such as empirical induction, deduction, abduction, or analogy, using one computational (or representational) mechanism, such as a decision tree, decision rules, a semantic network, frames, a neural net, or a classifier system. Such methods include those for empirical inductive generalization, quantitative law discovery, conceptual clustering, genetic algorithm based learning, explanation-based learning, learning by abduction, and case-based learning.

With the growing understanding of the capabilities and limitations of monostrategy methods, there has been an increasing interest in multistrategy systems that integrate multiple inference types and/or computational mechanisms in one learning system. Such systems can learn from a wider scope of input, and be applied to a wider range of problems than monostrategy methods. Although research on monostrategy methods continues to be of great importance to the field, there is a rapidly increasing interest in multistrategy learning. The beginning of this trend was already noticeable in Volume III, which contained a separate section on this area. Volume IV is now entirely devoted to multistrategy learning, reflecting a significant expansion and growing importance of research in this area. The immediate impetus for the preparation of this volume was the *First International Workshop on Multistrategy Learning* (MSL-91), organized by George Mason University in Harpers Ferry, West Virginia, November 7–9, 1991 (Michalski and Tecuci, 1991).

This volume contains tutorial presentations and research contributions representative of the current research by leading researchers in multistrategy learning. Individual chapters are substantially rewritten and improved versions of the papers that have been selected from among those presented at MSL-91. The book is divided into five parts. Part I addresses underlying principles and theoretical issues, as well as related topics of human learning, which is intrinsically multistrategy. Part II describes methods of theory revision through multistrategy learning. Part III presents architectures for multistrategy learners that emphasize a cooperation between different strategies or their selection according to the task. Part IV discusses issues of integrating symbolic and subsymbolic learning and compares the performances of these two paradigms on a selected class of learning problems. Part V addresses special topics and applications of multistrategy learning. Finally, the Bibliography provides a comprehensive source of references on multistrategy learning and selected background material from the entire field of machine learning. It contains over 600 entries, which are indexed by specific categories and subcategories.

Many individuals and several organizations contributed, directly or indirectly, to the preparation of this book. The editors would like to express their deep gratitude to the Office of Naval Research, especially Dr. Alan Meyrowitz, for the vision and understanding of the importance of research on multistrategy learning, for providing an early research grant to the first editor to study this area, and subsequently for supporting the organization of the First International Workshop on Multistrategy Learning (MSL-91).

We thank Dr. Andrew Sage, Dean of the GMU School of Information Technology and Engineering, and Dr. Larry Kershberg, Chairman of the GMU Department of Information Systems and Software Engineering, for their support and interest in the Workshop. We also acknowledge the help and continuing support of the members and the staff of the GMU Center for Artificial Intelligence.

Important contributions were made by Jerzy Bala, Eric Bloedorn, Tom Dybala, Michael Hieb, Ibrahim Imam, Ken Kaufman, Jayshree Sarma, Haleh Vafaie, and Janusz Wnek, Ph.D. students at the GMU Center for Artificial Intelligence. They provided indispensable assistance in preparing and organizing MSL-91, reviewing the papers, and providing comments to the authors. Our discussions with them on multistrategy learning helped shape the final version of the book.

We are very grateful to the MSL-91 participants for their discussions and comments at the Workshop. The idea of this book originated during these discussions and exchanges.

Our deep and heartfelt gratitude goes to all the contributors to this volume. They have made a special effort to improve and update their MSL-91 papers and to present them in a highly comprehensive and easy-to-read manner. We also thank all the reviewers whose diligent and careful reviews were crucial for achieving the high quality of all the contributions.

In presenting this new volume, we hope that it will stimulate interest in this novel and exciting area of machine learning.

References

Michalski, R.S., Carbonell, J.G., and Mitchell, T.M. (Eds.), *Machine Learning: An Artificial Intelligence Approach Volume I*, Tioga/Morgan Kaufmann, Los Altos, CA, 1983.

Michalski, R.S., Carbonell, J.G., and Mitchell, T.M. (Eds.), *Machine Learning: An Artificial Intelligence Approach*, Volume II, Morgan Kaufmann, Los Altos, CA, 1986.

Kodratoff, Y., and Michalski, R.S. (Eds.), *Machine Learning: An Artificial Intelligence Approach*, Volume III, Morgan Kaufmann, San Mateo, CA, 1990.

Michalski, R.S., and Tecuci, G. (Eds.), *Proceedings of the First International Workshop on Multistrategy Learning*, organized by George Mason University, Harpers Ferry, West Virginia, November 7–9, 1991.

PART
ONE

GENERAL ISSUES

1

INFERENTIAL THEORY OF LEARNING:

Developing Foundations
for Multistrategy Learning

Ryszard S. Michalski
(George Mason University)

Abstract

The development of multistrategy learning systems should be based on a clear understanding of the roles and the applicability conditions of different learning strategies. To this end, this chapter introduces the *Inferential Theory of Learning* that provides a conceptual framework for analyzing and explaining logical capabilities of learning strategies, i.e., their *competence.* Viewing learning as a process of modifying the learner's knowledge by exploring the learner's experience, the theory postulates that any such process can be described as a search in a *knowledge space* defined by the employed knowledge representation. The search operators are instantiations of *knowledge transmutations,* which are generic patterns of knowledge change. Transmutations may use any type of inference—deduction, induction, or analogy.

Several fundamental transmutations are presented in a novel and general way. These include generalization and specialization, abduction and prediction, abstraction and concretion, and similization and dissimilization. Generalization and specialization change the *reference set* of a description (the set of entities being described or referred to). Abstractions and concretions change the level of detail in describing the reference set. Explanations and predictions derive additional knowledge about the reference set (explanatory or predictive). Similizations and dissimilizations hypothesize knowledge about a reference set based on its similarity or dissimilarity with another reference set. Using concepts of the theory, a *multistrategy task-adaptive learning* (MTL) methodology is outlined and illustrated by an example. MTL dynamically adapts strategies to the *learning task* defined by the input information, the learner's background knowledge, and the learning goal. It aims at synergistically integrating a whole range of inferential learning strategies, such as empirical generalization, constructive induction, deductive generalization, explanation, prediction, abstraction, and similization.

> *For every belief comes either through syllogism or from induction.*
> Aristotle, Prior Analytics, Book II, Chapter 23 (p. 90)
> ca. 330 BC

1.1 INTRODUCTION

The last several years have marked a period of great expansion and diversification of methods and approaches to machine learning. Most of this research has been concerned with single learning strategy methods, which employ one underlying type of inference within a single representational or computational paradigm. Such *monostrategy* methods include inductive learning of decision trees or rules from examples, explanation-based generalization, quantitative empirical discovery, artificial neural net learning, genetic algorithm-based learning, conjunctive conceptual clustering, and reinforcement learning. The research progress on these methods has been reported in many sources, for example, Laird (1988); Touretzky, Hinton, and Sejnowski (1988); Goldberg (1989); Rivest, Haussler, and Warmuth (1989); Schafer (1989); Segre (1989); Fulk and Case (1990); Kodratoff and Michalski; (1990); Porter and Mooney (1990); Birnbaum and Collins (1991); Warmuth and Valiant (1991); Sleeman and Edwards (1992); and Utgoff (1993).

Monostrategy systems are intrinsically limited to solving only certain classes of learning problems defined by the type of input information they can learn from, the type of operations they are able to perform on the given knowledge representation, and the type of output knowledge they can produce. With the growing understanding of the capabilities and limitations of monostrategy learning systems, there has been an increasing interest in *multistrategy learning* systems that integrate two or more inferential and/or computational strategies.[1] Because of a complementary nature of many learning strategies, multistrategy systems have a potentially greater *competence*, i.e., a greater ability to solve diverse learning problems, than monostrategy systems. On the other hand, because multistrategy systems are more complex, their implementation presents a significant research challenge. Therefore, the effectiveness of their applicability to a given domain depends on the resolution of the above trade-off.

------

[1] By an "inferential strategy" is meant the primary type of inference underlying a learning process; by a "computational strategy" is meant the type of knowledge representation employed and the associated computational method for modifying it in the process of learning.

It is worth noting that human learning is intrinsically multistrategy—people can learn from a great variety of input, engage any kind of prior knowledge relevant to the problem, and perform all types of inference using a multitude of knowledge representations. Therefore, multistrategy learning and computer modeling of human learning have a natural interrelationship: research on human learning can provide valuable clues to multistrategy learning, and conversely, research on multistrategy learning can be a source of guides and ideas for cognitive studies of learning. The area of multistrategy learning has, thus, significant importance, regardless of its potential for powerful practical applications.

To date, a number of experimental multistrategy learning systems have been developed. Among such early systems (sometimes called "integrated learning systems"), one may mention UNIMEM (Lebowitz, 1986), Odysseus (Wilkins, Clancey, and Buchanan, 1986), Prodigy (Minton et al., 1987), DISCIPLE (Kodratoff and Tecuci, 1987), Gemini (Danyluk, 1987, 1989; 1994—Chapter 7 of this book), OCCAM (Pazzani, 1988), IOE (Dietterich and Flann, 1988), and KBL (Whitehall, 1990; Whitehall and Lu, 1994, Chapter 6). Most of these systems have integrated some method for symbolic empirical induction with explanation-based learning. Some, such as DISCIPLE, have also included a simple method for analogical learning. The integration of the strategies has usually been done in a predefined, problem-independent way without well-defined theoretical foundations.

This book describes a representative sample of recent research on multistrategy learning. Among the multistrategy systems described are EITHER, for revising incorrect propositional Horn-clause domain theories using deduction, abduction, or empirical induction (Mooney and Ourston, 1994, Chapter 5); CLINT, for interactive theory revision represented as a set of Horn clauses (De Raedt and Bruynooghe, 1994, Chapter 9); and WHY, for learning concepts using both causal models and examples (Baroglio, Botta, and Saitta, 1994, Chapter 12).

A remarkable aspect of human learners is that they are able to apply a great variety of learning strategies in a flexible and multigoal-oriented fashion and can dynamically accommodate the demands of changing learning situations. Developing an adequate and general computational model of such abilities emerges as a new fundamental long-term objective for machine learning research. To achieve this objective, it is necessary to investigate the principles and trade-offs characterizing diverse learning strategies; to understand their capabilities and interrelationships; to determine conditions for their most effective applicability; and, ultimately, to develop a general theory of multistrategy learning. Such a theory should provide conceptual foundations for constructing learning systems that integrate a whole spectrum of learning strategies in a domain-dependent way. These learning systems would automatically adapt a learning strategy or a combination of strategies to any given learning situation.

This chapter reports early results toward the above objective; specifically, it describes the *Inferential Theory of Learning* that views learning as a search through a *knowledge space* guided by a learning goal. The search operators are instantiations of certain generic types of knowledge change, called knowledge *transmutations* (or knowledge *transforms*). Transmutations change various aspects of knowledge: some generate intrinsically new knowledge (inductive or analogical transmutations), some generate derived knowledge (deductive transmutations), and others only manage knowledge. The Inferential Theory of Learning strives to characterize logical capabilities of learning systems, that is, their *competence*. It addresses such questions as what types of knowledge transformations occur in different learning processes; what is the validity of knowledge obtained through different types of learning, how is prior knowledge used; what knowledge can be derived from the given input and the prior knowledge; how learning goals and their structure influence learning processes; and how learning processes can be classified and evaluated from the viewpoint of their logical capabilities. The theory stresses the use of multitype inferences, the role of the learner's prior knowledge, and the importance of learning goals.

The above aims distinguish the Inferential Theory of Learning (ITL) from the Computational Learning Theory (COLT), which focuses on the *computational complexity* and *convergence* of learning algorithms, particularly those for empirical inductive learning. COLT has not been much concerned with multistrategy learning, the role of the learner's prior knowledge, or the learning goals (e.g., Fulk and Case [1990]; Warmuth and Valiant [1991]). The above should not be taken to mean that the issues studied in COLT are unimportant, only that they are different. A "unified" theory of learning should take into consideration both the competence and the complexity of diverse learning processes.

The first part of the chapter presents a novel characterization of basic types of inference and several fundamental knowledge transmutations. It analyzes such transmutations as generalization, abstraction, similization and their counterparts, specialization, concretion, and dissimilization, respectively. The second part outlines ideas about the application of the theory to the development of a methodology for *multistrategy task-adaptive learning* (MTL).

Learning processes are analyzed at the level of abstraction that makes the theory relevant to characterizing machine learning algorithms as well as to developing insights into the conceptual principles of learning in biological systems. The presented framework tries to formally capture many intuitive perceptions of various forms of human inference and learning and suggests solutions that could be used as a basis for developing cognitive models. In a number of cases, the presented ideas resolve several popular misconceptions—such as induction is the same as generalization, induction is always data-intensive, and abduction is fundamentally different from induction—and clarifies the distinction between generalization and abstraction. The presented theory also suggests some new types of transmutations, e.g., inductive specialization, analogical generalization, concretion, and dissimilization.

A number of ideas in the theory stem from the research on the core theory of human plausible reasoning (Collins and Michalski, 1989).

To provide an easy introduction and a general perspective on the subject, many results are presented in an informal fashion, using conceptual explanations and examples rather than formal definitions and proofs. Various details and a formalization of many ideas await further research. To make the chapter easily accessible to both AI and Cognitive Science communities, as well as to readers who do not have much practice with predicate logic, expressions in predicate logic are usually accompanied by a natural language interpretation. Also, to help the reader keep track of different symbols and abbreviations, they are compiled into a list in the Appendix. This chapter is an improved version of the original paper (Michalski, 1993b) and represents a significant extension or refinement of ideas described in earlier publications (Michalski, 1983, 1990a, 1991, 1993a).

1.2 BASIC TENETS OF THE THEORY

Learning has traditionally been characterized as an improvement of the learner's behavior due to experience. Although this view is appealing because of its simplicity, it does not provide many clues about how to actually implement a learning system. To build a learning system, one needs to understand, in computational terms, what behavior changes to perform in response to any given experience, how to efficiently implement these changes, how to evaluate them, how to employ learner's prior knowledge, etc. (By "experience" is meant here the totality of information generated in the course of performing some actions, not a physical process.)

To provide answers to such questions, the Inferential Theory of Learning (ITL) assumes that learning is a goal-guided process of improving the learner's knowledge by exploring the learner's experience and prior knowledge. It attributes behavior change, e.g., a better performance in problem solving, to changes in the system's knowledge. The system's knowledge includes both conceptual knowledge that represents the learner's understanding of the world and control knowledge that allows the learner to exhibit various skills.

Such a process can be viewed as a search through a *knowledge space* defined by the knowledge representation used. The search can employ any type of inference—deduction, induction, or analogy. It involves "background knowledge," that is, the relevant parts of the learner's prior knowledge. Consequently, the information flow in a learning process can be characterized by the general schema shown in Figure 1.1.

In each learning cycle, the learner analyzes the input information in terms of its background knowledge and its goals and performs various inferences to generate "new" knowledge. Learning terminates if new knowledge satisfies the learning

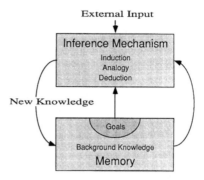

Figure 1.1:   An illustration of a general learning process

goal. The learning goal (or a system of goals) is defined by the performance system within which the learning system operates. A general default learning goal is to increase the "total" knowledge of the system.

The term new knowledge is understood here very generally. The new knowledge can consist of *derived* knowledge, *intrinsic* (or *intrinsically new*) knowledge, or both. The new knowledge is called derived if it is generated by deduction from prior learner's knowledge and the input (it is a part of the "deductive closure" of all knowledge available).

The new knowledge is called intrinsic (or intrinsically new) if it cannot be derived by deduction from the learner's prior knowledge and the input. Such intrinsically new knowledge can be provided by an external source (a teacher or observation) or generated by induction, analogy, or contingent deduction. A related concept is *pragmatically* new knowledge, which is knowledge that cannot be obtained by deduction from prior knowledge *using available computational resources*—time and/or space. Thus, pragmatically new knowledge includes both intrinsically new knowledge and knowledge that is theoretically deducible but not with the available computational resources.

The truth-status of derived knowledge depends on the validity of the background knowledge. The derived knowledge is true if the premises for deduction are true. The truth-status of intrinsically new knowledge is typically uncertain (it is certain only if the knowledge is obtained not by inference but is communicated by a source whose knowledge has been validated). Therefore, intrinsically new knowledge typically needs to be validated by an interaction with an external information source, for example, through experiments.

A question arises about whether learning occurs when the only change is in the organization of knowledge or in the confidence in the learner's prior knowledge. The answer is yes to both parts of the question and is based on the following arguments.

The theory assumes that any segment (or module) of the learner's knowledge has three aspects: its *content*, its *organization*, and its *certainty*. The content is what is conveyed by a declarative knowledge representation (e.g., by a sentence or a set of sentences in predicate calculus that represents the knowledge segment). The knowledge organization is reflected by the structure of the knowledge representation and determines the way in which the knowledge segment is used (e.g., the order in which components of a logical expression are evaluated). The *certainty* of a segment is the degree to which the learner believes that this particular segment is true. It is a subjective measure of knowledge validity, in contrast to the objective validity determined by an objective measure, such as an experiment. As a subjective measure, the learner's certainty may or may not agree with the objective validity.

To illustrate above distinctions, consider the following example. The knowledge content of a telephone book ordered alphabetically by the subscriber's name is the same as that of a book in which phone numbers are ordered numerically. The difference is only in the knowledge organization. Because change in the knowledge organization does not change the truth-status of knowledge (is truth-preserving), the result of such a change constitutes a special case of derived knowledge. Observe that different knowledge organizations facilitate different tasks, without changing the potential capability of performing these tasks. If a change in the knowledge organization improves the learner's performance of some tasks, then such a change is a form of learning. The certainty of the knowledge contained in the phone book is the overall certainty that entries in the book are correct.

The total change of a learner's knowledge is determined by the changes in all three aspects—the knowledge content, its organization, and its certainty. The theory states that learning occurs if there is any increase in the total knowledge of a learner or, more specifically, if the learner's total knowledge changes in the direction determined by the learning goal. Thus, even when the only change is in the certainty of some previously acquired knowledge segment (e.g., by obtaining a confirming evidence), the theory views this as learning because this increases the learner's total knowledge.

If the results of a given learning step ("Output") satisfy the learning goal, they are assimilated within the learner's background knowledge and become available for use in subsequent learning processes. A learning system that is able to take the learned knowledge as an input to another learning process is called a *closed-loop* system; otherwise, is it called an *open-loop* system. It is interesting to note that human learning is universally closed-loop, but many machine learning programs are open-loop.

The basic premise of the Inferential Theory of Learning is that in order to learn, an agent has to be able to perform *inference* and has to possess the ability to *memorize* knowledge. The ability to memorize knowledge serves two purposes: to supply the background knowledge (BK) needed for performing inference and to record "useful" results of inference. Without either of the two components—the ability to reason and the ability to store and retrieve information from memory—no learning can be accomplished. Thus, one can write an "equation":

Learning = Inferencing + Memorizing

where the term "inferencing" is viewed very generally: it includes any possible type of inference, knowledge transformation or manipulation, and a search for a specified knowledge entity.

The double role of memory—as a supplier of background knowledge and as a depository of results—is often reflected in the organization of a learning system. For example, in an artificial neural net, background knowledge is determined by the network's structure (the number and the type of units used and their interconnections) and by the initial weights of the connections. The learned knowledge resides in the new values of the weights. In a decision tree learning system, the BK includes the set of available attributes, their legal values, and an attribute selection procedure. The knowledge created is in the form of a decision tree. In a "self-contained" rule learning system, all background knowledge and learned knowledge would be in the form of rules. A learning process would involve modifying prior rules and/or creating new ones.

The key idea of ITL is to characterize all learning processes as goal-guided searches through a *knowledge space*. The knowledge space is defined by the knowledge representation language and the available search operators. The operators are instantiations of knowledge transmutations that a learner is capable of performing. Transmutations change various aspects of knowledge; some of them generate new knowledge, and others only manage knowledge. Transmutations can employ any type of inference. Each transmutation takes some input information and/or background knowledge and generates some new knowledge.

Any learning process is then viewed as a sequence of knowledge transmutations that transform the initial learner's knowledge to knowledge satisfying the learning goal (generally, a system of goals). Thus, ITL characterizes any learning process as a transformation:

Given:
- Input knowledge   (I)
- Goal   (G)
- Background knowledge   (BK)
- Transmutations   (T)

Determine:
- Output knowledge, O, that satisfies goal G, by applying transmutations from the set T to input I and the background knowledge BK.

The input knowledge, I, is the information that the learner receives from the outside during the learning process. The goal, G, specifies criteria to be satisfied by the output knowledge, O, in order to terminate a given act of learning. The background knowledge, BK, is a part of the learner's total prior knowledge that is relevant to a given learning process. (Although a formal definition of "relevant" knowledge goes beyond the scope of this chapter, as a working definition, the reader may assume that it is prior knowledge that is found useful at any stage in a learning process.)

The knowledge space is a space of representations of all possible input, the learner's background knowledge, and all the knowledge that the learner can potentially generate. In methods for empirical inductive learning, the knowledge space is usually called a *description space*. Transmutations are generic classes of knowledge operators that a learner performs in the knowledge space. They are classes of knowledge transformations that correspond to some cognitively comprehensible and meaningful types of knowledge change. A change in knowledge that does not represent some identifiable and comprehensible knowledge transformation would not be called a transmutation. A learning process can be viewed as a sequence of knowledge transmutations.

For illustration, let us informally describe some transmutations. An *inductive generalization* takes descriptions of some objects from a given class (e.g., concept examples) and hypothesizes a general description of the class. As shown in (Michalski, 1983), such a process can be characterized as an application of "inductive generalization rules." A *deductive generalization* derives a more general description from a more specific one by deducing it from the background knowledge and the input. A form of deductive generalization is *explanation-based generalization* (Mitchell, Keller, and Kedar-Cabelli, 1986) that takes a concept example in an "operational description space" and a concept description in an "abstract description space and deduces a generalized concept description by employing domain knowledge that relates the "abstract" and "operational" description spaces. Given some facts and background knowledge about similar facts, an *analogical generalization* hypothesizes a general description of the given facts by analogy to the generalization of similar facts. An *abstraction* takes a description of some entity and transforms it to a description that conveys less information about it but preserves information relevant to the learner's goals. An *explanation transmutation*, given some facts, generates an explanation of them by employing background knowledge that asserts that certain premises entail the given facts.

Given some input and prior knowledge, a new piece of knowledge may be determined in a number of ways, e.g., through a deductive derivation, an inductive generalization, or a *similization* transmutation (a form of analogy; see Section 1.8). An abstraction transmutation may re-express the derived piece of knowledge in a more abstract form. If the derived knowledge is hypothetical, a *generation* transmutation may generate additional facts, which are then used by a deductive transmutation to confirm or disconfirm the derived knowledge. If the knowledge is confirmed, it may be added to the original knowledge base by an *insertion* trans-mutation. The modified knowledge structure can be re-created in another knowl-edge base by a *replication transmutation*. The ultimate learning capabilities of a given learning system are determined by the types and the complexity of transmu-tations that the system is capable of performing and by the components of its knowledge that can or cannot be changed.

Another tenet of the theory is that knowledge transmutations can be analyzed and described *independently* of the computational mechanism that executes them. This is analogous to the analysis of an information content of an information source independently of the ways that information is represented or transmitted. Thus, ITL characterizes learning processes in an abstract way that does not depend on how transmutations are physically implemented. Transmutations can be implemented in a great variety of ways, using different knowledge representations and/or different computational mechanisms. In symbolic learning systems, knowl-edge transmutations are usually implemented in a more or less explicit way and executed in steps that are conceptually comprehensible. For example, the INDUCE learning system performs inductive generalization according to well-defined gener-alization rules, which represent conceptually understandable units of knowledge transformation (e.g., Michalski, 1983). Similarly, in inductive logic programming (Muggleton, 1992), individual steps correspond to well-defined operations on Horn clauses.

In subsymbolic systems (e.g., neural networks), transmutations are performed implicitly in steps that may not correspond to any conceptually simple operations. For example, a neural network may generalize an input example by performing a sequence of small modifications of weights of internode connections. These weight modifications are difficult to explain in terms of explicit inference rules. Neverthe-less, they can produce a global effect equivalent to generalizing a set of examples, thus performing a generalization transmutation.

The above effect can be demonstrated by *diagrammatic visualization* (DIAV). In DIAV, concepts are mapped into sets of cells in a planar diagram representing a multidimensional space spanned over multivalued attributes. Operations on con-cepts are visualized by changes in the configurations of the corresponding sets of cells. This way, one can visualize the effect of individual steps of a symbolic program as well as a neural network. Examples of a diagrammatic visualization of inductive generalizations performed by a neural network, genetic algorithm, and two different symbolic learning systems are presented in Wnek and Michalski (1991b; 1994, Chapter 19 of this book).

As indicated above, a learning process depends on the input information (input), background knowledge (BK), and the learning goal. These three compo-nents constitute what we call a *learning task* (or *environment*). An input can be sensory measurements or knowledge from a source (e.g., a teacher) or the previous learning step. The input can be in the form of stated facts, concept instances, previously formed generalizations, conceptual hierarchies, certainty measures, or any combinations of such types.

A learning goal is a necessary component of any learning process, although it may be present only implicitly. Given an input and a non-trivial background knowledge, a learner could potentially generate an unbounded number of inferences. To limit the proliferation of choices, a learning process has to be constrained and/or guided by the learning goal (or goals). In human learning, there is usually a whole structure of interdependent goals. Learning goals determine what parts of prior knowledge are relevant, what knowledge is to be acquired and in which form, how the learned knowledge is to be evaluated, and when to stop learning.

There can be many different types of learning goals. Goals can be classified into domain-independent and domain-dependent. Domain-independent goals call for a certain generic type of learning activity, independent of the topic of discourse. Examples of such goals are to concisely describe and/or generalize given observations, to discover a regularity in a collection of facts, to find a causal explanation of a given regularity, to acquire control knowledge to perform some activity, to reformulate given knowledge into a more effective form, to confirm a given piece of knowledge, etc. If a learning goal is complex, a learner needs to develop a plan specifying a structure of knowledge components to learn and the order in which they should be learned. A domain-dependent goal calls for acquiring a specific piece of knowledge about the domain, for example, to answer a question such as, "What is the distance to the nearest galaxy?" A learner may pursue several goals simultaneously, and the goals may be conflicting. When they are conflicting, their relative importance controls the amount of effort extended to pursue any of them. The importance of specific goals depends on the importance of higher-level goals they are instances of. Thus, learning processes may be controlled by a hierarchy of goals and the estimated degrees of their importance.

Most research in machine learning has so far given relatively little attention to learning goals and how they affect learning processes. This is quite understandable because most research was concerned with single strategy learning systems in which the learning goal is implicitly defined (or constrained) by the type and form of knowledge the system is designed to learn. For example, a decision tree learning program can only learn decision trees from examples; it cannot learn, e.g., specific rules from general rules.

The importance of goals specifically arises in multistrategy learning systems that can learn different types of knowledge and from different types of input. There have been several investigations of the role and the use of goals in learning and inference (e.g., Stepp and Michalski [1983]; Hunter [1990]; Ram [1991]; Ram and Hunter [1992]). Among important research problems related to this topic are to develop methods for goal representation, for using goals to guide a learning process; to understand the interaction and conflict resolution among domain-independent and domain-specific goals; and to develop plans for learning complex tasks. These issues are of significant importance to understanding multistrategy learning, and interest in them will likely increase in the future.

In sum, the Inferential Theory of Learning states that learning is a process of deriving goal-dependent knowledge by using input information and background knowledge. Such a process can be viewed as a search through a knowledge space, using transmutations as search operators. When a learning process produces knowledge satisfying a learning goal, it is stored and made available for subsequent learning processes.

Transmutations represent generic patterns of knowledge change (knowledge generation, transformation, manipulation, etc.) and can employ any type of inference. To clearly explain their function, it is necessary to analyze different types of inference and their interrelationships. To this end, Sections 1.3 to 1.5 discuss fundamental types of inference and give examples of transmutations that employ them. Section 1.6 summarizes different types of transmutations currently recognized in the theory. Subsequently, Sections 1.7 and 1.8 analyze in detail several basic transmutations, such as generalization, abstraction, and similization and their counterparts, specialization, concretion, and dissimilization. Sections 1.9 and 1.10 outline the application of the concepts of the theory to the development of a methodology for multistrategy task-adaptive learning.

1.3 TYPES OF INFERENCE

Any type of inference may generate a piece of knowledge that can be useful for some purpose and, thus, worth learning. Therefore, a complete theory of learning must include a complete theory of inference.

An attempt to schematically illustrate all basic types of inference is presented in Figure 1.2. The first classification is to divide inferences into two fundamental types: deductive and inductive.

In defining these types, conventional approaches (like those in formal logic) do not distinguish between the input information and the reasoner's background knowledge. Such a distinction is, however, important for characterizing learning processes. Clearly, from the viewpoint of a learner, there is a difference between knowledge that the learner already possesses and the information received from the senses. Thus, making such a distinction is useful for reflecting cognitive aspects of reasoning and learning and leads to a more adequate description of learning processes. To define basic types of inference in a general and language-independent way, let us consider an entailment:

$$P \cup BK \models C \tag{1}$$

where P stands for a set of statements, called the *premise*; BK stands for the reasoner's *background knowledge*; $\models$ denotes logical entailment; and C stands for a

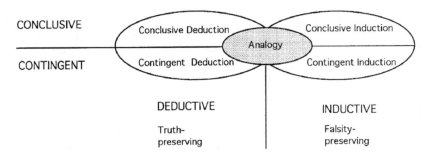

Figure 1.2:   A classification of basic types of inference

set of statements, called the *consequent*. It is assumed that P is logically consistent with BK.

Statement (1) can be interpreted as follows: P and BK logically entail C, or alternatively, C is a logical consequence of P and BK. Deductive inference is deriving consequent C, given P and BK. Inductive inference is hypothesizing premise P, given C and BK. Deduction can thus be viewed as tracing forward the relationship (1) and induction as tracing backward this relationship. Deduction is the process of determining a logical consequence of given knowledge, and its basic form is truth-preserving (C must be true if P and BK are true). In contrast, induction is hypothesizing a premise that together with BK entails the input, and its basic form is falsity-preserving (if C is not true, then P cannot be true). Because (1) succinctly captures the relationship between these two fundamental types of inference, we call it the *fundamental equation* for inference.

Inductive inference underlies several major knowledge generation transmutations, among them *inductive generalization* and *abductive derivation* (or, *explanation*). These two differ in the type of premise P that they generate and in the type of BK they employ. To put it simply, the differences between the two types of inductive inference are as follows (a more precise characterization is given in Sections 1.4 and 1.5; see also examples below): Inductive generalization produces a premise P that is a generalization of C; i.e., P characterizes a larger set of entities than the set described by C. As shown later, inductive generalization can be viewed as tracing backward a tautological implication specifically, the rule of *universal specialization*: $\forall x, P(x) \Rightarrow P(a)$. In contrast, abductive derivation produces a description that characterizes "reasons" for C. This is done by tracing backward an implication that represents some domain knowledge. If the domain knowledge represents a causal dependency, then such abductive derivation produces a *causal explanation*. Other less known types of inductive transmutations include *inductive specialization* and *inductive concretion* (see Sections 1.5 and 1.6).

In a general view of deduction and induction that also captures their approximate or common sense forms, the standard (conclusive) logical entailment ⊨ is replaced by a *plausible* (*contingent*) entailment $\models$. Such an entailment states that C is only a *plausible, probabilistic*, or *partial* consequence of P and BK. The difference between these two types of entailments leads to another major classification of types of inference.

Specifically, inferences can be *conclusive* (*sound, strong*) or *contingent* (*plausible, weak*). Conclusive inferences assume standard logical entailment in (1), and contingent inferences assume *plausible* entailment in (1). *Conclusive deductive* inferences (also called *formal* or *demonstrative*) produce true consequences from true premises. *Conclusive inductive* inferences produce hypotheses that conclusively entail premises. *Contingent deductive* inferences produce consequents that may be true in some situations and not true in other situations; they are weakly truth-preserving. *Contingent inductive* inferences produce hypotheses that weakly entail premises; they are weakly falsity-preserving.

The intersection of deduction and induction, that is, a truth- and falsity-preserving inference, is an equivalence-based inference (also called a *reformulation*; see Section 1.6). Such an inference transforms a given statement (or set of statements) into another logically equivalent statement.

Analogy can be viewed as an extension of such an equivalence-based inference, namely, as a "similarity-based" inference. It occupies the central area in the diagram because analogy can be viewed as a combination of induction and deduction. The inductive step consists of hypothesizing that a similarity between two entities in terms of some descriptors extends to their similarity in terms of some other descriptors. Based on this similarity and the knowledge of the values of the additional descriptors for the source entity, a *deductive* step derives their values for the target entity. An important knowledge transmutation based on analogical inference is *similization*. For example, if A$'$ is similar to A, then from A $\Rightarrow$ B, one can plausibly derive A$'$ $\Rightarrow$ B. In order that such an inference can work, there is a tacit assumption that the similarity between A and A$'$ is *relevant* to B. This idea is explained and illustrated by examples in Section 1.9.

Let us now illustrate various knowledge transmutations based on the above two basic forms of inference. The following is an example of a conclusive deductive transmutation:

Input	$a \in X$	(*a* is an element of X.)
BK	$\forall x \in X, q(x)$	(All elements of X have property q.)
	$(\forall x \in X, q(x)) \Rightarrow (a \in X \Rightarrow q(a))$	(If all elements of X have property q, then any element of X, e.g., *a*, must have property q.)
Output	$q(a)$	(*a* has property q.)

If Input stands for premise P and Output for the consequent C, then the fundamental equation (1) is clearly satisfied. The Output was obtained by "tracing forward" a tautological implication stated in BK, known in logic as the rule of universal specialization.

Before we give other examples, we need to introduce two important concepts, specifically, a *reference set* and a *descriptor*. A reference set of a statement or a set of statements is the entity or a set of entities that this statement(s) describes or refers to. A descriptor is an attribute, a relation, or a transformation whose instantiation (value) is used to characterize the reference set or the individual entities in it. For example, consider a statement: "Nicholas is of medium height, has Ph.D. in Astronomy from the Jagiellonian University, and likes travel." The reference set here is the singleton "Nicholas." The sentence uses three descriptors: a one-place attribute, *height(person)*; a binary relation, *likes(person, activity)*; and a four place relation, *degree-received(person, degree, topic, university)*.

Consider another statement: "Most people on Barbados and Dominica have beautiful dark skin." Here as the reference set one can take "Most people on Barbados and Dominica," and the descriptors are *skin-color(person)* and *skin-attractiveness(person)*. What is the reference set and what are descriptors in a statement or set of statements are a matter of interpretation and depend on the context in which the statement(s) is used. However, once the interpretation is decided, other concepts can be applied consistently.

Based on the above concepts, different inductive transmutations can briefly be characterized as follows:

- *Inductive generalization* inductively extends the reference set of the input statement(s).

- *Inductive specialization* inductively reduces the reference set.

- *Abductive derivation* (or *explanation*) hypothesizes a premise that entails the given input description according to some domain rule or rules.

- *Inductive concretion* hypothesizes additional details about the reference set described in the input statement (e.g., by hypothesizing values of more specific descriptors or hypothesizing more precise values of the original descriptors; see Section 1.7).

Let us illustrate these transmutations by simple examples. The following is an example of conclusive inductive generalization:

Input	$q(a)$	(a has property q.)
BK	$a \in X$	(a is an element of X.)
	$(\forall x \in X, q(x)) \Rightarrow (a \in X \Rightarrow q(a))$	(If all elements of X have property q, then any element of X, e.g., a, must have property q.)

Output	$\forall x \in X, q(x)$	(Maybe all elements of X have property q.)

This above transmutation is an inductive generalization because the property q that was initially known to characterize only an element, a, has been hypothetically reassigned to characterize a larger set—all elements in X. This hypothesis was obtained by tracing backward the rule of universal specialization. If Input is the consequent C, and the Output is the premise P, then the fundamental equation (1) is satisfied because the union of sentences in Output and BK entails the Input. Because the entailment is strong, this is a conclusive induction. The inference is falsity-preserving because if the Input were not true (a did not have the property q), then the hypothetical premise (Output) would have to be false. Because output from induction is uncertain, it is indicated here and henceforth by the qualifier "*Maybe*."

Let us now turn to an example of inductive specialization:

Input	$\exists x \in X, q(x)$	(There is an element in X that has property q.)
BK	$a \in X$	(a is an element of X.)
	$(a \in X \Rightarrow q(a)) \Rightarrow (\exists x \in X, q(x))$	(If some element a from X has property q, then there exists an element in X with property q.)
Output	$q(a)$	(Maybe element a has property q.)

The input statement can be restated as "One or more elements of X have property q." The reference set here is one or more unidentified elements in X. The inductive specialization hypothesizes that a specific element, a, from X has property q. Clearly, if this hypothesis and BK were true, the consequent would also have to be true. Again, the hypothesis was created by tracing backward an implicative rule in BK.

The following is an example of abductive derivation:

Input	$q(a)$	(a has property q.)
BK	$\forall x, x \in X \Rightarrow q(x)$	(If x is an element of X, then x has property q.)
Output	$a \in X$	(Maybe a is an element of X.)

The *Input* states that the reference set, a, has the property q. The abductive derivation hypothesizes the statement "Maybe a belongs to X," which can be viewed as an explanation of the input $q(a)$, assuming BK. The fundamental equation (1) holds because if Output is true, then Input must also be true in the context of BK. Again, if Input were not true, then Output could not be true; thus, the inference preserves falsity. As in the example of inductive generalization, Output was obtained by tracing backward an implicative rule in BK. Notice, however, an important difference from the two previous examples, namely, that the implicative rule in the case of abductive derivation represents *domain knowledge* (that may or may not be true) but in the cases of inductive generalization and inductive specialization represents a universally true relationship (a tautological implication).

Inductive concretion is illustrated by the following rule:

Input	q(a)	(a has property q.)
BK	$\forall x \in X, q'(x) \Rightarrow q(x)$	(If x is from X and has property q', then it has property q.)

Output	q'(a)	(Maybe a has property q'.)

To give an example of an inductive concretion, suppose that q and q' are two attributes characterizing some entity a and that q' is more specific than q. Suppose, for example, that a is a personal computer, q its brand—*Mac*, and q' its brand and model—*Mac Quadra*. X stands for a set of personal computers. The background knowledge states that if x is a *Mac Quadra*, then it is also a *Mac*. Given that the computer is a *Mac*, a concretion transmutation hypothesizes that perhaps it is a *Mac Quadra*. Without more background knowledge, such a hypothesis would just be a pure guess. With more BK, e.g., that the computer belongs to someone for whom the speed of the computer is important, and with the belief that *Mac Quadra* is the fastest model of *Mac*, such a hypothesis would be plausible. Because q' is a more specific property than q, q' conclusively implies q, and the presented example of concretion is a form of conclusive induction.

To summarize, the above examples illustrated several important types of inductive transmutation—inductive generalization, inductive specialization, abductive derivation, and concretion (other inductive transmutations are mentioned in Section 1.6). By reversing the direction of inference in these examples, that is, by replacing Output by Input and conversely, one obtains the opposite transmutations, specifically, *deductive specialization, deductive generalization, prediction*, and *abstraction*, respectively. Prediction is viewed as opposite of explanation (abductive derivation) because it generates effects of the given premises ("causes"). While abductive derivation traces backward given domain rules, prediction traces them forward. Abstraction is viewed as opposite of concretion because it transfers a more detailed description into a less detailed description of the given reference set.

The presented characterization of the above transmutations differs from the traditional views of these inference types, and may need more justification. The next two sections give a more systematic analysis of the proposed ideas. We start with abduction and its relation to contingent deduction.

1.4 ABDUCTION VS. CONTINGENT DEDUCTION

The literature on abduction (abductive derivation) sometimes describes it as a process of creating the "best" explanation of a given fact(s). According to this view, abduction is an inference that traces backward the "strongest" implicative rule (or chain of rules) that implies the given fact. A difficulty with such a characterization of abduction is that there can be more than one explanation of a given

fact, and it is not always easy to determine which explanation among the alternative ones is the "best." If producing an alternative but not the "best" explanation is
not abduction, then what is and what is not abduction depends on the measure of
"goodness" of explanation rather than on logical properties of inference.

Some authors restrict abduction to processes of creating causal explanations;
i.e., they limit it to inferences that trace backward "causal implications." The example of abduction given in the previous section was based on the rule "If an entity
belongs to X, then it has property q." This rule is not a causal implication but a
logical dependency. Consequently, according to such a view, the above example
would not qualify as abduction. It may also be pointed out that Peirce, who originally introduced the concept of abduction, did not have any measure of "goodness
of explanation," nor did he restrict abduction to reasoning that produces only
"causal" explanations (Peirce, 1965). Examples of some contemporary views of
abduction are in Console, Theseider, and Torasso (1991) and Zadrozny (1991).
Because abduction is related to causal reasoning, the development of such reasoning in humans is also relevant to the study of abduction (Schultz and Kestenbaum,
1985).

The proposed view of abduction extends the above views. It considers abduction as a form of knowledge-intensive induction that hypothesizes explanatory
knowledge about a given reference set. This process involves tracing backward
domain-dependent implications. Based on the type of implications involved, the
hypothesized knowledge may be a logical explanation or a causal explanation. If
there are different implications with the same consequent, tracing backward any of
them is an abduction. The results of these abductions may have different credibility,
depending on the "backward strength" of the implications involved (see below).

This view of abduction extends its conventional meaning in yet another sense.
It is sometimes assumed that abduction produces only ground facts, meaning that
the reference set is a specific object. As stated earlier, our view is that abduction
generates explanatory knowledge that characterizes a given reference set. If the
reference set consists of a collection of entities, abduction produces an explanation
of this set. Below is an example of the latter form of abduction (variables are
written with small letters):

Input	$\forall x, In(x,S)$ & $Banana(x) \Rightarrow NotSweet(x)$	(All bananas in shop S are not sweet.)
BK	$\forall x, Banana(x)$ & $FromB(x) \Rightarrow NotSweet(x))$	(Bananas from Barbados are not sweet.)

Output	$\forall x, In(x,S)$ & $Banana(x) \Rightarrow FromB(x)$	(Maybe all bananas in S are from Barbados.)

In this example, the hypothesized output is not a ground statement but a
quantified expression. The output was generated by tracing backward an implica-

tive rule in BK and making a replacement in the right-hand-side of the input expression.

Let us now analyze more closely the view of abduction as an inference that traces backward implicative rules. It is easy to see that this view makes some tacit assumptions that, if violated, would allow abduction to produce completely implausible inferences. Consider, for example, the following inference:

Input	Color(My-Pencil, Green)	(My pencil is green.)
BK	Type(object, Grass) $\Rightarrow$ Color(object, Green)	(If an object is grass, then it is green.)

Output	Type(My-Pencil, Grass)	(Maybe my pencil is grass.)

The inference that my pencil may be grass because it is green clearly strikes us as faulty. The reason for this is that reversing the implication in BK produces the implication

Color(object, Green) $\Rightarrow$ Type(object, Grass)   (If an object is green, then it is grass.)

which holds only with an infinitesimal likelihood.

This example demonstrates that abduction, if defined as tracing backward an implication, may produce a completely implausible hypothesis. This will happen if the "reverse implication" has insufficient "strength." This simply means that standard abductive inference makes a tacit assumption that there is a sufficient "reverse strength" of the implications used to perform abduction. To make this issue explicit, we employ the concept of "mutual implication" as a basis for abductive reasoning.

Definition. A *mutual implication*—or, for short, an *m-implication*—describes a logical dependency between statements in both directions:

$$A \Leftrightarrow B: \alpha, b \qquad\qquad (2)$$

where A and B are statements (well-formed logical expressions), and a and b, called *merit parameters*, express the *forward strength* and the *backward strength* of the m-implication, respectively. In a general form of m-implication, $A \Leftrightarrow B$ may be a quantified expression.

A standard interpretation of these two parameters is that $\alpha = p(B|A)$, and $\beta = p(A|B)$. However, to make the concept of m-implication applicable for expressing different kinds of dependencies, including those occurring in human plausible reasoning, it is assumed that merit parameters can also have other interpretations. They could be only estimates of conditional probability, ranges of probabilities, degrees of dependency based on a contingency table (e.g., Goodman and Kruskal [1979]; Piatetsky-Shapiro [1992]), qualitative characterizations of the "strength" of dependency, or some other measure.

An m-implication can be used for reasoning by "tracing" it in either direction. Tracing it forward (from the left to the right) means that if A is known to be true, then B can be asserted as true, with the degree of strength α, if no other information relevant to B is known that affects this conclusion. Tracing an m-implication backward means that if B is known to be true, then A can be asserted as true, with the degree of strength β, if no other information relevant to A is known that affects this conclusion. The m-implication reduces to a logical implication if α is 1, and β is unknown (in which case, it is written as A $\Rightarrow$B).

If either of the parameters α or β takes value 1 (which represents "full strength"), then the m-implication is *conclusive* (or *demonstrative*) in the direction for which the merit parameter equals 1; otherwise, it is called *mutually-contingent* (or *m-contingent*). In some situations, it is convenient to express an m-implication without stating precise values of merit parameters, with the assumption, however, that these values are above some "threshold of acceptance" (to ignore weak dependencies). For this purpose, we use symbols <—> (or —>), without listing α and β. Thus, A $\Leftrightarrow$ B: α, β, in which α and β are unspecified but above some threshold of acceptance, is alternatively written A <—> B or A—> B if only α is above the threshold. The concept of mutual implication was originally postulated in the theory of plausible reasoning (Collins and Michalski, 1989), which was developed by analyzing protocols recording examples of human reasoning.

Based on the above definition, one can say that abduction produces a plausible conclusion only if it traces backward a mutual implication in which β is sufficiently high. Thus, if abduction is based—as usually done—on the standard form of implication (in which β is unknown), then it is quite a haphazard reasoning. Section 1.8 generalizes the concept of m-implication into m-dependency and shows that such a dependency provides a formal basis for analogical inference.

The concept of m-implication raises a problem of how merit parameters can be combined and propagated in reasoning through a network of m-implications. A comprehensive study of ideas and methods for the case of the probabilistic interpretation of merit parameters is presented by Pearl (1988). He uses "Bayesian networks" for updating and propagating beliefs represented as probabilities.

The fundamental difficulty in solving this problem generally is that all logics of uncertainty, such as multiple-valued logic, probabilistic logic, and fuzzy logic, are not *truth-functional*, which means that there is no definite function for combining uncertainties. The reason for this is that the certainty of a conclusion from uncertain premises does not depend solely on the certainty (or probability) of the premises; it also depends on their semantic interrelationship. The ultimate solution of this open problem will require methods that take into consideration both merit parameters and the meaning of the sentences. The results of research on human plausible reasoning conducted by Collins and Michalski (1989) show that people derive a combined certainty of a conclusion from uncertain premises by taking into consideration semantic relations among the premises, based on a hierarchical knowledge representation, and also other types of merit parameters, such as typicality, frequency, and dominance.

Conclusive inferences trace m-implications only in the direction characterized by the merit parameter equal to 1 and assume that the input statements are true and perfectly match the premises. In contrast, contingent inferences use m-implications in the direction for which the strength parameter may be less than 1 and allow the input statements to be only partially true or to imperfectly match the premises. The results of contingent inferences are associated with a "degree of certainty." In natural language, such a degree is usually expressed by a qualitative measure—e.g., "maybe," "probably," "likely," and "with a high degree of confidence"—or indicated by a contingent quantifier—e.g., "most," "frequently," "usually," and "90% of... ." Suppose, for example, given is the statement "Most elements of X have property q." This statement can be interpreted as an m-implication $\forall x, x \in X \Rightarrow q$ (x): α, where α is a range of relative frequencies of x in X with property q that are consistent with the meaning of "most." If "a is a member of X," then deriving the statement "a has likely property q" is a contingent deduction.

Consider another statement: "Fire usually causes smoke." This statement can be represented as a mutual implication In(x, Smoke) $\Leftrightarrow$ In(x, Fire): α, β (where x is quantified over a set of places). If one sees fire in some place, then one may derive a conclusion (with certainty α) that there may be smoke there too. Conversely, observing smoke, one may hypothesize (with certainty β) that there may be fire there. Assuming that both merit parameters are smaller than 1, the above conclusions are uncertain. The first inference can be viewed as a contingent deduction and the second inference as a contingent induction. This form of contingent induction is contingent abduction because the mutually-contingent m-implication involved here represents domain knowledge (is not a tautological implication), and the conclusion "there may be fire there" serves as an explanation of the observation "there is a smoke."

The fact that both conclusions are uncertain might suggest that there is no real difference between contingent deduction and contingent abduction. A way to characterize the difference between the two types of inference is to check if the entailment $\models$ in (1) could be interpreted as a causal dependency, i.e., if P could be viewed as a cause and C as an effect. Contingent deduction derives a plausible consequent, C, of the causes represented by P. Abduction derives plausible causes, P, of the consequent C. Because we assume that "fire causes smoke" and not conversely, then the above rule allows us to make a qualitative distinction between inferences tracing this m-implication in different directions. Contingent deduction can thus be viewed as tracing forward and contingent abduction as tracing backward "causal" m-implications.

The above distinction, however, is generally insufficient. The problem is that there are mutual implications that do not represent causal dependencies. For example, consider the statement "Prices at Tiffany tend to be high." This statement can be expressed as a non-causal m-implication:

$$\text{Purchased-at(item, Tiffany)} \Leftrightarrow \text{Price(item, High)}: \alpha, \beta \qquad (3)$$

If one is told that an item, e.g., a crystal vase, was purchased at Tiffany, then one may conclude, with confidence α, that the price of it was high (if no other information about the price of the vase was known). The conclusion is uncertain if $\alpha < 1$ (which reflects, e.g., the possibility of a sale). If one is told that the price of an item was high, then one might hypothesize, with confidence β (usually quite low), that perhaps the item was purchased at Tiffany. The confidence β depends on our knowledge about how many expensive shops other than Tiffany are in the area where the item was purchased. Both above inferences are uncertain (assuming α, β < 1), and there is no clear causal ordering underlying the m-implication. Which inference is then contingent deduction, and which is contingent abduction?

We propose to resolve this problem by observing that in a standard (conclusive) deduction, an m-implication is traced in the "strong" direction (with the degree of strength 1), and in abduction, it is traced in the "weaker" direction. Extending this idea to reasoning with mutually-contingent implications that are not causal dependencies leads to the following rule:

If an m-implication is a non-casual mutually contingent domain dependency, then reasoning in the direction of the greater strength of the implication is contingent deduction, and reasoning in the direction of the weaker strength is contingent abduction.

If a non-causal m-implication has equal strength in both directions, there is no distinction between contingent deduction and contingent abduction. Going back to the example with Tiffany, one may observe that α is usually significantly higher than β, unless Tiffany is the only expensive store in the area under consideration. Thus, the forward reasoning based on (3) can be viewed as a contingent deduction and the backward reasoning as a contingent abduction. The distinction between contingent deduction and contingent abduction in the case of non-causal implications is thus a matter of degree.

To summarize, contingent deduction and contingent abduction can be distinguished by the direction of causality in the involved m-implications. In case of non-causal implications, these two forms can be distinguished on the basis of the strength of the merit parameters. Both forms of inference are truth- and falsity-preserving to the degree specified by the forward and backward merit parameters of the involved m-implications.

1.5 ADMISSIBLE INDUCTION AND INDUCTIVE TRANSMUTATIONS

Section 1.3 described induction as one of two fundamental forms of inference, opposite to deduction, and indicated that it includes several different forms. Inductive inference can produce hypotheses that can be generalizations, specializations, concretions, or other forms. Another aspect of such general formulation of induction is that induction is not limited to inferences that use small amounts of background knowledge, i.e., to *knowledge-limited* or *empirical* inductive inferences, but includes inferences that employ considerable amounts of background knowledge, i.e., *knowledge-intensive* or *constructive* inductive inferences. Inductive generalization based on the "changing constants to variables" rule (Michalski, 1993) is an example of empirical induction because it requires little background knowledge. Abduction can be viewed as an example of knowledge-intensive induction because it requires domain knowledge in the form of implicative relationships.

An important aspect of inductive inference is that given some input information (a consequent C) and some BK (which by itself does not entail the input), the fundamental equation (1) can be satisfied by a potentially infinite number of hypotheses. Among these, only a few may be of any interest. One is usually interested only in "simple" and most "plausible" hypotheses. If a learner has sufficient BK, then this knowledge both guides the induction process and provides constraints on the hypotheses considered. Because of BK, people are able to overcome limitations of empirical induction (Dietterich, 1989). The problem of selecting the "best" hypothesis among candidates appears in any type of induction. To limit a potentially unlimited set of hypotheses, some extra-logical criteria are introduced. This idea is captured by the concept of an *admissible induction*.

Definition. Given a consequent C and background knowledge BK, an admissible induction hypothesizes a premise P that is consistent with BK and satisfies

$$P \cup BK \models C \tag{4}$$

and the *hypothesis selection criterion.*

The selection criterion specifies how to determine a hypothesis among all candidates satisfying (4). Such a criterion may be a combination of several elementary criteria. In such a combination, some criteria may be stated explicitly and some implied by the representation language or the computational method used. In different contexts or for different forms of induction, the selection criterion has been called a *preference criterion* (Popper, 1972; Michalski, 1983), a *bias* (Utgoff, 1986; Grosof and Russell, 1989), *or a comparator* (Poole, 1989).

Ideally, the selection criterion should not be problem-independent or dictated by a specific learning mechanism but should specify properties of a hypothesis that reflect the *learner's goals*. This condition is not always satisfied by machine learning programs.

In some machine learning programs, the selection criterion is hidden in the description language employed (a "description language bias"). For example, a description language may be incomplete in the sense that it allows only hypotheses expressed in the form of conjunctive descriptions. If the "true" hypothesis is not expressible this way, the program cannot learn the concept. In human learning and in more advanced machine learning programs, the representation languages are complete. The linguistic constraints only influence what types of relationships are easy to express and what types are difficult (e.g., Michalski [1983]; Muggleton [1988]).

The selection criterion can also be based on the specific characteristics of the knowledge representational system used. For example, in decision tree learning, the selection criterion may seek a tree with the minimum number of nodes. This requirement may not, however, always produce the most desirable concept descriptions. Also, because of the limited representational power of decision trees, forcing a hypothesis into a form of a decision tree may introduce some unnecessary conditions to the concept representation (Michalski, 1990b).

There are three generally desirable characteristics of a hypothesis: *plausibility, utility*, and *generality*. The plausibility characteristic expresses a desire to find a "true" hypothesis. Because the problem is logically underconstrained, the "truth" of a hypothesis cannot be guaranteed in principle. To satisfy equation (4), a hypothesis has to be *complete* and *consistent* with regard to the input facts (Michalski, 1983). Experiments have shown, however, that in situations where the input contains errors or noise, an inconsistent and/or incomplete hypothesis will often lead to a better overall predictive performance than a complete and consistent one (e.g., Bergadano et al. [1992]).

In general, the plausibility of a hypothesis depends on the learner's BK. The core theory of plausible inference (Collins and Michalski, 1989) postulates that the plausibility depends on the structural aspects of the organization of human knowledge (Hieb and Michalski, 1992) and on various merit parameters. The utility criterion requires a hypothesis to be simple to express and easy to apply to the expected set of problems. The generality criterion seeks a hypothesis that can predict a large range of new cases. A "complete" hypothesis selection criterion should take into consideration all the above requirements.

The above view of induction is very general. It subsumes views usually expressed in the literature. It is, however, consistent with many long-standing thoughts on this subject, going back to Aristotle (e.g., Adler and Gorman [1987]; Aristotle [1987]). Aristotle and many subsequent thinkers, e.g., Bacon (1620), Whewell (1857), Cohen (1970), and Popper (1972), viewed induction as a fundamental inference underlying all processes of creating new knowledge. They did not limit it—as is sometimes done—to only inductive empirical generalization.

As mentioned earlier, induction underlies a number of different knowledge transmutations, such as inductive generalization, inductive specialization, abductive explanation, and concretion. The most common form is inductive generalization, which from properties of a sample of entities of a given class hypothesizes properties of the entire class. Inductive generalization is central to many learning processes.

Inductive specialization creates hypotheses that refer to a smaller reference set than the one referred to in the input. Typically, a generalization is inductive and specialization is deductive. However, depending on the meaning of the input and BK, generalization may also be deductive and specialization inductive (see Figure 1.3 below). An abductive explanation generates hypotheses that explain the observed properties of a reference set and is opposite to deductive *prediction*, which characterizes expected properties of the reference set. Concretion generates more specific information about a given reference set and is opposite to abstraction (see Section 1.7).

Examples of the above transmutations are presented in Figure 1.3. In these examples, to indicate that some m-implications are not conclusive (not logical implications) but are sufficiently strong to warrant consideration, the symbol <—> is used. Given an input and BK, there are usually many possible inductive transmutations of them; here, we list one of each type, the one that is normally perceived as the most "natural."

To indicate that Output of the transmutations in Figure 1.3 is hypothetical, their symbolic expressions are annotated by certainty parameter α, which is represented by qualifier "maybe" in the linguistic interpretation of the statements. The first, third, and fourth examples in Figure 1.3 represent conclusive induction (in which the hypothesis with BK strongly implies the input); the second and the last two examples represent contingent induction. The second example would be a conclusive induction if the rule in BK was

$\forall x, y$ (Pntng(x,y) & Btfl(x) $\Leftrightarrow$ Exp(x): $\alpha=$ usually, $\beta = 1$

("All beautiful paintings are usually expensive, but expensive paintings are always beautiful"), which does not reflect the facts in real life. In the examples, the subset symbol "$\subset$" is used with the assumption that cities, states, apartments, and buildings are viewed as sets of space parcels.

1.6 SUMMARY OF TRANSMUTATIONS

As stated earlier, transmutations are patterns of knowledge change and can be viewed as generic operators in knowledge spaces. A transmutation may change one or more aspects of knowledge, i.e., its content, organization, and/or its certainty. Transmutations can generate intrinsically new knowledge (by induction or analogy), produce derived knowledge (by deduction), modify the degree of belief in

Empirical inductive generalization

Input	Pntng(GF, Dawski) $\Rightarrow$ Btfl(GF)	(Dawski's paintings, "A girl's face" and
	Pntng(LC, Dawski) $\Rightarrow$ Btfl(LC)	"Lvov's cathedral," are beautiful.)
BK	$\forall x, P(x) \Rightarrow P(a)$	(The universal specialization rule.)

Output	$\forall x$,Pntng(x, Dawski) $\Rightarrow$ Btfl(x): α	(Maybe all Dawski's
		pntngs are beautiful.)

Constructive induction (generalization + deduction)

Input	Pntng(GF, Dawski) $\Rightarrow$ Btfl(GF)	(Dawski's pntngs, "A girl's face" &
	Pntng(LC, Dawski) $\Rightarrow$ Btfl(LC)	"Lvov's cathedral," are beautiful.)
BK	$\forall x,y$, Pntng(x,y)&Btfl(x) <—> Exp(x)	(Btfl pntngs tend to be
		expensive & opposite.)

Output	$\forall x$,Pntng(x, Dawski) $\Rightarrow$ Exp(x): α	(Maybe Dawski's pntngs
		are expensive.)

Inductive specialization

Input	Lives(John, Virginia)	(John lives in Virginia.)
BK	Fairfax $\subset$ Virginia	(Fairfax is a "subset" of Virginia.)
	$\forall x,y,z$, y $\subset$ z&Lives(x,y)	
	$\Rightarrow$Lives(x,z)	(Living in x implies living in superset of x.)

Output	Lives(John, Fairfax): α	(Maybe John lives in Fairfax.)

Inductive concretion

Input	Going-to(John, New York)	(John is going to New York.)
BK	Likes(John, driving)	(John likes driving.)
	$\forall x,y$, Driving(x,y) $\Rightarrow$ Going-to(x,y)	("Driving to" is a special
		case of "going to.")
	$\forall x,y$, Likes(x,driving) $\Rightarrow$ Driving(x,y)	(Liking to drive m-implies
		driving to places.)

Output	Driving(John, New York): α	(Maybe John is driving to New York.)

Abductive explanation

Input	In(House, Smoke)	(There is smoke in the house.)
BK	In(x, Smoke) <—> In(x, Fire)	(Smoke usually indicates
		fire & conversely.)

Output	In(House, Fire): α	(Maybe there is fire in the house)

Constructive induction (generalization + abduction)

Input	In(John'sApt, Smoke)	(Smoke is in John's apartment.)
BK	In(x, Smoke) <—> In(x, Fire)	(Smoke usually indicates
		fire &conversely.)
	John'sApt $\subset$ GKBld	(John's apt. is in the Golden Key building.)

Output	In(GKBld, Fire): α	(Maybe there is fire in the Golden Key bldg.)

Figure 1.3:   Examples of inductive transmutations

some components of knowledge, or change knowledge organization. Formally, a transmutation can be viewed as a transformation that takes as arguments a set of sentences (S), a set of entities (E), and background knowledge (BK) and generates a new set of sentences (S') and/or a new set of entities (E') and/or new background knowledge (BK'):

$$T: S, E, BK \longrightarrow S', E', BK' \tag{5}$$

Transmutations can be classified into two categories. In the first category are *knowledge generation* transmutations that change the content of knowledge and/or its certainty. Such transmutations represent patterns of inference. For example, they may derive consequences from given knowledge, suggest new hypothetical knowledge, determine relationships among knowledge components, confirm or disconfirm given knowledge, perform mathematical operations on quantitative knowledge, and organize knowledge into certain structures. Knowledge generation transmutations are performed on statements that have a truth status.

In the second category are *knowledge manipulation* transmutations that view input knowledge as data or objects to be managed. These transmutations change only knowledge organization. They can be performed on statements (well-formed logical expressions) or on terms (denoting sets). They include inserting (deleting) knowledge components into (from) given knowledge structures, physically transmitting or copying knowledge to/from other knowledge bases, or ordering knowledge components according to some syntactic criteria. Because they do not change the knowledge content, they are truth-preserving and, thus, can be viewed as based on deductive inference.

The distinction between transmutations—generic types of knowledge change—and types of inference—methods of deriving knowledge from other knowledge—is an important contribution of the theory. A significant consequence of it is a realization that every knowledge generation transmutation can, in principle, be performed by any type of inference—deduction, induction, or analogy (except for similization and dissimilization, which are inherently associated with analogical inference). In actual use, different transmutations are typically associated with only one type of inference. For example, generalization and agglomeration are typically done through induction and specialization and abstraction through deduction. Generalization, however, can be deductive (as, e.g., in explanation-based generalization) or analogical (when a more general description is derived by an analogy to some other generalization transformation). Specialization is typically deductive, but it can also be inductive or analogical.

Another contribution of the theory is an observation that transmutations can be grouped into pairs of opposite operators, that is, operators that change knowledge in the conceptually opposite direction (except for derivations that span a range of transmutations; the endpoints of this range are opposites; see explanation later).

Each pair of transmutations can thus perform a bi-directional operation on knowledge.

Below is a summary of knowledge transmutations that have been identified in the theory as those that frequently occur in human reasoning or machine learning algorithms. The transmutations are described informally to convey their basic meaning in a simple way. A rigorous and general description of these transmutations is a subject of future research (see Sections 1.7 and 1.8 for a more detailed analysis of generalization, abstraction, and similization).

The first nine groups represent knowledge generation transmutations, and the remaining groups represent knowledge manipulation transmutations. This list is not exhaustive; future efforts may likely identify other important transmutations. It should be noted that these transmutations can be applied to all kinds of knowledge—specific facts, general statements, metaknowledge, control knowledge, goals, and others.

1. *Generalization/specialization*
The generalization transmutation extends the reference set of a description; that is, it generates a description that characterizes (or refers to) a larger reference set than the original set. Typically, the underlying inference is inductive. Generalization can also be deductive when the more general description is deductively derived from the more specific one using background knowledge. It can also be analogical when the more general description is hypothesized through analogy to a generalization performed on a similar reference set. The opposite transmutation is *specialization*, which decreases the reference set. Specialization usually employs deductive inference, but there can also be an inductive or analogical specialization.

2. *Abstraction/concretion*
Abstraction reduces the amount of detail in a description of a given reference set. To do so, the description language may be changed to one that uses higher level concepts or operators that ignore details irrelevant to the reasoner's goal(s). Typically, abstraction is a truth-preserving operation, and therefore, the underlying inference is deduction. An opposite transmutation is *concretion*, which generates additional details about the reference set. Concretion is often done by induction.

3. *Similization/dissimilization*
Similization derives new knowledge about a reference set on the basis of the similarity between this set and another reference set, about which the learner has more knowledge. The opposite operation is *dissimilization*, which derives new knowledge on the basis of the lack of similarity between the compared reference sets. These transmutations are based on the patterns of inference presented in the theory of plausible reasoning by Collins and Michalski (1989). To illustrate a similization, assume that one knows that England grows roses and that England and Holland have similar climates. A similization transmutation is to hypothesize that Holland

may also grow roses. The underlying background knowledge here is that there exists a dependency between the climate of a place and the type of plants growing in that location. With this example, a dissimilization transmutation would be to infer that bougainvilleas probably do not grow in Holland because Holland has a very different climate from the Caribbean Islands where they are very popular. Similization and dissimilization are forms of analogical inference, which can be characterized as a combination of inductive and deductive inference (see Section 1.7).

4. *Explanation/prediction*
Explanation derives "explanatory knowledge" that strongly or plausibly implies given knowledge ("explanatory target") by exploring domain-specific background knowledge. A special case of explanation is a causal explanation that derives causes of the given facts by exploring causal relationships. A cognitive constraint on explanation is that the implicative relation between the explanatory knowledge and the explanatory target should be more or less direct and not through a long chain of inferences. An opposite transmutation is prediction that derives consequences of given knowledge. A discussion of different types of explanation is in Michalski (1993a). Depending on the type of inference used for deriving explanatory or predictive knowledge, explanations and predictions can be deductive, inductive, or analogical.

5. *Selection/generation*
The selection transmutation selects a subset from a set of entities (e.g., a set of knowledge components) that satisfies some criteria. For example, choosing a subset of relevant attributes from a set of candidates and determining the most plausible hypothesis among a set of candidate hypotheses are selection transmutations. The opposite transmutation is *generation*, which generates entities satisfying some criteria. For example, generating an attribute to characterize a given entity and creating an alternative hypothesis are forms of generation transmutation.

6. *Agglomeration/decomposition*
The agglomeration transmutation takes individual entities and groups them into units or a structure of units (e.g., hierarchy) according to some criterion. If it also hypothesizes that the units represent general patterns that also include unobserved entities, then it is called *clustering*. The grouping can be done according to a variety of principles, e.g., to maximize some mathematical notion of similarity as in conventional clustering or to maximize "conceptual cohesiveness" as in conceptual clustering (e.g., Stepp and Michalski [1983]). The opposite transmutation is a *decomposition* that takes a unit or a structure of units and determines individual entities.

7. *Characterization/discrimination*
A *characterization* transmutation determines a *characteristic* description of a class of entities that specifies properties of the class. A sufficiently specific characteristic

description will differentiate the given class from any other classes of entities. The basic form of a characteristic description is a conjunction of properties shared by all the entities in the class. The opposite transmutation is *discrimination*, which produces a description that discriminates the given class from a predetermined set of other classes (Michalski, 1983).

8. *Association/disassociation*
An association transmutation determines a dependency between given entities based on the observed facts and background knowledge. The dependency may be logical, causal, statistical, temporal, etc. Associating a concept instance with a concept name is an example of an association transmutation. The opposite transmutation is *disassociation*, which asserts a lack of dependency. For example, determining that a given instance is not an example of a given concept is a disassociation transmutation.

9. *Derivations: Reformulation/intermediate transmutations/randomization*
Derivations are transmutations that derive one piece of knowledge from another piece of knowledge based on some dependency between them but do not fall into the special categories described above. Because the dependency between knowledge units (statements or sets of semantically related statements) can range from a logical equivalence to a random relationship, derivations can be classified on the basis of the strength of dependency into a wide range of types. The extreme points of this range are *reformulation* and *randomization*. Reformulation transforms a knowledge unit into a logically equivalent unit. For example, mapping a geometrical object represented in a right-angled coordinate system into a radial coordinate system is a reformulation. In contrast, randomization transforms one knowledge unit into another one by making random changes. For example, the *mutation* operation in a genetic algorithm represents a randomization. Mathematical or logical transformations of knowledge also represent forms of derivation. A weak intermediate derivation is the *crossover* operator used in genetic algorithms, which derives new knowledge by exchanging two segments of related knowledge units.

10. *Insertion/deletion*
The insertion transmutation inserts a given knowledge component (e.g., a component generated by some other transmutation) into a given knowledge structure. An example of insertion is memorizing some fact. The opposite transmutation is *deletion*, which removes some knowledge component from a given structure. An example of deletion is forgetting.

11. *Replication/destruction*
Replication reproduces a knowledge structure residing in some knowledge base in another knowledge base. Replication is used, e.g., in *rote learning*. There is no change in the contents of the knowledge structure. The opposite transmutation is *destruction*, which removes a knowledge structure from a given knowledge base. The difference between destruction and deletion is that destruction removes a copy

of a knowledge structure that resides in some knowledge base, and deletion removes a component of a knowledge structure residing in the given knowledge base.

12. *Sorting/unsorting*
The sorting transmutation changes the organization of knowledge according to some syntactic criterion. For example, ordering decision rules in a rule base from the shortest (having the smallest number of conditions) to the longest is a sorting transmutation. An opposite operation is *unsorting*, which returns to the previous organization.

A summary of the above transmutations, together with the underlying types of inference, is presented in Figure 1.4. As mentioned earlier, depending on the way a transmutation is performed (which is determined by the amount of available background knowledge and the information in the input), any knowledge generation transmutation can involve any type of inference, i.e., deduction, induction, or analogy. This is illustrated by linking each transmutation with all three forms of inference. Exceptions to this rule are similization and dissimilization transmutations, which are based on analogy. A vertical link between lines stemming from the nodes denoting similarity/dissimilarity transmutations signifies that these transmutations combine deduction with induction: for an explanation, see Section 1.8.

Transmutations that employ induction, analogy, or contingent deduction increase the amount of intrinsically new knowledge in the system (knowledge that cannot be deduced conclusively from other knowledge in the system). Learning that produces intrinsically new knowledge is called *synthetic* (some authors call it "learning at the knowledge level" [Newell, 1981; Dietterich, 1986]).

Transmutations that employ only conclusive deduction increase the amount of *derived* knowledge in the system. Such knowledge is a logical consequence of what the learner already knows. Learning that changes only the amount of derived knowledge in the systems is called *analytic* (Michalski and Kodratoff, 1990). Transmutations are not independent processes. An implementation of one complex transmutation may involve performing other transmutations.

As mentioned earlier, the theory views transmutations as *types* of knowledge change and inferences as different *ways* in which these changes can be accomplished. This is a radical departure from the traditional view of these issues. The traditional view blurs the proposed distinctions; for example, it typically equates generalization with induction and specialization with deduction.

The proposed view stems from our efforts to provide an explanation of different operations on knowledge observed in people's reasoning and relate this explanation to formal types of inference in a consistent way. Experiments performed with human subjects have shown that the proposed ideas agree well with typical intuitions people have about different types of transmutations. Further research is needed to formalize these ideas precisely.

Knowledge Generation Transmutations

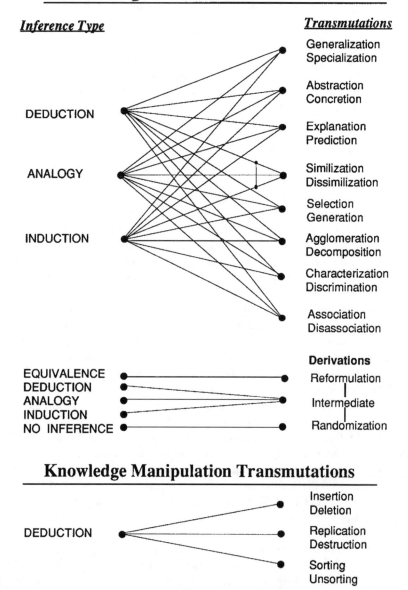

Figure 1.4: A summary of transmutations and the underlying types of inference

Learning is viewed as a sequence of goal-oriented knowledge transmutations. For example, a generation transmutation may generate a set of attributes to characterize given entities. Another generation transmutation may create examples expressed in terms of these attributes. A general description of these examples is created by generalization transmutation. By repeating different variants of a generalization transmutation, a set of alternative general descriptions of these examples can be determined. A selection transmutation would choose the "best" candidate description according to a criterion specified by the given learning goal. If a new example contradicts the description, a specialization transmutation would produce a new description that takes care of the inconsistency. The description obtained may be added to the knowledge base by an insertion transmutation. A replication transmutation may then copy this description into another knowledge base, e.g., may communicate the description to another learner. The next sections analyze some knowledge generation transmutations in greater detail, specifically, generalization, abstraction, and similization, and their opposites, specialization, concretion, and dissimilization, respectively.

1.7 GENERALIZATION VS. ABSTRACTION

This section analyzes two fundamental knowledge generation transmutations, generalization and abstraction, and their opposites, specialization and concretion. Generalization and abstraction are sometimes confused with each other; therefore, we provide an analysis of the differences between them. We start with generalization and specialization.

1.7.1 Generalization and Specialization

As stated earlier, our view of generalization is that it is a knowledge transmutation that extends the reference set of a given description. Depending on the background knowledge and the way it is used, generalization can be inductive, deductive, or analogical. Such a view of generalization is more general than the one traditionally expressed in the machine learning literature, which recognizes only one form of generalization, namely, inductive generalization.

Based on experiments with human subjects, we claim that the presented view more adequately captures common intuitions and the natural language usage of the term "generalization." To express the proposed view more rigorously, let us start with a more precise definition of the reference set than given previously.

Suppose S is a set of statements in predicate logic calculus. Suppose further that an argument of one or more predicates in statements in S stands for a set of entities and that S is interpreted as a description of or a referral to this set.

Under this interpretation, this set of entities is called the *reference set* for S. If the reference set is replaced by a set-valued variable, then the resulting expression is called a *descriptive schema* and is denoted by D[R], where R stands for the reference set.

For example, suppose given is a statement

S: In(John'sApt, Smoke)   (Smoke is in John's apartment.)

This statement can be interpreted as a referral to the set {John'sApt}. Thus, we have

D[R]:   In (R, Smoke)

R: John'sApt.

A given statement, if one ignores the context in which it is used, can often be interpreted in more than one way, from the viewpoints of what its reference set is and of what the corresponding descriptive schema is. For example, consider the statement: "George Mason lived at Gunston Hall." It can be interpreted as a description of "George Mason" (a singleton set), which specifies the place where he lived. It can also be interpreted as a description of "Gunston Hall," which specifies a special property of this place, namely, that George Mason lived there. The appropriate interpretation of a statement depends on the context in which it is used. For example, in the context of a discussion about George Mason, the first interpretation would apply, but if Gunston Hall is the object of a discussion, the second interpretation would apply.

Suppose that given are two sets of statements, S1 and S2, and that they are interpreted as having reference sets R1 and R2 and descriptive schemes D1 and D2, respectively; i.e., S1 = D1[R1], and S2 = D2[R2].

Definition.   The statement set S2 is more *general* than statement set S1 if and only if

R2 $\supset$ R 1   and

D2[R2] $\cup$ BK $\Rightarrow$ D1[R1]   (5')

        or

D1[R1] $\cup$ BK $\Rightarrow$ D2[R2]   (5'')

If condition (5') holds, S2 is an *inductive* generalization of S1; if condition (5'') holds, S2 is a *deductive* generalization of S1. By requiring that the compared statements satisfy an implicative relation in the context of given background knowledge, the definition allows one to compare the generality of statements that use different descriptive concepts or languages. Let us illustrate the above definition using examples from Section 1.5.

Example 1. (Empirical inductive generalization)

S1:   Pntng(GF, Dawski) & Btfl(GF)   (Dawski's painting, "A girl's
                                                          face," is beautiful.)

D1[R1]:   Pntng(R1, Dawski) & Btfl(R1)
R1:   GF   (GF is a singleton, {Girl's face}.)

S2: $\forall$x, Pntng(x, Dawski) $\Rightarrow$ Btfl(x)   (All ll Dawski's paintings
                                                          are beautiful.)

           Alternatively: Btfl(All_DPs)   (All_DPs denotes the set of
                                                          all Dawski's paintings.)

D2[R2]:   Btfl(R2)   (Paintings from the set R2 are beautiful.)
R2:   All_DPs   (It denotes all Dawski's paintings.)
BK: GF $\subset$ All_DPs

The interpretation of the predicate Btfl(R) is that the property Btfl applies to every element of the set R. Because R2 $\supset$ R1, and D2[R2] $\Rightarrow$ D1[R1], then S2 is more general than S1.

Example 2. (Deductive generalization)

S1:   Lives(John, Fairfax)   (John lives in Fairfax.)
D1[R1]:   Lives(John, R1)
R1:   Fairfax

S2:   Lives(John, Virginia)   (John lives in Virginia.)
D2[R2]:   Lives(John, R2)
R2:   Virginia
BK: Fairfax $\subset$ Virginia   (Fairfax is a part of Virginia.)

S2 is more general than S1 because R2 $\supset$ R1, and D1[R1] $\cup$ BK $\Rightarrow$ D2[R2].

In human reasoning, generalization is frequently combined with other types of transmutation, producing various composite transmutations. Here is an example of such a composite transmutation.

Example 3. (Inductive generalization and abduction)

S1:   In(John'sApt, Smoke)   (There is smoke in John's apartment.)
D1[R1]:   In (R1, Smoke)
R1:   John'sApt
BK: In(x, Smoke) <—> In(x, Fire)   (Smoke usually indicates fire
                                                          and conversely.)

John'sApt $\subset$ GKBld   (John's apartment is a part of
the Golden Key building.)

S2:   In(GKBld, Fire)
D2[R2]:   In(R2, Fire)
R2:   GKBldng

In this example, a generalization transmutation of the input produces a statement "Smoke is in the Golden Key building." An abductive derivation (or explanation) applied to the same input would produce a statement "There is fire in John's apartment." By applying abductive derivation to the output from generalization, one obtains a statement "There is fire in Golden Key building."

The above definition defined a generalization relation only between two sets of statements. Let us now extend this definition to the case where the input may be a collection of sets of statements. Such a case occurs in learning rules that generalize a set of examples (each example may be described by one or more statements).

Definition. The statement set, S, is a *generalization of a collection of statement sets* $\{S_i\}$, i=1,2,...,k, if and only if S is more general than each S_i.

To summarize, a generalization transmutation is a mapping from one description (input) to another description (output) that extends the reference set of the input.

A transmutation opposite to generalization is *specialization,* which reduces the reference set of a given set of statements. A typical form of specialization is deductive, but there can also be an inductive specialization (Figure 1.3). A reverse of the inductive specialization in Figure 1.3 is a deductive generalization:

Input	Lives(John, Fairfax)	(John lives in Fairfax.)
BK	Fairfax $\subset$ Virginia	(Fairfax is a "subset" of Virginia.)
	$\forall x,y,z, y \subset z$ & Lives(x,y) $\Rightarrow$ Lives(x,z)	(Living in y implies living in a superset of y.)

Output   Lives(John, Virginia)   (John lives in Virginia.)

In the above example, Fairfax and Virginia are interpreted as reference sets (sets of land parcels). The Input states that a property of Fairfax is that "John lives there." The property "Living in a set of land parcels" means occupying some elements of this set. This is an example of an *existential property* of a set, which is defined as a property that applies only to some unspecified elements of the set. Another example of an existential property would be a statement "Fairfax has an excellent library." If a set has an existential property, then so do its supersets. This is why the above inference is deductive.

In contrast, a *universal property* of a set applies to all elements of the set. If a set has such a property, so do all its subsets but not every superset. Thus, if in the above example, a universal property was used, e.g., "Soil(good, Fairfax)," a generalization transmutation to "Soil(good, Virginia)" would be inductive.

Generalization/specialization transmutations are related to another fundamental pair of transmutations, namely, abstraction/concretion. Generalization and abstraction often co-occur in commonsense reasoning, in particular, in inductive learning; therefore, they are easy to confuse with each other. It should also be noted that by changing the interpretation of a statement because of the change in the context of discourse, that is, by assigning the role of the reference set and descriptive schema to different statement components, deductive generalization could sometimes be *reinterpreted* as abstraction and inductive specialization as concretion. Thus, these two pairs of transmutations depend on the context in which statement(s) are interpreted. Abstraction and concretion are analyzed below.

1.7.2 Abstraction and Concretion

As stated earlier, abstraction reduces the amount of information conveyed by the descriptive schema of a given reference set. The typical purpose of abstraction is to reduce the amount of information about the reference set in such a way that the information relevant to the learner's goal is preserved, and the irrelevant information is discarded. For example, abstraction may translate a description from one language to another language in which the properties of the reference set relevant to the reasoner's goal are preserved, but other properties are not. An opposite operation to abstraction is *concretion*, which generates additional details about a given reference set.

A simple form of abstraction is to replace a specific attribute value (e.g., the length in centimeters) in the description of an entity with a less specific value (e.g., the length stated in linguistic terms, such as short, medium, or long). A complex form of abstraction would be, for example, to take a description of a computer in terms of electronic circuits and connections and, based on background knowledge, change it into a description in terms of the functions of its major components. Typically, abstraction is a form of deductive transmutation because it preserves the important information in the input and does not hypothesize any information (the latter may occur when the input or BK contain uncertain information).

Let us express this view of abstraction more formally. An early formal definition of abstraction was proposed by Plaisted (1981), who considered it as a mapping between languages that preserves instances and negation. A related but somewhat different view was presented by Giordana, Saitta, and Roverso (1991), who consider abstraction as a mapping between abstract models. In the view presented here, abstraction is a mapping between descriptions which creates a less detailed description from a more detailed description of the same set of entities (the reference set). Unlike generalization, it does not change the reference set; it only changes the level of precision in describing it.

Suppose that given are two sets of expressions, S1 and S2, that can be interpreted as having descriptive schemes D1 and D2, respectively, and the same reference set, R.

Definition. S2 is more *abstract* than S1 *in the context* of background knowledge BK and with *the degree of strength* α if and only if

$$D1[R] \cup BK \Rightarrow D2[R]: \alpha, \text{ where } \alpha \geq Th \tag{6}$$

and there is a homomorphic mapping between the set of properties specified in D1 and the set of properties specified in D2. The threshold Th denotes a limit of acceptability of transformation as abstraction.

The condition about homomorphic mapping is needed to exclude arbitrary deductive derivations. The most common form of abstraction is when (6) is a standard (conclusive) implication ($\alpha = 1$). In this case, the set of strong inferences (deductive closure) that can be derived from the output (abstract) description and BK is a proper subset of strong inferences that can be derived from the input description and BK. This case can be called a *strong* abstraction, in contrast to *weak* abstraction, which occurs when $\alpha < 1$. The introduction of the concept of weak abstraction is to allow abstractions that are not completely truth-preserving (as, e.g., in making drawings that only approximate the reality).

Comparing (5) and (6), one can see that an abstraction transmutation can be a part of an inductive generalization transmutation. The importance of abstraction for inductive generalization is that it ignores details that differentiate entities in the same class and, thus, allows the creation of a description of the whole class.

1.7.3 An Illustration of the Difference between Abstraction and Generalization

In commonsense usage, abstraction and generalization are sometimes confused with each other. To illustrate the difference between them, let us use a simple example. Consider a statement $d(\{r_i\},v)$, saying that descriptor d takes value v for entities from the set $\{r_i\}$. The reference set of this statement is $R = \{r_i\}$, $i = 1,2,...,$ and the descriptive schema is $D[R] = d(R,v)$. Let us write the above statement in the form

$$d(R) = v \tag{7}$$

Changing (7) to $d(R) = v'$, where v' represents a less precise characterization than v (e.g., is a parent node in a type hierarchy of values of the attribute d), is an abstraction transmutation. Changing (7) to a statement $d(R') = v$, in which R' is a superset of R, is a generalization transmutation.

For example, transferring the statement "color(my-pencil) = light-blue" into "color(my-pencil)=blue" is an abstraction operation. To see this, notice that [color(my-pencil) = light-blue] & (light-blue ⊂ blue) ⇒ [color(my-pencil) = blue]. Transforming the original statement into "color(all-my-pencils) = light-blue" is a generalization operation. Finally, transferring the original statement into "color(all-my-pencils) = blue" is both generalization and abstraction. In other words, associating the same property with a larger set is a generalization; associating less information with the same set is an abstraction.

An opposite transmutation to abstraction is *concretion*, which increases the amount of information that is conveyed by a statement(s) about the given reference set.

To summarize, the two pairs of mutually opposite transmutations, {generalization, specialization} and {abstraction, concretion}, differ in the aspects of knowledge they change. If a transmutation changes the size of the reference set of a description, then it is *generalization* or *specialization*. If a transmutation changes the amount of information (detail) conveyed by a description of a reference set, then it is *abstraction* or *concretion*. In other words, generalization (specialization) transforms descriptions along the set-superset (set-subset) direction and is typically falsity-preserving (truth-preserving). In contrast, abstraction (concretion) transforms descriptions along the more-to-less-detail (less-to-more-detail) direction and is typically truth-preserving (falsity-preserving). Generalization often uses the same description space (or language) for input and output statements, whereas abstraction often involves a change in the description space (or language). Abstraction and generalization often co-occur in learning processes.

1.8 SIMILIZATION VS. DISSIMILIZATION

The similization transmutation uses analogical inference to derive new knowledge. A dissimilization transmutation is based on the lack of analogy. As mentioned in Section 1.2, analogical reasoning can be considered as a combination of inductive and deductive inference. Before we demonstrate this claim, let us observe that an important part of our knowledge about the world is the knowledge of dependencies among various entities. These dependencies can be of different strengths or types, for example, functional, monotonic, correlational, general trend, statistical distribution, and relational. For example, we know that the dimensions of a rectangle exactly determine its area (this is a unidirectional functional dependency), that smoking often causes lung cancer (this is a weakly causal dependency), or that improving education of citizens is good for the country (this is an unquantified belief).

Such dependencies are often bi-directional, but the "strength" of the dependency in different directions may vary considerably. For example, from the fact that Martha is a heavy smoker, one may develop an expectation that she will likely develop a lung cancer later in her life; from learning that Betty has lung cancer, one may hypothesize that perhaps she was a smoker. The "strength" of these conclusions, however, is not equal. Betty may have lung cancer for other reasons, or she was married to a smoker. The dependencies can be known at different levels of specificity. In the past, the dependency between smoking and lung cancer was only suspected without much evidence backing it up; now we have a much more precise knowledge of this dependency and a lot of evidence indicating it.

Section 1.4 introduced the notion of mutual implication (eq. 2) for expressing a class of such relationships. Here we will extend the notion of mutual implication into a more general *mutual dependency*, which allows one to express a much wider class of relationships. The concept of mutual dependency is then used for describing similization and dissimilization transmutations.

As defined earlier, mutual implication expresses a relationship between two predicate logic statements (well-formed formulas; closed predicate logic sentences with no free variables). A mutual dependency expresses a relationship between two *sentences* that are both either predicate logic statements or term expressions (open predicate logic sentences in which some of the arguments are free variables).

To state that there is a mutual dependency (*m-dependency*) between two sentences S1 and S2, we write

$$S1 \Leftrightarrow S2: \alpha, \beta \tag{8}$$

where merit parameters α and β represent an overall *forward strength* and *backward strength* of the dependency, respectively. Merit parameters α and β represent the average certainty with which a value of S1 determines a value of S2 and conversely.

If S1 and S2 are statements (well-formed formulas), then m-dependency is an m-implication. If S1 and S2 are term expressions, then mutual dependency expresses a relationship between functions (because term expressions can be interpreted as functions). If term expressions in a mutual dependency are discrete functions, then the mutual dependency is logically equivalent to a set of mutual implications. A special case of m-dependency is *determination*, introduced by Russell (1989) and used for characterizing a class of analogical inferences. Determination is an m-dependency between term expressions in which α is 1, and β is unspecified, that is, a unidirectional functional m-dependency.

The concept of m-dependency allows us to describe the similization and dissimilization transmutations. These transmutations involve determining a *similarity* or *dissimilarity* between entities and then hypothesizing some new knowledge from this. The concept of similarity has been sometimes misunderstood in the past and viewed as an objective, context-independent property of objects. In fact, the similarity between any two entities is highly context-dependent. Any two entities (objects or sets of objects) can be viewed as boundlessly similar or boundlessly dissimilar, depending on what descriptors are used to characterize them or, in other words, what properties are used to compare the entities. Therefore, to talk meaningfully about a similarity between entities, one needs to indicate, explicitly or implicitly, the relevant descriptors. To express this, we use the concept of the *similarity in the context* of a given set of descriptors (introduced by Collins and Michalski [1989]). To say that entities E1 and E2 are similar to each other in context (CTX) of the descriptors in the set D, we write

E1 SIM E2 in CTX(D)   (9)

This statement says that values of the descriptors from D for the entity E1 and for the entity E2 differ no more than by some assumed tolerance threshold. For numerical descriptors, the threshold "Th" is expressed as a percentage, relative to the larger value. For example, if Th=10%, the values of the descriptor cannot differ more than 10%, relative to the larger value. Descriptors in D can be attributes, relations, functions, or any transformations applicable to the entities under consideration. The threshold expresses the required degree of similarity for triggering the inference.

The similization transmutation is a form of analogical inference and is defined by the following schema:

Input	E1 $\Rightarrow$ A
BK	E1 SIM E2 in CTX(D)
	D $\Rightarrow$ A: α > RT

Output	E2 $\Rightarrow$ A (10)

where α > RT states that the strength of the forward term dependency D $\Rightarrow$ A should be above a *relevance threshold*, RT, in order to trigger the inference. RT is a control parameter for the inference.

Given that entity E1 has property A and with the knowledge that there is a similarity between E1 and E2 in terms of descriptors defined by D, the rule hypothesizes that entity E2 may also have property A. This inference is allowed, however, if there is a dependency between the descriptors defined by D and the property A. The reason for the latter condition can be illustrated by the following example.

Suppose we know that some person who is handsome got their Ph.D. from MIT. It would not be reasonable to hypothesize that perhaps another person whom we find handsome also got her/his Ph.D. from MIT. The reason is that we do not expect any dependency between looks of a person and the university from which that person got the Ph.D. degree.

A dissimilization transmutation draws an inference from the knowledge that two entities are very different in the context of some descriptors. A dissimilization transmutation follows the schema

Input	E1 $\Rightarrow$ A
BK	E1 DIS E2 in CTX(D)
	D $\Rightarrow$ A: α > RT

| *Output* | E2 $\Rightarrow$ ~A | (11) |

where DIS denotes a relation of dissimilarity, other parameters are like in (10), and ~A denotes "not A ".

Given that some entity E1 has property A and knowing that entities E1 and E2 are very different in terms of descriptors that are in a mutual dependency relation with A, the transmutation hypothesizes that maybe E2 does not have the property A.

The following simple example illustrates a dissimilarity transmutation. Suppose we know that apples grow in Poland and are asked if oranges grow there. Knowing that apples are different from oranges in a number of properties, including the climate in which they normally grow, and that a climate of the area is m-dependent on the type of fruit grown there, one may hypothesize that perhaps oranges do not grow in Poland.

We will now illustrate the similization transmutation by a real-world example and then demonstrate that it involves a combination of inductive and deductive inference. To argue for a national, ultra-speed electronic communication network for linking industrial, governmental, and academic organizations in the U.S., its advocates used an analogy that "Building this network is an information equivalent of building national highways in the '50s and '60s." There is little physical similarity between building highways and electronic networks, but there is an end-effect similarity in that they both improve communication. Because building highways helped the country and, thus, was a good decision, then by analogy, building the national network will help the country and is a good decision.

Using the schema (10), we have

Input	Decision(Bld, NH) $\Rightarrow$ Effect-on(US, good)
BK	Decision(Bld, NH) SIM Decision(Bld, NN) in CTX (FutCom)
	FutCom (US, x) $\Rightarrow$ Effect-on(US, x): α > RT

| *Output* | Decision(Bld, NN) $\Rightarrow$ Effect-on(US. good) | (12) |

where NH stands for National Highways, NN stands for National Network, Decision(Bld, x) is a statement expressing the decision to build x, FutCom(area, state) is a descriptor expressing an evaluation of the future state of communication in the "area" that can take values "will improve" or "will not improve," and Effect-on (US, x) is a descriptor stating that "the effect on the U.S. is x."

We will now show how the general schema (10) can be split into an inductive and a deductive step.

An inductive step:

Input	E1 SIM E2 in CTX(D)
BK	D $\Leftrightarrow$ A: α > RT

Output   E1 SIM E2 in CTX(D, A)   (13)

From the similarity between two entities in terms of descriptor D and a mutual dependency between the descriptor and some new descriptor A, the schema hypothesizes a similarity between the entities also in terms of A. The deductive step uses the hypothesized relationship of similarity to derive new knowledge.

A deductive step:

Input	E1 SIM E2 in CTX(D, A)
BK	E1 $\Rightarrow$ A(a)

Output   E2 $\Rightarrow$ A(a)   (14)

where A(a) states that descriptor A is instantiated to take a specific value a.

Using the above schemes, we can now describe the previous example of similization in terms of an inductive and a deductive step.

An inductive step:

Input	Dec(Bld, NH) SIM Dec(Bld, NN) in CTX (Fut)
BK	FutCom(US, x) $\Rightarrow$ Effect-on(US, y): α > T

Output   Dec(Bld, NH) SIM Dec(Bld,NN)
             in CTX(FutCom,Effect-on)   (15)

A deductive step:

Input	Dec(Bld, NH) SIM Dec(Bld, NN) in CTX (FutCom, Effect-on)
BK	Dec(Bld, NH) $\Rightarrow$ Effect-on(US, good)

Output   Dec(Bld, NN) $\Rightarrow$ Effect-on(US, good)   (16)

From knowledge that the decision to build national highways is similar to the decision to build national networks in the context of communication in the U.S. and that communication in the U.S. has an effect on the U.S., the inductive step hypothesizes that there may be a similarity between two decisions also in terms of their effect on the U.S. The deductive step uses this similarity to derive a conclusion that building NN will have a good effect on the U.S. because building highways had a good effect. The validity of the deductive step rests on the strength of the hypothesis generated in the inductive step.

As mentioned earlier, an opposite of similization is dissimilization. The dissimilization reasoning pattern, as described by eq. 11, can also be split into an inductive or deductive step. More details on dissimilization are in Collins and Michalski (1989).

To summarize, similization, given some piece of knowledge, hypothesizes another piece of knowledge based on the assumption that if two entities are similar in terms of some properties (or transformations characterizing their relationship), then they may be similar in terms of other properties (or transformations). This holds, however, only if these other properties are sufficiently related by an m-dependency to the properties used for defining the similarity.

1.9 MULTISTRATEGY TASK-ADAPTIVE LEARNING

The ideas presented in previous sections provide a conceptual framework for *multistrategy task-adaptive learning* (MTL), which aims at integrating a whole range of learning strategies. An underlying idea of MTL is that a learning system should by itself determine the learning strategy, i.e., the types of inference to be employed and/or the representational paradigm that is most suitable for the given learning task (Michalski, 1990; Tecuci and Michalski, 1991a, 1991b). As introduced in Inferential Learning Theory, a learning task is defined by three components: what information is provided to the learner (i.e., *input* to the learning process), what information is already known by the learner that is relevant to the learning goal (i.e., *background knowledge* [BK]), and what it is that the learner wants to learn (i.e., the *goal* or *goals* of learning). Given an input, an MTL system analyzes its relationship to BK and the learning goals and, on that basis, determines a learning strategy or a combination of learning strategies. If an impasse occurs, a new learning task is assumed, and the learning strategy is determined accordingly.

The above characterization of MTL covers a wide range of systems, from "loosely coupled" systems that use the same representational paradigm and employ different inferential strategies as separate modules to "tightly coupled" (or "deeply integrated") systems in which individual strategies represent instantiations of one general knowledge and inference mechanism to *multirepresentational* multistrategy systems that can synergistically combine and adapt both the knowledge representation and inferential strategies to the learning task.

A general schema for Multistrategy Learning is presented in Figure 1.5. The input to a learning process is supplied either by the External World through Sensors or from a previous learning step.

The Control module directs all processes. The Actuators perform actions on the External World that are requested by the Control module, e.g., an action to get additional information. The input is filtered by the Selection module, which estimates the relevance of the input to the learning goal. Only information that is sufficiently relevant to the goal is passed through. The current learning goal is

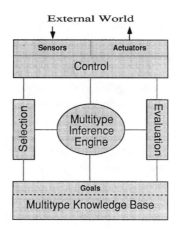

Figure 1.5: A general schema of a multistrategy task-adaptive learning (MTL) system

decided by the Control Module according to the information received from an external "master" system, e.g., teacher, or from the analysis of goals residing in the learner's knowledge base. The knowledge base is called Multitype Knowledge Base to emphasize the fact that it may contain, in the general case, different types of knowledge (various forms of symbolic, numeric, and iconic knowledge), which can be specified at different levels of abstraction.

Learning goals are organized into a *goal dependency network* (GDN), which captures the dependency among different goals. Goals are represented as nodes and the dependency among goals by labeled links. The labels denote the type and the strength of dependency. If a goal G1 subsumes goal G2, then node G1 has an arrow pointing to node G2. For example, the goal "Learn rules characterizing concept examples" subsumes the goal "Find concept examples" and is subsumed by the goal "Use rules for recognizing unknown concept instances." The idea of a GDN network was introduced by Stepp and Michalski (1983) and was originally used for conceptual clustering. In a general GDN for learning processes, the most general and domain-independent goal (represented by a node with no input links) is to store any given input and any plausible information that can be derived from it. More specific goals, though also domain-independent, are to learn certain types of knowledge.

For example, domain-independent goals may be to learn a general rule that characterizes facts supplied by the input, to reformulate a part of the learner's knowledge into a more efficient form, to determine knowledge needed for accomplishing some task, to develop a conceptual classification of given facts, to validate given knowledge, etc. Each of these goals is linked to some more specific subgoals. Some subgoals are domain-dependent, which call for determining some specific piece of knowledge, e.g., "learn basic facts about the Washington monument."

Such a goal in turn subsumes a more specific goal to "learn the height of the Washington monument."

Any learning step starts with the goal either defined directly by an external source or determined by the analysis of the current learning situation. The control module dynamically activates new goals in GDN as the learning process proceeds. The Multitype Inference Engine performs various types of inferences/transmutations required by the Control module in search of the knowledge specified by the current goal. Any knowledge generated is evaluated and critiqued by the Evaluation module from the viewpoint of the learning goal. If the knowledge satisfies the Evaluation module, it is assimilated into the knowledge base. It can then be used in subsequent learning processes.

Developing a learning system that would have all the features described above is a very complex problem and, thus, a long-term goal. Current research explores more limited approaches to Multistrategy-task adaptive learning. One such approach is based on building *plausible justification trees* (see Chapter 4 by Tecuci). Another approach, called *dynamic task analysis*, is outlined below. The learning system analyzes the dynamically changing relationship between the input, the background knowledge, and the current goal and, based on this analysis, controls the learning process. The approach uses a knowledge representation that is specifically designed to facilitate all basic forms of inference. The representation consists of collections of type (or generalization) hierarchies, part hierarchies (representing part-of relationships), and precedence hierarchies (representing ordered sets). The nodes of the hierarchies are interconnected by "traces" that represent observed or inferred knowledge. This form of knowledge representation, called DIH ("**D**ynamically **I**nterlaced **H**ierarchies"), allows the system to conduct different types of inference by modifying the location of the nodes connected by traces. This representation stems from the theory of human plausible reasoning proposed in Collins and Michalski (1989). Details are described in Hieb and Michalski (1993).

To give a very simple illustration of the underlying idea, consider a statement "Roses grow in the Summer." Such a statement would be represented in DIH as a "trace," linking the node *Roses* in the type hierarchy of *Plants* with the node *grow* in the type hierarchy of *Action*s and with the node *Summer* in the hierarchy of *Seasons*. By "moving" different nodes linked by the trace in different directions, different transmutations are performed. For example, moving the node *Roses* downward to Yellow *roses* would be a specialization transmutation; moving it upward to *Garden flowers* would be a generalization transmutation. Moving the node *Summer* horizontally to *Autumn* would be a similization transmutation.

In the dynamic task analysis approach, a learning step is activated when the system receives some input information. The input is classified into an appropriate category such as a fact, an example, a rule, etc. Depending on the category and the current goal, relevant segments of MKB are evoked. The next step determines the type of relationship that exists between the input information and BK. The method distinguishes among five basic types of relationship. The classification of the types presented below is only conceptual. It does not imply that a learning system needs to process each type by a separate module. In fact, because of the underlying knowledge representation (DIH), all these functions are integrated into one seamless system in which they are processed in a synergistic fashion. Here are the basic types of the relationship between the input and BK.

1. *The input represents pragmatically new information.*
An input is pragmatically new to the learner if no entailment relationship can be determined between it and BK, i.e., if it cannot be determined if it subsumes, it is subsumed by, or it contradicts BK within goal-dependent time constraints. The learner tries to identify parts of BK that are siblings of the input under the same node in some hierarchy (e.g., other examples of the concept represented by the input). If this effort succeeds, the related knowledge components are generalized, so that they now account for the input and, possibly, other information stored previously. The resulting generalizations and the input facts are evaluated for "importance" (to the goal) by the Evaluation module, and those that pass an *importance criterion* are stored. If the above effort does not succeed, the input is stored, and the control is passed to case 4. Generally, case 1 involves some form of synthetic learning (empirical learning, constructive induction, analogy) or learning by instruction.

2. *The input is implied by or implies BK.*
This case represents a situation when BK accounts for the input or is a special case of it. The learner creates a derivational explanatory structure that links the input with the involved part of BK. Based on the learning task, this structure can be used to create new knowledge that is more adequate ("operational," more efficient, etc.) for future handling of such cases. If the new knowledge passes an "importance criterion," it is stored for future use. This mechanism is related to the ideas on the utility of explanation based-learning (Minton, 1988). If the input represents a "useful" result of a problem solving activity, e.g., "given state x, it was found that a useful action is y" then the system tests its generality. If such a rule is sufficiently general so that it is likely to be evoked sufficiently often, then storing it is cost-effective. Such a mechanism is related to chunking used in SOAR (Laird, Rosenbloom, and Newell, 1986). If the input information (e.g., a rule supplied by a teacher) implies some part of BK, then an "importance criterion" is applied to it. If the criterion is satisfied, the input is stored, and an appropriate link is made to the part of BK that is implied by it. In general, this case handles situations requiring some form of analytic learning.

3. *The input contradicts BK.*
The system identifies the part of BK that is contradicted by the input information and then attempts to specialize this part. If the specialization involves too much

restructuring, or the confidence in the input is low, no change to this part of BK is made, but the input is stored. When some part of BK has been restructured to accommodate the input, the input also is stored but only if it passes an "importance criterion." If contradicted knowledge is a specific fact, this is noted, and any knowledge that was generated on the basis of the contradicted fact is to be revised. In general, this case handles situations requiring a revision of BK through some form of synthetic learning or inconsistency management.

4. *The input evokes an analogy to a part of BK.*
This case represents a situation when the input does not match any background fact or rule exactly, nor is it related to any part of BK in the sense of case 1; however, there is a similarity between the fact and some part of BK at some level of abstraction. In this case, matching is done at this level of abstraction, using generalized attributes or relations. If the fact passes an "importance criterion," it is stored with an indication of a similarity (analogy) to a background knowledge component and with a specification of the aspects (abstract attributes or relations) defining the analogy. For example, an input describing a lamp may evoke an analogy to the part of BK describing the sun because both lamp and sun match in terms of an abstract attribute "produces light."

5. *The input is already known to the learner.*
This case occurs when the input matches exactly some part of BK (a stored fact, a rule, or a segment). In such a situation, a measure of confidence and frequency parameter associated with this part is updated.

To summarize, an MTL learner may employ any type of inference and transmutation during learning. A deductive inference is employed when an input fact is consistent with, implies, or is implied by the background knowledge; analogical inference is employed when the input is similar to some part of past knowledge at some level of abstraction; and inductive inference is employed when there is a need to hypothesize a new knowledge. The above cases have been distinguished to indicate different types of learning that may occur in an MTL learner. By using proper knowledge representation (such as DIH), they all can be performed in a seamless way using one integrated mechanism.

1.10 AN ILLUSTRATION OF MTL

To illustrate the above-sketched ideas in terms of the inferential theory of learning, let us use a well-known example of learning—the concept of a "cup" (Mitchell, Keller, and Kedar-Cabelli, 1986). The example is deliberately oversimplified, so that major ideas can be presented in a simple way.

Figure 1.6 presents several inferential learning strategies as applicable to different learning tasks (defined by a combination of the input, BK, and the desired output). For each strategy, the figure shows the input and the background knowledge required by a given learning strategy and the produced output knowledge. The strategies are presented as independent processes only in a conceptual sense. In the actual implementation of MTL, all strategies are to be performed within one integrated inference system. The system specializes to any specific strategy using the same general computational mechanism based on Dynamic Interlaced Hierarchies (Hieb and Michalski, 1993).

In Figure 1.6, the name "obj" (in small letters) denotes a variable; the name "CUP1" (in capital letters) denotes a specific object. It defines a cup as an object that is an open vessel that is stable and liftable. The top part of the figure presents

- An *abstract concept description* (*Abstract CD*) for the concept "cup"

OD and CD stand for object description and concept description, respectively. CUP1 stands for a specific cup; obj denotes a variable. BK' denotes some limited background knowledge, e.g., a specification of the value sets of the attributes and their types.

An abstract concept description characterizes a concept in abstract terms, i.e., in terms that are assumed not to be directly observable or measurable. Here, it states that a cup is an open vessel that is stable and liftable. Individual conditions are linked to the concept name by arrows.

- The *domain rules*

These rules (formally, m-implications) relate abstract terms to observable or measurable properties ("operational" properties). These rules permit the deriving (deductively) of abstract properties from operational properties or the hypothesizing (abductively) of operational properties from abstract ones. For example, the abstract property "open vessel" can be derived from the observed (operational) property that the object is "up-concave" or that the object is "stable" if it has "flat bottom."

- A *specific object description* (*Specific OD*) of an example of a cup

Such a description characterizes a specific object (here, a cup) in terms of operational properties. By an example of a concept is meant a specific OD that is associated with the concept name.

- An *abstract object description* (*Abstract OD*)

Such a description characterizes a specific object in abstract terms. It is not a generalization of an object because its reference set is still the same object. Here, this description characterizes the specific cup, CUP1, in terms of abstract properties.

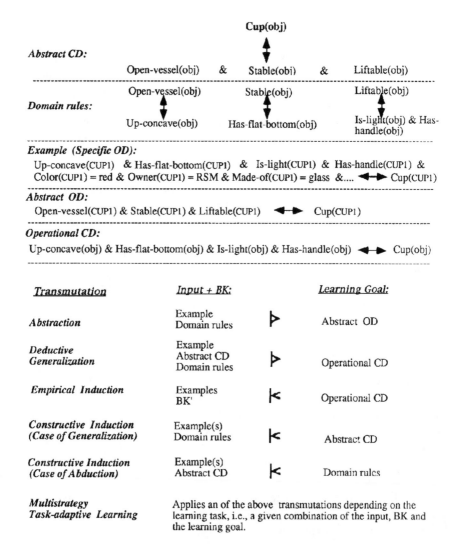

Abstract CD:

Cup(obj)

Open-vessel(obj)   &   Stable(obj)   &   Liftable(obj)

Domain rules:

Open-vessel(obj)   Stable(obj)   Liftable(obj)

Up-concave(obj)   Has-flat-bottom(obj)   Is-light(obj) & Has-handle(obj)

Example (Specific OD):

Up-concave(CUP1) & Has-flat-bottom(CUP1) & Is-light(CUP1) & Has-handle(CUP1) &
Color(CUP1) = red & Owner(CUP1) = RSM & Made-of(CUP1) = glass &.... ◀--▶ Cup(CUP1)

Abstract OD:

Open-vessel(CUP1) & Stable(CUP1) & Liftable(CUP1) ◀--▶ Cup(CUP1)

Operational CD:

Up-concave(obj) & Has-flat-bottom(obj) & Is-light(obj) & Has-handle(obj) ◀--▶ Cup(obj)

<u>Transmutation</u>	<u>Input + BK:</u>		<u>Learning Goal:</u>
Abstraction	Example Domain rules	▷	Abstract OD
Deductive *Generalization*	Example Abstract CD Domain rules	▷	Operational CD
Empirical Induction	Examples BK'	◁	Operational CD
Constructive Induction *(Case of Generalization)*	Example(s) Domain rules	◁	Abstract CD
Constructive Induction *(Case of Abduction)*	Example(s) Abstract CD	◁	Domain rules
Multistrategy *Task-adaptive Learning*	Applies an of the above transmutations depending on the learning task, i.e., a given combination of the input, BK and the learning goal.		

OD and CD stand for object description and concept description, respectively. CUP1 stands for a specific cup; obj denotes a variable. BK' denotes some limited background knowledge, e.g., a specification of the value sets of the attributes and their types. Symbol <--> stands for mutual implication in which the merit parameters (the backward and the forward strength) are unspecified. Symbols |> and |< denote deductive and inductive transmutations, respectively.

Figure 1.6:   An illustration of inferential strategies

- An *operational concept description* (*Operational CD*)

This description characterizes the concept in observable or measurable terms ("operational" terms). Such a description is used for recognizing the object from observable or measurable properties of the object. Notice that the argument of the predicates here is not some specific cup but the variable "obj."

The bottom part of the figure specifies several basic learning strategies (corresponding to the primary inferential transmutation involved) and presents learning tasks to which they apply. For each strategy, the input to the process, the background knowledge (BK), and the goal description are specified.

The input and BK are related to the goal description by a symbol indicating the type of the underlying inference: |> for deduction and |< for induction. A description of an object or a concept is associated with a concept name by a mutual dependency relation <—> (without defining the merit parameters). The mutual dependency can be viewed as a generalization of the *concept assignment operator* "::>" that is sometimes used in machine learning literature for linking a concept description with the corresponding concept name.

Using the m-implication allows one to express the fact that if an unknown entity matches the left-hand-side of the m-implication, then this entity can be classified to a given concept, and conversely, if one knows that an entity represents a concept on the right-hand-side, then one can hypothesize properties stated on the left-hand-side of the m-implication. The mutual implication sign also signifies that the general concept description is a hypothesis rather than a proven generalization.

1.11 SUMMARY

This chapter presented the Inferential Theory of Learning that provides a unifying theoretical framework for characterizing logical capabilities of learning processes. It also outlined its application to the development of a methodology for multistrategy task-adaptive learning (MTL). The theory analyzes learning processes in terms of generic patterns of knowledge transformation, called transmutations (or transforms). Transmutations take input information and background knowledge and generate some new knowledge. They represent either different patterns of inference ("knowledge generation transmutations") or different patterns of knowledge manipulation ("knowledge manipulation transmutations"). Knowledge generation transmutations change the logical content of input knowledge. Knowledge generation transmutations perform managerial operations that do not change the knowledge content. Transmutations can be performed using any kind of inference—deduction, induction, or analogy. The theory views any form of learning as a search in knowledge spaces. The search operators are instantiations of knowledge transmutations.

Several fundamental knowledge generation transmutations have been described in a novel way and illustrated by examples: generalization, abstraction, and similization and their opposites. They were shown to differ in terms of the aspects of knowledge that they change. Specifically, generalization and specialization change the reference set of a description, abstraction and concretion change the level-of-detail of a description of the reference set, and similization and dissimilization hypothesize new knowledge about a reference set based on the similarity or lack of similarity between the source and the target reference sets. By analyzing diverse learning strategies and methods in terms of abstract, implementation-independent transmutations, the Inferential Theory of Learning offers a very general view of learning processes. Such a view provides a clear understanding of the roles and the applicability conditions of diverse inferential learning strategies and facilitates the development of a theoretically well-founded methodology for building multistrategy learning systems.

The theory was used to outline a methodology for multistrategy task-adaptive learning (MTL). An MTL system determines by itself which strategy or which combination of strategies, is most suitable for a given learning task. A learning task is defined by the input, background knowledge, and the learning goal. MTL aims at integrating such strategies as empirical and constructive generalization, abductive derivation, deductive generalization, abstraction, and analogy.

Many ideas presented here are at an early stage of development, and a number of topics need to be explored in future research. More work is needed on the formalization of the proposed transmutations, on a clarification of their interrelationships, and on the identification and analysis of other types of knowledge transmutations. Future research needs to address also the problem of the role of goal structures, their representation, and the methods for their use for guiding learning processes.

Open problems also include the development of an effective method for measuring the amount of knowledge change resulting from different transmutations and the amount of knowledge contained in various knowledge structures in the context of a given BK. Other important research topics are to systematically analyze existing learning algorithms and paradigms using concepts of the theory, that is, to describe them in terms of knowledge transmutations employed. A research problem of significant practical value is to use the theory for determining criteria for the most effective applicability of different learning strategies in diverse learning situations.

The proposed approach to multistrategy task-adaptive learning was only briefly sketched. Further research is needed to demonstrate its feasibility. Future research should also investigate different approaches to the implementation of multistrategy task-adaptive learning, investigate their relationships, and implement experimental systems that synergistically integrate all major learning strategies. It is hoped that the presented research, despite its early state, provides useful insights into the complexities of research in multistrategy learning and will stimulate the reader to undertake some of the indicated research topics.

ACKNOWLEDGMENTS

The author thanks Thomas Arciszewski, David Duff, Mike Hieb, David Hille, Ibrahim Imam, Marcus Maloof, Elizabeth Marchut-Michalski, Ray Mooney, Lorenza Saitta, David A. Schum, Gheorghe Tecuci, Brad Whitehall, Janusz Wnek, his students from Machine Learning and Inference classes, and unknown reviewers for many constructive suggestions and criticisms that substantially helped in the preparation of the final version of this chapter.

This research was done in the Center for Artificial Intelligence at George Mason University. The Center's research is supported in part by the National Science Foundation under Grant No. IRI-9020266; in part by the Office of Naval Research under Grant No. N00014–91-J-1351; and in part by the Advanced Research Projects Agency under Grant No. N00014–91-J-1854, administered by the Office of Naval Research, and Grant No. F49620–92-J-0549, administered by the Air Force Office of Scientific Research.

References

Adler, M.J. and Gorman, W. (Eds.), The Great Ideas: A Syntopicon of Great Books of the Western World, Vol. 1, Ch. 39 (Induction), pp. 565–571, Encyclopedia Britannica, Inc., Chicago, 1987.

Aristotle, Posterior Analytics, in *The Works of Aristotle*, Volume 1, Hutchins, R.M. (Ed.), Encyclopedia Britannica, Inc., Chicago, 1987.

Bacon, F., *Novum Organum*, in Great Books of the Western World, Hutchins, R.M. (Ed.), Vol. 30, Encyclopedia Britannica, Inc., Chicago, 1987.

Baroglio, C., Botta, M. and Saitta, L., WHY: A System That Learns Using Causal Models and Examples, in *Machine Learning: A Multistrategy Approach, Volume IV*, Michalski, R.S. and Tecuci, G. (Eds.), Morgan Kaufmann Publishers, San Mateo, CA, 1994.

Bergadano, F., Matwin, S., Michalski, R.S. and Zhang, J., "Learning Two-tiered Descriptions of Flexible Concepts: The POSEIDON System," *Machine Learning*, Vol. 8, pp. 5–43, 1992 (originally published in *Machine Learning and Inference Reports,* No. MLI-3, Center for Artificial Intelligence, George Mason University, September 1990).

Birnbaum, L. and Collins, G. (Eds.) *Proceedings of the 8th International Conference on Machine Learning*, Chicago, June 1991.

Bloedorn, E. and Michalski, R.S., Data-Driven Constructive Induction, *Proceedings of the 3rd. International Conference on Tools for Artificial Intelligence*, IEEE Computer Society Press, San Jose, CA, 1991.

Carbonell, J.G., Michalski R.S. and Mitchell, T.M., "An Overview of Machine Learning," in *Machine Learning: An Artificial Intelligence Approach,*" Michalski, R.S., Carbonell, J.G. and Mitchell, T.M. (Eds.), Morgan Kaufmann Publishers, San Mateo, CA, 1983.

Cohen, L.J., *The Implications of Induction*, London, 1970.

Collins, A. and Michalski, R.S., "The Logic of Plausible Reasoning: A Core Theory," *Cognitive Science*, Vol. 13, pp. 1–49, 1989.

Console, L., Theseider, D. and Torasso, P., On the Relationship between Abduction and Deduction, *Journal of Logic and Computation*, Vol. 1, No. 5, October 1991.

Danyluk, A.P., "The Use of Explanations for Similarity-Based Learning," *Proceedings of IJCAI-87*, pp. 274–276, Morgan Kaufmann Publishers, San Mateo, CA, 1987.

————, "Recent Results in the Use of Context for Learning New Rules," Technical Report No. TR-98–066, Philips Laboratories, 1989.

————, Gemini: An Integration of Analytical and Empirical Learning, in *Machine Learning: A Multistrategy Approach, Volume IV*, Michalski, R.S. and Tecuci, G. (Eds.), Morgan Kaufmann Publishers, San Mateo, CA, 1994.

De Raedt, L. and Bruynooghe, M., "Interactive Theory Revision," in *Machine Learning: A Multistrategy Approach, Volume IV*, Michalski, R.S. and Tecuci, G. (Eds.), Morgan Kaufmann Publishers, San Mateo, CA, 1994.

Dietterich, T.G., "Limitations on Inductive Learning," *Proceedings of the 6th International Workshop on Machine Learning*, Morgan Kaufmann Publishers, San Mateo, CA, pp. 124–128, 1989.

————, "Learning at the Knowledge Level," *Machine Learning*, Vol. 1, No. 3, pp. 287–316, 1986 (reprinted in J.W. Shavlik and T.G. Dietterich (Eds.) *Readings in Machine Learning*, Morgan Kaufmann Publishers, San Mateo, CA, 1990).

Dietterich, T.G. and Flann, N.S., "An Inductive Approach to Solving the Imperfect Theory Problem," *Proceedings of the 1988 Symposium on Explanation-based Learning*, pp. 42–46, Stanford University, 1988.

Fulk, M. and Case, J., *Proceedings of the 3rd Annual Workshop on Computational Learning Theory*, University of Rochester, NY, August 6–8, 1990.

Giordana, A., Saitta, L. and Roverso, D., "Abstracting Concepts with Inverse Resolution," *Proceedings of the 8th International Workshop on Machine Learning*, pp. 142–146, Morgan Kaufmann, San Mateo, CA, June 1991.

Goldberg, D.E., *Genetic Algorithms in Search, Optimization, and Machine Learning*, Addison-Wesley, Reading, MA, 1989.

Goodman, L.A. and Kruskal, W.H., *Measures of Association for Cross Classifications*, Springer-Verlag, New York, 1979.

Grosof, B.N. and Russell, S. "Declarative Bias for Structural Domains," *Proceedings of the Sixth International Workshop on Machine Learning*, Morgan Kaufmann Publishers, San Mateo, CA, 1989.

Hieb, M. and Michalski, R.S., "A Knowledge Representation System Based on Dynamically Interlaced Hierarchies: Basic Ideas and Examples," *Reports of Machine Learning and Inference Laboratory*, Center for Artificial Intelligence, George Mason University, 1993.

Hunter, L., "Planning to Learn," *Proceedings of the Twelfth Annual Conference of the Cognitive Science Society*, pp. 26–34, Lawrence Erlbaum Associates, Hillsdale, NJ, 1990.

Kodratoff, Y. and Michalski, R.S. (Eds.), *Machine Learning: An Artificial Intelligence Approach, Volume III*, Morgan Kaufmann Publishers, San Mateo, CA, 1990.

Kodratoff, Y., and Tecuci, G., "DISCIPLE-1: Interactive Apprentice System in Weak Theory Fields," *Proceedings of IJCAI-87*, pp. 271–273, Morgan Kaufmann Publishers, San Mateo, CA, 1987.

Laird, J.E. (Ed.), *Proceedings of the Fifth International Conference on Machine Learning*, University of Michigan, Ann Arbor, MI, June 12–14, 1988.

Laird, J.E., Rosenbloom, P.S. and Newell A., "Chunking in SOAR: The Anatomy of a General Learning Mechanism," *Machine Learning*, Vol. 1, No. 1, pp. 11–46, 1986.

Lebowitz, M., "Integrated Learning: Controlling Explanation," *Cognitive Science*, Vol. 10, No. 2, pp. 219–240, 1986.

Michalski, R.S., "Theory and Methodology of Inductive Learning," *Machine Learning: An Artificial Intelligence Approach*, pp. 83–134, Michalski, R.S., Carbonell, J.G. and Mitchell T. M., (Eds.), Morgan Kaufmann Publishers, San Mateo, CA, 1983.

————, "A Methodological Framework for Multistrategy Task-adaptive Learning," *Proceedings of the Fifth International Symposium on Methodologies for Intelligent Systems*, Elsevier, NY, 1990a.

————, Learning Flexible Concepts: Fundamental Ideas and a Method Based on Two-tiered Representation, in *Machine Learning: An Artificial Intelligence Approach Volume III*, pp. 63–111 Kodratoff, Y. and Michalski, R.S. (Eds.), Morgan Kaufmann Publishers, San Mateo, CA, 1990b.

————, "Toward a Unified Theory of Learning: An Outline of Basic Ideas," *Proceedings of the First World Conference on the Fundamentals of Artificial Intelligence*, De Glas, M., and Gabbay, D. (Eds.), Paris, France, July 1–5, 1991.

————, "Toward a Unified Theory of Learning: Multistrategy Task-adaptive Learning," in *Readings in Knowledge Acquisition and Learning: Automating the Construction and Improvement of Expert Systems*, Buchanan, B.G. and Wilkins, D.C. (Eds.) pp. 7–38, Morgan Kaufmann Publishers, San Mateo, CA, 1993a (originally published in *Reports of Machine Learning and Inference Laboratory*, MLI-90–1, Center for AI, George Mason University, January 1990.)

————, "Inferential Theory of Learning as a Conceptual Framework for Multistrategy Learning," *Machine Learning Journal* (Special Issue on Multistrategy Learning), Vol. 11, Nos. 2 and 3, 1993b.

Michalski, R.S. and Kodratoff, Y., "Research in Machine Learning: Recent Progress, Classification of Methods and Future Directions," in *Machine Learning: An Artificial Intelligence Approach Volume III*, pp. 3–30, Kodratoff, Y. and Michalski, R.S. (Eds.), Morgan Kaufmann Publishers, San Mateo, CA, 1990.

Minton, S., "Quantitative Results Concerning the Utility of Explanation-based Learning," *Proceedings of AAAI-88*, pp. 564–569, AAAI Press, Menlo Park, CA, 1988.

Minton, S., Carbonell, J.G., Etzioni, O., Knoblock, C.A. and Kuokka, D.R., "Acquiring Effective Search Control Rules: Explanation-based Learning in the PRODIGY System," *Proceedings of the 4th International Machine Learning Workshop*, pp. 122–133, Morgan Kaufmann Publishers, San Mateo, CA, 1987.

Mitchell, T.M., Keller, T. and Kedar-Cabelli, S., "Explanation-based Generalization: A Unifying View," *Machine Learning*, Vol. 1, No. 1, 47–80, 1986.

Mooney, R.J. and Ourston, D., A Multistrategy Approach to Theory Refinement, in *Machine Learning: A Multistrategy Approach, Volume IV*, Michalski, R.S. and Tecuci, G. (Eds.), Morgan Kaufmann Publishers, San Mateo, CA, 1994.

Muggleton, S., "A Strategy for Constructing New Predicates in First-order Logic," *Proceedings of EWSL-88*, Glasgow, Scotland, pp. 123–130, 1988.

Muggleton, S. (Ed.), *Inductive Logic Programming*, Academic Press, San Diego, CA, 1992.

Newell, "The Knowledge Level," *AI Magazine*, No. 2, 1–20, 1981.

Pazzani, M.J., "Integrating Explanation-based and Empirical Learning Methods in OCCAM," *Proceedings of EWSL-88*, pp. 147–166, Glasgow, Scotland, 1988.

Peirce, C.S., "Elements of Logic," in *Collected Papers of Charles Sanders Peirce* (1839–1914), Hartshorne, C. and Weiss, P. (Eds.), Harvard University Press, Cambridge, MA, 1965.

Pearl, J., *Probabilistic Reasoning in Intelligent Systems: Networks of Plausible Inference*, Morgan Kaufmann Publishers, San Mateo, CA, 1988.

Piatetsky-Shapiro, G., "Probabilistic Data Dependencies," *Proceedings of the ML92 Workshop on Machine Discovery*, Zytkow, J.M. (Ed.), Aberdeen, Scotland, July 4, 1992.

Plaisted, D., "Theorem Proving with Abstraction," *Artificial Intelligence*, Vol. 16, 47–108, 1981.

Polya, G., *Mathematics and Plausible Reasoning*, Vols. I and II, Princeton University Press, Princeton, NJ, 1968.

Poole, D., "Explanation and Prediction: An Architecture for Default and Abductive Reasoning," *Computational Intelligence*, No. 5, pp. 97–110, 1989.

Popper, K.R., *Objective Knowledge: An Evolutionary Approach*, Oxford University Press, New York, 1972.

Porter, B.W. and Mooney, R.J. (Eds.), *Proceedings of the 7th International Machine Learning Conference*, Austin, TX, 1990.

Ram, A., "A Theory of Questions and Question Asking," *The Journal of the Learning Sciences*, Vol.1, Nos. 3 and 4, pp. 273–318, 1991.

Ram, A. and Hunter, L., "The Use of Explicit Goals for Knowledge to Guide Inference and Learning," *Applied Intelligence*, No. 2, pp. 47–73, 1992.

Rivest, R., Haussler D. and Warmuth, M., *Proceedings of the Second Annual Workshop on Computational Learning Theory,* Santa Cruz, CA, July 31–August 2, 1989.

Russell, S., *The Use of Knowledge in Analogy and Induction,* Morgan Kaufmann Publishers, San Mateo, CA, 1989.

Schafer, D., (Ed.), *Proceedings of the 3rd International Conference on Genetic Algorithms,* George Mason University, Fairfax, VA, June 4–7, 1989.

Schultz T.R. and Kestenbaum N.R., Causal Reasoning in Children, *Annals of Child Development,* Vol. 2, Whitehurst, G.J. (Ed.), pp. 195–249, JAI Press Inc., Greenwich, CT, 1985.

Segre, A.M. (Ed.), *Proceedings of the Sixth International Workshop on Machine Learning,* Cornell University, NY, June 26–27, 1989.

Sleeman, D. and Edwards, P., *Proceedings of the Ninth International Workshop,* Aberdeen, UK, July 1–3, 1992.

Stepp, R.S. and Michalski, R.S., "How to Structure Structured Objects," *Proceedings of the International Machine Learning Workshop,* Urbana, IL, June 22–24, 1983.

Tecuci, G. "Plausible Justification Trees: A Framework for Deep and Dynamic Integration of Learning Strategies," *Machine Learning Journal* (Special Issue on Multistrategy Learning), Vol. 11, 1993. See also chapter 4 of this book.

Tecuci, G. and Michalski, R.S., "A Method for Multistrategy Task-adaptive Learning Based on Plausible Justifications," in Birnbaum, L., and Collins, G. (Eds.), *Machine Learning: Proceedings of the Eighth International Workshop,* Morgan Kaufmann Publishers, San Mateo, CA, 1991a.

Tecuci G. and Michalski R.S., "Input 'Understanding' as a Basis for Multistrategy Task-adaptive Learning," *Proceedings of the 6th International Symposium on Methodologies for Intelligent Systems,* Ras, Z. and Zemankova, M., (Eds.), Lecture Notes on Artificial Intelligence, Springer Verlag, New York, 1991b.

Touretzky, D., Hinton, G. and Sejnowski, T. (Eds.), *Proceedings of the 1988 Connectionist Models Summer School,* Pittsburgh, PA, June 17–26, 1988.

Utgoff, P., "Shift of Bias for Inductive Concept Learning," in *Machine Learning: An Artificial Intelligence Approach, Volume II,* Michalski, R.S., Carbonell, J.G., and Mitchell, T.M. (Eds.), Morgan Kaufmann Publishers, San Mateo, CA, 1986.

Utgoff, P. (Ed.), *Proceedings of the Tenth International Conference on Machine Learning,* Amherst, MA, June 27–29, 1993.

Warmuth, M. and Valiant, L. (Eds.) *Proceedings of the 4th Annual Workshop on Computational Learning Theory,* Morgan Kaufmann Publishers, San Mateo, CA, 1991.

Whewell, W., *History of the Inductive Sciences,* 3 vols., 3rd edition, London, 1857.

Whitehall, B.L., "Knowledge-based Learning: Integration of Deductive and Inductive Learning for Knowledge Base Completion," *Ph.D. Thesis,* Computer Science Department, University of Illinois at Champaign-Urbana, 1990.

Whitehall, B.L. and Lu, S.C-Y., Theory Completion Using Knowledge-Based Learning, in *Machine Learning: A Multistrategy Approach, Volume IV*, Michalski, R.S. and Tecuci, G. (Eds.), Morgan Kaufmann Publishers, San Mateo, CA, 1994.

Wilkins, D.C., Clancey, W.J. and Buchanan, B.G., *An Overview of the Odysseus Learning Apprentice*, Kluwer Academic Press, New York, 1986.

Wnek, J. and Michalski, R.S., "Hypothesis-Driven Constructive Induction in AQ17: A Method and Experiments," *Proceedings of the IJCAI-91 Workshop on Evaluating and Changing Representation in Machine Learning*, Morik, K., Bergadano, F. and Buntine, W. (Eds.), pp. 13–22, Morgan Kaufmann, San Mateo, CA, 1991a.

———, "An Experimental Comparison of Symbolic and Subsymbolic Learning Paradigms: Phase I—Learning Logic-style Concepts," *Proceedings of the First International Workshop on Multistrategy Learning*, Michalski, R.S. and Tecuci, G. (Eds.), Harpers Ferry, VA, Nov. 7–9, 1991b.

———, "Comparing Symbolic and Subsymbolic Learning: Three Studies," in *Machine Learning: A Multistrategy Approach, Volume IV*, Michalski, R.S. and Tecuci, G. (Eds.), Morgan Kaufmann Publishers, San Mateo, CA, 1994.

Zadrozny, W. "The Logic of Abduction (Preliminary Report)," *First International Workshop on Principles of Diagnosis*, Stanford, CA, 1990.

APPENDIX: A TABLE OF SYMBOLS AND ABBREVIATIONS

$\cup$	Set-theoretical union
$\subset$	Subset relation
$\supset$	Superset relation
$\models$	Logical (conclusive) entailment
$\approx\!\!\models$	Plausible (contingent) entailment
$\sim$	Logical "NOT"
&	Logical "AND"
$\Rightarrow$	Logical implication or unidirectional mutual implication
$A \Leftrightarrow B: \alpha, \beta$	Mutual dependency (or m-dependency) between A and B (If A and B are statements, i.e., well-formed logical expressions, then m-dependency becomes mutual implication; if A and B are terms, then m-dependency represents a mutual relationship between terms. Parameters α and β, called merit parameters, express the forward and backward strength of the dependency, respectively.)
$A <\!\!-\!\!> B$	Mutual dependency in which merit parameters are not specified
$\forall x, P(x)$	Universal quantification (for every x, P is true)

|>	Deductive knowledge transmutation
|<	Inductive knowledge transmutation
BK	Background knowledge
SIM	Similarity relation
DIS	Dissimilarity relation
CTX(D)	The context for measuring the similarity or dissimilarity between two entities (It is specified by the descriptor set D.)
D[R]	Descriptive schema of the reference set R
R	The reference set of a description
ITL	Inferential theory of learning
m-dependency	Mutual dependency (see above)
m-implication	Mutual implication (see above)
MTL	Multistrategy task-adaptive learning
OD	Object description
CD	Concept description

2

THE FICTION AND
NONFICTION OF FEATURES

Edward J. Wisniewski
(Northwestern University)

Douglas L. Medin
(University of Michigan)

Abstract

This chapter discusses feature construction in human learning. It suggests that people use a multistrategy approach to construct features in the sense that they rely on a variety of sources of knowledge to derive features. In particular, feature construction is modifiable and interacts with knowledge sources such as previous training items and expectations about a category. In contrast, feature selection models do not incorporate construction processes into their learning algorithms, and construction processes in explanation-based learning are not usually general, flexible, or modifiable. We discuss the significance of these findings for machine learning systems.

2.1 INTRODUCTION

Feature construction is the process of mapping existing features onto new ones (Matheus and Rendell, 1989). In this chapter, the terms *feature* and *feature construction* are used broadly. The term *feature* is used in an informal sense to mean any property or characteristic that is true of an object or class of objects and that may vary in terms of its abstractness. To illustrate, consider a drawing of a person, shown in Figure 2.1. The features that describe the drawing can exist at

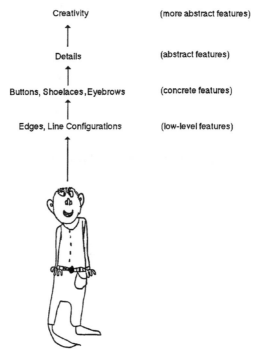

Creativity　　　　　　(more abstract features)

Details　　　　　　(abstract features)

Buttons, Shoelaces, Eyebrows　　　　(concrete features)

Edges, Line Configurations　　　　(low-level features)

Figure 2.1:　Levels of features

multiple levels of abstraction. At one level, the drawing can be viewed as a set of low-level features (e.g., edges, configurations of lines). At a higher level of abstraction, these features can be viewed as more concrete ones, such as "buttons," "shoelaces," and "eyebrows." At an even higher level, these features can be viewed as examples of an abstract feature such as "detailed." A feature such as "detailed" might in turn be viewed as indicating "creativity." In similar fashion, feature construction is any process that maps features from one level onto another level (e.g., "edges" and "line configurations" onto "buttons").

Learning systems can broadly be divided into those that select features and those that construct them (Michalski, 1983). Feature selection models assume that training items are described by a space of well-defined features. Learning involves selecting some subset of this space that typically allows the system to distinguish members of a category from nonmembers (e.g., Mitchell, 1982; Quinlan, 1986; Fisher, 1987; Nosofsky, 1988; J.R. Anderson, 1990). In contrast, feature construction models augment the space of features that describe the training items by inferring or creating additional features. These systems are typically called *constructive induction systems* (e.g., Michalski, 1980; Matheus and Rendell, 1989; Pagallo, 1989). They use a variety of methods to construct features, including those that are knowledge-driven, data-driven, hypothesis-driven, or multistrategy (see Wnek and Michalski, 1991, for a review). A number of constructive induction systems create new features by *combining* existing features in various ways. For example, some systems create new features by conjoining existing ones (e.g., Gluck, Bower, and Hee, 1989; Pagallo, 1989). Other systems create new features by taking the product of existing ones (e.g., Sutton and Matheus, 1991).

Although not traditionally viewed as such, explanation-based learning (e.g., Dejong and Mooney, 1986; Mitchell, Keller, and Kedar-Cabelli, 1986) also involves feature construction. Explanation-based learning (EBL) systems typically infer additional features of a training item (e.g., "one can grasp the item") as a side effect of deductively proving that the item meets some functional specification (e.g., "one can drink from the item").

This chapter explores feature construction processes in human learning. A key idea will be that learning about a category not only involves using feature construction processes but also *learning* these processes. Thus, feature selection models (which presuppose the existence of features) are limited in their applicability. Furthermore, feature construction processes are acquired and modified through an interaction of multiple sources of knowledge. This finding contrasts with traditional EBL systems that do not acquire and modify such processes in the course of learning over a series of training items.

The context in which we have investigated human learning is somewhat similar to the one used to investigate explanation-based learning. Therefore, we will compare feature construction in human learning with that in explanation-based learning.[1] The context involves giving people abstract concepts to operationalize, which apply to a series of training items, presented sequentially. In the course of learning, people formulate and generalize explanations. This situation is fairly analogous to one involving EBL systems operating over multiple training items (e.g., Flann and Dietterich, 1989; Mooney and Ourston, 1989; Yoo and Fisher, 1991).

This analysis begins by describing feature selection models and the need for feature construction. EBL systems and their use of feature construction is then briefly described. Next, we describe a standard learning task (incremental rule learning) for exploring feature construction. We highlight certain findings from our studies, noting their implications for selection models and for EBL systems. In the final section, we speculate about the details and desirable qualities of feature construction processes.

---

[1] Comparing our findings to constructive induction systems is less appropriate because they primarily use empirical methods for constructing features and generally do not rely on background knowledge (but see Callan and Utgoff, 1991; Fawcett and Utgoff, 1991; Wnek and Michalski, 1991, for exceptions).

2.2 FEATURE SELECTION MODELS OF LEARNING

In both cognitive psychology and machine learning, researchers often investigate learning by providing intelligent systems with a finite space of predetermined, well-defined features that describe one or more training items. Learning is viewed as selecting an appropriate subset of features from this space to form a concept or representation of a category of items. Typically, this selection process is driven by statistical properties of the features (e.g., the relative frequency of features within a category and its contrasting categories). The concept or representation of the category can then be used to classify novel items (i.e., items not present in the initial training set).

A classic example of a feature-selection model is ID3 (Quinlan, 1983, 1986), which learns rules (in the form of decision trees) for category membership. As shown in Figure 2.2, ID3 is given a training set of members and nonmembers of a category, described as lists of features. Learning involves determining a subset of features that distinguish the members of the category from the nonmembers. For example, in Figure 2.2, members of the category are described by the rule "hair color = red OR [hair color = blond AND eye color = blue]." Nonmembers are described by the rule "hair color = dark OR [hair color = blond AND eye color = brown]." ID3 can then use these rules to classify novel items as members or nonmembers of the category.

In cognitive psychology, a classic example of a feature-selection model is the prototype model. Smith and Medin (1981) describe a variant of this model that they suggest is a more general version of a number of existing models (e.g., Collins and

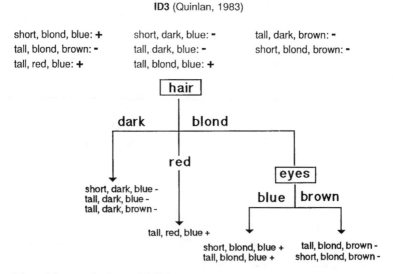

ID3 (Quinlan, 1983)

short, blond, blue: **+**	short, dark, blue: **-**	tall, dark, brown: **-**
tall, blond, brown: **-**	tall, dark, blue: **-**	short, blond, brown: **-**
tall, red, blue: **+**	tall, blond, blue: **+**	

Figure 2.2:   A feature selection model: ID3

Prototype Model (general version)

Item 1	Item 2	Item 3	Item 4
wings	wings	wings	wings
feathers	feathers	feathers	feathers
flies	walks	flies	flies
sings	clucks	sings	sings
small	large	small	small
•	•	•	•
•	•	•	•
•	•	•	•

Prototype

Weight	Feature
1.00	wings
1.00	feathers
.75	flies
.75	sings
.75	small
•	
•	
•	

Figure 2.3:   A feature selection model: General Prototype Model

Loftus, 1975; Hampton, 1979; McCloskey and Glucksberg, 1979). As illustrated in Figure 2.3, input to the model consists of category members that are described as lists of features. Learning involves selecting the modal value of each feature. (The model also weights these features by some function of their perceptual or conceptual salience and their relative frequency among the category members.) This set of features corresponds to a prototype or summary representation of the category. One can then use the prototype to decide whether a novel item belongs to a category. In particular, category membership is a weighted sum of the features shared by the item and the prototype. An item is considered a member of the category if this sum exceeds a threshold.

There are a number of classes of feature-selection models. In addition to prototype and rule-based models, they include exemplar models (e.g., Medin and Schaffer, 1978; Heit, in press; Hintzman, 1986; Nosofsky, 1988, 1991), recent models of incremental conceptual clustering (e.g., Fisher, 1987; J.R. Anderson, 1990), as well as some connectionist models (e.g., Anderson, et al., 1977; Hinton, 1987; Gluck and Bower, 1988).

2.2.1 The Fiction in Selection Models

At the heart of all feature selection models is the assumption that learning operates over a set of clearly specified features that are *a given*. In some contexts, this assumption may be reasonable. For example, experts in a domain may be able to provide a learning system with training items and their associated features. In fact, experts provided AQ11 (Michalski and Chilausky, 1980) with descriptions of individual soybean plants and their diseases. Given these descriptions, the system learned general rules for diagnosing soybean diseases that outperformed those of the experts.

In most contexts, however, it is generally true that features are not "just out there," ready for a learning system to operate over them. There have to be processes that produce these features. For example, most people would agree that the drawings shown in Figure 2.6 consist of features such as "arm," "hand," "fingers," "head," and so on. These features resulted from an interaction of a perceptual system and knowledge structures. Roughly speaking, a perceptual system delivered certain low-level features such as lines and configurations of lines, and these features matched knowledge structures corresponding to "arm," "hand," "fingers," "head," and so on (see Ullman, 1979; Marr, 1982; Biederman, 1987 for details). This process results in subjectively interpreting the drawing as having these features.

Feature selection models do not consider processes that construct features. In defense of this practice, one could argue that feature construction should be done by a separate module. That is, one might assume that features were given to the learning component by a perceptual system interacting with knowledge structures. The details of this process would not be relevant to learning. Other researchers (like those studying vision) would flesh them out. Eventually, a learning system operating in the real world would interface with such a process.

On the other hand, one could argue that features are not solely derived from a process that lies outside the learning component. Rather, the learning component itself influences and modifies these processes. This chapter will suggest that learning about a category often involves *learning the processes that construct features* and is influenced by multiple sources of knowledge that sometimes interact in complex ways. The view that features are a given in learning may be a fiction.

2.3 FEATURE CONSTRUCTION MODELS OF LEARNING

Recently, machine learning researchers have incorporated feature construction processes into their models. Although it has not been typically thought of in this way, explanation-based learning or EBL systems form one broad category of feature construction models. These systems use background knowledge in the form of a domain theory to infer or construct additional features of a training item. EBL systems construct features in the course of applying domain theory rules to a training item. In this sense, one can view the application of a domain theory rule as a feature construction process. As illustrated in Figure 2.4, input to an EBL system typically consists of a training item, described as a set of well-specified features ("light weight," "white color," "handle," and so on), and a *functional specification* of the item (e.g., "item is drinkable-from"). The domain theory consists of a set of

domain theory rules

Rule 1: IF item is liftable AND item is open AND item is stable
AND item is a container THEN item is drinkable-from

Rule 2: IF item is light AND item has a handle THEN item is liftable

Rule 3: IF item is concave THEN item is open

Rule 4: IF item is concave AND item has an upward orientation
THEN item is a container

Rule 5: IF item has a flat bottom THEN item is stable

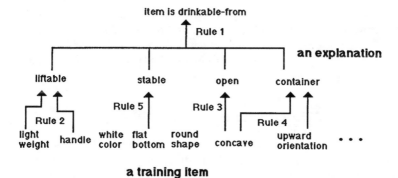

a training item

Figure 2.4:   Explanation-based learning

well-defined rules (e. g., "If item has a handle, then item is liftable"). The system uses the rules to deductively prove or *explain* why the particular item meets the functional specification.

As shown in Figure 2.4, the explanation is actually a tree whose root is the functional specification and whose leaves are a subset of the features of the training item. The intermediate nodes of the tree are additional features that EBL has constructed of the item by using its domain theory rules. After formulating a specific explanation for why an item meets the functional specification, EBL then generalizes the explanation so that it can apply to novel items with similar characteristics (see Dejong and Mooney, 1986; Mitchell, Keller, and Kedar-Cabelli, 1986; Dejong, 1988 for details).

2.3.1 The Fiction in Construction Models

At the heart of EBL systems are three basic assumptions. First, EBL systems assume that feature construction processes are invoked in a straightforward manner. The features specified in the left-hand side of a domain theory rule are compared to those that describe a training item. If there is a match, the system invokes the rule, and the features specified on the right-hand side of the rule are inferred of the training item. Second, the models typically assume that feature construction processes are not influenced by their previous use (but see Tecuci [1991] as one exception). Suppose, for example, that a domain theory rule had been involved in a large number of explanations of previous training items. An EBL system would not be biased to favor or select this rule in forming an explanation of the current training item. Third, because the models tend to operate in well-defined domains, they assume that construction processes remain unchanged during learning over a set of items. For example, a rule like "If item has a handle, then item is liftable" (shown in Figure 2.4) would not be modified in the course of forming explanations for a series of items.

EBL systems go beyond feature selection models in that they incorporate feature construction processes into the learning process. As shown later, however, the preceding assumptions generally do not hold for feature construction in human learning. The view of straightforward, unmodifiable feature construction in EBL may be a fiction.

2.4 THE NONFICTION OF FEATURE CONSTRUCTION

How are features constructed during learning? Features that describe a particular learning item arise from feature construction processes that are potentially influenced by multiple sources of knowledge. Figure 2.5 presents the sources of knowledge that may influence feature construction on a given learning trial. One source of knowledge is information about the current training item itself. A second source is previous training items and the features associated with them. A third source is prior expectations about the category, formed before having experience with its members. A person's general, background knowledge also influences feature construction.

According to this view, the features that describe a particular learning item arise from construction processes that are influenced by a variety of knowledge

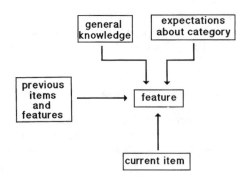

Figure 2.5:   Multiple sources of knowledge that influence feature construction

sources during learning. The knowledge sources affect which processes are selected and whether they are invoked. Furthermore, part of learning involves acquiring these processes. In particular, these processes may be operationalized, adjusted, and modified during learning. The following sections present evidence for this view.

2.4.1 Studying Feature Construction in Human Learning

A number of our studies have investigated feature construction processes using an incremental rule learning task. In this task, training items are presented sequentially (one at a time). The items belong to one of two categories. Participants decide into which category a particular item belongs and then give a reason or explanation for category membership. Then they receive feedback from the experimenter on whether they have correctly classified the item. In response to feedback, participants have the option of modifying their rules. The categories used in these studies are children's drawings of people (taken from Harris, 1963 and Koppitz, 1984). They were produced by children who were administered the "draw a person test" (Koppitz, 1984). One of the pairs of categories is shown in Figure 2.6.

Figure 2.6:   Categories of children's drawings used in incremental rule learning

These studies also varied the prior expectations that people bring to the learning task, by varying the *meaningfulness* of the labels that were associated with the categories. In one form of the task, some subjects are given meaningful labels that apply to the categories, whereas others are given labels having little meaningful content. This task allows us to compare feature construction under conditions in which people have or do not have prior expectations about the categories. The meaningful labels activate expectations (or simple domain theories) about the categories. (They are also somewhat analogous to the functional specifications given to EBL systems.) For example, being told that one will see drawings done by either emotionally-disturbed or well-adjusted children is likely to elicit the belief that one of these categories will display unusual characteristics. People not given this label are unlikely to have this prior belief. In another form of the task, different groups of subjects are given *different* meaningful labels for the *same* categories (see below). This task reveals the effects of different expectations and simple theories on feature construction in identical items.

A number of researchers have argued that adult learning almost always occurs in a context involving such expectations (e.g., Nisbett and Ross, 1980; Murphy and Medin, 1985; Forbus and Gentner, 1986; Wisniewski and Medin, 1991a). For example, consider the first time you encountered a computer. It is unlikely that you learned about computers without relying on any expectations. You had probably read or been told that computers were used for text writing and programming. Also, seeing a computer for the first time may have reminded you about televisions, typewriters, and calculators. Undoubtedly, these expectations influenced your learning about computers. For example, they may have determined which features were likely to be relevant.

One general finding of these studies was that the different sources of knowledge (i.e., expectations, previous training items, and the current training item) clearly affected feature construction. Furthermore, these sources interacted in various ways to determine features. A second finding was that feature construction processes sometimes were complex, flexible, and modifiable. These results are described below.

2.4.2 The Effect of Expectations on Feature Construction

A number of our studies have shown that the expectations that people bring to a learning situation influence the features that they construct (e.g., Wisniewski and Medin, 1991a). In one study, people learned about two categories of drawings done by children. The drawings are shown in Figure 2.6. The participants were divided into two groups. Both groups learned about the same two categories. However, before seeing the drawings, the two groups were given different information about the categories. One group (the Creative/Noncreative group) was told that the drawings were of people done by either creative or noncreative children. The second group (the Farm/City group) was told that drawings were of people done by either farm or city children.

This information activated certain expectations that the two groups had about the categories. Before seeing the categories, the two groups were asked how they thought the categories might be different. The Creative/Noncreative group generally believed that the drawings of the creative children would be more detailed and show more imagination than those of the noncreative children. For example, one person stated that "creative kids will draw more detail—like eyelashes, teeth, curly hair, shading and coloring in—noncreative kids will draw more stick-figurish people." On the other hand, the Farm/City group generally believed that the drawings would reflect the kinds of people that farm and city kids were exposed to in their different environments and, consequently, that these people could be identified by differences in clothing. For example, one person stated that "farm kids will draw people with overalls, straw or farm hats. City kids will draw people with ties, suits."

These expectations clearly influenced the features that people constructed during learning. For example, there was evidence that the two groups sometimes interpreted the *same* part of a drawing *differently* and that the different interpretations were related to their different expectations. For example, in drawing 3 (shown in Figure 2.6), a person in the Creative/Noncreative group interpreted the vertical line of dots as "buttons." The person mentioned this feature as evidence of "detail," which implied that the drawing was done by a creative child. On the other hand, a person in the Farm/City group interpreted the same part of the drawing as a "tie." The person mentioned this feature as evidence that the drawing depicted a "business person," which implied that the drawing was done by a child from the city. As a second example, a person in the Creative/Noncreative group stated that drawing 5 (shown in Figure 2.6) depicted "someone dancing." This feature "showed imagination" and implied that the drawing was done by a creative child. In contrast, a person in the Farm/City group interpreted the drawing as someone "climbing in a playground." This feature implied that the person in the drawing was from the city and, therefore, that the drawing was done by a child from the city.

These expectations also influenced the construction of more abstract features. For example, participants with different expectations sometimes interpreted the same drawing as depicting different stereotypical people. To take one case, five subjects in the Creative/Noncreative group interpreted drawing 8 as a person from a culture different from that of America, e.g., a Frenchman (which implied that the drawing was done by a creative child). In contrast, six people in the Farm/City group interpreted this drawing as a person from a city, e.g., a bellboy (which implied that the drawing was done by a city child).

In these examples, it appears that features are ambiguous at different levels of abstraction. For example, most people would agree that drawing 3 displays a vertical line of dots, but at a higher level of abstraction, it may be unclear whether the dots are buttons or part of a tie. Similarly, most people would agree that the person in drawing 8 is wearing a hat, but at a higher level of abstraction, it may be unclear whether the hat indicates that the person is from a city or a different culture.

Clearly, people's prior expectations about the learning situation helped them to disambiguate these features. The finding is not limited to the domain of children's drawings. For example, consider the interpretation of x-rays in medical diagnosis. Whether a white area on an x-ray indicates a lung tumor, a bone, or an artifact of the procedure can depend on a variety of prior expectations, including the patient's case history, the type of x-ray (e.g., the x-ray is a chest x-ray), the physician's knowledge of the location of bones, and the likelihood that the x-ray was underexposed.

These findings suggest that the learning component influences *which* feature construction processes operate. Different expectations of the learner can activate different feature construction processes, and the particular features that people construct depend on which processes are activated. In the x-ray example, a physician who is trying to learn the nature of a patient's illness will interpret a similar white area as a lung tumor, bone, or artifact, depending on his or her prior expectations. The features involved in learning are determined to some extent by prior expectations. Importantly, these expectations do not merely indicate which features are relevant but also which features are present. Contrary to the assumptions of the selection model, one often cannot *begin* with the features and *then* invoke learning. The context of the learning situation itself determines the features.

2.4.3 The Modifiability of Feature Construction Processes

Feature construction processes can *change* over the course of experience with a series of category items. During learning, people sometimes operationalize, adjust, and modify their feature construction processes. In contrast, EBL systems do not change such processes when operating over a series of training items (e.g., Flann and Dietterich, 1989; Mooney and Ourston, 1989; Yoo and Fisher, 1991).

Informal observations from several of our studies suggest that learning involves operationalizing abstract expectations or features. However, the manner in which people operationalize abstract features differs from the way that EBL operationalizes such features. In particular, operationalization in human learning sometimes relies on both a domain theory *and* knowledge about previous training items. In contrast, operationalization in EBL relies only on an existing domain theory.

To illustrate this difference, consider a learner who believes that drawings done by emotionally disturbed children will be unusual. Furthermore, assume that the learner is *uncertain* about the *specific* features of the drawings that would provide evidence for "unusual." In this example, the process that constructs the feature "unusual" is unspecified for such drawings. Now, the learner is shown a drawing that depicts someone with "four fingers." This feature *may* be evidence that the drawing is unusual. On the other hand, there are a wide variety of plausible explanations (not involving emotional illness) for why a child might draw four fingers instead of five: the child may not be very observant, may be a poor drawer, and so on. In this situation, the learner may have to examine a number of items to determine if the feature "four fingers" is actually associated with emotionally disturbed drawings. A learner's confidence that "four fingers" is evidence for "unusual" may increase with the number of emotionally disturbed drawings that have four fingers. As a result, operationalizing "unusual" as "four fingers" depends both on a domain theory (which initially indicated that the feature "unusual" was relevant) and on knowledge that previous training items with four fingers were drawings done by emotionally disturbed children. In this way, theory-driven and empirically driven learning are *tightly coupled* (Wisniewski and Medin, 1991b).

In contrast, EBL systems operationalize abstract features (e.g., functional specifications) by applying a set of well-defined rules to a training item and deductively proving that the item instantiates the abstract feature. The operationalization process is completely specified in a set of rules that do not change during learning. These assumptions, however, will not hold for situations in which people have general but not specific knowledge about a domain.

One situation that prompts people to modify their feature construction processes occurs when they receive feedback that they have incorrectly classified a drawing. In the first study mentioned above, people modified their feature construction processes about 20% of the time after receiving negative feedback.[2] In many of these cases, people *reinterpreted* the features that they had used in making their incorrect decisions. Then, they used these reinterpreted features as evidence for the correct category. For example, one person interpreted a drawing as a "television character" and suggested that the drawing was done by a city child because city children watch more television. However, told that the drawing was done by a farm child, the person reinterpreted the drawing as a "character created from a farm child's imagination." Presumably, the person has modified these feature construction processes in some way and would now be less likely to interpret a very similar drawing as a "television character" and more likely to interpret the drawing as a "character from a farm child's imagination."

Another way that people modified feature construction processes after receiving negative feedback was by adjusting or fine tuning these processes. For example, one person classified a drawing as done by a creative child because it was more detailed. However, told that the drawing was done by a noncreative child, the person stated that "drawings done by creative children would be *even more*

---

[2]There were other common responses to negative feedback besides modifying feature construction processes. About 30% of the time, people mentioned other features in the drawing as evidence for the correct category. About 14% of the time, they simply noted that the features that they had assumed provided evidence for a category were not diagnostic of that category.

detailed." One interpretation of this example is that a person has changed or adjusted the criteria for interpreting a drawing as "more detailed." As another example, one person stated that a drawing was done by a city child because "it looks very detailed, has colored-in places." Told that the drawing was done by a farm child, the person re-examined the details of the drawing and stated "drawings with detail in specific clothing is more of a rule for city kids—not detail in body movement as this one had." As in the first example, the person has adjusted or altered the use of the feature "detail." Presumably, now for a drawing to be classified as done by a city child, it must show "detailed clothing" as opposed to "detail in body movement."

One issue concerns whether people later apply these modified feature construction processes to other category items. If people did so, it would provide stronger evidence that feature construction processes were modified in the course of learning. This issue is difficult to examine in the current learning task. For one thing, it is almost impossible to predict *how* people will modify these processes, and, therefore, whether such processes will apply to later drawings.

2.4.4 The Effect of Expectations and Previous Category Items

Some preliminary findings suggest that multiple knowledge sources have synergistic effects on feature construction. In particular, a feature is more likely to be constructed given *both* expectations and previous category items than given either of these knowledge sources *alone*.

An unpublished study used drawings that were actually done by emotionally disturbed and well-adjusted children. Some clinical psychologists have found that the drawings of emotionally disturbed children include certain features more often than the drawings of well-adjusted children. These *emotional indicators* include "asymmetrical body parts," "missing body parts," "cross eyes," "teeth," and "very small head relative to the body" (see Koppitz, 1984 for details). Furthermore, people report that they expect these emotional indicators to occur more often in the drawings of emotionally disturbed children than in those of well-adjusted children.

In this study, the drawings that were done by emotionally disturbed children were divided into two types. The *Unambiguous* drawings had a number of clear, unambiguous emotional indicators. For example, in Figure 2.7, the unambiguous drawing 1 clearly has "asymmetrical body parts." Unambiguous drawing 3 clearly has "missing body parts." In the *Ambiguous* drawings, it was not clear that the drawings had such emotional indicators. Thus, in Figure 2.7, one could interpret ambiguous drawing 2 as having "asymmetrical body parts" (i.e., one arm is wider than the other), but the presence of this feature is not nearly as clear and salient as it is in the corresponding unambiguous drawing. Likewise, in Figure 2.7, one could interpret ambiguous drawing 4 as having "missing body parts" (i.e., a missing foot), but the presence of this feature is also not clear and salient.

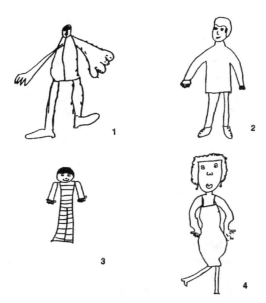

Figure 2.7:   Ambiguous and unambiguous training items

The synergistic effects of multiple sources of knowledge on feature construction were examined by varying the expectations associated with the category items and the order in which people saw the drawings. Participants were divided into two groups. The Expectation group was told that they would be learning how to classify drawings that were done by either "emotionally disturbed children" or "well-adjusted children." These instructions should activate people's expectations that the emotional indicators would be likely to occur in the drawings of emotionally disturbed children. The No Expectation group was simply told that they would be learning how to classify drawings as belonging to either "group 1" or "group 2." Therefore, their expectations about emotional indicators should not be activated.

Importantly, within the Expectation and No Expectation groups, we varied the *order* of the Unambiguous and Ambiguous drawings. Specifically, for half of the participants in each group, the Unambiguous drawings *preceded* the Ambiguous drawings during learning. For the other half in each group, the Unambiguous drawings *followed* the Ambiguous drawings.

Our study then focused on the features that people constructed in the *Ambiguous* drawings. One preliminary finding is that people mention the most emotional indicators in the ambiguous drawings when they have expectations, *and* they have seen the unambiguous drawings. That is, having data from the preceding unambiguous items *together with* having expectations had the greatest effect on the construction of emotional indicators in new training items. When people only had expectations, they constructed fewer emotional indicators in the drawings. When

Figure 2.8:   Effects of feature conjunctions on feature construction

they had only seen the preceding unambiguous items, they constructed even fewer emotional indicators. When people had neither source of knowledge, they very rarely constructed emotional indicators in the ambiguous drawings.

2.4.5 More Complex Effects of Knowledge Sources

It seems plausible that feature construction processes are influenced in even more complex ways than already noted. For example, suppose that a person expects to see drawings done by emotionally disturbed children and well-adjusted children. The person examines a number of emotionally disturbed drawings containing both a "limb asymmetry" and a "missing body part" and arrives at the belief that this *conjunction* of features distinguishes emotionally disturbed drawings from well-adjusted drawings. Now, consider two novel items presented to the person (shown in Figure 2.8). Notice that drawing 1 contains a clear, unambiguous "asymmetry between the arms" but an ambiguous "missing foot." Drawing 2 contains the identical ambiguous "missing foot" but does not contain a limb asymmetry.

Our intuition suggests that the person will be more likely to interpret drawing 1 as having a missing foot than drawing 2. Furthermore, the person may tend to classify drawing 1 as emotionally disturbed but classify drawing 2 as well adjusted. In interpreting drawing 1 as having a missing foot, the person has been influenced by expectations about emotionally disturbed drawings, conjunctions of particular features that have occurred in previous category items, and another feature within drawing 1 (i.e., a limb asymmetry).

2.5 FEATURE CONSTRUCTION REVISITED

In contrast to feature construction in explanation-based learning, people's feature construction processes can be flexible and modifiable. Is this capability a desirable one for a machine learning system? It would seem that this capability should be an important component of a learning system. One reason is that there are probably many domains about which people lack *specific* knowledge. On the other hand, they probably have some *general* knowledge that is useful in learning about the domain. People learn about the specific aspects of the domain through an interaction of this general knowledge and exposure to learning situations associated with the domain. Other intelligent systems would be faced with similar situations.

It is highly unlikely that intelligent systems could have straightforward mapping rules for every potential domain. As an example, consider a rule that constructs the feature "more detailed." A straightforward rule that maps concrete features such as "buttons," "eyebrows," "shoelaces," and "belt buckle" onto "more detailed" will *only* apply to pictures of people drawn by creative children. It will not apply if the content of the picture or the artist is varied. For example, the features that map onto "more detailed" for drawings of people done by creative *adults* may be different from those for the drawings of creative children. Likewise, the features that map onto "more detailed" for drawings of *trees* done by creative children will be different than those for drawings of people.

Furthermore, it appears that feature construction may occur through a somewhat complex interaction of different knowledge sources. To illustrate these interactions, consider the effects of simple expectations, low-level data of a training item, and the features of previous training items on feature construction.

Simple expectations may initially activate knowledge structures (such as schemas or frames), and low-level data from the training item may constrain which knowledge structures are plausible. These data include shape descriptors and the relations between them, which are delivered by the perceptual system (Marr and Nishihara, 1978; Biederman, 1987). For example, consider a previous example in which a person interpreted the vertical dots of drawing 3 (shown in Figure 2.6) as a "tie." Expecting to see drawings done by city and farm children may have activated knowledge structures corresponding to clothing items that distinguish people who live in urban environments from people who live in rural environments. These structures might correspond to "suits," "ties" (indicating an urban person), and "overalls" and "straw hats" (indicating a rural person). Low-level features such as the vertical orientation of the dots and their location in the center of the upper torso would be consistent with the knowledge structure corresponding to "tie" but not with the other structures. The low-level features would also be consistent with the knowledge structure "buttons," but this structure would not be active because it does not distinguish people from urban versus rural environments.

Knowledge about the features from previous training items will also affect feature construction. This knowledge may strengthen or weaken the activation of knowledge structures, depending upon whether features corresponding to those structures have frequently or infrequently occurred in previous category members and nonmembers. Thus, if a person has seen many ties in previous drawings done by city children, the person may be more likely to look for a tie in the next drawing. Furthermore, the person may be more likely to interpret data consistent with multiple interpretations (e.g., "button" and "tie") as a tie.

Of course, the picture is even more complex than suggested. First, perceptual constraints and prior expectations need not interact in order for people to construct features. Clearly, perceptual information can activate features in the absence of prior expectations (e.g., one can identify a barn without expecting to see a farm). Second, one type of constraint may dominate the other. For example, no matter how strongly you expected to see an elephant, other constraints would cause you to interpret the drawings in Figure 2.6 as people (e.g., the presence of fingers, two legs, etc.). Third, data may actually activate expectations that then exert their own influences. For example, a drawing of a person holding a pitchfork could remind a person of farms. The person might then expect to see drawings done by farm children. These expectations in turn would bias feature construction processes in subsequent drawings. (In general, the drawings in our studies did not activate such prior expectations in the No Expectation groups.)

Given the possible interactions between different knowledge sources, it may be best to view the presence of a feature as having some amount of support or evidence. In contrast, most learning systems assume that all features are unambiguous and are present with certainty. Our results suggest that the amount of support for a feature can vary. As people experience more training items and receive feedback, they may adjust the support. Sometimes the support for a feature becomes very low, and it is effectively disregarded. A new feature may take its place. Evidence for this claim comes from the finding that people sometimes reinterpreted data as new features that supported the correct category and abandoned previous interpretations that supported the incorrect category.

2.6 SUMMARY

Our results suggest that part of learning involves determining feature construction processes. Features are not simply present in training items, and learning does not consist solely of selecting the relevant features. Furthermore, feature construction is a flexible, modifiable process that can be affected by multiple knowledge sources. Standard EBL systems do not show this flexibility and modifiability, primarily because they have generally operated in well-defined domains. However, most domains that people learn about are not well specified. The flexibility and modifiability of feature construction processes are an important prerequisite for any intelligent system learning in these domains.

The present research has primarily demonstrated that different sources of knowledge work together in determining the features over which learning takes place. Many issues still need to be explored. In particular, we have been somewhat vague about how the various sources of knowledge are actually combined and weighted in determining features. In future work, we plan to carefully manipulate these sources of knowledge in order to derive more quantitative predictions about learning. In any event, we hope that this chapter contributes to a clearer understanding of how features are constructed during learning.

ACKNOWLEDGMENTS

This research was supported in part by the National Institute of Child Health and Development under Fellowship Award 5 F32 HD07279-02 given to the first author and by the National Science Foundation under Grant 9110245 given to the second author. We thank Arthur Markman and Ryszard Michalski for their trenchant comments on a previous draft.

References

Anderson, J.A., Silverstein, J.W., Ritz, S.A., and Jones, R.S., "Distinctive Features, Categorical Perception, and Probability Learning: Some Applications of a Neural Model," *Psychological Review*, Vol. 84, pp. 413–451, 1977.

Anderson, J.R., *The Adaptive Character of Thought*, Erlbaum, Hillsdale, NJ, 1990.

Biederman, I., "Recognition-by-components: A Theory of Image Understanding," *Psychological Review*, Vol. 94, pp. 115–147, 1987.

Callan, J.P., and Utgoff, P.E., "A Transformational Approach to Constructive Induction," *Proceedings of the Eighth International Workshop on Machine Learning*, Evanston, IL, Morgan Kaufmann, San Mateo, CA, pp. 122–126, 1991.

Collins, A., and Loftus, E.F., "A Spreading Activation Theory of Semantic Processing," *Psychological Review*, Vol. 82, pp. 407–428, 1975.

Dejong, G., "An Introduction to Explanation-based Learning," In *Exploring Artificial Intelligence*, H. E. Shrobe (Ed.), Morgan Kaufmann, San Mateo, CA, 1988.

Dejong, G., and Mooney, R.J., "Explanation-based Learning: An Alternative View," *Machine Learning*, Vol. 1, pp. 145–176, 1986.

Fawcett, T.E., and Utgoff, P.E., "A Hybrid Method for Feature Generation," *Proceedings of the Eighth International Workshop on Machine Learning*, Evanston, IL, Morgan Kaufmann, San Mateo, CA, 1991.

Fisher, D.H., "Knowledge Acquisition via Incremental Conceptual Clustering," *Machine Learning, Vol.* 2, pp. 139–172, 1987.

Flann, N.S., and Dietterich, T.G., "A Study of Explanation-based Methods for Inductive Learning," *Machine Learning*, Vol. 4, pp. 187–226, 1989.

Forbus, K.D., and Gentner, D., "Learning Physical Domains: Towards a Theoretical Framework," In *Machine Learning: An Artificial Intelligence Approach*, Vol. 2, R.S. Michalski, J.G. Carbonell, and T.M. Mitchell (Eds.), Tioga, Palo Alto, CA, 1986.

Gluck, M.A., and Bower, G.H., "Evaluating an Adaptive Network Model of Human Learning," *Journal of Memory and Language*, Vol. 27, pp. 166–195, 1988.

Gluck, M.A., Bower, G.H., and Hee, M.R., A Configural-cue Network Model of Animal and Human Associative Learning, *Proceedings of the Eleventh Annual Conference of the Cognitive Science Society*, Ann Arbor, MI, Lawrence Erlbaum Associates, Hillsdale, NJ, pp. 323–332, 1989.

Hampton, J.A., "Polymorphous Concepts in Semantic Memory," *Journal of Verbal Learning and Verbal Behavior*, Vol. 18, pp. 441–461, 1979.

Harris, D.B., *Children's Drawings as Measures of Intellectual Maturity,* Harcourt Brace and World, New York, 1963.

Heit, E., "Categorization Using Trains of Examples," *Cognitive Psychology*, Vol. 24, pp. 341–380, 1992.

Hinton, G.E., "Connectionist Learning Procedures," Technical Report No. CMU-CS-87-115, Carnegie Mellon University, Pittsburgh, PA, 1987.

Hintzman, D.L., "Schema Abstraction in a Multiple-Trace Memory Model," *Psychological Review*, Vol. 93, pp. 411–428, 1986.

Koppitz, E.M., *Psychological Evaluation of Human Figure Drawings by Middle School Pupils*, Grune and Stratton, Inc., Orlando, FL, 1984.

Lebowitz, M., "Integrated Learning: Controlling Explanation," *Cognitive Science*, Vol. 10, pp. 219–240, 1986.

Marr, D., *Vision*, W.H. Freeman and Company, New York, 1982.

Marr, D., and Nishihara, H.K., "Representation and Recognition of the Spatial Organization of Three-dimensional Shapes," *Proceedings of the Royal Society of London,* Vol. B 200, pp. 269–294, 1978.

Matheus, C.J., and Rendell, L.A., Constructive Induction on Decision Trees, *Proceedings of the International Joint Conference on Artificial Intelligence*, 645–650, Detroit, MI, Morgan Kaufmann, San Mateo, CA, 1989.

McCloskey, M., and Glucksberg, S., "Decision Processes in Verifying Category Membership Statements: Implications for Models of Semantic Memory," *Cognitive Psychology,* Vol. 11, pp. 1–37, 1979.

Medin, D.L., and Shaffer, M.M., "A Context Theory of Classification Learning," *Psychological Review*, Vol. 85, pp. 207–238, 1978.

Medin, D.L., Wattenmaker, W.D., and Michalski, R.S., "Constraints and Preferences in Inductive Learning: An Experimental Study of Human and Machine Performance," *Cognitive Science*, Vol. 11, pp. 299–339, 1987.

Michalski, R.S., "Pattern Recognition as Rule-guided Inductive Inference," *IEEE Transactions on Pattern Analysis and Machine Intelligence*, Vol. PAMI-2, No. 4, pp. 349–361, 1980.

————, "A Theory and Methodology of Inductive Learning," In *Machine Learning: An Artificial Intelligence Approach*, Vol. 1, R.S. Michalski, J.G. Carbonell, and T.M. Mitchell (Eds.), Tioga, Palo Alto, CA, 1983.

Michalski, R.S., and Chilausky, R.L., "Learning by Being Told and Learning from Examples: An Experimental Comparison of the Two Methods of Knowledge Acquisition in the Context of Developing an Expert System for Soybean Disease Diagnosis," *Policy Analysis and Information Systems*, Vol. 4, No. 2, pp. 125–161, 1980.

Mitchell, T.M., "Generalization as Search," *Artificial Intelligence*, Vol. 18, pp. 203–226, 1982.

Mitchell, T.M., Keller, R.M., and Kedar-Cabelli, S.T. "Explanation-Based Generalization: A Unifying View," *Machine Learning*, Vol. 1, pp. 47–80, 1986.

Mooney, R.J., and Ourston, D., "Induction over the Unexplained: Integrated Learning of Concepts with Both Explainable and Conventional Aspects," *Proceedings of the Sixth International Workshop on Machine Learning*, pp. 5–7, Ithaca, NY, 1989.

Murphy, G.L., and Medin, D.L., "The Role of Theories in Conceptual Coherence," *Psychological Review*, Vol. 92, pp. 289–316, 1985.

Nisbett, R., and Ross, L., *Human Inference: Strategies and Shortcomings of Social Judgment*, Prentice Hall, Inc., Englewood Cliffs, NJ, 1980.

Nosofsky, R.M., "Similarity, Frequency, and Category Representations," *Journal of Experimental Psychology: Learning, Memory, and Cognition,* Vol. 14, pp. 54–65, 1988.

Nosofsky, R.M., "Exemplars, prototypes, and similarity rules," In *From Learning Theory to Connectionist Theory: Essays in Honor of W.K. Estes*, Vol. 1, A. Healy, S. Kosslyn, and R. Shiffrin (Eds.), Erlbaum, Hillsdale, NJ, pp. 149–167, 1991.

Pagallo, G., Learning DNF by Decision Trees, *Proceedings of the International Joint Conference on Artificial Intelligence*, 639-644, Detroit, MI, Morgan Kaufmann, San Mateo, CA, 1989.

Quinlan, J.R., "Learning Efficient Classification Procedures and Their Application to Chess End Games," In *Machine Learning: An Artificial Intelligence Approach*, Vol. 1, R.S. Michalski, J. G. Carbonell, and T.M. Mitchell (Eds.), Tioga, Palo Alto, CA, pp. 463–482, 1983.

————, "Induction of Decision Trees," *Machine Learning*, Vol. 1, pp. 81–106, 1986.

Smith, E., and Medin, D.L., *Categories and Concepts*, Harvard University Press, Cambridge, MA, 1981.

Sutton, R.S., and Matheus, C.J., "Learning Polynomial Functions by Feature Construction," *Proceedings of the Eighth International Workshop on Machine Learning*, Evanston, IL, Morgan Kaufmann, San Mateo, CA, pp. 208–212, 1991.

Tecuci, G.D., "Learning as Understanding the External World," *Proceedings of the First International Workshop on Multistrategy Learning*, Harpers Ferry, WV, pp. 49–65, June 7–9, 1991.

Ullman, S., *The Interpretation of Visual Motion*, MIT Press, Cambridge, MA, 1979.

Wisniewski, E.J., and Medin, D.L., "Harpoons and Long Sticks: The Interaction of Theory and Similarity in Rule Induction," In *Concept Formation: Knowledge and Experience in Unsupervised Learning*, D.H. Fisher, M.J. Pazzani, and P. Langley (Eds.), Morgan Kaufmann, San Mateo, CA, pp. 237–238, 1991a.

————, "Is It a Pocket or a Purse: Tightly Coupled Theory and Data Driven Learning," *Proceedings of the Eighth International Machine Learning Worskshop*, Evanston, IL, Morgan Kaufmann, San Mateo, CA, pp. 564–568, 1991b.

Wnek, J., and Michalski, R.S., "Hypothesis-driven Constructive Induction in AQ17: A Method and Experiments," *Proceedings of the IJCAI-91 Workshop on Evaluating and Changing Representations in Machine Learning*, K. Morik, F. Bergadano, W. Buntine (Eds.), pp. 13–22, Sydney, Australia, Morgan Kaufmann, San Mateo, CA, 1991.

Yoo, J., and Fisher, D.H., "Concept Formation over Explanations and Problem-solving Experience," In *Concept Formation: Knowledge and Experience in Unsupervised Learning*, D.H. Fisher, M.J. Pazzani, and P. Langley (Eds.), Morgan Kaufmann, San Mateo, CA, pp. 279–303, 1991.

3

INDUCTION AND THE
ORGANIZATION OF KNOWLEDGE

Yves Kodratoff
(CNRS & Université Paris-Sud)

Abstract

This chapter investigates various forms of the induction principle in view of a discussion of the importance of a well-known objection to induction, namely, Hempel's paradox. This paradox arises because an inductive hypothesis can be confirmed by its instances (e.g., confirming that all crows are black by actually seeing a black crow) as well as by "negative" information (e.g., confirming that all crows are black by actually seeing a non-black non-crow entity such as a white shoe). In spite of its apparent simplicity, this paradox is still an important question that should be considered by systems performing unsupervised learning because they are prone to confirm their hypotheses by such irrelevant negative information. It is argued here that avoiding Hempel's paradox can be achieved with a tight integration of the statistical findings together with a clear organization of knowledge. Progressive organization of knowledge plays an essential role in the inductive growth of new scientific theories. In this sense, multistrategy learning, which integrates numerical induction and the building of knowledge structures, is imperative in order to avoid confirmation by nonrelevant information.

3.1 INTRODUCTION

Over the past 60 years, the problem of the growth of science has been a significant element in the philosophical debate. Everyone agrees that science justifies its theories in a deductive way, as emphasized, for instance, by Popper (1959) and Nagel (1961). Nevertheless, there is little general agreement on where these theories come from and how they propagate in the scientific medium. This explains the implicit or explicit role played in this debate by the problem of induction.

There is a strong strand of probabilistic justification of induction, as represented by Carnap (1950). Hempel (1965) starts his analysis of scientific explanation by describing some (symbolic) inductive inconsistencies. Van Fraassen (1980, 1985) refines Hempel's criteria for statistical justification. The exact formulation of probabilistic induction, particularly that of probabilistic causal generalization is still a matter of debate, as illustrated by the Eels/Dupré debate about contextual unanimity for drawing justified inductions (Eels and Sober, 1983; Dupré, 1984, 1990; Eels, 1986, 1987). Nevertheless, the probabilistic induction view aroused a good deal of criticism. For instance, Popper (1963) "refutes" Carnap's views on the growth of scientific knowledge, mainly because of Carnap's definition of induction. Watkins (1968) criticizes Popper and Carnap by showing some of the contradictions stemming from the two kinds of skepticism that appear when one accepts that statements about the world are uncertain. All this shows clearly that the problem of induction is still far from being resolved. Another chapter in this volume (Michalski, 1994, Chapter 1) presents new ideas about the definition of induction. In the present chapter, we present no new formalization of induction; we will stress the requirement that induction takes place within already existing, well-defined structures of knowledge.

For the purposes of this chapter, let us recall that inference is a very general reasoning process that covers both deduction and induction.[1] Let us note A |= B, where one can infer B from A.

For any inference rule A |= B, |= is said to be **truth-preserving** if whenever A is true, then B is also true.

Deduction is classically defined as the mode of inference that preserves truth, i.e., inference A |= B, is a deduction if and only if B is true whenever A is true. There are many deductive rules, the most famous of which is *modus ponens* (A and A $\Rightarrow$ B) |= B. Other examples of deductive rules are the suppression of double negations, $\neg\neg$A |= A, or mathematical induction (F($\mathbf{0}$) and $\forall$a [F(a) $\Rightarrow$F($\mathbf{suc}$(a))]) |= $\forall$x [F(x)], etc.

Induction does not preserve truth value and is often defined as the process by which one infers theories from facts (Peirce, 1965). Nevertheless, this definition is not precise enough. It will be refined by seeing it as built from elementary inductive processes, such as abduction, and several other processes described in the next section.

---

[1] We could also speak of analogical inference but do not wish to start a discussion of this topic here.

3.2 A DESCRIPTION OF SOME INDUCTIVE PROCESSES

The best known elementary inductive processes used in machine learning are **generalization** and **abduction** (Michalski and Kodratoff, 1990; see also Michalski [1994], Chapter 1 in this book). Without any pretense about being exhaustive,[2] let us present here five other forms of induction. They are **causality determination**, **attribution of properties**, **spatial or temporal inclusion**, and **clustering and chunking** and their relation to **numeric induction**. The first process is essentially symbolic; the next are mixed symbolic-numeric; the last, though seemingly purely numeric, yields knowledge organization.

Let us first recall some well-known facts about abduction and generalization, which are the most classical inductive processes.

3.2.1 Abduction

The classical rule for abduction, as given by Peirce, is an inductive version of *modus ponens*, i.e., a kind of inversion of *modus ponens* in which instead of deducing B from A and A $\Rightarrow$ B, one induces A from B and A $\Rightarrow$ B.[3] For instance, knowing that $\forall$x[Drunk(x) $\Rightarrow$ Stumbling(x)], one deduces that a drunk will stumble. On the contrary, one induces from seeing a particular person stumbling that he might be drunk.

There are generally many abductions possible from one fact because several theorems can conclude this fact. For instance, $\forall$x[Wounded(x) $\Rightarrow$ Stumbling(x)] and $\forall$x[Sunstruck(x) $\Rightarrow$ Stumbling(x)] are also possible.

Abduction is obviously of a symbolic nature.

3.2.2 Generalization

Technically, generalization is the process by which, starting with a term t_1, one finds a substitution σ and a term t_2 such that $\sigma\, t_2 = t_1$ (for instance, see Kodratoff, 1983; Kodratoff & Ganascia, 1986). Michalski (1990) presents it also as the process that infers $\forall$x [F(x)] from F(a).

In practice, generalization is a fairly complex knowledge representation mechanism. It builds trees of dependencies, called taxonomies of generality, the links of which are IS_A links. In these trees, each parent is more general than its children. Generalization will then consist of observing some of the children and

---

[2] For instance, we do not study here the types of inductive inferences obtainable by using a sub-part of mathematical induction (despite its name, purely deductive), such as inducing on a finite number of instances and inducing on incomplete base-cases.

[3] An important application of induction and abduction is the completion of failed proofs (Cox and Pietrzykowski, 1986; Duval and Kodratoff, 1990). Abduction is used as follows: A proof fails because one fails to prove B; it is noted that A $\Rightarrow$ B; and one makes the abduction of A, which of course proves B and, therefore, allows the proof to be completed.

concluding that the parent holds. In order to avoid odd generalizations, a certain proportion of the children must be observed before inducing to their parent. In this sense, generalization is partially a numeric process.

Many more details about generalization can be found in Michalski (1983, 1984, 1994; Chapter 1 in this book), Dietterich and Michalski (1981), Kodratoff (1983, 1988, 1990), Vrain (1990).

As with abduction, specialists in generalization have developed many symbolic ways of justifying their inductions by deductions (Kodratoff, 1988, 1990; Kodratoff and Ganascia, 1986; Pazzani, 1989; Vrain, 1990).

3.2.3 Causality Determination

When several phenomena seem to occur simultaneously, one might hypothesize that some are the cause of the others. For instance, one might observe that many drunkards stumble, which is nothing but the conjunction of [Drunk(Joe) & Stumbling(Joe)] & ... & [Drunk(Bob) & Stumbling(Bob)]. Choosing which phenomenon causes the other can be done by deduction. There, the causal relationship is provable. It can be also done by induction. In this case, there is no deductive proof allowing the conjunctions to be transformed into implications; for instance, [Drunk(Joe) $\Rightarrow$ Stumbling(Joe)] & ... & [Drunk(Bob) $\Rightarrow$ Stumbling(Bob)].

This leads to the interesting problem of whether or not a conjunction (hence, a set of plain observations) can be transformed into an implication, i.e., if a conjunction can confirm an implication. In order to allow such a confirmation, Hempel (1965) had to build a mechanism that has been revisited recently by Gemes (1990). This philosophical debate concerns the syntax of causality. Eels and Dupré have likewise discussed the meaning of probabilistic causality (Eels and Sober, 1983; Dupré, 1984, 1990; Eels, 1986, 1987).

Section 3.3 further discusses the links between causality and statistics. At present, let us just emphasize the importance of causality in the organization of knowledge. In general, causalities are not isolated relations; rather, they generate chains of implications, linking deep causes to their shallow consequences. Different causal chains intersect each other at different places, thus generating a kind of net of causality within the knowledge, with the property that no two sub-chains can contradict each other. Thus, knowledge takes the form of a complex net in which everything has more or less distant causal links with everything else.

Finding such causal links allows the implication to be qualified by a "CAUSES" semantic marker, similar to the IS_A qualifying generalizations. The idea of noting explicitly the semantics of causal links is nothing new. For instance, the system PROTOS (Bareiss, Porter, and Wier, 1990) makes explicit use of such implications, which are implemented as links, labelled CAUSES, in a semantic network.

3.2.4 Attribution of Properties

When several simultaneous observations are made, one might hypothesize that one of them is a concept, and the others are the properties of this concept. Choosing which is the concept and which are the properties can be done by deduction, but it can also be by induction, where one again transforms some conjuncts into implications. For instance, one might observe a black crow, named Jacko, written crow(Jacko) & black(Jacko). This observation contains no information about what is the property and what bears it. By hypothesizing that the concept is crow(Jacko), which bears the property black(Jacko), one transforms the conjunct into an implication crow(Jacko) $\Rightarrow$ black(Jacko).

This process is also a very powerful way of structuring knowledge because it clusters the properties around the concepts they describe. When meeting a crow, one knows in advance that it will have a whole set of properties that are a kind of definition of what a crow is (i.e., the recognition function of a crow). A concept usually belongs to a taxonomy of concepts, such as *crow* is a child of the concept *bird,* but it is not a property of the more general concept.[4] Therefore, there is no confusion between generality and concept-property relationships.

Implications arising from the attribution of a property carry a "HAS_PROPERTY" semantic link between their premise and their conclusion.

3.2.5 Spatial or Temporal Inclusion

Spatial (or temporal) inclusion means that for all events happening within the spatially (or temporally) included region, it is implied that it also happens in the including one as well. For instance, $\forall x$[happens_in_Paris$(x)\Rightarrow$happens_in_France(x)] expresses that everything happening in Paris happens also in France, which is of course only partially true because there are many towns named Paris in the United States.

This information structures the knowledge in PART_OF trees of dependency, well-known for being different from the IS_A ones built by the generalization process. Spatial and temporal inclusions are of a mixed symbolic-numeric nature because the limits of the domains are better described in numeric terms, but the properties that hold inside these domains are better described in symbolic terms.

3.2.6 Clustering and Chunking

Clustering brings together several pieces of knowledge, such as objects of the world, concepts, properties, or relations. That pieces of knowledge are clustered is

---

[4] In natural language, however, ambiguity arises between words that are both nouns (concepts) and adjectives (properties). We suppose here that this problem has been resolved explicitly in the knowledge base.

in itself useful information. In general, clustering techniques are inductive numeric techniques, such as in data analysis (an early French reference is Benzecri et al. [1973]). For a thorough discussion of the links between symbolic and numeric approaches, one can consult Michalski and Stepp (1983) and Kodratoff and Diday (1991).

Chunking keeps as a unit a sequence of operations that has proven useful during a problem-solving episode. It is essentially a deductive process, but when many chunks are gathered and many problem-solving episodes are studied, then some statistical properties of the chunks can be looked for. This is why it can be seen as merging numeric and symbolic approaches, as exemplified by the system SOAR (Laird et al., 1986, 1987), which implements chunking in a problem-solving environment, and by PRODIGY (Carbonell, Knoblock, and Minton, 1990), which computes macro-operators.

Once more, let us stress the fact that these inferences bring structure into knowledge because clustering sets boundaries around instances of the same concept, and chunking sets up links between successive actions or concepts.

3.2.7 Numeric Induction

Let us expose two different definitions of probabilistic induction. The first one is nothing but a rephrasing of Carnap (1950), who states that he conceives inductive logic as the theory of an exact concept of the measure of evidential support,[5] that is to say, measuring properly how much an event favors a theory. This definition can be made somewhat more formal, as follows: Let $\{X\}$ be a set of experimental events, and let x be the current representative of this set. If $A(x)$ is true (or false) for a sub-set[6] $\{X'\}$ of $\{X\}$, such that $\{X'\}$ is statistically meaningful for $\{X\}$, then one can induce that $A(x)$ is true (or false) for $\{X\}$. Obviously, this amounts to defining properly what statistically meaningful means, and that is a problem for statistics. To simplify, let us state that statistical meaningfulness is defined by comparing the sizes of $\{X'\}$ and $\{X\}$ and by evaluating the "spatial distribution" of $\{X'\}$ inside $\{X\}$. This type of numeric induction does not require any special pattern in the way the knowledge of $\{X'\}$ is distributed in $\{X\}$, but rather, it sets distributions of distances of the instances of $\{X'\}$ relatively to the instances of $\{X\}$. Therefore, it can be said that it structures knowledge only in a very broad sense because it does require a distribution of $\{X'\}$ in $\{X\}$, but the structure is defined in a mathematical sense only, not "visually" as the other structures are.

---

[5] Actually, he says that it is an "explicatum for probability$_1$," and we have used his definitions of the words explicatum and probability$_1$.

[6] Statistical deduction demands it to be true for all sub-sets and not just for one of the sub-sets.

The second definition can be obtained through a simplified definition of probabilistic causality, as stated by Suppes (1984); for instance, B is said to be the cause of A if and only if (1) B occurs earlier than A, and (2) the conditional probability of A occurring when B occurs is greater than the unconditional probability of A occurring. This second definition, as opposed to the first one, makes statistical induction a primary way of structuring knowledge by including in it causal links.

It could be possible to add a specific statistical definition for each of the structuring mechanisms reviewed in this section. It would then define probabilistic abduction, generalization, etc. In other words, it is quite possible to look upon statistics as a way of structuring knowledge, thus obtaining non-statistical effects from statistical knowledge. It is therefore a good place to point out clearly that this chapter is not written "against" numerical knowledge. Rather, it claims that statistical knowledge and symbolic knowledge are intertwined, and it attempts to clarify what belongs to statistics and what is the use of symbols.

> As a conclusion, it can be said that induction creates a net of implications among otherwise independent pieces of knowledge.

This net of implication must obviously be consistent to be considered scientific knowledge, a simple requirement that forces the existence of quite strong structures within the net because implication chains pointing at any A are forbidden to lead to $\neg A$. A well-known example of such chains is the branches of a taxonomy of generality, as natural sciences often produce.

It must also be stressed that these implications have different semantics depending on their origin. For instance, an implication originating from an induction on causality will transfer causal relations and no property inheritance, but an implication coming from an induction about generality will transfer no causality but property inheritance. In other words, knowledge is represented by a network of implications. These implications are labelled by their semantics, such as IS_A, CAUSES, HAS_PROPERTY, PART_OF, depending on which kind of induction each link originates from.

The next section will discuss why and how uncertainty does not destroy these structures.

3.3 THE SYMBOLIC/NUMERIC DEBATE

When it is confronted with real world problems, the symbolic approach to Artificial Intelligence (AI) needs to represent and to handle uncertainty. When uncertain information is dealt with, at least three problems occur.

The first problem is the combination of uncertainties during a reasoning phase. There have been many proposals for the solution of this problem, the most famous being based upon Bayesian combinations (Shafer, 1979), belief coefficients (Buchanan and Shortliffe, 1984), and fuzzy sets theory (Zadeh, 1965). These techniques have received a very large amount of attention. They will not be elaborated upon here.

The second problem comes from the fact that A and $\neg A$ are, to some extent, simultaneously true; the knowledge base contains some kind of contradiction; and the reasoning process must be able to deal with these contradictions. We already presented this problem in great detail in Kodratoff, Perdrix, and Franova (1985); Duval and Kodratoff (1989); and Kodratoff et al. (1990).

Before stating the third problem, let us recall here that one should not confuse the uncertainty, or the belief coefficient, attached to an implication or to the concepts concerned by the implication, such as explained in Kodratoff and Ganascia (1984). For example, some uncertainty may be attached to the fact that John smokes and has a cancer; i.e., the facts *smokes(John)* and *cancer(John)* may be known with some degree of uncertainty. We can also consider that these facts are known for sure and question the certainty about the implication itself, *smokes(John)* $\Rightarrow$ *cancer(John)*. In the following, we shall speak of the uncertainty of the implication when only that uncertainty is considered. We shall speak of the uncertainty of the concepts, or of the features, when only that type of uncertainty is considered.

The third problem concerns uncertainty about the implications themselves. As soon as it is accepted that an implication can be uncertain, we are confronted with the idea that there are no real implications in the world but, rather, uncertain equivalences because both directions of the implication are possible; that is, $A \Rightarrow B$ with a certainty of $y\%$, and $B \Rightarrow A$ with a certainty of $z\%$, where y and z are the certainty coefficients associated with the implications. It is clear that these two coefficients have no special relationship because the uncertainty in one direction has little to do with the uncertainty in the other direction.[7] Claiming that all kinds of knowledge are in this form does not lead one to deny uncertain induction. In our example, it is known that smoking does not mechanically entail cancer; therefore, one believes, say, that $\forall x[smokes(x) \Rightarrow cancer(x)]$ with a certainty of $y = 10\%$ and then that *smokes(John)* $\Rightarrow$ *cancer(John)* with this same certainty. We can also imagine that cancer, before it is even medically observable, brings the patient to such a state that it drives him to smoking. Because this is a somewhat shaky explanation, a very low confidence will be attributed to $\forall x[cancer(x) \Rightarrow smokes(x)]$, say, $z = 0.1\%$. This illustrates two things. First, it illustrates how unrelated y and z are. It may even happen that $z = 0\%$ (as could well be the case in our example) without y being equal to 100%. Second, it also illustrates that each fact—here, facts about smoking and cancer—can give place to both a deduction and an induction. On meeting Jane who has a cancer, one can induce, as often people do,

---

[7] Obviously, the uncertainty of the negation of $A \Rightarrow B$, $\neg[A \Rightarrow B] = A \ \& \ \neg B$, has something to do with the uncertainty of $A \Rightarrow B$. On the other hand, the uncertainties of $A \Rightarrow B$ and $B \Rightarrow A$ are completely disconnected.

that she smokes by using $\forall x[\text{smokes}(x) \Rightarrow \text{cancer}(x)]$ in the reverse direction. There is still no estimate of the value of this induction because it depends on how many smokers have cancers, which is quite different from the probability of getting a cancer because of smoking. It is also possible to deduce that she smokes with a certainty of 0.1% by using $\forall x[\text{cancer}(x) \Rightarrow \text{smokes}(x)]$.

We shall now argue that the existence of uncertainty does not change the fact that one direction of the implication is of a deductive nature, but the other is of an inductive nature.

3.3.1 Well-Structured Knowledge Leads to a Kind of Certainty

Even when knowledge is uncertain, there are cases of some implications that are 100% sure. For instance, $\forall x\ [\text{woman}(x) \Rightarrow \text{human}(x)]$ with a certainty of 100% is a certain implication. Based on the fact that *human* and *woman* are not perfectly defined concepts because there are monsters at the fringe of humanity, that the difference between some men and some women is not always clear-cut does not prevent one from claiming that as soon as a woman has been recognized, a human has been also. As seen later, this is not an isolated phenomenon but a tendency characteristic of scientific approaches.

The organization of knowledge tends to transform uncertain theorems into certain ones and to transfer the uncertainty to the concepts. As long as knowledge is badly structured, uncertainty may remain attached to the implications, but it is the role of organization to ensure this transfer from the implications to the concepts they link. Natural sciences are a very good example of a highly structured science that deals with highly uncertain knowledge because living beings show great variability in their characteristics. Nevertheless, this old science contains strong structures and has organized its knowledge by "chasing" uncertainty out of the implications and putting it back into the definitions of the features of the concepts. For example, the color of a fungus is "green to gray, possibly yellow," or a flower shows "six to ten petals," all very uncertain features.

Let us present a detailed occurrence of such certain implications about very uncertain knowledge. We know of an actual story where a mycologist met a very rare puzzle, that of finding a sample that could just as well have been *amanita spissa* as *amanita phalloides* ("death cup"). Normally, they are easy to differentiate, but this exemplar was particularly unusual, showing blurred differentiating characteristics; i.e., it could be seen as a particularly uncertain example. Nevertheless, its foot was a bit too fleshy for the normally fragile foot of *phalloides* and was thus in accordance with the somewhat fleshy foot of *spissa*. The two fungi show another large difference, which one can be unwilling to check: *phalloides* is lethal to ingest, but *spissa* is edible and delicious. Our man hesitated to acknowledge a *spissa*, but one of his fellow mycologists insisted that it was one. Both mycologists were 100% certain that *phalloides* implies death and fragile foot, but *spissa* implies pleasure and fleshy foot. Their belief in any of these theorems would therefore not be changed by any particular exemplar. One of them, however, did not agree that the foot was fleshy enough to identify a *spissa* unambiguously, but his colleague insisted that the foot was indeed fleshy. More generally, both of them were certain of the theorems to be used, but they were uncertain about the recognition of the concepts used in the theorems. In this story, the second fellow ate the fungus, remained healthy, and won his argument.

This story is a good illustration of everyday induction in which no new striking discoveries are performed, but the definition of features is refined by experience. The first mycologist learned what fleshy means in the context of differentiating a death cup from another fungus. In this form of "humble induction," certain implications are never questioned, but concept definitions are what the inductions are about. In other words, the implications are still rote learning, but the concept definitions are those that require real intelligence to learn. This point is very important and seemingly overlooked in philosophical discussions about the growth of science.

The above argument shows that when organization has taken place, the implications are certain, and there is thus no discussion about what an induction is and what a deduction is. Nevertheless, even when the organization is still incomplete, as in new science, or when a new problem is being tackled, statistical arguments are mixed with symbolic ones in order to determine what is induction and what is deduction.

3.3.2 The Type of Inference Is Not Decided by Statistics

The type of inference—deductive or inductive—depends on factors other than the purely statistical.[8] More precisely, $A \Rightarrow B$ with a certainty of $y\%$, and $B \Rightarrow A$ with a certainty of $z\%$, and $y \gg z$ does not really entail that $A \Rightarrow B$ is the deduction and that $B \Rightarrow A$ is the induction. This can be true when an induction is much more reasonable than some very uncertain deductions.

As a first illustration of that point, consider again the uncertainties of $\forall x[\text{smokes}(x) \Rightarrow \text{cancer}(x)]$ with a belief of 10% and $\forall x[\text{cancer}(x) \Rightarrow \text{smokes}(x)]$ with a belief of 0.1%. Suppose also that 70% of the cancer sufferers are also smokers. By seeing a cancer sufferer, the implication $\forall x[\text{smokes}(x) \Rightarrow \text{cancer}(x)]$ can be used the other way round, as an induction, to induce that a given person, Jane, who has cancer, was also a smoker. In this reasoning, it is acknowledged that smoking causes cancer but also that it is not the only source of cancers. For instance, inhaling asbestos also causes cancer for non-smoking persons. This shows

---

[8] This is notwithstanding the temporal condition already included in the definition of probabilistic causality, as seen in Section 3.2.7.

the indisputable inductive form of the inference from cancer to smoking. Nevertheless, because many people show both smoking and cancer, the induction is quite reasonable and has some 70% chance of success in this example. On the contrary, if the deduction about cancer causing smoking is used and if the belief in that deductive inference is 0.1% certain, as in this example, then this deduction will have very little chance against the induction.

More generally, when knowledge is still so uncertain that the implications themselves are uncertain, uncertain equivalences are actually dealt with. In other words, what is causal is not yet known. In this example, the causes of cancer and, even more so, the causes of why people smoke tobacco, are still very shaky. As soon as it can be sure, say, that cancer does not cause smoking, then this example at once does not apply, but, immediately, deducing from smoking to cancer becomes certain as well as inducing from cancer to smoking.

This phenomenon occurs quite often when a science is still evolving on a particular topic. In most cases, however, scientists possess large amounts of background knowledge that help them orient their inferences. Again in the above example, accepting that cancer causes smoking requires that the human race, which has been evolving for most of its history without using tobacco, developed this characteristic for no reason at all. This hypothesis, therefore, goes against background knowledge and has been used here merely as an illustration.

3.4 A PARADOX OF INDUCTION

Hempel's paradox (1965) is very typical of the arguments that have been drawn against the mere possibility of uttering a symbolic induction without being self-contradictory because it disputes the possibility of induction ever being "experimentally" justified.

The paradox relies on the logical equivalence of a theorem and its contraposition. Suppose that some black crows are observed, from which the induction $\forall x$ $[\text{crow}(x) \Rightarrow \text{black}(x)]$ is made. This is an inductive hypothesis that will need confirmation from new observations. Meeting new black crows will obviously confirm $\forall x \, [\text{crow}(x) \Rightarrow \text{black}(x)]$.

Nevertheless, using the two equivalences $(A \Rightarrow B) \equiv (\neg A \vee B)$ and $\neg\neg A \equiv A$, one notes easily that $(A \Rightarrow B) \equiv (\neg\neg A \Rightarrow \neg\neg B) \equiv (\neg\neg\neg A \vee \neg\neg B) \equiv (\neg A \vee \neg\neg B)$ $\equiv ((\neg A) \vee \neg(\neg B)) \equiv (\neg B \Rightarrow \neg A)$. Therefore, $\forall x \, [\text{crow}(x) \Rightarrow \text{black}(x)]$ is equivalent to $\forall x \, [\neg\text{black}(x) \Rightarrow \neg\text{crow}(x)]$ (they are said to be contrapositions to each other). Because they are equivalent, anything that confirms one confirms the contraposition as well. This means that all non-black non-crow entities, say, a white shoe, confirm that crows are black. This contradicts the intuition about what a confirmation should be, hence the paradox.

Two types of argument have mainly been put forward against this paradox.

The first type is of a numerical nature and claims that the "distance" between crows and shoes is very large. Therefore, white shoes do confirm black crows but, in a very weak way, a function of the distance between the concepts.

The second type is of a symbolic nature. It rejects inferences that lead to contrapositions. It can for instance reject the validity of $\neg\neg A \equiv A$, thus claiming that the logic of induction is of intuitionist nature. Notice that the so-called "inference systems" (as opposed to the deduction systems) use only *modus ponens*— from A and $A \Rightarrow B$, infer B—but reject the use of *modus tollens*—from $\neg B$ and $A \Rightarrow B$—infer $\neg A$—which means refusing to consider contrapositions of facts in the inference system.

Let us now develop arguments based on the organization of knowledge. We shall not attempt to refute Hempel's paradox but rather to specify when it applies and when it does not.

First Argument.   Contraposing certain theorems about uncertain features is not paradoxical.

This argument takes advantage of the standard scientific practice of transferring uncertainty from the theorems onto the definition of the predicates involved, as illustrated in Section 3.3.1. The theorems are then certain, and the induction (or the confirmation, depending on which stage is being considered) that takes place when meeting instances is relative to the definition of concepts and not to the validity of the theorems. The mushroom example of Section 3.3.1 illustrates how contraposition acts upon the uncertain concepts linked by the certain theorem. In the example, it was very clear that the observation of a dubiously fleshy mushroom foot allows the definition of a fragile foot to be refined. It does not allow the definition of any type of non-fleshy feet to be refined. In other words, each time a concept is misclassified, it allows the description of all the concepts it could be confused with to be refined and not the description of the concepts it cannot be confused with. Seeing an example of a fleshy foot does not draw upon all kinds of feet, only mushroom feet and only those that can possibly be confused with the fleshy foot in question. This phenomenon, a kind of focusing on the fly, allows the danger of paradoxical confirmation to be restricted by selecting from among all the possible concepts whose properties could be confirmed by contraposition, those of real interest, i.e., those that actually show confusion about the characteristic under observation.

This argument rules all certain theorems about uncertain features out of the possibility of showing Hempel's paradox. Notice however, that it does not rule out the possibility of learning about this knowledge by refining one's knowledge about the concepts, if not about the theorems that are fixed.

Second Argument.   Not all uncertain theorems are prone to lead to a paradox.

This second argument makes use of the semantics associated with the implications. Whenever the semantics of the implication are causality, generality, or temporal or spatial inclusion, there is nothing paradoxical about using its contraposition to confirm a theorem.

Let us consider *causality relationships.*

When $A \Rightarrow B$ means A causes B, it is a standard scientific practice to use instances of $\neg B \& \neg A$ in order to confirm $A \Rightarrow B$.

For instance, *smoking $\Rightarrow$ cancer* is typically an uncertain implication because the exact causes of cancer are not yet fully understood. Nevertheless, doctors are convinced now that smoking is one of the indisputable causes of cancer. The causality itself is 100% sure, but not all exemplars of smokers show a cancer. This is the very reason why arguments using contraposition are actually in use. Each time a non-cancerous non-smoker is met, it confirms that *smoking $\Rightarrow$ cancer*. If all non-smokers were non-cancerous, the proof by contraposition would be very strong, as long as smoking being the cause of cancer is not absurd.[9]

These examples show that Hempel's paradox is simply nonexistent in scientific thinking, as well as in common sense thinking, whenever the implications carry the meaning of causality.

Let us make clear, however, that any non-causal conjunction in the premise of the implication makes it sensitive again to contraposition. For instance, *human & smoking $\Rightarrow$ cancer* is confirmed by any non-human non-cancerous, and a paradox arises because the "part" *human $\Rightarrow$ cancer* is not causal. In other words, the present argument holds only when a careful pruning of the non-causal facts has been performed on the premises of the implication.

This pruning is not always performed by existing ML systems, and this argument shows that keeping spurious facts in an explanation is much more harmful than usually acknowledged.

There is still some need to examine two extreme cases: What if the causal link is reasonable but wrong, and what if the causal link is absurd?

Wrong causal links are dealt with very simply. Suppose $A \Rightarrow B$ is wrongly hypothesized, then it is confirmed by observing both $\neg B$ and $\neg A$ and disconfirmed by observing $\neg B$ and A or B and $\neg A$. For instance, hypothesizing *smoking $\Rightarrow$ AIDS* is confirmed by all smokers and AIDS-sick persons together with all non-smoking AIDS-free persons. It is disconfirmed by meeting many non-smokers who have caught AIDS and by even many more smokers who are AIDS-free. It follows that if

---

[9] As an aside, notice that common sense reasoning has the same attitude. Consider "food-nuts" who use non-scientific arguments to justify their macrobiotic diet and who believe that it prevents cancer. They believe in the theorem $\forall x[\text{macrobiotic}(x) \Rightarrow \text{no-cancer}(x)]$, and each time they meet a non-macrobiotic person who has cancer, it confirms their belief in this theorem. Their mistake does not occur because they use some instances of a contraposition in order to confirm their theorem. Their mistake occurs because they refuse to acknowledge that there are many more instances of non-macrobiotic and non-cancerous persons than of non-macrobiotic and cancerous persons.

an ML system conjectures wrongly, it will find disconfirmation in the data, as it should.

An absurd causal link is much more devious. If it is hypothesized, then it will be confirmed by no positive instances, but its contraposition will be confirmed by many. For instance, hypothesizing *smoking* $\Rightarrow$ *blue_hair* is directly confirmed by nobody, but all non-smokers have non-blue hair, and they all confirm the contraposition. It is disconfirmed by non-smokers with blue hair (there are none) and smokers with non-blue hair. Finally, it is confirmed by all non-smokers and disconfirmed by all smokers. If there happen to be many more non-smokers than smokers, then there will be strong statistical evidence supporting the crazy hypothesis. More generally, a crazy hypothesis is confirmed or disconfirmed depending on the size of the support of its premise versus the size of the support of the negation of its premise. Obviously, this has little to do with science because scientists tend to avoid uttering hypotheses with no positive support at all. On the other hand, it is very relevant and dangerous for an ML system that would generate inductive hypotheses that have no direct confirmation.

It is also obvious that organized knowledge will not generate such absurd hypotheses. For instance, blue-colored hair is known to be caused by a special dye only, and dyeing has no causal link with smoking.

In conclusion, we acknowledge that Hempel's paradox occurs in the case of irrelevant causal links, but there are many ways of avoiding this danger, knowledge organization being one of them.

Consider now *generality relationships and temporal or spatial inclusion.*

Let us denote the set of all the instances showing a property A by {A}. In the case of generality relations, spatial inclusion, or temporal inclusion, the implication $A \Rightarrow B$ carries the meaning that {A} is included in {B}. Existing structures naturally allow the attention to be focused on siblings of the same grandparent.

Again, using the contrapositions of the implication is standard scientific practice. It is called "using negative examples of the concept" in order to refine the definition of the concept. Usually, negative examples are siblings of the same grandparent.

For instance, the implication *crow* $\Rightarrow$ *bird* is indeed confirmed by meeting all kinds of animals that are neither crows nor birds.

Finally, consider the *attribution of properties.*

This is the typical case for which Hempel's paradox does apply. Nevertheless, it does not strike one very strongly because the organization of knowledge allows the attention to be focused on limiting it.

Consider the theorem that states that *amanita phalloides* has a fragile foot (refer also to Section 3.3.1), *phalloides* $\Rightarrow$ *fragile_foot*. Accept now that this theorem is uncertain, and let us simplify the taxonomy of fungi by considering *amanita* as a direct child of *fungus*. Obviously, meeting any kind of fungus with a non-fragile foot should not confirm this theorem. In the real world, looking at an isolated fragile foot of *phalloides* is of no interest. Actually, this fragile foot is compared to one (or several) non-fragile ones but not to all non-fragile ones. For instance, it is not compared with the fibrous foot of *lepiota procera* ("parasol mushroom") because the gill size, form, and attachment of the tribe *lepiota* are totally different from that of the tribe *amanita*, etc. In the example already given in Section 3.3.1, the fragile foot of *phalloides* was compared to the fleshy foot of *spissa* because of the very special fuzziness of the exemplar considered; normally, the two fungi are easy to differentiate by other features. Again, let us suppose that the theorem *spissa* ⇒ *fleshy_foot* is uncertain. Because of the focus of attention and because only these two fungi are compared, ¬*phalloides* means only *spissa*, and ¬*fragile_foot* means only *fleshy_foot*. Thus, confirming *spissa* ⇒ *fleshy_foot* confirms *phalloides* ⇒ *fragile_foot* as well. It is indeed paradoxical, but it happens only for those cases upon which one is focusing attention, thus relatively seldom.

Third Argument. Only concepts that are siblings in a taxonomy of generality can show the paradox.

It is quite a simple argument based on the fact that concepts are organized in taxonomies of generality. Therefore, theorems about their properties are not exactly of the form

$$\forall x \, [\text{concept}(x) \Rightarrow \text{property}(x)]$$

but rather of the form

$$\forall x \in \{\text{class}\} \, [\text{concept}(x) \Rightarrow \text{property}(x)]$$

The contraposition of this last theorem is

$$\forall x \in \{\text{class}\} \, [\neg\text{property}(x) \Rightarrow \neg\text{concept}(x)]$$

This rules out all the concepts that do not belong to the same class, thus avoiding most of the embarrassing cases. For instance, based on the supposition that *crow* is a direct descendent of *bird* (actually, *crow* is a direct descendent of the genus *corvus*), the induced theorem reads

$$\forall x \in \{\text{bird}\} \, [\text{crow}(x) \Rightarrow \text{black}(x)]$$

The contraposition of this theorem reads

$$\forall x \in \{\text{bird}\} \, [\neg\text{black}(x) \Rightarrow \neg\text{crow}(x)]$$

Concepts, disjoint from a direct parent of the concept under study, do not intervene in the confirmation of the properties of this concept. This rids us of the "white shoe" problem. Only direct siblings of the same parent constitute a problem. When a taxonomy of generality is not detailed enough, then Hempel's paradox shows again. In the above instance, it is still a puzzling fact that a red cardinal confirms in any sense that a crow is black. Refining the taxonomies makes the problem smaller, but still, uncertain theorems about properties show the paradox.

Notice how much this argument relies on the organization of knowledge. It is obviously possible to "rewrite" $\forall x \in \{\text{bird}\}$ [crow$(x) \Rightarrow$ black(x)] under a non-organized form, such as $\forall x$ [bird(x) & crow$(x) \Rightarrow$ black(x)] or $\forall x$ [bird$(x) \Rightarrow$ [crow$(x) \Rightarrow$ black(x)]]. If this is done, i.e., if the notion of class, *bird*, containing the concept *crow*, is forgotten, then the paradox shows again. From the ML point of view, this means that systems that do not associate their semantics with generalization and particularization of concepts will fall into Hempel's paradox.

This discussion of Hempel's paradox shows that acquiring new knowledge must take place among structures of knowledge. In other words, to avoid confirming wrongly a hypothesis by instances of its contraposition requires careful organization of the acquired knowledge, together with the induction module.

This also brings up the point that many inductive programs, such as ID3 (Quinlan, 1983), and AGAPE (Kodratoff and Ganascia, 1983), that do not structure the domain knowledge while learning can be suspected of the defect of being able to confirm hypotheses by spurious examples that simply confirm the contraposition of the hypothesis.

More recently, new inductive techniques, such as neural networks and genetic algorithms, generate unstructured knowledge, and it would be interesting to check if they fall in the same trap.

On the other hand, more recent integrated approaches, as advocated for in Michalski and Kodratoff (1990), can be seen as illustrations of the requirements put forward in this chapter. For example, the integrated system MOBAL (Morik, 1988) learns within an object-oriented framework explicitly for the purpose of avoiding Hempel's paradox (Kietz, 1988).

3.5 CONCLUSIONS

We would like first to reject the obvious objection that our reasoning contains a logical loop because structures seem to be needed to learn structures. Non-paradoxical new causal structures can be learned easily. Similarly, certain implications about uncertain concepts and generality taxonomies can be learned directly. Only uncertain properties can be confirmed wrongly by instances of their contrapositions.

This discussion suggests a new definition for statistical model of confirmation of inductive hypotheses and also a non-statistical model.

An inductive hypothesis is statistically well entrenched when many instances of this hypothesis have actually been met. When the hypothesis is about causality (taking care to avoid absurd hypotheses and non-causal premises), contrapositions count as instances of the hypothesis, the same as for generality. When the hypothesis is relative to the property of a concept, instances of the contraposition are no longer a valid confirmation, and care must be given to differentiate direct instances and contraposition instances.

An inductive hypothesis is logically confirmed when its negation cannot be proven with a high belief and when it does not contradict a relevant causal model.

Induction brings uncertain results. It is therefore very tempting to reduce induction to uncertain reasoning, as proposed by Carnap (1950) and recently accepted by Holland et al. (1986). That Carnap reduces induction to uncertain deduction is very clear from the preface of his book, where he describes his "basic conceptions: (1) all inductive reasoning,..., is reasoning in terms of probability; (2) hence inductive logic, the theory of inductive reasoning, is the same as probability logic." In Section 43 of his book (this section is called "Inductive and Deductive Logic"), he asserts again that inductive logic can be considered as being built from deductive logic by adding to it the notion of degree of confirmation. In Carnap (1968), he states "from my point of view, it seems preferable to take as the essential point in inductive reasoning the determination of probability values." The present chapter strongly opposes this opinion by showing the deep difference between induction and deduction whenever the knowledge is already structured, or some new structures are built around old ones; "the essential point in inductive reasoning" is seen here as the building of new structures of knowledge.

The reason behind Popper's (1959) opposition to including induction in the process of the growth of science is "the question how it happens that a new idea occurs to a man...may be of great interest to empirical psychology; but it is irrelevant to the logical analysis of scientific knowledge.... Accordingly, I shall distinguish sharply between the process of conceiving a new idea and the methods...of examining it logically...there is no such thing as a logical method for having new ideas, or a logical reconstruction of this process." In Popper (1972), he still states that "a universal theory...is certainly not inferred inductively or with the help of 'inductive assumptions'." Because a good part of ML is about a reconstruction of the process of inventing new ideas, either ML is a complete failure, or Popper's view of the growth of science should be questioned. Anyhow, symbolic induction and its link with the creation of new structures in knowledge provide a way of reconstructing the process of discovery in a rational way. This kind of process does not hamper the subsequent Popperian steps of verification. It simply seems that we are better armed to propose models and simulations of the discovery process than in Popper's time. A good example of such behavior is provided by Zytkow and Simon (1986), who reconstructed the discovery of Dalton's law and were subsequently able to criticize the way Lavoisier refuted the theory of phlogiston.

The main tool for the organization of knowledge is presently the building of taxonomies of generality, as pointed out by Michalski (1983). Clustering (Michalski and Stepp, 1983), chunking (Laird et al., 1986, 1987), or building macro-operators as in PRODIGY (Carbonell, Knoblock, and Minton, 1990) are also well-known in the ML community. This chapter shows that other organizational techniques such as part-of hierarchies, time inclusion, causality, attribution of properties, and also perhaps Explanation Patterns (Schank, 1986; Schank and Kass, 1990) should also be considered as tools for justifying the inductive techniques built around them.

We also show that symbolic and numeric approaches to induction are very different, even if some techniques, such as temporal inclusion or clustering, belong to both. We have shown that even in the presence of uncertain knowledge, that is, even if $A \Rightarrow B$ with a certainty of $y\%$, and $B \Rightarrow A$ with a certainty of $z\%$, the structure of knowledge forbids it to be an uncertain equivalence. Actually, the structure of knowledge gives to $A \Rightarrow B$, besides the classical $(\neg A \vee B)$, semantics, which tell, in principle independently of the values of y and z, which of $A \Rightarrow B$ and $B \Rightarrow A$ is a deductive and which an inductive inference.

That the two approaches are different calls for the building of symbolic/numeric tools for machine learning, but there is still a large amount of work to be done in order to combine them to increase the efficiency of a learning system.

The main principle of numeric techniques is to give a numeric representation of knowledge and to apply the semantics of numbers in order to simulate reasoning processes. The semantics of the domain is really included in the way computations are performed, but this is done in an implicit way. The numeric computations increase the speed of reasoning but forbid any explanation of intermediary steps. Only the specialist in this kind of computation, as opposed to the field specialist, can understand what is going on inside the system. The approach of AI, which emphasizes the symbolic side of reasoning, demands that the representation of knowledge be explicit, and that the reasoning be carried out according to the semantics of the application field. Explanations are then obtained quite easily, but the reasoning becomes very lengthy to perform. Actual systems obviously need fast computation techniques, but they also need good explanation facilities for their validation and updating. A challenge for AI systems is to merge the two approaches without losing too much either in efficiency or in explainability.

ACKNOWLEDGMENTS

This work has been supported partially by PRC/GRECO-IA of "CNRS" and "Ministre de la Recherche et de la Technologie." Early presentations of these results to the AI group of GMD Bonn, and at the First International Workshop on Multistrategy Learning, were the source of fruitful changes in the chapter. My thanks to Maria Zemankova for drawing my attention on Dupré's and Gemes' recent philosophical papers.

References

Bareiss, E.R., Porter, B.W., Wier, C.C. "Protos: An Exemplar-Based Learning Apprentice," in *Machine Learning: An Artificial Intelligence Approach, Volume III*, Y. Kodratoff, R.S. Michalski (Eds.), Morgan Kaufmann, San Mateo, CA, pp. 112–127, 1990.

Benzecri, J.P. (with many co-authors). *L'analyse des Données*, Dunod, Paris, 1973.

Buchanan, B.G., Shortliffe, E.H. *Rule-Based Expert Systems: The MYCIN Experiments of the Stanford Heuristic Programming Project*, Addison-Wesley Publishing Company, Reading, MA, 1984.

Carbonell, J.G., Knoblock, C.A., Minton, S., "PRODIGY: An Integrated Architecture for Planning and Learning," in *Architectures for Intelligence*, K. VanLehn (Ed.), Erlbaum, Hillsdale, NJ, pp. 241–278, 1990.

Carnap, R., *Logical Foundations of Probability*, Univ. of Chicago Press, Chicago, 1950.

Cox, P.T., Pietrzykowski, T., "Causes for Events: Their Computation and Applications," *Proceedings of the Eighth International Conference on Automated Deduction*, Oxford, Lecture Notes in Computer Science n–230, Springer Verlag, Berlin, pp. 608–621, 1986.

Dietterich, G.T., Michalski, R.S. "Inductive Learning of Structural Descriptions: Evaluation Criteria and Comparative Review of Selected Methods," *Artificial Intelligence Journal 16*, pp. 257–294, 1981.

Dupré, J. "Probabilistic Causality Emancipated," in *Midwest Studies in Philosophy IX: Causation and Causal Theories*, P.A. French, T.E. Uehling, Jr., H.K. Wettstein (Eds.), Univ. of Minnesota Press, Minneapolis, pp. 169–175, 1985.

————. "Probabilistic Causality: A Rejoinder to Ellery Eels," *Philosophy of Science 57*, 690–698, 1990.

Duval, B., Kodratoff, Y. "A Tool for the Management of Incomplete Theories: Reasoning about Explanations," in *Machine Learning, Meta-Reasoning and Logics*, P. Brazdil and K. Konolige (Eds.), Kluwer Academic Press, New York, pp. 135–158, 1989.

Eels, E. "Probabilistic Causal Interaction," *Philosophy of Science 53*, 52–64, 1986.

————. "Probabilistic Causality: Reply to John Dupré," *Philosophy of Science 54*, 105–114, 1987.

Eels, E., Sober, E. "Probabilistic Causality and the Question of Transitivity," *Philosophy of Science 50*, 35–57, 1983.

Gemes, K. "Horwitch, Hempel, and Hypothetico-deductivism," *Philosophy of Science 57*, 699–702, 1990.

Hempel, C.G., *Aspects of Scientific Explanation*, The Free Press, New York, 1965.

Holland, J.H., Holyoak, K.J., Nisbett, R.E., Thagard, P.R., *Induction*, The MIT Press, Cambridge, MA, 1986.

Kietz, J.U. "Inkrementelle und Reversible Acquisition von Taxonomischem Wissen," Studienarbeit, TU Berlin, Computer Science Department, 1988.

Kodratoff, Y., "Generalizing and Particularizing as the Techniques of Learning," *Computers and Artificial Intelligence 2*, 417–441, 1983.

Kodratoff, Y. *Introduction to Machine Learning*, Pitman, London, 1988.

———. "Learning Expert Knowledge by Improving the Explanations Provided by the System" in *Machine Learning: An Artificial Intelligence Approach, Volume III*, Y. Kodratoff, R.S. Michalski (Eds.), Morgan Kaufmann, San Mateo, CA, pp. 433–465, 1990.

Kodratoff, Y., Diday, E. (Eds.) *Induction Symbolique et Numérique é Partir des Données*, Cepadues édition, Toulouse, 1991.

Kodratoff, Y., Ganascia, J.G., "Improving the Generalization Step in Learning," in *Machine Learning: An Artificial Intelligence Approach, Volume II*, R.S. Michalski, J.G. Carbonell, T.M. Mitchell (Eds.), Morgan Kaufmann, San Mateo, CA, pp. 215–244, 1986.

Kodratoff, Y., Ganascia, J.G. "Learning as a Non-deterministic but Exact Logical Process," in *The Mind and the Machine*, S. Torrance (Ed.), Ellis Horwood, London pp. 182–191, 1984.

Kodratoff, Y., Perdrix, H., Franova, M., "Traitement Symbolique du Raisonnement Incertain," Actes Congre s AFCET *Matériels et Logiciels pour la 5 me Génération*, Paris, pp. 33–45, 1985.

Kodratoff, Y., Rouveirol, C., Tecuci, G., Duval, B., "Symbolic approaches to uncertainty," in Z.W. Ras, and M. Zemankova (Eds.), *Intelligent Systems: State of the Art and Future Directions*, Ellis Horwood, London, 1990.

Laird, J.E., Newell, A., Rosenbloom P.S. "SOAR: An Architecture for General Intelligence," *Artificial Intelligence 33*, pp. 1–64, 1987.

Laird, J.E., Rosenbloom, P.S., Newell, A. "Chunking in SOAR: The Anatomy of a General Learning Mechanism," *Machine Learning 1*, pp. 11–46, 1986.

Lakatos, I. *The Methodology of Scientific Research Programmes*, Cambridge University Press, Cambridge, UK, 1978.

Michalski, R.S., "A Theory and Methodology of Inductive Learning," in *Machine Learning: An Artificial Intelligence Approach, Volume 1*, R.S. Michalski, J.G. Carbonell, T.M. Mitchell (Eds.), Tioga, Palo Alto, CA, pp. 83–134, 1983.

Michalski, R.S., "Inductive Learning as Rule-guided Transformation of Symbolic Descriptions: A Theory and Implementation," in *Automatic Program Construction Techniques*, A. Biermann, G. Guiho, and Y. Kodratoff (Eds.), Macmillan Publishing Company, New York, pp. 517–552, 1984.

———. "Toward a Unified Theory of Learning: Multi-strategy, Task-Adaptive Learning," Report MLI 90–1, George Mason Univ., Fairfax, VA, 1990.

Michalski, R.S., "Inferential Learning Theory as Conceptual Basis for Multistrategy Learning," in *Machine Learning: A Multistrategy Approach, Volume IV*, R.S. Michalski and G. Tecuci (Eds.), Morgan Kaufmann Publishers, San Mateo, CA, 1994.

Michalski, R.S., Kodratoff, Y. "Research in Machine Learning: Recent Progress, Classification of Methods, and Future Direction," in *Machine Learning: An Artificial Intelligence Approach, Volume III*, Y. Kodratoff and R.S. Michalski (Eds.), Morgan Kaufmann, San Mateo, CA, pp. 3–30, 1990.

Michalski, R.S., Stepp, R.E., "Learning from Observation: Conceptual Clustering," in *Machine Learning: An Artificial Intelligence Approach*, Michalski, R.S., Carbonell, J.G., Mitchell, T.M. (Eds.), Morgan Kaufmann, San Mateo, CA, pp. 331–363, 1983.

Morik, K. "Acquiring Domain Models," in *Knowledge Acquisition Tools for Expert Systems 2*, Boose, J. and Gaines, B. (Eds.), Academic Press, San Diego, CA, 1988.

Nagel, E. *The Structure of Science, Problems in the Logic of Scientific Explanation*, Routledge and Kegan, London, 1961.

Pazzani, M., "Creating High Level Knowledge Structures from Simple Elements," in *Knowledge Representation and Organization in Machine Learning*, Morik K. (Ed.), Lecture Notes in AI, n–347, Springer-Verlag, Berlin, pp. 258–288, 1989.

Peirce, C.S. "Elements of Logic" in *Collected Papers of Charles Sanders Peirce (1839–1914)*, C.H. Hartshone and P. Weiss (Eds.), Harvard University Press, Cambridge, MA, 1965.

Popper, K.R. *The Logic of Scientific Discovery,* Harper and Row, New York, 1959.

———. *Conjectures and Refutations: The Growth of Scientific Knowledge,* Harper and Row, New York, 1963.

———. *Objective Knowledge,* Clarendon Press, Oxford, UK, 1972.

Quinlan, J.R. "Learning Efficient Classification Procedures and Their Application to Chess End Games," in *Machine Learning: An Artificial Intelligence Approach*, R.S. Michalski, J.G. Carbonell, T.M. Mitchell (Eds.), Morgan Kaufmann, Tioga, Palo Alto, CA,, pp. 463–482, 1983.

Schank, R., *Explanation Patterns: Understanding Mechanically and Creatively*, Erlbaum, Hillsdale, NJ, 1986.

Schank, R.C., Kass, A. "Explanations, Machine Learning, and Creativity," in *Machine Learning: An Artificial Intelligence Approach, Volume III*, Y. Kodratoff and R.S. Michalski (Eds.), Morgan Kaufmann, San Mateo, CA, pp. 31–48, 1990.

Shafer, G.A. *Mathematical Theory of Evidence*, Princeton University Press, Princeton NJ, 1979.

Suppes, P. "Conflicting Intuitions about Causality," in *Midwest Studies in Philosophy IX, Causation and Causal Theories*, University of Minnesota Press, Minneapolis, MN, pp. 151–168, 1984.

Van Fraassen, B.C., *The Scientific Image*, Clarendon Press, Oxford, UK,1980.

———. "Empiricism in the Philosophy of Science," in *Images of Science*, P.M. Churchland and C. A. Hooker (Eds), The University of Chicago Press, Chicago, pp. 245–308, 1985.

Vrain, C. "OGUST: A System Which Learns Using Domain Properties Expressed as Theorems," in *Machine Learning: An Artificial Intelligence Approach, Volume III*, Y. Kodratoff and R.S. Michalski (Eds.), Morgan Kaufmann, San Mateo, CA, pp. 360–382, 1990.

Watkins, J.W.N. "Hume, Carnap, and Popper," in *The Problem of Inductive Logic*, I. Lakatos (Ed), North Holland, Amsterdam, pp. 271–282, 1968.

Zadeh, L.A. "Fuzzy Sets," *Information and Control 8*, 338–353, 1965.

Zytkow, J.M., Simon, H.A. "A Theory of Historical Discovery: The Construction of Componential Models," *Machine Learning 1*, pp. 107–136, 1986.

4

AN INFERENCE-BASED FRAMEWORK
FOR MULTISTRATEGY LEARNING

Gheorghe Tecuci
(George Mason University and
Romanian Academy)

Abstract

This chapter describes a general framework for multistrategy learning. One idea of this framework is to view learning as an inference process and to integrate the elementary inferences that are employed by the single-strategy learning methods. Another idea is to base learning on building and generalizing a special type of explanation structure called plausible justification tree that is composed of different types of inference and relates the learner's knowledge to the input. In this framework, learning consists of extending and/or improving the knowledge base of the system so that to explain the input received from an external source of information. The framework is illustrated with a specific method that integrates deeply and dynamically explanation-based learning, determination-based analogy, empirical induction, constructive induction, and abduction.

4.1 INTRODUCTION

The Knowledge Base (KB) of an intelligent system could be regarded as an internal model of the system's application domain. The more adequately this model approximates the domain, the better is the system's behavior. Therefore, a general learning goal of the system is to continually improve its domain model, either from the point of view of competence or from the point of view of performance. The system is improving its competence if it learns to solve a broader class of problems and to make fewer mistakes in problem solving. Also, it is improving its performance, if it learns to solve more efficiently the problems from its area of competence.

Research in machine learning has developed several single-strategy learning methods, such as empirical induction, explanation-based learning, learning by abduction, learning by analogy, and case-based learning, that are based on a primary type of inference and illustrate different ways in which a system can learn (Michalski, Carbonell, and Mitchell, 1983; Michalski, Carbonell, and Mitchell, 1986; Kodratoff and Michalski, 1990; Shavlik and Dietterich, 1990). Each of these learning methods could be characterized by the learning task performed. The learning task is defined by the input from which the system learns, the knowledge base (which contains the knowledge that the system can use during learning and which represents the domain model), and the learning goal (which indicates what the system tries to learn). That is, the learning task defines both the applicability conditions and the results of the corresponding learning method. For instance, in the case of empirical induction, where the primary type of inference is inductive generalization/specialization, the input may consist of *many (positive and/or negative) examples* of some concept C, the KB usually contains only a *small amount of knowledge* related to the input, and the goal is to *learn a description of C* in the form of an inductive generalization of the positive examples that does not cover the negative examples. This description extends the domain model and may improve the competence of the system. In the case of explanation-based learning, where the primary type of inference is deduction, the input may consist of only *one example* of a concept C, the KB should contain *complete knowledge about the input*, and the goal is to *learn an operational description of C* in the form of a deductive generalization of the input example. This description is a reorganization of some knowledge pieces from the domain model and may improve the performance of the system. In the case of learning by analogy (and case-based learning), the input may consist of *a new entity I*, the KB should contain an *entity S that is similar to I*, and the goal is to *learn new knowledge about the input I* by transferring it from the known entity S. In the case of learning by abduction, the input may be *a fact F*, the KB should contain *causal knowledge related to the input*, and the goal is to *learn a new piece of knowledge* that would account for the input. Learning by analogy, case based-learning, and learning by abduction extend the domain model with new pieces of knowledge and usually improve the competence of the system.

This brief characterization of the learning tasks of different single-strategy learning methods shows that these methods have limited applicability because each requires a special type of input and background knowledge and learns a specific type of knowledge.

On the other hand, the complementary nature of these requirements and results naturally suggests that by properly integrating the single-strategy methods, one could obtain a synergistic effect in which different strategies mutually support each other and compensate for each other's weaknesses. As a result, one may build a multistrategy learning system that may be applicable to a wider spectrum of problems. Each of the multistrategy learning systems that have been built in the last several years illustrates a specific way in which several single-strategy methods could be integrated in order to perform a learning task that could not be performed by a single-strategy method (e.g., Lebowitz, 1986; Danyluk, 1987; Minton and Carbonell, 1987; Pazzani, 1988; Tecuci, 1988; Flann and Dietterich, 1989; Hirsh, 1989; Bergadano and Giordana, 1990; Genest, Matwin, and Plante, 1990; Shavlik and Towell, 1990; Tecuci and Kodratoff, 1990; Whitehall, 1990; Wilkins, 1990; Cohen, 1991; De Raedt, 1991; Gordon, 1991; Mooney and Ourston, 1994; Morik, 1994; Ram and Cox, 1994; Reich, 1994; Saitta, Botta, and Neri, 1993; Widmer, 1994).

After the development of many methods and techniques for the integration of learning strategies, the research in machine learning started to address the problem of defining general principles and frameworks for the design of advanced multistrategy learning systems. One such framework for a multistrategy learning system consists of a cascade of single strategy learning modules in which the output of one module is an input to the next module. Another framework consists of a global control module and a toolbox of single strategy learning modules, all using the same knowledge base. The control module analyzes the relationship between the input and the knowledge base and decides which learning module to activate.

This chapter presents another general framework for multistrategy learning. One idea of this framework is to regard learning as an inference process and to integrate the elementary inferences (like deduction, analogy, abduction, generalization, specialization, abstraction, concretion), that are employed by the single-strategy learning methods. As a consequence, instead of integrating learning strategies at a macro level (as is done in most of the current multistrategy systems), one could integrate the different elementary inferences that generate individual learning strategies. Another idea of the framework is to base learning on building and generalizing a special type of explanation structure, called plausible justification tree, that is composed of different types of inference and relates the learner's knowledge to the input. In this framework, learning consists of extending and/or improving the knowledge base of the system to explain the input received from an external source of information.

The next section presents this general framework for multistrategy learning. The rest of the chapter illustrates the general framework with a specific concept learning and theory revision method that deeply and dynamically integrates explanation-based learning, determination-based analogy, empirical induction, constructive induction, and abduction.

4.2 INFERENCE-BASED MULTISTRATEGY LEARNING

As mentioned, the KB of an intelligent system could be regarded as a model of the system's application domain. During problem solving, the system uses this model in order to answer questions about the application domain or to find solutions to different problems. For instance, it can answer if a certain fact is true in the real world by simply checking if the fact is explicitly represented in the model or derives form facts that are explicitly represented.

One could regard learning as a reverse process in which the system receives information about the external world as, for example, a new fact (or a solution to a certain problem) and tries to improve its domain model to be able to infer the received input, as well as similar ones (or to solve the input problem and similar ones).

Based on this observation, one could define a general learning scenario in which the system has an incomplete and partially incorrect knowledge base (domain model) and receives new input information about the application domain.

The input may take different forms. It may be a ground fact. It may consist of one or several positive and/or negative examples of a concept. It may also consist of one or several positive (and negative) examples of problem solving episodes, each episode specifying a problem and its solution.

The goal of the system is to improve its KB to consistently integrate the information contained in the input. More precisely, after learning from an input I, the KB should be such that a generalization of I is inferable from the KB.

The general learning strategy is based on understanding the input in terms of the current KB. This means that the system will try to build a plausible justification tree that demonstrates that the input is a plausible consequence of the knowledge from the KB.

A plausible justification tree is like a proof tree, except that the inferences that compose it may be the result of different types of reasoning (not only deductive but also analogical, abductive, probabilistic, fuzzy, etc.).

Let us suppose, for instance, that the learner's input is a new fact

$$P_n(a,b) \tag{1}$$

where "P_n" is a predicate, and "a," "b" are object names or object properties.

To "understand" this input, the learner would try to build a plausible justification tree such as the one from Figure 4.1. The root of the tree is the input fact, the leaves are facts from the KB, and the intermediate nodes are intermediate facts generated during the "understanding" process. The branches connected to any given node link this node with facts, the conjunction of which *certainly* or *plausibly implies* the fact at the node, according to the learner's KB. The notion "plausibly implies" means that the target (parent node) can be inferred from the premises (children nodes) by some form of plausible reasoning, using the learner's KB. The

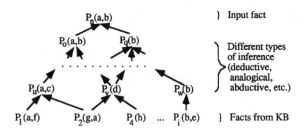

Figure 4.1:   A plausible justification tree for the input $P_n(a,b)$

branches, together with the nodes they link, represent individual inference steps that could be the result of different types of reasoning.

For example, the inference step[1]

$$P_1(a,f) \ \& \ P_2(g,a) \Rightarrow P_u(a,c) \tag{2}$$

(see Figure 4.1) may be the result of deduction based on the following deductive rule from the KB:

$$\forall s \ \forall t \ \forall z \ \forall p \ (P_1(s,t) \ \& \ P_2(z,s) \Rightarrow P_u(s,p)) \tag{3}$$

Also, the inference step

$$P_2(g,a) \ \& \ P_4(h) \rightarrow P_v(d) \tag{4}$$

may be the result of analogy with the following implication from the KB:

$$P_2(g',a') \ \& \ P_4(h') \Rightarrow P_v(d') \tag{5}$$

Indeed, suppose that the system determined that g, a, h, and d are similar to g', a', h', and d', respectively. By analogy, the system concludes that from $P_2(g,a)$ & $P_4(h)$ one can plausibly infer $P_v(d)$ and, hence, inference step 4.

The inference step

$$P_i(b,e) \Rightarrow P_w(b) \tag{6}$$

may be the result of abduction based on the following causal relationship from the KB:

$$\forall r \ (P_i \ (r,e) \Rightarrow P_w(r)) \tag{7}$$

Indeed, let us suppose that the predicate $P_w(b)$ would need to be true in order to build the plausible justification tree in Figure 4.1. Because $P_w(b)$ matches the

---

[1]Throughout this chapter we use : : > to denote concept assignment, $\Rightarrow$ to denote certain (deductive) implication, $\rightarrow$ to denote plausible implication, and - - > to denote plausible determination.

right hand side of rule 7, one may trace backward this rule and hypothesize that $P_i(b,e)$ is true.

An inference step could also result from a combination of empirical generalization and deduction, which is called inductive prediction (see Section 4.4.4). To illustrate this, let us suppose that the KB contains the following examples of the concept $P_n(x,y)$:

$$P_o(c,f) \ \& \ P_q(f) \ \& \ P_j(b,e) : : > P_n(c,f) \tag{8}$$
$$P_o(d,g) \ \& \ P_q(g) \ \& \ P_k(b) : : > P_n(d,g)$$

These examples can be generalized empirically to the rule

$$\forall x \ \forall y \ (P_o(x,y) \ \& \ P_q(y) \rightarrow P_n(x,y)) \tag{9}$$

Rule 9 could then be used to produce the following plausible inference step:

$$P_o(a,b) \ \& \ P_q(b) \rightarrow P_n(a,b) \tag{10}$$

In a more complex case, available examples may not be generalizable so easily to rule 9, and the system may have to use constructive induction.

Thus, the tree in Figure 4.1 shows that $P_n(a,b)$ is a plausible consequence of facts that are explicitly represented in the system's KB.

The understanding process proceeds in the same way when the input is an example of a concept or a specific solution to some problem.

Indeed, let us suppose that the input is the following example of the concept $P_n(x,y)$:

$$P_1(a,f) \ \& \ P_2(g,a) \ \& \ P_3(b) \ \& \ P_4(h) \ \&...\& \ P_j \ (b,c) : : > P_n(a,b) \tag{11}$$

Then the system will try to "understand" it by building the plausible justification tree in Figure 4.1 in which the leaves are facts from the left hand side of equation 11, the intermediate nodes are intermediate facts generated during the "understanding" process, and the top is the right hand side of the equation. Thus, the plausible justification tree shows that equation 11 is indeed an example of the concept $P_n(x,y)$.

Let us now suppose that the input is the following example of a problem solving episode:

$$\textit{to achieve the goal: } P_n(a,b) \tag{12}$$
$$\textit{perform the actions: } P_u(a,c), P_w(b), ... , P_m(c)$$

In this case, the top of the justification tree is the goal $P_n(a,b)$. The intermediate nodes are the actions $P_u(a,c), P_w(b), ... , P_m(c)$, facts that are preconditions of these actions, facts that are effects of these actions, or other generated facts that plausibly imply these preconditions or derive from these effects. The leaves are facts from the knowledge base that are either preconditions of some of the actions $P_u(a,c), P_w(b), ... , P_m(c)$ or plausibly imply these preconditions. Therefore, in this case, the plausible justification tree is a plan that shows that in the context of the current KB, the system could achieve the goal $P_n(a,b)$ by performing the actions $P_u(a,c)$, $P_w(b)$, ... , $P_m(c)$.

An important result of building the plausible justification tree is the generation of new pieces of knowledge that extend the KB to infer the input.

In the case of the justification tree in Figure 4.1, these new pieces of knowledge are

$P_2(g,a)$ & $P_4(h) \rightarrow P_v(d)$	(generated through analogy)
$P_i(b,e)$	(generated through abduction)
$P_o(a,b)$ & $P_q(b) \rightarrow P_n(a,b)$	(generated through inductive prediction)

By asserting these pieces of knowledge into the KB, the system is able to deductively infer the input. The new pieces of knowledge are supported by the fact that they allow building a logical connection (the plausible justification tree) between a KB that represents parts of the real world and a piece of knowledge (the input) that is known to be true in the real world.

In general, a learning system should try to learn as much as possible from any input it receives. In the case of the considered learning scenario, it may do so by generalizing the plausible justification tree as much as allowed by the knowledge used to build it in the first place. By this, it will generalize the hypothesized knowledge so that the resulting KB will entail not only the received input but also similar ones.

One way to generalize the plausible justification tree is presented in Section 4.4.6. It consists of replacing each implication with a plausible generalization and then unifying the connections between these generalized implications.

To illustrate this process, take, for instance, inference step 2; i.e., $P_1(a,f)$ & $P_2(g,a) \Rightarrow P_u(a,c)$. This inference step can be generalized locally into rule 3 that allowed it; i.e., $\forall s \, \forall t \, \forall z \, \forall p \, (P_1(s,t)$ & $P_2(z,s) \Rightarrow P_u(s,p))$. The branches of the tree in Figure 4.1, corresponding to the original inference step 2, are then replaced by the appropriate components of this rule. This is a *deductive generalization.*

Let us now consider inference step 4; i.e., $P_2(g,a)$ & $P_4(h) \rightarrow P_v(d)$. This step was made by analogy with implication (eq. 5); i.e., $P_2(g',a')$ & $P_4(h') \Rightarrow P_v(d')$. The generalization of this analogical inference is based on the idea that a similarity of an entity to a given entity generates an equivalence class of all entities similar to the given entity. Following this idea, one may generate a conjunctive generalization that covers all the inferences that could be derived by analogy with equation 5:

$$P_2(g'',a'') \text{ \& } P_4(h'') \rightarrow P_v(d'') \tag{13}$$

where g'', a'', h'', and d'' represent classes that contain g and g', a and a', h and h', and d and d', respectively. This is a *generalization based on analogy.*

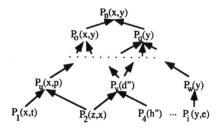

Figure 4.2:   A generalization of the justification tree from Figure 4.1

The abductive step 6, $P_i(b,e) \Rightarrow P_w(b)$, is replaced by $P_i(r,e) \Rightarrow P_w(r)$, according to the general rule 7; i.e., $\forall r \ (P_i(r,e) \Rightarrow P_w(r))$. This generalization is justified because a system abducing $P_i(b,e)$ in order to explain $P_w(b)$ might also abduce $P_i(r,e)$ in order to explain $P_w(r)$ for any r. This is a *generalization based on abduction*.

Finally, the inference step 10, $P_o(a,b) \& P_q(b) \rightarrow P_n(a,b)$, was done by applying rule 9, i.e., $\forall x \forall y \ (P_o(x,y) \& P_q(y) \rightarrow P_n(x,y))$, which was obtained by empirical generalization. Then the corresponding branch is replaced by rule 9. This is an *empirical inductive generalization*.

As one can notice, the generalization of an implication depends on the type of inference that generated it and on the system's knowledge. This idea opens a new research direction in the theory of generalization by suggesting that a specific type of generalization may be associated with each type of inference. Consequently, a learning system may perform not only deductive and empirical generalizations but also generalizations based on analogy, abduction, etc.

As mentioned above, after all the inference steps are locally generalized, the system unifies their connections. In particular, it makes the following unifications: ($x=s=a''$, $z=g''$, $y=r$). In this way, the system builds the general plausible justification tree from Figure 4.2.

During the generalization of the plausible justification tree, some of the previously learned knowledge may also be generalized as, for instance, the analogical implication 4 $P_2(g,a) \& P_4(h) \rightarrow P_v(d)$, which was generalized to rule 13, $P_2(g'',a'')$ $\& \ P_4(h'') \rightarrow P_v(d'')$.

Other general knowledge pieces have been generated during the building of the plausible justification tree in Figure 4.1. An example of such a knowledge piece is rule 9.

The generalized plausible justification tree shows how a generalization of the input is inferable from the KB. However, this tree was built by making plausible inferences and plausible generalizations and is therefore less plausible.

The system may improve the generalized justification tree, as well as the knowledge pieces learned during its building, by learning from additional input (other facts of the form $P_n(a_k, b_k)$, concept examples, or examples of problem solving episodes).

For each new positive example E_i, the system will generalize the plausible justification tree in Figure 4.2 to cover a plausible justification of E_i. Also, some of the knowledge pieces from the KB may be generalized to cover inferences from the plausible justification of E_i.

For each new negative example N_j, the system will specialize the general plausible justification tree to no longer cover a plausible justification tree that would show that N_j is a positive example. This may also require the specialization of some knowledge pieces from the KB such as rule 9 or rule 13.

After all the examples have been processed, the system may extract several (operational or abstract) concept definitions from the final general justification tree. For instance, if the final general justification tree is the one from Figure 4.2, then its leaves represent an operational definition of $P_n(x,y)$:

$$P_1(x,t) \ \& \ P_2(z,x) \ \& \ P_4(h'') \ \&...\& \ P_i(y,e) : : > P_n(x,y) \tag{14}$$

Also, the top part of the justification tree represents the most abstract characterization of $P_n(x,y)$:

$$P_o(x,y) \ \& \ P_q(y) : : > P_n(x,y) \tag{15}$$

Other learnable knowledge pieces are various abstractions of the input examples. For instance, one abstraction is obtained by instantiating the variables in the above abstract characterization (eq. 15) to specific arguments in a certain example:

$$P_o(a,b) \ \& \ P_q(b) : : > P_n(a,b) \tag{16}$$

Other abstractions would correspond to lower levels of the generalized justification tree.

As a result of this learning process, the system may increase its problem solving abilities both in terms of competence and performance. Indeed, if the input is a new fact, then the system will be able to predict that certain similar facts are true in the real world. If the input is a sequence of positive (and negative) examples of some concept, then the system will be able to predict if a new instance is (or is not) an example of the learned concept. Also, if the system retains operational definitions such as equation 14, then it may be able to make these predictions faster. If the input is an example of a problem solving episode, represented by a problem P and its solution S, then the system will be able to solve problems similar to P by proposing solutions similar to S.

Table 4.1 synthesizes the main steps of this learning methodology.

By generalization of the KB, one means any transformation that results in an increase of knowledge inferable from the KB. The KB may be generalized by generalizing knowledge pieces or by simply adding new knowledge pieces.

Table 4.1:   The learning methodology

- For the first positive example I_1:
  - ○ Build the "best" plausible justification tree T_1 of I_1.
  - ○ Build the plausible generalization T_u of T_1.
  - ○ Generalize the KB to entail T_u.
- For each new positive example I_i:
  - ○ Generalize T_u to cover a plausible justification tree T_i of I_i.
  - ○ Generalize the KB to entail the new T_u.
- For each new negative example I_i:
  - ○ Specialize T_u to no longer cover any plausible justification tree T_i of I_i.
  - ○ Specialize the KB to entail the new T_u without entailing the previous T_u.
- After all the examples have been processed:
  - ○ Extract different concept definitions from T_u.

Similarly, by specialization of the KB, one means any transformation that results in a decrease of knowledge inferable from the KB. The KB may be specialized by specializing knowledge pieces or by simply removing knowledge pieces from the KB.

It is important to stress that the types of inference from the plausible justification trees (see Figure 4.1 and Figure 4.2) and the order in which they are performed depend on the relationship between the input and the KB. Consequently, a learning method developed in the presented framework will integrate dynamically different types of elementary reasoning mechanisms. Moreover, as will be shown in Section 4.7, if a particular learning task corresponds to a single-strategy method, then the behavior of the system should correspond to the application of such a method. Such an adaptive integration of different learning strategies (that seems also to be a characteristic of human learning) has been called multistrategy task-adaptive learning, or MTL for short (Michalski, 1990, 1994; Tecuci and Michalski, 1991a, 1991b).

The next sections present a specific Multistrategy Task-adaptive Learning method that was developed in this framework. The method, called MTL-JT (Multistrategy Task-adaptive Learning based on building plausible Justification Trees), deeply and dynamically integrates explanation-based learning, determination-based analogy, empirical induction, constructive induction, and abduction in order to learn from one or several positive (and negative) concept examples.

4.3 THE LEARNING TASK OF MTL-JT

The learning task of MTL-JT is presented in Table 4.2. As one can notice, it is both a theory revision task and a concept learning task. The main steps of the

Table 4.2: The learning task of MTL-JT

Input: one or several positive (and negative) examples of a concept
The examples are represented as conjunctions of first-order predicates, are considered noise-free, and are presented in sequence.

Knowledge Base: incomplete and partially incorrect
The KB may include a variety of knowledge types (facts, examples, implicative or causal relationships, determinations, etc.) represented with first-order predicates.

Goal: to improve the KB and learn different concept definitions from the input example(s)
The learned concept definitions may be operational or abstract, and the KB is improved by both generalizing and specializing it to entail these definitions.

MTL-JT method are those presented in Table 4.1. A detailed presentation of the method is given in Tecuci (1993).

One may notice the generality of the learning goal. In a specific application of this learning method, this goal would need to be specialized. For instance, some of the learnable concept definitions may not be useful and, consequently, will not be learned.

In order to illustrate this learning task and the corresponding learning method, we shall consider the case of a learning system in the area of geography. The purpose of the system is that of acquiring geographical data and rules in order to answer questions about geography.

Let us consider, for instance, that the knowledge base is the one from Table 4.3. It contains several ground facts, two examples of fertile soil, a plausible determination rule, and four deductive rules.

Table 4.3: A sample of an incomplete and partially incorrect KB

Facts:
  terrain(Philippines, flat), rainfall(Philippines, heavy), water-in-soil(Philippines, high)

Examples (of fertile soil):
  soil(Greece, red-soil) : : > soil(Greece, fertile-soil)
  terrain(Egypt, flat) & soil(Egypt, red-soil) : : > soil(Egypt, fertile-soil)

Plausible determination:
  rainfall(x, y) --> water-in-soil(x, z)

Deductive rules:
  $\forall x$, soil(x, loamy) $\Rightarrow$ soil(x, fertile-soil)
  $\forall x$, climate(x, subtropical) $\Rightarrow$ temperature(x, warm)
  $\forall x$, climate(x, tropical) $\Rightarrow$ temperature(x, warm)
  $\forall x$, water-in-soil(x, high) & temperature(x, warm) & soil(x, fertile-soil) $\Rightarrow$ grows(x, rice)

Table 4.4:   Positive and negative examples of "grows(x, rice)"

Positive Example 1:
   rainfall(Thailand, heavy) & climate(Thailand, tropical) & soil(Thailand, red-soil) &
   terrain(Thailand, flat) & location(Thailand, SE-Asia) : : > grows(Thailand, rice)

Positive Example 2:
   rainfall(Pakistan, heavy) & climate(Pakistan, subtropical) & soil(Pakistan, loamy) &
   terrain(Pakistan, flat) & location(Pakistan, SW-Asia) : : > grows(Pakistan, rice)

Negative Example 3:
   rainfall(Jamaica, heavy) & climate(Jamaica, tropical) & soil(Jamaica, loamy) &
   terrain(Jamaica, abrupt) & location(Jamaica, Central-America) : : > ¬ grows(Jamaica, rice)

Let us also consider that the input consists of the sequence of concept examples from Table 4.4. The left hand side of each positive example (negative example) is the description of a country that grows rice (does not grow rice), and the right hand side is the statement that the respective country grows rice (does not grow rice).

The different types of knowledge pieces learned from the above KB and input examples are presented in Table 4.5.

One result of learning consists of several concept definitions (Michalski, 1990).

The first definition in Table 4.5 is an operational definition of "grows(x, rice)," expressed with the features present in the input examples. The second definition is an abstract definition of "grows(x, rice)," expressed with more general features, derived from those present in the input examples (because this rule was already known, the new knowledge is just that it represents an abstract definition). The third definition is an abstraction of Example 1 that was obtained by instantiating the previous abstract definition.

The other result of learning is the improvement of the KB to entail the learned concept definitions.

The KB was generalized by learning two new facts and a rule. It was also specialized by conjunctively adding a literal to the left hand side of the plausible determination.

As indicated in Table 4.5, the system also retains all the examples of the learned knowledge pieces in order to update them when new knowledge becomes available. These examples have been generated through different forms of plausible reasoning and have been validated during the learning process. Therefore, they also represent an improvement of the KB.

The next three sections illustrate the MTL-JT method, which follows the steps presented in Table 4.1.

Table 4.5:   The learned knowledge

Concept Definitions

Operational definition of "grows(x, rice)":
{ rainfall(x, heavy) & terrain(x, flat) & [climate(x, tropical) ∨ climate(x, subtropical)] &
[soil(x, red-soil) ∨ soil(x, loamy)] } : : > grows(x, rice)

Abstract definition of "grows(x, rice)":
water-in-soil(x, high) & temperature(x, warm) & soil(x, fertile-soil) : : > grows(x, rice)

Abstraction of Example 1:
water-in-soil(Thailand, high) & temperature(Thailand, warm) & soil(Thailand, fertile-soil)
                                                                                      : : > grows(Thailand, rice)

Improved KB

New facts:
water-in-soil(Thailand, high), water-in-soil(Pakistan, high)

New plausible rule:
∀x, soil(x, red-soil) → soil(x, fertile-soil)
with the positive examples: (x<-Greece), (x<-Egypt), (x<-Thailand).

Specialized plausible determination:
rainfall(x, y) & terrain(x, flat) --> water-in-soil(x, z)
with the positive examples: (x<-Philippines, y<-heavy, z<-high),
                              (x<-Thailand, y<-heavy, z<-high),
                              (x<-Pakistan, y<-heavy, z<-high).
with the negative example: (x<-Jamaica, y<-heavy).

4.4 LEARNING FROM THE FIRST EXAMPLE

4.4.1 Building the Plausible Justification Tree

As shown in Table 4.1, the first step of the learning method consists of building a plausible justification tree for the first example received by the system. In MTL-JT, the system builds an AND/OR tree by conducting a top-down uniform-cost search (Nilsson, 1971).

The developed AND/OR tree contains several AND trees, each having a cost that estimates its global plausibility. The cost of a partial AND tree is computed as a tuple (m, n), where m represents the number of the deductive implications in the tree, and n represents the number of the non-deductive implications (which, in the case of MTL-JT, could be obtained by analogy, inductive prediction, or abduction). The ordering relationship for the cost function is defined as follows:

$(m1, n1) < (m2, n2)$ *if and only if $n1<n2$ or ($n1=n2$ and $m1<m2$)*

According to this cost function, the best justification tree is the tree with the fewest number of non-deductive implications. In particular, it is a deductive tree (if one exists) and the deductive tree with the fewest implications (if several exist).

As a general strategy, the system always tries to justify a given predicate (for instance, "grows(Thailand, rice)" in Figure 4.3) by deduction. If it succeeds, then it tries to justify the resulting predicates (i.e., "water-in-soil(Thailand, high)," "temperature(Thailand, warm)," and "soil(Thailand, fertile-soil)"). However, if it fails, then it tries to justify the predicate by using as many plausible reasoning methods as possible. It will try these methods in order: (1) analogy, (2) inductive prediction, and (3) abduction. If one of them produces a plausible inference step, then the system tries the remaining ones in order to confirm or to contradict it. If no contradiction is found, the inference step is accepted. This method (although quite simple and definitely a necessary topic of future research) is related to that employed by humans. Indeed, Collins and Michalski (1989) argue that people solve problems by pursuing different "lines of reasoning." They estimate the "strength" of each line of reasoning and make their conclusion on the basis of this evaluation. If the lines lead to the same conclusion, they have a strong belief in the result. If the lines lead to different conclusions, and the associated "strengths" are roughly similar, people restrain from making any decisive conclusion.

It should be noticed that although at the level of a given inference step, the different reasoning methods are tried in a predefined order, globally (at the level of the resultant justification tree) there is no predefined order. For instance, in the case of the justification tree in Figure 4.3, the order of the inference steps was deduction, analogy, deduction, inductive prediction, and abduction. In general, this order depends on the relationship between the KB and the input. Therefore, the MTL-JT method is an example of a dynamic and deep (i.e., at the level of individual inference steps) integration of single strategy learning methods (each learning method corresponding to a specific type of inference).

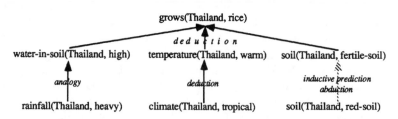

Figure 4.3:   The plausible justification tree T_1 of Example 1

The next sections present briefly the way the different inference steps in Figure 4.3 have been made.

4.4.2 Deduction

Two inference steps in Figure 4.3 are the results of deductions based on the deductive rules from Table 4.3, as illustrated in the following:

$\forall x$, climate(x, tropical) $\Rightarrow$ temperature(x, warm)
climate(Thailand, tropical)
_____

temperature(Thailand, warm)

4.4.3 Analogy

Analogical inference is the process of transferring knowledge from a known entity S to a similar but less known entity T. S is called the *source* because it is the entity that serves as a source of knowledge, and T is called the *target* because it is the entity that receives the knowledge. The central intuition supporting this type of inference is that if two entities, S and T, are similar in some respects, then they could be similar in other respects as well. Therefore, if S has some feature, then one may infer by analogy that T has a similar feature.

In MTL-JT, one uses a simple form of analogy based on plausible determinations defined as follows:

P(x, y) --> Q(x, z) (P plausibly determines Q) meaning
$\forall S$, $\forall T$ { *If* $\exists y$ [P(S, y) & P(T, y)]
     then it is probably true that $\exists z$ [Q(S, z) & Q(T, z)] }
where P and Q are first order logical expressions.

Otherwise stated, if the source S and the target T are characterized by the same feature P (i.e., $P(S, y_0)$=true and $P(T, y_0)$=true), then it is probably true that they are also characterized by a same feature Q. Therefore, if $Q(S, z_0)$=true, then one may infer by analogy that $Q(T, z_0)$=true.

We use the term "probably true" to express that the determination-based analogy we are considering is a weak inference method that does not guarantee the truth of the inferred knowledge. This is similar to the mutual dependency rules introduced in (Collins and Michalski, 1989; Michalski, 1994, Chapter 1 in this book), but different from the determination rules introduced in (Davies and Russell, 1977) that guarantee the truth of the inferred knowledge.

The analogical inference step in Figure 4.3 was made by using the plausible determination

rainfall(x, y) --> water-in-soil(x, z)

(i.e., the rainfall of an area determines the quantity of water in the soil of that area). Indeed, Philippines and Thailand are similar from the point of view of "rainfall" (in both cases this is heavy). Therefore, one may infer by analogy that the two countries are also similar from the point of view of "water-in-soil." Thus, the system concluded "water-in-soil(Thailand, high)" from the fact "water-in-soil(Philippines, high)."

One should notice that a plausible determination rule indicates only what kind of knowledge could be transferred from a source to a target (knowledge about "water-in-soil" in the case of the considered determination) and in what conditions (the same type of "rainfall"). It does not indicate, however, the exact relationship between the type of the rainfall (for instance, "heavy") and the quantity of water in soil ("high"). The exact relationship is indicated by the source entity ("Philippines"). Therefore, a plausible determination rule alone (without such a source entity) cannot be used in the inference process.

In general, the MTL methods are intended to incorporate different forms of analogy based on different kinds of similarities, such as similarities among causes, relations, and meta-relations.

4.4.4 Inductive Prediction

Inductive prediction consists of finding an inductive generalization of a set of examples of a concept and applying it in order to predict if a new instance is (or is not) a positive example of the concept.

The generalization of the examples could be obtained through a process of empirical or constructive generalization. The generalization process is empirical if it involves only descriptors from the description space of the examples and is constructive if it introduces new descriptors that do not belong to the description space of the examples. A detailed characterization of empirical and constructive generalization is given in (Michalski, 1994, Chapter 1 in this book).

In MTL-JT, one uses an inductive generalization method that determines the most specific generalization of a set of positive examples that does not cover any of the negative examples. Moreover, the system is retaining all the examples in order to update the generalization when new examples become available.

One inference step in Figure 4.3 was the result of inductive prediction. Indeed, in order to prove that "soil(Thailand, fertile-soil)" is true, the system looked into the KB for examples of "fertile-soil." Then it inductively generalized them to a rule that was used to predict the inference step from Figure 4.3, as indicated in Table 4.6.

It is important to stress that the system keeps the learned rule in the KB as an inductive generalization. Therefore, future applications of this rule are also inductive predictions. Let us also notice that the rule in Table 4.6 was obtained through

Table 4.6:   Making an inference through inductive prediction

---

Examples from KB:
    soil(Greece, red-soil) : : > soil(Greece, fertile-soil)
    terrain-type(Egypt, flat) & soil(Egypt, red-soil) : : > soil(Egypt, fertile-soil)

Inductive generalization:
    $\forall x$, soil(x, red-soil) $\rightarrow$ soil(x, fertile-soil)
    with the positive examples: (x<-Greece)(x<-Egypt)

Predicted inference:
    soil(Thailand, red-soil) $\rightarrow$ soil(Thailand, fertile-soil)

---

an empirical generalization process because it is expressed only in terms of the descriptors used in the examples.

4.4.5 Abduction

In general, abduction is defined as follows (Josephson, 1991):

D is a collection of data;
H explains D;
<u>*No other hypothesis is able to explain D as well as H does;*</u>
Therefore, H is probably true.

According to this definition, abduction involves two steps: generation of explanatory hypotheses and selection of the "best" hypothesis.

In MTL-JT, one considers two forms of abduction:

1. Tracing backward a deductive rule
    If D is to be explained and H $\Rightarrow$ D then hypothesize H.
    In particular, *if $H = H_1$ & H_2 & ... & H_n and H_2 & ... & H_n is true then hypothesize H_1.*
2. Hypothesizing an ISA relationship (i.e., d_1 ISA d_2)
    If $P(a, d_2)$ is to be explained and $P(a, d_1)$ is true then hypothesize that $P(a, d_1) \rightarrow P(a, d_2)$.

Choosing the "best" abductive hypothesis is the most difficult problem of abductive learning. This is somewhat simplified in the context of MTL-JT because the system is trying to make an inference step through as many plausible inference methods as possible, and abduction is the last one to try (as shown in Section 4.4.1). Therefore, if an inference "$H \rightarrow D$" has been made through some other form of reasoning, abduction is used only to confirm this inference or to contradict it (i.e., to prove "$H \rightarrow C$," where D & C = false).

In the absence of the above criterion, the system chooses the abductive hypotheses in the following order:

- Prefer the ISA abductions.
- Prefer to backtrace the rule H_1 & H_2 & ... & $H_n \Rightarrow D$ with the highest number of true antecedents.
- Prefer to backtrace the rule that has the highest number of known instances.
- Prefer the simplest hypothesis.

In the case of the plausible justification tree in Figure 4.3, the system made an ISA abduction confirming the previously made inductive prediction from Table 4.6. Indeed, "soil(Thailand, fertile-soil)" needed to be proven, and "soil(Thailand, red-soil)" was known to be true. Therefore, the system abduced the ISA relationship:

$$\text{soil(Thailand, red-soil)} \rightarrow \text{soil(Thailand, fertile-soil)} \qquad (17)$$

4.4.6 Generalization of the Plausible Justification Tree

Once a justification tree is successfully created, the system analyzes the individual implications associated with the elementary inference steps to determine if these implications could be generalized locally within the constraints of the KB that were used to make the inference steps. After the implications are generalized locally, the system unifies them globally and builds a generalized justification tree. This technique is an extension of the one elaborated by Mooney and Bennet (1986). The extension concerns the way individual implications are generalized, by using the knowledge from which they were derived. The idea is to replace each implication $A \rightarrow B$ (or $A \Rightarrow B$) with the least general generalization of all the similar implications that could be obtained from the knowledge that produced it (Tecuci & Michalski, 1991b).

A deductive implication is replaced by the deductive rule that generated it. This is a *deductive generalization*. For instance

water-in-soil(Thailand, high) & temperature(Thailand, warm) &
$$\text{soil(Thailand, fertile-soil)} \Rightarrow \text{grows(Thailand, rice)}$$

is replaced by

$\forall x1$, water-in-soil($x1$, high) & temperature($x1$, warm) & soil($x1$, fertile-soil)
$$\Rightarrow \text{grows}(x1, \text{rice})$$

An analogical implication is generalized by considering the knowledge used to derive it. In our example, the implication

rainfall(Thailand, heavy) $\rightarrow$ water-in-soil(Thailand, high) was obtained by analogy with "rainfall(Philippines, heavy)" and "water-in-soil(Philippines, high)" based on the plausible determination

rainfall(x, y) --> water-in-soil(x, z)

Because the system would infer "water-in-soil($x2$, high)" for any $x2$ such that "rainfall($x2$, heavy)," the analogical implication is generalized to

$\forall x2$, rainfall($x2$, heavy) $\rightarrow$ water-in-soil($x2$, high)

This is a *generalization based on analogy.*

An implication obtained through inductive prediction is generalized to the rule that produced it. Therefore, the predicted inference from Table 4.6 would be replaced with the *empirical inductive generalization* from Table 4.6.

An abductive implication obtained by tracing backward a deductive rule would be generalized to that rule. However, for an abduced ISA relationship, there is no knowledge that could be used to generalize it. Therefore, it would remain unchanged in the explanation structure.

An implication obtained through several forms of reasoning is generalized to the least general expression that covers the generalizations corresponding to individual reasoning methods. Therefore, the implication from Figure 4.3, which was obtained through both inductive prediction and abduction, is generalized to the least general generalization of the rule in Table 4.6 and of the abduced ISA relationship (eq. 17):

$\forall x4$, soil($x4$, red-soil) $\rightarrow$ soil($x4$, fertile-soil)

The generalization of the implications from Figure 4.3 forms the explanation structure S_1 from the top part of Figure 4.4. To transform this explanation structure into a general justification tree, one has to determine the most general unification of the connection patterns, which in this case is ($x1=x2=x3=x4=x$). By making these unifications, one obtains the tree from the bottom of Figure 4.4, which represents the most general plausible generalization of the justification tree from Figure 4.3.

As mentioned in Section 4.2, an interesting research direction suggested by the generalization of the plausible justification trees is to investigate different forms of generalizations, not only deductive and inductive but also analogical, abductive, etc.

4.4.7 Generalization of the KB

As indicated in Table 4.1, the system will generalize the KB to entail the tree T_u in Figure 4.4. In this case, it learned a new fact (by analogy)

water-in-soil(Thailand, high),

The explanation structure S_1:

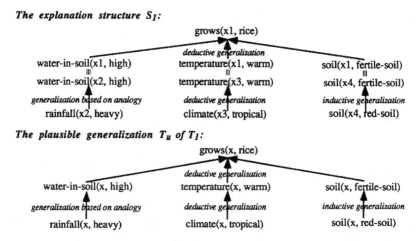

Figure 4.4:   Building the plausible generalization T_u of the justification tree T_1 in Figure 4.3

positive examples of the determination "rainfall(*x*, *y*) --> water-in-soil(*x*, *z*)"

> (*x*<-Philippines, *y*<-heavy, *z*<-high),
> (*x*<-Thailand, *y*<-heavy, *z*<-high)

and a rule (by empirical generalization)

> $\forall x$, soil(*x*, red-soil) $\rightarrow$ soil(*x*, fertile-soil)
> *with the positive examples:* (*x*<-Greece), (*x*<-Egypt), (*x*<-Thailand)

4.5 LEARNING FROM A NEW POSITIVE EXAMPLE

4.5.1 Generalization of the Plausible Justification Tree

Let us now consider that the system receives Example 2 in Table 4.4. As indicated in Table 4.1, the system tries to generalize the current justification tree T_u from Figure 4.4 to cover a justification of the new positive example. This process is illustrated in Figure 4.5.

First of all, the system determines the instance of the general tree T_u in Figure 4.4 corresponding to Example 2 in Table 4.4. Then it analyzes the leaf predicates and the inference steps from this tree. If the leaf predicates are true and the inference steps are plausible, then this tree is a plausible justification of the new positive example that is already covered by the general justification tree T_u in Figure 4.4. This ends the processing of the current example. However, this tree is not a correct justification of Example 2 because the leaf predicates "climate(Pakistan, tropical)" and "soil(Pakistan, red-soil)" are not true. Therefore, the system uses the deductive rules

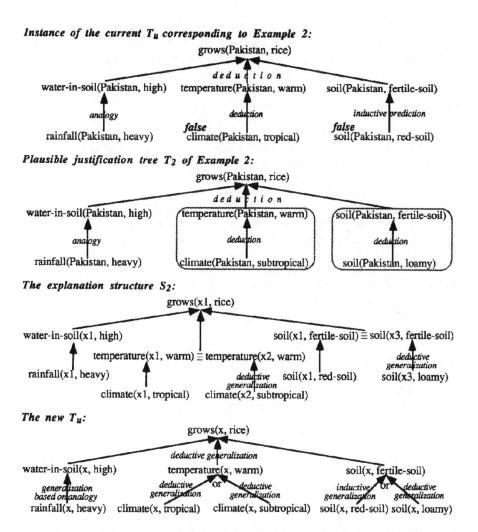

Figure 4.5: Generalization of T_u to cover the justification tree T_2 of Example 2

"$\forall x$, climate(x, subtropical) $\Rightarrow$ temperature(x, warm)"

and

"$\forall x$, soil(x, loamy) $\Rightarrow$ soil(x, fertile-soil)"

from Table 4.3 and builds a correct plausible justification tree T_2.

It is important to notice that this plausible justification tree of Example 2 has been built by using the plausible justification tree of the previous example (Example 1). This not only facilitates the process of building the justification tree but also the process of generalizing the general tree T_u, as will be shown in the following. Moreover, it shows some similarities between this method and human learning that involves the use of the explanations of previous examples in the process of building an explanation for a new example (Wisniewski and Medin, 1991).

The next step of the learning process is to build the explanation structure S_2 that has two general components to be unified:

- The tree T_u in Figure 4.4
- The generalization of the part of the tree T_2 in Figure 4.5 that is specific to it (this generalization being made according to the procedures described in Section 4.4.6)

As the result of the unification of the connection patterns from the explanation structure S_2, one obtains the general justification tree T_u from the bottom of Figure 4.5. This general tree covers both the justification tree of Example 1 and that of Example 2.

It should be noticed that although the justification trees of individual positive examples are AND trees, the generalization of these trees is, in general, an *AND/OR tree*. This is also the case with the tree T_u in Figure 4.5. Indeed, "grows(x, rice)" is an AND node, "climate(x, warm)" is an OR node, and "soil(x, fertile-soil)" is also an OR node.

4.5.2 Generalization of the KB

Besides generalizing the tree T_u, another result of learning from Example 2 consists of extending the KB with a new fact

water-in-soil(Pakistan, high)

and a new positive example of the plausible determination rule "rainfall(x, y) --> water-in-soil(x, z)"

(x<-Pakistan, y<-heavy, z<-high)

4.6 LEARNING FROM NEGATIVE EXAMPLES

4.6.1 Specialization of the General Justification Tree

Let us now consider that the system receives the Negative Example 3 from Table 4.4. As indicated in Table 4.1, the system tries to specialize the general justification tree T_u to no longer cover any justification of the negative example. At the same time, it may need to specialize the KB to entail the new T_u without entailing the previous T_u.

Again the system builds the instance of the general justification tree T_u in Figure 4.5, the instance corresponding to this new example (see Figure 4.6). This

Instance of T_u corresponding to the Negative Example 3:

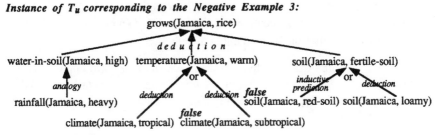

The new T_u :

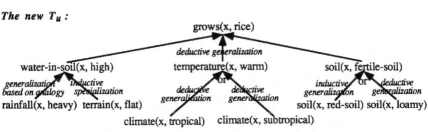

Figure 4.6:   Specialization of T_u to no longer cover a justification of the Negative Example 3

tree would lead to the wrong conclusion that the current input is a positive example of "grows(x, rice)." Therefore, the tree must contain some false leaf facts or false implications. These have to be detected, and both the general justification tree T_u in Figure 4.5 and the KB should be specialized to no longer contain them. One should notice that this is a limited specialization of the KB. Further specializing the KB to no longer entail *any* plausible justification of the negative example does not seem to be an obvious goal for a plausible reasoner that, by definition, may also reach some false conclusions.

Because the instance of T_u from the top of Figure 4.6 is an AND/OR tree, one should make sure to prove that enough of the leaf facts and implications are false. For instance, both "climate(Jamaica, subtropical)" and "soil(Jamaica, red-soil)" are false facts. However, because the nodes "temperature(x, warm)" and "soil(Jamaica, fertile-soil)" are OR nodes, the tree may still entail "grows(Jamaica, rice)." Therefore, one should show that an implication is false.

Deciding which is the false implication is a difficult problem. In the current version of MTL-JT, the implications hypothesized to be false are selected according to the following criteria:

- Select the weakest implications (first abduction, then inductive prediction, analogy, and deduction).
- Among the selected implications, select those for which the corrections of the KB and of the general justification tree cause the minimum loss of coverage of the known instances.

- Among the selected ones, select those for which the corrections produce a minimum increase in the complexity of the modified knowledge pieces.
- Choose arbitrarily from the remaining hypotheses.

In the considered example, hypothesizing which is the false implication was simple because the justification tree from the top of Figure 4.6 contains one analogical implication and three deductive implications. Therefore, the analogical implication was considered to be the false one:

$$\text{rainfall(Jamaica, heavy)} \not\rightarrow \text{water-in-soil(Jamaica, high)} \qquad (18)$$

The corresponding implication from the current general justification tree is

$$\text{rainfall}(x, \text{ heavy}) \rightarrow \text{water-in-soil}(x, \text{ high}) \qquad (19)$$

which was derived from the determination

$$\text{rainfall}(x, y) \dashrightarrow \text{water-in-soil}(x, z) \qquad (20)$$

Consequently, the system will try to specialize rule 20 to no longer cover equation 18 by taking into account the known instances of equations 19 and 20

$$\text{rainfall(Philippines, heavy)} \rightarrow \text{water-in-soil(Philippines, high)}$$
$$\text{rainfall(Thailand, heavy)} \rightarrow \text{water-in-soil(Thailand, high)}$$
$$\text{rainfall(Pakistan, heavy)} \rightarrow \text{water-in-soil(Pakistan, high)}$$

together with the known properties of the involved objects (Jamaica, Philippines, Thailand, and Pakistan).

The inductive learner of MTL-JT will suggest, in this case, specializing the determination (eq. 20) by adding the left-hand side predicate "terrain(x, flat)":

$$\text{rainfall}(x, y) \ \& \ \text{terrain}(x, \text{flat}) \dashrightarrow \text{water-in-soil}(x, z)$$

The same specialization is applied to the implication (eq. 19). Thus, the general justification tree is specialized as indicated at the bottom of Figure 4.6.

4.6.2 Specialization of the KB

As a result of learning from the Negative Example 3, the system discovered a negative example of the plausible determination rule in Table 4.3 and specialized it by conjunctively adding the left hand side predicate "terrain(x, flat)," as shown in Table 4.5.

Because Negative Example 3 is the last input example, the system extracts from the tree T_u in Figure 4.6 the operational and abstract definitions indicated in Table 4.5.

4.7 BASIC CASES

An important feature of the presented method is that it behaves as a single-strategy learning method whenever the learning task of MTL-JT is specialized to the learning task of the single-strategy method. This feature is important because it shows that the MTL-JT method is a generalization of the integrated learning strategies that not only takes advantage of the complementarity of the integrated strategies (as has been shown in the previous sections) but also inherits the features of these strategies.

The next sections show that the MTL-JT method may behave as

- Explanation-based learning, learning by abduction, or learning by analogy when the input consists of only one positive example
- Multiple-example explanation-based generalization when the input consists of a sequence of positive examples
- Empirical or constructive inductive generalization when the input consists of a sequence of positive and negative examples

4.7.1 Explanation-Based Learning

Let us suppose that in addition to the rules in Table 4.3, the KB also contains the following deductive rules:

$\forall x$, rainfall(x, heavy) $\Rightarrow$ water-in-soil(x, high)
$\forall x$, soil(x, red-soil) $\Rightarrow$ soil(x, fertile-soil)

In such a case, the justification trees in Figures 4.3 and 4.4 become logical proofs, and the result of learning from Example 1 is an operational definition of "grows(x, rice)." Thus, the MTL-JT method reduces to explanation-based learning (DeJong and Mooney, 1986; Mitchell, Keller, and Kedar-Cabelli, 1986).

4.7.2 Learning by Abduction

Let us now suppose that the relationship between "rainfall" and "water-in-soil" is not a plausible determination but a deductive implication

$\forall x$, rainfall(x, heavy) $\Rightarrow$ water-in-soil(x, high)

and the KB does not contain examples of the predicate "soil." In this case, in order to build the justification tree of Example 1, the system needs only to create the explanatory hypothesis

soil(Thailand, red-soil) $\rightarrow$ soil(Thailand, fertile-soil)

Therefore, the result of learning is the created explanatory hypothesis, and the MTL-JT method reduces to abductive learning.

4.7.3 Learning by Analogy

Let us suppose that the KB contains only the following knowledge that is related to Example 1:

Facts: rainfall(Philippines, heavy), water-in-soil(Philippines, high)

Determination: rainfall(x, y) --> water-in-soil(x, z)

Then the system can only infer "water-in-soil(Thailand, high)" by analogy with "water-in-soil(Philippines, high)," as shown in Section 4.4.3. Thus, in this case, the MTL-JT method reduces to analogical learning.

4.7.4 Multiple-Example Explanation-Based Generalization

If the input of the system consists only of positive examples that are deductively entailed by the KB, then the presented MTL-JT method behaves as the multiple example explanation-based generalization, or mEBG, that was developed, among others, by Kedar-Cabelli (1985), Pazzani (1988), and Hirsh (1989).

4.7.5 Empirical and Constructive Inductive Generalization

Let us assume that the KB does not contain the knowledge from Table 4.3, and the input consists of all the examples from Table 4.4. In this case, the input is new, neither confirming nor contradicting the KB. Therefore, each example is interpreted as representing a single implication that defines a tree, as shown in the top part of Figure 4.7.

The MTL-JT method will compute the least general generalization of the trees corresponding to the positive examples, generalization that does not cover the tree corresponding to the negative example. The result of learning is therefore an empirical generalization that represents an operational definition of "grows(x, rice)" (see Figure 4.7). Thus, in this case, the MTL-JT method behaves as empirical inductive generalization.

If, however, the KB contains the deductive rules

$\forall x$, climate(x, subtropical) $\Rightarrow$ temperature(x, warm)
$\forall x$, climate(x, tropical) $\Rightarrow$ temperature(x, warm)

then the result of learning is the generalization from the bottom of Figure 4.7. This is a constructive generalization because it contains the descriptor "temperature" that does not belong to the description space of the examples. Therefore, in this case, the MTL-JT method behaves as constructive inductive generalization.

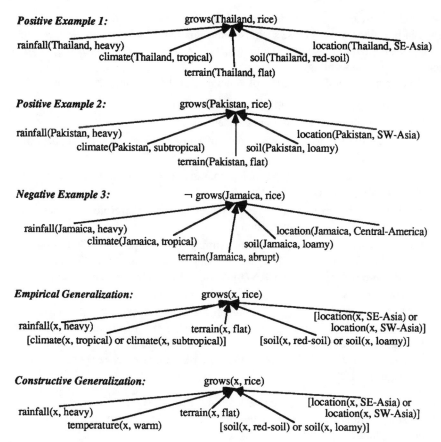

Figure 4.7: Empirical and constructive inductive generalizations of the input examples

4.8 DISCUSSION AND CONCLUSION

This chapter presented an inference-based framework for multistrategy learning and illustrated it with a specific multistrategy task-adaptive learning method called MTL-JT. The framework and the method evolved as a generalization and extension of DISCIPLE (Tecuci, 1988; Tecuci and Kodratoff, 1990), an early interactive multistrategy learning system that learns from a specific problem solving episode by building a plausible explanation of it, over-generalizing the explanation, and updating it as a result of an analysis of its instances.

This work is also related to the inferential theory of learning (Michalski, 1992) in that the learning strategies described in this theory could naturally be integrated into the presented framework.

Other researchers have also investigated the use of different types of inference in building explanations, such as determinations (Mahadevan 1989; Widmer, 1989) or qualitative reasoning (DeJong, 1989; Widmer, 1992), which suggests that this idea is very appealing.

There are several dimensions of generality of the presented framework:

- It allows learning from different types of input, such as one or several facts, examples, or problem solving episodes.
- It allows the KB to contain a variety of knowledge pieces that support different types of inference.
- It solves a general learning problem that includes theory revision and learning different types of concept definitions.
- It is extensible in that new types of inference and, therefore, learning strategies could naturally be integrated into it.
- It allows the use of different search strategies in the process of building plausible justification trees. The strategy employed in the MTL-JT method is a uniform-cost search of an AND-OR tree. However, one could employ any other search strategy (not only exhaustive but also heuristic).
- It has certain similarities with human learning, for example, the building of the justification tree of an example by using the justification trees of the previous examples (Wisniewski and Medin, 1991) and the use of multiple lines of reasoning in the justification of a plausible inference step (Collins and Michalski, 1989).

The multistrategy task-adaptive learning method MTL-JT is only one way in which such a framework could be instantiated. It points, however, to the potential of the presented framework.

An important feature of MTL-JT is that it behaves as a single-strategy learning method whenever the learning task of MTL-JT is specialized to the learning task of the respective single-strategy method. This shows that MTL-JT is a generalization of the integrated learning strategies that not only takes advantage of their complementarity but also inherits their features.

The presented framework and method have also revealed a new research direction in the theory of generalization by suggesting that with each type of inference may be associated a certain type of generalization. Consequently, one could perform not only deductive and inductive generalizations but also generalizations based on analogy, abduction, etc.

There are also several limitations and necessary developments of MTL-JT and of the general framework that need to be addressed by the future research.

One limitation was mentioned in Section 4.6.1: during learning from a negative example, the KB is not specialized enough to guarantee that it no longer entails any justification tree that would prove that the example is positive.

Also, MTL-JT does not deal with noisy input. This is an intrinsically difficult problem for a plausible reasoner that may itself make wrong inferences. However, because MTL-JT is a generalization of methods that could deal with noisy input, it inherits these capabilities. For instance, as in EBL, one may reject as noisy a negative example if one could build a deductive proof tree showing that the example is positive, or one may reject the negative example if the required specializations of the KB would determine a significant loss of coverage of instances of the knowledge pieces to be specialized.

The learning strategies integrated into MTL-JT (especially learning by analogy) are simple and should be replaced by more powerful ones.

Also, new symbolic and even subsymbolic methods (as, for instance, reinforcement learning or neural network learning) should be integrated into MTL-JT. This will require, of course, elaboration of generalization techniques specific to each new strategy.

MTL-JT may also be extended to learn from other types of input (like general pieces of knowledge or input already known).

Another important research direction regards the extension and the application of MTL-JT to knowledge acquisition from a human expert. In this case, the method would need to be extended with an important interactive component that would allow the system to ask different questions to the human expert in order to decide on the best learning actions to take (Tecuci, 1988, 1992a, 1992b). In general, the human expert would be asked to solve the problems that are intrinsically difficult for a learning system such as *the credit/blame assignment problem* (i.e., assigning credit or blame to the individual decisions that led to some overall result) or *the new terms problem* (i.e., extending the representation language with new terms when this cannot represent the concept or the rule to be learned).

ACKNOWLEDGMENTS

This research was done in the GMU Center for Artificial Intelligence. Research by the Center is supported in part by the National Science Foundation Grant No. IRI-9020266; in part by the Office of Naval Research Grant No. N00014-91-J-1351; and in part by the Defense Advanced Research Projects Agency Grant No. N00014-91-J-1854, administered by the Office of Naval Research.

References

Bergadano, F., and Giordana, A., "Guiding Induction with Domain Theories," in *Machine Learning: An Artificial Intelligence Approach*, Vol. 3, Y. Kodratoff and R.S. Michalski (Eds.), San Mateo, CA, Morgan Kaufmann, pp. 474–492, 1990.

Cohen, W., "The Generality of Overgenerality," in *Machine Learning: Proceedings of the Eighth International Workshop*, L. Birnbaum and G. Collins (Eds.), San Mateo, CA, Morgan Kaufmann, pp. 490–494, 1991.

Collins, A., and Michalski, R.S., "The Logic of Plausible Reasoning: A Core Theory," *Cognitive Science*, Vol. 13, pp. 1–49, 1989.

Danyluk, A.P., "The Use of Explanations for Similarity-based Learning," *Proceedings of the International Joint Conference on Artificial Intelligence*, San Mateo, CA, Morgan Kaufmann, pp. 274–276, 1987.

Davies, T.R., and Russell, S.J., "A Logical Approach to Reasoning by Analogy," *Proceedings of the International Joint Conference on Artificial Intelligence*, San Mateo, CA, Morgan Kaufmann, pp. 264–270, 1987.

DeJong, G., and Mooney, R., "Explanation-Based Learning: An Alternative View," *Machine Learning*, Vol. 1, pp. 145–176, 1986.

De Raedt, L., Interactive Concept Learning, *Ph.D. Thesis*, Catholic University of Leuven, 1991.

Flann, N., and Dietterich, T., "A Study of Explanation-based Methods for Inductive Learning," *Machine Learning*, Vol. 4, pp. 187–266, 1989.

Genest, J., Matwin, S., and Plante, B., "Explanation-based Learning with Incomplete Theories: A Three-step Approach," in *Machine Learning: Proceedings of the Eighth International Workshop*, B. Porter and R. Mooney (Eds.), San Mateo, CA, Morgan Kaufmann, pp. 286–296, 1990.

Gordon, D.F., "An Enhancer for Reactive Plans," in *Machine Learning: Proceedings of the Eighth International Workshop*, L. Birnbaum and G. Collins (Eds.), San Mateo, CA, Morgan Kaufmann, pp. 505–508, 1991.

Hirsh, H., "Incremental Version-space Merging: A General Framework for Concept Learning," *Ph.D. Thesis,* Stanford University, 1989.

Josephson, J., "Abduction: Conceptual Analysis of a Fundamental Pattern of Inference," *Technical Research Report 91-JJ,* Laboratory for Artificial Intelligence Research, The Ohio State University, 1991.

Lebowitz, M., "Integrated Learning: Controlling Explanation," *Cognitive Science,* Vol. 10, pp. 219–240, 1986.

Mahadevan, S., "Using Determinations in Explanation-based Learning: A Solution to Incomplete Theory Problem," in *Proceedings of the Sixth International Workshop on Machine Learning,* A. Segre (Ed.), San Mateo, CA, Morgan Kaufmann, 1989.

Michalski, R.S., "Toward a Unified Theory of Learning: Multistrategy Task-adaptive Learning," *Reports of Machine Learning and Inference Laboratory*, MLI 90-1, Center for Artificial Intelligence, George Mason University, 1990.

————, "Inferential Learning Theory: Developing Theoretical Foundations for Multistrategy Learning," in *Machine Learning: A Multistrategy Approach, Vol. 4,* R.S. Michalski and G. Tecuci (Eds.), San Mateo, CA, Morgan Kaufmann, 1994.

Minton, S., and Carbonell, J.G., "Strategies for Learning Search Control Rules: An Explanation-based Approach," *Proceedings of the International Joint Conference on Artificial Intelligence,* San Mateo, CA, Morgan Kaufmann, pp. 228–235, 1987.

Mitchell, T.M., Keller, T., and Kedar-Cabelli, S., "Explanation-based Generalization: A Unifying View," *Machine Learning,* Vol. 1, pp. 47–80, 1986.

Mooney, R., and Bennet S., "A Domain Independent Explanation-Based Generalizer," *Proceedings of the Fifth National Conference on Artificial Intelligence,* Menlo Park, CA, AAAI, pp. 551–555, 1986.

Mooney, R., and Ourston, D., "A Multistrategy Approach to Theory Refinement," in *Machine Learning: A Multistrategy Approach, Vol. 4,* R.S. Michalski and G. Tecuci (Eds.), San Mateo, CA, Morgan Kaufmann, 1994.

Morik, K., "Balanced Cooperative Modeling," in *Machine Learning: A Multistrategy Approach, Vol. 4,* R.S. Michalski and G. Tecuci (Eds.), San Mateo, CA, Morgan Kaufmann, 1994.

Nilsson, N., *Problem Solving Methods in Artificial Intelligence,* McGraw-Hill, 1971.

Pazzani, M.J., "Integrating Explanation-based and Empirical Learning Methods in OCCAM," *Proceedings of the Third European Working Session on Learning,* Glasgow, Scotland: Pitman, pp. 147–166, 1988.

Ram, A., and Cox, M., "Introspective Reasoning Using Meta-explanations for Multistrategy Learning," in *Machine Learning: A Multistrategy Approach, Vol. 4,* R.S. Michalski and G. Tecuci (Eds.), San Mateo, CA, Morgan Kaufmann, 1994.

Reich, Y., "Macro and Micro Perspectives of Multistrategy Learning," in *Machine Learning: A Multistrategy Approach, Vol. 4,* R.S. Michalski and G. Tecuci (Eds.), San Mateo, CA, Morgan Kaufmann, 1994.

Saitta, L., Botta, M., and Neri, F., "Multistrategy Learning and Theory Revision," *Machine Learning,* Vol. 11, pp. 153–172, 1993.

Shavlik, J.W., and Towell, G.G., "An Approach to Combining Explanation-based and Neural Learning Algorithms," in *Readings in Machine Learning,* J.W. Shavlik and T. Dietterich (Eds.), San Mateo, CA, Morgan Kaufmann, pp. 828–839, 1990.

Tecuci, G., DISCIPLE: A Theory, Methodology, and System for Learning Expert Knowledge, *Ph.D. Thesis,* University of Paris-South, 1988.

———, "Automating Knowledge Acquisition as Extending, Updating, and Improving a Knowledge Base," *IEEE Transactions on Systems, Man, and Cybernetics,* Vol. 22, No. 6, 1992a.

———, "Cooperation in Knowledge Base Refinement," in *Machine Learning: Proceedings of the Ninth International Conference (ML92),* D. Sleeman and P. Edwards (Eds.), San Mateo, CA, Morgan Kaufmann, 1992b.

———, "Plausible Justification Trees: A Framework for the Deep and Dynamic Integration of Learning Strategies," *Machine Learning,* Vol. 11, pp. 237–261, 1993.

Tecuci, G., and Kodratoff, Y., "Apprenticeship Learning in Imperfect Theory Domains," in *Machine Learning: An Artificial Intelligence Approach, Vol. 3,* Y. Kodratoff and R.S. Michalski (Eds.), San Mateo, CA, Morgan Kaufmann, pp. 514–551, 1990.

Tecuci, G., and Michalski, R.S., "A Method for Multistrategy Task-adaptive Learning Based on Plausible Justifications," in *Machine Learning: Proceedings of the Eighth International Workshop,* L. Birnbaum and G. Collins (Eds.), San Mateo, CA, Morgan Kaufmann, pp. 549–553, 1991a.

————, "Input Understanding as a Basis for Multistrategy Task-adaptive Learning," in *Proceedings of the International Symposium on Methodologies for Intelligent Systems,* New York, Springer-Verlag, pp. 419–428, 1991b.

Whitehall, B.L., "Knowledge-based Learning: Integration of Deductive and Inductive Learning for Knowledge Base Completion," *Ph.D. Thesis*, University of Illinois at Urbana-Champaign, 1990.

Widmer, G., "A Tight Integration of Deductive and Inductive Learning," *Proceedings of the Sixth International Workshop on Machine Learning,* A. Segre (Ed.), San Mateo, CA, Morgan Kaufmann, pp. 11–13, 1989.

————, "Learning with a Qualitative Domain Theory by Means of Plausible Explanations," in *Machine Learning: A Multistrategy Approach, Vol. 4,* R.S. Michalski and G. Tecuci (Eds.), San Mateo, CA, Morgan Kaufmann, 1994.

Wilkins, D.C., "Knowledge Base Refinement as Improving an Incorrect and Incomplete Domain Theory," in *Machine Learning: An Artificial Intelligence Approach, Vol. 3,* Y. Kodratoff and R.S. Michalski (Eds.), San Mateo, CA, Morgan Kaufmann, pp. 493–513, 1990.

Wisniewski, E.J., and Medin, D.J., "Is It a Pocket or a Purse? Tightly Coupled Theory and Data Driven Learning," in *Machine Learning: Proceedings of the Eighth International Workshop*, L. Birnbaum and G. Collins (Eds.), San Mateo, CA, Morgan Kaufmann, pp. 564–568, 1991.

PART

TWO

THEORY REVISION

5

A MULTISTRATEGY APPROACH
TO THEORY REFINEMENT

Raymond J. Mooney
(University of Texas at Austin)

Dirk Ourston
(British Petroleum Research)

Abstract

This chapter describes a multistrategy system that employs independent modules for deductive, abductive, and inductive reasoning to revise an arbitrarily incorrect propositional Horn-clause domain theory to fit a set of preclassified training instances. By combining such diverse methods, EITHER is able to handle a wider range of imperfect theories than other theory revision systems and guarantee that the revised theory will be consistent with the training data. EITHER has successfully revised two actual expert theories, one in molecular biology and one in plant pathology. The results confirm the hypothesis that using a multistrategy system to learn from both theory and data gives better results than using either theory or data alone.

5.1 INTRODUCTION

The problem of revising an imperfect domain theory to make it consistent with empirical data has important applications in the development of expert systems (Ginsberg, Weiss, and Politikas, 1988). Knowledge-base construction can be facilitated greatly by using a set of training cases to automatically refine an imperfect, initial knowledge base obtained from a textbook or by interview with an expert. The advantage of a refinement approach to knowledge-acquisition as opposed to a purely empirical learning approach is two-fold. First, by starting with an approximately correct theory, a refinement system should be able to achieve high-performance with significantly fewer training examples. Therefore, in domains in which training examples are scarce or in which a rough theory is easily available, the refinement approach has a distinct advantage. Second, theory refinement results in a structured knowledge-base that maintains the intermediate terms and explanatory structure of the original theory. Empirical learning, on the other hand, results in a decision tree or disjunctive-normal-form (DNF) expression with no intermediate terms or explanatory structure. Therefore, a knowledge-base formed by theory refinement is much more suitable for supplying meaningful explanations for its conclusions, an important aspect of the usability of an expert system.

This chapter describes a multistrategy approach to revising an arbitrarily incorrect propositional Horn-clause domain theory to fit a set of preclassified training instances. The system implementing it, EITHER (Explanation-Based and Inductive THeory Extension and Revision), is modular and contains independent subsystems for deduction, abduction, and induction. Each of these reasoning components makes an important contribution to the overall goal of the system. EITHER can also be viewed as integrating knowledge-intensive (deductive and abductive) and data-intensive (inductive) learning methods.

The remainder of this chapter is organized as follows. Section 5.2 presents an overview of the EITHER system and the problem it is designed to solve. Sections 5.3–5.6 discuss each of EITHER's reasoning strategies (deduction, abduction, and induction) as well as the minimal covering algorithms that coordinate the interaction of these components. Section 5.7 presents empirical results on two real knowledge bases that EITHER has refined. Section 5.8 discusses how EITHER compares to related work and Section 5.9 presents some conclusions and directions for future work.

5.2 EITHER OVERVIEW

The EITHER system combines deduction, abduction, and induction to provide a focused correction to an incorrect theory. The deductive and abductive parts of the system identify the failing parts of the theory and constrain the examples used for induction. The inductive part of the system determines the specific corrections to failing rules that render them consistent with the supplied examples.

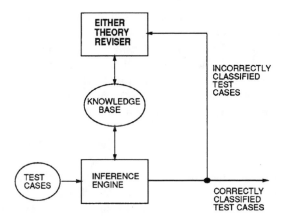

Figure 5.1:   EITHER components

5.2.1 Problem Definition

Stated succinctly, the purpose of EITHER is

Given: An imperfect domain theory for a set of categories and a set of
classified examples each described by a set of observable features

Find: A minimally revised version of the domain theory that correctly
classifies all the examples

Figure 5.1 shows the architecture for the EITHER system. So long as the
inference engine correctly classifies test cases, no additional processing is required.
In the event that a misclassified example is detected, EITHER is used to correct the
error.

Horn-clause logic (if-then rules) was chosen as the representational formalism
for the EITHER system. This provides a relatively simple and useful language for
exploring the problems associated with theory revision. Theories currently are
restricted to an extended propositional logic that allows numerical and multi-valued
features as well as binary attributes. In addition, domain theories are required to be
acyclic, and therefore, a theory defines a directed acyclic graph (DAG). For the
purpose of theory refinement, EITHER makes a closed-world assumption. If the
theory cannot prove that an example is a member of a category, then it is assumed
to be a negative example of that category. Due to the restrictions of propositional
logic, EITHER is primarily useful for classification—assigning examples to one of
a finite set of predefined categories.

Propositions that are used to describe examples (e.g., `color=black`) are called *observables*. To avoid problems with negation as failure, only observables can appear as negated antecedents in rules. Propositions that represent the final concepts in which examples are to be classified are called *categories*. It is currently assumed that the categories are disjoint. In a typical domain theory, all the sources (leaves) of the DAG are observables and all the sinks (roots) are categories. Propositions in the theory that are neither observables nor categories are called *intermediate concepts*.

It is difficult to precisely define the adjective "minimal" used to characterize the revision to be produced. Because it is assumed that the original theory is "approximately correct," the goal is to change it as little as possible. Syntactic measures such as the total number of symbols added or deleted are reasonable criteria. EITHER uses various methods to help ensure that its revisions are minimal in this sense. However, finding a revision that is guaranteed to be syntactically minimal is clearly computationally intractable. When the initial theory is empty, the problem reduces to that of finding a minimal theory for a set of examples.

A sample theory suitable for EITHER is a version of the cup theory (Winston et al., 1983) shown in Figure 5.2. Figure 5.3 shows six examples that are consistent with this theory, three positive examples of `cup` and three negative examples. Each example is described in terms of twelve observable features. There are eight binary features—`has-concavity`, `upward-pointing-concavity`, `has-bottom`, `flat-bottom`, `lightweight`, `has-handle`, `styrofoam`, and `ceramic`; three multi-valued features—`color`, `width`, and `shape`; and a single real-valued feature—`volume`. Given various imperfect versions of the cup theory and these six examples, EITHER can regenerate the correct theory. For example, if rule 4 is missing from the theory, examples 2 and 3 are no longer provable as cups. If the antecedent `width=small` is missing from rule 5, then negative example 5 becomes provable as a cup. EITHER can correct either or both of these errors using the examples in Figure 5.3.

The need for EITHER processing is signaled by incorrectly classified examples, as shown in Figure 5.1. In making corrections, EITHER operates in batch

```
1.         cup  ⇐  stable & liftable & open-vessel
2.      stable  ⇐  has-bottom & flat-bottom
3.    liftable  ⇐  graspable & lightweight
4.   graspable  ⇐  has-handle
5.   graspable  ⇐  width=small & styrofoam
6.   graspable  ⇐  width=small & ceramic
7. open-vessel  ⇐  has-concavity & upward-pointing-concavity
```

Figure 5.2:   The cup theory

	has-concavity	upward-pointing	has-bottom	flat-bottom	lightweight	has-handle	styrofoam	ceramic	color	width	volume	shape	
1. +	X	X	X	X	X		X		red	sm	8	hem	
2. +	X	X	X	X	X	X		X	blue	med	16	hem	
3. +	X	X	X	X	X	X		X	tan	med	8	cyl	
4. -	X	X	X	X	X				gray	sm	8	cyl	
5. -	X	X	X	X	X		X		red	med	8	hem	
6. -	X	X	X	X	X			X	blue	med	16	hem	

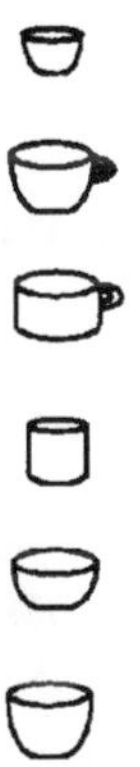

Figure 5.3:   Cup examples

mode, using as input a set of training examples. The incorrectly classified examples, or *failing* examples, are used to identify that there is an error and to control the correction. The correctly classified examples are used to focus the correction and to limit the extent of the correction. An important property of the EITHER algorithm is that it is guaranteed to produce a revised theory that is consistent with the training examples when there is no noise present in the data. That is, the following statements will be true for every example:

$$T \bigcup E \models C_E \tag{1}$$

$$\forall C_i (C_i \neq C_E \Rightarrow T \bigcup E \not\models C_i) \tag{2}$$

where T represents the corrected theory, E represents the conjunction of facts describing any example in the training set, C_E is the correct category of the example, and C_i is any arbitrary category. A proof of this consistency property is given in Ourston (1991).

5.2.2 Types of Theory Errors

Figure 5.4 shows a taxonomy for incorrect propositional Horn-clause theories. At the top level, theories can be incorrect because they are either overly general or overly specific. An overly general theory entails category membership for exam-

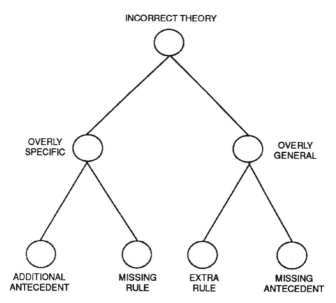

Figure 5.4:   Theory error taxonomy

ples that are not members of the category. One way a theory can be overly general is by having rules that lack required antecedents, providing proofs for examples that should have been excluded. Another way a theory can be overly general is by having completely incorrect rules. By contrast, an overly specific theory fails to entail category membership for members of a category. This can occur because the theory is missing a rule or because an existing rule has additional antecedents that exclude category members. Note that these definitions allow a theory to be both overly general *and* overly specific.

The following terminology is used in the remainder of this chapter. "The example is provable" is used to mean "the example is provable as a member of its own category." A *failing positive* refers to an example that is not provable as a member of its own category. A *failing negative* refers to an example that is provable as a member of a category other than its own. Notice that a single example can be both a failing negative and a failing positive.

5.2.3 EITHER Components

As shown in Figure 5.5, EITHER uses a combination of methods to revise a theory to make it consistent with the examples. It first attempts to fix failing positives by removing antecedents and to fix failing negatives by removing rules because these are simpler and less powerful operations. Only if these operations fail does the system resort to the more powerful technique of using induction to

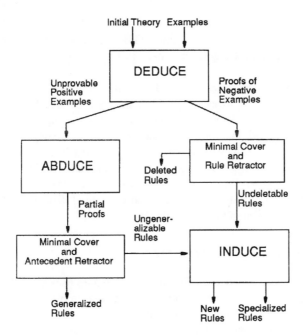

Figure 5.5:   EITHER architecture

learn rules to fix failing positives and to add antecedents to existing rules to fix failing negatives.

Horn-clause deduction is the basic inference engine used to classify examples. EITHER initially uses deduction to identify failing positives and negatives among the training examples. It uses the proofs generated by deduction to find a near-minimal set of rule retractions that would correct all the failing negatives. During the course of the correction, deduction is also used to assess proposed changes to the theory as part of the generalization and specialization processes.

EITHER uses abduction to initially find the incorrect part of an overly specific theory. Abduction identifies sets of assumptions that allow a failing positive to become provable. These assumptions identify rule antecedents that, if deleted, would properly generalize the theory and correct the failing positive. EITHER uses the output of abduction to find a near-minimal set of antecedent retractions that would correct all the failing positives.

Induction is used to learn new rules or to determine which additional antecedents to add to an existing rule. In both cases, EITHER uses the output of abduction and deduction to determine an appropriately labelled subset of the training examples to pass to induction in order to form a consistent correction. EITHER currently uses a version of ID3 (Quinlan, 1986) as its inductive component. The decision trees returned by ID3 are translated into equivalent Horn-clause rules (Quinlan, 1987). The remaining components of the EITHER system constitute generalization and specialization control algorithms that identify the types of corrections to be made to the theory.

One of the main advantages of EITHER's architecture is its modularity. Because the control and processing components are separated from the deductive, inductive, and abductive components, these latter components can be modified or replaced as better algorithms for these reasoning methods are developed.

The following sections describe each of EITHER's components and their interactions in details. The discussion focuses on the basic multistrategy approach employed in EITHER. Recent enhancements to the system are discussed in Ourston and Mooney (1991) and Mooney and Ourston (1991a, 1991b), and a complete description is given in Ourston (1991).

5.3 THE DEDUCTIVE COMPONENT

The deductive component of EITHER is a standard backward-chaining, Horn-clause theorem prover similar to Prolog. Our particular implementation is based on the deductive retrieval system from Charniak et al. (1987). Deduction is the first step in theory revision. The system attempts to prove that each example is a member of each of the known categories. Failing positives (examples that cannot be proven as members of the correct category) indicate overly specific aspects of the theory and are passed on to the abductive component. Failing negatives (examples that are proven as members of incorrect categories) indicate overly general aspects of the theory and are passed on to the specialization procedure. In order to satisfy the requirements of specialization, the deductive component finds all possible proofs of each incorrect category and returns all the resulting proof trees.

The deductive component also forms the basic performance system and is used during testing to classify novel examples. If during testing an example is provable as a member of multiple categories, the system picks the provable category that is most common in the training set. If an example fails to be provable as a member of any category, it is assigned to the most common category overall. This assures that the system always assigns a test example to a unique category.

The deductive component is also used to check for overgeneralization and overspecialization when certain changes to the theory are proposed. For example, when an antecedent retraction is proposed, all the examples are reproven with the resulting theory to determine whether any additional failing negatives are created. Analogously, when a rule retraction is proposed, all the examples are reproven to determine whether any additional failing positives are created. If so, then the proposed revision is not made, and the system resorts to learning new rules or adding antecedents. Better bookkeeping methods, such as truth-maintenance techniques, could potentially be used to avoid unnecessary reproving of examples. For example, existing proofs of all examples could be used to more directly determine the effect of a rule deletion, and partial proofs of negative examples could be used to more directly determine the effect of antecedent deletions. However, such methods would be fairly complicated and incur a potentially large overhead.

5.4 THE ABDUCTIVE COMPONENT

If an example cannot be proven as a member of its category, then abduction is used to find minimal sets of assumptions that would allow the example to become provable. The normal logical definition of abduction is

Given: A domain theory T and an observed fact O

Find: All minimal sets of atoms A, called *assumptions*, such that $A \cup T$ is logically consistent and $A \cup T \models O$.

The assumptions A are said to *explain* the observation. Legal assumptions are frequently restricted, such as allowing only instances of certain predicates (*predicate specific abduction*) or requiring that assumptions not be provable from more basic assumptions (*most-specific abduction*) (Stickel, 1988).

In EITHER, an observation states that an example is a member of a category (in the notation introduced earlier, $E \to C_E$). In addition, EITHER's abductive component backchains as far as possible before making an assumption (most-specific abduction), and the consistency constraint is removed. As a result, for each failing positive, abduction finds all minimal sets of most-specific atoms, A, such that

$$A \cup E \cup T \models C_E \tag{3}$$

where minimal means that no assumption set is a subset of another. The proof supported by each such set is called a *partial proof*. EITHER currently uses an abductive component that employs exhaustive search to find all partial proofs of each failing positive example (Ng & Mooney, 1989). Partial proofs are used to indicate antecedents that, if retracted, would allow the example to become provable. The above definition guarantees that if all the assumptions in a set are removed from the antecedents of the rules in their corresponding partial proof, the example will become provable. This is because not requiring a fact for a proof has the same generalizing effect as assuming it.

As a concrete example, assume that rule 4 about handles is missing from the cup theory. This will cause example 2 from Figure 5.3 to become a failing positive. Abduction finds two minimal sets of assumptions: {width=small$_6$} and {width=small$_5$, styrofoam$_5$}. The subscripts indicate the number of the rule to which the antecedent belongs because each antecedent of each rule must be treated distinctly. Notice that removing the consistency constraint is critical to the interpretation of assumptions as antecedent retractions. Assuming `width=small` is inconsistent when `width=medium` is known; however, retracting `width=small` as an antecedent from one of the graspable rules is still a legitimate way to help make this example provable.

5.5 THE MINIMUM COVER COMPONENTS

In EITHER, a cover is a complete set of rules requiring correction. There are two types of covers: the *antecedent cover* and the *rule cover*. The antecedent cover is used by the generalization procedure to fix all failing positives. The rule cover is used by the specialization procedure to fix all failing negatives. There is an essential property that holds for both types of cover: If all the elements of the cover are removed from the theory, the examples associated with the cover will be classified correctly. Specifically, if all the antecedents in the antecedent cover are removed, the theory is generalized so that all the failing positives are fixed, and if all the rules in the rule cover are removed, the theory is specialized so that all the failing negatives are fixed. In each case, EITHER attempts to find a *minimum* cover in order to minimize change to the initial theory. The details of the minimum cover algorithms are given in the next two subsections. EITHER initially constructs covers containing only rules at the "bottom" or "leaves" of the theory; however, if higher-level changes are necessary or syntactically simpler, non-leaf rules can also be included (Ourston and Mooney, 1991; Ourston, 1991).

5.5.1 The Minimum Antecedent Cover

The partial proofs of failing positives generated by the abductive component are used to determine the minimum antecedent cover. In a complex problem, there will be many partial proofs for each failing positive. In order to minimize change to the initial theory, EITHER attempts to find the minimum number of antecedent retractions required to fix *all* the failing positives. In other words, we want to make the following expression true:

$$E_1 \& E_2 \& \ldots \& E_n \tag{4}$$

where E_i represents the statement that the *i*th failing positive has at least one completed partial proof; that is,

$$E_i \Leftrightarrow P_{i1} \lor P_{i2} \lor \ldots \lor P_{im} \tag{5}$$

where P_{ij} represents the statement that the *j*th partial proof of the *i*th failing positive is completed; that is,

$$P_{ij} \Leftrightarrow A_{ij1} \& A_{ij2} \ldots \& A_{ijp} \tag{6}$$

where A_{ijk} means that the antecedent represented by the kth assumption used in the jth partial proof of the ith example is removed from the theory. In order to determine a minimum change to the theory, we need to find the minimum set of antecedent retractions (As) that satisfy this expression. To return to the example of the cup theory that is missing the rule for handles, both failing positives (examples 2 and 3) have the same partial proofs, resulting in the expressions

$$E_2 \Leftrightarrow (\texttt{width=small}_6) \vee [(\texttt{width=small}_5) \,\&\, \texttt{styrofoam}_5]$$
$$E_3 \Leftrightarrow (\texttt{width=small}_6) \vee [(\texttt{width=small}_5) \,\&\, \texttt{styrofoam}_5]$$

In this case, the minimum antecedent cover is trivial and consists of retracting the single antecedent $\texttt{width=small}_6$.

Because the general minimum set covering problem is NP-Hard (Gary and Johnson, 1979), EITHER uses a version of the *greedy covering algorithm* to find the antecedent cover. The greedy algorithm does not guarantee finding minimum cover but will come within a logarithmic factor of it and runs in polynomial time (Johnson, 1974). The algorithm iteratively updates a partial cover, as follows. At each iteration, the algorithm chooses a partial proof and adds the antecedent retractions associated with the proof to the evolving cover. The chosen partial proof is the one that maximizes *benefit-to-cost*, defined as the ratio of the additional examples covered when its antecedents are included divided by the number of antecedents added. The set of examples that have the selected partial proof as one of their partial proofs is removed from the examples remaining to be covered. The process terminates when all examples are covered. The result is a near-minimum set of antecedent retractions that fix all the failing positives.

Once the antecedent cover is formed, EITHER attempts to retract the indicated antecedents of each rule in the cover. If a given retraction is not an overgeneralization (i.e., it does not result in any additional failing negatives as determined by the deductive component), then it is chosen as part of the desired revision. If a particular retraction does result in additional failing negatives, then the inductive component is instead used to learn a new rule (see Section 5.6.1).

5.5.2 The Minimum Rule Cover

The proofs of failing negatives generated by the deductive component are used to determine the minimum rule cover. In order to minimize change to the initial theory, EITHER attempts to find the minimum number of leaf-rule retractions required to fix *all* the failing negatives. In analogy with the previous section, we would like to make the following expression true:

$$\neg E_1 \,\&\, \neg E_2 \,\&\, \ldots \,\&\, \neg E_n \tag{7}$$

where E_i represents the statement that the ith failing negative has a complete proof; that is,

$$\neg E_i \Leftrightarrow \neg P_{i1} \& \neg P_{i2} \& \ldots \& \neg P_{im} \tag{8}$$

where P_{ij} represents the statement that the jth proof of the ith failing negative is complete; that is,

$$\neg P_{ij} \Leftrightarrow \neg R_{ij1} \vee \neg R_{ij2} \ldots \vee \neg R_{ijp} \tag{9}$$

where $\neg R_{ijk}$ represents the statement that the kth leaf rule used in the jth proof of the ith failing negative is removed; i.e., a proof is no longer complete if at least one of the rules used in the proof is removed.

As with assumptions, EITHER attempts to find a minimum cover of rule retractions using greedy covering. In this case, the goal is to remove all proofs of all the failing negatives. Note that in computing retractions, EITHER removes from consideration those rules that do not have any disjuncts in their proof path to the goal because these rules are needed to prove *any* example. At each step in the covering algorithm, the eligible rule that participates in the most faulty proofs is added to the evolving cover until all the faulty proofs are covered.

As an example, consider the cup theory in which the width=small antecedent is missing from rule 5. In this case, example 5 becomes a failing negative. The minimum rule cover is the overly general version of rule 5

```
graspable   ⇐ styrofoam
```

because it is the only rule used in the faulty proof with alternative disjuncts (rules 4 and 6).

Once the rule cover is formed, EITHER attempts to retract each rule in the cover. If a given retraction is not an overspecialization (i.e., it does not result in any additional failing positives as determined by the deductive component), then it is chosen as part of the desired revision. If a particular retraction does result in additional failing negatives, then the inductive component is instead used to specialize the rule by adding additional antecedents (see Section 5.6.2).

5.6 THE INDUCTIVE COMPONENT

If retracting an element of the antecedent cover causes new failing negatives or if retracting an element of the rule cover causes new failing positives, then the inductive component is used to learn new rules or new antecedents, respectively. The only assumption EITHER makes about the inductive component is that it solves the following problem:

Given: A set of positive and negative examples of a concept C described by a set of observable features

Find: A Horn-clause theory T that is consistent with the examples; i.e., for
each positive example description, P, $P \cup T \models C$, and for each negative
example description, N, $N \cup T \not\models C$

As mentioned previously, EITHER currently uses ID3 as an inductive component by translating its decision trees into a set of rules; however, any inductive
rule-learning system could be used. An inductive system that directly produces a
multi-layer Horn-clause theory would be preferable, but current robust inductive
algorithms produce decision trees or DNF formulas. In EITHER, *inverse resolution*
operators (Muggleton, 1987; Muggleton and Buntine, 1988) are used to introduce
new intermediate concepts and produce a multi-layer theory from a translated decision tree (Mooney and Ourston, 1991a).

5.6.1 Rule Addition

If antecedent retraction ever over-generalizes, then induction is used to learn a
new set of rules for the consequent (C) of the corresponding rule. The rules are
learned so they cover the failing positives associated with the antecedent retraction
without introducing any new failing negatives. The positive examples of C are
those that have a partial proof completed by the given antecedent retraction (i.e.,
the failing positives covered by the given assumptions). The negative examples of
C are examples that become failing negatives when C is assumed to be true (i.e.,
this is a proof by contradiction that they are $\neg C$ because a contradiction is derived
when C is assumed).

Again consider the example of missing rule 4 from the cup theory. Based on
the antecedent cover, EITHER first attempts to remove width=small from rule 6;
however, this results in example 6 becoming a failing negative. Therefore, induction is used to form a new rule for graspable. The positive examples are the
original failing positives, examples 2 and 3. The negative examples are examples 4,
5, and 6, which become provable when graspable is assumed to be true. Because
has-handle is the only single feature that distinguishes examples 2 and 3 from
examples 4, 5, and 6, the inductive system (ID3) generates the required rule:

```
graspable  ⇐  has-handle
```

If an element of the antecedent cover is not an observable, then a rule is
learned directly for it instead of for the consequent of the rule in which it appears.
For example, if both rules for graspable are missing from the cup theory, then
most-specific abduction returns the single assumption set {graspable} for all the
failing positives (examples 1, 2, and 3). Because removing the graspable antecedent results in all the negative examples becoming failing negatives, EITHER
decides to learn rules for graspable. All the positive examples are used as positive

examples of `graspable`, and all the negatives are used as negative examples of graspable, and the system learns the approximately correct rules:

```
graspable ⇐ has-handle
graspable ⇐ width=small & styrofoam
```

5.6.2 Antecedent Addition

If rule retraction ever overspecializes, then induction is used to learn additional antecedents to add to the rule instead of retracting it. Antecedents are learned so they fix the failing negatives associated with the rule retraction without introducing any new failing positives. The positive examples of C are those examples that become unprovable (failing positives) when the rule is retracted. The negative examples of C are the failing negatives covered by the rule.

For example, again consider the case of missing the antecedent `width=small` from rule 5. Based on the rule cover, EITHER first removes the overly general rule 5

```
graspable ⇐ styrofoam
```

and tests for additional failing positives. Because example 1 becomes unprovable in this case, EITHER decides to add additional antecedents. Example 1 (the failing positive created by retraction) is used as a positive example, and example 5 (the original failing negative) is used as a negative example. Because `width` is the only feature that distinguishes these two examples, ID3 learns the rule

```
positive ⇐ width=small
```

This is combined with the original rule to obtain the correct replacement rule:

```
graspable ⇐ width=small & styrofoam
```

5.7 EMPIRICAL RESULTS

EITHER has revised two real expert-provided rule bases, one in molecular biology and one in plant pathology. This section presents details on our results in these domains. Further information on these tests, including the actual initial and revised theories, is given in Ourston (1991).

5.7.1 Single Category: DNA Results

EITHER was first tested on a theory for recognizing biological concepts in DNA sequences. The original theory is described in Towell, Shavlik, and Noordewier (1990); it contains 11 rules with a total of 76 propositional symbols. The purpose of the theory is to recognize *promoters* in strings of nucleotides (one of A, G, T, or C). A promoter is a genetic region that initiates the first step in the expression

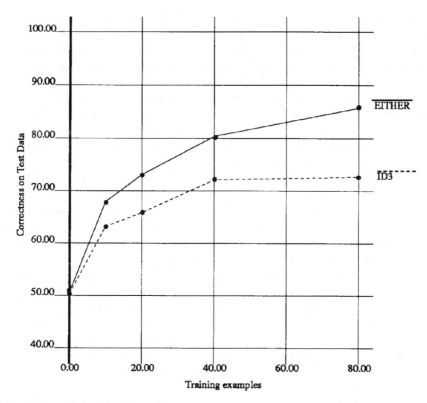

Figure 5.6:   Results for the DNA theory

of an adjacent gene (*transcription*) by RNA polymerase. The input features are 57 sequential DNA nucleotides. The examples used in the tests consisted of 53 positive and 53 negative examples assembled from the biological literature. The initial theory classified none of the positive examples and all of the negative examples correctly, thus indicating that the initial theory was entirely overly specific.

Figure 5.6 presents learning curves for this domain. In each test, classification accuracy was measured on 26 disjoint test examples. The number of training examples was varied from one to eighty, with the training and test examples selected at random. The results were averaged over 21 training/test divisions. ID3's performance is also shown in order to contrast theory refinement with pure induction.

The accuracy of the initial promoter theory is shown in the graph as EITHER's performance with 0 training examples—it is no better than random chance (50%). With no examples, ID3 picks a category at random and exhibits the same accuracy. However, as the number of training examples increases, EITHER's use of the existing theory results in a significant performance advantage compared to pure induction. A one-tailed Student t-test on paired differences showed that EITHER's superior accuracy compared to ID3 is statistically significant ($p < .05$) for every non-zero point plotted on the learning curves. Overall, EITHER improves the accuracy of the theory by 35 percentage points. An additional reason for including ID3 in the performance graphs is that it represents EITHER's performance without an initial theory because in this case, every example is a failing positive, and induction is used to learn a set of rules from scratch. Therefore, including ID3's learning curve provides a clear illustration of the advantage provided by theory-based learning. In fact, if a different inductive system were substituted for ID3, the absolute performance of both learning systems might change, but the relative advantage of EITHER compared to the purely inductive system should remain approximately the same.

Another way of looking at the performance advantage provided by an initial theory is to consider the additional examples required by ID3 in order to achieve equal performance with EITHER. For example, at 75% accuracy, ID3 requires over sixty additional training examples to achieve equal performance with EITHER. Therefore, in some sense, the information contained in the theory is equivalent to 60 examples.

The initial theory is primarily revised by deleting antecedents in various ways. In general, EITHER's changes made sense to the expert. In particular, the subconcept *conformation* was removed from the *promoter* concept in its entirety. This correction was validated by the biologist who encoded the theory (Noordewier), who indicated that conformation was a weakly justified constraint when it was originally introduced.

This domain theory was also used to test the KBANN system (Towell, Shavlik, and Noordewier, 1990), which translates the initial theory into an equivalent neural net and then applies the backpropagation algorithm (Rumelhart, Hinton, and Williams, 1986) to revise the network. KBANN's accuracy is somewhat better than EITHER's in this domain (a test set accuracy of 92% with 105 training examples). The likely explanation for the performance advantage is that the DNA task involves learning a concept of the form *N out of these M features must be present*. Experiments comparing backpropagation and ID3 report that backpropagation is better at learning *N out of M* functions (Fisher and McKusick, 1989). Some aspects of the promoter concept fit the *N out of M* format, where, for example, there are several potential sites where hydrogen bonds can form between the DNA and the protein; if enough of these bonds form, promoter activity can occur. EITHER attempts to learn this concept by learning a separate rule for each potential configuration by deleting different combinations of antecedents from the initial rules, which makes this a comparatively difficult learning task for a rule-based system. Finally, it should be noted that when KBANN translated its results into Horn clauses, the resulting theory was significantly more complicated than EITHER's (Towell and Shavlik, 1994, Chapter 15 in this book). This is because EITHER's goal is to produce a minimally revised Horn-clause theory, and KBANN has no such bias.

5.7.2 Multiple Categories: Soybean Results

In order to demonstrate EITHER's ability to revise multiple category theories, EITHER was used to refine the expert rules given in Michalski and Chilausky (1980). This is a theory for diagnosing soybean diseases that distinguishes between nineteen possible soybean diseases using examples that are described with thirty-five features. The original experiments compared expert rules to induction from examples. By revising the expert rules to fit the examples, we hoped to show that one could produce better results than using just the examples or just the rules.

The original expert rules associated probabilistic weights with certain disease symptoms. In addition, some groups of disease symptoms were regarded as *significant,* but other groups were regarded as *confirmatory.* The rules were translated to propositional Horn-clause format by only including the significant symptoms and by deleting any symptom from the theory that had a weight less than 0.8. After translation, the theory contained 73 rules with 325 propositional symbols.

Unfortunately, the classification performance of the Horn-clause version was seriously deficient compared to the original probabilistic rules. For example, the Horn-clause theory obtained a 12.3% classification performance compared to the accuracy of 73% reported in Michalski and Chilausky (1980). To circumvent the problem, a "flexible" matcher was used to classify the test examples based on the updated theory provided by EITHER. The flexible matcher accounts for two possible classification problems with a multi-category theory. The first problem occurs when a test example is provable as a member of more than one category. The second problem occurs when a test example is not provable as a member of any category. With the standard EITHER tester, such examples are assigned to the most common category. In contrast, the original soybean tests assigned a match score to each possible category and chose the category with the highest score. The flexible matcher used by EITHER is a simple approximation to the original technique. If an example is assigned to multiple categories, the tester selects the category that makes the most use of the example's features. This is done by choosing the category whose proof of category membership contains the greatest number of features. If an example is assigned to no category, the flexible matcher chooses the category that comes closest to being provable. This is done by choosing the category with a partial proof of category membership that has the least number of assumptions.

Learning curves for the soybean experiments are shown in Figure 5.7. In each test, accuracy was measured against 75 disjoint test examples. The number of training examples was varied from one to one hundred, with the training and test examples drawn at random from the entire example population. The results were averaged over 22 train/test divisions. Note that even with the flexible matcher, the

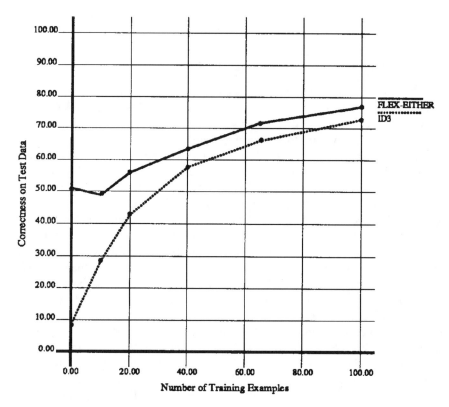

Figure 5.7:   Results for the soybean theory

accuracy of the original rules was only 51%, compared to 73% for the original results presented in Michalski and Chilausky (1980). Overall, the accuracy of the initial rules is increased by 26 percentage points, and EITHER maintains its initial performance advantage compared to pure induction over the entire training interval. A one-tailed Student t-test on paired differences showed that the superior performance of EITHER is statistically significant ($p < .05$) for every point plotted on the learning curves. Therefore, employing both rules and examples is better than using either one alone.

Because comparing a system with flexible matching (FLEX-EITHER) to one without it (ID3) is somewhat inequitable, we also tested a version of ID3 that uses the same flexible matcher as FLEX-EITHER. However, there was no significant difference between the performance of ID3 and FLEX-ID3 in this domain. Because ID3 has a bias for very simple, general descriptions, the case in which an example is not initially categorized into any category (and therefore requires partial matching) rarely occurred.

5.8 RELATED WORK

As discussed in Langley (1989), any incremental inductive learning system can be viewed as continually refining a knowledge base formed from previous examples. However, existing incremental inductive systems (Reinke and Michalski, 1988; Utgoff, 1989) employ "flat" representations such as decision trees and DNF expressions as opposed to multi-layer theories with intermediate concepts. In addition, attempts to initialize an incremental inductive system with a user-supplied domain theory have met with mixed results (Mahoney and Mooney, 1991; Thompson, Langley, and Iba, 1991).

Most systems for integrating explanation-based and empirical inductive methods cannot refine arbitrarily imperfect theories. Some systems are only capable of generalizing an overly specific (incomplete) theory (Wilkins, 1988; Danyluk, 1994, Chapter 7 in this book; Whitehall and Lu, 1994, Chapter 6 in this book), and others are only capable of specializing an overly general theory (Flann and Dietterich, 1989; Cohen, 1990; Mooney, in press). Many systems do not revise the theory itself but instead revise the *operational definition* of a concept (Bergadano and Giordana, 1988; Hirsh, 1990; Pazzani, Brunk, and Silverstein, 1991). Still other systems rely on active experimentation rather than a provided training set to detect and correct errors (Rajamoney, 1990).

Recent experiments with ANAPRON (Golding and Rosenbloom, 1991), a system that integrates case-based and rule-based reasoning, also demonstrate that combining initial rules and data performs better than either individually. However, this system stores specific cases as exceptions to rules rather than modifying the rules themselves.

KBANN (Towell and Shavlik, 1994, Chapter 15 in this book) and RTLS (Ginsberg, 1990) are theory revision systems that come the closest to handling as many types of imperfections as EITHER. However, neither integrates independent components for deduction, abduction, and induction. Modularity allows EITHER to easily take advantage of improvements in each of these areas of automated reasoning. Also, neither KBANN nor RTLS guarantees consistency with all the training data when given an arbitrary initial theory.

DUCTOR (Cain, 1991) is a recent EITHER-inspired system that integrates deduction, abduction, and induction. However, it does not generate all proofs and partial proofs, nor does it attempt to find a minimum cover of theory changes. Consequently, it is less focused on finding a *minimal* revision to the initial theory.

5.9 FUTURE RESEARCH

EITHER suffers from a number of shortcomings that we hope to address in future research. First, although it has been efficient enough to apply to several real theories, the current implementation can be quite slow at revising large rule bases (its takes 90 minutes on a Texas Instruments Explorer II to fit the soybean theory to 100 examples). Computation of all the partial proofs of failing positives is the primary bottleneck in the current system. By incorporating improved deductive and abductive components, we hope to dramatically improve system efficiency. Specifically, we plan to employ an abduction system that uses heuristic search to compute only a subset of the partial proofs with the fewest assumptions (Ng and Mooney, 1991). Another approach to improving efficiency is to only partially fit the theory to the training data. Existing experiments with a version of EITHER that computes only partial covers of the failing positive and failing negative examples have demonstrated that this technique can significantly increase efficiency without significantly affecting accuracy (Mooney and Ourston, 1991b). This method was originally developed to deal with noisy data.

Second, the current system cannot handle theories that employ *negation as failure*. Antecedents of the form not(P) complicate the revision process because generalizing or learning a rule that concludes P actually specializes the overall theory by preventing this antecedent from being satisfied. Conversely, specializing or eliminating a rule for P may actually generalize the overall theory. Therefore, the system will have to consider standard generalization operators as specializers in certain contexts and vice versa.

Third, the current system assumes all examples are instances of exactly one of the top-level categories. It cannot directly accept examples of intermediate concepts or deal with overlapping categories. A truly robust theory revision system should be able to accept examples of any of its concepts and use them to revise the rules for that concept directly or to revise other concepts indirectly.

Fourth, EITHER is basically restricted to revising propositional theories. We have already developed a prototype of a successor system called FORTE that is capable of revising first-order Horn-clause theories (Richards and Mooney, 1991). This system is undergoing continued development to improve its efficiency and capabilities.

Finally, EITHER is restricted to revising purely logical theories, and many rule bases employ some form of probabilistic reasoning. Some previous work has addressed the problem of refining the probabilities or certainty factors attached to rules (Ginsberg, Weiss, and Politikas, 1988; Ling and Valtorta, 1991); however, such numerical adjustments have not been integrated with more symbolic revisions such as learning new rules. We are currently developing a system that first "tweaks" certainty factors until no more improvement is possible and then resorts to learning new rules. The system cycles between "tweaking" and rule learning until it converges to 100% accuracy on the training data.

5.10 CONCLUSIONS

The development and testing of EITHER has demonstrated how deduction, abduction, and induction can be integrated successfully to revise imperfect domain theories. By combining such diverse methods, EITHER is able to handle a wider range of imperfect theories than other systems and guarantee that the revised theory will be consistent with the training data. Results on revising two actual expert theories has demonstrated EITHER's abilities and generality and confirmed the conjecture that learning from both theory and data gives better results than using either one alone.

ACKNOWLEDGMENTS

We would like to thank Mick Noordewier and Jude Shavlik for providing the DNA theory and data and helping us interpret the results, Jeff Mahoney for translating the soybean theory and data and implementing the flexible matcher, and Hwee Tou Ng for providing the abduction component. We would also like to thank the editors for their comments on an earlier draft of this chapter. This research was supported by the NASA Ames Research Center under Grant NCC 2-629 and by the National Science Foundation under Grant IRI-9102926. Equipment was donated by Texas Instruments Corporation.

References

Bergadano, F., and Giordana, A., "A knowledge intensive approach to concept induction," *Proceedings of the Fifth International Conference on Machine Learning*, pp. 305–317, Morgan Kaufmann Publishers, San Mateo, CA, 1988.

Cain, T., "The DUCTOR: A theory revision system for propositional domains," *Proceedings of the Eighth International Workshop on Machine Learning*, pp. 485–489, Morgan Kaufmann Publishers, San Mateo, CA, 1991.

Charniak, E., Reisbeck, C., McDermott, D., and Meehan, J., *Artificial Intelligence Programming (2nd Edition)*, Lawrence Erlbaum and Associates, Hillsdale, NJ, 1987.

Cohen, W.W., "Learning from textbook knowledge: A case study," *Proceedings of the Eighth National Conference on Artificial Intelligence*, pp. 743–748, AAAI Press, Menlo Park, CA, 1990.

Danyluk, A.P., "GEMINI: An integration of analytical and empirical learning," *Machine Learning: A Multistrategy Approach, Vol. IV,* R.S. Michalski and G. Tecuci (Eds.), Morgan Kaufmann Publishers, San Mateo, CA, 1994.

Fisher, D.H., and McKusick, K.B., "An empirical comparison of ID3 and backpropagation," *Proceedings of the Eleventh International Joint Conference on Artificial Intelligence,* pp. 788–793, Morgan Kaufmann Publishers, San Mateo, CA, 1989.

Flann, N.S., and Dietterich, T.G., "A study of explanation-based methods for inductive learning," *Machine Learning, 4:* 187–226, 1989.

Gary, M., and Johnson, D., *Computers and Intractability: A Guide to the Theory of NP-Completeness,* Freeman, New York, NY, 1979.

Ginsberg, A., "Theory reduction, theory revision, and retranslation," *Proceedings of the Eighth National Conference on Artificial Intelligence,* pp. 743–748, AAAI Press, Menlo Park, CA, 1990.

Ginsberg, A., Weiss, S.M., and Politikas, P., "Automatic knowledge base refinement for classification systems," *Artificial Intelligence, 35:* 197–226, 1988.

Golding, A.R., and Rosenbloom, P.S., "Improving rule-based systems through case-based reasoning," *Proceedings of the Ninth National Conference on Artificial Intelligence,* pp. 777–782, AAAI Press, Menlo, Park, CA, 1991.

Hirsh, H., *Incremental version space merging: A general framework for concept learning,* Kluwer, Hingham, MA, 1990.

Johnson, D.S., "Approximation algorithms for combinatorial problems," *Journal of Computer and System Sciences, 9:* 256–278, 1974.

Langley, P., "Unifying themes in empirical and explanation-based learning," *Proceedings of the Sixth International Workshop on Machine Learning,* pp. 2–4, Morgan Kaufmann Publishers, San Mateo, CA, 1989.

Ling, X., and Valtorta, M., "Revision of reduced theories," *Proceedings of the Eighth International Workshop on Machine Learning,* pp. 519–523, Morgan Kaufmann Publishers, San Mateo, CA, 1991.

Mahoney, J.J., and Mooney R.J., "Initializing ID5 with a Domain Theory: Some Negative Results," Technical Report AI91-154, Artificial Intelligence Laboratory, University of Texas at Austin, March 1991.

Michalski, R.S., and Chilausky, R.L., "Learning by being told and learning from examples: An experimental comparison of the two methods of knowledge acquisition in the context of developing an expert system for soybean disease diagnosis," *Policy Analysis and Information Systems, 4*: 125–160, 1980.

Mooney, R.J., "Induction over the unexplained: Using overly-general domain theories to aid concept learning" *Machine Learning, 10:* 79–110, 1993.

Mooney, R.J., and Ourston, D., "Constructive induction in theory refinement," *Proceedings of the Eighth International Workshop on Machine Learning*, pp. 178–182, Morgan Kaufmann Publishers, San Mateo, CA, 1991a.

————, "Theory Refinement with Noisy Data," Technical Report AI91-153, Artificial Intelligence Laboratory, University of Texas at Austin, 1991b.

Muggleton, S., "Duce, an oracle-based approach to constructive induction," *Proceedings of the Tenth International Joint Conference on Artificial Intelligence,* pp. 287–292, Morgan Kaufmann Publishers, San Mateo, CA, 1987.

Muggleton, S., and Buntine, W., "Machine invention of first-order predicates by inverting resolution," *Proceedings of the Fifth International Conference on Machine Learning*, pp. 339–352, Morgan Kaufmann Publishers, San Mateo, CA, 1988.

Ng, H.T., and Mooney, R.J., "Abductive Explanation in Text Understanding: Some Problems and Solutions," Technical Report AI89-116, Artificial Intelligence Laboratory, University of Texas at Austin, October 1989.

————, "An efficient first-order horn-clause abduction system based on the ATMS," *Proceedings of the Ninth National Conference on Artificial Intelligence*, pp. 494–499, AAAI Press, Menlo Park, CA, July 1991.

Ourston, D., *Using Explanation-Based and Empirical Methods in Theory Revision*, Ph.D. Thesis, University of Texas, Austin, TX, 1991.

Ourston, D., and Mooney, R.J., "Changing the rules: A comprehensive approach to theory refinement," *Proceedings of the Eighth National Conference on Artificial Intelligence*, pp. 815–820, AAAI Press, Menlo Park, CA, 1990.

————, "Improving Shared Rules in Multiple Category Domain Theories," *Proceedings of the Eighth International Machine Learning Workshop*, pp. 534–538, Morgan Kaufmann Publishers, San Mateo, CA, 1991.

Pazzani, M.J., Brunk, C., and Silverstein, G., "A knowledge-intensive approach to learning relational concepts," *Proceedings of the Eighth International Workshop on Machine Learning*, pp. 432–436, Morgan Kaufmann Publishers, San Mateo, CA, 1991.

Quinlan, J.R., "Induction of decision trees," *Machine Learning, 1*: 81–106, 1986.

————, "Generating production rules from decision trees," *Proceedings of the Tenth International Joint Conference on Artificial Intelligence,* pp. 304–307, Morgan Kaufmann Publishers, San Mateo, CA, 1987.

Rajamoney, S.A., "A computational approach to theory revision," *Computational Models of Scientific Discovery and Theory Formation*, J. Shrager and P. Langley (Eds.), pp. 225–254, Morgan Kaufmann Publishers, San Mateo, CA, 1990.

Reinke, R.E., and Michalski, R.S., "Incremental learning of concept descriptions," *Machine Intelligence (Vol. 11)*, J.E. Hayes, D. Michie, and J. Richards (Eds.), Oxford University Press, Oxford, England, 1988.

Richards, B.L., and Mooney, R.J., "First order theory revision," *Proceedings of the Eighth International Workshop on Machine Learning*, pp. 447–451, Morgan Kaufmann Publishers, San Mateo, CA, 1991.

Rumelhart, D.E., Hinton, G.E., and Williams, J.R., "Learning internal representations by error propagation," *Parallel Distributed Processing* (Vol. 1), D.E. Rumelhart and J.L. McClelland (Eds.), MIT Press, Cambridge, MA, 1986.

Stickel, M.E., "A Prolog-like inference system for computing minimum-cost abductive explanations in natural language interpretation," Technical Note 451, SRI International, Menlo Park, CA, 1988.

Thompson, K., Langley, P., and Iba, W., "Using background knowledge in concept formation," *Proceedings of the Eighth International Machine Learning Workshop*, pp. 554–558, Morgan Kaufmann Publishers, San Mateo, CA, 1991.

Towell, G., and Shavlik, J.W., "Refining symbolic knowledge using neural networks," *Machine Learning: A Multistrategy Approach, Vol. IV*, R.S. Michalski and G. Tecuci (Eds.), Morgan Kaufmann Publishers, San Mateo, CA, 1994.

Towell, G., Shavlik, J.W., and Noordewier, M.O., "Refinement of approximate domain theories by knowledge-based artificial neural networks," *Proceedings of the Ninth National Conference on Artificial Intelligence,* pp. 861–866, AAAI Press, Menlo Park, CA, 1990.

Utgoff, P.E., "Incremental induction of decision trees," *Machine Learning, 4*: 161–186, 1989.

Whitehall, B.L., and Lu, S.Y., "Theory completion using knowledge-based learning," *Machine Learning: A Multistrategy Approach, Vol. IV*, R.S. Michalski and G. Tecuci (Eds.), Morgan Kaufmann Publishers, San Mateo, CA, 1994.

Wilkins, D.C., "Knowledge base refinement using apprenticeship learning techniques," *Proceedings of the Seventh National Conference on Artificial Intelligence,* pp. 646–651, Morgan Kaufmann Publishers, San Mateo, CA, 1988.

Winston, P.H., Binford, T.O., Katz, B., and Lowry, M., "Learning physical descriptions from functional definitions, examples, and precedents," *Proceedings of the Third National Conference on Artificial Intelligence*, pp. 433–439, Morgan Kaufmann Publishers, San Mateo, CA, 1983.

6

THEORY COMPLETION USING
KNOWLEDGE-BASED LEARNING

Bradley L. Whitehall[1]
(United Technologies Research Center)

Stephen C-Y. Lu
(University of Illinois at Urbana-Champaign)

Abstract

To learn effectively, a system needs to use all the knowledge that is available. This chapter describes *knowledge-based inductive learning*, an approach that uses an incomplete domain theory and examples to induce knowledge missing in the theory. Many problems in engineering and other areas can provide a learning system with knowledge in these two forms. Knowledge-based inductive learning removes much of the operational burden from a user of a learning system by determining where knowledge is missing in the incomplete domain theory, selecting a relevant subset of the provided examples to use in induction, and inducing new rules or modifying existing rules to extend the domain theory. When new rules must be constructed, the system determines certain values for the rule consequence in addition to inducing the rule antecedents. The knowledge-based inductive learning approach is illustrated with KBL1, a system designed and implemented to work with domains requiring a representation of real numbers and mathematical formulas, such as engineering. Empirical results obtained from KBL1 illustrate that using a domain theory to guide induction over examples is beneficial and that when there

---

[1]The research described in this chapter was completed while at the University of Illinois.

are few examples available compared to the size of the problem space, the resulting rules are more accurate than those from pure empirical learning techniques.

6.1 INTRODUCTION

Constructing knowledge-based systems is difficult. The knowledge engineer must compose into a working system heuristics provided by the domain expert and rules developed by studying previously solved examples. As with many projects, the so-called 20/80 rule appears to be true in knowledge-base construction. That is, 80% of a system's functionality can be obtained in the first 20% of the knowledge engineer's effort. Completing the remaining 20% of functionality of the knowledge base requires 80% of the knowledge engineer's time. Tools are needed to assist the knowledge engineer in obtaining the remaining functionality of the knowledge base with less effort.

Until recently, machine learning research has produced algorithms that create rules for knowledge-based systems that require either a large number of examples or a complete domain theory (often in the form of rules). Pure empirical learning systems require a set of examples that sufficiently cover the problem space in order for the algorithm to produce a description (rules or decision tree) of the problem class (Dietterich and Michalski, 1983; Quinlan, 1986; Stepp and Michalski, 1986; Fisher, 1987). Explanation-based learning (EBL) systems require a complete, correct, and tractable domain theory (DeJong and Mooney, 1986; Mitchell et al., 1986). As stated previously, it is difficult for a knowledge engineer to produce such a knowledge base. In some domains, it might be impossible because the domain is constantly evolving. In many real-world situations, only a limited number of examples and an incomplete domain theory are available. In such cases, where traditional learning techniques perform poorly, a learning algorithm that can use knowledge from *both* examples and rules can do much better. For a learning system to be useful, it must produce rules that can be incorporated into the existing knowledge. *Knowledge-based inductive learning* (KBL) is an approach that combines the strengths of empirical learning with the strengths of explanation-based learning to overcome previous limitations.

A number of multistrategy learning systems that assist a knowledge engineer when some knowledge already exists have been researched over the past couple of years. This chapter describes one such system, KBL, and identifies some of the problems confronting these multistrategy learning systems. Starting with an initial corpus of knowledge, these systems use that knowledge to discover or extract additional knowledge from solved problems (examples). These knowledge-based inductive learning systems use the given knowledge to provide guidance in determining what to learn, what examples are most useful, and which attributes of the problems are the most relevant. Although the provided knowledge is useful, it is not flawless. The learning system must constantly guard against believing the knowledge base when there is overwhelming empirical support against it.

Recent research has investigated the combining of EBL and SBL techniques (Pazzani, 1985; Flann and Dietterich, 1986; Lebowitz, 1986; Pazzani et al., 1986; Danyluk, 1987; Pazzani, 1987; Wilkins, 1987; Fawcett, 1989; Mooney and Ourston, 1989; Tecuci and Kodratoff, 1989). Each of the previous systems combines an empirical algorithm with a deductive method. In contrast with the traditional combining methods, knowledge-based inductive learning defines a much smaller grain size between the processes, allowing them to interact more tightly.

KBL performs all the following functions:

- Select examples for the induction without user intervention.
- Determine where knowledge is missing, and induce both the consequent (binding for the missing variable value) and the antecedents of the new rule.
- Partition events into classes to avoid overgeneralization of the new rules.
- Handle real numbers and discover mathematical formulas.

There are a number of issues that all systems combining EBL and empirical techniques must account for during learning:

- What knowledge will be used to identify where knowledge is missing?
- What are the relevant examples for the problem?
- Which attributes of the problems are most relevant for the problem?

In the rest of this chapter, the approach taken by knowledge-based inductive learning systems to each of these questions is described. The next section provides an overview of knowledge-based inductive learning, focusing on how KBL is failure driven and uses the problem context to guide induction. Section 6.3 describes the major components of KBL1, an implemented KBL system. In section 6.4, results comparing the KBL approach with ID3 are presented. ID3 is used in the comparison because it finds accurate rules quickly. The last section presents conclusions.

6.2 KNOWLEDGE-BASED INDUCTIVE LEARNING

In manual knowledge acquisition, the domain expert critiques the results (i.e., failures) of the inference engine to complete the domain theory. In KBL, the inference engine indicates that learning needs to occur by providing the learning system with a problem that it cannot solve (Figure 6.1). KBL uses the current unsolved problem to direct the learning process. The system uses examples provided by the expert and knowledge in the form of rules. The rule knowledge can be obtained through manual knowledge acquisition techniques or by expert consultation with an interactive knowledge acquisition system, i.e., TEIRESIAS (Davis, 1982).

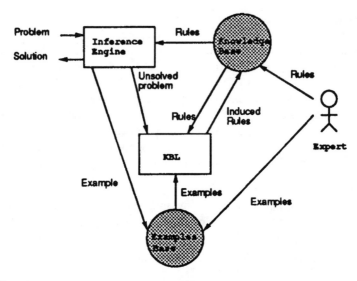

Figure 6.1:   Knowledge-based inductive learning approach to knowledge base construction

The KBL process starts with a problem the inference engine cannot solve using available knowledge. The problem is a set of ground facts and an un-instanciated top-level goal. KBL first constructs a partial-proof tree[2] (see Figure 6.4 for an example partial proof tree). The system uses the partial-proof tree to guide the induction process. The generalized leaves of the partial proof tree are used to form a *context*. The context is used to find similar problems in a database of examples that will be used during induction.

The induction process can repair an existing rule or induce a new one to enable the inference engine to solve the previously unsolvable problem. The knowledge base is modified to reflect the change. In short, KBL systems require the following inputs

- An incomplete domain knowledge.
- A set of examples with solutions (example base). (These examples should capture knowledge that is not expressed in the domain knowledge. Examples may also be added from the performance element as problems are solved.)
- A language specification that identifies the number of arguments to each predicate and the valid argument types.
- A problem that cannot be solved with the incomplete domain knowledge.

---

[2] The proof tree is not complete because then a solution would have been found.

Induction guided by a partial-proof tree is one major part of KBL, but unsolved problems usually have many partial proofs. One useful heuristic for selecting a partial proof according to its expected utility is the size of the inductive leap required to complete the proof. *Rule-structured induction* uses this heuristic to guide the induction. The induction process uses the heuristically selected partial-proof tree to select relevant examples appropriate for rule induction. This facilitates knowledge acquisition within the knowledge base by focusing the induction and structuring it to fit the existing knowledge.

6.2.1 Rule-Structured Induction

Unlike learning systems that are told *what* to learn, KBL systems must determine where knowledge is missing. Similarity-based learning systems are informed what to learn by the class membership of the provided examples. Explanation-based learning systems are provided with the goal concept; the goal concept is the consequent of the rule to be learned. KBL systems must determine the correct goal for the consequent of the learned rule, i.e., by determining which subgoal is missing a rule. Because there is no a priori information about which knowledge is missing from the knowledge base, inductive inference must be used to identify (heuristically) the consequent of the needed new rule.

One approach to identifying missing knowledge is to assume that any unsatisfied subgoal is caused by a missing rule. This is an erroneous approach because if backtracking were allowed, the unsatisfied subgoal might have been avoided by using a different rule farther up in the proof structure. Yet, if a complete proof cannot be constructed, knowledge must be missing for (at least) one of the unsolved subgoals. If the system backtracks until no partial proof is identified, then the induction mechanism will learn rules for the top-level goal, and the system will not take advantage of the knowledge in the system.

In general, determining where a knowledge base needs to be repaired or extended is difficult. *Rule-Structured Induction* (RSI) is an inductive approach to determining where knowledge is missing from a domain theory and thus directs the construction of partial-proof trees. RSI frees a knowledge engineer from determining the locations most suitable for learning in the existing rule structure. The goal of RSI is to generalize the knowledge base as little as possible while the current problem is solved. The system has a bias against inducing a new rule when an existing rule can be modified slightly to solve the problem. The rules selected for generalization have the most subgoals satisfied and require small inductive leaps to allow the unsatisfied subgoals to be proved for the problem. Rule-structured induction is guided by the following goals:

- To use the (derived) context for the problem. (The context highlights important aspects of the problem that should be used in constructing new rules and modifying old rules).

- To generalize the knowledge base as little as possible to solve the current problem.
- To take advantage of the knowledge in existing rules by generalizing or specializing existing rules before adding new rules.

6.2.1.1 Defining a Rule Structured Induction Task

Inducing rules within an existing structure is similar to the problem confronting an incremental learning system. The system is provided an event not covered by the current set of rules. The goal is to extend the set of rules to cover the new event. The version spaces method (Mitchell, 1982) does this for events in an attribute space that only allows conjunctive descriptions. The problem is more complex when events have relational predicates, disjunctive concepts are allowed, or the rules compose a hierarchical structure.

Before defining the RSI approach, a hierarchical rule structure must be defined.

Definition 1.   A hierarchical rule structure, R, is a set of rules in which the consequence of one rule is used in the antecedent of another rule. Rule chaining can occur to any finite depth.

A hierarchical rule set is denoted by

$$R_0 \leftarrow C_{01} \wedge R_i \wedge \cdots \wedge R_n$$
$$R_0 \leftarrow C_{02} \wedge R_q \wedge \cdots \wedge R_s$$
.
.
.
$$R_i \leftarrow C_{ij} \wedge R_t \wedge R_v \wedge \cdots \wedge R_p$$
.
.
.

where each C_{ij} is a conjunction of literals

$$c_{ij1} \wedge c_{ij2} \wedge \cdots \wedge c_{ijq}$$

C_{ij} is the primitive portion of the rule; that is, all the c_{ijk} literals have predicates that do not occur as the consequent of any rule. R_i is a literal whose predicate is the consequent of at least one rule. R_0 is the highest level goal of the system. The R_is of a rule set will be called the *chaining* literals of the rule because they can be grounded by chaining through a number of rules. The R_is for a single consequent do not have to be unique. A PROLOG program is an example of a hierarchical rule structure.

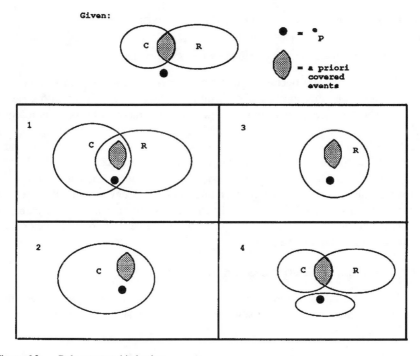

Figure 6.2:   Rule-structured induction

For generalizing within a rule structure, there is an event e_p that the user has indicated belongs to the class of events defined by a hierarchical rule structure, R. However, the set of rules, R, does not cover the event. The rules in R must be generalized to cover e_p.

As shown in Figure 6.2, there are four general methods to modify a set of rules to cover a new event.[3] The diagram shows a case of a single chaining literal referenced on the left-hand side of the concept rule. The concept rule is *Positiveclass* $\leftarrow C \wedge R$.

The four possible solutions are

1. Generalize both the selected concept rule constants in C and the chaining rule R to cover the new event e_p.

2. Generalize C to cover e_p and drop R from the concept rule.

---

[3] *To cover* means extending the knowledge base so that rules will fire for the facts of the unsolved problem.

3. Generalize R to cover e_p and drop C from the concept rule.

4. Create a new rule for the concept, *Positiveclass* $\leftarrow e_p$, thus introducing a new disjunct for the concept described by the positive class.

These are the only operations that can be performed to generalize the coverage of a rule. Note that initially C or R might already cover e_p (Figure 6.2 shows the case where neither initially covers e_p). The combinatorics become more complex when the concept rule has more chaining rules in its antecedent. If the concept is defined by a number of rules, the learning system must choose among these options for each of the rules and determine the best generalization overall. When a number of rules for a concept exist, the system could remove the current rules and perform a batch inductive learning technique to learn a new set of rules. For the system to do this, all the events currently covered by the rules must be available. If a system chooses this option, the chaining rules could be used to infer higher-level (constructed) features for the events.

6.2.1.2 Assigning Heuristic Goodness Values

To perform rule-structured induction, a numeric value is assigned to each rule indicating the amount of generalization required for it to solve the current problem. Four factors are used in computing the numeric value.

1. Number of subgoals that exactly match the current problem. If many antecedents of a rule are grounded with the attributes of the current problem, less generalization is required to make the rule applicable for the problem.

2. Number of subgoal predicates matched with unmatched arguments. In this situation, the attributes (predicates) in the rule are present in the problem, but their values do not match the values in the antecedents. For example, an antecedent term could be (part-estimated-weight 5), but the problem description has (part-estimated-weight 3). Generalization is required if these subgoals are to be used to solve this problem. Guided by the desire to generalize as little as possible, the algorithm prefers using rules with subgoals almost covering the problem. There are degrees of matching. If the current subgoal requires a value for attribute X between 1 and 100, but the value of X is 101, a small leap of faith is required to extend the range for the subgoal. If instead the value for X is 1,000, then one should be hesitant to extend the range for this attribute and should consider looking at another rule.

3. Number of unmatched subgoal predicates. An unmatched predicate could either be a chaining predicate or a primitive predicate. When a primitive predicate does not match any of the predicates in the current problem, the only generalization technique permitting the rule to fire is to drop the rule antecedent. When a chaining predicate does not match the current problem, none of the rules that have the subgoal as the head can be used to prove the subgoal. In this situation, there are two options: (1) create a new rule for the goal or (2) generalize a rule in the structure for this goal. RSI can be applied to the subgoal to determine if one of the deeper-level rules needs to be modified. The system looks deeper into the structure for the appropriate generalization. If no lower-level rule is modified, the system induces a new rule for the subgoal. A chaining failure (defined later) is the only type of failure that signals RSI to induce new rules.

4. Prefer to generalize longer rules. Rules with many subgoals are more specific than rules with a few. To minimize the impact of the generalization, the learning system should work with rules unlikely to apply in situations other than the current problem and closely related problems.

In addition to the general guidelines provided above, user preferences also guide where the generalizations can occur. The user might prefer adding new rules to modifying existing ones. For example, suppose the existing knowledge base has worked for a large class of problems that make up the bulk of the load for this system. When seeing a new problem, one would be hesitant to change the existing, well-tested rules. In some situations, the user might prefer to add or change rules at higher levels in the proof tree rather than make generalizations to subgoals lower in the tree. To accommodate these different preferences, the user provides parameter values that determine which rule should be generalized.

RSI requires five parameter values that are used to assign a numeric score to each rule. These scores determine which rule modification to the knowledge base best meets the preferences of the user. Each term of the rule antecedent is compared with the terms of the current problem description. A value is assigned for each expression depending upon the type of match (below). The value of a rule is the ratio of the sum of the values for the antecedent terms to a perfect score for a rule with the same number of antecedents. The rule with a ratio closest to 1 is considered the best. The five parameter values are

1. **Perfect match value.** The antecedent term matches a term of the problem description, e.g., (color red) vs. (color red).
2. **Slight extend value.** The predicate matches, but a nominal value range needs to be extended or a real number range needs to be extended slightly (a threshold parameter); e.g., (part-length ?x)(< 5 ?x)(< ?x 10) vs. (part-length 4.5).
3. **Extreme extend value.** The predicate matches, but a real number range needs to be extended by more than the provided threshold for a slight extension; e.g., (part-length ?x)(< 5 ?x)(< ?x 10) vs. (part-length 50).

```
Factor(R, Eₚ, Θ)
; R - rule
; Eₚ - current problem
; Θ - bindings
Sum = 0
Count = 0
Do for each A in Antecedents(R)
    ; Accumulate the match value for each antecedent
    Sum = Sum + Find-match(AΘ, Eₚ)
    Count = Count + 1
Enddo
; Return the normalized sum value
Return(Sum / (Count × perfect-match-value))

Find-match(A, E)
; A - antecedent
; E - problem description
; Determine the type of match and return that
; value for the antecedent
If A ∈ E
    V = * perfect-match-value *
Else If A matches e ∈ E within tolerance
    V = * slight-extend-value *
Else If Predicate(A) = Predicate(e), e ∈ E
    V = * extreme-extend-value *
Else If Chaining-pred?(Predicate(A))
    V = * chaining-failure-value *
Else
    V = * primitive-failure-value *
Endif
Return(V)
```

Figure 6.3:   Algorithm used to compute the numerical value (Factor) for a rule

4. **Chaining failure value.** The subgoal is a chaining predicate where the rules for the predicate are not grounded.

5. **Primitive failure value.** A primitive predicate does not match any of the attributes of the problem and would have to be dropped for the rule to work for the problem.

Figure 6.3 contains the algorithm used to compute the numerical value (factor) for a rule. The Find-match algorithm called by Factor determines the degree of match using the five parameter values and returns the appropriate overall score.

6.2.1.3 Global Considerations for Rule Generalization

What has been presented so far shows how RSI can heuristically target a rule to generalize from a set of rules. The rule with a ratio of generalization values to perfect matches for all components closest to 1 is designated the best rule to generalize. Generalizing this rule to solve the problem requires less inference, as measured by syntactical changes. Generalizing rules in isolation, however, is insufficient. The system must consider how changing a rule at one level affects the performance of other rules in the system. A simple change at one level might cause complex changes to occur at other levels, thus complicating the proof structure or even making it incorrect for other examples. To help avoid this problem, the system searches through the possible changes and determines the best alternative. This is a search through an AND/OR tree for the path that satisfies the top-level (problem) goal but requires the fewest number of modifications to the existing knowledge base. At the root of the tree is the goal for the problem. A number of rules can be used to prove the goal, only one of which is required. Each rule consists of a number of antecedents, each of which must be proved for the rule to prove the goal. A simple backward chaining mechanism such as that described in Winston (1984) can be used for this search. This search can be converted into a search through an OR tree, allowing heuristic search techniques such as branch and bound to be applied (Barr and Feigenbaum, 1981, page 42).

To summarize RSI, the system identified where knowledge is missing by searching the rules in the knowledge base to find a proof that is as complete as (heuristically) possible. The system chooses rules to generalize based upon the parameters provided by the user. Those values determine preferences for different methods of extending the knowledge base. When a chaining failure occurs, the system applies learning for the failed subgoal. Although the system is biased against inducing completely new rules when existing rules can be generalized, there are times when that is the best repair for the system. Specifically, if the values for all the rules of a subgoal are below a (parameterized) threshold, say 0.75, then the system will not try to modify any of the existing rules. The parameter values in this case indicate that none of the current rules are close enough to solving the current problem to warrant the effort of repairing them. The induction of a new rule is always an alternative for a chaining failure and, depending upon the search procedure used, could be performed even when there are other modifications possible to deeper rules. If many changes are involved in repairing the deeper level, it might be advantageous to create a new rule.

6.2.2 Induction Process

With traditional empirical learning systems, the user must supply the relevant examples with the relevant attributes to the system. The KBL induction module selects the relevant examples based upon the partial-proof tree determined by RSI and uses the knowledge base to focus attention on the attributes most likely to be important to the problem. Also, because of the representation required to solve engineering problems, the system must discover the consequent of the rule in addition to inducing the antecedents. Rules induced by KBL have the form

(pred1 ?x ?y) ← **TESTS** (= ?y **VALUE**)

The RSI module finds `pred1`, and the induction module must determine **VALUE**. (The form (= ?y *value*) sets the value of variable ?y to *value*.) The reason for chaining on `pred1` is to set ?y to **VALUE**. The induction algorithm discovers the consequent of the rule by setting **VALUE** to a constant value, a bound variable, or a formula using other bound variables. The **TESTS** portion of a rule defines the conditions that must be true in the current context in order to apply the rule. The following subsections describe the five components of the induction process.

6.2.2.1 Gather Examples

A KBL system selects relevant examples from an example base rather than depend upon the user to provide them. The examples from the provided example base that match the *context* of the current problem are used for the rule learning. The context is the portion of the partial-proof tree that has been solved (all variables in the leaves are grounded). The ungrounded version of the context makes up the constraints. The system applies those constraints to the example base and collects the examples that contain attributes that unify with the constraints. Figure 6.4 contains a simple partial-proof tree. The context from that partial-proof tree is (a1 ?y) (a2 ?y) (b1 ?w). Any example in the example base that has attributes a1 and a2 with the same value and an attribute b1 defined will match the given constraints for this context. KBL assumes that a solution for an example matching the context is similar to the solution needed to correct the problem.

6.2.2.2 Compute Solutions

The system now has a set of example/solution pairs from the example base that match the context. To perform induction, the examples must be classified. Before they can be classified, the value of the unsolved subgoal must be determined. In the example of Figure 6.4, the system is trying to induce a rule for b2, as indicated by ???. The set of examples collected have solutions for (foo ?x)—the top level goal. The induction module must derive from the value for ?x of foo a value for ?z of b2 so that the value can be used to assign class membership to the examples. In general, the best the system can do is constrain the solution to a range of possible values. Fortunately, this method is adequate to allow induction to continue.

To get the set of values to which the missing variable can be bound, the system must work backwards from the solution to the point in the tree where the

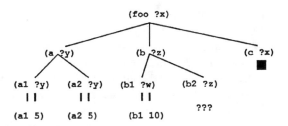

Figure 6.4:   Example partial-proof tree

variable is bound. The first place where the variable is used (traversing the tree in pre-order) indicates where it is assigned a new value.[4] References to the variable later in the proof tree are only accessing the bound value of the variable. These references are used to constrain the actual values that would allow a proof of the problem to be solved.

6.2.2.3 Collect Relevant Attributes

Real-world problems can have many attributes, easily hundreds. The system must, therefore, focus on the attributes that are relevant to the unsolved goal. In traditional empirical learning, systems use all the attributes (or the user selects the relevant attributes). Focusing on relevant attributes helps the system produce sensible results. In addition, it helps reduce the problem space. As more attributes are used in the induction of a new rule, more examples need to be used to identify areas outside the scope of the new rule (i.e., more negative examples are required).

Relevant attributes can be identified in at least two ways. Knowledge can be provided indicating which attributes are more likely to be useful when inducing rules for a predicate (as in Drastal et al., 1989). Alternatively, the KBL1 system looks for other rules with the same predicate in their consequent as the subgoal under consideration. The system focuses on the attributes used by these other rules.

6.2.2.4 Discover Rule Consequent

After the system computes the solution to the unsolved goal of each example (or a range of values that bound the solution), the consequent of the rules must be determined. If the missing variable could only be assigned a single, constant value, the task would be easy. The events are partitioned into classes for each value seen. At the worst, this creates overly specific rules. Engineering problems, however, require a more expressive language, one that allows variables to be bound to the

---

[4] If the variable is bound before this point in the partial proof tree, then this procedure does not need to occur. The exact value will already exist in the binding list.

values of other variables or mathematical formulas. The induction module must discover the relationship between the missing values and the other variables. The system searches for the proper expression to place in the rule consequent: constant, variable, or mathematical formula. Not all the examples need to be covered by one expression. Sets of examples are formed (partitioned) based on the different expressions covering them. The examples for one partition can, later, act as near misses for the other classes during induction. The search used for the expressions relating examples is similar to that used in scientific discovery systems (Falkenhainer and Michalski, 1986; Langley et al., 1987). The main difference is that for complex domains, the system has a bias of finding simpler formulas that cover some subset of the examples in preference to finding one complex formula that covers all the examples.[5]

As an example, the system could discover that $?z$ of Figure 6.4 is equal to $2 * ?y$ for some examples and $3 * ?y$ for others. The system could learn two rules, where $?z$ is set to the appropriate value in each rule.

6.2.2.5 Induce New Rule

With partitioned examples and a known consequent for the rules of each partition, the system is ready to induce the antecedents. A traditional empirical learning from examples system can be used to induce the appropriate conditions for firing a rule. The induction system should be biased to produce specific rules instead of general rules. The system can detect overly specific rules when constructing the partial-proof tree and further generalize those rules. In order to detect overly general rules, an oracle must indicate an incorrect result, or the system must search for contradictions between existing rules and provided examples.

6.3 DEMONSTRATION OF KBL1

The KBL approach has been used with a number of engineering domains, including an expert system for designing traffic light times (Linkenheld et al., 1989). To demonstrate the KBL1 system, a simple domain for computer-aided process planning is used (Figure 6.5). PROLOG style rules are used to define the domain knowledge, where variables are prefixed by ?. The top-level goal is TOP, and the idea is to determine the type of machining required for the object provided. The two variables to TOP are bound to the type of feature found and the machining needed to produce that feature. The predicate TYPE is used to determine the type of feature for the facts that are given to describe the part. For this simple example, the only types of parts are slots and holes. The predicates SLOT and HOLE are proposi-

---

[5] Details on this process can be found in Whitehall (1990) and Whitehall et al. (1990).

```
(TOP ?X ?W) ← (TYPE ?Y ?X) (SIZE ?Z) (MACHINE ?W ?Z ?Y)
(TYPE ?Y ?X) ← (SLOT ?X) (= ?Y (BINDING SLOT))
(TYPE ?Y ?X) ← (HOLE ?X) (= ?Y (BINDING HOLE))
(SIZE ?Z) ← (WIDTH ?X) (< ?X 5) (= ?Z (BINDING NARROW))
(SIZE ?Z) ← (WIDTH ?X) (≥ ?X 5) (= ?Z (BINDING WIDE))
(MACHINE ?W NARROW HOLE) ← (= ?W (BINDING DRILL))
(MACHINE ?W WIDE HOLE) ← (= ?W (BINDING 2-PASS-DRILL))
(MACHINE ?W WIDE SLOT) ← (= ?W (BINDING 2-PASS-END-MILL))
(MACHINE ?W NARROW SLOT) ← (= ?W (BINDING END-MILL))
```

Figure 6.5:   Simple CAPP knowledge base

tional because their arguments have no meaning. The presence of SLOT indicates a slot is being processed, and HOLE indicates that a hole should be machined. In a more complex domain theory, subgoal TYPE would be used to obtain the type of feature, instead of just having propositional values indicate the appropriate type. The subgoal SIZE is used to determine the size of the feature, either narrow or wide, as determined by the measured width of the feature. The subgoal MACHINE determines what the actual processing must be, drilling or end-milling, and if a one or two pass process is required. The = predicate is used to set the first argument to the value of the second argument. The second argument is evaluated, and BINDING just returns the value of its argument (similar to quote in LISP).

To evaluate KBL1's ability to learn, the following two rules were removed from the complete domain theory of Figure 6.5:

```
(TYPE ?Y ?X) ← (SLOT ?X) (= ?Y (BINDING SLOT))
(MACHINE ?W NARROW SLOT) ← (= ?W (BINDING END-MILL))}
```

The initial facts for a problem are provided to KBL1, (SLOT SLOT-E) (WIDTH 4). For this example, the feature is a slot, called slot-e, and has a width of 4. These facts are entered so that the rules of the knowledge base can use them. The examples stored in the example base are provided next. The examples have the form *facts describing feature / result of goal TOP*.

1. (SLOT SLOT-1) (WIDTH 3) / (TOP SLOT-1 END-MILL)
2. (SLOT SLOT-2) (WIDTH 2) / (TOP SLOT-2 END-MILL)
3. (SLOT SLOT-3) (WIDTH 4) / (TOP SLOT-3 END-MILL)
4. (SLOT SLOT-3A) (WIDTH 4) / (TOP SLOT-3A END-MILL)
5. (SLOT SLOT-3B) (WIDTH 4) / (TOP SLOT-3B END-MILL)
6. (SLOT SLOT-4) (WIDTH 6) / (TOP SLOT-4 2-PASS-END-MILL)
7. (SLOT SLOT-5) (WIDTH 10) / (TOP SLOT-5 2-PASS-END-MILL)
8. (HOLE HOLE-1) (WIDTH 3) / (TOP HOLE-1 DRILL)
9. (HOLE HOLE-2) (WIDTH 10) / (TOP HOLE-2 2-PASS-DRILL)

When KBL1 was presented with the goal (TOP ?a ?b), all nine of the examples were collected to help the system induce a rule for subgoal TYPE. But because a rule for MACHINE was also missing, the system could not derive solutions for all the examples as outlined in Section 6.2.2.2. Solutions were only found for examples 6, 7, 8, and 9, so they were used to induce the rule

```
(TYPE ?Y1 ?X2) ⇐ (SLOT ?X2)(WIDTH ?X1)(≤ 4 ?X1)(≤ ?X1 10)(= ?Y1
    (BINDING SLOT))
```

With the new rule, KBL1 continued working to find a solution for the problem. KBL1 stopped backward chaining when a rule was needed for MACHINE. The examples 3, 4, and 5 were matched by this partial-proof tree and used to induce the rule

```
(MACHINE ?W1 ?Z1 ?Y1) ⇐ (SLOT ?X2) (WIDTH ?X1) (≤ 4 ?X1) (≤ ?X1 4)
    (= ?W1 (BINDING END-MILL)))
```

With the second rule, the system has completed the proof for the problem.

The rules demonstrated in this example are more complex than one might expect because most-specific generalization is used in creating the rules. If more examples were present, the rules would be more general. The first rule (for TYPE) has information about WIDTH that is not necessary and will disappear as more examples are provided. The rule for MACHINE says that the object must be a slot (because it has the SLOT attribute) and narrow (because WIDTH has the value of 4) as required.

6.4 EMPIRICAL RESULTS

This section presents some empirical results that compare the accuracy and speed of learning for ID3[6] and the KBL approach. A simple domain was constructed for these experiments, as shown in Figure 6.6. The problems consist of 10 binary-valued attributes (problem space has 1,024 events). The topmost goal, A, has three binary-valued arguments (eight decision classes (A 0 0 0) through (A 1 1 1)), where the first variable is determined by the rules for A1 from Figure 6.6, the second variable by the rules for A2. The third variable's value (A3) is determined by the rules

```
(A3 ?X) ⇐ (B2 1) (B6 1) (B9 0) (= ?X 1)
(A3 ?X) ⇐ (B2 0) (B6 1) (B8 1) (= ?X 0)
(A3 ?X) ⇐ ( = ?X 0)
```

---

[6] The version of ID3 used for these tests handles multiple classes.

```
(A ?X ?Y ?Z) ⇐ (A1 ?X) (A2 ?Y) (A3 ?Z)
(A1 ?X) ⇐ (B1 1) (B2 1) (= ?X 1)
(A1 ?X) ⇐ (= ?X 0)
(A2 ?X) ⇐ (B2 0) (B5 1) (B6 1) (= ?X 1)
(A2 ?X) ⇐ (B2 1) (B7 0) (B6 1) (= ?X 0)
(A2 ?X) ⇐ (B2 1) (B4 0) (= ?X 1)
(A2 ?X) ⇐ (= ?X 0)
```

Figure 6.6:   KBL binary test domain

These latter rules for predicate A3 were not included in the domain theory at the start of the experiment. This domain has only nonstructured attributes, in order to allow ID3 to process the data.

KBL and ID3 use the training examples in very different ways. KBL uses the examples in the example base (the training examples) only when the performance element fails to solve a problem. Thus, if a problem is never presented to the system requiring knowledge from the examples, that knowledge is never extracted from the examples and put into rule form. In contrast, ID3 initially looks at all the examples and extracts knowledge from those examples. These differences complicate the comparison of the systems. For the domain theory given to KBL1 (Figure 6.6), learning will always occur on the first problem presented. Subsequent learning occurs in KBL1 as examples not covered by the extended theory are encountered. The next section describes the testing procedures used to compare ID3 and KBL1 and accounts for the different uses of knowledge.

6.4.1 Testing Method

In each experiment, the learning system was given a set of training examples randomly selected from the problem space. ID3 constructed a decision tree with these training examples. KBL1 stored the examples in the example base. Next, 25 episodes of the procedure (defined next) were performed. An example was randomly chosen from the problem space (without replacement) and tested on each system. If ID3's decision tree correctly classified the event, the decision tree was unchanged; otherwise, a new decision tree was constructed using the initially provided training set and all examples seen thus far. If the current domain theory of KBL1 could not assign a decision value for the event, learning occurred to extend the knowledge base. Each presented example was added to the example base. When either system learned, examples representing all the points from the problem space were tested against the new decision tree or domain theory to measure the accuracy of the system. The accuracy reported is the absolute accuracy (number of positive examples classified correctly divided by the size of the problem space) of the state of the knowledge (decision tree or domain theory) after the learning occurred. The number of examples in the initial training set was varied in the experiments presented below. For each training set size, 20 runs were performed. The results presented are averaged over the 20 runs for each set of experiments.

By testing each system in an incremental manner, the systems could be compared. KBL systems do not learn in batch mode. They must be presented with unsolved problems to extract the useful knowledge from the examples. This method allows the comparison of learning accuracy as well as a simple comparison of the rate of learning. All the results are presented with two graphs, as done in Figure 6.7. The top graph presents the accuracy of the system as new events are seen. The bottom graph describes how quickly the system learns. This graph indicates what percentage of the runs have not achieved their maximum accuracy at the specified learning episode (the percentage of trials still improving after seeing the examples). For example, at episode 5, 60% of the 20 runs for the KBL system have not reached their best results, but 100% of the ID3 runs have not reached their maximum performance. The graph on the bottom is only useful in the context of

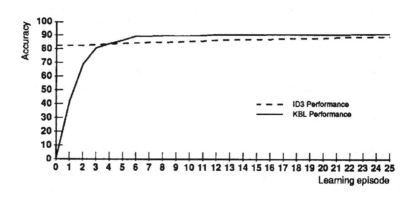

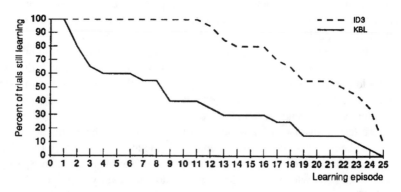

Figure 6.7:   System given 50 initial cases

the top graph. A system might be able to learn quickly but have low accuracy; the two must be considered together. When two systems tend to have closely related performance, the bottom graph indicates trends showing which system is approaching its peak performance more rapidly.

6.4.2 Learning Results

In this section, the results of using the procedure described above with initial training sets of 50, 25, 35, and 100 examples are shown. The results of these experiments are presented in Figures 6.7 through 6.10. The graphs indicate there is a relationship between the size of the initial example base and system performance. As shown in Figure 6.10 (when the training set contains 100 examples), ID3 has slightly higher accuracy than KBL1 when many examples exist. This is to be expected because the number of examples is a significant portion of a problem

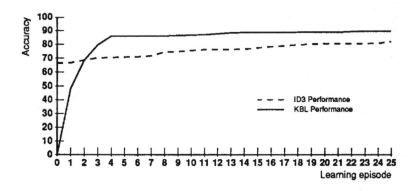

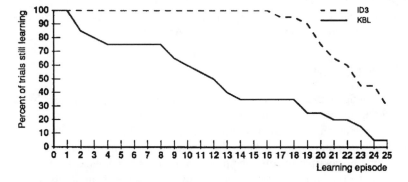

Figure 6.8:   System given 25 initial cases

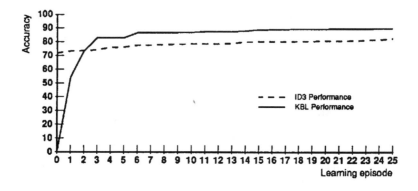

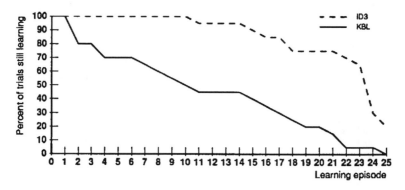

Figure 6.9:   System given 35 initial cases

space (approximately 10%). As fewer examples are initially provided to the systems, KBL1 performs better than ID3. Figure 6.7 presents the data when the initial data set contains 50 examples. Not only does KBL1 have higher accuracy, but it also obtains that accuracy after seeing just a few examples. The trend continues as fewer examples are initially provided (Figures 6.8 and 6.9).

6.5 CONCLUSION

Knowledge-based inductive learning assists a knowledge engineer by inducing rules for an incomplete domain theory. The learning system is called when the inference engine fails to solve a problem. Using rule-structure induction, KBL heuristically determines where knowledge is missing and modifies the knowledge base as little as possible to solve the problem. KBL uses a context for the problem defined by the partial-proof tree to select relevant examples from a larger example base, thus not requiring the system user to provide the specific examples for a

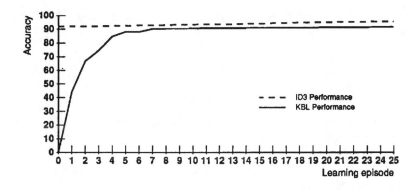

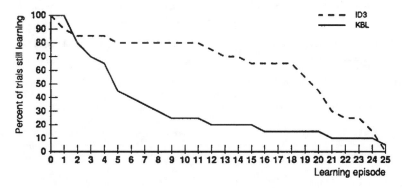

Figure 6.10:   System given 100 initial cases

learning task. Knowledge-based inductive learning makes use of knowledge in the form of rules and in the form of examples. Many domains (e.g., engineering tasks) have both types of knowledge in limited amounts and quality. KBL1 uses this knowledge and can handle real numbers and discover mathematical formulas for rules. It is shown that allowing domain knowledge to help guide induction is not only feasible, but it also allows the system to learn with fewer examples than required by pure empirical techniques.

ACKNOWLEDGMENTS

We would like to thank all the members of the Knowledge-Based Engineering Systems Research Laboratory at the University of Illinois for their input on this project. Funding for this research was partially supported by the Defense Advanced Research Projects Agency under Grant N00014-87-K-0874, National Science

Foundation under Grant DMC 86-57116, and a research contract from Digital Equipment Corporation.

References

Barr, A., and Feigenbaum, E. *The Handbook of Artificial Intelligence*, volume 1. William Kaufmann, Inc., Los Altos, CA, 1981.

Danyluk, A.P. The use of explanations for similarity-based learning. In *Proceedings of the Tenth International Joint Conference on Artificial Intelligence*, pages 274–276, San Mateo, Calif.: Morgan Kaufmann, 1987.

Davis, R. Applications of meta-level knowledge to construction, maintenance and use of large knowledge bases. In R. Davis and D. Lenat, editors, *Knowledge-Based Systems in Artificial Intelligence*, pages 229–490. New York: McGraw-Hill, 1982.

DeJong, G., and Mooney, R. Explanation-based learning: An alternative view. *Machine Learning*, 1(2):145–176, 1986.

Dietterich, T.G., and Michalski, R.S. A comparative review of selected methods for learning from examples. In R.S. Michalski, J.G. Carbonell, and T.M. Mitchell, editors, *Machine Learning: An AI Approach*, volume 1, pages 41–82, San Mateo, Calif.: Morgan Kaufmann, 1983.

Drastal, G.; Czako, G.; and Raatz, S. Induction in an abstraction space: A form of constructive induction. In *Proceedings of the Eleventh International Joint Conference on Artificial Intelligence*, pages 708–712, San Mateo, Calif.: Morgan Kaufmann, 1989.

Falkenhainer, B., and Michalski, R.S. Integrating qualitative and quantitative discovery: The ABACUS system. *Machine Learning*, 1(4): 367–401, 1986.

Fawcett, T.E. Learning from plausible explanations. In *Proceedings of the Sixth International Machine Learning Workshop*, pages 37–39. San Mateo, Calif.: Morgan Kaufmann, 1989.

Fisher, D.H. Knowledge acquisition via incremental conceptual clustering. *Machine Learning*, 2(2):139–172, 1987.

Flann, N.S. and Dietterich, T.G. Selecting appropriate representations for learning from examples. In *Proceedings of the Fifth National Conference on Artificial Intelligence*, pages 460–466, San Mateo, Calif.: Morgan Kaufmann, 1986.

Langley, P.; Simon, H.A.; Bradshaw, G.L.; and Zytkow, J. M. *Scientific Discovery: Computational Explorations of the Creative Process*. Cambridge, Mass.; MIT Press, 1987.

Lebowitz, M. Integrated learning: Controlling explanation. *Cognitive Science*, 10(2): 219–240, 1986.

Linkenheld, J.; Garrett, J.H., Jr.; and Benekohal, R. A knowledge-based system for the design of signalized intersections. In *First Conference on Expert Systems in Environmental and Urban Planning*, Boston, Mass., 1989.

Mitchell, T.M. Generalization as search. *Artificial Intelligence*, 18: 203–226, 1982.

Mitchell, T.M.; Keller, R.M.; and Kedar-Cabelli, S.T. Explanation-based generalization: A unifying view. *Machine Learning,* 1(1): 47–80, 1986.

Mooney, R., and Ourston, D. Induction over the unexplained: Integrated learning of concepts with both explainable and conventional aspects. In *Proceedings of the Sixth International Machine Learning Workshop*, pages 5–7. San Mateo, Calif.: Morgan Kaufmann, 1989.

Pazzani, M.J. Explanation and generalization-based memory. In *Proceedings of the Seventh Annual Conference of the Cognitive Science Society,* pages 323–328, Lawrence Erlbaum Associates, Inc., Hillsdale, NJ, Irvine, Calif, 1985.

———. Inducing causal and social theories: A prerequisite for explanation-based learning. In *Proceedings of the Fourth International Machine Learning Workshop*, pages 230–241, San Mateo, Morgan Kaufmann, 1987.

Pazzani, M.J.; Dyer, M.; and Flowers, M. The role of prior causal theories in generalization. In *Proceedings of the Fifth National Conference on Artificial Intelligence,* pages 545–550, San Mateo, Calif.: Morgan Kaufmann, 1986.

Quinlan, J.R. Induction of decision trees. *Machine Learning*, 1(1), pages 81–106, 1986.

Stepp, R.E., and Michalski, R.S. Conceptual clustering: Inventing goal-oriented classifications of structured objects. In R.S. Michalski, J.G. Carbonell, and T.M. Mitchell, editors, *Machine Learning: An AI Approach*, volume 2, pages 471–498. San Mateo, Calif.: Morgan Kaufmann, 1986.

Tecuci, G., and Kodratoff, Y. Multi-strategy learning in nonhomogeneous domain theories. In *Proceedings of the Sixth International Machine Learning Workshop*, pages 14–16, San Mateo, Calif.: Morgan Kaufmann, 1989.

Whitehall, B.L. *Knowledge-Based Learning: Integration of Deductive and Inductive Learning for Knowledge Base Completion.* Ph.D. thesis, Computer Science Department, University of Illinois, 1990. Also published as technical report no. UIUCDCS-R-90-1637.

Whitehall, B.L.; Stepp, R.E.; and Lu, S.C.-Y. Equation generation for clustering. In *Proceedings of The Third International Conference on Industrial and Engineering Applications of Artificial Intelligence & Expert Systems*, pages 999–1004, Charleston, SC: The Association for Computing Machinery, New York, NY, 1990.

Wilkins, D.C. *Apprenticeship Learning Techniques for Knowledge Based Systems.* Ph.D. thesis, Stanford University, 1987.

Winston, P.H. *Artificial Intelligence*, second edition, Reading, Mass.: Addison Wesley Publishing Company, 1984.

7

GEMINI:

An Integration of Analytical and Empirical Learning

Andrea P. Danyluk
(NYNEX Science and Technology, Inc.)

Abstract

This chapter presents Gemini, a system that integrates analytical and empirical learning. Analytical learning and empirical learning have been applied with success in a number of domains. Gemini combines the two in a feedback loop, allowing intercommunication for the mutual benefit of the two methods. Empirical learning relies on large quantities of data from which it extrapolates general knowledge. This is used in Gemini to augment an incomplete knowledge base. Analytical techniques, which make use of domain knowledge, can help to guide the empirical learning. This chapter describes the architecture of the Gemini system and then discusses the analytical and empirical components, giving the algorithms implemented in each. The chapter concludes with an analysis of the strengths and weaknesses of the system, as well as a discussion of directions for future research.

7.1 INTRODUCTION

Analytical and empirical learning have been investigated for a number of years. In that time, they have been applied with success to quite a few domains. Neither approach is entirely without limitations, however. Because analytical and empirical learning are complementary in nature, many researchers have been finding it beneficial to use one as a solution to any problems with the other. Gemini is a multistrategy learning system that has been designed in keeping with this idea. It integrates analytical and empirical learning in a feedback loop for the *mutual* benefit of the two methods.

The analytical learning method incorporated into Gemini is a form of **explanation-based learning (EBL)**. The goal of EBL is not to learn new knowledge but, rather, to reformulate an existing knowledge base to make it more efficient. For example, the goal may be to make a system capable of more efficiently recognizing concepts that it is already capable of recognizing. An EBL system for this task begins with a complete and consistent knowledge base for a particular domain. Given an environment-provided example of a specific domain concept, the system extracts the concept's salient features. The system analyzes the example by using the domain theory to generate an explanation describing why the instance is a member of the concept to be learned. The concept's salient features, extracted from the explanation, are then the basis of a new concept definition that no longer needs to be derived by an explanatory analysis. Although EBL has been applied with success to a variety of problems, it suffers from three very strong and unrealistic assumptions. It assumes that the domain theory is complete, correct, and tractable to use.

Empirical methods, on the other hand, require essentially no initial knowledge. The goal is to acquire knowledge that the system does not yet possess. In general, the system is provided with many examples from which it extrapolates general definitions or rules. For instance, the goal might be to acquire descriptions that will allow the system to recognize concepts it does not yet know. Examples of the concept might be compared against each other to extract a general definition of the concept. Empirical learning may suffer because of its lack of an explicit domain theory, however. The method requires that human intervention play a large role in tailoring input examples and their representation so that the system may converge on a good concept definition.

Gemini integrates analytical and empirical learning in such a way that the two methods compensate for each other's weaknesses. It invokes empirical learning to induce concept definitions missing from an EBL domain theory. However, it also uses heuristics that exploit contextual information from previously derived EBL explanations in order to guide the empirical induction of the missing knowledge.

Gemini was designed with system autonomy as a key concern. The contextual heuristics that guide induction of missing domain theory rules make use of *generally available* explanatory knowledge, and they can therefore be machine-generated rather than hand-crafted for each domain. Information from earlier cases is efficiently stored by the learning system for later use. When examples are needed for the creation of missing knowledge, Gemini can automatically extract them from its memory. Gemini was primarily designed as a testbed for the evaluation of contextual heuristics that guide the induction of missing domain knowledge. As a result, many implementation decisions were made to support that goal.

This chapter gives a high-level overview of the Gemini system. Gemini has been applied to four domains: network fault diagnosis, two domains describing military radio fault diagnosis, and terrorist event news stories. These domains span a wide range of classification tasks. Examples in this chapter are taken from two domains: network fault diagnosis and terrorist event news stories. These are described in the following section after an introduction to the architecture of the system. Analytical learning and empirical learning are implemented in Gemini as separate phases. Individual sections describe analytical and empirical learning as implemented in Gemini. The chapter concludes with a discussion of related work and directions for the future.

7.2 A HIGH LEVEL VIEW OF GEMINI

7.2.1 Architecture

Gemini is composed of three major subsystems: one performing analytical learning (G-EBL, or Gemini EBL) and two carrying out different types of empirical learning. One form carried out by Gemini is a type of **conceptual clustering** that creates a hierarchically organized memory of input seen by the system (G-CC, or Gemini Conceptual Clustering). It essentially learns relationships among the input examples. The second type of empirical learning carried out by Gemini is **learning from examples** in order to fill gaps in partial explanations produced by G-EBL (G-RI, or Gemini Rule Induction).

Gemini's architecture is shown in Figure 7.1. Input to G-EBL is the name of a goal concept and an example of that concept. G-EBL attempts to construct an explanation describing why the example is an instance of the goal concept. Built into the system is domain knowledge in the form of a rule base that is used by G-EBL in constructing explanations. Gemini does not assume that the domain knowledge is complete. It is possible that for any given input, Gemini will be able to construct only a partial explanation (or none at all).

G-RI constructs new rules when a gap is detected in the domain knowledge used by G-EBL. During explanation construction, a gap is detected when it is known that a subgoal must be inferred, but it is not possible given the rules in the rule base (i.e., the domain knowledge is overly specific). G-RI treats the uninferred subgoal as the name of a concept to be learned. The input example is assumed to be a positive example of that concept. In order to create a general concept definition, additional examples, both positive and negative, are retrieved from Gemini's processing history, along with their derived explanation information. The examples are found in a memory (the GBM, or generalization-based memory) that is constructed by G-CC. The learned rule is generalized by invoking heuristics that indi-

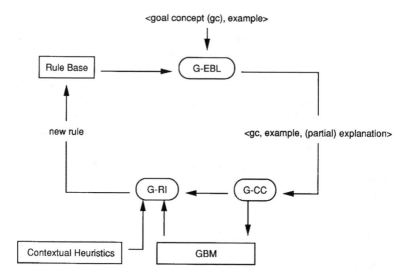

Figure 7.1:   Gemini's architecture

cate ways to remove unnecessary information based upon contextual information extracted from the (perhaps partial) explanations constructed by G-EBL.

All three major components of Gemini share access to a static semantic memory that defines hierarchical relationships among entities in a given domain. More specifically, the static semantic memory is a directed acyclic graph representing relationships among feature values of input instances. Details about the static semantic memory are given later with respect to the manner in which it is used by Gemini's procedural components.

7.2.2 Domains of Application

As discussed earlier, Gemini has been applied to four different classification domains. Two of those will be used to illustrate points in this chapter. One domain is **network fault diagnosis**. This domain involves the diagnosis of an ethernet/token ring network. A fault in the network is signaled by the inability of one user to reach another user connected to the same network. The knowledge used by the performance system is encoded on a level that enables isolation of the fault to a particular segment of the network but does not allow deeper analysis of the problem.

A second domain is the analysis of **terrorist event news stories**. This domain is modeled loosely around the following performance task: Given information from a news story describing a terrorist event, suggest an action that a law enforcement agency might take in response, given a database of earlier events. One might conjecture that in order to devise a proper response, a planner would require the most pertinent information about a specific case, as well as information about related occurrences. Analytical learning provides focus on the most relevant aspects of an input, and the conceptual clustering style of empirical learning organizes input cases together with others considered to be most similar.

7.3 ANALYTICAL LEARNING IN GEMINI

7.3.1 Input

This section describes Gemini's analytical learning component, G-EBL. Input to G-EBL is a goal concept and an example of that concept. Input examples are described by their attributes. Each attribute is a feature/value pair. A feature's value may be a complex entity that is in turn described by its attributes. In the current implementation of Gemini, input examples are represented as frames. Attributes are represented by slots in those frames. Slot fillers may be values; pointers to sub-frames that describe the attribute in more detail; or nil, which indicates that a value is not known.

A typical goal concept in the domain of network fault diagnosis is a problem diagnosis, such as *poss-fiber-optic-cable-prob* (a possible fiber optic cable problem). A corresponding input example represents the state of the network at the time of diagnosis. For instance, the input example in Figure 7.2 represents the state of a network with a possible fiber optic cable problem. Some attributes in this example give the status of particular parts of the network: *cond-tgt-node-responds-to-ping?* indicates whether the target node of an initiated communication responds (i.e., whether it appears to be "alive"). Other attributes give descriptive information. All attribute values in this domain are either true (T) or false (F). Nil would indicate that a value was unknown. The input example in Figure 7.2 is shown with the actual attribute names and values used by Gemini. Attributes for this domain were extracted from a prototype expert system for network fault diagnosis developed at CMU (Eshelman, 1988). They correspond to questions asked of the user directly rather than to inferences made by the system.

Another example can be taken from the domain of terrorist event news stories. Here, actual news stories are transcribed by hand into Gemini's representation. For instance, consider the following excerpt from a *New York Times* news story describing an act of terrorism in 1986:

> PARIS, Feb. 4—A bomb ripped through a crowded bookstore in the Latin Quarter tonight, wounding four people, the police said. ... The bomb that exploded tonight was planted in the basement record section of the Gibert Jeune bookstore on the Place St. Michel. The blast occurred at 7:40 P.M. with scores of customers in the store.

A part of the representation for this news story is shown in Figure 7.3. In this domain, attribute values are more descriptive than the binary values used in the

Attribute Name	Value
complaint-user-cant-connect?	T
cond-is-it-a-single-remote-MAU?	F
cond-rptrs-are-in-fault-domain?	F
cond-segnet-user-can-initialize?	F
cond-TD-gets-PC-init-failure?	T
cond-tgt-node-responds-to-ping?	T
td-all-nodes-gone-fault-domain?	F
td-can-ping-nodes-but-not-user?	F
td-can-ping-rtr-fm-Edinboro?	T
td-can-ping-rtr-from-MAU?	T
td-can-ping-source-net?	T
td-can-user-reach-another-net?	F
td-local-fbr-rptr-low-lite-on?	T
td-local-fbr-rptr-low-signal?	F
td-local-fbr-rptr-pwr-lite-off?	F
td-local-loopback-test?	T
td-remot-fbr-rptr-pwr-lite-off?	F
td-remote-fbr-rptr-low-lite-on?	F
td-remote-loopback-test?	T
td-rt-console-hung/no-msg?	F
td-rt-console-has-error-msg?	F
td-the-user-is-on-a-TRN?	T
td-the-user-is-on-an-Ethernet?	F
td-user-cant-communicate-at-all	F
td-user-says-cant-initialize?	T
td-user-wall-connection-OK?	T
td-usr-gets-init-retry-failure?	T

Figure 7.2:   Sample input for network fault diagnosis

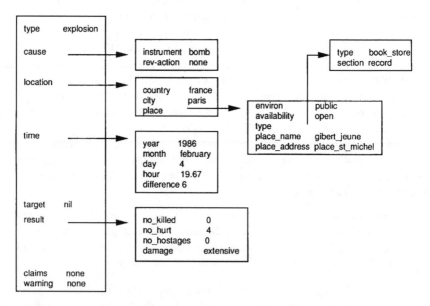

Figure 7.3:   Sample input for terrorist event news stories

network fault diagnosis domain. A number of attribute values are pointers to more in-depth information about a particular feature.

Every input example is given to Gemini as an instance of a specific goal concept. In the terrorist event domain, the goal concept is always taken to be *terrorist_event*. EBL is used to explain why the action is a terrorist event as opposed to some other type of news event.

7.3.2 Output

The output of Gemini's analytical learning component is an explanation (perhaps partial) describing why the input example is an instance of the goal concept. The explanation generated by Gemini linking the network fault given in Figure 7.2 to the diagnosis of a possible fiber optic cable problem is given in Figure 7.4. In the network fault domain, *user* refers to a user of a network who has attempted to communicate with another node in the network but has failed. The explanation tree in Figure 7.4 may be read bottom-up as follows:

> If the target of the failed communication responds in general, but the user who initiated the failed communication is not able to reach any node in the network, then the problem appears to lie in the source of the failed connection; if this is the case, and the user is on a token ring network, then ...

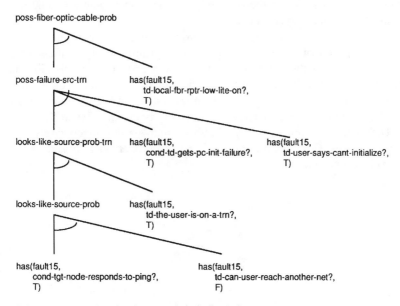

Figure 7.4: Sample explanation for network fault diagnosis

7.3.3 System Knowledge

In order to construct Gemini's explanations, G-EBL requires domain knowledge, which in Gemini is a knowledge base of *if-then* rules. (They are encoded as *if-then* rules and then parsed.) Gemini's rules have the expressiveness of predicate logic and could just as easily be represented in that way. We use *if-then* rules, however, because of their similarity to English and, thus, the ease in reading them.

The conditions of a Gemini rule refer to specific input example features and/or (sub)goals that must be proven. Conditions referring to actual input features contain variables to enable the specification of relationships among the input example attributes; all variables are implicitly universally quantified. A (sub)goal is a predicate to be proven true of the input example as a whole.

As an example, consider the following rule from the network fault diagnosis domain:

```
IF
    ISA (X,fault) ∧
    HAS (X,complaint-user-cant-connect?,T) ∧
    HAS (X,td-can-user-reach-another-net?,T)
THEN
    ASSERT (looks-like-dest-prob)
```

The rule states, "If X is a fault situation in which a user is complaining that a connection cannot be established with a particular destination, but the same user is able to reach other nodes on the network, then the problem appears to lie with the destination of the unestablished connection."

G-EBL shares access with the empirical learning components to a static semantic memory that defines hierarchical relationships among entities in a given domain. Because feature values for the network fault diagnosis domain are restricted to true and false, no static semantic memory is needed to define relationships among those values. A static semantic memory is useful, however, for the terrorist event domain. A fragment of that memory is shown in Figure 7.5.

The static semantic memory allows Gemini's rules to concisely refer to classes of values. Consider the following rule from Gemini's domain knowledge for terrorist event stories:

```
IF
    ISA (X, place) ∧
    GEN (X, type, public_place) ∧
    HAS (X, availability, open) ∧
    ASSERT (not_significant_warning)
THEN
    ASSERT (crowded_target)
```

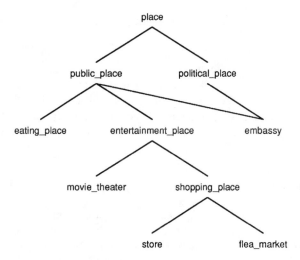

Figure 7.5:   Fragment of static semantic memory for terrorist event news stories

This rule states, "If the place of occurrence, X, is public and is open when the event occurs, and Gemini can assert that there was no significant warning, then infer that the target is crowded." Here, a condition of the rule refers to any public place. Whether the place specified in the input example is a specialization of this concept can be inferred from the static semantic memory.

7.3.4 Gemini's EBL Algorithm

Gemini's explanations are generated by backward-chaining (depth-first) from the input goal concept. Because Gemini's domain knowledge may be incomplete, Gemini will sometimes fail to generate an explanation. This may occur in one of two ways. The rule base is incomplete if (1) complete rules are missing or (2) conditions on a rule are too specific and will therefore not allow the rule to be applied to all relevant cases.

Disjunctive conditions are represented as separate rules in Gemini. Thus, the first of the above two incompleteness types may result in either of the following:

- There are *some* missing disjuncts—i.e., the domain knowledge contains rules for making the necessary conclusion, but the set of rules is too specific.
- There is *no way* to infer a particular subgoal given the domain knowledge —i.e., all disjuncts are missing. The subgoal to be proven cannot be found in the conclusion of any rule.

The second of these is easy to detect and is implemented in Gemini. All other types of incompleteness require consideration of the rule, or rules, that were applied but failed. Any of these is potentially responsible for the failure of the explanation.

Gemini has largely been developed as a testbed for evaluating rule induction heuristics as described in Danyluk (1992). A control is imposed on the experiments in the following manner: A full explanation is generated, and then the rule to be learned is removed from the explanation *by hand*, making it incomplete. The system is then tested to see what contextual heuristics are useful in learning the missing rule. Thus, at this point, Gemini does not generate partial explanations on its own.

7.4 BUILDING A MEMORY OF INPUT EXAMPLES IN GEMINI

The primary objective of empirical learning in Gemini is to create new rules to augment EBL's incomplete domain theory. In order to induce a new rule, Gemini requires examples, which it selects from a collection of examples it has analyzed in the past. Gemini imposes order on past examples by organizing them into a taxonomy. What Gemini is learning by doing so are various relationships among input entities. This results in easier retrieval when the examples are required. The memory, called a **generalization-based memory**, is generated by a form of **conceptual clustering** (Michalski and Stepp, 1983), an empirical learning method. This section discusses the conceptual clustering performed by Gemini, which we refer to as G-CC. The other type of empirical learning, learning from examples to generate new rules, is discussed in the following section.

7.4.1 Input

G-CC receives Gemini's input examples as its primary input and, in addition, is given their corresponding explanations. Recall that before entering the clustering component of the system, an explanation, either partial or complete, has been constructed for an input example by G-EBL. This provides additional information about the attributes' relative importance.

Similarities among the attributes of the input examples play a large role in determining their relationships. However, if they were used as the sole factor, then Gemini would have no means by which to distinguish between similarities that were truly significant and those that were only coincidental. As an example, consider three possible scenarios from the terrorist event news story domain. Say that one story reported an assassination attempt on the leader of country X. A second told of a bombing in country Y during a talk given by the leader of country X. A third story reported of a bombing in a store in country Y. If one were to determine relationships based only on surface similarity, one would find a relationship between the first two events because they share the attribute of the leader of country X. One would also find a relationship between the second two events because they involve bombings in country Y. A system would have no good way to determine which of those relationships was more significant than the other, if at all, yet people find a qualitative difference between the levels of similarity. Explanations generated by G-EBL can help focus on specific sets of relevant features.

7.4.2 Output

Relationships among input examples are recorded in a generalization-based memory (GBM) (Lebowitz, 1986) that is the output of G-CC. In general, a GBM is a directed acyclic graph in which terminal nodes are specific instances; internal nodes represent generalizations that classify the input instances that are their children. As an example, consider the small fragment of a GBM shown in Figure 7.6 taken from the domain of terrorist event news stories. Here, two stories are alike in that they have similar targets. One of them, however, is also similar to another in that these two share the terrorist method.

As mentioned earlier, a structure such as that given in Figure 7.6 might not adequately distinguish between significant similarities and spurious correlations. Explanations (complete or partial) provide additional information about the relative importance of various attributes. Those actually playing a role in an explanation might be considered more relevant and, thus, more significant than those that do not. For example, because specific targets were indicated in the first two stories of Figure 7.6, the features about those people presumably play a role in the respective explanations. The actual method of attack might not appear as a significant feature in these cases. In the third event, because there was no specific target known, the method of attack might appear as a feature in an explanation. The difference in emphasis on various features might result in a memory such as that shown in Figure 7.7, where the third event is not related to the others at all. In creating the GBM, Gemini considers both attribute similarity and analytic similarity and can choose to focus on one or the other.

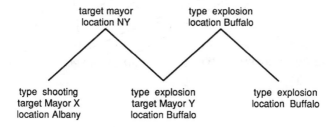

Figure 7.6:   Fragment of a memory of terrorist event news stories

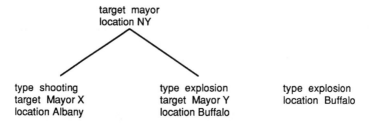

Figure 7.7:   Memory after explanation

7.4.3 System Knowledge

Gemini's empirical learning components share access with G-EBL to the static semantic memory that defines hierarchical relationships among entities in the domain. It is this that enables Gemini to find similarities such as the one pictured in Figure 7.6. In that case, two terrorist targets were considered to be similar because they were both specific instances of mayors, even though they were different individuals. Given two feature values, Gemini is able to determine whether they are related by searching the static semantic memory for a common generalization of the two. If there is none, then they are not considered to be similar. If there is a common generalization, the closeness of the similarity must be determined. In Gemini, this is a function of the distance from the feature values to their generalization in the static semantic memory.

Consider the fragment of a static semantic memory shown in Figure 7.8. Because it is a graph rather than a tree, it is possible for two values to share multiple common generalizations. In such cases, additional contextual information

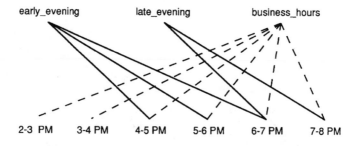

Figure 7.8:   Fragment of static semantic memory with context markers

is useful in selecting the generalization that is most appropriate. Say, for instance, that two events had taken place at the hours of 6:00 PM and 8:00 PM, respectively. These times of occurrence are similar in that they are both *late_evening* hours. However, they are also *business_hours* for places of entertainment such as movie theaters and restaurants. Now say the two events had taken place at movie theaters, presumably crowded at the time of the attack. Because the events took place in a business context, the most informative generalization for the two time values would probably be *business_hours* rather than *late_evening*. In general, the presence of certain attributes, either alone or in combination, indicates a context in which to view other attributes. In Gemini, this type of context information is explicitly given in the rule base for a domain. Consider the following variation of the rule shown earlier in the section on Gemini's rules:[1]

"If the event occurs at a place of business and
    the place is open at the time of attack,

Then the place of occurrence is crowded.
{Mark time with *business* context}"

If this rule applies to the input, it explicitly causes all time-related input attributes to be generalized within the business context. Thus, in addition to the static semantic memory, G-CC requires that context information be indicated in the rule base used by G-EBL. This ability to view an attribute in a particular way is unique to Gemini.

7.4.4 Learning Algorithm

A number of other systems build memories called GBMs (for instance, UNIMEM [Lebowitz, 1987]). Though this chapter uses the term GBM to describe the general structure created, the algorithm implemented to create the memory was developed specifically for Gemini and is unique to it. It overcomes a number of constraints of other GBM-building algorithms, as will be discussed later.

Gemini builds its memory of input examples "from the bottom up," considering the relationships among all input examples. The algorithm is incremental, comparing an input against each example already in the memory. This pairwise matching results in many possible generalizations, from which a "best" generalization is selected. Because the pairwise matching of input examples is the basis of the clustering algorithm, it is discussed first. The clustering algorithm itself, which makes decisions about the generalizations to retain, is described after that.

---

[1] This rule has been rewritten in English for conciseness and clarity.

7.4.4.1 Pairwise Matching of Gemini Input Examples

This chapter has already introduced the notion that two input examples may be similar in a number of ways. Among these are the following:

- They may share a large subset of attributes.
- They may share attributes that, although not identical, can be described by more general values.
- They may share attributes that are similar when viewed in the same context.
- They may have identical or nearly identical corresponding explanations.
- They may share a large subset of relevant attributes, where relevance is determined by the explanations.

The implementation of G-CC has taken a number of these into consideration. The algorithm for pairwise comparison of input examples is given in Figure 7.9. Input to the algorithm are two examples, Example1 and Example2, with their corresponding explanations. The algorithm builds a third structure, Example3, that is a generalization of the two inputs. When an input enters the system, it is matched against each example previously seen, using the pairwise matching algorithm, and for each match, a generalization is created. Later, a single best match is selected based upon scores given to the generalizations.

The first phase of the algorithm compares the examples for similarity of their attribute values. For each attribute, the values in Example1 and Example2 are compared. Exact matching is attempted before any generalization is performed. If two attribute values match exactly, the corresponding value in Example3 is the same. If not, generalization via the static semantic memory is attempted.

The first phase of the algorithm results in a new example that is a least generalization of the two inputs. In addition, it produces a measure of the quality of the match. Results with lower total match scores are more similar and, thus, better. Results with smaller numbers of unknowns are more specified and are thus better as well. Often, there is a trade-off between the match score and the number of unknowns. In Gemini, the match score takes higher priority, with the stipulation that the number of unknowns be below a reasonable (user-specified) threshold.

The next phase of the pairwise matching algorithm considers similarity of explanations. Although the explanations could be compared in a number of ways, it is generally effective to simply consider the sets of input attributes referenced in the explanations. These are referred to as explanation features. Given two sets of explanation features, this step of the algorithm takes their intersection and stores that with the new generalized example.

Once two examples are compared and their generalization is created, G-CC must determine whether the match is sufficiently good to possibly be noted in the memory. This is accomplished by considering three factors: (1) the total match score, (2) the total number of unknowns and complete mismatches, and (3) the

```
INPUT: Example1, Explanation1, Example2, Explanation2.
OUTPUT: Example3—annotated with explanation information,
        match statistics.

PHASE I—Determine attribute similarity.

For each attribute in Example1 or Example2
  * Create attribute of that name for Example3;
  * IF attribute value unknown in Example1 or Example2
      THEN /* no attribute match established */
          the value in Example3 is unknown;
          the match score for the attribute is unknown
  * IF attribute values in Example1 & Example2 identical
      THEN /* exact match */
          the value in Example3 is matched value;
          the match score for the attribute is 0 (i.e., no general-
              ization required)
  * IF attribute values in Example1 & Example2 have
    common generalizations
      THEN
          select at most one generalization (context markers get
            highest priority);
          the value in Example3 is the generalized value;
          match score for the attribute is determined by distance
              (number of edges) between the two initial values
  * IF no match
      THEN /* treat the same as an unknown */
          the attribute value in Example3 is unknown;
          the match score for the attribute is unknown
Generate final count of unknowns in Example3;
Generate final total of attribute match scores in Example3.

PHASE II—Determine explanation similarity.

Find intersection of Example1's explanation features and
    Example2's explanation features.
```

Figure 7.9:   Pairwise input example comparison

percentage of explanation features matched. All three of these must be within thresholds specified by a user.

7.4.4.2 Gemini's Clustering Algorithm

The complete algorithm for building a memory of input examples is given in Figure 7.10. When a new input is to be incorporated into the memory, it is com-

INPUT: example i, with corresponding explanation; GBM
OUTPUT: updated Generalization-Based Memory.

ALGORITHM:

1. For every terminal node n in existing memory
   * Compare input example i against n
     using the pairwise matching algorithm
   * Find measure of their similarity

2. Select best match *best* (Better distance measures have highest
   priority);

3. IF *best* falls within acceptable bounds for retaining the match
      THEN
         make i a terminal node in the GBM;
         create a new internal node g that is a generalization of
            i and the best matching n;
         create arcs from g to its specializations i and n
      ELSE
         make i a terminal node in GBM, but do not attach it to any
            existing part of the GBM.

4. Recursively invoke the algorithm: Treat generalization g
      as input; treat generalizations one level up from leaves
      as leaves.

Figure 7.10:   Gemini's clustering algorithm

pared pairwise against each previously seen example, as discussed above. A single
best match is then selected. If the best match is an acceptable one, the generalized
example is stored in the memory as a parent of the two inputs that generated it.
Generalizations are compared similarly to create deeper hierarchies.

Because even the best match found for an input example might be unacceptable, parts of the memory might become disjoint. That is, the memory might be a
set of graphs rather than a single connected structure. Conceptually, one might
view the graphs as entities unrelated except for the fact that they are taken from a
single domain.

The concept of building a memory of input examples for later use is not new.
Memories of this type were constructed previously in systems such as UNIMEM
(Lebowitz, 1987) and CYRUS (Kolodner, 1983). There are a number of differences
between the Gemini implementation and others. The major differences result from
the fact that new input examples enter Gemini's memory from the bottom (i.e.,
with a comparison against *all* other input examples), while, in general, examples

are placed in memory following a path from the most general concept down to the leaves. Thus, in Gemini, the placement of a new example is less dependent upon the order of previous input seen. A second distinction between Gemini and others is the use of information extracted from explanations. G-CC does, however, also have a greater time complexity, requiring $O(n^2)$, where n is the number of input examples, in the worst case to incorporate an input; UNIMEM, for instance, requires only $O(\log n)$.

7.5 RULE LEARNING IN GEMINI

7.5.1 Input

During the course of deriving an explanation that an input example is an instance of a particular concept, G-EBL may find that it is unable to complete the explanation. On the assumption that there is no noise in the input and that the domain knowledge is not incorrect, this indicates that the domain knowledge is incomplete. A gap in Gemini's rule base is detected by G-EBL when it is unable to deduce a subgoal that would have to be true for an explanation to be complete. As an example, consider the partial explanation shown in Figure 7.11. This is almost identical to the explanation shown earlier in Figure 7.4, except that one of its subgoals has not been inferred. This might occur in one of two ways. First, it would occur if the domain knowledge contained no rules at all with *looks-like-source-prob* in their conclusions. It might also occur if there were rules that concluded *looks-like-source-prob*, but the conditions of those rules did not fit the current input (i.e., they were too specific). The task of the learning component discussed in this section is to determine the relationship between the uninferred subgoal and the input features (and/or inferred subgoals) that would imply it. The task is to learn a rule that, when instantiated, would not only complete the current explanation but would be correctly applicable to future cases as well.

The rule induction component, G-RI, uses a variation on methods of learning from examples in order to construct rules missing from the rule base. In learning from examples, a system is given a concept to learn and is also given positive and/or negative examples of the concept. The system's goal is to find a set of attributes that describes all the positive examples but does not include any negative ones.

G-RI receives two principal input: (1) the input example for which a complete explanation could not be constructed and (2) the best partial explanation derived for the example. As discussed earlier, the problem of selecting a best partial explanation is a difficult one and was not addressed in the design of Gemini. If during generation of an explanation Gemini encounters a subgoal for which no rules exist in the domain knowledge, that partial explanation is selected as the one to be completed. Otherwise, selection of a best explanation is performed by hand at this

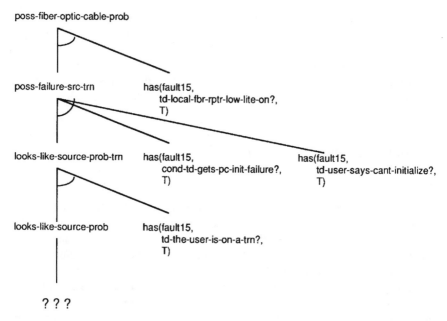

poss-fiber-optic-cable-prob

poss-failure-src-trn   has(fault15,
                                            td-local-fbr-rptr-low-lite-on?,
                                            T)

looks-like-source-prob-trn   has(fault15,   has(fault15,
                                            cond-td-gets-pc-init-failure?,   td-user-says-cant-initialize?,
                                            T)   T)

looks-like-source-prob   has(fault15,
                                            td-the-user-is-on-a-trn?,
                                            T)

???

Figure 7.11:   A partial explanation derived by Gemini

point. This is in keeping with Gemini's principle role as a testbed for evaluating contextual heuristics that guide induction of a rule to complete an explanation. Human control over the selection of best partial explanations fixes one of the possible variables in a study of contextual heuristics.

7.5.2 Output

G-RI creates a new rule for G-EBL's domain knowledge. The generation of a missing rule involves the determination of both its premise and conclusion. When G-EBL is unable to complete an explanation, it is because at least one necessary subgoal is not provable using the partial knowledge, as illustrated in Figure 7.11. In the figure, to make the inference *looks-like-source-prob*, G-RI must find the set of input attributes that correctly imply it. The conclusion of the missing rule is the unproven predicate. The conditions must be extracted from the input example.

A missing rule will not always conveniently fall at the leaves of an explana- tion tree. Gemini may fail to prove a subgoal higher in the tree, as in Figure 7.12a. In this case, the conditions of the rule may refer to subgoals. Because Gemini generates explanations by chaining backward from the goal concept, it stops as soon as a subgoal cannot be proven. That is, it does not continue generating the "lower" parts of the explanation. In Figure 7.12a, we include the lower part of the

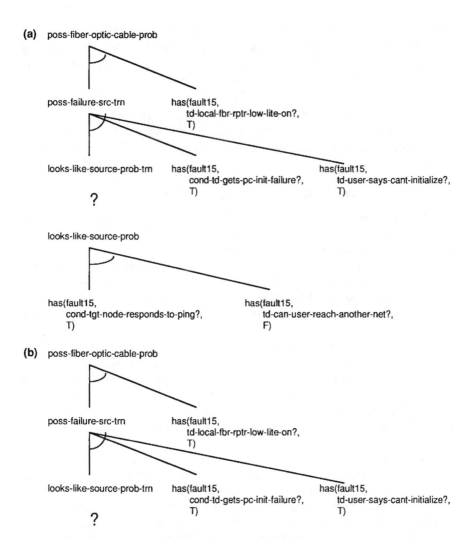

Figure 7.12:   Explanation missing a rule in the middle; (a) gives the complete explanation except for the missing rule; (b) give Gemini's view.

partial explanation simply to illustrate the missing rule's context. Figure 7.12b shows Gemini's view of the partial explanation.

The G-RI algorithm learns a single rule at a time. This does not, however, restrict learning to partial explanations with only one gap. If an input example's explanation is missing multiple rules, the rules are learned *one at a time* as follows; for *each* unproven subgoal:

1. Take the input example to be a positive instance of that subgoal.
2. Given the example and its partial explanation (however shallow it may be), use contextual heuristics as usual to retrieve other positive and negative examples from the GBM for learning.

Because the partial explanation in this situation is missing multiple inferences, it will presumably contain less contextual information than a more complete explanation. In general, more examples will be required to fully generalize the learned rule.

7.5.3 System Knowledge

The problem of learning a rule to fill a gap in an explanation is treated as concept learning from examples. Specifically, Gemini treats an uninferred subgoal as a concept to be learned. The input example for which the partial explanation was derived is assumed to be a positive instance not only of the final goal concept but of the subgoal to be learned as well. Gemini's task is to select those input attributes (or other subgoals inferred from them) that best describe the uninferred subgoal. If there are disjunctive ways to do so, only the disjunct covering the given example is learned.

In order to find the missing premise for a rule, G-RI considers other examples in addition to the one for which the partial explanation has been derived. The reason for this is that we would like the rule learned to be generalized so that it would apply to more than the specific case under consideration. Examples for inductive learning of the subgoal concept description are extracted by G-RI from the GBM. Gemini has a knowledge base of contextual heuristics that indicate what examples to retrieve and whether to consider them as positive or negative, even if exact information about their subgoal concept membership is not readily available.

Rule induction in Gemini can be broken down into two phases. In the first phase, known positive examples of the missing subgoal are retrieved from the GBM, and induction from positive examples is performed. That is, earlier examples are retrieved that were also missing the ability to conclude the current unprovable subgoal. In the second phase, contextual heuristics are applied to retrieve additional examples and to further generalize the new rule.

It is possible to identify known positive examples of the missing subgoal for the first phase for two reasons:

1. For some applications, induction can be postponed until a "critical mass" of examples exists.
2. Examples are stored in the GBM with their *first-derived* explanations. Even if a rule was previously created for the missing subgoal, the created rule might

be too specific to apply to the current case. The earlier example might need to be retrieved to re-learn the rule and make it more general.

Many examples may be required to generalize a new rule sufficiently. To minimize the need to wait for additional examples from the environment, Gemini makes use of examples already seen. In the absence of explicit labeling of earlier examples as positive or negative for a currently missing subgoal, G-RI makes use of explanatory information. Gemini contains a knowledge base of heuristics that indicate the type of examples to retrieve and whether those examples should be treated as positive or negative for induction of the missing concept definition. A second type of heuristic simply states sets of features that should receive particular emphasis in the new rule. The heuristics base their advice on information derived from explanations.

As an illustration of the type of heuristic that labels previously seen examples as positive or negative for the current missing concept, consider the terrorism story given earlier. Say the explanation for this story, given in Figure 7.13, could only be derived partially because the rule to infer a crowded target was missing. Now say the system had previously seen an example based on the following fictional news story: "PARIS, Bastille Day—An assassination attempt was made on the President here today... The sniper ..." Because of its very different nature, the explanation for this earlier example would bear essentially no resemblance to the current case. Thus, the system could treat it as a negative example of the concept to be learned. Furthermore, to emphasize the difference, all features indicating similarity between the examples could be removed from the new rule. This contextual heuristic can be summarized as follows:

```
"If a previously seen example differs from the current one
in its explanation leaves, subgoals, and rules, then:
(1) treat it as a negative example of the currently missing
    subgoal;
(2) eliminate all features from the new definition that
    would indicate similarity to this negative case."
```

As an example of the second type of heuristic, consider the following:

```
"If features under consideration are already in the partial
explanation, exclude them from the missing rule because they
are probably not required at multiple points in the explanation."
```

Contextual heuristics are intended only as a general guide for induction. As such, they are not required (or expected) to be complete. Danyluk (1992) describes the origin of contextual heuristics and an algorithm for generating them, as well as experiments that validate and compare their efficacy.

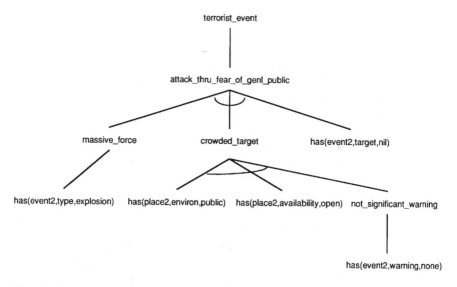

Figure 7.13:   An explanation of a terrorist event news story

7.5.4 The Rule Induction Algorithm

Gemini's rule induction algorithm is an integration of two principle ideas:

1. Learning from a conservatively selected set of positive examples provides focus on a single missing disjunct.
2. Contextual knowledge is often useful in further tailoring a missing rule.

The algorithm (shown in Figure 7.14) begins by finding other positive examples of the missing concept (the unproven subgoal) in memory. Recall that before induction, the current example has already been stored in the GBM. G-RI looks at earlier examples "close" to the current one in the GBM.[2] Of the closely related examples, those previously missing the same unproven subgoal are retrieved. Next, it performs induction over the positive examples to find attributes that describe the missing subgoal. If the new rule is to be useful for completing the partial explanations of all the selected examples, its premise must refer to attributes shared by all of them. Sharing attributes is not restricted to having identical values for them. Values may be sufficiently similar if they have a common generalization in the static semantic memory.

---

[2] Closeness is a user-defined parameter.

```
INPUT: example that could not be explained; corresponding
       partial explanation.
OUTPUT: new rule.
```

ALGORITHM:

1. Select from memory a set of closely related positive examples
   of the concept to be learned;

2. Perform a type of induction from positive examples to find the set
   of attributes common to all examples selected. Essentially,
   least generalization from examples performed;

3. Invoke contextual heuristics to retrieve additional examples and
   to explicitly focus on or discard conditions on concept
   membership.

4. Reason forward from rule premise and change rule to reflect
   inferences made.

Figure 7.14:   The rule induction algorithm

The rule produced as a result of the first part of the algorithm might require additional generalization. Contextual knowledge may provide clues as to the generalization to perform. As introduced in the previous section, a good rule of thumb might be to eliminate from the new rule premise references to all features already in the relevant partial explanations. Gemini invokes a number of heuristics.

The discussion of G-RI thus far has concentrated on finding a set of input attributes that describe an unproven subgoal. However, this is not always appropriate because the rule is not necessarily missing at the leaves of an explanation tree. To handle this case, G-RI attempts to reason forward from the attributes in the new rule premise. If subgoals are inferred (other than those already in the partial explanation trees), they replace their defining attributes in the rule premise. For example, say that G-RI was presented with the partial explanation in Figure 7.12b. Say that the rule learned as a result was

```
IF
  ISA (X,fault) ∧
  HAS (X,cond-tgt-node-responds-to-ping?,T) ∧
  HAS (X,td-can-user-reach-another-net?,F) ∧
  HAS (X,td-the-user-is-on-a-trn?,T)
THEN
  ASSERT (looks-like-source-prob-trn)
```

which states that "if there is a fault, X, in which the target is 'alive,' the initiator of the communication cannot reach any other nodes on the net, and the initiator is on a token ring network, then there appears to be a problem with the initiator, or the source, on the token ring network." G-RI attempts to reason forward from the premise, using the existing rules, and finds that from the values of *cond-tgt-node-responds-to-ping?* and *td-can-user-reach-another-net?* it can conclude *looks-like-source-prob*. The rule is modified to reflect the inference as follows:

```
IF
 ISA (X,fault) ∧
 HAS (X,td-the-user-is-on-a-trn?,T) ∧
 ASSERT (looks-like-source-prob)
THEN
 ASSERT (looks-like-source-prob-trn)
```

Gemini's rule induction algorithm differs from other approaches in a number of ways. The major difference lies with the knowledge base of contextual heuristics that guide generalization of a rule. Unlike previous work using auxiliary knowledge, this knowledge base

- Does not have to be complete for successful induction.
- Makes use of the structure of explanations rather than the semantics of any specific domain.

7.6 RELATED WORK

Gemini is similar to a number of other systems that integrate analytical and empirical learning, particularly systems that focus on using empirical learning to augment an incomplete knowledge base. The most notable similarity is to EITHER (Mooney and Ourston [1994]), Chapter 5 of this book). EITHER is capable of handling more types of imperfect domain theories than Gemini is. However, EITHER relies primarily on inductive methods alone to augment the domain theory. It requires that positive and negative examples be explicitly given to the system and is not able to make use of existing explanatory information in the way that Gemini does.

Another system that is closely related to Gemini is KBL1 (Whitehall and Lu [1994]), Chapter 6 of this book). Gemini was implemented for classification domains, but KBL1 works in engineering domains. Like Gemini, it makes use of the context of a partial explanation to select examples for induction. It uses the context in only one way, however, and Gemini makes use of a number of contextual heuristics for selection. KBL1 is able to focus on particular attributes for a new rule based on their existence in other rules leading to the same consequent. Although this is a reasonable heuristic, it will often fail, especially if it is assumed that earlier rules may be incorrect. One important way in which KBL1 is more autonomous than Gemini is that it is able to select its own best partial explanation for which a new rule is learned.

Other earlier work closely related to Gemini includes ADEPT (Rajamoney, 1989), OCCAM (Pazzani, 1988), and ODYSSEUS (Wilkins, 1988). All these make use of auxiliary knowledge to augment the incomplete domain theory. Although Gemini uses auxiliary knowledge in the form of contextual heuristics, it does not impose stringent requirements on that knowledge.

7.7 CONCLUSIONS

Gemini is a multistrategy learning system that combines empirical and analytical learning in a feedback loop. Gemini makes use of a type of induction to learn rules missing from EBL domain knowledge. The inductive component receives guidance in the form of contextual heuristics that make use of the explanations generated by G-EBL.

Three major subsystems make up Gemini. One performs explanation generation, and the others perform two distinct types of empirical learning. A type of conceptual clustering is used to build a memory of input examples. This is useful to the rule induction component in that it provides it with the positive examples from which to learn in the first step of induction.

Gemini makes use of a knowledge base of contextual heuristics in order to generalize new rules. These are especially useful if large numbers of examples are not available for standard induction. More on the evaluation of the efficacy of heuristics, as well as other details about the system, can be found in Danyluk (1992).

Gemini has many strengths. Among them is that Gemini uses auxiliary knowledge in the form of contextual heuristics to help guide induction of missing rules, but it does not impose stringent requirements on the auxiliary knowledge. In general, one of Gemini's strengths is that it has been designed with system autonomy as a principle goal. Currently, Gemini does require that a user select a single "best" explanation from many possible partial explanations. This could be automated by a method such as Whitehall and Lu's (1994), for example, for selecting good partial explanations. Yet another of Gemini's strong points is that it attempts to learn not only correct rules but rules that maintain the conceptual structure of the knowledge base to which the rules are being added. Gemini learns rules missing at the leaves of explanation trees as well as rules missing in the middle of explanations. Furthermore, Gemini's goal is to learn a new rule in the context of an explanation, so that the conceptual integrity of the remaining knowledge base is preserved.

Although Gemini has many strengths, it also has limitations. For instance, Gemini has been tested in four domains, but all those are classification domains. Gemini has not been designed to work in more complex domains, such as those that involve information about time, for example. As already pointed out above, the selection of partial explanations is currently done by hand. Although this has been adequate for Gemini's role as a testbed for evaluating contextual heuristics, it would not be acceptable if Gemini were required to be a truly autonomous system.

Future work on Gemini can be taken in two directions: (1) Gemini can be enhanced to overcome its limitations or (2) Gemini can be extended and used in new ways. For the second of these, one interesting area to investigate is Gemini's application to the problem of domain theory intractability. One of the problems of EBL is that the domain theory is assumed to be tractable to use. For very complex domains, this is problematic. Gemini could be applied in the following manner. Explanation generation could proceed "as far as possible" (i.e., until resources had been exhausted). Then all subgoals in the partial explanation that had not yet been expanded could be treated as concepts to learn. Gemini could be applied to learn new rules for those subgoals. The new rules would essentially "summarize" the remainder of the explanation that could not previously be generated. Another interesting use of Gemini would be as a knowledge engineering tool. A complete knowledge base could be made partial by selectively eliminating rules. Gemini could be used to re-learn those. An expert would then be able to analyze both the original rule and that learned by Gemini.

ACKNOWLEDGMENTS

This research was supported in part by the Defense Advanced Research Projects Agency under contract N00039–84-C-0165. The work was a part of the author's doctoral research at Columbia University, New York, NY.

References

Danyluk, A.P., "Extraction and Use of Contextual Attributes for Theory Completion: An Integration of Explanation-Based and Similarity-Based Learning," Ph.D. Thesis, Columbia University Department of Computer Science, 1992. (Also appears as Technical Report CUCS-005–92).

Eshelman, L., Personal Communication, 1988.

Kolodner, J.L., "Maintaining Organization in a Dynamic Long-Term Memory," *Cognitive Science*, Vol. 7, No. 4, pp. 243–280, 1983.

Lebowitz, M., "Concept Learning in a Rich Input Domain: Generalization-Based Memory," *Machine Learning: An Artificial Intelligence Approach, Volume II*, R.S. Michalski, J.G. Carbonell, and T.M. Mitchell (Eds.), Morgan Kaufmann, Los Altos, California, 1986.

————, "Experiments with Incremental Concept Formation: UNIMEM," *Machine Learning*, Vol. 2, No. 2, pp. 103–138, 1987.

Michalski, R.S. and Stepp, R.E., "Automated Construction of Classifications: Conceptual Clustering Versus Numerical Taxonomy," *IEEE Transactions on Pattern Analysis and Machine Intelligence*, Vol. 5, No. 4, pp. 396–409, 1983.

Mooney, R. and Ourston, D., "A Multistrategy Approach to Theory Refinement," *Machine Learning: A Multistrategy Approach, Volume IV*, R.S. Michalski and G. Tecuci (Eds.), Morgan Kaufmann, San Mateo, California, 1994.

Pazzani, M.J., "Learning Causal Relationships: An Integration of Empirical and Explanation-Based Learning Methods," Ph.D. Thesis, UCLA Department of Computer Science, 1988.

Rajamoney, S.A., "Explanation-based Theory Revision: An Approach to the Problems of Incomplete and Incorrect Theories," Ph.D. Thesis, University of Illinois Computer Science Department, 1989.

Whitehall, B. and Lu S., "Theory Completion Using Knowledge-Based Learning," *Machine Learning: A Multistrategy Approach, Volume IV*, R.S. Michalski and G. Tecuci (Eds.), Morgan Kaufmann, San Mateo, California, 1994.

Wilkins, D.C., "Knowledge Base Refinement Using Apprenticeship Learning Techniques," *Proceedings of the Seventh National Conference on Artificial Intelligence*, AAAI Press, Menlo Park, California, pp. 646–651, 1988.

8

THEORY REVISION BY ANALYZING EXPLANATIONS AND PROTOTYPES

Stan Matwin
(University of Ottawa)

Boris Plante
(CSA Recherche Ltée, Québec)

Abstract

The chapter addresses the problem of revising a theory when it treats a training example incorrectly, either by failing to explain a positive example or by covering a negative one. The method employed is knowledge-scant—it relies only on knowledge given in the original domain theory or in the example—and is based on an analysis of the failed explanation. This analysis evaluates predicates in the theory and in examples used in the explanation and identifies ones that can be used in new rules to fill the gap in the theory responsible for misclassification of the example. The process employs a constructive inductive procedure that discriminates the features of the incorrectly-classified example from features of prototypical instances that the theory classifies correctly. Fruitful induction introduces new terms to the language of the original theory. Revision of the theory is accomplished by adding a second tier of rules on top of those that represent the original theory. When subsequently called upon during an explanation activity, rules defined in the second tier supersede those in the first tier that they cover. A two-tiered structure alleviates the problem of correctly placing in the representation. It also provides a convenient middle-ground between purely case-based and purely rule-based representations of the theory.

8.1 INTRODUCTION

The method presented here demonstrates how a multistrategy approach addresses the problem of theory modification in Explanation-Based Learning. More specifically, the chapter considers the situation where an EBL system must modify its theory to accommodate examples that are outside—but not very far outside—the scope of its knowledge. The main contribution of this work is a deductive and inductive, example-driven algorithm that repairs the theory as it fails to correctly cover examples.

The focus is on examples that are misclassified by the existing theory in one of two ways. Either they are instances of positive concepts that the theory failed to explain, or they are negative concepts that the theory explained in error. These misclassified examples fail either by not satisfying a single predicate in the proof or by mismatching the arguments of several predicates. Consequently, they are close to the border of the existing theory and, therefore, are referred to as *marginal examples* of the concept.

The method requires

- A domain theory, possibly incomplete or inconsistent, expressed in first order logic.
- A set of training examples divided into prototypical and marginal examples.

Some of the examples must cause the theory to fail as a result of its incompleteness or inconsistency. The method described here modifies the theory to repair the error made evident by these examples.

The approach presented here requires no additional knowledge to reason, e.g., about the purpose of particular subgoals in explanations. We have presented a knowledge-rich solution to the same problem elsewhere (Genest et al., 1990). Here, it is shown that a knowledge-scant technique can be highly effective if the available knowledge is restructured according to its utility in explaining prototypical and marginal examples (the deductive part of our method performs this restructuring for the inductive part). A knowledge-scant approach has the additional advantage of being independent of the domain.

The method revises the theory each time it treats a marginal instance incorrectly either by failing to explain a positive example or by explaining a negative one. The system first modifies the theory by introducing new arguments to predicates. If the theory still fails to deal with the marginal example correctly, a further attempt is made to repair it by constructive modification, i.e., by enlarging the theory with new predicates that extend its language. The important issue of identifying which rule in the theory is to be modified is addressed by the use of a two-tiered concept representation (Bergadano et al., 1992) (see next section). In this framework, all theory modifications are considered as rules that either extend or contract the existing theory. These rules are used only if one wishes to double-check the categorization provided by the first tier.

The chapter begins by introducing the idea of a two-tiered representation of concept descriptions. The architecture of our system is discussed based on the categories of predicates produced by analyzing explanations. It is shown how a simple induction that contrasts features of prototypes with those of marginal concepts produces focused theory modifications. Following a review of selected related work, the conclusion outlines the operation of our method within the realm of two-tiered concept representations.

8.2 TWO-TIERED CONCEPT REPRESENTATION AND DYNAMICALLY MODIFIED THEORIES

The idea of a two-tiered knowledge representation has already been employed successfully in inductive learning (Bergadano et al., 1992). EBL can well be rendered in this same framework. In contrast to the classical representation of a theory as an unstructured ruleset, a two-tiered representation is composed of a first tier of rules that explain typical instances of a concept. To this is added a second tier of rules that apply only in certain given contexts. Reasoning in this formalism can thus be simpler than in a representation that stores a single large and undifferentiated ruleset.

The first tier of rules characterizes the central tendency of the concept. They capture its principle, its most relevant properties, and the basic intention behind it. The second tier handles special cases of the concept, anomalies, exceptions, and context-dependencies. It deals with them either by extending the first tier (theory *extension*) or by specializing it (theory *contraction*). When an unknown entity is encountered, an attempt is made to explain it by means of first tier rules. Depending on the outcome of that trial, the entity may then be subjected to the second tier's extensions or contractions.

A two-tiered structure mirrors the natural process by which a theory is first acquired and then dynamically modified. To illustrate how the method is applied, an expert system for identifying mammals is described. We believe that a system has to be dynamic: it has to be able to change itself if the knowledge changes during its life cycle. A machine learning module in an expert system can play an important role in helping the system evolve over time.

The life cycle of an expert system can be summarized as follows:

- *Knowledge engineering*: construction of rules that represent zoological knowledge at the time of the expert system's construction.
- *Knowledge verification*: gathering of data to support or edit this zoological knowledge.

- *Knowledge evolution:* adaptation of knowledge to take into account new data not known when the system was created (the machine learning module attempts to make revisions automatically).

In our example, it is assumed that an expert system to recognize mammals has been developed solely on the basis of terrestrial examples. These terrestrial mammal examples are called *positive prototypes.* The system can correctly recognize examples of all terrestrial mammals known at the time it was engineered. However, there are other, non-terrestrial mammals, so the system is based on incomplete knowledge. Examples unknown at knowledge engineering time will all be *marginal* from the point of view of the existing theory. Mammals such as the whale, bat, kangaroo, and duck-billed platypus, which differ from known terrestrial mammals, are *positive marginals.* Thus, positive prototypes are used to build the theory, and positive marginals are examples not known when the theory was built. Usually, the positive marginals will be close to the borders of the theory; in many respects, a bat is similar to that terrestrial mammal the mouse.

The knowledge base of the system must be modified to take into account the existence of non-terrestrial mammals. The case, therefore, is one of a theory that is underspecified because of the lack of knowledge at the time it was enunciated. On the other hand, a theory may also be overly general; this is revealed when a negative example is encountered that it covers. The theory must then be specialized (contracted) to exclude such *negative marginals.* The method presented here automates this task of knowledge modification.

The theory, the prototypes, and the marginals are viewed as data for a machine learning module that operates without additional background knowledge, as illustrated in Fig. 8.1. We believe that a data driven method can identify the reason for marginality in the theory and examples.

Because the new marginal positive instances are different from the prototypes, they introduce new language into the theory. This happens in two ways:

- New arguments in a predicate, referred to as "marginality by arguments."
- New predicates never used by the theory, referred to as "marginality by predicates."

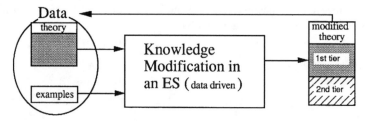

Figure 8.1:   An ML module using theory and examples as data

8.3 AN EXAMPLE: MAMMAL THEORY

Knowledge of terrestrial mammals allows us to categorize typical mammals and develop a theory to describe them. The prototypical mammals of horse, mouse, cat, dog, and bear can all be characterized by three subconcepts that characterize terrestrial mammals—locomotion, sexual life (child care), and blood system—as shown in Figure 8.2.

In view of the theory of mammals in Figure 8.2, a bat, a whale, and a kangaroo are positive marginals because they are mammals not covered by the existing theory. However, the theory is overspecialized: different examples exhibit definitions of different subconcepts of the theory that are too specific. For instance, the subconcept of locomotion is too specific to include a bat and a whale, but the subconcept of baby care is too specific to include a kangaroo. The previous theory is incomplete, and its language must be extended sufficiently to permit talk about wings and fins for locomotion (i.e., the bat and the whale). Because locomotion already includes the subconcept of forelimbs in the predicate `ante-limbs`, it is enough to add new values for `wings` and `fins` to it. In order to describe a kangaroo, a new subconcept of embryonic development must be added to the theory via the predicate `embryo_dev`. The arguments of `embryo_dev` will discriminate between prototypical and marginal mammals (`embryo_dev(X, placenta)` for prototypes and `embryo_dev(kangaroo, marsupium)` for the marginal `kangaroo`).

mammal(X)	<--	blood_system(X,type_m) & sexual_life(X,type_m) & locomotion(X,type_m)
blood_system(X,type_m)	<--	blood(X,hot) & heart(X,4_chambers)
sexual_life(X,type_m)	<--	fertilization(X,internal) & baby_care(X,type_m)
locomotion(X,type_m)	<--	ante_limbs(X,legs) & post_limbs(X,legs) & move(X,ground)
baby_care(X,type_m)	<--	birth(X,well_formed)& reproduction(X,viviparous)& feed(X,milk) & milk_organ(X,type_m)

Figure 8.2:   A theory for mammals

With these extensions, the kangaroo can be described as

```
breath(kangaroo,air) & heart(kangaroo,4_chambers) &
fertilization(kangaroo,internal) & blood(kangaroo,hot) &
ante_limbs(kangaroo,legs) & post_limbs(kangaroo,legs) &
move(kangaroo,ground) & reproduction(kangaroo,viviparous) &
embryo_dev(kangaroo,marsupium) & milk_organ(X,type_m) &
covered(kangaroo,hair) & mastication(kangaroo,tooth) &
feed(kangaroo,milk)
```

Other examples will all be adjusted with the new predicates; e.g., the positive prototypes will contain `embryo_dev(X, placenta)` in their description. Moreover, some predicates not previously used by the theory may be useful to describe examples, e.g., `breath(kangaroo,air)`.

8.4 OVERALL APPROACH TO THEORY MODIFICATION

The system uses both marginal and prototypical examples of the concept. Table 8.1 shows four categories of examples.

Positive prototypes represent typical positive instances of the concept, but positive marginals represent positive examples not explained by the existing theory. Negative marginals are negative examples explained by the existing theory. Gaps or errors in the theory responsible for misclassification are also referred to as errors of omission (positive marginal) and commission (negative marginal). Based on the terminology of Bergadano et al. (1992), omission errors call for a theory modification by adding an *extending* rule, and commission errors call for a *contracting* rule.

Figure 8.3 presents the overall architecture of our system.

The system uses an algorithm divided into a batch deductive step and an interactive inductive step. The skeleton of the main part of the algorithm is presented in Figure 8.4.

Deduction first explains positive examples and produces a prototype table that partitions their features into ones required by the explanation and ones it does not use. This module also categorizes different predicates involved in the example and the explanation by classifying them according to their role in the latter. The results of classification are referred to as PCPs, Proof-Categorized Predicates. The induc-

Table 8.1:   Four Categories of Concept Instances

Type of Instance	Concept's Membership	Coverage by Theory	Action
Positive prototype	+	Explained positive	Not needed
Positive marginal	+	Unexplained positive	Extend theory
Negative prototype	−	Unexplained negative	Not needed
Negative marginal	−	Explained negative	Contract theory

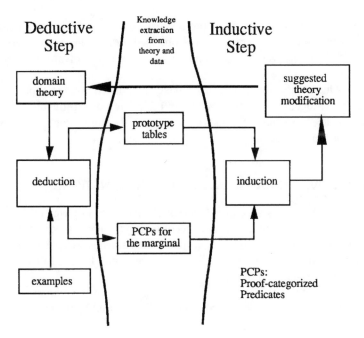

Figure 8.3:   General overview of the approach to theory revision

```
input (theory);
input (examples);
for each example do              {deductive step}
  select(example);
  prove(example, theory, explanations);
  if example is positive then
     if example is proved then
       update(prototype_table)
     else
       categorize(proof_predicates, explanations, PCPs)
     end
  else                          {a negative marginal}
     if example is proved then
       categorize(proof_predicates, explanations, PCPs)
     end
  end;
endfor;
for each marginal              {inductive step}
  select(marginal)
  inductive_phase(marginal, PCPs, prototype_table,
     theory_modification)
endfor.
```

Figure 8.4:   General description of the theory revision algorithm

tive module uses information about prototypes, as well as the PCPs, to suggest a
theory modification. That modification is obtained by focusing inductively on one
of the several alternatives deemed appropriate as a result of an analysis of the
proof.

The deductive technique used here makes a knowledge-scant approach possible. The PCPs, together with the Prototype Table, are powerful enough to predict
which predicate in a single marginal example is sufficient to contract or extend a
domain theory rule adequately.

8.5 DEDUCTIVE PHASE: ANALYSIS OF EXPLANATIONS

This section defines several categories of predicates in terms of their role in
an explanation, or proof, of an example according to a domain theory. I denotes the
instance whose membership in the concept is being proven. T(I) denotes the set of
all operational predicates in the theory required by a proof that I satisfies the goal
of concept membership.

The first useful category is the set CP of all predicates common to the proof
and the example, i.e., the set of all example predicates used by the proof T(I):

$$CP = \{\ p_i\ |\ p_i \in I \text{ and } p_i \in T(I)\ \}$$

Another category is the set of unused predicates NP, i.e., the set of all example
predicates not used by the proof T(I):

$$NP = \{\ p_i\ |\ p_i \in I \text{ and } p_i \notin T(I)\}$$

When proof of a positive marginal fails, an important category of predicates
are the failure consequents FC. To define these predicates, antecedents of a rule that
had p_i as its consequent are denoted by $ANTC(I,p_i)$. FC then represents the set of
rules (identified by their consequents) in the proof tree using a low-level predicate
not satisfied by the example:

$$FC = \{\ p_i\ |\ \text{exists } p_j\colon p_j \in ANTC(I,p_i) \text{ and } p_j \notin I \text{ and } p_j \in [\ T(I)\}$$

Again, for positive marginal examples, the set FP represents failure predicates
responsible for a rule failure, i.e., the set of all predicates in the leaves of the theory
not satisfied by the example:

$$FP = \{p_i\ |\ p_i \text{ is operational and } p_i \notin I \text{ and exists } p_j\colon p_i \in ANTC(I,p_j) \text{ and } p_j \in FC\}$$

Finally, the set AP (*"already there"*) contains all predicates in a failed rule
that are not responsible for the failure because they are satisfied by the example:

$$AP = \{\ p_i\ |\ p_i \in I \text{ and } p_i \in ANTC(I,p_j) \text{ and } p_j \in FC\}$$

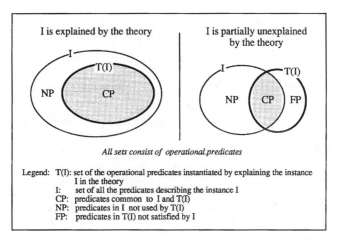

All sets consist of operational predicates

Legend: T(I): set of the operational predicates instantiated by explaining the instance
            I in the theory
         I: set of all the predicates describing the instance I
         CP: predicates common to I and T(I)
         NP: predicates in I not used by T(I)
         FP: predicates in T(I) not satisfied by I

Figure 8.5:   Examples explained and unexplained by a theory

Figure 8.5 represents the relationships between these different sets of predicates.

Our deduction module analyzes the knowledge in the instances and in the theory and categorizes predicates according to their membership in the sets defined above. Figure 8.6 shows the proof tree and the different PCPs identified in a partial explanation of the kangaroo by the mammal theory of Figure 8.2.

How is this tree built?

First, the goal `mammal(X)` is invoked with the instantiation `{X/kangaroo}`. This in turn invokes the three non-operational predicates that are antecedents of its first rule in the existing theory (Figure 8.2). The subconcept `blood_system(kangaroo,type_m)` invokes its two antecedents `blood(kangaroo,hot)` and `heart(kangaroo,4_chambers)`. These two predicates are both operational and satisfied in the example, so they are placed in the set `CP` by the procedure `categorize(proof_predicates, explanations, PCPs)` in the theory revision algorithm (Figure 8.4).

The operational predicate `birth(kangaroo,well-formed)` is not satisfied by the facts of the example; so, the attempted proof fails, and this predicate is placed in the set `FP`. The subconcept consequent responsible for calling it (`baby_care(kangaroo,type_m)`) is put in the set `FC`. All other antecedents of `baby_care(kangaroo,type_m)` are placed in the set `AP` because they are satisfied by the example. Note that `T(I) = CP + FP`; all the operational predicates that the theory requires to prove the goal are either in the proof (`CP`), or they are missing (`FP`).

Several cases must now be considered. First, if there are multiple explanations of the example, the single explanation that has the best chance to be repaired is selected according to the cognitively justified heuristic investigated in Gick and

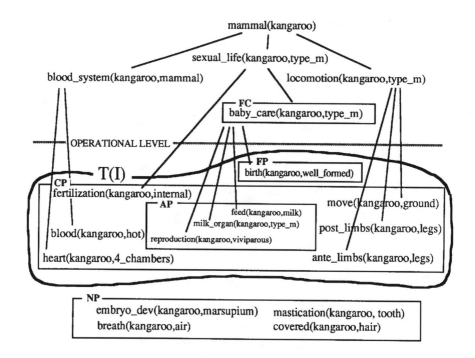

Figure 8.6:   An explanation tree with its predicates labeled by PCPs

Matwin (1991). Consequently, in our method, it suffices to consider a single explanation. Second, the algorithm checks whether more than one rule failed in the explanation (i.e., whether there is more than one element in the set FC). For explanations in which multiple rules failed, induction on arguments is employed to deal with the failure (see Section 8.6.1). Finally, the case when a single rule has failed can be considered (i.e., there is a single FC). If there are several FP sets (i.e., if the corresponding FC is the head of a disjunctive rule), all FP sets, together with their corresponding AP and NP sets, are passed on to the inductive phase. This creates the opportunity to inductively prune the AP sets if the FP sets are similar. Pruning is accomplished by intersecting the AP sets to produce a more general rule, but it does not select a best rule to repair (however, negative marginals may later bring about specialization of the rule and justifiably force a preference of one rule over another). For instance, suppose that there are two FC sets, each of which is equal to {a}, and in both cases, FP = {d}. In one case, AP = {b, c}, and in the other, it equals {b, e}. This corresponds to the situation

```
a <- b, c, d
a <- b, e, d
```

where the rule with head a has failed. The two AP sets can be pruned from {b, c} and {b, e} down to {b} alone by intersecting them.

Figure 8.6 illustrates the case of a single selected failed explanation. An obvious and simple theory modification would be to change the baby_care rule in the theory by adding a disjunct:

```
baby_care(X,type_m)  <--
feed(X,milk) & milk_organ(X,type_m) & reproduction(X,viviparous) &
covered(kangaroo,hair) & mastication(kangaroo,tooth) &
breath(kangaroo,air) & embryo_dev(kangaroo,marsupium)
```

However, even this simple example shows that the result is unsatisfactory: the repaired rule contains predicates not related to baby_care and is unnecessarily specific to the kangaroo example. The rule is overspecialized: it will likely fail for mammals other than the kangaroo. The general method would be to create a new disjunct with the predicate in FC as the consequent and the predicates in NP and AP in the antecedent. Such a rule, however, would be *ad hoc* and unconstructive and would "overfit" the theory with respect to this particular marginal example. Worse, the antecedent contains several irrelevant features imported from the example.[1] This simple illustration shows that an analysis of explanation alone is not adequate to revise an existing domain theory successfully.

8.6 INDUCTIVE PHASE

Because analytical methods alone are not sufficient to repair a theory, one naturally turns to induction over prototypes to identify features of the marginal that are responsible for it not being explained correctly. Our induction algorithm consists of two steps, described below. Section 8.6.2 discusses the case of marginals whose proofs fail because the theory lacks the necessary language (predicates) to describe them adequately: Such instances are referred to as *marginal by predicate*. The other class of marginals is composed of those that could be described by the language of the theory were it not for the arguments of certain predicates. Those examples are referred to as *marginal by arguments*. The first step is to check if a given marginal fails the theory because of its arguments. Finding new arguments can be considered valuable in itself, even if the arguments have never been used by the theory, because increasing the number of argument values increases a theory's expressiveness.

---

[1] It must be noted, however, that overfitting by including predicates from AP may prevent overgeneralization in the later, inductive phase.

8.6.1 Induction on Arguments: First Conservative Step

The set FP contains all the reasons why a positive marginal failed, and it is time- and space-efficient to use it as a guide to the first step of induction. In many cases, a marginal differs from prototypes just by the values of its arguments; so, before trying to expand the theory with a new predicate, a conservative repair procedure limited to the arguments is attempted. For each predicate in FP, it is verified whether the marginal has a *new argument* for it.

For instance, in the theory of mammals, a bat is marginal because of its arguments. This theory involves the concept of locomotion expressed in terms of the anterior and posterior limbs and the environment in which the animal moves. Suppose the marginal example of a bat had the following description:

```
breath(bat,air) & blood(bat,hot) & heart(bat,4_chambers) &
fertilization(bat,internal) & ante_limbs(bat,wings) &
post_limbs(bat,legs) & move(bat,air) & feed(bat,milk)
embryo_dev(bat,placenta) & reproduction(bat,viviparous) &
milk_organ(X,type_m) & covered(bat,hair) & mastication(bat, tooth)
```

Because the instantiated locomotion rule requires "legs on the ground" for prototype mammals, based on our deductive step, there will be two predicates in FP. FP={ante_limbs(bat,legs), move(bat,ground)}) fails the existing mammal theory. Induction on arguments will attempt to repair the two members of the set FP by extending the rule for locomotion with two similar predicates from NP={ante_limbs(bat,wings), move(bat,air)}. The second tier of mammal theory will accept an exception for locomotion. The extending rule has the form

```
replacing(mammal,locomotion(X,type_m))
<-- post_limbs(X,legs) & ante_limbs(X,wings) & move(X,air)
```

Because the other subconcepts of the domain theory of mammals (blood_system and sexual_life) are satisfied for this new example, the bat will be covered by this extension of the concept mammal.

Induction on arguments is applied first because it is a straightforward and easy to use method. Limiting repair to arguments allows the system to repair more than one rule. In the case of an example that is marginal by arguments, each member of FP can be repaired within the realm of the existing language and new arguments. In this situation, one has confidence in the theory, and one simply enhances its applicability by adding arguments that occurred in the marginal. After repairs, a failure is still possible but only when there are multiple elements in FC. In such a case, the marginal instance is considered to be distinct by more than argument values, and the second deductive step will try to extend the language by importing new predicates.

8.6.2 Constructive Induction: Second Innovative Step

In this learning step, induction attempts to identify new predicates hitherto absent from the language in which the domain theory is expressed. The basic idea is to contrast the features of examples that are *marginal by predicates* with the features of prototypical examples. For that reason, all non-used predicates are collected during the explanation of any class 1 example in a Prototype Table PT. More specifically, PT contains all the predicates not in the proof (NP) that are common to all class 1 examples. The table is indexed by predicate name, and each of its entries contains all instantiations of a given predicate that have been encountered when processing a prototypical positive example. Elsewhere (Plante 1991), we discuss the Prototype Table as a set of equivalence classes, and we compare the approach with Version Spaces. More details on Prototype Tables can be found in Plante and Matwin (1990).

When dealing with a positive marginal, the method presented here first tries to find any predicates that (1) occur in the set NP for the marginal and (2) also occur in PT but with arguments different from the ones in NP. Such predicates are referred to as *promising predicates*, or PPs. They discriminate in a focused way between a value of a prototypical feature and a different value of this feature for a marginal instance. First, predicates from PP are present in *all* prototypes without participating in explanations of prototypes. Second, as predicates in PP discriminate between the marginal and all prototypes, elements of PP should be good candidates to explain the marginality of the example.

If there is no PP, the method looks for predicates that simply occur in NP but are not in PT. Such predicates are referred to as *marginal predicates*, or MPs. In either case, the theory modification is achieved by adding a disjunct to a rule with a consequent in FC. The antecedent of the rule consists of the predicates from AP, PP, and MP. PP is preferred over MP because the predicates in MP may well be irrelevant. Consequently, the set MP provides a fallback technique to be used in cases where the real reason for marginality is not in PP (see the example of whale in this section).

Let us consider our kangaroo example. The set NP is presented in Figure 8.6 and Figure 8.7. How can we find PP? Supposing that all prototypes were described using the same extensions to the language, the table PT shown in case 1 of Figure 8.7 will be created by the `update(prototype_table)` procedure in the deductive phase of the algorithm (Figure 8.4). We observe that only one predicate in the set NP is different from PT: the baby kangaroo is developed in the marsupium. This predicate is placed in the set PP.

As a result, the following rule

```
replacing(mammal,baby_care(X,type_m))
<-- feed(X,milk) & milk_organ(X,type_m) &
      reproduction(X,viviparous) & embryo_dev(X,marsupium)
```

Case 1 :kangaroo	Case 2: blue_whale

• **Prototype Table PT:**
  breath: {air}
  covered: {hair}
  mastication:{tooth}
  develop: { placenta}
 	
• **PCP:**
FC: {baby_care(kangaroo,type_m)}
AP: {feed(kangaroo,milk),
      milk_organ(kangaroo,type_m),
      reproduction(kangaroo,viviparous)}
FP: birth(kangaroo,well_formed)
NP: {breath(kangaroo,air),
      embryo_dev(kangaroo,
      marsupium),covered(kangaroo,hair),
      mastication(kangaroo,tooth)}
 	
• **Repair by arguments:** []
 	
• **PP:**   {develop(embryo,marsupium) }
• **MP:** []
	• **Prototype Table PT:**
	  breath: {air}
	  covered: {hair}
	  mastication: {tooth}
	  develop: { placenta}
	
	• **PCP:**
	FC: {locomotion(blue_whale,type_m)}
	AP: {}
	FP: {ante_limbs(blue_whale,legs),
	      move(blue_whale,ground),
	      post_limbs(blue_whale,legs)}
	NP: {breath(blue_whale,air),
	      embryo_devblue_whale,
	      placenta),tail(blue_whale,bilobed)
	      ante_limbs(blue_whale,fins),
	      move(blue_whale,water)}
	
	• **Repair by arguments:**
	      {ante_limbs(blue_whale,fins),
	      move(blue_whale,water)}
	
	• **PP:** []
	
	• **MP:** {tail(blue_whale,bilobed)}

Figure 8.7:   PP and MP for two positive marginal examples

is placed in the second tier to extend the domain theory and cover the example of a kangaroo. The second tier extending rule is only applicable if the first tier rule is used in the context of the mammal theory, ensuring that the modification of the "baby_care" concept is only applicable to mammals. The specification of the context in which theory modification applies is indicated by the first argument of the operation replacing.

The Prototype Table avoids the inconsistency that other forms of rule modification can bring about: the new rule provides another explanation of the prototype. We can observe that this does not happen here—PT suggests rules based on predicates that were not used in the explanation of prototypes; thus, no new proofs for prototypes are possible. PT compensates for a lack of knowledge about the marginal by using abundant knowledge about prototypes. This combined deductive-inductive approach allows us to repair a faulty rule based on a single misclassified marginal example. Suppose, however, that the unexplained example is distinct from the prototypes by more than just a single argument (see case 2 in Figure 8.7); the corresponding example looks as follows:

```
ante_limbs(blue_whale,fins) & blood(blue_whale,hot) &
breath(blue_whale,air) & heart(blue_whale,4_chambers) &
tail(blue_whale,bilobed) & feed(blue_whale,milk) &
```

```
move(blue_whale,water) & embryo_dev(blue_whale,placenta) &
milk_organ(X,type_m) & fertilization(blue_whale,internal) &
reproduction(blue_whale,viviparous)
```

Again, the first step of the inductive phase used PT to discard some predicates from NP. In our case, predicates breath(blue_whale, air) and embryo_dev (blue_whale, placenta) are deemed not useful because they occur in PT with the same arguments as in NP. Because whales have no mastication and no hair, predicates regarding these characteristics are absent from NP. Of the three predicates in FP, two—ante_limbs(blue_whale,legs) and move(blue_whale, ground)—were repaired in the first step of the inductive phase when they were found in NP with different arguments. The third predicate in FP is post_limbs (blue_whale,legs). This predicate is absent from NP, so the second inductive step of the inductive phase identifies a marginal predicate to replace it, one not used by any prototype. The following rule will be suggested using the MP set because in the case of blue_whale, PP is empty (Figure 8.7):

```
replacing(mammal,locomotion(X,type_m))
  <-- ante_limbs(blue_whale,fins) & move(blue_whale,water) &
      tail(blue_whale,bilobed)
```

We shall now discuss how the theory is revised when a negative marginal is encountered. Recall that in this case a negative example is incorrectly explained by the theory (commission error). There is no failure to explain, and consequently, the FP, AP, and FC sets are empty. Only CP and NP have members. By way of illustration, suppose that while using the existing theory of mammals, an extra-terrestrial, or ET, is discovered. It is known that ET is not a mammal. Observation indicates that it satisfies all three top-level subconcepts of mammals (locomotion, blood_system, sexual_life). However, observation also suggests that ET has to plug into an electrical outlet once every 24 hours to get energy. From the knowledge of mammals, it is known that they draw their energy from the food they eat. Consequently, ET can be distinguished from a mammal because of its reliance on electricity as an energy source. The relevant knowledge about mammals and the negatively marginal ET can be summed up as shown in Figure 8.8.

Figure 8.8 presents two ways of representing the examples. In case 1, all descriptions of instances are augmented with the predicate energy. In case 2, the predicate energy is only present in the marginal instance of ET. Both cases support a repair to the theory through the introduction of a "contracting" rule. For the second case (which provides less knowledge about the prototypes than the first), this is the only way to fix the theory. This solution simply uses a negation of the PP or MP predicate: in our example, this means **not** energy(electric). A second solution, applicable only in case 1, will confirm the discriminating feature suggested by the difference between PT and PCP in the concept definition. In our example, that means energy(X, food) will be present in the concept definition. The first solu-

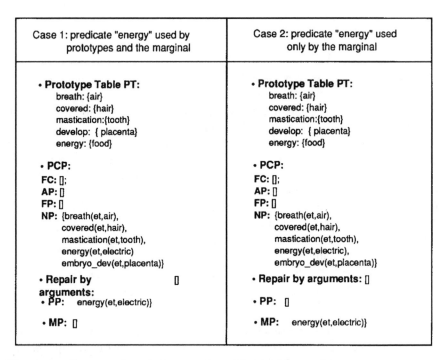

Case 1: predicate "energy" used by prototypes and the marginal	Case 2: predicate "energy" used only by the marginal

• **Prototype Table PT:**
    breath: {air}
    covered: {hair}
    mastication:{tooth}
    develop: { placenta}
    energy: {food}
 	
• **PCP:**
FC: [];
AP: []
FP: []
NP: {breath(et,air),
    covered(et,hair),
    mastication(et,tooth),
    energy(et,electric)
    embryo_dev(et,placenta)}
• **Repair by**   []
arguments:
• **PP:**   energy(et,electric)}
 	
• **MP:** []
	• **Prototype Table PT:**
	    breath: {air}
	    covered: {hair}
	    mastication:{tooth}
	    develop: { placenta}
	    energy: {food}
	
	• **PCP:**
	FC: [];
	AP: []
	FP: []
	NP: {breath(et,air),
	    covered(et,hair),
	    mastication(et,tooth),
	    energy(et,electric),
	    embryo_dev(et,placenta)}
	• **Repair by arguments:** []
	
	• **PP:** []
	
	• **MP:** energy(et,electric)}

Figure 8.8:   Two ways of representing examples and the resulting PP and MP

tion may lead to overgeneralization. With the second solution, the inconsistency problem is still avoided when more knowledge about the examples becomes available.

We can make some general observations on this process. Because of the characteristics of the Prototype Table, any predicate instance taken from it lies outside the prototype. We can observe that methods of theory revision using the PP and MP sets extend the language of the theory with new predicates learned from examples. With the PP-based method, there is also an assurance that the new predicates are not irrelevant: they were present in all the prototypes but with different arguments.

In the ET case analyzed in Figure 8.8, any rule placed in the second tier is a constraining rule for the mammal theory. In this context, the source of energy is constrained without having to modify the theory for other mammals:

```
restriction(mammal, energy(X, Y)) <-- energy(X, food)
```

or

```
restriction(mammal, energy(X, Y)) <-- not energy(X, electric)
```

The first alternative is added when we use the second solution permitted by case 1 in Figure 8.8, but the second rule is added when we use the case two representation. Another example of theory repair to eliminate a negative marginal is described in Matwin and Plante (1991).

8.7 RELATED WORK

In this section, we will review recent related work in chronological order.

Hall (1988) was one of the first to discuss the problem of dealing with an incomplete domain theory in EBL. He did not consider the case of inconsistent theory. Hall's approach applies mainly to applications of EBL to design and is not a general learning system. It is based on two algorithms: *precedent analysis* and *rule re-analysis*. Precedent analysis seems to yield results similar to our PT table, but rule re-analysis seems to be equivalent to PP/MP. Hall's discussion and experiments suggest that the method works best for "near misses," which correspond to our "marginals"; the performance degrades for explanations that diverge far from a correct proof.

Wilkins (1988) deals with incomplete knowledge. His system, ODYSSEUS, creates a new domain theory rule. The antecedent of this rule is the unexplained fact, and the consequent is as high as possible in the theory. Another theory is then used to confirm the modification.

Ginsberg's (1988) RTLS system performs full operationalization of the theory; i.e., it produces all possible proofs as if the theory has been exposed to all the possible examples (we avoid this). RTLS then proceeds inductively to repair the gaps. The approach is computationally expensive and quite different in spirit from the work presented here.

In OCCAM (Pazzani, 1988), incompleteness of the domain theory is addressed by *tentative generalizations* from examples. These generalizations are obtained directly from the examples. Only positive examples and class 2 marginals (omissions) are considered. The approach is knowledge-rich: the theory is modified by extensive inference about the purposes of subgoals in explanations. OCCAM focuses on the assignment of blame for a failure, and the discussion of how the domain theory is revised is unspecific. OCCAM solves the problem of confirmation of theory modifications (which we address by simply using our method incrementally and modifying the theory as needed). OCCAM also considers the case where inconsistency is introduced by theory modification. This is done by seeking confirmation or weakening competing hypotheses by new examples. Inconsistency is also addressed by our method without needing an extensive set of examples. Moreover, the problem does not arise when our method is used in conjunction with a two-tiered concept representation (see next section).

Danyluk (1989) investigates the bias that incomplete explanations provide for empirical methods attempting to generalize a theory. The proposed repair is performed at the lowest level in the theory. The case of commission errors is not addressed. The biases analyzed seem to be equivalent to the constraints imposed on the inductive part of our method, described in Section 8.4.1 and Section 8.4.2, where induction is performed on unused parts of explanations of prototypical examples.

Mooney's and Ourston's (1991) EITHER system repairs shared rules by identifying the repair spots with a syntactic heuristic. We apply a more "semantic" two-tiered approach, where an incomplete explanation is to be selected for repair; the syntactic selection criterion, however, is cognitively justified (Gick and Matwin, 1991). EITHER seems to work best on marginals (all the examples shown are marginals), though this is not stated.

Cain's (1991) DUCTOR system seems very much like Ourston's EITHER; from the description, it is not clear how the rule is identified that is to blame for an explained negative. DUCTOR does the most specific covering of positives during discrimination, just as we do. Like EITHER, DUCTOR requires re-explanation of failing positive and provable negative examples with each rule modification. This potentially costly process is in contrast with the approach proposed here, where rule modification requires no re-explanation.

This chapter attempts to cast the theory modification problem in a multi-strategy context, relying on the two-tiered representation of deductively acquired concept description. Bergadano et al. (1992) provide an extensive discussion of the two-tiered approach in general and present strong empirical evidence of its power in the case of concept descriptions that are acquired inductively.

8.8 FUTURE WORK

The approach presented here can suffer from overspecialization in cases when the marginality is the result of several features. Using again our `blue_whale` example, we observe that the method described runs into a difficulty when the PP and MP sets are large. If the description of the whale also included the predicates `filtration(blue_whale, plates)` and `covered(blue_whale,nude)`, the sets PP and MP would not be empty, and the rule would be more complex because all these predicates are good examples of the marginality of blue whale:

```
replacing(mammal,locomotion(X,type_m))
<-- ante_limbs(X,fins) & move(X,water) & filtration(X, plates) &
covered(X,nude) & tail(X,bilobed)
```

Two possibilities for pruning this rule for the locomotion may be suggested. The first technique could be a third step of induction: a semantic justification. If additional background knowledge is available (e.g., the goal of the tail is to allow faster or more directed movement of an animal), the new predicate `tail` can be justifiably linked with the subconcept locomotion. If, however, the same background knowledge tells us that the argument plates are used for eating, the entire filtration predicate may likely be discarded from the second-tier rule, adjusting the subconcept locomotion.

The second technique performs induction based on PCP again. The origin of predicates in the second tier would be recorded; i.e., they would be labeled with their PCP categorization (AP, MP, PP, or the result from induction on arguments). Second-tier rules would also be associated with the FP members that produced them. Keeping the origin of the different predicates in the second-tier rule can help us later to prune it safely. Induction on a second tier rule representing a subconcept can be done if other marginals failed this subconcept in the same way (i.e., with the same FP). For example, the killer whale will fail locomotion by failing the same predicates as the blue_whale: post_limb(killer_whale,legs), ante_limb (killer_whale, legs), and move(killer_whale,ground). Our inductive module will produce an extending rule:

```
replacing(mammal,locomotion(X,type_m))
<-- ante_limbs(X,fins) & move(X,water) & covered(X,nude) &
tail(X,bilobed)
```

At this time, two rules in the second tier are very similar: they share the same FP, the same AP, and the same predicates repaired by arguments. Such rules then become candidates for induction. A killer whale, however, has no plates; so, instead of building two different rules for the blue and killer whales, the predicate filtration can be dropped to accommodate two kinds of whale with just one locomotion rule. filtration(X, plates) is dropped because it has the label MP, and two other predicates (covered(X, nude) and tail(X, bilobed)) have the same label. Because second tier rules based only on the AP predicates already present in the first tier are unsuitable, these two remaining MP predicates are relied upon to justify marginality with respect to the prototypes. Because some whales have hair, later during the induction, there may be an opportunity to drop the other predicate covered(X, nude) from the rule. This would leave tail as the only non-AP predicate left.

In our approach, the induction process is driven by the quality of predicates that are dropped during generalization. All AP predicates are a judicious choice for the subconcept because they occur also in a similar first tier rule. MP predicates can be irrelevant, but PP predicates are more relevant than MP predicates. Induction can only prune predicates in MP and PP. A modified rule may also contain predicates from FP that are repaired by the change of argument; they are not pruned.

8.9 CONCLUSION

The method presented here uses an analysis of prototypical examples and misclassified marginal examples to revise a concept theory from a single instance. Inductively collected knowledge about prototypes permits revision of the theory when it fails to eliminate negative examples, a case where deductive methods alone are unhelpful. Overgeneralization is avoided by requesting that prototypical features be present in positive marginals rather than having atypical features be absent from the negative marginals. Inconsistency is avoided by filling the theory gaps with predicate instances that do not occur in prototypes.

The method uses the declarative bias of the theory to identify categories of predicates involved in the proof and to select prototypical features that are not involved in explanations. An empirical bias is then used to build a rule that modifies a theory from a single example.

The method has been designed to fit within the context of two-tiered concept representation. The original domain theory remains unchanged, and all modifications are placed in the second tier, which is only called upon as a result of first tier failure during a proof. Only under this circumstance will explanations be redone using additional rules, possibly overruling the classification produced by the first tier.

The two-tiered approach used here is a kind of middle ground between the rule-based and case-based approaches. A general part of a theory is modified to deal with special, marginal examples. It is difficult to repair a good general theory with rules for a few rare marginal examples. A case-based approach in which the second tier would consist of exemplars of marginals provides one solution. However, a case-based method would keep the marginal cases in their entirety and would lead to a fairly specific second tier. Our approach keeps in the second tier only those parts of the case that modify the first tier theory to deal correctly with a marginal. This produces a more general two-tiered theory, capable of dealing with marginals that realize the CP set via rules other than those that explain predicates used during learning. As a result, our approach is more general than a simple case-based representation but more specific than a purely rule-based approach.

We are also able to avoid the problem of determining where to place a modifying rule in the theory. Rules for omission errors (extending rules) are not hard to place because the proof failure hints at where the fix should be applied. Commission errors (contracting rules) are more difficult because there is no proof failure to point to a locus, so where should the fix go? The two-tiered approach used here deals with this by placing the fix in the second tier. Moreover, it only affects the second tier of the concepts involved in the offending example. For instance, a restriction on liftability requesting that handles be on the side is limited to cups and does not apply to the concept of liftability in general.

The approach is domain independent. It has been applied to the problem of modifying theories for recognizing mammals, fish, and birds. These theories were presented with marginals such as the bat, the whale, and the duck-billed platypus. The method correctly modified the theories, neither overgeneralizing nor overfitting (Plante 1991).

Finally, the approach used here is cognitively justified. The use of FC, FP, and NP predicates corresponds to a cognitive heuristic discovered and investigated by Chi et al. (1989).

A more complete account of this work is presented in Plante (1991).

ACKNOWLEDGMENTS

The work described here has been supported by the Natural Sciences and Engineering Research Council of Canada; the Government of Ontario (URIF Program); Cognos, Inc., under the Ontario Technology Fund program; and the Canada Centre for Remote Sensing. Terry Copeck's suggestions helped improve the readability of the chapter.

References

Bergadano, F., Matwin, S., Michalski, R. and Zhang, J., "Learning Two-Tiered Descriptions of Flexible Concepts: The POSEIDON System," *Machine Learning*, Vol. 8(1), pp. 5–43, 1992.

Cain, T., "The DUCTOR: A Theory Revision System for Propositional Domains," *8th International Workshop on Machine Learning*, pp. 485–489, Morgan Kaufmann, San Mateo, CA, 1991.

Chi, M.T., Bassok, M., Lewis, M., Reimann, W.P. and Glaser, R., "Self-Explanations: How Students Study and Use Examples in Learning to Solve Problems," *Cognitive Science*, (13), pp. 145–182, 1989.

Danyluk, A., "Finding New Rules for Incomplete Theories: Explicit Biases for Induction with Contextual Information," *6th International Machine Learning Workshop*, pp. 34–36, Morgan Kaufmann, San Mateo, CA, 1989.

Genest, J., Matwin, S. and Plante, B., "Explanation-Based Learning with Incomplete Theories: A Three-Step Approach," *Proceedings of the 7th International Conference on Machine Learning*, pp. 286–294 Morgan Kaufmann, San Mateo, CA, 1990.

Gick, M. and Matwin, S. "The Importance of Causal Structure and Facts in Evaluating Explanations," *Proceedings of the 8th International Workshop on Machine Learning*, pp. 51–54 Morgan Kaufmann, San Mateo, CA, 1991.

Ginsberg, A., "Theory Revision via Prior Operationalization," *Proceedings of the 7th National Conference on Artificial Intelligence*, pp. 590–595, AAAI Press, Menlo Park, CA, 1988.

Hall, R., "Learning by Failing to Explain: Using Partial Explanations to Learn in Incomplete or Intractable Domains," *Machine Learning*, Vol. 3(1): 45–78, 1988.

Matwin, S. and Plante, B., "A Deductive-Inductive Method for Theory Revision," *Proceedings of the 1st International Workshop on Multistrategy Learning*, pp. 160–174, George Mason University, Fairfax, VA, 1991.

Mooney, R. and Ourston, D., "Constructive Induction in Theory Refinement," *8th International Workshop on Machine Learning*, pp. 178–182 Morgan Kaufmann, San Mateo, CA, 1991.

Pazzani, M., "Explanation-Based Learning with Weak Domain Theories," *6th International Machine Learning Workshop*, pp. 72–74, Morgan Kaufmann, San Mateo, CA, 1989.

Plante, B., "Revision d'une Théorie du Domaine pour des Cas Marginaux en Employant une Analyse de la Preuve et des Exemples Prototypiques," *Master Thesis*, University of Ottawa, 1991.

Plante, B. and Matwin, S., "Learning Flexible Concepts through Theory Revision," *5th International Symposium on Methodologies for Intelligent Systems*, pp. 412–419 Knoxville, TN, 1990.

Wilkins, D., "Knowledge Base Refinement Using Apprenticeship Learning Techniques," *Proceedings of the 7th National Conference on Artificial Intelligence*, pp. 646–653, AAAI Press, Menlo Park, CA, 1988.

9

INTERACTIVE THEORY REVISION

Luc De Raedt
Maurice Bruynooghe
(Katholieke Universiteit Leuven)

Abstract

This chapter describes a multistrategy learning system, called CLINT, for interactive theory revision. CLINT operates in the framework of first order predicate logic and is representative of the inductive logic programming paradigm. The system integrates several learning strategies and techniques: abduction, induction, shifting of the bias, postponing, and handling of integrity constraints.

9.1 INTRODUCTION

Roughly speaking, interactive theory revision is the process where one starts from a given theory and some new evidence that is not explained by the theory. The aim is then to modify the given theory such that the evidence is explained by the revised theory. In *interactive* theory revision, one may query the user for additional information. Theory revision is one of the major problems in artificial intelligence. The need for theory revision arises in many practical applications. Two very important ones are learning apprentices and intensional knowledge base updating.

Learning apprentices are interactive aids for building and refining a knowledge base (cf. Smith et al. [1985]) during normal operation of the system. Theory revision is needed in this kind of system when the user detects errors made by the system. By signaling this to the apprentice, the system can revise its theory to avoid making similar mistakes again in the future. Today, there exist several learning apprentices, e.g., LEAP (Mitchell, Mahadevan, and Steinberg, 1985), the one of Smith et al. (1985), DISCIPLE (Tecuci and Kodratoff, 1990), BLIP (Morik, 1989;

Wrobel, 1989) and ODYSEUS (Wilkins, 1989). Most of these learning apprentices are quite complex knowledge based systems, integrating many features and subsystems. The system DISCIPLE has, for instance, three integrated learning modules, a knowledge base consisting of action models and object knowledge, and an expert system shell. All of the mentioned approaches (except LEAP) have a theory revision component. This reveals that theory revision is a major subtask in learning apprentices.

Intensional knowledge base updating (see, e.g., Bry [1990], Guessoum and Lloyd [1990], De Raedt and Bruynooghe [1992a]) is a technique used in deductive databases to update the database in an intelligent way. In classical approaches to database updating, the user has to specify the modifications needed to realize updates. In intensional knowledge base updating, the user only needs to declare the desired effect of the update. Intensional knowledge base updating techniques will then translate this update request into the required modifications to the database. Intensional knowledge base updating techniques allow the user to *declaratively* specify the update (*what* to modify) instead of *procedurally* (*how* to modify). As we will see, theory revision is a generalization of intensional knowledge base updating (cf. also De Raedt and Bruynooghe [1992a])

Our investigation aims at a firm framework for interactive theory revision that is applicable to learning apprentices and intensional knowledge base updating. As an incarnation of our framework, we have developed the concept-learning environment CLINT (Concept-Learning in an INTeractive way) (see also De Raedt and Bruynooghe [1992b] and De Raedt [1992]). It can be used as a module for learning apprentice and intensional knowledge base updating systems. Two principal design goals of theory revision in our context are

- *User-friendliness*: A system is user-friendly if it can be used in a simple manner by users that are not familiar with the underlying techniques.

- *Opportunism*: A system is opportunistic if it takes the initiative to revise its theory whenever there is an opportunity to do so.

This means that the theory revisor should be *easy to teach* and *eager to learn*. Few of the existing theory revisors meet these requirements. Probably the systems that meet these requirements best are DISCIPLE (Tecuci and Kodratoff, 1990) and MARVIN (Sammut and Banerji, 1986). However, the approaches to theory revision in DISCIPLE and MARVIN concentrate only on concept-learning, which is—as we shall see—a special case of theory revision. One aspect in which they can be extended is the use of integrity constraints and abduction.

To meet the above goals, we incorporated several learning strategies and techniques in CLINT: inductive concept-learning, abduction, shifting of the bias, postponing, and integrity handling. In this chapter, we will present the basic components of CLINT in an intuitive way. For a more technical and detailed presentation of CLINT, we refer to De Raedt (1992) and De Raedt and Bruynooghe (1991, 1992c).

The knowledge representation used by CLINT is a first order logic that corresponds to pure PROLOG without functors. Therefore, CLINT fits very well in the inductive logic programming paradigm (Muggleton 1991, 1992), which attempts to upgrade classical inductive learning techniques that employ a less expressive framework (typically a propositional logic or attribute value pairs) toward a first order logical framework. This choice of representation is well-suited for our two applications because the knowledge base of learning apprentices and deductive databases can effectively be represented using logic (cf., e.g., Gallaire, Minker, and Nicolas [1984]). Furthermore, using logic, one can easily analyze theoretical issues such as convergence because logic has a well-understood semantics.

This chapter is organized as follows. In Section 9.2, we introduce the logical framework of CLINT; in Section 9.3, we present CLINT's abductive and inductive techniques; in Section 9.4, two extensions of this basic technique are presented: the shifting of bias and the postponing of examples; in Section 9.5, we introduce the notion of integrity constraints and show how they are used by CLINT. Finally, in Sections 9.6 and 9.7, we conclude and briefly discuss related work.

9.2 THE LOGICAL FRAMEWORK

CLINT uses a logical framework (Bratko, 1986; Genesereth and Nilsson, 1987) to represent its theory. Within this framework, a concept p (in logic, concepts are named *predicates*) is defined by a set of *Horn clauses*, which are logical expressions of the following form:

$$p(t_1,...,t_n) \Leftarrow q_1(u_{1,1},...,u_{1,k_1})\&...\&q_m(u_{m,1},...,u_{m,k_m})$$

The terms t_i and $u_{i,j}$ are either constants or variables, and $p,q_1,...,q_m$ are predicates. Variables are represented by capitals and constants by a sequence of lower-case characters. Variables are always universally quantified in Horn clauses. Therefore—as in the programming language PROLOG—we do not write the quantifier $\forall$ explicitly. $p(t_1,...,t_n)$ is called the head of the clause (the conclusion) and $q_1(u_{1,1},...,u_{1,k_1})\&...\&q_m(u_{m,1},...,u_{m,k_m})$ the body (the consequence). Roughly speaking, a Horn clause states that the head is true whenever the body is. Using this formalism, one can define the concept of a legal pair of cards as follows:

```
legal(X,Y)      ⇐ card(X) & card(Y) & red(X) & black(Y) (1)
legal(X,joker)  ⇐ card(X) (2)
```

Clause (1) states that a pair of cards is legal if the first card is red, and the second one is black. Clause (2) states that any pair of cards where the second card is a joker is legal. Clause (1) holds for *all* X and Y and clause (2) for *all* X. This is because variables in clauses are always universally quantified. We will distinguish—as in deductive databases—between two kinds of predicate definitions: extensional definitions and intensional ones. Extensional predicate definitions consist of a set of ground facts, which are clauses where all terms t_i are constants, and $m = 0$; e.g., `legal(joker,joker)` $\Leftarrow$. Facts are unconditional statements about the world; therefore, facts are always true. Intensional definitions consist of a set of clauses where all terms t_i and $u_{i,j}$ are variables, and all variables in the head of the clause also occur in the body of a clause, e.g., clause (1). A theory is a set of intensional and extensional definitions. In CLINT, the user has to declare whether a predicate is intensional or extensional. For intensional predicates, clauses are learned in an inductive way and for extensional ones in an abductive way. A second dimension to be declared by the user is related to the correctness of the given predicate definition in the theory. *Basic* predicates are assumed to be correct and will never be modified; *learning* predicates may be correct or incorrect, and they may be modified.

Although clause (2) does not conform to our requirements for clauses in an intensional definition, an extensional definition of the constant `joker`, i.e.,

```
joker(joker) ⟸
```

together with a trivial rewriting, i.e.,

```
legal(X,Y) ⟸ card(X) & joker(Y)
```

makes it confirm. For reasons of convenience, we will often use clauses such as (2) as a shorthand in intensional predicate definitions.

As in concept-learning, CLINT uses examples. There are two kinds of examples: positive examples and negative ones. An example is a ground fact, together with its truth-value in the intended interpretation. The intended interpretation contains the truth-value of all formulae in the target theory, which is the desired theory where all predicates are correctly defined. Positive examples are true in the intended interpretation, whereas negative examples are false in this interpretation. Given the target theory T_1 consisting of clauses (1) and (2) and correct definitions for the concepts `red`, `black`, and `card`, the example `legal(spades-7,hearts-ace)` is negative, and `legal(diamonds-8,joker)` is positive. An example e is *covered* by a theory T if and only if e is logically implied by T. This can be verified by running the query $\Leftarrow e$ on theory T using a sound and complete theorem prover. (PROLOG is sound but not always complete; algorithms that are both sound and complete for this subset of logic are well known in the context of deductive databases.) If the query succeeds, e is covered; otherwise, it is not. In theory T_1, `legal(diamonds-8,joker)` is covered, but `legal(spades-7,hearts-ace)` is not.

CLINT also employs a notion of *bias* related to the description language of concepts. A concept-description language imposes syntactical restrictions on the clauses allowed in the definition of intensional predicates. For example, the language L_0 states that all variables occurring in the body of the clause also have to appear in the head of the clause. CLINT uses this notion to restrict the space of predicate definitions that has to be searched when revising its theory.

Because CLINT is an interactive theory revisor, it relies on the user to answer membership and existential questions. A membership question asks the user for the truth-value (or classification) of an example in the intended interpretation. An existential question $p(a_1,...,a_n)$ asks the user for all substitutions (an assignment of terms to variables) θ such that $p(a_1,....,a_n)\theta$ does not contain variables, and $p(a_1,...,a_n)\theta$ is true in the intended interpretation. Existential questions are generated by the abductive procedure in CLINT. Given theory T_1 specified above as the target theory, the membership question `legal(spades-7,hearts-ace)` would be answered negatively, and the existential question `legal(joker,X)` would be answered with `{X = joker}`.

By now, we can define the basic problem addressed by CLINT:

Given:

- A theory T containing definitions of intensional and/or extensional predicates.
- A set of positive and negative examples.
- A language definition L.
- A user willing to answer membership and existential questions about the intended interpretation.

Find: A revised theory T' obtained by adding/retracting facts for extensional learning predicates to/from T and adding/retracting clauses expressible in language L for intensional predicates to/from T, such that T' covers all positive and none of the negative examples.

Notice that P and N may contain examples of multiple predicates. It is one of the distinctive characteristics of CLINT that it is able to learn multiple related predicate-definitions.

9.3 INDUCTION AND ABDUCTION

Analyzing CLINT's problem-specification reveals two kinds of opportunities for learning: a positive example not covered by the current theory and a negative one covered by the current theory. In the first case, CLINT will remove an incorrect clause from the theory. In the second case, CLINT will derive a number of clauses/facts that cover the example and add them to the theory.

9.3.1 A Covered Negative Example

This case is treated by CLINT similarly as in the Model Inference System of Shapiro (1983). Basically, CLINT computes a proof-tree (an AND-tree) explaining why the negative example is implied by the theory. Afterwards, it asks membership-questions about the nodes in the proof-tree in order to find an incorrect clause. A clause c is incorrect if there is a substitution θ such that $body(c)\theta$ is true, and $head(c)\theta$ is false in the intended interpretation. Once the incorrect clause has been detected, it is removed from the theory, and (positive) examples that were covered by that clause are reconsidered. The positive examples that are no longer covered by the theory are passed to the generalization procedure of CLINT described in the next subsection. This procedure is illustrated in Example 1.

Example 1: Finding an incorrect clause. Consider theory T_1 and assume that the example `legal(diamonds-7, spades-8)` is negative. Using theory T_1, one could derive the proof-tree shown in Figure 9.1. Given that the predicate `card` is known to be correct (it is declared *basic*) and the other predicates are declared *learning*, the system can discover that clause (1) is incorrect when the membership questions `red(diamonds-7)` and `black(spades-8)` are answered positively. In that case, there is a substitution `{X = diamonds-7, Y = spades-8}` making the body of clause (1) true and its head false. Therefore, clause (1) must be incorrect. ◊

9.3.2 An Uncovered Positive Example

CLINT uses two different strategies to make uncovered positive examples implied: an abductive procedure and the inductive one of De Raedt and Bruynooghe (1992b). We first present the inductive procedure and then the abductive one.

9.3.2.1 Induction

The inductive procedure is only invoked on examples for intensional predicates and only when abduction fails. The reason is that adding facts for extensional predicates is less intrusive toward the original theory than adding rules. The inductive procedure of CLINT proceeds in two different steps: in the first step, CLINT computes a starting clause covering the positive example and none of the negative ones; in the second step, CLINT generalizes this starting clause by generating examples and asking membership questions of the user.

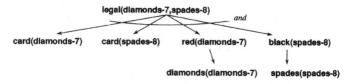

Figure 9.1: A proof tree

To compute the starting clause that covers a (positive) example p, CLINT uses a function SC that takes three arguments: the example p, a language L, and a theory T. The result of $SC(p,T,L)$ is the set of most specific clauses c expressible in L using T such that $T \cup \{ c \}$ covers p. The term *most specific* clause deserves some explanation. This notion is based on the *is more general than* relation that is frequently used in machine learning (cf. Mitchell [1982] and Michalski [1983]). In inductive logic programming, a clause c_1 is more specific than a clause c_2 if and only if there is a substitution θ such that $c_1\theta \subset c_2$ (this definition was introduced by Plotkin [1970]). c_1 is then a specialization of c_2 and c_2 a generalization of c_1. For example, clause `legal(X,X)` $\Leftarrow$ `card(X)` & `red(X)` is more specific than `legal(X,Y)`$\Leftarrow$ `card(X)` & `card(Y)` because $\{$`legal(X,Y)`, $\neg$`card(X)`, $\neg$`card(Y)`$\}$ $\{X = Y\}$ $\subset$ $\{$`legal(X, X)`, $\neg$`card(X)`, $\neg$`red(X)`$\}$. Roughly speaking, a clause is more specific than another clause if all examples covered by the first clause are also covered by the second one. This means that the more specific clause imposes more restrictions on the concept than the more general one. The *is more specific than* relation is important for concept-learning because it allows structuring the search and pruning it in an intelligent way (cf. Mitchell, 1982). Indeed, when a positive example is not covered by a clause, no specialization of that clause will cover the example. Also, when a negative example is covered by a clause, all generalizations of the clause will cover the example. In the first situation, all specializations of the clause can be pruned and, in the second one, all generalizations. The function SC is illustrated in example 2.

Example 2: The function SC. Consider theory T_2, which contains correct definitions of the following predicates in the domain of cards:

- `card(X)`, `red(X)`, `black(X)`, `diamonds(X)`, `hearts(X)`, `spades(X)`, `clubs(X)`, `face(X)`, `number(X)`: the predicate p(X) succeeds when X is a p-card

- `same_color(X,Y)`, `same_suit(X,Y)`, `same_rank(X,Y)`, `successor_rank(X,Y)`, `lower_rank(X,Y)`: the predicate p(X,Y) succeeds when X has the p as/of Y

Given this situation:

```
SC (legal(diamonds-10,spades-jack),T₂,L₀) = {
    legal(X,Y) ⇐ diamonds(X) & red(X) & card(X) & number(X)
    spades(Y) & black(Y) & card(Y) & face(X) &
    successor_rank(X,Y) & lower_rank(X,Y)}
```

No clause is expressible in L_0 that is more specific than this one and that will cover the example when added to T_2.   ◊

For the moment, we will assume that $SC(p,T,L)$ always contains a clause that does not cover any negative example. As will be shown in Section 9.4, this assumption does not hold in general. Upon receipt of a positive example p, CLINT will compute a consistent clause $sc \in SC(p,T,L)$ and pass this clause to its second step, the generalization procedure.

Observe that the function SC allows coping with the problem of indirect relevance of Michalski (1983). This is easily seen by looking at an example: suppose the aim is to learn the predicate `father` from the example `father (jeff,paul)`. Notice that the example does not mention any property about `jeff` and `paul`. These properties have to be derived from the theory. In order to achieve this, CLINT uses its language. The generated starting clause then contains the properties about the arguments that are important for the example given the theory and the language; e.g., `father(X,Y)` $\Leftarrow$ `male(X) & male(Y) & parent(X,Y)`.

In the generalization step of the algorithm, CLINT starts from an old clause c (initially, c is the starting clause generated by the first step of the inductive procedure) and constructs a least general generalization c' of c,[1] such that c' covers an example e that is not covered by c, and c' does not cover any of the known negative examples. When c' and e fulfill these conditions, CLINT will verify whether it already knows the intended interpretation of e or not. If not, it will generate a membership question concerning e to the user. If e turns out to be a positive example, the old clause c is replaced by the new one c', and the process is repeated for the new clause. If e is negative, the system will memorize the example and will search for other generalizations of the old clause c. This process continues until there are no more generalizations of the old clause that fulfill the requirements. CLINT will then add the old clause c to its theory. It has been shown (cf. De Raedt [1992]) that the clause added to the theory is maximally general w.r.t. the given theory and negative examples. This means that all generalizations of the clause also cover negative examples. An example that illustrates the different steps can be found below:

Example 3: Induction. Assume that theory T_2 of example 2 is used. In the next session with CLINT, user-input is in roman, or text, and system output is `typewritten`.

> ?-learn.
> `Next example ?` legal(spades-queen,hearts-8).
> `Class ?` positive.

---

[1] In the implementation of CLINT, generalizations of clauses are obtained by dropping literals in the clause. Because the implementation also uses an explicit representation of equality, this generalization operator is complete for Horn-clause logic without functors. Explicit equality means that a clause such as `p(X,X,Z)` $\Leftarrow$ `q(X,Z) & r(Z)` would be rewritten as `p(X,Y,Z)` $\Leftarrow$ `q(X,Z) & q(Y,Z) & X = Y & r(Z)`.

Starting clause in L_0:
   legal(X,Y) ⇐ spades(X) & black(X) & card(X) & face(X) &
      hearts(Y) & red(Y) & card(Y) & number(Y) & lower_rank(Y,X)
Is legal(clubs-jack,hearts-7) true ? {spades(X)} deleted yes.
Generalized clause:

   legal(X,Y) ⇐ black(X) & card(X) & face(X) &
      hearts(Y) & red(Y) & card(Y) & number(Y) & lower_rank(Y,X)
Is legal(clubs-jack,diamonds-7) true ? {hearts(Y)} deleted yes.

Generalized clause:

   legal(X,Y) ⇐ black(X) & card(X) & face(X) &
      red(Y) & card(Y) & number(Y) & lower_rank(Y,X)

Is legal(hearts-jack,diamonds-7) true ? {black(X)} deleted no.
Is legal(spades-king,spades-7) true ? {red(Y)} deleted no.
Is legal(spades-9,diamonds-8) true ? {face(X)} deleted no.
Is legal(spades-queen,diamonds-jack) true ? {number(Y)} deleted no.
No further generalizations
Clause added to theory:

   legal(X,Y) ⇐ black(X) & face(X) & red(Y) & number(Y)

The conditions card(X), card(Y), *and* lower_rank(Y,X) *are redundant. Therefore, they are deleted from the final clause.* ◊

Note that CLINT is able to learn disjunctive concepts by invoking the procedure to recover from an uncovered positive example more than once.

9.3.2.2 Abduction: Acquiring Facts

The inductive procedure of CLINT presented above is not sufficient to address the full theory revision problem. The procedure has two important limitations: it does not allow the adding of facts to the theory, and when it learns one predicate, it does not take into account other predicates. Both limitations can easily be seen when considering the following example. Suppose the theory contains the definition of daughter as daughter(X,Y) ⇐ parent(X,Y) & female(Y) and the definitions of female and parent, which are extensional predicates. When the theory revisor then receives the uncovered positive example daughter(luc,soetkin), CLINT's inductive procedure cannot find an adequate solution. The most desirable solution adds the facts parent(luc,soetkin) and female(soetkin) to the theory. This solution can be computed in an abductive manner.

The abductive procedure starts from a positive example $p(a_1,...,a_n)$. If p is an extensionally declared predicate, CLINT merely adds $p(a_1,...,a_n)$ to the current theory. If p is intensionally declared and there is a clause $p(t_1,...,t_n) \Leftarrow q_1 \& ... \& q_m$ in the theory, CLINT will first find the substitution θ such that $p(t_1,...,t_n)\theta = p(a_1,...,a_n)$. It will then attempt to interactively solve the goal $\Leftarrow q_1\theta \& ... \& q_m\theta$. This is realized by solving the literals $q_i\theta$ one after the other. To solve a literal $q_i\theta$, the system first verifies whether $q_i\theta$ is implied by the current theory or is known to be negative. If $q_i\theta\rho_i$ is implied by the theory for some substitution ρ_i, CLINT will attempt to solve the remaining part of the goal; i.e., $\Leftarrow q_{i+1}\theta\rho_1...\rho_i \& ... \& q_m\theta\rho_1...\rho_i$. If nothing is known about $q_i\theta$, then the membership or existential question $q_i\theta\rho_1...\rho_{i-1}$ is asked of the user. If the user answers positively, the rest of the goal, i.e., $\Leftarrow q_{i+1}\theta\rho_1...\rho_i \& ... \& q_m\theta\rho_1...\rho_i$, is solved. In this case, ρ_i is the answer from the user. If $q_i\theta$ is negative, the system backtracks to other possibilities ρ_j for earlier literals and, when this is impossible, to other clauses for p. When the goal is empty, CLINT has found a substitution $\rho_1...\rho_m$ such that $\Leftarrow (q_1 \& ... \& q_m)\theta\rho_1...\rho_m$ is true. However, there may still be literals in this goal (the literals obtained by querying the user) that are not yet covered by the current theory. Therefore, CLINT will pass all these uncovered positive examples belonging to this goal to its inductive and/or abductive procedure. It is only when the abductive procedure fails to result in an empty goal that the inductive procedure is called; so for intensionally declared predicates, both procedures may be invoked on uncovered positive examples. The abductive technique will—as all CLINT's techniques—never ask questions about basic predicates. Notice that using the abductive procedure of CLINT allows alleviating the earlier sketched problems. The abductive procedure is illustrated in example 4.

Example 4: Abductive procedure. Assume that theory T_2 is used but that the predicate `same_suit` is an intensionally declared learning predicate defined by

```
same_suit(X,Y) ⇐ spades(X) & spades(Y)
same_suit(X,Y) ⇐ clubs(X) & clubs(Y)
same_suit(X,Y) ⇐ diamonds(X) & diamonds(Y)
```

Assume that the predicate `legal` is defined by

```
legal(X,Y) ⇐ same_suit(X,Y) & face(X) & number(Y)
?-learn.
Next example ? legal(hearts-king, hearts-7).
Class ? positive.
Invoking abduction ...
```

As `face(hearts-king)` *and* `number(hearts-7)` *are implied by the theory, the system needs only to verify*

```
Is same_suit(hearts-king,hearts-7) true ? yes.
same_suit(hearts-king,hearts-7) is an uncovered positive example
Invoking abduction ... abduction fails
```

The abductive procedure fails because the predicates spades, diamonds, *and* clubs *are basic predicates, which are completely correct*

```
Invoking induction ...
Starting clause in L₀:
```

```
same_suit(X,Y) ⇐ hearts(X) & red(X) & card(X) &
    hearts(Y) & red(Y) & card(Y) & same_color(X,Y) &
    lower_rank(Y,X) & face(X) & number(Y)
```

```
Is same_suit(hearts-9,hearts-7) true ? {face(X)} deleted yes.
Generalized clause:
```

```
same_suit(X,Y) ⇐hearts(X) & red(X) & card(X) &
    hearts(Y) & red(Y) & card(Y) & same_color(X,Y) &
    lower_rank(Y,X) & number(Y)
```

```
Is same_suit(hearts-king,hearts-queen) true ? {number(Y)} deleted
  yes.
Generalized clause:
```

```
same_suit(X,Y) ⇐ hearts(X) & red(X) & card(X) &
    hearts(Y) & red(Y) & card(Y) &
    same_color(X,Y) & lower_rank(Y,X)
```

```
Is same_suit(hearts-7,hearts-jack) true ? {lower_rank(Y,X)} deleted
  yes.
Generalized clause:
```

```
same_suit(X,Y) ⇐ hearts(X) & red(X) & card(X) &
    hearts(Y) & red(Y) & card(Y) & same_color(X,Y)
```

Suppose the system knows the following two negative examples: same_suit(hearts-7,diamonds-8) *and* same_suit(diamonds-8,hearts-7). *This is sufficient to exclude all further generalizations. This yields*

```
No further generalizations
Clause added to theory:
same_suit(X,Y) ⇐ hearts(X) & hearts(Y)
```

9.4 SHIFT OF BIAS AND POSTPONING

During the presentation of CLINT's inductive procedure, we have assumed that the set $SC(p,T,L)$ always contains a consistent clause, i.e., a clause that does not cover any of the negative examples. This assumption does not hold in general. Two problems may occur, as illustrated in example 5.

Example 5: Inconsistent starting clauses. Let the target definition of the predicate `legal` be `legal(X,Y) ⇐ successor_rank(X,Z) & successor_rank(Z,Y)`. Two situations may prevent CLINT's inductive procedure from finding this clause:

- The considered concept-description language may not contain the target clause. For example, the language L_0 does not contain the clause because `z` is a variable not occurring in the head.
- The current theory of CLINT may not be sufficient for learning the predicate. For instance, when the predicate `successor_rank` is not known, the above clause can never be derived.   ◊

To remedy these problems, the inductive learning strategy of CLINT was extended with two enhancements.

The first enhancement *shifts the bias* of the concept-description language when the set $SC(p,T,L_i)$ does not contain any consistent clause. This is realized by considering a series of concept-description languages, $L_0,L_1,L_2,...,L_M$. Each language L_i imposes certain syntactic restrictions on the clauses derived by CLINT. Furthermore, the languages are ordered according to growing expressiveness. This means that all clauses that can be expressed in L_i can also be expressed in L_{i+1}. When $SC(p,T,L_i)$ does not contain any consistent clause, it means that there is no consistent clause expressible in L_i given the current state of the theory T that covers the positive example p. In this case, CLINT will shift its bias to L_{i+1} and consider $SC(p,T,L_{i+1})$. This process continues until CLINT finds a consistent clause in some language L_j or detects that none of the languages allows finding a consistent clause covering the example. In the first case, the starting clause sc passed to CLINT's generalization procedure is a clause $sc \in SC(p,T,L_i)$, such that sc is consistent with the negative examples, and i is minimal. The minimality condition implies that all clauses $c \in SC(p,T,L_j)$ with $j < i$ cover negative examples. In the latter case, the treatment of the example p will be postponed (cf. below).

De Raedt and Bruynooghe (1990) defined several series of languages. To give the reader an intuitive understanding of the nature of these languages, let us consider the following series: In L_0, all variables occurring in the body of a clause also occur in the head of a clause and vice versa. In L_1, a limited number of local variables (local variables are variables that occur in the body of the clause but not in its head) are allowed to occur in the body of the clauses, but each local variable may occur only once in the clause. In L_2, we then also allow for multiple occurrences of the local variables introduced in L_1. One can easily see that in this way, it is possible to derive a series of languages. The above series defines only one possible series of languages, and in this respect, it is important to realize that the considered series *biases* the system. Other language series will give different results. For a formal presentation of the languages used by CLINT, we refer to De Raedt (1992) and De Raedt and Bruynooghe (1990).

When there is no consistent clause in $SC(p,KB,L_i)$ for all $i: 0 < i < M + 1$, it means that CLINT's inductive procedure fails. In that case, CLINT assumes that the reason for the failure is because of an incomplete theory, and therefore, it will *postpone* the treatment of the example (cf. De Raedt [1992]). Postponing an example means that the theory is temporarily left as it is but that the system remembers that there is still an uncovered positive example. Afterwards, when the system has modified the theory because of some other examples, it will reinvoke its inductive procedure on the example. Usually, however, CLINT finds a consistent starting clause and passes the found starting clause to its generalization procedure. Shifting the bias and postponing are illustrated in example 6.

Example 6: Shifting bias—postponing. Suppose the relevant part of the theory is

```
female(mary)   ⇐        parent(mary,rose)  ⇐
female(kaatje) ⇐        parent(leo,rose)   ⇐
female(lieve)  ⇐        parent(rose,luc)   ⇐
female(rose)   ⇐        parent(mary,stef)  ⇐

male(luc)      ⇐        parent(stef,jan)   ⇐
male(leo)      ⇐        parent(leo,stef)   ⇐
male(stef)     ⇐        parent(etienne,luc) ⇐
male(etienne)  ⇐        parent(stef,kaatje) ⇐
```

?-learn.
Next example ? grandparent(mary, luc).
Class ? positive.
Starting clause in L_0:
grandparent(G,C) ⇐ male(C) & female(G)
No further generalizations
Clause asserted in the knowledge base

CLINT is unable to further generalize this clause because all generalizations are outside the language L_1. L_1 contains only clauses of which all variables occurring in the body of the clause also occur in the head and vice versa. Because the clause is incorrect, the user supplies an example that is incorrectly handled by the induced theory.

?-learn.
```
Next example ? grandparent(rose, jan).
Class ? negative.
Is male(jan) true ? yes.
Is female(rose) true ? yes.
Retracting incorrect clause:
     grandparent(G,C) ⇐ male(C) & female(G)
```

This shows the procedure that handles covered negative examples at work.

```
grandparent(mary,luc) is no longer covered
Starting clause in L0:

     grandparent(G,C) ⇐ male(C) & female(G)


Starting clause covers negative example
Shifting bias
```

If at this point there would be no further languages in the series, i.e., $M = 0$, then CLINT would postpone this positive example.

```
Starting clause in L1:
     grandparent(G,C) ⇐ male(C) & female(G) & parent(G,I)
          & parent(J,C)
```

L_1 allows for 1 local variable in each literal. Local variables may have only one occurrence in clauses of L_1.

```
Starting clause covers negative example
Shifting bias
Starting clause in L2:
     grandparent(G,C) ⇐ male(C) & female(G) & parent(G,I)
          & parent(J,C) & female(I) & equal(I,J)
```

L_2 also allows for relations among the local variables introduced in L_2.

```
Is grandparent(leo,luc) true ? {female(G)} deleted yes.
Generalized clause:

     grandparent(G,C) ⇐ male(C) & parent(G,I) & parent(J,C)
          & female(I) & equal(I,J)


Is grandparent(leo,jan) true ? {female(I)} deleted yes.
Generalized clause:

     grandparent(G,C) ⇐ male(C) & parent(G,I) & parent(J,C)
          & equal(I,J)


Is grandparent(leo,kaatje) true ? {male(C)} deleted yes.
```

Generalized clause:

```
grandparent(G,C) ⇐ parent(G,I) & parent(J,C) & equal(I,J)
```

No further generalizations
Clause added to theory.

9.5 USING INTEGRITY CONSTRAINTS

9.5.1 Motivation

In this section, we will show how CLINT's algorithms can be extended to cope with integrity constraints. The introduction of integrity constraints into inductive learning was motivated (see De Raedt and Bruynooghe [1992a]) by analyzing the differences between *incremental concept-learning* and *intensional knowledge base updating* (see, e.g., Bry [1990]; and Guessoum and Lloyd [1990]). One of the conclusions of this comparison was that integrity constraints are very useful for inductive concept-learning (and, therefore, also for theory revision) because they allow making the learning process very knowledge intensive. Whereas the use of integrity constraints is common in database technology (see, e.g., Gallaire, Minker, and Nicolas [1984]; and Reiter [1990]), it is new for concept-learning. Using integrity constraints, one can easily specify properties about the target theory. For example, the user can tell the system that a parent should be either a mother or a father. In our framework, such properties or integrity constraints are stated as general first order logic clauses, i.e., clauses of the form $p_1 \& ... \& p_k \Rightarrow q_1 \vee ... \vee q_m$, e.g., parent(X,Y) ⇒ father(X,Y) ∨ mother(X,Y). Constraints are input by the user and assumed to be correct in the intended interpretation. Therefore, constraints have to be satisfied by the derived theory. A constraint $p_1 \& ... \& p_k \Rightarrow q_1 \vee ... \vee q_m$ is satisfied by the theory if and only if the query $\Leftarrow p_1 \& ... \& p_k \& \neg q_1 \& \neg ... \& \neg q_m$ fails. When this goal succeeds for a substitution θ, we will say that the constraint is violated for θ. Notice that examples are a special kind of constraint: a positive example p corresponds to a constraint of the form $\Rightarrow p$ and a negative example n to a constraint $n \Rightarrow$.

Integrity constraints are specially useful in Learning Apprentice Systems because one needs to learn multiple concepts from examples, and integrity constraints provide the user with the possibility of specifying the relations among different predicates to be learned. These constraints act as restrictions on the definitions of the predicates in the theory.

Other reasons for introducing integrity constraints are summarized below (see also the literature on databases): (1) constraints are not restricted to definite Horn-clauses, but clauses in the theory, i.e., concept-definitions, are; (2) when adding constraints to the theory as inference rules, one would obtain a much more complicated theory with many redundancies, thus decreasing the efficiency of deductions;

and (3) certain constraints should in no case be used as inference rules. Think for example about the following rule: `human(X) & age(X,Y)` $\Rightarrow$ `Y < 150`. One does not want to use such rules to derive facts for the predicate $<$. This reveals that integrity constraints allow making the theory revision process very knowledge intensive. For a further discussion of integrity constraints, we refer to the database literature.

9.5.2 Integrity Constraints in CLINT

CLINT has been enhanced with two different techniques to handle constraints: the *lazy* method and the *eager* one (De Raedt, Bruynooghe, and Martens, 1991). The eager technique requires less examples than the lazy one, but it is more complicated. Therefore, we will only explain the lazy method in detail and give a more intuitive presentation of the eager one. For a more detailed presentation, we refer to De Raedt (1992).

The general principle for using constraints for theory revision is rather simple. When a constraint $p_1 \& ... \& p_k \Rightarrow q_1 \vee ... \vee q_m$ is violated for a substitution θ, we have one of the following:

- The definition of one of the predicates p_i in the body of the constraint is too general (i.e., T covers $p_i\theta$ but should not).
- The definition of one of the predicates q_j in the head of the constraint is too specific (i.e., T does not cover $q_j\theta$ but should).

This observation reveals that violated constraints can be used to generate examples that are not satisfied by the theory. When there is only one literal in a constraint, it is clear that the violated instance of the literal itself is an example that is not satisfied by the theory. However, if there is more than one literal in a violated constraint, the responsible examples have to be identified by performing credit-assignment on a violated instance of the constraint. In interactive theory revisors, the credit-assignment procedure queries the user for the truth-value in the intended interpretation of the instances of the literals in the violated constraint.

As an example of credit-assignment, consider the following constraint:

```
is_allowed_to_drive(X,Y) & isa(Y,car) ⇒ license(X,car)
```

Let us assume that the constraint is violated for θ = {X=luc, Y=dyane}. The source of the violation can be located by asking the user for the intended interpretation of the corresponding facts. The error is then the fact for which the intended interpretation is different from the truth-value according to the theory; so, we have that `is_allowed_to_drive` or `isa` is too general, or `license` is too specific.

This example and the above discussion motivate the following straight-forward *lazy* method to cope with constraints in the context of CLINT.

When a constraint is violated, credit is assigned to the literals in a violated instance of the constraint. This allows deriving examples that are not satisfied by the given theory. These examples are passed to CLINT, which treats them as specified in previous sections. Once CLINT finishes learning from these examples, it verifies whether the constraints are satisfied by the resulting theory. Violations at that point are treated in the same manner. This process of verifying constraints, deriving examples from violated instances of constraints, and revising theory from examples by CLINT is repeated until the theory satisfies all constraints. The user is then queried for additional constraints (or examples).

There is, however, one complication with this approach: the treatment of postponed examples. When an example is postponed for a predicate p, one should not expect the constraints mentioning the predicate p to be satisfied. Also, the predicates (and the constraints) that depend on the postponed predicate may be affected. (A predicate p depends on a predicate q w.r.t. a given theory if and only if there is a clause in the definition of p that mentions q, or there is a clause in the definition of p that mentions a predicate r that depends on q.)

Constraints that depend on a predicate for which a postponed example exists are postponed. (A constraint c depends on a predicate p if and only if there is a literal of p in c, or there is a literal in c of a predicate q that depends on p.) Postponed constraints are reactivated when all examples causing their postponement are reactivated. Formally speaking, a constraint c is postponed by CLINT when c is an example that is postponed, or there is a postponed example $p(t_1,...,t_n)$ such that c depends on p. When a constraint is not postponed, it is *active*. Notice that the class of active constraints evolves when examples become postponed or active.

The straightforward algorithm outlined above can now easily be modified to take these considerations into account: After a theory revision phase by CLINT using the inductive and/or abductive procedures, all *active constraints* are verified. Given a violated active constraint, credit is assigned to the literals in a violated instance of the constraint in order to find an example that is not satisfied, i.e., not handled correctly, by the current theory. This is realized by asking the user for the truth-value of literals in a violated instance of the constraint. Note that if the violated constraint contains only one literal (as in the case of examples),[2] its truth-value is known. Then, the user need not be bothered with questions. In any case, credit-assignment allows identifying a violated example. This example is then passed to the abductive and inductive procedures of CLINT, described in previous sections. These procedures will then recover from the error. Notice also that these procedures will verify the predicates, depending on the example, and will possibly reconsider the postponed examples.

---

[2] Similarly, if a constraint contains only one learning predicate, that predicate must cause the violation.

The eager method differs from the lazy one in the sense that it also verifies whether the starting clauses (and all generalizations of such clauses) satisfy the restrictive constraints for the considered concept. A constraint is restrictive for a predicate if the predicate occurs in the body of the constraint. When adding the considered clause to the theory results in a violation of a restrictive constraint, credit-assignment is performed in order to find the cause of the violation, and the responsible examples are passed to CLINT's inductive and abductive procedure. Using the eager method results in detecting violations at an earlier stage and, therefore, usually requires less examples. On the other hand, the eager method is computationally more expensive because the constraints have to be verified more often (for each candidate-clause to be added to the theory). The use of integrity constraints in CLINT is illustrated in the next examples.

Example 7: Integrity constraints—lazy method. Suppose we start from the same theory as in example 6. Suppose the user inputs the constraint `parent(X,Y)` $\Rightarrow$ `father(X,Y)` $\vee$ `mother(X,Y)`. This constraint is violated for its instance `parent(mary,rose)` $\Rightarrow$ `father(mary,rose)` $\vee$ `mother(mary,rose)`.

Querying the user for the truth value of `parent(mary,rose)` (true) and `father(mary,rose)` (false) reveals that `mother(mary,rose)` must be true. This uncovered positive example is then supplied to CLINT. CLINT induces the correct definition for `mother`, i.e., `mother(M,C)` $\Leftarrow$ `female(M)` & `parent(M,C)`, by asking some membership questions. After adding the learned clause to the theory, CLINT verifies the relevant integrity constraints. At this point, the constraint is violated for `parent(leo,rose)` $\Rightarrow$ `father(leo,rose)` $\vee$ `mother(leo,rose)`, which results in learning the correct definition for father.   ◊

Example 8: Illustrating integrity constraints—eager method. Reconsider theory T_2 of example 2 and assume that the following constraints are known to the system:

```
legal(X,Y) & number(X)  ⇒  false (3)
legal(X,Y)  ⇒  black(X) (4)
```

Constraint (3) states that the first card of a legal tuple may not be a number; constraint (4) states that all first cards of a legal tuple must be black. This illustrates well that supplying integrity constraints to CLINT amounts to giving hints to the learner. Let us assume that the same predicate is being learned as in example 3 and that all other predicates in the theory are declared basic.

?-learn.
Next example ? legal(spades-queen, hearts-8).
Class ? positive.
Starting clause in L_0:

```
legal(X,Y) ⇐ spades(X) & black(X) & card(X) & face(X) &
    hearts(Y) & red(Y) & card(Y) & number(Y) & lower_rank(Y,X)
```

Is legal(clubs-jack,hearts-7) true ? {spades(X)} deleted yes.
Generalized clause:

```
legal(X,Y) ⇐ black(X) & card(X) & face(X) &
    hearts(Y) & red(Y) & card(Y) & number(Y) & lower_rank(Y,X)
```

Is legal(clubs-jack,diamonds-7) true ? {hearts(Y)} deleted yes.
Generalized clause:

```
legal(X,Y) ⇐ black(X) & card(X) & face(X) &
    red(Y) & card(Y) & number(Y) & lower_rank(Y,X)
```

At this point, the question for legal(hearts-jack,diamonds-7) *is avoided because the resulting generalization violates constraint (4), and any violation of (4) (and also [3]) must be because of the predicate* legal *because the other ones are declared basic.*

Is legal(spades-king,spades-7) true ? {red(Y)} deleted no.

The question for the truth-value of legal(spades-9,diamonds-8) *is avoided because the resulting generalizations violate constraint (3).*

Is legal(spades-queen,diamonds-jack) true {number(Y)} deleted no.
No further generalizations
Clause added to theory:

```
legal(X,Y) ⇐ black(X) & face(X) & red(X) & number(X)          ◊
```

9.6 EXTENSIONS OF CLINT

There exist several extensions of CLINT that have not been presented in this chapter. Let us briefly mention the most important ones:

- *Program-synthesis*: To make CLINT an effective tool for synthesizing PRO-LOG programs from examples, one needs to give it the ability to handle functors. Using functors in CLINT can, however, lead to serious problems because termination is no longer guaranteed. This is a basic problem because it is in general undecidable whether a certain example is implied by a logic theory. To alleviate this problem, an *h*-easy or *h*-complex approach can be followed (cf. De Raedt [1992]). The *h*-easy technique imposes a depth-bound on the depth of a proof of any query, whereas the *h*-complex approach restricts the considered terms to the ones satisfying a certain complexity measure. Negation by failure can be dealt with in a similar fashion.

- *Predicate invention*: CLINT is unable to invent new predicates because it only learns definitions of predicates mentioned by the user. However, using the Constructive Induction by Analogy technique (cf. De Raedt and Bruynooghe [1992b]), it can propose interesting new predicates to the user by analogy to previously learned ones. For example, when it has learned the predicate `father(X,Y)` ⇐ `male(X)` & `parent(X,Y)`, it can later propose the predicate `p(X,Y)` ⇐ `female(X)` & `parent(X,Y)` to the user and ask him/her to name `p`. This may result in the introduction of new predicates in the theory. The basic CIA-technique derives schemata (cf. Wrobel [1989]) from learned clauses and matches these schemata with future starting clauses in order to make a guess at the target conceptor to introduce new predicates.

- *Abduction using types*: The abductive procedure presented above relies very much on the syntax of the clauses in the theory. When `father(X,Y)` ⇐ `male(X)` & `parent(X,Y)` is present, CLINT can relate the predicates `father`, `male`, and `parent`. However, when these predicates are defined in an extensional way, CLINT fails to do so. Therefore, we have enhanced CLINT (cf. De Raedt, Feyaerts, and Bruynooghe [1991]) with an abductive procedure using types. The procedure derives the type-graph from the predicates as in BLIP (Morik, 1989; Kietz, 1989). The type-graph contains information about the relations among different predicates. For example, the type of the first argument of `father` is a subtype of the type of `male` and of the type of the first argument of `parent`. The second argument of `father` is a subtype of the second argument of `parent`. Because of these relations, it is possible to ask about `male(luc)`, `parent(Y,soetkin)`, and `parent(luc,X)` upon receiving a new example `father(luc,soetkin)`. Also in this approach, one would question `male(soetkin)` or `female(soetkin)`.

9.7 RELATED WORK AND CONCLUSIONS

An important point to note is that we have shown (cf. De Raedt [1992]) that CLINT converges to a correct theory in the limit whenever there exists a correct definition of the theory expressible in terms of the languages of CLINT and the initial theory. This means that when the target theory can be expressed using the languages of CLINT and the background knowledge, and the user supplies a sufficient number of examples and constraints, CLINT will find a correct definition of the target theory after processing a finite number of constraints/examples.

We believe that CLINT is very well suited for use as a module in the learning apprentice context. It could, e.g., be used as a learning module of the DISCIPLE system of Tecuci and Kodratoff (1990). Doing so would extend DISCIPLE in several ways because the use of integrity constraints, abduction, postponing, and the shifting of bias of DISCIPLE's explanations would become possible. Alternatively, one could integrate CLINT with BLIP of Morik (1989) and Wrobel (1989), which is a passive learning apprentice that does not query the user. By integrating CLINT and BLIP, one would realize a learning apprentice, where the user can choose—at each moment—between the interactive and the non-interactive mode.

Using CLINT in intensional knowledge base updating is also feasible. This can be illustrated using family relations, e.g., `mother(X,Y)` $\Leftarrow$ `parent(X,Y)` & `female(Y)`, and integrity constraints such as `parent(X,Y)` $\Rightarrow$ `human(Y)`, where `human(X)` $\Leftarrow$ `male(X)` and `human(X)` $\Leftarrow$ `female(X)`. Given an update request to add the fact `mother(lieve,soetkin)`, where `soetkin` is a newborn baby, the system would query for `parent(lieve,soetkin)` and also for `human(soetkin)`, leading it to asking for the sex of the baby. In this way, an effective translation of the update specification is computed. CLINT extends state of the art in intensional knowledge base updating because it inductively derives non-unit clauses and adds them to the theory. CLINT also extends the state of the art in inductive predicate learning by the introduction of constraints. It has to be noted, though, that many of the intensional knowledge base updating techniques use a more general logical framework, including negation as failure (e.g., Bry [1990], Guessoum and Lloyd [1990]). CLINT has also been extended in this respect, see De Raedt (1992). CLINT also differs from the other techniques in the sense that CLINT is interactive, which significantly reduces the combinatorics of the techniques but also makes it more user-friendly.

The work presented here is related to the inductive logic programming paradigm (cf. Muggleton [1992]). Nevertheless, we want to stress that our approach (just like the one of Shapiro [1983]) differs from the mainstream in this paradigm (such as GOLEM of Muggleton and Feng [1992]; LINUS of Lavrac, Dzeroski, and Grobelnik [1991]; and FOIL of Quinlan [1990]) in the sense that our approach aims at deriving (or revising) a whole theory of interrelated predicates in an interactive way. The mainstream of inductive logic programming attempts to upgrade the classical empirical concept-learning setting toward a relational setting (an early approach along these lines is the INDUCE system of Michalski [1980]). These empirical approaches to inductive logic programming focus on learning a *single* predicate from a *given* set of examples. They are able to handle large training sets of examples and to cope with noisy data. In contrast to these empirical approaches to inductive logic programming, we believe that CLINT can be regarded as a true multistrategy concept-learner because it integrates different strategies, techniques, and knowledge sources for learning. This cannot be said of the majority of the other approaches in inductive logic programming, such as Shapiro (1983), Sammut and Banerji (1986), Muggleton and Feng (1992), and Quinlan (1990). The approaches of Muggleton and Feng (1992), Quinlan (1990), and Sammut and Banerji (1986) use basically only one learning strategy—induction—which explains why they cannot be seen as theory revising systems. On the other hand, the early approach of MIS (Shapiro, 1983) can be seen as a theory revisor because it uses both abduction and induction. From a certain perspective, CLINT is a state-of-the-art descendant of MIS that extends MIS in several respects (e.g., the shift of bias, the postponing, and the use of integrity constraints). Rather than searching general to specific as the MIS, CLINT searches specific to general. We also believe that CLINT better exploits the available knowledge and generates more interesting questions than the MIS. Like CLINT and MIS, the system WHY of Baroglio, Botta, and Saitta (1994) (Chapter 12 of this book) also combines induction with abduction to learn predicate definitions from examples.

Another important inductive logic programming system is the system CIGOL of Muggleton and Buntine (1988) that is based on the inverse resolution principle. This system combines features of empirical and interactive inductive logic programming: it queries the user for the truth-value of Horn clauses, it is able to handle examples of multiple predicates, and it is heuristically guided in order to find the most compact predicate definitions and to cope with noise. CIGOL also addresses the issue of predicate invention, which is the automatic introduction of new predicates in the theory by the system. In this way, CIGOL aims at finding the most compact theory that explains the observations. The approach taken in CLINT differs significantly from CIGOL because CLINT only generates simple questions to the user, CLINT is theoretically well-understood (because it converges to theories in the limit), and CLINT has the ability to use integrity constraints and to shift its bias. However, CLINT does not address noise or predicate invention like CIGOL.

9.7.1 MacCLINT: A Public Domain Implementation of CLINT

A user-friendly implementation of CLINT on Apple Macintosh II is available upon request from the authors. To obtain this implementation, send an e-mail request to lucdr@cs.kuleuven.ac.be. MacCLINT has a nice windowing interface and is a stand-alone application developed by Wim Van Holder using MacPRO-LOG.

ACKNOWLEDGMENTS

Maurice Bruynooghe and Luc De Raedt are supported by the Belgian National Fund for Scientific Research. The ideas developed in this chapter were strongly influenced by Yves Kodratoff, Bern Martens, Katharina Morik, and Gheorghe Tecuci. We would also like to thank R.S. Michalski and G. Tecuci for inviting us to write this chapter and Wim Van Holder for his implementation of CLINT on the Apple Macintosh. This implementation was supported by Apple Belgium.

References

Baroglio, C., Botta, M., and Saitta, L. WHY: A System That Learns from First Principles. In R.S. Michalski and G. Tecuci (Eds.), *Machine Learning: A Multistrategy Approach*, volume 4, Morgan Kaufmann, San Mateo, CA, 1994.

Bratko, I. *Prolog Programming for Artificial Intelligence*. Addison-Wesley, Reading, MA, 1986.

Bry, F. Intensional Updates: Abduction Via Deduction. In D. Warren and P. Szeredi (Eds.), *Proceedings of the 7th International Conference on Logic Programming*, pages 561–578. The MIT Press, Cambridge, MA, 1990.

De Raedt, L. *Interactive Theory Revision: An Inductive Logic Programming Approach*. Academic Press, San Diego, CA, 1992. This is a revision of the author's Ph.D. thesis.

De Raedt, L. and Bruynooghe, M. Indirect Relevance and Bias in Inductive Concept-learning. *Knowledge Acquisition*, 2: 365–390, 1990.

De Raedt, L. and Bruynooghe, M. CLINT: A Multistrategy Interactive Concept-learner and Theory Revision System. In *Proceedings of the 1st International Workshop on Multistrategy Learning*, pages 175–191, 1991.

————. Belief Updating from Integrity Constraints and Queries. *Artificial Intelligence*, 53: 291–307, 1992a.

————. Interactive Concept-learning and Constructive Induction by Analogy. *Machine Learning*, 8: 107–150, 1992b.

————. An Overview of the Interactive Concept-learner and Theory Revisor CLINT. In S. Muggleton (Ed.), *Inductive Logic Programming*, pages 163–192 Academic Press, San Diego, CA, 1992c.

De Raedt, L., Bruynooghe, M., and Martens, B. Integrity Constraints and Interactive Concept-learning. In *Proceedings of the 8th International Workshop on Machine Learning*, pages 394–398. Morgan Kaufmann, San Mateo, CA, 1991.

De Raedt, L., Feyaerts, J., and Bruynooghe, M. Acquiring Object-knowledge for Learning Systems. In Yves Kodratoff (Ed.), *Proceedings of the 5th European Working Session on Learning*, volume 482 of *Lecture Notes in Artificial Intelligence*, pages 245–264. Springer-Verlag, New York, 1991.

Gallaire, H., Minker, J., and Nicolas, J.M. Logic and Databases: A Deductive Approach. *ACM Computing Surveys*, 16: 153–185, 1984.

Genesereth, M., and Nilsson, N. *Logical Foundations of Artificial Intelligence*. Morgan Kaufmann, San Mateo, CA, 1987.

Guessoum, A., and Lloyd, J.W. Updating Knowledge Bases. *New Generation Computing*, 8: 71–88, 1990.

Kietz, J.U. Incremental and Reversible Acquisition of Taxonomies. In M. Linster, B. Gaines, and J. Boose (Eds.), *Proceedings of the 2nd European Knowledge Acquisition for Knowledge Based Systems Workshops*, pages 24.1–24.11. Paris, 1988.

Lavrac, N., Dzeroski, S., and Grobelnik, M. Learning Non-recursive Definitions of Relations with LINUS. In Yves Kodratoff (Ed.), *Proceedings of the 5th European Working Session on Learning*, volume 482 of *Lecture Notes in Artificial Intelligence*, pages 265–287. Springer-Verlag, New York, 1991.

Michalski, R.S. Pattern Recognition as Knowledge-guided Computer Induction. *IEEE Transactions on Pattern Analysis and Machine Intelligence*, 2: 349–361, 1980.

————. A Theory and Methodology of Inductive Learning. In R. S Michalski, J.G. Carbonell, and T.M. Mitchell (Eds.), *Machine Learning: An Artificial Intelligence Approach*, volume 1, pages 83–134, Morgan Kaufmann, San Mateo, CA, 1983.

Mitchell, T.M. Generalization as Search. *Artificial Intelligence*, 18: 203–226, 1982.

Mitchell, T.M., Mahadevan, S., and Steinberg, L.I. LEAP: A Learning Apprentice for VLSI Design. In *Proceedings of the 9th International Joint Conference on Artificial Intelligence*, pages 573–580. Morgan Kaufmann, San Mateo, CA, 1985.

Morik, K. Sloppy Modeling. In Katharina Morik (Ed.), *Knowledge Representation and Organization in Machine Learning*, volume 347 of *Lecture Notes in Artificial Intelligence*, pages 70–134. Springer-Verlag, New York, 1989.

Muggleton, S. Inductive Logic Programming. *New Generation Computing*, 8(4): 295–317, 1991.

Muggleton, S., editor. *Inductive Logic Programming*. Academic Press, San Diego, CA, 1992.

Muggleton, S., and Buntine, W. Machine Invention of First Order Predicates by Inverting Resolution. In *Proceedings of the 5th International Conference on Machine Learning*, pages 339–351. Morgan Kaufmann, San Mateo, CA, 1988.

Muggleton, S., and Feng, C. Efficient Induction of Logic Programs. In S. Muggleton, Ed., *Inductive Logic Programming,* pages 281–298. Academic Press, San Diego, CA, 1992.

Plotkin, G. A Note on Inductive Generalization. In *Machine Intelligence*, volume 5, pages 153–163. Edinburgh University Press, Edinburgh, UK, 1970.

Quinlan, J.R. Learning Logical Definition from Relations. *Machine Learning*, 5: 239–266, 1990.

Reiter, R. On Asking What a Database Knows. In J.W. Lloyd (Ed.), *Computational Logic*, pages 96–113. Springer-Verlag, New York, 1990.

Sammut, C., and Banerji, R. Learning Concepts by Asking Questions. In R.S. Michalski, J.G. Carbonell, and T.M. Mitchell (Eds.), *Machine Learning: An Artificial Intelligence Approach*, volume 2, pages 167–192. Morgan Kaufmann, San Mateo, CA, 1986.

Shapiro, E.Y. *Algorithmic Program Debugging*. The MIT Press, Cambridge, MA, 1983.

Smith, R.G., Mitchell, T.M., Winston, H.A., and Buchanan, B.G. Representation and Use of Explicit Justifications for Knowledge Base Refinement. In *Proceedings of the 9th International Joint Conference on Artificial Intelligence*. Morgan Kaufmann, San Mateo, CA, pages 673–680, 1985.

Tecuci G., and Kodratoff, Y. Apprenticeship Learning in Non-homogeneous Domain Theories. In Y. Kodratoff and R.S. Michalski (Eds.), *Machine Learning: An Artificial Intelligence Approach*, volume 3, pages 514–551. Morgan Kaufmann, San Mateo, CA, 1990.

Wilkins, D.C. Knowledge Base Refinement Using Apprenticeship Learning Techniques. In K. Morik (Ed.), *Knowledge Representation and Organization in Machine Learning*, volume 347 of *Lecture Notes in Artificial Intelligence*, pages 249–257. Springer-Verlag, New York, 1989.

Wrobel, S. Demand Driven Concept-Formation. In K. Morik (Ed.), *Knowledge Representation and Organization in Machine Learning*, volume 347 of *Lecture Notes in Artificial Intelligence*, pages 289–318. Springer-Verlag, New York, 1989.

PART
THREE

COOPERATIVE
INTEGRATION

10

LEARNING CAUSAL PATTERNS:

Making a Transition from Data-Driven to Theory-Driven Learning

Michael Pazzani
(University of California, Irvine)

Abstract

This chapter describes an incremental learning algorithm, called causal theory driven learning, that creates rules to predict the effect of actions. Causal theory driven learning exploits knowledge of regularities among rules to constrain learning. We demonstrate that this knowledge enables the learning system to rapidly converge on accurate predictive rules and to tolerate more complex training data. An algorithm for incrementally learning these regularities is described, and we provide evidence that the resulting regularities are sufficiently general to facilitate learning in new domains. The results demonstrate transfer from one domain to another can be achieved by deliberately overgeneralizing rules in one domain and biasing the learning algorithm to create new rules that specialize these over-generalizations in other domains.

10.1 INTRODUCTION

In order to understand the environment, people must learn to predict the effects of their own actions and the actions of others. This prediction process requires the learner to associate state changes with actions. Many researchers have shown that even in very young children, this learning process is constrained by general knowledge of the actions that are likely to be responsible for state changes. Bullock, Gelman, and Baillargeon (1982) and Shultz and Kestenbaum (1985) provide excellent overviews of the types of general constraints that are exploited during the learning of specific causal rules.

Pazzani (1991) proposes a computational learning model that is intended to explain why learning some predictive relationships is more difficult than others for human learners. Here, we report on experiments that show that this learning model provides an advantage over a purely data-driven learner under a variety of circumstances. The learning model relies on an explicit representation of general knowledge of causality. Here, we also propose an algorithm for learning this general knowledge of causality. We computationally explore the hypothesis that much of the general knowledge of causality (and some simple specific causal rules) can be learned by simple correlational processes. Once this general knowledge of causality is acquired, the later acquisition of more complex specific causal rules is constrained and facilitated by the general knowledge of causality that has been acquired. As general knowledge of causality is acquired, the learner shifts learning strategies from a data-driven strategy that attempts to find regularities in a set of examples to a causal theory driven strategy that looks for instantiations of its general knowledge.

In particular, a learner will be described that starts with only temporal knowledge of causality (i.e., temporal contiguity and temporal priority). This knowledge is sufficient to induce simple causal rules. We hypothesize that more general causal knowledge is acquired by finding common patterns in the simple causal rules. This more general knowledge represents additional spatial and configural patterns that are present in causal rules.

To make the problem more concrete, consider the sequence of events in Table 10.1. This is the output of Talespin (Meehan, 1981), a program designed to generate short stories describing actors attempting to achieve goals. We will use Talespin to simulate a world in which the learner must observe actions and predict their results.

The output is divided into a number of discrete time intervals. In each time interval, some actions may be observed, and the state of the world may change. Although this simulated input is necessarily a simplification of the complex world

Table 10.1: An example of the output produced by Talespin, divided into 14 time intervals

---

(0) Karen was thirsty. (1) She pushed the door away from the cupboard. The cupboard was open. (2) She took a small red plastic cup from the cupboard. Mike pushed the light switch. She had the cup. The cup was not in the cupboard. The light was on. (3) She pushed the door to the cupboard. The cupboard wasn't open. (4) The auburn cat pushed a large clear glass vase to the tile floor. Karen pushed the handle away from the cold faucet. The cold water was flowing. The vase was broken. (5) She moved the cup to the faucet. The cup was filled with the water. (6) She pushed the handle to the faucet. The cold water wasn't flowing. (7) Karen dropped the cup to the tile floor. The cup wasn't filled with the water. (8) She pushed the door away from the cupboard. The cupboard was open. (9) She took a small clear glass cup from the cupboard. She had the cup. The cup was not in the cupboard. (10) Karen pushed the handle away from the cold faucet. The cold water was flowing. The phone was ringing. (11) She moved the cup to the faucet. Lynn picked up the phone receiver. The cup was filled with the water. The phone wasn't ringing. (12) Karen pushed the handle to the faucet. The cold water wasn't flowing. (13) She drank the water. The cup wasn't filled with the water. Karen wasn't thirsty.

---

in which a child learns causal rules, we have added a number of complexities to Talespin to make it more realistic but still allow systematic experimentation by varying parameters such as the amount of noise in the data. For example, two actions may occur in the same time interval (e.g., Time 4). Therefore, the agent must be able to determine which effect is associated with which action. This problem is complicated by the fact that some actions may have more than one effect (e.g., Time 9), and some actions may have no effect. In addition, the same action may have different effects (e.g., dropping an object in Times 4 and 7). Finally, some state changes may be observed, although the action that caused the state change may not be observed (e.g., the phone ringing during Time 10).

This learning problem can be summarized as follows:

Given: A sequence of time intervals where each time interval consists of a set of actions and a set of state changes.

Create: A set of rules that predict when a state change will occur.

This chapter first discusses the representation of examples, causal rules, and general knowledge of causality. Next, we review a learning method called causal theory driven learning (CTDL) that makes use of general knowledge of causality to constrain the search for causal rules. Finally, we discuss an extension to causal theory driven learning that allows the general knowledge of causality to be learned from initial observations and demonstrate that the induced knowledge facilitates learning in new domains.

10.1.1 Representation of Examples

To avoid problems of natural language understanding, we will assume that the training examples are in some internal representation. Our learning model will make use of Conceptual Dependency (CD) (Schank & Abelson, 1977), the internal representation used by the Talespin program. A role-filler notation is used to represent CD structures. CD structures have a head and a set of roles and fillers. The filler for a role is a CD structure that must have a head and may have zero or more roles. Common heads are ACT (for actions), STATE (for unary predicates), RELATION (for binary predicates), and PP (for physical objects). For ACTs, the roles used are type, actor, object, from, and to. STATEs have type, actor, and mode roles. RELATIONs have type, actor, val, and mode roles.[1] PPs have a wide variety of roles, such as type, subtype, size, and color. Every individual PP has a special role, unique-id, used to indicate the referent in Talespin's world.

In Talespin, each change of the world is indicated by the assertion of a new STATE or RELATION (indicated by a mode of POS) or the retraction of a STATE or

---

[1] The actor role of STATEs and actor and val roles of RELATIONs may be misnomers. This is terminology used by Talespin. A better name for these roles might be argument1 and argument2.

Table 10.2: A rule indicating that picking up a phone receiver results in the phone not ringing

```
IF   ACT type GRASP
        object PP type RECEIVER
                   component-of ?X
                   (PP type PHONE)
THEN          STATE type RING
                   actor ?X
                   mode NEG
```

RELATION (indicated by a mode of NEG). STATEs and RELATIONs are assumed to hold for all future time intervals until explicitly retracted (cf. Elkan, 1990).

10.1.2 Representation of Causal Rules

The task required by the learner is to predict the state changes that will occur when an action is observed. In order to achieve this task, a set of causal rules is learned. Each rule contains a general description of a class of actions and a description of a state change. Table 10.2 illustrates the representation of a simple rule that indicates that a phone stops ringing after the phone receiver is picked up.[2] A question mark before a symbol (e.g., ?X) indicates that the symbol is a variable. In this rule, the variable is needed to indicate that the phone whose receiver is lifted is the phone that stops ringing. The CD structure after a variable in the antecedent (i.e., PP type PHONE) indicates that the object bound to the variable is constrained to also match that structure.

A variety of tasks could be achieved using rules such as that in Table 10.2. The rule can be used for planning (specifying an action to perform to achieve the goal of stopping the telephone from ringing) or for abductive inference (infer what action may have occurred to account for a phone that stopped ringing). Here, we will consider only a prediction task. When an action is observed, all state changes that are the consequent of rules whose antecedents match that action will be predicted. There are two types of prediction errors that can be made. Errors of omission occur when a state change is observed but not predicted. Errors of commission occur when a state change is predicted but is not observed.

The learner needs to monitor the accuracy of the causal rules that are acquired. This is implemented by associating a confidence that is the ratio of two counters with each rule. One counter is incremented each time the rule makes a prediction; the other is incremented whenever the rule makes an incorrect prediction. In addition, any exceptions to a rule (i.e., actions on which the rule made an

---

[2] Note that this rule is true in Talespin's world. In the real world, the situation is more complex.

incorrect prediction) are stored in memory indexed by the rule.[3] The exceptions are used only for learning and are not used during prediction.

In order to generate a story, Talespin contains a simulator that determines the effects of actions. This simulator is essentially a large Lisp conditional expression that asserts state changes when an action occurs. The causal rules learned can be viewed as a declarative representation of Talespin's simulator.

10.1.3 A Data-Driven Learning Process for Acquiring Causal Rules

A variety of data-driven (i.e., associative) learning theories have been proposed that can address the problem. For example, DIDO (Scott and Markovitch, 1989) performs a similar task (i.e., determining the effects of its own operators rather than observed actions). With a suitable change of representation, neural network systems (e.g., Sutton, 1988) could also be applied to this problem. Here, we briefly describe a data-driven learning method based upon UNIMEM (Lebowitz, 1987). In our learning model, data-driven learning will be used to form initial causal rules. More general principles of causality will be derived from these rules (as described in Section 10.3) and used by the causal theory-driven learning process (described in Section 10.2).

Each time interval is represented by a set of actions and a set of state changes. The learner must acquire rules to indicate which actions are predictive of each state change. An unsupervised learning task is performed at each time interval. First, the observed actions are compared to existing causal rules, and a set of state changes are predicted. Next, the predicted state changes are compared to the observed state changes. The confidence and exceptions are updated for those state changes that were correctly predicted and for those state changes that were predicted but not observed. If there are any unpredicted state changes, the learner is run on all pairings of observed actions with unpredicted state changes.

The learner processes each time interval as it is observed. Because this is an unsupervised learning task, the learner must perform two subtasks (Fisher, 1987). First, because of the variety of training examples, the examples must be aggregated into clusters of similar examples. In this work, we rely on a UNIMEM-like approach to clustering and concentrate on the second subtask: creating a general description of the aggregated examples. This general description is the rule used to make predictions about new examples.

The first example in a new cluster becomes the initial rule. The rule is constructed by using the action as the antecedent and the state as the consequent. If the same object (as indicated by its `unique-id`) fills more than one role in the action or the state, a variable is introduced. Variables represent equality constraints. For

---

[3] There is a maximum number of exceptions that can be indexed by each rule. In this paper, each rule maintains the five most recent exceptions.

example, the variable ?X in Table 10.2 indicates the phone that stops ringing must be identical to the phone whose receiver is picked up. Whenever a new example is added to a cluster, the rule is generalized by dropping any roles that differ between the rule and the example. In addition, if the example does not conform to an equality constraint, the equality constraint is dropped.

10.2 BACKGROUND

Causal theory-driven learning brings additional knowledge to the learning process. Data-driven learners exploit inter-example relationships (i.e., regularities among several training examples). Causal theory driven learning has knowledge of intra-example relationships (i.e., constraints between the role fillers of an action and state change). We call these constraints *causal patterns*. The causal patterns warrant the causal theory-driven learning program to ignore certain regularities between examples. As a consequence, CTDL searches a smaller hypothesis space and would be expected to learn accurate rules from fewer examples (provided that the smaller hypothesis space contains an accurate hypothesis).

At least two learning systems have been developed that make use of general causal knowledge to constrain learning. LUCK (Shultz, 1987) makes use of a general theory of causality to identify the cause responsible for an effect. CTDL (Pazzani, 1987) learns causal rules that are consistent with a general theory of causality. Pazzani (1991) discusses how *causal patterns* can be used to encode a human's general knowledge of causal relationships. In particular, the causal patterns represent spatial and temporal conditions under which human observers report that an action appears to result in a state change.

10.2.1 Representation of Causal Patterns

The causal theory driven learning procedure can only learn causal rules that conform to one of the causal patterns. Here, we discuss two types of causal patterns:

Exceptionless: An exceptionless causal pattern applies when all the examples in a cluster are followed by the same state change (or when there is only one example).

Dispositional: A dispositional causal pattern applies when some examples in a cluster are followed by a state change, but others are not. It postulates that a difference in a particular role filler is responsible for the different results.

Table 10.3 displays one exceptionless causal pattern: an action performed on a component of an object may result in a state change to that object. The causal

Table 10.3: An exceptionless causal pattern: An action performed on a component of an object may result in a state change to that object

CAUSE	ACT object PP component-of ?O
EFFECT	STATE actor ?O

Table 10.4: A dispositional causal pattern

CAUSE	ACT object ?O
EFFECT	STATE actor ?O
DISPOSITION	object

rule in Table 10.2 (picking up a phone results in the phone not ringing) conforms to this pattern.

For each exceptionless pattern, there may be a dispositional pattern. A dispositional pattern limits the search for differences between positive and negative examples to one or more roles of the action. Table 10.4 displays a dispositional causal pattern. In this pattern, there is a single dispositional role: object. This pattern indicates that when similar actions performed on an object have different results, and they are performed on different objects, the differing roles of the object are responsible for the different result. This pattern would be useful in creating a rule that describes the difference between the result of a cat knocking over a large clear glass vase during Time 4 in Table 10.1 and Karen dropping a small red plastic cup in Time 7. Such a rule would indicate that glass objects break when they fall, but plastic objects do not. Note that correlation between examples is needed to determine that the composition rather than the color of the object is important. However, this correlation is constrained to the object role. Therefore, CTDL will not entertain a hypothesis that indicates that objects break when dropped by cats but not by humans.

10.2.2 The Process of Theory-Driven Learning

Pazzani (1990) describes the causal theory-driven learning process in detail. Here we only provide an overview that is needed to understand how CTDL uses new causal patterns acquired through the process described in Section 10.3. Both the data-driven and causal theory-driven learning strategies use the same clustering process. Causal theory-driven learning occurs whenever a new example is added to a cluster, and the current rule did not make a correct prediction. If a causal pattern matches the situation, CTDL will form a causal rule that is consistent with both the data and the causal pattern.

10.2.3 Experiments with CTDL

In this section, experiments with CTDL in OCCAM are reported. OCCAM is a multistrategy learning system that includes an explanation-based, a causal theory-driven, and a data-driven learning component. We compare CTDL to the data-driven learning (DDL) algorithm in OCCAM.[4] We test the following hypotheses:

1. CTDL will tolerate more complex training data than DDL. In this experiment, multiple actions (and state changes) will occur at the same time.

2. The CTDL and DDL algorithms will degrade gracefully with noisy training data. Here, we consider one type of noise that was created by making the operators in Talespin's world nondeterministic. With a certain probability, an action may have no effect. For example, glass objects may break only 75% of the time they are knocked off a counter onto the floor.

3. A combination of CTDL and DDL will tolerate incomplete and incorrect sets of causal patterns. Here we will compare the performance of CTDL and DDL combined to the performance of DDL alone. In this combination, DDL is run only if CTDL fails to find a rule (i.e., no causal pattern matches the experiences).

We will use Talespin to generate test and training examples for these learning algorithms. In this world, actors may have one of three goals (thirsty, hungry, or bored) and perform actions to achieve these goals. The thirsty goal is satisfied by drinking a glass of milk or water from the refrigerator or water from the faucet. Table 10.1 shows a typical thirsty story. The hungry goal is satisfied by eating a piece of fruit from either the counter or the refrigerator. The bored goal is satisfied by playing catch with either a ball or a balloon. Random actions may occur during any story (cats knocking objects over, phones or door bells ringing, etc.), and actors may have accidents (dropping objects, throwing balls into windows, throwing a balloon into a rose bush). A total of approximately 60 rules are needed to predict the state changes in all these domains. The fact that 10 causal patterns can facilitate learning indicates that there is a structure in Talespin's world that can be exploited to constrain the learning process.

10.2.3.1 Simultaneous Actions

In most realistic situations, more than one action is occurring at the same time. In order to run this experiment, we modified Talespin so that with a certain probability, P, two contiguous time intervals are merged into one. This merging is

---

[4] In previous publications on OCCAM, the DDL algorithm was called SBL, and the CTDL algorithm was simply called TDL (theory-driven learning).

done recursively so that, for example, there is a P^2 probability that three contiguous time intervals are merged. Ten runs were made of DDL and CTDL on the same randomly generated sequences of Talespin output of 500 time intervals (corresponding to roughly 25 stories). The errors of omission and commission of each algorithm are measured by testing on 600 action-state change pairs after every 20 time intervals for the first 100 examples and every 50 time intervals for the remaining 400 training time intervals.

DDL takes a conservative approach and learns one rule for each action that occurs in the same time interval as a state change. When an error of commission later occurs, the "confidence" in each rule is lowered (by incrementing an exception counter), but the rule is not deleted. Such rules are not deleted because some actions do not always have the same effect (e.g., sometimes a glass cup does not break when it is dropped). In this experiment, to be more fair to DDL, we will measure errors of commission in two manners. With the first measure, errors of commission will be reported as the percent of total predicted state changes that were not observed. A second measure takes the confidence in the prediction into account by multiplying the total number of predictions and the total number of unsubstantiated predictions by the confidence of the rule that made the prediction.

CTDL will not learn a rule if a training example does not conform to a known causal pattern. As a consequence, CTDL is predicted to be less sensitive to a complex learning environment in which multiple actions occur simultaneously. Figure 10.1 shows the mean percentage of errors for DDL and CTDL as a function of the number of training examples when P=0.35. The graph in Figure 10.1

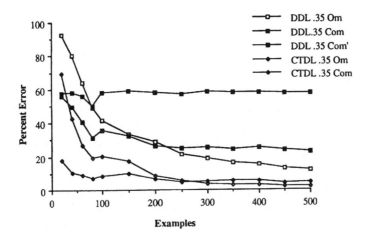

Figure 10.1:   A comparison of CTDL and DDL when there is a 0.35 probability that time two actions occur simultaneously. Errors of omission and commission are plotted as a function of the number of training examples. Com' indicates that the errors of commission calculation takes account of the confidence of the prediction.

demonstrates that CTDL converges on an accurate set of rules more rapidly than DDL.

With this complex training data, CTDL has fewer errors of omission and commission than DDL. Taking the confidence of the prediction into account (the line labeled DDL .35 Com' in the figure) lessens the difference between the DDL and CTDL. This indicates that the predictions of DDL made with greater confidence are more likely to be correct. To simplify the graph, CTDL errors of commission weighted by the confidence are not displayed. CTDL typically has higher confidence values, so the two measures of errors of commission are very close in value. The results of this experiment confirm the prediction that CTDL will be less sensitive than DDL when multiple actions occur at the same time.

10.2.3.2 Learning from Noisy Data

In learning causal rules, we consider one type of noise. With a certain probability, an action will not have any effect. In Talespin's world, this is a natural type of noise. For example, glass objects do not always break when struck, and balloons don't always pop when they fall onto a grass lawn. The CTDL and DDL algorithms were designed to tolerate training data with this type of noise. In particular, DDL only finds commonalities between examples in which there is a state change. When there is noise in the training data, there are fewer positive examples, so more errors of omission would be expected as the amount of noise increases. Exceptionless causal patterns in CTDL operate similarly. However, dispositional patterns attempt to find a role filler (or conjunction of role fillers) that differentiates the actions accompanied by state changes from those that are not. In this case, noise in the training data may cause CTDL to blame an incorrect role filler. Because the algorithm attempts to find a role filler that appears in the fewest stored negative examples (rather than a role filler that appears in no negative examples), it is expected to tolerate some amount of noise. Nonetheless, one would predict a greater percentage of errors of commission with increased noise.

In order to test these predictions, an experiment was run in which 20% and 40% of the state changes were deleted randomly from the training data. We measured the accuracy (on noise-free test data) in the same manner as the first experiment. Figure 10.2 displays the results of these experiments. To avoid clutter, DDL and CTDL with 20% noise are not shown for errors of omission. The values typically fell between the algorithm with no noise and the algorithm with 40% noise.

The graphs show that, as expected, the algorithms degrade gracefully with this type of noise. The algorithms were not intended to deal with other forms of noise (e.g., noise in the role fillers or state changes sometimes occurring without a cause). We expect that the algorithms would require modification before tolerating other types of noise. However, this noise does not arise naturally in this domain.

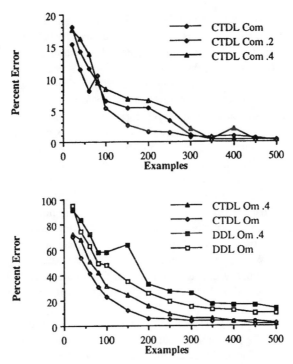

Figure 10.2:   Errors of omission and commission when learning from noisy data as a function of the number of training examples. DDL does not make errors of commission on this data

10.2.3.3 Incorrect Causal Patterns

CTDL is one of the learning components of OCCAM (Pazzani, 1990). When a new time interval is observed, if the state change was already expected (i.e., the observed outcome could be predicted by an existing rule), then no learning is necessary. Otherwise, OCCAM first tries EBL, then CTDL, then DDL. The rationale here is that EBL is expected to produce accurate rules from fewer training examples than CTDL, and CTDL produces more accurate rules than DDL. Thus, this particular combination of learning methods is intended to maximize the learning rate. In addition, the learning system is intended to be widely applicable because it can fall back on a data-driven learning algorithm in novel domains. Furthermore, the data-driven and causal theory-driven learning methods create rules that can be used by the explanation-based methods. Therefore, as OCCAM learns, it can switch from a knowledge-free to a knowledge-intensive learner. In Section 10.3, we describe how the empirical learning algorithm can learn causal patterns to be used by CTDL. Here, we describe an experiment that demonstrates that a combination of CTDL and DDL can be used when the causal patterns are incomplete and incorrect. This is particularly important because newly created causal patterns are likely to be incorrect, and the system will initially have an incomplete collection of causal patterns.

There are 10 causal patterns used by OCCAM. Six of these patterns were replaced by incorrect versions. Incorrect versions of three patterns were formed by replacing the dispositional roles with other (i.e., irrelevant) roles. Such a change might cause CTDL to search for differences between actors while a correct rule has a difference in the object role. If no such difference exists, then DDL will be used. Three other patterns were modified by changing the location of a variable. For example, a pattern requiring the object of an action to be the actor of a state was changed so that the actor of the action was required to be the actor of a state. Such a change would make the pattern match situations that are not causally related and not match sequences that are causally related. In the latter case, DDL will be tried immediately. In the former case, CTDL will initially create a rule that makes inaccurate predictions. When further examples are seen, the pattern will no longer be matched (e.g., the equality constraints that were coincidentally true in the initial few examples do not hold in later examples), and DDL will be used to form a new rule.

We ran 10 trials of CTDL with these incorrect causal patterns combined with DDL and measured the percentage errors. All time intervals always had exactly one action, and there was no noise in the training data. Runs were made of DDL and CTDL on 10 randomly generated sequences of Talespin output of 500 time intervals (corresponding to roughly 25 stories). The errors of omission and commission of each algorithm are measured by testing on 600 action-state change pairs after every 20 examples for the first 100 examples and every 50 examples for the remaining 400 training examples. Figure 10.3 shows the mean percentage of errors for DDL alone, CTDL alone (with correct causal patterns), and CTDL with incorrect and incomplete patterns combined with DDL (labeled Bad CTDL in the legend) as a function of the number of training examples. In the combined system, approximately 45% of the final rules were learned with CTDL, and the remainder were learned with DDL. The fact that the combined method has fewer errors of omission than DDL indicates CTDL is able to determine when it is not applicable and allows DDL to learn accurate rules. However, the fact that the percentage of errors of commission of the combined methods is higher than that of CTDL (with a correct theory) indicates that it takes CTDL several examples to determine that an accurate rule cannot be formed that conforms to a causal pattern. This also indicates that the changes made to create the incorrect patterns were not so random that the patterns did not match any training examples.

Whether CTDL should always be preferred to DDL in a simple noise-free learning environment depends upon the relative cost of errors of omission and errors of commission. However, in more complex learning environments, CTDL

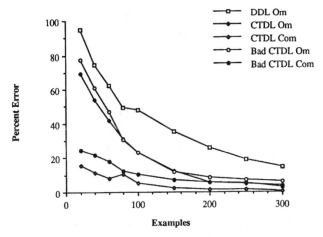

Figure 10.3: Errors of CTDL with incorrect causal patterns (Bad CTDL), CTDL, and DDL as a function of the number of training examples

exhibits both fewer errors of omission and commission. Furthermore, using the methods in combination, but preferring CTDL, yields faster learning rates than just DDL. This combination can be applied even when the causal patterns are incomplete and incorrect.

10.3 LEARNING CAUSAL PATTERNS

The previous section has shown how causal patterns can be represented and used to constrain the hypothesis space. Here, we discuss how causal patterns can be learned from examples. The motivation for this work is to enable CTDL to be adapted more easily to new domains. An initial subset of the data is used to acquire general information to apply to the acquisition of specific knowledge in the remainder of the data.

DDL implicitly makes use of a single causal pattern: "if a state change occurs in the same time interval as an action, then the action caused the state change." This simple causal pattern doesn't contain any constraints between causes and effects. This allows the system to create rules without any more specific causal patterns. By noticing common patterns in established rules, new causal patterns can be created. In the future, hypotheses that conform to one of these patterns are preferred.

10.3.1 An Algorithm for Creating Causal Patterns

We have explored a variety of algorithms for inducing new causal patterns. A number of approaches based upon aggregating rules into clusters of similar rules and forming generalizing among the rules failed. The weak link here was the aggregation algorithm. Although UNIMEM's clustering algorithm produces reasonable clusters of events to generalize to form rules, it did not seem to produce reasonable clusters of rules to generalize to form causal patterns. The rules in such clusters were typically so dissimilar that there was not a generalization in the hypothesis language (conjunctions of role fillers with equality constraints). We also experimented with adapting other clustering algorithms (e.g., COBWEB [Fisher, 1987]) to this task without success (because COBWEB cannot represent equality constraints and because COBWEB deals with data represented as attribute-value pairs).

The goal of creating causal patterns is to form a general pattern that can be instantiated (by the CTDL algorithm) to form a new rule. Here, we describe an "eager" approach to creating new causal patterns. In effect, whenever a rule is created with DDL, the approach determines the most specific causal pattern that could be instantiated to create the same rule with CTDL. If the rule learned by DDL is revised, then the pattern is revised.

After forming a rule, an exceptionless causal pattern can be formed by retaining only the equality constraints of the rule (and the heads of the CD structures to make a syntactically correct causal pattern).[5] In addition, a dispositional pattern can be created by adding dispositional roles for every role filler in the rule. Roles explicitly encoding a type hierarchy are not used as dispositional roles because these hierarchical roles are treated specially by the CTDL algorithm. Causal patterns formed in this manner are a deliberate overgeneralization of the training data. Future causal rules that have the same equality constraints as a causal pattern are preferred to those that do not.

An incremental algorithm was implemented to create new causal patterns whenever a rule is created by DDL. If a pattern with the same equality constraints already exists, a new pattern is formed by finding the union of the dispositional roles. A dependency is recorded between each causal pattern and the rule (or rules) that resulted in the formation of the pattern. Whenever a rule is revised, the causal pattern that was formed from the rule is also revised. For example, if a role is dropped from a rule (and no other rule with the same causal pattern uses that role), then a dispositional role is removed from the causal pattern. If an equality constraint is dropped from a rule, and the rule is the only support of a causal pattern, the causal pattern is deleted, and a new causal pattern is formed from the rule (or merged into an existing pattern with the same equality constraints).

---

[5] If there are no equality constraints between the action and a state change, no causal pattern is created. In effect, this algorithm assumes that some object must be involved somehow in both an action and a state change. The algorithm learns additional constraints in terms of which roles of the action can be associated with roles of the state change. CTDL takes advantage of these constraints to search a reduced hypothesis space.

An example of creating and revising a causal pattern will help to illustrate the algorithm. Assume the first example seen is "Lynn (age 6, blond hair) took a banana from the counter. Lynn has the banana." The rule and causal pattern in Table 10.5 is created. The equality constraints of the rule are preserved in the causal pattern. Every role that has a filler in the rule becomes a dispositional role. For example, the actor's age is present in the rule. Therefore, a disposition role is created to indicate that the age of the actor may be used to distinguish actions that result in a state change from those that do not.

A second similar example—"Mom (brown hair, age 29) gave Karen (age 4, blond hair) a balloon. Karen has the balloon."—causes the rule and pattern to be revised. In the rule, the constraint that the `actor` of the `act` be the same as the `to` of the `act` and the `val` of the `relation` is dropped. This occurs because in the first example, Lynn is both the actor and the destination, but in the second example, the actor and destination of the action differ. In addition, a number of role-filler constraints are dropped such as the hair color of the actor (but not the to) and the age of the actor. The revisions to the rule also force revisions to the causal pattern. For example, the variable in the actor role of the cause is removed. In addition, dispositional roles corresponding to constants in the original rule (e.g., the actor's age) are dropped.

The goal of the above algorithm is to create causal patterns by data-driven means from an initial subset of the training data so that causal theory-driven learn-

Table 10.5: The initial rule and causal pattern formed from a single example. Those parts that are underlined are deleted when the second example is seen.

	Rule		Pattern	
IF	ACT type ATRANS	CAUSE	ACT	actor ?a
	actor ?A: PP type PERSON			object ?b
	age 6			to ?a
	gender FEMALE	EFFECT	RELATION	actor ?b
	hair BLOND			val ?a
	object ?B: PP type FRUIT	DISPOSITION:	actor age	
	subtype BANANA		actor gender	
	color YELLOW		actor hair	
	to ?A: PP type PERSON		object color	
	age 6		to age	
	gender FEMALE		to gender	
	hair BLOND		to hair	
	from PP type COUNTER		from color	
	color WHITE		from composition	
	composition TILE			
THEN	RELATION type POSSES			
	actor ?B			
	val ?A			
	mode POS			

ing may be used on later parts of the training data. Because of the combination of CTDL and DDL, the combined system gradually shifts from using DDL to using CTDL to learn new rules. As a result, when the system is trained on one domain, it learns a new domain more quickly, provided that the rules in the new domain conform to the same general patterns as the rules in the old domain.

10.3.2 Experimental Results

We ran an experiment to test whether causal patterns applied in one domain can facilitate learning in a new domain. We ran 10 trials of training the system of 15 randomly generated stories of actor's satisfying the bored goal followed by 15 randomly generated stories about the hungry goal. Appendix I contains a typical hungry and a typical bored story. The combined system was using CTDL and DDL and creating new causal patterns. Next, all the rules (but not the causal patterns) were deleted. We then measured the percentage error on 400 training examples of CTDL using the induced causal patterns, CTDL using the hand-coded causal patterns, and DDL from stories about achieving thirsty goals. This particular training sequence was selected because the thirsty stories are the most complex and varied. The error was measured by testing 200 randomly generated examples taken from thirsty stories.

Figure 10.4 shows the percentage error of the three learning systems. CTDL with learned rules is called LCTDL in this graph. LCTDL does not perform as well as CTDL. An examination of the patterns learned indicates that some patterns were more specific than hand-coded patterns. In particular, some learned patterns included more equality constraints than the hand-coded ones. If these spurious equality constraints were deleted, several specific rules could be merged into a more general pattern identical to the hand-coded ones. As a consequence, fewer situations will match these specific patterns, resulting in more errors of omission for LCTDL. In addition, the examination of the learned causal patterns indicates that they contain more dispositions than the hand-coded rules. As a result, the LCTDL relies more on correlation and less on the knowledge encoded in the causal pattern to find differences between positive and negative examples.

The graph does indicate that LCTDL has fewer errors of omission than DDL. This demonstrates that the induced rules, like the hand-coded rules, capture regularities between rules that can be used to constrain future learning. Learning causal patterns in one domain accelerates learning in a new domain by enabling OCCAM to use CTDL rather than DDL in the new domain.

10.3.3 Psychological Implications of CTDL

Early work on children's understanding of causality (Piaget, 1930) pointed out differences in causal explanations among various age groups. In spite of more recent evidence (Leslie and Keeble, 1987) that very young infants are able to

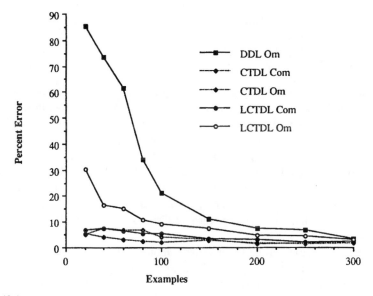

Figure 10.4: A comparison of DDL, CTDL, and LCTDL (CTDL with learned causal patterns)

perceive causal relationships, there is no question that older children are better at attributing causality than younger children. A current research topic in developmental psychology addresses the question of how much of this causal knowledge is innate and how much is learned empirically (Siegler, 1975; Bullock, Gelman, and Baillargeon, 1982; Carey, 1984; Shultz et al., 1986). The amount of initial knowledge required to induce causal patterns provides additional evidence in support of the view that much of the general knowledge of causality is learned empirically. In particular, in addition to representational biases, the only initial knowledge of causality required by this computational model is temporal contiguity. From this knowledge, it is possible to learn simple predictive rules. The additional knowledge of causality (e.g., spatial contiguity) is derived from common patterns in the predictive rules. Once learned empirically, this knowledge is available to constrain future learning.

10.3.4 The Role of Conceptual Dependency in CTDL

Causal theory-driven learning is intended to be independent of the representation of causal patterns and training data. For example, the causal pattern "If an action on an object is accompanied by a state change for the object, then the action results in the state change" might be represented as follows:

$$\forall a,s,t_a,t_s,l_a,l_s \ (Act(a)\&States(s)\&Time(a,t_a)$$
$$\&Time(s,t_s)\&(t_s\text{-}\varepsilon<t_a<t_s)\&Loc(a,l_a)$$
$$\&Loc(s,l_s)\&Near(l_a,l_s))$$
$$\Rightarrow Result(a,s)$$

However, it is well known that the representation of the training data can have a major impact on the speed and accuracy of learning programs. OCCAM makes use of Conceptual Dependency to represent its training examples. Conceptual Dependency was designed primarily to facilitate inference for natural language understanding. The Talespin program was implemented without any thought that a learning program would attempt to learn rules that describe the effects of actions in its world. Therefore, in this research, we have not engineered the representation to suit the needs of the learning program. Nonetheless, there are several important properties of CD that simplify the learning task. Here, we identify some of these properties.

First, CD attempts to be explicit and canonical. For example, the representation of "punch" would be to apply a force, and the object applying the force is the hand of the actor. The representation of kick is to apply a force with the foot. Therefore, if one sees an example in which someone punches something and breaks his hand and an example where someone kicks something and breaks his foot, a regularity can be detected easily. However, if instead the training examples are not explicit (e.g., kick does not refer to foot) and canonical (kick and punch are not represented in terms of applying a force), then detecting this regularity is greatly complicated. For example, a poor choice of representation for learning might be

```
1. kick(john1,wall) & twisted(foot4) & foot_of(john1,foot4,left)
2. punch(bob7,wall) & sprained(hand3) & hand(hand3) &
   right(hand3) part_of(bob7,hand3)
```

Note that the learning task is not impossible. With suitable axioms, sprained and twisted could be related, and the relationship between the actors and the body parts could be identified. However, these tasks will require inference. Furthermore, the clustering process would be complicated greatly. By attempting to be explicit and canonical, CD allows these regularities to be detected and generalized by a straightforward matching process. Learning with such a representation succeeds only when the designer of the representation has foreseen which items need to be explicitly represented so that meaningful generalizations can be made by deleting role fillers and introducing equality constraints.

A second useful property of CD is that a syntactic regularity between two representations implies that there is a semantic relationship between the objects being represented. The roles in CD are intended to have a constrained meaning. In representations without explicit role names, the same effect might be achieved by having a systematic interpretation of the position of arguments to predicates. Without such a system interpretation, there is no reason to believe that there would be regularities between rules, and CTDL would have one pattern for each rule. For example, a poor choice of representation for learning would be

```
1. kick(john1,wall,foot4) &
   injured(foot4)
2. punch(wall,hand3,bill1) &
   injured(hand3)
3. butt(head6,goat3,wall) &
   injured(head6)
```

Note that, once again, additional knowledge could be supplied to relate these actions via an inference process (e.g., instrument(head6), instrument(hand3), etc.). However, CD allows regularities between rules to be discovered by a simple matching process that finds equality constraints between roles.

10.3.5 Limitations

Causal theory-driven learning is intended to be applicable to learning causal rules between simple, overt, physical actions and their immediate effects. In these cases, there are constraints on the possible sorts of predictive relationships between actions and state changes. Indeed, we deal with only a limited form of causality in which the effect of an action is immediately apparent (cf. Shoham, 1990). In this class of relationships, the conceptual dependency link, result (Schank & Abelson, 1977), is appropriate. More complex causal relationships, involving feedback or many intermediate states (e.g., the relationships between the tax rate and the rate of unemployment), are beyond the scope of CTDL. In such a domain, a suitable system of representation for monetary actions has not been worked out, so that it is not possible to express constraints on the relationships between possible monetary actions and their effect. Furthermore, CTDL does not capture the sense of "cause" that means "make more likely to occur," as in snow causes automobile accidents.

The algorithm that we have implemented for learning causal patterns has some additional limitations. In particular, it only creates exceptionless and dispositional causal patterns. OCCAM also contains "historical" patterns[6] in which a sequence of events is necessary to achieve a state change (e.g., shaking a can of soda followed by opening the can results in the soda squirting out). The reason for this limitation is that the data-driven learning algorithm that creates causal rules does not attempt correlations between pairs of actions in different time interval and state changes. A more general instance of this same problem is that CTDL is not

---

[6] This is not a problem in our experiments because historical patterns are not needed to make predictions in Talespin.

capable of making predictions about objects with unobservable internal states.[7] In such a case, there may be an arbitrary time interval between an action that changes the internal state of an object and a subsequent action whose effect is dependent on the internal state. Unfortunately, this implies that CTDL is limited in its ability to reason about the goals and plans of agents.

10.4. RELATED WORK

Causal theory driven learning is in some ways similar to a variety of previous work. In particular, the exceptionless causal patterns of CTDL are similar to determinations (Davies and Russell, 1987) and rule models (Davis, 1978). The causal theory driven learning procedure is similar to SPARC (Dietterich, 1980) in that both procedures create rules by instantiation of skeletal rules (called causal patterns in CTDL). Finally, CTDL is related to other systems that learn with background knowledge such as META-DENDRAL (Buchanan and Feigenbaum, 1978) and explanation-based learning (EBL) (DeJong and Mooney, 1986; Mitchell, Keller, and Kedar-Cabelli, 1986) with overly general domain theories (e.g., Mooney and Ourston, 1989; Cohen, 1990).

10.4.1 Determinations

Determination rules have been proposed as a form of knowledge that supports analogical reasoning and justifies why one generalization may be given a great deal of credence, and another generalization may be viewed suspiciously, although both generalizations may have the same number of positive examples and negative examples. For example, one determination rule states that nationality determines language. This determination allows the generalization that all Americans speak English to be created after encountering a single example of an American speaking English. The generalization that all Americans smoke cigarettes would not be created after encountering a single example of an American smoking a cigarette because there is no determination rule that states that nationality determines smoking behavior. For creating new rules from a single training example, the following form of a determination rule is most useful (Russell and Grosof, 1989):

$$\forall yz.\{\exists x.P(x,y) \wedge Q(x,y)\} \Rightarrow$$
$$\{\forall w.P(w,y) \Rightarrow Q(w,z)\}$$

For example, the determination rule that nationality determines language would be represented as

---

[7] Pearl and Verma (1991) discuss an approach to discovering hidden variables. However, it only takes advantage of temporal constraints on causal relationships.

$\forall yz.\{\exists x.Nationality(x,y) \land Language(x,y)\} \Rightarrow$
$\{\forall w.Nationality(w,y) \Rightarrow Language(w,y)\}$

Causal patterns, like determination rules, are a weaker form of background knowledge than the domain theory of EBL. In particular, the rules learned by EBL follow deductively from the domain theory. With causal patterns and determinations, the rules learned follow from the background knowledge *and* the training examples. However, unlike learning from determinations, CTDL does not require that the new rule *deductively* follow from the causal patterns and the examples. Rather, the causal patterns are heuristics that suggest rules subject to empirical validation and refinement. Furthermore, a rule learned by CTDL may tolerate exceptions, provided that no refinement of the rule has fewer exceptions.

A procedure for inducing determination rules for binary predicates from training data is described in Russell (1989). In effect, it operates by instantiating P and Q to binary predicates, finding pairs from the joint domain of P and Q and calculating how often the determination rule holds. A determination factor from 0 to 1 is computed rather than require that the determination rule be universally true. This algorithm has been used to demonstrate that interesting and potentially useful determinations exist. However, because the learning algorithm is not incremental, it has not been demonstrated that the acquisition of such determinations from an initial subset of the data facilitates acquiring accurate rules in the remaining data.

10.4.2 TEIRESIAS

TEIRESIAS (Davis, 1978) is a system designed to help an expert formulate rules for a rule based expert system. One way it assists an expert is by having rule models. A rule model encodes the type of preconditions typically associated with a rule that makes a particular type of conclusion. For example, rules that identify the category of an organism typically have preconditions describing the site of a culture, an infection, and a portal of entry of an organism. When a new rule is entered, TEIRESIAS suggests that it mention preconditions typically associated with the rule's conclusion. The rule models in TEIRESIAS can be created by finding commonalities among rules with similar conclusions. Although it has not been demonstrated, these rule models should be able to provide constraints that facilitate automated learning of new rules.

10.4.3 SPARC

In some respects, CTDL is similar to SPARC (Dietterich, 1980; Dietterich and Michalski, 1986), a system that learns rules that describe patterns in sequential data. SPARC approaches this problem by having abstract, parameterized skeletal rules that can be instantiated to form specific rules. For example, one skeletal rule represents periodic sequences of length N. This schema can be instantiated if commonalities are found between examples that are N items apart in a sequence. Once a rule is created, it is tested to determine how well it fits the data. CTDL also can be viewed as creating new rules by instantiating skeletal rules (i.e., causal patterns). In addition, like SPARC, CTDL instantiates a template with values obtained by constrained correlation among training instances. A primary difference between CTDL and SPARC is that CTDL is accompanied by an algorithm that induces rule templates from training data.

10.4.4 META-DENDRAL

META-DENDRAL (Buchanan and Feigenbaum, 1978; Buchanan and Mitchell, 1978) is a program that learns cleavage rules to predict which bonds in a molecule will be broken in a mass spectrometer. It starts with a half-order theory that is overly general (i.e., it predicts more bonds will break than actually occur). A program called RULEGEN uses the half-order theory to propose rules that are then tested to see if they are true in many positive examples. Next, a program called RULEMOD refines and revises the rules to ensure that few negative examples are covered by a rule. In addition, RULEMOD removes redundant rules.

In CTDL, like SPARC, the prior knowledge is abstract knowledge that can be instantiated to form specific rules. In contrast, RULEGEN uses its knowledge in a generate-and-test fashion. It would be possible to use the causal patterns of CTDL in a generate-and-test manner. The patterns could generate rules for all combinations of action and state types. These rules would then be tested against the data and incorrect rules deleted. However, by making use of at least one example, the number of rules generated and then tested is considerably reduced.

10.4.5 EBL with Overly General Theories

The causal patterns may be viewed as an overly general domain theory. In fact, the algorithm for creating causal patterns deliberately overgeneralizes the data by only including equality constraints. It might be possible to use the overly general domain theory to explain why a particular action resulted in a state change. Then some explanation-based algorithm designed to deal with overly general domain theories could be used to create rules. Here, we discuss how IOU (Mooney and Ourston, 1989) and A-EBL (Cohen, 1990) might approach this problem. IOU (Mooney and Ourston, 1989) operates by first forming a definition via m-EBG (Flann and Dietterich, 1989) for the positive examples. Next, IOU removes any negative examples from the training set that are correctly classified by the results of m-EBG. Finally, IOU deletes those features from the remaining negative and all positive examples and runs an induction algorithm on the features. The final concept is formed by conjoining the result of induction over the unexplained features with the result of m-EBG. The explanations produced by causal patterns would be overly general explanations. Therefore, the result of m-EBG would typically result in errors of commission. This result is specialized by an induction process that would eliminate (most of) the errors of commission. The primary difference between IOU and CTDL is that CTDL uses dispositional causal patterns to focus the search for a difference between the positive and negative examples. Because CTDL searches a more restricted hypothesis space, one would expect that it would converge on an accurate rule from fewer examples than IOU.

The A-EBL system (Cohen, 1990) is also designed to handle overly general domain theories. It operates by finding all proofs of all positive examples and uses a greedy set covering algorithm to find a set of operational definitions that cover all positive examples and no negative examples. Unlike IOU, A-EBL will not specialize an operationalized proof to avoid covering any negative examples. A-EBL would not be able to address the problem of learning accurate rules from causal patterns. A-EBL is best suited to those theories that are overly general because the theory has superfluous, incorrect disjunctions. In contrast, causal patterns are overly general because they contain too few preconditions. As a result, no disjunction of the operationalized proofs will exclude the negative examples. Instead, the operationalized proofs need to be specialized by some induction process.

10.4.6 Multistrategy Learning

There are a variety of approaches to combining multiple learning strategies in an integrated learning system. For example, in Gemini (Danyluk, 1991), an empirical and an analytical learning method have predefined, specific tasks. The result is an integrated strategy in which each learning method has a separate and distinct role. Other systems, such as Meta-AQUA (Cox and Ram, 1991), treat the selection of learning strategies as an additional problem to be solved by the learner. That is, the system reasons about what learning strategy is appropriate for each learning problem.

In OCCAM, there are three learning strategies, and each learning strategy can perform the same task (acquiring a predictive relationship). The strategies differ according to the amount of knowledge that they acquire. EBL requires the most detailed, specific knowledge (i.e., a set of causal rules capable of explaining how an action produces a state change). CTDL requires more general knowledge of causality and finds causal rules that are instantiations of this more general knowledge. DDL places no such restrictions on the causal rules that are learned. The control strategy of OCCAM is quite simple. It uses the most knowledge-intensive learning strategy that is capable of finding a causal rule to account for an unexpected state change. However, when the less knowledge-intensive strategies are successful, they acquire knowledge that can be used in the future by the more knowledge-intensive strategies. As a consequence, as OCCAM learns, it shifts from data-driven learning methods to knowledge-intensive methods.

In more recent work (Pazzani and Kibler, 1992), a tighter integration of learning methods is proposed in which an explanation-based and a data-driven learning algorithm both attempt to produce rules. An information-based evaluation function (Quinlan, 1990), uniformly applied to the hypotheses produced by each method, determines which hypothesis to accept. Furthermore, the hypothesis produced by one method may be refined further by either method.

10.5 CONCLUSIONS

We have shown how intra-example constraints may be represented and used to constrain the problem of learning a collection of predictive rules. The resulting system converges on accurate concepts more rapidly than a similar system that does not make use of these constraints. Finally, we have shown how these constraints may be discovered in an initial subset of the data and used to facilitate later learning.

ACKNOWLEDGMENTS

This research is supported by a National Science Foundation Grant IRI-8908260 and by the University of California, Irvine, through an allocation of computer time. Comments by Kamal Ali and Caroline Ehrlich on an earlier draft of this chapter were helpful in improving the presentation.

References

Buchanan, B., and Feigenbaum, E. Dendral and Meta-Dendral: Their applications dimension. *Artificial Intelligence*, 11, 5–25, 1978.

Buchanan, B., and Mitchell, T. Model-directed learning of production rules. In D. Waterman and F. Hayes-Roth (Eds.), *Pattern-directed inference systems* (pp. 297–312). New York: Academic Press, 1978.

Bullock, M., Gelman, R., and Baillargeon, R. The development of causal reasoning. In W. Friedman (Ed.), *The developmental psychology of time* (pp. 209–254). New York: Academic Press, 1982.

Carey, S. *Conceptual change in childhood*. Cambridge, MA: MIT Press, 1984.

Cohen, W. Learning from textbook knowledge: A case study. *Proceedings of the Eighth National Conference on Artificial Intelligence* (pp. 743–748). Menlo Park, CA: AAAI, 1990.

Cox, M., and Ram, A. Using introspective reasoning to select learning strategies. *Multi-strategy Learning Workshop* (pp. 217–230). Harpers Ferry, VA, November 7–9, 1991.

Danyluk, A. Gemini: An integration of analytical and empirical learning. *Multi-strategy Learning Workshop* (pp. 191–206). Harpers Ferry, VA, 1991.

Davies, T., and Russell, S. A logical approach to reasoning by analogy. *Proceedings of the Tenth International Joint Conference on Artificial Intelligence* (pp. 264–270). Milan, Italy, San Mateo: Morgan Kaufmann, 1987.

Davis, R. Knowledge acquisition in rule-based systems: Knowledge about representation as a basis for system construction and maintenance. In D. Waterman and F. Hayes-Roth (Eds.), *Pattern-Directed Inference Systems*. New York: Academic Press, 1978.

DeJong, G., and Mooney, R. Explanation-based learning: An alternate view. *Machine Learning, 1*, 47–80, 1986.

Dietterich, T. Applying general induction methods to the card game Eleusis. *Proceedings of the First National Conference on Artificial Intelligence* (pp. 218–220). Menlo Park, CA: AAAI, 1980.

Dietterich, T., and Michalski, R. Learning to predict sequences. In R.S. Michalski, J.G. Carbonell, and T.M. Mitchell (Eds.), *Machine Learning: An artificial intelligence approach* (Vol. 2) (pp. 63–106). San Mateo, CA: Morgan Kaufmann, 1986.

Dietterich, T., London, B., Clarkson, K., and Dromey, G. Learning and inductive inference. In P. Cohen & E. Fiegenbaum (Eds.), *The handbook of artificial intelligence* (Vol. 3) (pp. 323–511). San Mateo, CA: Morgan Kaufmann, 1982.

Elkan, C. Incremental, approximate planning. *Proceedings of the Eighth National Conference on Artificial Intelligence* (pp. 145–150). Menlo Park, CA: AAAI, 1990.

Fisher, D. Knowledge acquisition via incremental conceptual clustering. *Machine Learning, 2*, 139–172, 1987.

Flann, N., and Dietterich, T. A study of inductive methods for explanation-based learning. *Machine Learning, 4*, 187–226, 1989.

Lebowitz, M. Experiments with incremental concept formation: UNIMEM. *Machine Learning, 2*, 103–138, 1987.

Leslie, A., and Keeble, S. Do six-month-old infants perceive causality? *Cognition, 25*, 265–288, 1987.

Meehan, J. Talespin. In R. Schank and C. Riesbeck (Eds.), *Inside computer understanding: Five programs plus miniatures*. Hillsdale, NJ: Lawrence Erlbaum Associates, 1981.

Mitchell, T., Keller, R., and Kedar-Cabelli, S. Explanation-based learning: A unifying view. *Machine Learning, 1*, 47–80, 1986.

Mooney, R., and Ourston, D. Induction over the unexplained: Integrated learning of concepts with both explainable and conventional aspects. *Proceedings of the Sixth International Workshop on Machine Learning* (pp. 5–7). San Mateo, CA: Morgan Kaufmann, 1989.

Pazzani, M. *Creating a memory of causal relationships: An integration of empirical and explanation-based learning methods*. Hillsdale, NJ: Lawrence Erlbaum Associates, 1990.

————. A computational theory of learning causal relationships. *Cognitive Science, 15*, 401–424, 1991.

Pazzani, M., and Kibler, D. The role of prior knowledge in inductive learning. *Machine Learning, 9*, 57–94, 1992.

Pearl, J., and Verma, T. A theory of inferred causation. In *Proceedings of the Second International Conference on Principles of Knowledge Representation and Reasoning* (pp. 441–452). San Mateo, CA: Morgan Kaufmann, 1991.

Piaget, J. *The child's conception of physical causality*. London: Kegan Paul, 1930.

Quinlan, R. Learning logical definitions from relations. *Machine Learning, 5*, 239–266, 1990.

Russell, S. *Analogical and inductive reasoning*. London: Pitman Press, 1989.

Russell, S., and Grosof, B. Declarative bias: An overview. In P. Benjamin (Ed.), *Change of representation and inductive bias*. Norwell, MA: Kluwer Academic Press, 1989.

Schank, R., and Abelson, R. *Scripts, plans, goals, and understanding*. Hillsdale, NJ: Lawrence Erlbaum Associates, 1977.

Scott, P., and Markovitch, S. Learning novel domains through curiosity and conjecture. *Proceedings of the Eleventh International Joint Conference on Artificial Intelligence* (pp. 669–674). San Mateo, CA: Morgan Kaufmann, 1989.

Shoham, Y. Nonmonotonic reasoning and causality. *Cognitive Science, 4*, 213–252, 1990.

Shultz, T. *Learning and using causal knowledge*. Paper presentation at the Meeting for Research in Child Development. Baltimore, MD, April 1987.

Shultz, T., Fisher, G., Pratt, C., and Rulf, S. Selection of causal rules. *Child Development, 57*, 143–152, 1986.

Siegler, R.S. Defining the locus of developmental differences in children's causal reasoning. *Journal of Experimental Child Psychology, 20*, 512–525, 1975.

Sutton, R. Learning to predict by the methods of temporal differences. *Machine Learning 3*, 9–44, 1988.

APPENDIX I. TYPICAL STORIES INVOLVING HUNGER AND BOREDOM

Karen was hungry. She asked Mom, "Would you give me the yellow long banana?" Mom picked up it. She had it. The phone was ringing. Dad picked up the receiver. The phone wasn't ringing. He had the receiver. He pushed the light switch. The light was on. The black cat pushed a large red plastic vase to the tile floor. Mom gave Karen the banana. Karen had it. Mom didn't have it. Karen peeled it. She ate it. She wasn't hungry. Karen threw the peel to the basket. She didn't have the peel. Mom pushed the light switch. The light wasn't on.

Lynn was bored. Lynn asked Karen, "Would you throw me the balloon?" She asked Mom, "Would you give me the balloon?" Mom pushed the door away from the cupboard. The cupboard was open. The auburn cat pushed a large clear glass vase to the tile floor. The vase was broken. She took the balloon from the cupboard. She had the balloon. The cupboard didn't have the balloon. She pushed the door to the cupboard. The cupboard wasn't open. She exhaled into the balloon. It was inflated. Mom picked up the balloon. She had it. She exhaled into it. It was inflated. She let go of it. She didn't have it. It was flying. It wasn't inflated. She picked it up. She had it. She exhaled into the balloon. It was inflated. She tied it. It was sealed. She gave Lynn the balloon. Lynn had it. Mom didn't have it. Lynn went to the outside. Karen went to the outside. Lynn threw Karen the balloon. Karen had it. Lynn didn't have it. Karen threw Lynn the balloon. Lynn had it. Karen didn't have it. Lynn threw Karen the balloon. Karen had it. Lynn didn't have it. Karen dropped the balloon to the green pointed grass. The balloon burst. She didn't have it.

11

BALANCED COOPERATIVE
MODELING

Katharina Morik
(University of Dortmund)

Abstract

Machine learning techniques are often used for supporting a knowledge engineer in constructing a model of part of the world. Different learning algorithms contribute to different tasks within the modeling process. Integrating several learning algorithms into one system allows it to support several modeling tasks within the same framework. In this chapter, we focus on the distribution of work between several learning algorithms on the one hand and the user on the other hand. The approach followed by the MOBAL system is that of **balanced cooperation**; i.e., each modeling task can be done by the user or by a learning tool of the system. The MOBAL system is described in detail. We discuss the principle of multifunctionality of one representation for the balanced use by learning algorithms and users.

11.1 INTRODUCTION

The overall purpose of knowledge acquisition as well as the one of machine learning has often been described as constructing a model of part of the world, on purpose. Knowledge acquisition includes knowledge elicitation, i.e., interviewing experts and using written material in order to get at the knowledge about a domain, as well as building up a knowledge base. Building a knowledge base for a particular application is a modeling process.[1] The process of forming a knowledge base can be performed by a knowledge engineer using knowledge acquisition environments. These are special editors and interfaces for knowledge acquisition. In this case, the knowledge acquisition is performed manually. This is knowledge acquisition in the narrow sense. Machine learning can support the knowledge engineer by creating parts of the knowledge base automatically. In this case, at least parts of the knowledge acquisition are performed automatically. If we use the term "knowledge acquisition" in the narrow sense, machine learning is alternative to knowledge acquisition. Both (manual) knowledge acquisition and machine learning are ways to support a human user in building a knowledge base. Knowledge acquisition environments support the user by structured editors and interviewing tools. The user has to type in rules as well as some cases or examples. Machine learning supports the user by acquiring rules automatically. The user has to provide for cases or examples.

We can describe the tasks of the modeling process in more detail and derive requirements that a system has to fulfill if it is to support this process. Building up a knowledge base means, of course, to enter knowledge items, e.g., facts and rules. If a system is to support the knowledge engineer constructing a model, it must **accept new items** and integrate them into the knowledge base. During the modeling process, the knowledge engineer needs to inspect the model built so far. Hence, the system must present the state of the domain model and allow the user to **inspect** it. The inspection may show that some parts of the knowledge base are not as they should be. Therefore, the system must also support **revisions** of all modeling decisions of the user. For instance, some rules may need to be refined. Even the designed representation language may need some revisions. Therefore, a system must support the **refinement** of rules or rule sets and the introduction of **new features** or concepts.

The first two requirements are fulfilled by most of the knowledge acquisition environments. Revisions are frequently supported only by a text editor. Then, it is up to the user to check consistency and integrity of the revised domain model. The user is supported only in performing the addition of new items and the inspection of the domain model. One of the first knowledge acquisition environments, however, the system TEIRESIAS, asked the user for missing rules and correcting rules as well as to enhance the representation language (Davis, 1982).

Machine learning algorithms are most often used for automating the construction of rules as additional items of the knowledge base. Automatic refinement and automatic construction of new features or concepts (constructive induction) are also now being provided by some machine learning systems. Moreover, inspection can

---

[1] For details of the modeling process, see Morik (1989, 1991).

also make good use of machine learning. Hence, for all the modeling tasks listed above, there exists a machine learning tool which automatizes at least parts of it.

A system that integrates several learning tools, each responsible for performing a different modeling subtask, is a multistrategy learning system (Michalski, 1994, Chapter 1 in this book). Questions concerning the **cooperation of tools** are whether one tool can use the results of another, whether several tools can use the same knowledge items, and whether a tool can call another one. MOBAL is such a multistrategy learning system, where the learning tools cooperate by means of input-output data to solve the global modeling task. A multistrategy learning system also needs some information about the domain and the desired domain model given by the user. The **cooperation with the user** is necessary even for the most advanced learning system. This is not a disadvantage. On the contrary, the user should guide the learning and be in control of the modeling process. On one hand, we appreciate machine learning to automate some tasks. On the other hand, we still want the users to perform their tasks—supported by the system. The question is how to organize the cooperation of user and system tools such that both system and user contribute to model-building. For MOBAL, a synergistic effect can be stated that is the result of both the user and the learning tools contributing to the global modeling task.

11.2 COOPERATION

There are different ways to use machine learning algorithms for knowledge acquisition. They correspond to a different distribution of work between system and user. The work share has consequences for the knowledge representation.

11.2.1 Work Share between System and User

We may distinguish the following three prototypical ways of distributing the work between system and user in modeling a domain:

1. The one-shot learning where the user prepares examples and background knowledge and then runs an algorithm on the data (examples are ID3 [Quinlan, 1983], FOIL [Quinlan, 1991], and KLUSTER [Morik and Kietz, 1989; Kietz and Morik, 1991]).

2. The interactive learning where the user prepares examples and background knowledge and then interacts with a learning system (examples are DISCIPLE [Kodratoff and Tecuci, 1989] and CLINT [De Raedt, 1991]).

3. Balanced interaction of system and user where learning contributes to preparing background knowledge, to enhancing the domain knowledge, and to inspecting the (learned) knowledge (an example is MOBAL, described in this chapter).

These options of how to use machine learning correspond to different **tasks** handled by a learning system. A learning task can be described by a certain type of input and the produced output. An additional characteristic of the learning task is whether the learning is performed incrementally (which can be the case in the second and third options). Of course, the same learning task can be applied to various domains. In the first option, the user calls a learning algorithm for one particular task. Most often, this task is to learn a set of rules from examples of complementary classes. The second two options have the learning system cover a broader range of tasks. Each learning task corresponds to a learning tool that solves it—regardless of whether implemented as separate modules or in one module.

Whereas in the first two options the user is requested to give some particular **information**, in the third option, the user can give any information, and the system uses it. Of course, the information must be sensible. However, the user is free to enter, e.g., facts or rules or term sorts or predicate sorts. That is, the distribution of work between system and user is strictly prescribed in the first two options, whereas it is flexible in the third one.

The **control** of the modeling process is in the users' hands in the first option. They call the learning tool. In the second option, the system is in control. The system prompts the user to give the needed information. In the third option, control is mixed. The users can call tools explicitly as in the first option. If they don't want that, the flow of control between the tools is organized by the system. The users are never prompted to input a (counter-)example or a declaration of background knowledge. However, by setting some parameters, they can state that they want to be asked by the system what is to be done at certain decision points.

In the first option, **revisions** of the learning results are performed by the user in an edit-and-compile cycle with no more support than a text editor can give. If new, negative examples are acquired from the application, a new example set must be constructed, consisting of the new and some already known examples. The learning algorithm then constructs new rules that probably are better than the ones learned before. In the second option, some revision of rules is performed by a learning tool because of negative examples. In the third option, learning techniques are used for refinement and the construction of new features or concepts. More-over, revisions of all modeling decisions that have been made are supported by some knowledge editing tools.

The prototypical ways of using learning (1–3 above) illustrate the aspects of work share between system and user:

- Which tasks are performed by the user; which tasks are performed by the system?
- Which information is given by the user; which information is constructed or derived by the system?
- Is the user, the system, or both in control of the modeling process?
- Which revisions are supported by the system; which revisions are automatically done by a learning tool?

If the user as well as the system can perform a task, construct knowledge items of a certain kind, run (learning) tools, and revise given knowledge, then we call such a system **balanced cooperative**. MOBAL is such a balanced cooperative system. It will be described in detail in the next section.

11.2.2 Multifunctionality

The use of the system has consequences for the knowledge representation. In the first way of using a tool, the representation can easily be tailored for the needs of the one algorithm. The representation of a multistrategy learner (options 2 and 3) has to integrate different representations of different tools, or the one representation is to be designed with respect to several, possibly conflicting needs. The Machine Learning Toolbox integrates several learning systems, each with its own representation (Morik, Causse, and Boswell, 1991). The integration problem is then to transfer *given* representation formalisms into a canonical one. In contrast, the MOBAL system is a multistrategy learner that integrates various tools using a *uniform* representation. The integration problem with respect to knowledge representation is then to develop a formalism that is powerful enough to suit all tools well and that is still tractable.

Balanced cooperative modeling additionally demands that all knowledge sources (examples, background knowledge, declarations, rules) have to be represented such that the system, as well as the user, can easily input, modify, and inspect the knowledge. This constrains the representation to be designed. If revisions of all knowledge entities have to be processed and their consequences have to be maintained by the system, this constrains the design of a representation even further.

11.3 COOPERATION IN MOBAL

All the knowledge needed for problem solving in a particular domain can be input by the user. In this case, all the information is given by the user who performs all modeling tasks and completely controls the modeling process. The user is supported by an inference engine and a human-computer interface (see below). However, the user does not need to input almost everything. For each knowledge item that the user might input, there exists a corresponding learning tool that can acquire parts of that knowledge. The basic input that the system expects from the user are facts and rule models (see next section). Of course, a system cannot create a model without any given information! But also to those basic items, there exist corresponding capabilities of MOBAL, namely, the inference engine (deriving facts) and the model acquisition tool (producing rule models). Between the extremes of modeling by the user alone and automatic modeling on the basis of user given examples by the system, all variations of work share are possible. In particular, an interactive layout of the representation language, followed by automatic rule learning on the basis of example facts, is a good start. The user entering some rules that have to be valid in the domain may then lead to knowledge revision and concept formation. Then, applying rule learning again and perhaps entering new rule models enhances the domain model further. It is a matter of users' style whether the topology is entered in the layout phase or is created by the system on the basis of learned and entered rules. MOBAL does not prescribe any strategy but aims at supporting a user's individual working routine.

11.3.1 MOBAL's Representation

The MOBAL system is an environment for building up, inspecting, and changing a knowledge base. Before we present the learning tools, we describe the items that constitute a domain model in MOBAL.

The knowledge items integrated by the inference engine of MOBAL (Emde, 1991) are

- **Facts**, expressing, e.g., relations, properties, and concept membership of objects (`owner(luc,diane1)` and `not(owner(luc,mercedes))` are facts).
- **Rules**, expressing, e.g., relations between concepts, necessary and sufficient conditions of concepts, and hierarchies of properties (`owner(X,Y)&involved (Z,Y) --> responsible(X,Z)` is a rule).
- **Sorts**, expressing a structure of all the objects (constant terms) of the domain model.
- **Topology of predicates**, expressing the overall structure of the rules of the domain model.
- **Rule models**, expressing the structure of the rules to be learned.

The items are represented in a restricted higher-order logic that was proven to be tractable (Wrobel, 1987). The user need not know all about the meta-predicates and the meta-rules in which they appear. The user also does not need to know the internal representation format. The windows of the human-computer interface provide presentations, both as graphics and as text, of the knowledge base that are understandable without knowing the internal data structures. The user beginning an application regularly starts with facts and rules that are easy to understand. In the following, the knowledge items are described.

11.3.1.1 Facts

Facts are used to state relations, properties of objects, and concept membership. Facts are represented as function-free literals without variables. The arguments of a predicate are of a particular *sort*. A fact `p(o1,o2,o3)` is only well-formed if the constant terms `o1`, `o2`, and `o3` belong to the sorts of the first, second, or third argument place of `p`, respectively. For instance, the term at the first place of the predicate `involved` must be a member of the sort of events; the term at the second place must be a member of the vehicle sort. The form of a fact is $p(t_1,...,t_n)$, where p is a n-ary predicate and t_j is a constant term or a number of the sort s_j.

The mapping from a fact to a truth value may obey a fuzzy logic because in principle, the inference engine handles continuous truth values (Emde, 1991). However, usually, it is difficult for a user to assign a fuzzy truth value to a fact. Therefore, only the truth values `unknown`, `true`, `false`, and `contradictory` are used. A derived or input fact without explicit negation is interpreted as `true`. Every fact that is to be interpreted as `false` must be negated explicitly. This explicit negation has some advantages compared with the closed world assumption. It enables the user to input incomplete examples, to build up the model incrementally. The closed world assumption requires the user to know in advance which statements are necessary to complete the description of an example, but, as was stated above, modeling does not start with such a precise idea. Therefore, leaving out some statements in one example does not mean the negation of these statements. Hence, MOBAL interprets missing information simply as `unknown`.

Explicit negation also allows the user to explicitly contradict a derived fact of the system. Supposed, the inference engine has derived the fact

```
owner(luc, diane1)
```

and the user knows that this is not true. The user then inputs

```
not(owner(luc, diane1))
```

As a result, the fact `owner(luc, diane1)` becomes `contradictory`.

An explicit contradiction does not lead to the counter-intuitive behavior of standard logic that all formulas become true. Instead, the contradictory parts of the knowledge-base are excluded from inference processes. Hence, facts that are not contradictory keep their truth values. Contradictions are resolved by a knowledge revision component (Wrobel, 1989).

11.3.1.2 Rules

In MOBAL, rules correspond to Horn clauses. In addition, the applicability of rules is maintained. For each variable occurring in a rule, its domain is represented as a *support set* (Emde, Habel, Rollinger, 1983; Wrobel, 1989). In the normal case, the support set is a tuple of the sets of all objects. The rule `owner(X,Y) & involved(Z,Y) --> responsible(X,Z)` has a support set giving the domains for `X,Y,Z`. In the regular case, these are `all`. The support set then is `all x all x all`. It is also possible to restrict the applicability of a rule to a more special support set. This can be done by exceptions of a variable's domain, by a tuple of exceptions of the support set, or by an expression of a variable's domain by a concept. The above rule is only valid for events that are members of the concept `minor_violation`.

The domain of variable z is restricted to instances of minor (traffic law) violations: all x all x minor_violation is the correct support set for that rule.[2]

More formally, let all denote the set of all objects of a universe of discourse, D_i denote all or subsets of this set, T_j be an n-tuple of constant terms, and $t_1...t_k$ be constant terms (corresponding to particular objects in D), covered by a concept C. Then the form of a support set for a rule with the variables $X_1,...,X_n$ is

$$(X_1,...,X_n) \text{ in } D_1 \times ... \times D_n \text{ except } \{T_1,...,T_j\}$$

where the except part can be empty.

The T_j are tuples of objects that should not be instances of the variables $X_1,...,X_n$ of the rule because the rule would then lead to a contradiction. In a tuple T_j, each term can be of a different subset of all. In our example, such a tuple is (luc, renault2, event3).

A particular D_i can be restricted by a set of exceptions, $\{t_1,...,t_k\}$, written D_i except $\{t_1,...,t_k\}$; in our example, it is all except {event3, event12, event13}. The variable's domain D_i can also be restricted to a particular concept, such as minor_violation in the example above.

11.3.1.3 Sorts

Sorts are used to guarantee the (semantic) well-formedness of predicates in facts and rules. Sorts can be named and given by the user in a predicate declaration: owner/2: <person>, <vehicle>. This means that the two-place predicate owner accepts only terms of sort person as the first argument and terms of sort vehicle as the second argument. It is not well-formed to state owner(john, michael). A sort covers a subset D_i of all. The sorts that are built automatically by the sort taxonomy tool have constructed names, such as arg1(owner) denoting the set of terms occurring at the first place of the predicate owner.

Sorts with the same set of terms form a class. For instance, arg1(owner) and arg1(responsible) have the same constant terms, e.g., [luc, yves, cathy]. Together, they form a class: class21: [arg1(owner), arg1(responsible)] [luc, yves, eve].

Classes are organized in a lattice. The most general class is all; the most special class is the empty class. There are subclasses and intersection classes. The lattice of classes gives an overview of all sorts and classes, their subset relations, and their intersections. In this way, the structure of an application domain can be presented with respect to the objects of that domain. Figure 11.1 shows an excerpt of the lattice of sorts for the traffic law domain.

---

[2]In Germany, the owner of a car has to pay a fine for a minor violation, even if he was not driving the car.

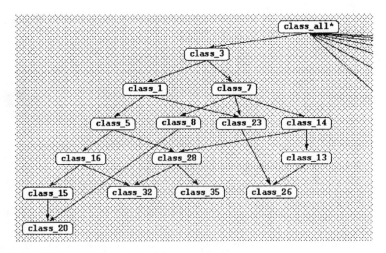

Figure 11.1:   Excerpt of a lattice of sort classes

11.3.1.4 Topology of Predicates

The topology of predicates is used to guarantee the (semantic) well-formedness of rules. Sets of predicates form a named node of a graph. For instance, the node called Beurteilung (English: evaluation), represented as

```
tnode: Beurteilung -Preds: [illegal_parking, responsible,
unsafe_vehicle_violation] -Links: [places,circumstances,laws]
```

contains the predicates illegal_parking, responsible, and unsafe_vehicle_violation. In the graph, the subnodes of this node are called

```
[Orte, Umstaende, Verbote/Gebote, Fahrzeug, Verhalten]
```

(English: [places,circumstances,laws, vehicle, behavior]). In a well-formed rule, if the predicate symbol of the conclusion is a member of a node TN (e.g., evaluation), the premises can only use predicate symbols from a subnode of TN (e.g., places,circumstances,laws,vehicle,behavior) or TN itself. For instance, it is not well-formed to conclude, from the assurance contract of a vehicle's owner, the evaluation of the owner's parking behavior.

The topology graph, where the nodes represent sets of predicate symbols that can be premises of the supernodes, gives an overview of possible rules in an application domain. Figure 11.2 shows the topology graph for the traffic law domain.

The topology graph can be viewed as a generalization of determinations (Davies and Russell, 1987). There, it is stated that a rule that relates some particular predicates is sensible. The topology generalizes this to sets of predicates: rules

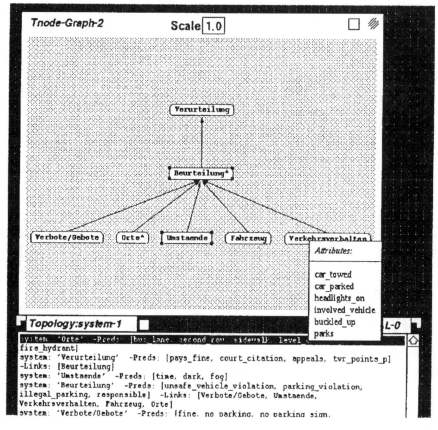

Figure 11.2:   Topology graph

that use predicates of the same topology node TN or a predicate in TN for the conclusion and predicates of subnodes of TN for the premises are sensible.

11.3.1.5 Rule Models

A rule model is a rule in which predicate variables are used instead of actual predicates of an application domain.[3] A predicate variable can be instantiated by a predicate symbol of the same arity. There is a substitution Σ for predicate variables. Let RS be a rule model; then RSΣ is a (partially) instantiated one. If all predicate

---

[3] Rule models of MOBAL are completely different from the rule models of TEIRESIAS (Davis, 1982). Whereas MOBAL's rule models show the syntactic structure of rules, the ones of TEIRESIAS show semantically the rules involved in derivation paths of certain facts.

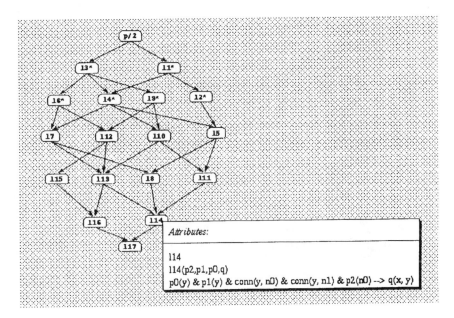

Figure 11.3:   Generality structure of rule models

variables are substituted by predicate symbols, the rule RSΣ is predicate ground. Hence, a fully instantiated rule model is a rule.

The rule model `R1(X,Y)& R2(Z,Y) --> Q(X,Z)` can be instantiated Σ: `{R1/owner, R2/involved, Q/responsible }`, thus becoming our example rule. Rule models are ordered with respect to their generality such that the generality of fully instantiated rule models is given by theta-subsumption (Plotkin 1970). RS1 is more general than RS2 iff for all Σ there exists a substitution of terms σ such that $RS2\Sigma \subseteq RS1\Sigma\sigma$. The above rule model is, for instance, more general than the rule model `R1(X,Y)&R2(Z,Y)&R3(X,Y) --> Q(X,Z)` because every fully instantiated rule of the first one is a subset of the second one.[4] Σ is not allowed to replace different predicate variables by the same predicate symbol. Rule models are labeled by generated names, such as r1 or l2. The generality structure is presented as a graph, where the labels of rule models are the nodes, and the generality relations are the links (see Figure 11.3).

Rule models can also be instantiated partially. All possible instantiations of all rule models together form the *hypothesis space* for rule learning in MOBAL. The

---

[4] The more general rule model must be instantiated to become a subset of the more special one. This is the underlying meaning of theta-subsumption: a more general rule must be instantiated to become a subset of a more special rule.

hypothesis space is structured by the generality structure of rule models. This is used by the rule discovery tool (see below) in order to prune branches of rule models where no instantiation can lead to an accepted rule.

The following rule models can be used to model neighborhood relations. The domain predicate symbol `conn` states a neighborhood relation; the predicate variables `p0`, `p1`, `p2`, `p3`, and `q` can be instantiated to characterize the related objects. The most general rule model is the statement of a two-place predicate that always is true. The next general rule model has in addition a one-place premise.

```
r0(q)  :  → q(x,y).
r1(p0,q)  :  p0(y)  → q(x,y).
r2(p1,p0,q)  :  p0(y) & p1(y)  → q(x,y).
r3(q)  :  conn(y,n0)  → q(x,y).
r4(p0,q)  :  p0(y) & conn(y,n0)  → q(x,y).
r5(p1,p0,q)  :  p0(y) & p1(y) & conn(y,n0)  → q(x,y).
r6(q)  :  conn(y,n0) & conn(y,n1)  → q(x,y).
r7(p0,q)  :  p0(y) & conn(y,n0) & conn(y,n1)  → q(x,y).
r8(p1,p0,q)  :  p0(y) & p1(y) & conn(y,n0) & conn(y,n1)  → q(x,y).
r9(p0,q)  :  conn(y,n0) & p0(n0)  → q(x,y).
r10(p1,p0,q)  :  p0(y) & conn(y,n0) & p1(n0)  → q(x,y).
r11(p2,p1,p0,q)  :  p0(y) & p1(y) & conn(y,n0) & p2(n0)  → q(x,y).
r12(p0,q)  :  conn(y,n0) & conn(y,n1) & p0(n0)  → q(x,y).
r13(p1,p0,q)  :  p0(y) & conn(y,n0) & conn(y,n1) & p1(n0)  → q(x,y).
r14(p2,p1,p0,q)  :  p0(y) & p1(y) & conn(y,n0) & conn(y,n1) & p2(n0)
    → q(x,y).
r15(p1,p0,q)  :  conn(y,n0) & conn(y,n1) & p0(n0) & p1(n1)  → q(x,y).
r16(p2,p1,p0,q)  :  p0(y) & conn(y,n0) & conn(y,n1) & p1(n1) & p2(n1)
    → q(x,y).
r17(p3,p2,p1,p0,q)  :  p0(y)&p1(y)&conn(y,n0)&conn(y,n1)& p2(n0)&p3(n1)
    → q(x,y).
```

11.3.2 MOBAL's Learning Tools

The MOBAL system includes several learning tools:

- A rule discovery tool (RDT) that is a model-based, first-order logic learning algorithm inducing rules from facts.
- A concept formation tool (CLT) that induces necessary and sufficient conditions for concepts from positive and negative examples.
- A model acquisition tool (MAT) that abstracts rule models from rules.
- A sort taxonomy tool (STT) that clusters constant terms occurring as arguments in facts.
- A predicate structuring tool (PST) that abstracts rule sets to an overall structure of the knowledge base.

To describe each of the learning tools in detail requires much more space than we have in this chapter. Because we want to concentrate on the use of the tools—either by the user or by another tool—it is sufficient to describe them as black boxes and only indicate the principle of how they work.

11.3.2.1 Rule Discovery Tool

The rule discovery tool RDT helps the user to find regularities in facts. The *task* is that of learning from observations or discovering regularities in order to predict new events.

Input: a set of facts, a set of rule models

Output: a set of rules that are most general inductive generalizations of the facts

The necessary *input* to this model-based inductive algorithm are facts and rule models. It is not necessary that the facts be complete descriptions of examples. If rules are already learned or given by the user, they are taken into account by the algorithm. In particular, they are not re-discovered, and they are not contradicted by a hypothesis for learning. Moreover, the inference engine performs forward inferences from (learned or given) rules, hence "saturating" the knowledge base for learning.

The learning *strategy* is top-down induction; i.e., the most general generalization is specialized until a rule is found that obeys a user-given acception criterion.

The rule discovery tool can be *called* in different ways. It can be called with a time limit so that the rule discovery tool learns within this CPU time limit and then stops. This allows using it incrementally. The aim is that it can learn in the background during the modeling activity of the user. It then tries to learn about the predicate the user inputs as the predicate symbol of a fact. If the user wishes to focus on a particular predicate or a list of predicates, the rule discovery tool looks for rules with these predicates in the conclusion. The set of predicates can be given by clicking on a node of the topology graph. The rule discovery tool can also be called from the concept formation tool with a particular set of facts. The list of rule models is given by a parameter. The default is to use all rule models that are part of the domain model. The evaluation criteria for accepting a hypothesis can be set by the user. The basic building blocks for defining criteria are prepared. A default setting is given, but the user can define particular criteria and input them as parameter settings.

The *learning result* is a set of rules. The rules are not bound together in order to build sufficient and necessary conditions for concept membership, nor is there an ordering of rules such as is in decision trees. Also, relations that hold between features are not distinguished from relations that hold between concepts or between features and concepts. The user may interpret the learned rules as characterizing concepts or as background knowledge. The learning result is used by the inference engine; hence, the rule discovery tool performs *closed-loop learning*.

The basic idea behind this learning in predicate logic is to instantiate given rule models systematically and test the instantiations (i.e., rules) against ground facts. First, the most general rule model is instantiated. If an instance (i.e., a rule) is not accepted with respect to the acception criterion and still enough facts are available, the next special rule model is instantiated. This procedure is similar to Shapiro's refinement operator (Shapiro, 1981). However, whereas the refinement operator builds up a complete hypothesis space, the hypothesis space of MOBAL's rule discovery is restricted by the rule models. Because the rule models regularly do not cover the forms of all possible Horn clauses, they restrict the hypothesis space.

For a rule model, each possible instantiation is tested. An instantiation is possible if the predicates that substitute predicate variables of the rule model have a compatible arity, sort restriction, and topology restriction. That is, the resulting rule hypothesis must be well-formed with respect to the sorts and the topology of predicates (see above). This restricts the hypothesis space further. For instance, the most general rule models can be `P(X)-->Q(X)`, `R(X,Y)-->Q(X,Y)`. All 1-ary domain predicates with the same sort of an argument type that are in the same or linked topology node are tried as instances of the first rule model. If, for an instantiation Q/q and P/p there are many matching facts but not all of them justify the hypothesis, then the next special rule model is tried, e. g., `p(X)&R(X,Y)-->q(X)`. All compatible 2-ary predicates are tried as instantiations of R. Specializing hypotheses stops if a rule already exists or becomes accepted or if there are not enough facts that could match the (more special) hypothesis. As is easily seen, MOBAL's rule discovery is much quicker than, e.g., FOIL (Quinlan, 1991), if the rule models are well-suited for the desired learning results. If a rule model is missing that would correspond to the desired result, the rule discovery will not find the wanted rule.[5]

11.3.2.2 Concept Formation Tool

The concept formation tool CLT learns from positive and negative examples. The *task* is to define a concept on the basis of some concept instances:

Input: a set of positive examples, a set of negative examples, a set of rule models

Output: a set of rules giving the sufficient and necessary conditions of a concept

---

[5] For a detailed description of RDT, see Kietz and Wrobel (1991).

The new concept can serve as a feature for some other concepts. In other words, MOBAL's concept formation tool can be used to construct new features. Its *input* is a set of rule models; the name of the concept to be learned; and facts, among which are those with the target concept name as predicate symbol. If this fact is positive, it contributes to a positive example. If this fact is negated, it contributes to a negative example. The concept can be a relational one; i.e., a two-place predicate can be defined by the concept formation tool. As is the case for the rule discovery, for the concept formation, the user can also input an acception criterion as a parameter. The list of rule models to be used for concept formation need not be identical with the list used for rule discovery.

The concept formation tool can be *called* by the user or by the knowledge revision module.[6]

The *learning result* is a set of rules that represent the sufficient and necessary conditions for concept membership. The sufficient conditions are rules with the concept in the conclusion. The necessary conditions are rules with the concept as a premise.

The concept formation tool uses the rule discovery algorithm in a focused manner. Sufficient and necessary conditions for a concept are to be discovered.[7]

11.3.2.3 Model Acquistion Tool

The model acquisition tool MAT abstracts rule models from rules. The *task* is to generate rule models.

Input: a set of rules, a set of rule models

Output: new, non-redundant rule models

Because users prefer to input rules instead of rule models, the *input* to the model acquisition tool are rules. The learning *strategy* is that of abstraction over rules. The rules are abstracted by turning predicate symbols from the application domain into predicate variables. It is checked whether a new rule model corresponds to an already extisting one. If there are constant terms in the rule, these can either be turned into variables, too, or be introduced into the rule model. Rule models, including a constant term as argument of a predicate, may be of good use if the desired learning result is to clarify all properties and relations concerning a particu-

---

[6] Only the learning tools are described in this chapter. The knowledge revision KRT is a tool that handles contradictions and selects a rule to be deleted or to be refined. The rule refinement is then performed either by the user or by the system. If a concept is missing that restricts the support set appropriately, KRT calls the concept formation to learn that concept.

[7] For a detailed description of CLT, see Wrobel (1989).

lar object or attribute value. The *result* is a rule model that is not redundant to any given one.[8]

11.3.2.4 Sort Taxonomy Tool

The sort taxonomy tool STT organizes the objects (constant terms) of an application domain into sorts and classes of sorts. The *task* is to structure the constant terms or objects of a domain. In other words, the task is to learn types for a typed logic. If the fact base of MOBAL changes and the non-incremental mode has been selected, then the user can call the update of the sort taxonomy.

Input: a set of facts

Output: a lattice of classes of sorts

The *input* to the algorithm is a set of facts. The *output* of it is a lattice of classes of sorts. The sort taxonomy tool can be used either incrementally or as a single-step learner. The lattice gives an overview of the actual state of the fact base. It is used by the user for inspection and by the system to check the sort compatibility of new facts and rules (rule hypotheses).[9]

The learning *strategy* is that of bottom-up induction, where the learned classes are described by their extensions. The basic idea of the algorithm is to produce sets of constant terms on the basis of their occurrence at particular argument places of predicates. These sets are inspected with respect to subset relations, identity, or intersections. The sets are sort extensions. Equivalence classes are built for these sorts. The classes are organized in a lattice based on their subset relations or intersections. The most time consuming part of the algorithm is the calculation of intersections. The user can select whether intersections are to be built or not. The algorithm is efficient because it corresponds to learning in propositional logic.

11.3.2.5 Predicate Structuring Tool

The predicate structuring tool PST organizes the predicate symbols of an application domain into linked sets of predicate symbols. The *task* is to structure the predicates of a domain.

Input: a set of rules

Output: an acyclic directed graph

The *output* of it is an acyclic directed graph, the topology. The topology graph gives an overview of the rule base. It is used by the user for inspection and by the system to check the topology compatibility of rule hypotheses.

------

[8] For a detailed description of a previous version of MAT, see Thieme (1989).

[9] For a more detailed description, see Kietz (1988).

The learning *strategy* is that of abstraction over rule sets. The basic idea of the algorithm is to create a rule graph and then perform abstraction on it. A rule graph is a graph where the predicates of rule conclusions are in one node, and the predicates of the premises are in its subnodes. Because a predicate can only be in one node, the graphs for several rules can be combined easily to form the one rule graph for all rules of the rule base. This graph can be cyclic. It is transformed into an acyclic one by the first abstraction: for each cycle, a node is created with all the predicate symbols that occur in the cycle. The graph is further reduced by merging all nodes with the same successors or predecessors. In the *icterus* application, the rule graph had 127 nodes for about 200 rules, but the abstracted topology had only 50 nodes, thus giving a good overview of the rule base.[10]

11.3.3 Cooperating Learning Tools

The brief description of MOBAL's learning tools already indicated their task and their use by user and system. The cooperation of the tools is

- To use the results of another tool.
- More particular, to call another tool.
- To use the same knowledge as does another tool.

In MOBAL, the rule discovery tool uses the results of model acquisition, the predicate structure, and the sort taxonomy, as provided by MAT, STT, and PST, if the user has not given the rule models, predicate declarations, or topology of predicates. In this way, the tools produce structures that on the one hand allow the user to inspect the evolving domain model. On the other hand, the tools produce prerequisites for another tool, namely, the rule discovery tool. Moreover, in doing so, the tools take the burden of structuring that otherwise would be on the back of the user. The results of STT and PST in particular illustrate the multifunctionality of represented knowledge. Figure 11.4 shows the interaction of the learning tools. The lines between tool names indicate the use of knowledge produced by a tool. The arrows denote a tool calling another one.

The concept formation tool CLT calls the rule discovery with the name of the target concept and the list of rule models. Concept formation can be called by the user or by the knowledge revision. If a support set of a rule has too many exceptions (the criterion for "too many" given by the user or by default), the concept formation tool is called to define either a concept for the good rule applications or for the exceptions. The good and contradictive rule applications serve as positive and negative examples for CLT. In this way, the knowledge revision prepares the set of examples for CLT. The support sets are multifunctional in that they prohibit wrong inferences and can be used as examples for introducing new concepts.

---

[10] For a detailed description of PST, see Klingspor (1991).

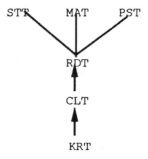

Figure 11.4:   Learning tools cooperating

The same knowledge, namely, facts, is used for rule discovery, concept formation, and the construction of the sort taxonomy, where STT can use any set of facts, and CLT needs positive and negative facts concerning a particular predicate, the target concept. Indirectly, via forward inferences (saturation), rules are used for rule discovery, concept formation, and the construction of a sort taxonomy. In addition, rules are used in rule discovery for not learning a known rule again. If background knowledge were represented differently from the (learned) rules—as is the case in many learning systems—the rule discovery could not use its learning results for further learning. MOBAL's uniform representation of background knowledge and learning results enables RDT to use new facts that were derived from learned rules as additional descriptions (examples). In particular, negated facts can be derived from learned rules with a negative conclusion and serve as counter-examples for further learning.

11.3.4 MOBAL Cooperating with the User

The user is supported in modeling by several capabilities of MOBAL. As was pointed out above, we include inspection, testing (validation), and revisions in the modeling process. The tools of MOBAL serve the overall modeling activity of the user. In addition to the learning tools described above, there is an inference engine, a programmer's interface, a user interface, and a knowledge-revision tool. In the following, first the user interface is sketched. Then, it is shown how each knowledge item can be input by the user or inferred by a tool. Finally, the opportunities of MOBAL for revising are indicated.

11.3.4.1 The Interfaces

In general, all items are *input* using an edit-window named "scratchpad" where the user can edit the items before entering them into the system. A help window associated with the scratchpad shows the format of each item for input. If the data are available, they can also be read into the system as text files in the scratchpad format. Using the programmer's interface, which offers high-level system calls, MOBAL can be coupled with another system directly. Data can be exchanged between the systems using the commands of the programmer's interface.

All items can be displayed as text in windows. The windows reflect changes of the knowledge base immediately. The content of a window can be *focused* so that only items containing a particular predicate symbol or constant term are displayed. Several windows can be opened in parallel for facts, rules or rule models.

The windows are easily used for some *operations*. A double click with the mouse on a particular item pops up a menu where the user can select an operation (e.g., delete) or display the item *graphically*.

The user interface eases the inspection of the evolving domain model, but the overview, the consequences of changes, and the detection of contradictions are delivered by the tools and provide the real support for inspection.

11.3.4.2 Balanced Adding of Items

In this section, the balanced cooperation of system and user is described with respect to adding knowledge items. It is shown that for each type of knowledge there exists a tool that creates items of this type, and there is an interface that supports the user in adding items of this type.

The user may input *predicate declarations* with named *sorts*. This is sometimes useful when it is easy to forget what argument type was supposed to occur where in a predicate. The predicate declaration then serves as a reminder of, e.g., where to put the person name in the predicate owner. If, however, the facts are already electronically available, the user need not input predicate declarations. The sort taxonomy tool STT will do the job.

The user may input a *topology of predicates* in order to structure the domain model beforehand, e.g. with respect to steps of problem solving which uses the (learned) rules.[11] For instance, the leave nodes of the topology may consist of predicates that refer to the given data (observations) in an application. Intermediate nodes may refer to intermediate problem solving results. The root node may consist of predicates that refer to possible results of problem solving (possible solutions). In this way, the topology is a task structure for the performance element that uses the built-up knowledge base in an application. If, however, the user does not know the overall domain structure, the predicate structuring tool PST can construct it on the basis of the rules.

The user may input *rules* and set the parameter such that the model acquisition tool MAT is called in order to obtain rule models from them. The user may

---

[11]Learning serves the acquisition of a rule base for a particular application where the rules are put to use!

also set the parameter to "direct rule input" so that MAT is not called for an input rule. The user may also input some rule models and call RDT for discovering rules. Thus, here again, there is a flexible work share of system and user.

The user must input some *facts*. Facts are necessary for learning, inferring, and building the sort taxonomy, but facts can also be added by the system's inferences. By selecting an inference depth for forward and for backward inferences (parameter of the inference engine), the user can force the inference engine to derive as many facts as possible within the selected inference depth (inference path length).

Hence, for each knowledge item there is a system tool adding it to the knowledge base, and there is the option that the user enters it. Balanced modeling is the flexible use of the tools for supporting the user to add items or to have the system adding items to the knowledge base.

11.3.4.3 Revisions

Revisions of all knowledge items are supported by MOBAL, and the consequences are immediately propagated. If a rule or fact is deleted, all its consequences are deleted too. Consequences are the facts derived from this rule or fact. Also updating the sort taxonomy and the abstracted topology reflects the change. It is not (yet) maintained, however, that a particular rule was learned because of facts that were deleted afterwards. This requires more bookkeeping and would slow down the inference engine.

The interface allows the user to react to the displayed knowledge base. If, for instance, the user detects a (derived) fact that he wants to reject, he can either delete it in the fact window, or, better, he can input this fact with the explicit negation. In this case, the negated fact serves as a constraint and influences learning. No rule covering the rejected fact can be learned any more. The knowledge revision detects contradictions of facts and displays graphically the inference paths leading to the contradiction. The user or the system may perform the blame assignment and repair the rule base. Also, the explicit representation of exceptions in support sets, and the call of CLT to form a new concept if too many exceptions of a rule have occurred helps to refine the domain model. The integration of concept formation into knowledge revision is comparable with the approach of Raymond Mooney and Dirk Ourston (1994, Chapter 5 in this book). MOBAL integrates inspecting, inputing, and revising a domain model.

11.4 CONCLUSION

There are some typical ways of using MOBAL. The extremes are the automatic and the manual mode. In the automatic mode, the system automatically constructs a sort taxonomy and learns rules, given facts and rule models. The predicate structuring tool then constructs the topology of predicates using the learned rules. In the manual mode, the user inputs rules, declares the predicates, builds up the topology, and inputs some facts. The user calls the learning tools in order to enhance the knowledge base. Here STT and PST are called for inspection purposes; the revision options of the inference engine and knowledge revision are frequently used. Usually, modeling is performed using the system manually and automatically. The applications of MOBAL are

- Traffic law domain—a self-made knowledge base with a rich structure and not too many facts (the knowledge base evolved in the automatic mode).
- Icterus—facts and rules provided by Dr. Mueller-Wickop and the knowledge base built up in the manual mode, using the tools for inspection only.
- Maldecensus testis—data provided by the Foundation of Research and Technology, Hellas (FORTH), the data not reflecting the diagnosis model that was manually input by us in collaboration with a medical expert (Prof. Charisis).
- SPEED—knowledge about the supervision of security policy in distributed systems provided by Alcatel-Alsthom Recherche, Marcoussis (AAR), (the domain offers a rich structure where CLT successfully invented a new concept for rule refinement).

Two detailed studies of applying MOBAL have been made in collaboration with FORTH (Morik et al., 1993) and AAR (Sommer et al., 1993). It is difficult to exploit evaluation criteria that are used for other types of learning systems. There, the performance of a learning system is compared with the performance of an expert. In the paradigm of balanced cooperative learning, however, an expert is not to be replaced by the system. In contrast, the expert is supported by the system in order to become most efficient. Because of the interactivity and the interaction of the tools, learning curves that indicate the classification found by the system do not make sense. The evaluation for the single tools is done by theoretical analysis. The evaluation of the overall system is done by the users. Fargier has written an experience report on using MOBAL for the AAR domain (Fargier, 1991). Becoming acquainted with a system as complex as MOBAL takes some time. Setting the evaluation criteria, for instance, seems to be a skill that requires some experience with MOBAL. If users are familiar with attribute-value learning systems such as ID3, for instance, they tend to not input relations and not use all the options that MOBAL offers. In this case, the users have already done beforehand what could have been learned using MOBAL. More naive users (with respect to computers) easily exploit the opportunities of MOBAL. The main advantage of MOBAL was the ease of inputing background knowledge or learning parts of the background knowledge. Users also employed the inspection and revision abilities of MOBAL. Moreover, MOBAL offers all advantages of a first order logic learning tool as opposed to a propositional logic one.

As a conclusion, MOBAL indeed accepts new items and integrates them into the knowledge base, supports the user in inspecting the knowledge base, detects contradictions, and refines the rules. All these tasks can be performed by the user or by a tool of the system. The users choose when to let the system do a task and when to do the task themselves. In both cases, the same knowledge representation and operations are applied. Therefore, MOBAL is a balanced cooperative system.

ACKNOWLEDGMENTS

Work reported in this chapter has partially been conducted within the project MLT, which is funded by the ESPRIT programme of the European Community under P2154.

The MOBAL system is being developed at the German National Research Center for Computer Science by (in alphabetical order) Joerg-Uwe Kietz, Volker Klingspor, Katharina Morik, Edgar Sommer, and Stefan Wrobel. It is a successor to the BLIP system that was developed at the Technical University, Berlin. The author of this chapter wishes to thank colleagues from the Berlin, as well as colleagues from the Bonn, days.

References

Davies, T.R., and Russell, S.J. A Logical Approach to Reasoning by Analogy, *Procs. of IJCAI-87*, San Mateo, Calif.: Morgan Kaufmann, 1987.

Davis, R. *Knowledge-Based Systems in Artificial Intelligence Part 2—TEIRESIAS: Applications of Meta-Level Knowledge*, New York: McGraw-Hill, 1982.

Emde, W.; Habel, C.; and Rollinger, C.-R. The Discovery of the Equator or Concept-driven Learning, *Procs. of IJCAI-83*, San Mateo, Calif.: Morgan Kaufmann, pp. 455–458 1983.

Fargier, H. Using MOBAL for Security Policy Management: Overview and Remarks, MLT Technical Note AAR/P2154/40/1, Alcatel Alsthom Recherche, 1991.

Kietz, J.-U. Incremental and Reversible Acquisition of Taxonomies. Linster, M., Boose, J. & Gaines, B. (eds), *Procs. of EKAW-88*, GMD-Studien 143, 1988.

Kietz, J.-U., and Morik, K. Constructive Induction: Learning Concepts for Learning. *Arbeitspapiere der GMD*, No. 543, 1991.

Kietz, J.-U., and Wrobel, S. Controlling the Complexity of Learning through Syntactic and Task-oriented Models. In Muggleton, S. (ed.) *Inductive Logic Programming*, London: Academic Press, pp. 335–359 1992.

Klingspor, V. MOBAL's Predicate Structuring Tool. *Deliverable 4. 3. 2/G* of the MLT project, MLT-Report, No. GMD/P2154/22/1, 1991.

Kodratoff, Y., and Tecuci, G. The Central Role of Explanations in DISCIPLE. In Morik, K. (ed.); *Knowledge Representation and Organization in Machine Learning*, New York: Springer-Verlag, pp. 135–147 1989.

Michalski, R.S. Inferential Theory of Learning: Developing Foundations for Multistrategy Learning. In R.S. Michalski and G. Tecuci (eds.), *Machine Learning: A Multistrategy Approach*, Vol. IV, San Mateo, Calif.: Morgan Kaufmann, 1994.

Morik, K. Sloppy Modeling. In Morik, K. (ed.), *Knowledge Representation and Organization in Machine Learning*, New York: Springer-Verlag, pp. 107–134 1989.

Morik, K. Underlying Assumptions of Knowledge Acquisition and Machine Learning. *Knowledge Acquisition Journal, 3*, 137–156, 1991.

Morik, K., and Kietz, J.-U. A Bootstrapping Approach to Conceptual Clustering. In Serge, A. (ed.), *Procs. of 6th IWML*, San Mateo, Calif.: Morgan Kaufmann, 1989.

Morik, K.; Causse, K.; and Boswell, R. A Common Knowledge Representation Integrating Learning Tools. In R.S. Michalski and G. Tecuci (eds.), *1st International Workshop on Multistrategy Learning*, West Virginia, 1991.

Morik, K.; Potamias, G.; Moustakis, V.; and Charisis, G. Knowledgeable Learning Using MOBAL-A Case Study on a Medical Domain. In Kodratoff, Y., Langley, P. (eds.), *Real-World Applications of ML, Workshop Notes*, Vienna, 1993.

Plotkin, G.D. A Note on Inductive Generalization. In B. Meltzer and D. Michie (eds.), *Machine Intelligence*, Chapter 8, pp. 153–163, Elsevier Publishers, 1970.

Quinlan, R. Learning Efficient Classification Procedures and Their Application to Chess End Games. In R.S. Michalski, J.G. Carbonell, and T. Mitchell (eds.), *Machine Learning—An Artificial Intelligence Approach, Vol. I*, Palo Alto, CA: Tioga, pp. 463–482 1983.

———. Learning Logical Definitions from Relations. *Machine Learning Journal, 3*, 239–266, 1990.

Shapiro, E.Y. Inductive Inference from Facts. *Yale Research Report*, No. 192, Yale University, 1981.

Sommer, E.; Morik, K.; André, J.M.; Uszinsky, M. What On-Line Machine Learning Can Do for Knowledge Acquisition—A Case Study. *Arbeitspapiere der GMD*, No. 757, 1993.

Thieme, S. The Acquisition of Model Knowledge for a Model-driven Machine Learning Approach. In K. Morik (ed.), *Knowledge Representation and Organization in Machine Learning*, New York: Springer-Verlag, pp. 177–191 1989.

Wrobel, S. Higher-order Concepts in a Tractable Knowledge Representation. In K. Morik (ed.), *Procs. German Workshop on AI*, Heidelberg: Springer-Verlag, pp. 129–138 1987.

———. Demand-Driven Concept Formation. In K. Morik (ed.), *Knowledge Representation and Organization in Machine Learning*, New York: Springer-Verlag, pp. 289–319 1989.

12

WHY:

A System That Learns Using Causal Models and Examples

Cristina Baroglio
Marco Botta
Lorenza Saitta
(Università di Torino)

Abstract

The system WHY, which learns and updates a diagnostic knowledge base using domain knowledge and a set of examples, is presented. The *a priori* knowledge consists of a causal model of the domain, stating the relationships among basic phenomena, and a body of phenomenological theory, describing the links between abstract concepts of the causal model and their possible manifestations in the world. The phenomenological knowledge is used deductively, the causal model is used abductively, and the examples are used inductively. The problems of imperfection and intractability of the theory are handled by allowing the system to make assumptions during its reasoning. In this way, robust knowledge can be learned with limited complexity and limited number of examples. The system works in a first order logic environment and has been applied to an industrial problem of mechanical troubleshooting.

12.1 INTRODUCTION

The development of tools for building up, maintaining, and refining the knowledge base of an expert system is becoming a major task in the field of automated knowledge acquisition. In fact, the ability of the system to build up reliable and robust knowledge bases, to increase its performance level with its experience, to adapt itself to changes in the environment, and to incorporate new pieces of knowledge would greatly increase the acceptability of expert systems in a wide range of applications.

The class of expert systems addressed in this chapter is concerned with diagnostic (or classification) tasks. It is widely recognized that this type of expert system, in order to work on real-world applications, needs more complex knowledge representation schemes than a simple set of {Pattern → Decision} rules; in diagnostic systems, for instance, several authors have advocated the necessity of using deep models of the structure and behavior of the entities involved in the given domain (Davis, 1984; Genesereth, 1984; Reiter, 1984; de Kleer and Seely Brown, 1986).

A shift of the attention toward methodologies with the potential of achieving a deeper understanding of the world is even more appropriate in learning. In fact, this shift is actually going on. Early systems relied on inductive techniques (Mitchell, 1982; Michalski, 1983; Quinlan, 1986); pure induction can detect regularities in a large amount of data, but it can neither explain why these regularities occur nor guarantee their meaningfulness. Nevertheless, inductive systems have been proved viable tools for solving some real-world problems (Michalski and Chilausky, 1980; Quinlan, 1986; Cestnik and Bratko, 1988; Bergadano, Giordana, and Saitta, 1988).

The two papers by Mitchell, Keller, and Kedar-Cabelli (1986) and DeJong and Mooney (1986) proposed a new, deductive approach to learning and had the great merit of focusing the attention on the fundamental role *a priori* knowledge can play in this process. Deductive learning offers grounds for the knowledge it derives at the cost of supplying a complete and consistent theory of the domain. Because this last requirement cannot be met in real applications, attempts have been made to take the best of the inductive and deductive approaches by integrating them into a single framework (Lebowitz, 1986; Bergadano and Giordana, 1988; Pazzani, 1988).

The deductive approach has been called *Explanation-based* because it essentially relies on "explaining," by means of the domain theory, why known examples are instances of the corresponding concepts. This definition deserves further clarification if looked at more closely. In fact, even though we may have a naïve intuition of what we would be willing to accept as an explanation of a phenomenon, the exact explication of this notion has generated a strong debate in philosophy of science since the seminal paper by Hempel and Oppenheim (1948) proposing the Deductive-Nomological (D-N) model of explanation. Today, disagreeing views come from the pragmatist, deductivist, and mechanist schools.

The view of deductive learning as explanation-based relies upon the implicit assumption that explanations are logical arguments. To this view, the completeness and consistency of the domain theory are essential. However, although on the one hand, people agree on the impossibility of supplying a system with a perfect theory, on the other, the identity between explanations and logical arguments has been seriously questioned (see, for instance, Salmon [1989] for an in-depth discussion). Finally, even though a perfect theory could possibly be encoded, its use would, most likely, turn out to be intractable.

For the mentioned reasons, the explanation-based approach should be widened to accommodate a more comprehensive notion of explanation; at the same time, an epistemological analysis of domain theories should enlighten their nature and suggest what kind(s) of knowledge can possibly satisfy the two requirements of being tractable while keeping its explanatory power. In this chapter, we suggest that a *causal model* of the domain, coupled with *abductive* reasoning, can be used to satisfy both requirements.

The notions of explanation and causal relation have been debated widely, and different definitions have emerged in various disciplines. AI scientists have also contributed to the discussion (de Kleer and Seely Brown, 1986; Cox and Pietrzykowski, 1987; Poole, 1988; Levesque, 1989; Torasso and Console, 1989; Michalski, 1990, 1991; Console and Saitta, 1992). In this chapter, we will rely on the following intuitive productivist interpretation of the causal relation: A is the cause of B if a physical mechanism can be specified, which shows how the occurrence of A brings about B. It is out of the scope of this chapter to locate this definition w.r.t. the current thoughts. We only notice that it is strongly oriented to domains in which the entities are physical objects governed by Physics and Chemistry laws.

That causality plays a fundamental role in explaining the world is without doubt (Salmon, 1989). Then, we do not need to argue about the second requirement, mentioned above, for the *a priori* knowledge to have explanatory import. In order to discuss the first requirement (tractability), we need to do it in connection with the discussion of the abductive reasoning scheme. The word abduction does not refer here to the task of finding some "best" explanation but instead to the following reasoning scheme: from (*if* α *then* β) and β, plausibly assert α (Peirce, 1958; Levesque, 1989; Console and Saitta, 1992). Abduction regresses, through chains of cause-effect relations, from observations to a set of axioms, the *first causes*, which are the ultimate hypotheses we are disposed to accept. Obviously, the definition of the first causes is task-dependent and can be suggested by an expert of the domain.[1] First causes are also called, in the literature on principled diagnosis, "abducible predicates" (Eshghi and Kowalski, 1989; Torasso and Console, 1989).

The reason for the potentially limited complexity of abduction, in comparison with a deductive approach, mostly resides in the possibility of making *assumptions* about the state of the world. In this way, the causal model focuses the search for a problem solution toward fundamental phenomena, first by producing a "deep skeleton" to which "surface" details can be added later. Nevertheless, one has to be aware that the inferred results are only *valid under a set of assumed hypotheses*.

Causal models are particularly useful in updating and refining a knowledge base because they greatly help locate defective parts of the knowledge and suggest motivated changes (Botta and Saitta, 1988; Botta, Giordana, and Saitta, 1990). Finally, the occurrence of unexpected phenomena and changes in the world can be faced by exploiting causal models. In fact, a causal model is supposed to capture fundamental laws governing the domain, and hence, it is often well assessed, well understood, and robust with respect to noise and environmental time evolutions.

Some authors have recently proposed using plausible reasoning or abduction in learning, mainly as a modification of explanation-based techniques (DeJong, 1990; Geffner, 1990; Hartley and Coombs, 1990; Morris and O'Rorke, 1990; Michalski, 1991; Tecuci, 1991; Botta, Ravotto, and Saitta, 1992). An interesting approach to the use of deep models in learning has been put forward by Mozetic and Holzbaur (1991), who proposed a layered representation, at different abstraction levels, for reducing complexity.

Even though a causal model C of the domain plays, in the approach proposed in this chapter, a prominent role, other types of knowledge also contribute. In fact, the causal model is usually too abstract to allow practical diagnostic rules to be learned only on its basis. Then, we consider, beside C, a *phenomenological* theory $\mathcal{P}$, which contains a set of rules aimed at describing the manifestations of abstractly defined concepts, i.e., re-expressing them in terms of "operational" predicates (Keller, 1988). For instance, the concept of "incandescent object" can be linked to its manifestation by saying that the object is bright. Notice that establishing this relation does not increase our understanding of the incandescence phenomenon because it allows an incandescent object to be recognized but does not tell us, for instance, how to make an object incandescent on purpose. In fact, the knowledge $\mathcal{P}$, even if necessary in order to fill the gap between abstract entities and their possible

---

[1] The term "first cause" has to be intended in a pragmatical sense: in the literature on principled diagnosis it represents a set of phenomena (events or states) that the expert judges adequate explanations w.r.t. the problem at hand.

manifestations, can just explain *how* things happen but not *why*. Then, pragmatically, a phenomenon will be considered *justified* only if it is explained by C. The distinction between C and $\mathcal{P}$ is also reflected in the different representation formalisms and in the associated reasoning mechanisms (abductive for C and deductive for $\mathcal{P}$). In support to the usefulness of keeping apart $\mathcal{P}$ and C, we notice that the same malfunction (recognizable from the symptoms specified by $\mathcal{P}$) may often have different causes (specified by C) and that only the knowledge of the true cause allows an effective repair. Morris and O'Rorke (1990) suggest using abduction for refining theories that do not give correct predictions. To do this, the theory is split into a "core" theory, which cannot be modified, and the remainder. A possibility for making such a split could be to adopt a partition similar to that between C and $\mathcal{P}$.

We shall now describe how the above mentioned ideas have been implemented in the system WHY, an evolution of the learning system ML-SMART (Bergadano, Giordana, and Saitta, 1988) in which inductive and deductive techniques have already been integrated (Bergadano and Giordana, 1988). WHY has been applied to a real-world problem of mechanical diagnosis (Saitta et al., 1991). However, a simpler example of a heat transfer problem will be used in this chapter for the sake of comprehensibility.

Several aspects differentiate the system WHY from others devoted to similar learning tasks. First of all, WHY is able to deal with first order logic languages, representing both the domain theory and the target knowledge, by keeping track of the (possibly multiple) bindings between variables in formulas and components of instances. Second, the system can be used for acquiring and refining a target knowledge base as well as for revising the *a priori* knowledge supplied to it. In this last task, the system works in a semi-automated way, allowing a direct interaction with the expert, who can suggest modifications to the background or to the target knowledge; the expert will receive an immediate feedback to his/her suggestions because WHY evaluates the effects of the modifications and presents them back to the expert for validation. In order to ease this interactive aspect, WHY is provided with a friendly interface toward the user based on a frame system supporting a menu-like interaction protocol. Another innovative aspect of WHY is the integration of the performance module into the learner, so that they both use the same knowledge structures, and the same reasoning process can serve both classification and learning.

The chapter is organized as follows: Section 12.2 describes the representation formalisms used for the various types of knowledge handled by WHY. Section 12.3 describes the basic reasoning mechanisms in isolation, whereas Section 12.4 illustrates how these reasoning schemes can be combined to build up justifications and to generate decision rules. In Section 12.5, the knowledge refinement process is outlined, whereas Section 12.6 is devoted to a description of the performance module. Section 12.7 contains some conclusions.

12.2 KNOWLEDGE REPRESENTATION

WHY handles four bodies of knowledge: the causal model, C; the phenomenological theory, P, the target knowledge base, KB, and the control knowledge.

The representation schemes for all the kinds of knowledge share a first order logic language L in Horn clause form. In the following, a double arrow $\Rightarrow$ will denote material implication, whereas the simple arrow $\rightarrow$ will create a causal link. Moreover, lowercase letter predicates are operational (i.e., directly observable on the data) and grouped in a set $P^{(o)}$, whereas capital letter predicates are non-operational (i.e., need to be deduced) and belong to a set $P^{(n)}$.

12.2.1 Target Knowledge Base

The target knowledge base consists of an unordered set of decision rules:

$$\text{r} \equiv \forall e \ | \exists \ \mathbf{x} | \ \varphi(e,\mathbf{x}) \ \Rightarrow \ \text{h}(e) | \tag{1}$$

where $\mathbf{x}$ denotes a set of variables, e an event to be interpreted, h a concept belonging to a set H_0 of concepts, and φ a formula of L. In (1), formula $\varphi(e,\mathbf{x})$ may contain both operational and non-operational predicates.

The set S(h) of rules, whose conclusion is h, is an *intensional* description of the concept h. During the learning process, each $\varphi(e,\mathbf{x})$ also has an *extensional* representation, consisting of all the training examples satisfying φ; the extension of φ is stored as a relation in a relational database (Bergadano, Giordana, and Saitta, 1988). More precisely, let F be a set of (structured) events and $\varphi^{(o)}(x_1, x_2, \dots, x_k)$ an operational formula. Given an event $e \in$ F, every possible binding satisfying $\varphi^{(o)}$ between k-tuples of components of e and the k-tuple of variables $x_1, x_2, \dots, x_k$ is represented in a (k+2)-ary relation $\varphi^* = <$F, H, $X_1, X_2, \dots, X_k>$, where field F contains the identifier of an example; H is its correct classification (the concept, which e is an instance of); and $X_1, X_2, \dots, X_k$ are the names of the constants (components of e) bound to variables $x_1, x_2, \dots, x_k$, respectively.

12.2.2 Phenomenological Theory

The phenomenological theory P is represented as a set of Horn clauses and describes taxonomies, structural information, general knowledge, and links between abstract concepts and their manifestations. For instance, the following four rules are typical examples of the kinds of information represented by P.

table(x) $\Rightarrow$ FURNITURE(x)

(taxonomic knowledge)

NEAR(z,y) $\wedge$ part-of(x,z) $\Rightarrow$ NEAR(x,y)

(general knowledge)

cord(x) $\land$ plug(y) $\land$ connected-to(y,x) $\Rightarrow$ ELECTRICAL-CABLE(x,y)

(structural knowledge)

bright(x) $\Rightarrow$ INCANDESCENT(x)

(manifestation)

Other examples of rules in $\mathcal{P}$ are given in the next subsection (the rule set $\mathcal{P}_1$). As we shall see, the causal network C subdivides the phenomenological theory $\mathcal{P}$ into subsets, allowing the reasoner to consider only limited parts of it at any given time.

12.2.3 Causal Model

The logical representation of the causal model C consists of an acyclic graph. In Figure 12.1, a very simple model of heat transfer phenomena is reported. Nodes in the network are either *primary* (ellipses) or *accessory* (rectangles and clouds). Primary nodes correspond to processes or system states, and a subset of these nodes contains the *first causes* (shaded nodes), which do not have entering edges. Effects of the same cause are AND-ed; causes of the same effect are OR-ed.

Accessory nodes represent two types of additional information: *constraints* (rectangles) and *contexts* (clouds). Constraints are attached to edges and correspond to conditions that are to be necessarily verified in order to be able to instantiate the

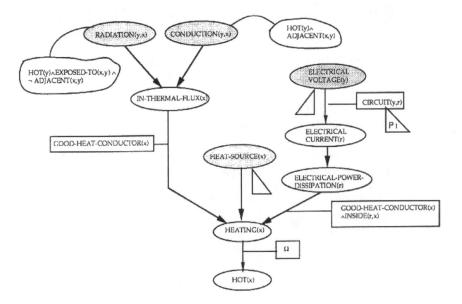

Figure 12.1:   Simplified model of heat transfer phenomena

corresponding cause-effect relation. Contexts are attached to primary nodes and represent the environmental conditions allowing the instantiation of the related phenomenon. One of the differences between constraints and contexts is that constraints are intended to describe physical properties of the involved bodies or structural information, i.e., properties that do not depend on time and can be considered permanently true. Contexts state conditions that may only temporarily be true; they usually involve parts of the considered system larger than the one currently under analysis. For example, conditions may refer to system components different from the one for which the causal network has currently been activated: in Figure 12.1, the explanation of why a body x is hot may involve the presence of a hot body y adjacent to it from which heat can flow toward x through heat conduction.

Primary nodes of the network may or may not be observables, i.e., evaluable either directly on the data (if their description involves operational predicates only) or indirectly, using the phenomenological theory $\mathcal{P}$. Constraints and contexts must be observable; as an exception, contexts may also be described in terms of primary causal nodes, introducing recursion in the net. This is the case of HOT(y) in the contexts of RADIATION(y,x) and CONDUCTION(y,x) in Figure 12.1.

Finally, a triangle associated with a node contains that part of the phenomenological theory $\mathcal{P}$ that describes the manifestations associated with the node. As an example, triangle $\mathcal{P}_1$ contains, among others, the following rules, allowing the predicate CIRCUIT(y,r) to be evaluated:

TERMINALS(y) $\land$ RESISTANCE(r) $\land$ connected-to(y,r) $\Rightarrow$ CIRCUIT (y,r)
{A circuit is constituted by a resistance and a terminal connected together.}

plug(y) $\Rightarrow$ TERMINALS(y)
{A plug is a terminal.}

ELECTRICAL-CABLE(x,y) $\Rightarrow$ TERMINALS(y)
{An electrical cable is a terminal.}

cord(z) $\land$ plug(y) $\land$ connected-to(y,z) $\Rightarrow$ ELECTRICAL-CABLE(z,y)
{An electrical cable is constituted by a plug and a cord connected together.}

The occurrence of predicates belonging to $\mathcal{P}$ in nodes of C is not the unique link between $\mathcal{P}$ and C; in fact, the name of a node of C can occur in the body of some clauses defining non-operational predicates in $\mathcal{P}$. This is also the way links between C and concepts in H_0 are established; as a matter of fact, concepts are non-operational predicates defined in $\mathcal{P}$. Suppose, for instance, that we want to use the network in Figure 12.1 to characterize objects that are dangerous to be touched because they may burn. We can define the class UNSAFE-TO-TOUCH(x) as follows (names of nodes occurring in C are underlined in $\mathcal{P}$):

$\underline{HOT}(x) \Rightarrow$ UNSAFE-TO-TOUCH(x)

{Hot objects are unsafe to touch.}

$\underline{HOT}(y) \wedge obj(x)$ part-of(y,x) $\Rightarrow$ UNSAFE-TO-TOUCH(x)

{Objects that have a hot component part are unsafe to touch.}

12.2.4 Theory Incompleteness

When encoding a domain theory, incompleteness may affect almost any part of it (DeJong, 1990), and we may not be aware of where and what knowledge is missing. On the other hand, there are cases in which either we know exactly where some information is missing, but we do not know which one, or we want to hide information on purpose (for instance, for tractability reasons). In these cases, we would like to warn the system about this lack of information. To this aim, a special predicate Ω (unknown) is introduced. For example, the rule

$$\text{electrical-plate}(x) \wedge \Omega \Rightarrow \text{HEAT-SOURCE}(x) \tag{2}$$

states that an electrical plate *may* be a heat source if some other unspecified condition is verified (for instance, if it is plugged in). As an extreme case, Ω may coincide with the whole body of a clause, as in the following example:

$$\Omega \Rightarrow Q(x) \tag{3}$$

Rule (3) denotes that we are unable (or do not want) to specify how predicate $Q(x)$ can be operationalized. Sometimes, we are in an intermediate situation: the expert can tell that predicate $Q(x)$ is expressible in terms of a combination of other predicates $\{R_1, R_2, ... , R_n\}$, either operational or non-operational, but he/she does not know exactly which combination. Then, we associate the set $\{R_1, R_2, ... , R_n\}$ to Ω in a *dependency* rule (Bergadano, Giordana, and Ponsero, 1989)

$$\{R_1, R_2, ... , R_n\} \Rightarrow Q(x) \tag{4}$$

that can be used to define a reduced hypothesis space.

The presence of Ω in a constraint denotes a weakening in the causal relation associated with the corresponding edge: in this case, the cause *may* produce the effect but not necessarily. For example, in Figure 12.1, an object x can become hot upon heating only if a sufficient time is elapsed or if it is not melting.

12.2.5 Control Knowledge

The system WHY is a knowledge-intensive learner, which has a body of declarative knowledge to control its behavior. The control acts at two main levels: the high-level control chooses, among available reasoning schemes (abduction, induction, deduction), the most suitable one for each learning step. The low-level control determines the behavior of a single learning strategy. The control knowledge is implemented as a set of frames containing the description of a situation and the action(s) suitable to handle that situation. As an example of such a rule, let us consider the following:

(Ks_abd_cont_path (pd)
        (situation (and (not_empty_extension pd)
                (equal (status pd) 'open)))
        (action perform_abduction_on_pd))
{if a node on a causal path has a non-empty extension and has not been explored yet, then perform an abduction step toward that node}

which describes the set of conditions that must be met in order to perform an abductive step on a given path descriptor *pd* (see Section 12.4.2).

12.3 BASIC REASONING MECHANISMS

Three basic reasoning schemes are integrated in the system WHY: induction, deduction, and abduction. Each one of these is briefly illustrated in the following.

12.3.1 Inductive Specialization

Inductive specialization is used to fill the possible gaps in the domain theory and is performed by invoking the inductive module of the WHY system. This module searches, using a general-to-specific strategy, in a space of first order logical formulas and outputs a set of decision rules, whose left-hand sides are the selected formulas. A body of control knowledge, in declarative form, is used to guide the search toward the most promising paths and to evaluate candidate formulas for inclusion in the final rule set. Criteria for evaluating formulas include (but are not limited to) their completeness and consistency.

Multiple bindings between variables in the formulas and parts in the examples are allowed.

12.3.2 Deduction

Deduction is performed by WHY's deductive module in a way similar to that described in Bergadano and Giordana (1988). The module handles a first order theory expressed in Horn clause form and is based on Robinson and Siebert's LOGLISP (Robinson and Siebert, 1982). The deductive mechanism deals with many examples at the same time and has the possibility of also performing a forward deduction, i.e., of building the operationalization tree starting from the operational predicates (leaves of the tree) true of the considered examples.

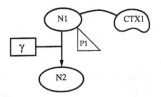

Figure 12.2:   Scheme of the relations among nodes in the causal network. Two basic reasoning steps
are defined: prediction from causes to effects and abduction from effects to causes.

12.3.3 Abduction

Abductive reasoning is needed to exploit the causal model. In Figure 12.2, a typical part of the causal network is reported for the sake of illustrating the basic reasoning steps.

Reasoning with the causal model can be performed by moving from effects to causes (abduction) or from causes to effects (prediction) in order to assert the truth status of each node:

- Prediction of effects from causes:

$$N_1 \wedge CTX_1 \wedge \gamma \rightarrow N_2$$

- If node N_1 is true in the context CTX_1 and the constraints γ are verified, then node N_2 deterministically (if Ω does not occur in γ) or plausibly (if Ω occurs in γ) follows.

- Abduction of causes from effects:

$$N_2 \wedge \gamma \rightarrow N_1 \wedge CTX_1$$

- If effect N_2 has been observed (or hypothesized) and the constraints γ are verified, then we can hypothesize that N_2 was originated by N_1 in the context CTX_1. In this abductive step, Ω does not have any influence.

Notice that the truth status of a node can also be determined by the result of its evaluation on the data (rules P_1, for instance), independently of the presence of its causes and/or effects. This fact constitutes another connection between phenomenological and causal reasoning.

The above reasoning steps are quite complex to be implemented in a first order logic environment because of the variables' bindings. How to maintain these bindings and the truth status of each node (possibly different for each binding of each instance) will be described in Section 12.4.

The "context" nodes play a particular role in the causal reasoning. Suppose that we are trying to explain why a given object x is hot. The causal network tells us that there are a number of causes justifying this phenomenon; however, some of these are acceptable only if the environment supplies the conditions to support them. For instance, heat conduction requires that there is an object y, different from x, which is, in turn, hot and adjacent to x. When the causal reasoning is invoked on a given part of the system (in Figure 12.1, the object x), contexts act as defaults and are always assumed true. Then, each of the first causes, hypothesized to explain the phenomenon, has its context hypothesized at the same time. It is up to the general control strategy to decide whether to accept the assumed context by default or to verity it, possibly re-entering the causal network. This strategy closely matches the one often used by human experts and also has the advantage of breaking recursion in the causal reasoning.

12.3.4 Handling Assumptions

Making assumptions is a fundamental aspect of the reasoning process in an uncertain environment and, in particular, at a point when only an incomplete theory is available. In WHY, assumptions can be made during both the phenomenological and the causal reasoning, but the ways they are handled in the two cases differ.

Let us consider a set of Horn clauses in $\mathcal{P}$, sharing the same head:

$$\varphi_k(\mathbf{x}) \Rightarrow P(\mathbf{x}) \qquad (1 \leq k \leq n)$$

According to Clark's completion (Clark, 1978), we can assume that

$$P(\mathbf{x}) \Leftrightarrow \varphi_1(\mathbf{x}) \vee \ldots \ldots \vee \varphi_n(\mathbf{x}) \qquad (5)$$

As an example, let us assume that only yellow or blue or red objects are considered in our world; then, we can assert that

$$\text{HAS-COLOR}(\mathbf{x}) \Leftrightarrow \text{yellow}(\mathbf{x}) \vee \text{blue}(\mathbf{x}) \vee \text{red}(\mathbf{x})$$

If the predicate Ω does not occur in any of the $\varphi_k(\mathbf{x})$'s, then with rule (5), predicate $P(\mathbf{x})$ can be proved false if and only if all the $\varphi_k(\mathbf{x})$ $(1 \leq k \leq n)$ are false. Things are different if Ω does occur because Ω, by default, is always assumed to be true. If Ω occurs in the body of a clause, such as in (2), the effect is that the predicate in the head of the clause will never be true but can only be *assumed* true if the other predicates in the body of the rule are true. If a clause such as (3) occurs, then the Clark's completion of $\mathcal{P}$ will contain it as a disjunct:

$$\mathcal{P}(\mathbf{x}) \Leftrightarrow \varphi_1(\mathbf{x}) \vee \ldots \ldots \vee \varphi_n(\mathbf{x}) \vee \Omega. \qquad (6)$$

According to (6), $P(\mathbf{x})$ is never false because of Ω. The number of assumptions in a formula φ made during reasoning is an important strategic parameter and is kept in the extension of the formula itself. In particular, this information is maintained for each instance and possible binding between variables in φ and objects in an instance.

In the causal network, the symbol Ω may occur only in constraints and contexts. Constraints predicates, which cannot be proved true, are assumed to be false (except for Ω).

12.4 INTEGRATING MULTIPLE STRATEGIES

The overall learning process can be separated into two main steps: the first one is aimed at building up an initial set of decision rules, whereas the goal of the second step is that of possibly revising either the target knowledge base or the domain theory. An abstract description of the initial rule learning process will be portrayed in this section, whereas a description of the refinement methodology will be given in the next one. Initial rule learning encompasses three major phases—elicitation, justification, and rule construction—as outlined in the following:

Elicitation:

Elicit from the expert a body of background knowledge, partitioned into a causal network and a phenomenological theory, $T = C \cup P$, using the USER INTERFACE.
Let F_0 be a set of training examples.

Justification:

Phase 1—Build up an AND/OR forest G, called the *justification forest*, by applying a forward *deduction* algorithm to the phenomenological theory P.
Insert in the data base the extension, evaluated on the set F_0, of each node in G.
Activate some nodes of the causal network C.

Phase 2—Apply the *abductive* algorithm CAUSAL to find paths in the causal network, regressing from the activated nodes toward first causes.
Insert in the data base the extension, evaluated on the set F_0, of each node in each causal path activated in C.

Phase 3—Verify hypothesized contexts, possibly recursively re-entering the causal network.

Rule Learning:

Generate decision rules for the concepts in H_0 by collecting operational predicates that are true (or assumed true) along the activated causal paths, and insert the rules in KB.

If   The rules have an "acceptable" (according to a given criterion)
        degree of completeness and consistency

Then   Stop

Else   Go to **KNOWLEDGE REFINEMENT**

A graphical user interface helps the expert configure the system: he/she has to define the causal network and the phenomenological theory and to provide an initial training set of instances. The justification phase is the core of the learning process because it builds up all the data structures needed in successive steps. The main goal of this phase is that of finding causal explanations (justifications) of why instances are examples of a given concept. The third phase consists of extracting decision rules that are justified by the given domain knowledge. This phase may be skipped if the initial set of rules is directly supplied by the expert.

For the sake of exemplification, we shall use the task, mentioned in Section 12.2, of characterizing possibly UNSAFE-TO-TOUCH objects, given a set of 14 examples and 18 counterexamples of this concept taken from everyday life (irons, pots, lamps, knives, etc.). Examples of the objects are given in Appendix A.

12.4.1 Construction of the Justification Forest

In order to describe how the system works, some definitions have to be introduced first. Let $T = C \cup P$ be the domain theory. Let, moreover, Σ be the set of primary nodes in the causal network C and Σ_0 the subset of nodes corresponding to first causes. Two kinds of justifications will be considered: the first one (analogous to the one introduced in EBL) refers to *instances* and is an explanation, in terms of cause/effect relations, of why an example f is an instance of a concept h.

Definition 1.   Given a theory $T = C \cup P$ and an instance f of a concept h (denoted by h(f)), we call *explanation* E(h,f) of f w.r.t. h the pair $\{\sigma_0(f), A\}$ such that

$$T \cup \sigma_0(f) \cup A \vDash h(f)$$

where $\sigma_0(f)$ is a first cause, and A is a set of assumptions, i.e., a set of predicates belonging to **P** that have to be assumed true in order to derive h(f). $\Diamond$

The second type of justification refers to *rules* and *instances* and explains why a given rule is correctly applied to an instance f of a concept h.

Definition 2.   Given a rule $r \equiv (\varphi(z, \mathbf{x}) \Rightarrow h(z)) \in KB$ and an instance f of h, let $\varphi^{(o)}(f)$ be the operationalization of φ true of f. Then, a *justification* J(r, f, ρ) of r w.r.t. f is a 4-tuple $\{\sigma_0(f), A, \psi^{(o)}, \rho)$ such that

a) $T \cup \sigma_0(f) \cup A \vDash (\psi^{(o)}(f, \mathbf{x}) \Rightarrow h(f))$.

b) $\sigma_0(f)$ is a first cause, and A is a set of assumptions.

c) $\psi^{(o)} = \rho \wedge \xi_1$ and $\varphi^{(o)} = \rho \wedge \xi_2$ (i.e., $\psi^{(o)}$ and $\varphi^{(o)}$ have a subformula ρ in common). $\Diamond$

We distinguish between *total justification*, in which $\rho \equiv \varphi^{(o)}$, and *partial justification*, in which $\xi_2 \neq \varnothing$. Definitions 1 and 2 can be generalized to the case of a set of examples F, obtaining E(h,F) and J(r,F,ρ), respectively.

The justification forest G is an extension of the classical explanation tree, used in EBL, to the case of simultaneous operationalization of several predicates on many examples. It is similar in structure to the justification tree used by Tecuci (1991), but it is built up by only using inductive specialization and deduction. The construction of G is performed by a forward deduction algorithm, which starts from the set of operational predicates $\mathcal{P}^{(o)}$ that are true of the data and applies forward the rules in $\mathcal{P}$ until either no more rules are applicable, or some primary node of the causal network has been reached (Botta et al., 1992).

In Figure 12.3, some steps of this process are illustrated. With the predicates *cord*, *plug*, *conn-to*, and *resistance* to start (Figure 12.3(a)) true of some examples (specified under the predicate), ELECTRICAL-CABLE, CIRCUIT, and RESISTANCE (among others) are stimulated; RESISTANCE and ELECTRICAL-CABLE are selected for verification because they have all the predicates in their body already proved, and their truth is established for the specified examples (Figure 12.3(b)); TERMINALS is stimulated and proved, and then CIRCUIT can be proved true of examples {1–6} (see Figure 12.3(c)). Part of the resulting justification forest built up for the 32 examples of unsafe and safe objects is reported in Figure 12.4.

Notice that for each example, more than one binding is possible. A major source of complexity in the construction of G is the need to maintain identity constraints among variables in AND nodes. In fact, the bindings between variables and components in the examples are performed independently from one another in the son nodes (being the forest built up bottom-up). As an example, all the pairs of objects connected to each other are stored in the extension of the node conn-to(u,v); however, only those pairs of connected objects that are a cord and a plug, respectively, are to be selected to form an electrical cable. Then, it may happen that an AND node is false, but their son nodes are true, taken in isolation. This detailed information about bindings is fundamental for the tasks of knowledge refinement and theory revision because it allows the point where an explanation fails to be exactly located.

Additional pieces of information are also added to each node: one is its possible connection with primary or secondary nodes of C, and another is a *truth status*, which can assume one among the values {True, Assumed True, Assumed False, False}. An "Assumed True" status may derive from the presence of a Ω within an operationalization or from the assumption of some predicate that was not specified in the data but could not be proved false. Obviously, the status is not a global

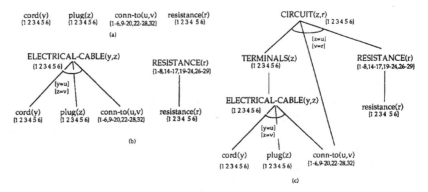

Figure 12.3:   Three steps in the construction of the justification forest

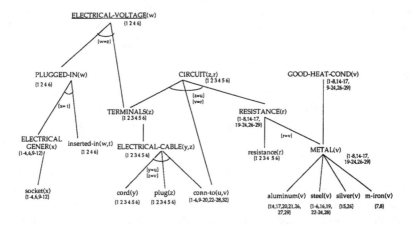

Figure 12.4:   Part of the justification forests for the considered set of 14 unsafe-to-touch and 18 safe-to-touch objects. The set of numbers associated with each node represents the set of examples satisfying the formula associated with the node.

property of the node because different assumptions might have been made for different examples. Then, the status is evaluated for every binding of each example and stored, as an additional field in each tuple, in the relation associated with the node.

12.4.2 Finding Causal Paths

During the preceding phase, a subset of the nodes in Σ have been activated. Now, we want to use abduction to hypothesize first causes, moving back from the activated nodes. The abductive process is performed by the following algorithm *ABDUCTION*. For the sake of simplicity, those parts of the algorithm handling the extensional representation of the causal nodes and the assumptions have been omitted.

Algorithm ABDUCTION

Let σ be an activated node from which a causal path starts.
Let **SUCCESS** be the set of paths successfully arrived at a first cause from σ
    and **FAIL** the set of failed paths.
Initially, **SUCCESS** = **FAIL** = $\varnothing$.
Let **PATHS** be a set of causal paths starting at node σ. Initially, **PATHS** $\equiv$
    $\{\sigma\}$.
Choose $path_i$ from **PATHS**, and let θ be the topmost node in $path_i$ in the
    network C.
For each node $\sigma_i \in \{$Immediate causes of $\theta\}$ **do**.
    Let φ be the formula corresponding to node θ.
    Let γ_i be the (possibly empty) constraint on the edge connecting σ_i to θ in C.
    Evaluate the formula $\psi = \varphi \wedge \gamma_i$.
    If No example verifies ψ **or** (σ_i has a manifestation ξ_i in $\mathcal{P}$ **and** No example
        verifies ξ_i)
        Then FAIL = **FAIL** $\cup \{path_i\}$
        Else Hypothesize σ_i with its associated context CTX_i (if any)
    If σ_i is a first cause
        Then SUCCESS = **SUCCESS** $\cup \{path_i\}$
        Else Add σ_i to $path_i$
Endfor

The above algorithm describes how a single step of abduction is performed. Sequences of abduction steps belonging to the same path are kept together in a single global description. When an exhaustive search for causal paths is too expensive, paths that currently have less assumptions are followed first. In the example of Figure 12.4, the following causal paths have successfully been completed (among others):

Path$_1$ = <HOT(x), HEATING(x), GOOD-HEAT-CONDUCTOR(x),
    CONDUCTION(y,x), IN-THERMAL-FLUX(x), *HOT(y),*
    ADJACENT(x,y)>

Path$_2$ = <HOT(x), HEATING(x), GOOD-HEAT-CONDUCTOR(x),
    INSIDE(r,x), ELECTRICAL-POWER-DISSIPATION(r),
    ELECTRICAL-CURRENT(r), CIRCUIT(y,r),
    ELECTRICAL-VOLTAGE(y)>

In the above paths, underlined predicates are primary nodes in C, whereas italic predicates belong to contexts. Path$_1$ covers 8 examples (see Appendix A), namely, four electrical irons (examples #1–4) that are hot because of the Joule effect produced by the electrical current flow and four pots (actually three pots and one lid) (examples #18, 19, 21, 25) that are hot because of the heat conduction from some heat source with which they are in contact. During causal justification, the context $HOT(y) \wedge ADJACENT(x,y)$, associated with the first cause CONDUC-TION(y,x), is hypothesized at the same time as the first cause. Then, CONDUC-TION(y,x) is also a potential explanation for the four irons. Because of this ambiguity, the hypothesized context is checked, and it turns out that it is false for the irons and true for the pots. During verification of the context, the predicate ADJA-CENT(y,x) is tested first because it does not involve recursion. In this way, for three of the irons, this verification fails immediately, and the re-activation of the causal reasoning on HOT(y) is necessary only for one of them. However, this recursive activation also fails because the iron is adjacent to an object that is cold. Then, the cause CONDUCTION(y,x) only covers the pots, whereas ELECTRI-CAL-VOLTAGE(y) only covers the electrical irons.

12.4.3 One-Step Learning

After the process of building up, for the training examples, the justification forest, and the set of causal paths, learning can start. In particular, an initial $\mathcal{KB}$ is extracted, and afterwards, it can be refined if it is the case.

From the causal paths, an initial set of decision rules is generated, one rule for each set of explained examples. For the sake of exemplification, let us consider the two sets of four pots (covered by Path$_1$) and four irons (covered by Path$_2$).

In order to complete a causal path, several predicates, not denoting primary causal nodes, have been verified and associated with the path. In particular, let δ be the conjunction of the necessary conditions (constraints in boxes in the causal network) and ψ the conjunction of the remaining ones (predicates occurring in primary nodes and contexts). For Path$_1$, the two sets are

δ_1 = GOOD-HEAT-CONDUCTOR(x)
ψ_1= HOT(y) $\wedge$ ADJACENT(x,y)

whereas for Path$_2$, we obtain (by operationalizing ELECTRICAL-VOLTAGE(y) by means of PLUGGED-IN(y) $\wedge$ TERMINALS(y))

δ_2 = GOOD-HEAT-CONDUCTOR(x) $\wedge$ INSIDE (r,x) $\wedge$ CIRCUIT(y,r)
ψ_2 = PLUGGED-IN(y) $\wedge$ TERMINALS(y)

Then, we shall consider the following heuristic decision rules:

$r_1 \equiv$ *GOOD-HEAT-CONDUCTOR(x)* $\wedge$ HOT(y) $\wedge$ ADJACENT(x,y) $\Rightarrow$
$\qquad \Rightarrow$ UNSAFE-TO-TOUCH(x)   (7)

{If the object x is a good heat conductor, and it is in contact with a hot object y, then x is unsafe to touch.}

$r_2 \equiv$ *GOOD-HEAT-CONDUCTOR(x)* $\wedge$ *INSIDE (r,x)* $\wedge$ *CIRCUIT(y,r)* $\wedge$
$\qquad$ PLUGGED-IN(y) $\wedge$ TERMINALS(y)
$\qquad \Rightarrow$ UNSAFE-TO-TOUCH(x)   (8)

{If the object x is a good heat conductor, and there is an electrical circuit inside it whose terminals are plugged in, then x is unsafe to touch.}

The distinction between the necessary conditions (in italic) and other conditions is kept as such in the heuristic rules because we want the performance module to manage them in different ways: in fact, during classification, as well as during learning, necessary conditions are assumed false if they cannot be proved true, whereas other conditions are assumed true if they cannot be proved false.

As we can notice, rules (7) and (8) contain non-operational predicates. This is allowed not only for making assumptions in classification but also for obtaining a more compact $\mathcal{KB}$. Let us consider, for instance, the predicate GOOD-HEAT-CONDUCTOR(x); we know that metals are good heat-conductors, so that rule (7) may correspond to a possibly large number of operational rules, each one obtained by substituting steel(x), aluminum(x), silver(x), etc...., in place of GOOD-HEAT-CONDUCTOR(x). These rules are essentially the same rule. It is, then, more convenient to allow non-operational predicates to occur in the left-hand sides of the rules (Segre, 1987; Hirsh, 1988). Another advantage can be obtained with this choice: we do not need to write a $\mathcal{KB}$ separate from the justification structure. It is sufficient to link, in $\mathcal{G}$, the non-operational predicate UNSAFE-TO-TOUCH(x) to the AND nodes corresponding to left-hand sides of the rule concluding that class. In this way, the process of classifying a new instance coincides with that of justifying it and also of locating the failure point when an error occurs.

In the example given above, rules (7) and (8) are consistent (they do not cover any counterexample), but they are not complete (only 8 examples are covered by them). It turns out that one more consistent rule can be obtained in this phase, covering a hot pan inside an oven. For the remaining objects (3 types of bulbs and 2 cups filled with hot coffee), no explanation can be obtained (all paths are cut because of the failure of necessary conditions) and, hence, no rule. This case requires a session of theory revision. Even if in the example presented it is not the case, it may also happen that explanations can be found only by making some assumptions. Then, the obtained rules may not be consistent. This case requires a session of rule refinement.

12.5 KNOWLEDGE REFINEMENT

Sometimes, it may happen that the extracted rules are not sufficiently complete, and consistent or new instances are taken into account, or inconsistency in
the theory is detected. The system allows operating either on the target knowledge
base (RULE REFINEMENT), on the domain knowledge (THEORY REVISION),
or on both. The basic operations allowed are summarized in the following:

Rule Refinement:

Locate on G the node(s) responsible for the error.
. **If** There is an omission error **Then** Generalize $\mathcal{KB}$.
If There is a commission error **Then** Specialize $\mathcal{KB}$, possibly by invoking
   induction.
Update the data base.
Update the justification forest.

Theory Revision:

If A justification should have been found and was not
   Then Invoke *induction* for filling a gap in $\mathcal{P}$, or ask the expert to
            generalize $\mathcal{P}$ and/or extend C.
If A justification was found and should not have been found
   Then Ask the expert to specialize $\mathcal{P}$ and/or modify C.
Evaluate the consequences of the suggested modifications.
Ask the expert to choose his/her preferred modifications and add them to $\mathcal{T}$.
Update all data structures.

Rule refinement can be activated by the rule learning phase if the system was
unable to find "good" rules or by the performance module if new instances are
misclassified. Theory revision implies a much deeper intervention in the knowledge
and is activated when some contradiction arises during the justification phase.

12.5.1 Target Knowledge Refinement

Knowledge refinement will only be briefly outlined here because it has
already been discussed elsewhere (Botta, Giordana, and Saitta, 1990). It is not
necessary that knowledge refinement be invoked on a $\mathcal{KB}$ acquired as described in
the previous subsection. On the contrary, the $\mathcal{KB}$ may come from a different source,
for instance, from an expert. Hence, let us suppose that someone suggested the
following rule:

$$r \equiv OBJ(x) \wedge body(y) \wedge part\text{-}of(y,x) \wedge closed(y) \wedge METAL(y) \wedge$$
$$CABLE(z) \wedge part\ of(z,x) \wedge medium\text{-}size(x)$$
$$\Rightarrow UNSAFE\text{-}TO\text{-}TOUCH(x) \qquad\qquad (9)$$

{If a medium-size object x has a closed, metallic body and a cable among its component parts, then x is unsafe to touch.}

By considering that CABLE(x) can be operationalized by thread(x) and by ELECTRICAL-CABLE(x,y), rule (9) has two alternative operationalizations on the set of 32 training examples:

$r_1 \equiv$ OBJ(x) $\wedge$ body(y) $\wedge$ part-of(y,x) $\wedge$ closed(y) $\wedge$ aluminum(y) $\wedge$
    thread(z) $\wedge$ part-of(z,x) $\wedge$ medium-size(x)
    $\Rightarrow$ UNSAFE-TO-TOUCH(x)   (10)
{If a medium-size object x has, among its component parts, a closed body made of aluminum and a thread, then x is unsafe to touch.}

$r_2 \equiv$ OBJ(x) $\wedge$ body(y) $\wedge$ part-of(y,x) $\wedge$ closed(y) $\wedge$ steel(y) $\wedge$ cord(z) $\wedge$
    plug(w) $\wedge$ connected-to(w,z) $\wedge$ part-of(z,x) $\wedge$ medium-size(x)
    $\Rightarrow$ UNSAFE-TO-TOUCH(x)   (11)
{If a medium-size object x has, among its component parts, a closed body made of steel and a cord with an attached plug, then x is unsafe to touch.}

Rule r_1 correctly covers a hot electrical iron but incorrectly covers a window shade-handle, which is safe to touch. On the other hand, r_2 correctly covers three plugged-in irons and incorrectly covers two unplugged irons. If we try to justify rule r, we notice that the window shade-handle belongs to the extension of CABLE (x) but not to that of ELECTRICAL-CABLE(x,y). Then, CABLE(x) is too general, and the counterexample can be cut by specializing (9) as follows:

OBJ(x) $\wedge$ body(y) $\wedge$ part-of(y,x) $\wedge$ closed(y) $\wedge$ METAL(y) $\wedge$ medium-
size(x) $\wedge$ part of(z,x) $\wedge$ ELECTRICAL-CABLE(z, r)
$\Rightarrow$ UNSAFE-TO-TOUCH(x)   (12)
{If a medium-size object x has, among its component parts, a closed, metallic body and an electrical cable, then x is unsafe to touch.}

Rule (12) still covers two unplugged irons. Using the algorithm for finding causal paths described in Section 12.4, we can prove that for the set of hot irons

$\mathcal{T} \models$ [OBJ(x) $\wedge$ body(y) $\wedge$ part-of(y,x) $\wedge$ METAL(y) $\wedge$ cord(z) $\wedge$ plug(w) $\wedge$
    $\wedge$ connected-to(w,z) $\wedge$ resistance(u) $\wedge$ socket(v) $\wedge$ connected-to(z,u) $\wedge$
    $\wedge$ inside(u,y) $\wedge$ inserted-in(w,v) $\Rightarrow$ UNSAFE-TO-TOUCH(x)]   (13)
{If an object x has, among its component parts, a metallic body with a resistance inside, and moreover, this resistance is connected to a cord with an attached plug, which is, in turn, plugged into a socket, then x is unsafe to touch.}

Comparing rule (13) and rule (12), we notice that there is an overlapping part

$\rho \equiv$ OBJ(x) $\wedge$ body(y) $\wedge$ part-of(y,x) $\wedge$ METAL(y) $\wedge$
       $\wedge$ ELECTRICAL-CABLE(z,r) $\wedge$ part-of(z,x)

that constitutes the justified part of rule (12). Notice that predicates closed(y), referring to the body, and medium-size(x) are not justified by the theory. In order to cut the two unplugged irons, rule (13) suggests a set of predicates to possibly be added to rule (12): {resistance(u), socket(v), connected-to(z,u), inside(u,y), inserted-in(w,v)}. By analyzing the extensions of these predicates, we notice that inserted-in(w,v) covers exactly the four irons that we want to cover and nothing else. However, by climbing the justification forest, we find the node PLUGGED-IN(w), which is more general (hence potentially covering more examples) and does not cover any counterexamples, so this last node is chosen to be added. Finally, we obtain the consistent rule

OBJ(x) $\wedge$ body(y) $\wedge$ part-of(y,x) $\wedge$ METAL(y) $\wedge$ ELECTRICAL
    -CABLE(z,r) $\wedge$ part of(z,x) $\wedge$ PLUGGED-IN(z)
$\Rightarrow$ UNSAFE-TO-TOUCH(x)   (14)
{If an object x has, among its component parts, a metallic body and a
plugged-in electrical cable, then x is unsafe to touch.}

The above described methodology for acquiring discrimination rules has also been applied to a real domain of mechanical diagnosis of 5 fault classes in horizontal centrifugal motor-pumps. In this application, the rules learned from only 30 examples (5 for each class) showed, on a test set of 170 examples, performances comparable to those of the rule base which was learned without causal model (but with domain theory) from 140 examples. Moreover, the rules obtained from the causal model were clearly comprehensible to the expert of the domain in terms of his understanding of the underlying phenomena.

12.5.2 Theory Revision

An interesting aspect of the system WHY is its ability to work in an interactive manner during several phases of its behavior. In order to facilitate this interaction, a friendly, menu-driven user interface has been implemented.

Interaction with the expert occurs at the beginning, when he/she is required to give an initial bulk of phenomenological theory and an abstract causal model. Because this knowledge can easily be revised later, it is not very critical that it be as complete and consistent as possible from the beginning. Because of the deep integration of the performance module in the learning process, the expert can let WHY run on his/her suggested modifications, analyze the results, and modify the theory accordingly. This kind of interaction is two-way: the feedback from WHY helps the expert to focus his/her attention on defective parts of the theory, whereas the expert can direct the system to explore the consequences of a subset of the current theory, saving computational efforts.

The human expertise can also be exploited in knowledge refinement because the expert can directly suggest heuristic rules or parts of them or can guide the system toward more promising rule specializations or generalizations, telling explicitly which predicates to try to remove or add. For instance, in this case, the expert is presented with the following menu:

Refine Menu

The expert selects a rule r to be refined. Rule r may exist in the knowledge base or can be a hint from the expert.

Current rule: r

Rule syntax: $\varphi \to h$

Rule assumptions: {set of conjuncts in φ that have been assumed}

Dependency rules: {if φ contains an Ω, a dependency rule may be associated with it in order to limit induction to a subspace of formulas}

Extension: {set of bindings for each example covered, containing the identifier of the instance, the correct class, the sets of instance parts satisfying φ, and the number of assumptions made for each binding)

General: {set of rules, more general than r, existing in $\mathcal{KB}$}

Specific: {set of rules, more specific than r, existing in $\mathcal{KB}$}

The expert can select from among the following choices:

Delete   =   Deactivate r.

Forest   =   Show the justification forest for r.

Save   =   Save r.

Spec   =   Activate a rule in **Specific** instead of r.

Gen   =   Activate a rule in **General** instead of r.

Ref-pred =   Modify r by refining a predicate {climbing a taxonomy or choosing an operationalization}.

Ref-ind   =   Specialize r by invoking induction.

The intervention of the expert during theory revision can be spontaneous, or it can be requested by WHY when some contradiction arises. As an example, let us consider the case of the three hot bulbs, which cannot be justified even by making assumptions. The reason is that there is no mention, in $\mathcal{T}$, of how electrical current can flow into the bulb filament. Because we know that the bulbs are positive instances of the concept UNSAFE-TO-TOUCH, and no explanation could be found, we are in the presence of an incompleteness in the theory. Then, WHY signals the problem and presents the expert with the part of the justification forest instantiated on the bulbs and with the set FAIL of failed causal paths. At the same time, it asks the expert if he/she wants to modify the causal model or the phenomenological theory. According to the expert's answer, an appropriate menu appears (similar to the REFINE MENU above).

In the considered case, the expert chooses to revise $\mathcal{P}$ because he knows that the problem is in the incomplete definition of the predicate TERMINALS. Then, he/she adds a new operationalization of TERMINALS, stating that the electrical contact of the bulb is TERMINALS:

$$\text{electrical\_contact}(x) \wedge \text{bulb}(y) \wedge \text{part-of}(x,y) \Rightarrow \text{TERMINALS}(x)$$

It is interesting to note that a first trial of refining an incomplete explanation for the bulbs by induction succeeded; in fact, WHY covered the three bulbs and no counterexamples by adding to the partial rule, extracted from the justification forest, the predicate bright(x), true for all three objects. However, this modification is doubtful because of the number of considered examples, whereas the same predicate, added after completing the theory, can be trusted.

12.6 CLASSIFICATION STRATEGY

As mentioned in the preceding sections, the performance module is fully integrated with the learning module in the system WHY. The target knowledge base $\mathcal{KB}$ is kept in an internal format that mirrors the way decision rules are acquired and allows a fast classification process to be performed. As an example, let us consider again rule (14), whose internal structure is reported in Figure 12.5.

As it can be noted, only those parts of the justification forest directly involved with the rule are linked with non-operational predicates. In this way, a simple

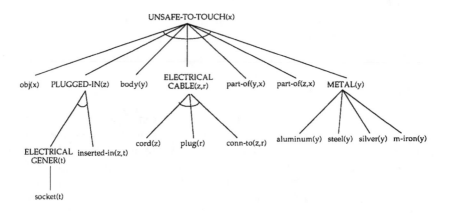

Figure 12.5:   Internal structure of a decision rule

bottom-up (or top-down) verification process can be performed by proving non-operational predicates only using operationalizations reported in the justification structure (and not all the possible ones defined in the phenomenological theory), as described by the following algorithm.

Classify:

Given an unknown instance f.

Starting from the leaves of the justification forest true of f, prove predicates in the forest following its structure.

At the end, some of the decision rules have possibly been verified.

Perform a tie-breaking process.

If it succeeds, and the classification is correct

Then Update the data base.

Update the justification forest.

Else Perform a refinement step according to expert's choice.

It should be noted that necessary conditions are marked in rule (14) and used in the classification process to reduce the set of competing rules to fire. Predicates that are used to prove necessary conditions cannot be assumed true.

When more than one rule has been verified, the number of other conditions assumed let the system decide which rule is winning the tie-breaking process and will be used to classify the instance. At this point, if an error occurs, the expert can decide to perform a refinement step either on the target knowledge base or on the domain knowledge, as described earlier.

12.7 CONCLUSIONS

The system WHY, which learns diagnostic rules from a set of examples (by induction), from a phenomenological theory (by deduction), and from a causal model (by abduction), has been presented. The system can work automatically and in an interactive mode. The exploitation of a causal model proved to be particularly useful during knowledge refinement in that it allowed gaps and errors in the knowledge base to be located easily and corrected, at the same time, keeping the computational effort within acceptable bounds.

The possibility of interacting with the system and of obtaining direct information about the effects of proposed theory updates has also been very much appreciated by human experts. For this reason, it is worth developing friendly interfaces for serving this goal.

An aspect not yet investigated up to now is the possibility of using the causal model to predict suitable sequences of examples to be presented to the learning system in order to obtain a faster convergence toward an effective knowledge base.

On the other hand, the design and implementation efforts required for developing a system of the type of WHY make it suitable in a multi-task environment, where the same *a priori* knowledge could be used, for instance, for developing intelligent systems for diagnosis, for design, for monitoring, and so on, within the same domain.

ACKNOWLEDGMENTS

This work has been supported by the Italian CNR Project "Progetto Finalizzato INFORMATICA."

References

Bergadano, F., and Giordana, A. "A Knowledge Intensive Approach to Concept Induction," *Proc. of the Machine Learning Conference*, 305–317, Ann Arbor, MI, Morgan Kaufmann, San Mateo, CA, 1988.

Bergadano, F., Giordana, A., and Ponsero, S. "Deduction in Top-down Inductive Learning," *Proc. of the Machine Learning Conference*, 23–25, Ithaca, NY, Morgan Kaufmann, San Mateo, CA, 1989.

Bergadano, F., Giordana, A., and Saitta, L. "Automated Concept Acquisition in Noisy Environment," *IEEE Transactions on Pattern Analysis and Machine Intelligence*, Vol. PAMI-10, 555–575, 1988.

Bergadano, F., Giordana, A., and Saitta, L. "Automated versus Manual Knowledge Acquisition: A Comparison in a Real Domain," *Proc. of the First Japanese Knowledge Acquisition for Knowledge-Based Systems Workshop*, 301–314, OHMSHA, Tokyo, Japan, 1990.

Botta, M., and Saitta, L. "Improving Knowledge Base System Performances by Experience," *Proc. of the EWSL-88*, 15–23, Glasgow, UK, Pitman, London, 1988.

Botta, M., Giordana, A., and Saitta, L. "Knowledge Base Refinement Using a Causal Model," *Intelligent Systems: State of the Art and Future Trends*, Ras, Z. and Zemankova, M. (Eds.), 337–356, Ellis Horwood Ltd., Chichester, UK, 1990.

Botta, M., Ravotto, S., and Saitta, L. "Use of Causal Models and Abduction in Learning Diagnostic Knowledge," *International Journal of Man-Machine Studies*, Vol. 36, 289–307, 1992.

Cestnik, B., and Bratko, I. "Learning Redundant Rules in Noisy Domains," *Proc. of the ECAI-88*, 348–350, Munich, W. Germany, Pitman, London, 1988.

Clark, K. "Negation as Failure," *Logic and Data Bases*, Gallaire, H. and Minker, J. (Eds.), 275–295, Plenum Press, New York, 1978.

Console, L., and Saitta, L. "Abduction, Induction and Inverse Resolution," *Proc. of the First Compulog-Net Workshop on Logic Programming in AI*, London, UK, 1992.

Cox, P.T., and Pietrzykowski, T. "General Diagnosis by Abductive Inference," *Proc. of the IEEE Symposium on Logic Programming*, 183–189, IEEE Computer Society, Washington, DC, 1987.

Davis, R. "Diagnostic Reasoning Based on Structure and Behavior," *Artificial Intelligence*, Vol. 24, 347–410, 1984.

DeJong, G., and Mooney, R. "Explanation Based Learning: An Alternative View," *Machine Learning*, Vol. 1, 47–80, 1986.

DeJong, G. "Plausible Inference vs. Abduction," *Proc. of the AAAI Symposium on Automated Abduction*, 48–51, AAAI Press, Menlo Park, CA, 1990.

de Kleer, J., and Seely Brown, J. "Theories of Causal Ordering," *Artificial Intelligence*, Vol. 29, 33–61, 1986.

Eshghi, K. and Kowalski, R. "Abduction Compared with Negation by Failure," *Proc. of the Sixth International Conference on Logic Programming*, 234–254, Lisbon, Portugal, 1989.

Geffner, H. "Causal Theories for Default and Abductive Reasoning," *Proc. of the AAAI Symposium on Automated Abduction*, 150–154, AAAI Press, Menlo Park, CA, 1990.

Genesereth, M. "The Use of Design Descriptions in Automated Diagnosis," *Artificial Intelligence*, Vol. 24, 411–436, 1984.

Hartley, R., and Coombs, M. "Abduction in Model Generative Reasoning," *Proc. of the AAAI Symposium on Automated Abduction*, 130–134, AAAI Press, Menlo Park, CA, 1990.

Hempel, C., and Oppenheim, P. "Studies in the Logic of Explanation," *Philosophy of Science*, Vol. 15, 135–75, 1948.

Hirsh, H. "Reasoning about Operationality for Explanation-based Learning," *Proc. of the Machine Learning Conference*, 214–220, Ann Arbor, MI, Morgan Kaufmann, San Mateo, CA, 1988.

Keller, R. "Defining Operationality for EBL," *Artificial Intelligence*, Vol. 35, 227–242, 1988.

Lebowitz, M. "Integrated Learning: Controlling Explanation," *Cognitive Science*, Vol. 10, No. 2, 219–240, 1986.

Levesque, H. "A Knowledge-level Account of Abduction," *Proc. of the IJCAI-89*, 1061–1067, AAAI Press, Menlo Park, CA, 1989.

Michalski, R.S., and Chilauski, R.L. "Learning by Being Told and Learning from Examples: An Experimental Comparison of the Two Methods of Knowledge Acquisition in the Context of Developing an Expert System for Soybean Disease Diagnosis," *International Journal of Policy Analysis and Information Systems*, Vol. 4, No. 2, 125–126, 1980.

Michalski, R.S. "A Theory and Methodology of Inductive Learning," *Artificial Intelligence*, Vol. 24, 111–161, 1983.

—————. *Toward a Unified Theory of Learning: Multistrategy Task-adaptive Learning*, Technical Report, Machine Learning and Inference Laboratory, MLI 90–1, Center for Artificial Intelligence, George Mason University, Fairfax, VA, 1990.

————. "Inferential Learning Theory as a Basis for Multistrategy Task-adaptive Learning," *Proc. of the First International Workshop on Multistrategy Learning*, 3–18, Harpers Ferry, WV, 1991.

Mitchell, T. "Generalization as Search," *Artificial Intelligence*, Vol. 18, 203–226, 1982.

Mitchell, T., Keller, R., and Kedar-Cabelli, S. "Explanation Based Generalization," *Machine Learning*, Vol. 1, 47–80, 1986.

Morris, S., and O'Rorke, P. "An Approach to Theory Revision Using Abduction," *Proc. of the AAAI Symposium on Automated Abduction*, 33–37, AAAI Press, Menlo Park, CA, 1990.

Mozetic, I., and Holzbaur, C. "Extending Explanation-based Generalization by Abstraction Operators," *Proc. of the EWSL-91*, 282–297, Porto, Portugal, 1991.

Pazzani, M.J. "Integrating Explanation-based and Empirical Learning Methods in OCCAM," *Proc. of the EWSL-88*, 147–165, Glasgow, UK, 1988.

Peirce, C. *Collected Papers of Charles Sanders Peirce*, Harvard University Press, Cambridge, MA, 1953.

Poole, D. "Representing Knowledge for Logic-based Diagnosis," *Proc. of the Int. Conf. on Fifth Generation Computer Systems*, 1282–1290, Tokyo, Japan, 1988.

Quinlan, R. "Induction of Decision Trees," *Machine Learning*, Vol. 1, 81–106, 1986.

Reiter, R. "A Theory of Diagnosis from First Principles," *Artificial Intelligence*, Vol. 32, 57–95, 1984.

Robinson, J.A., and Siebert, E.E. "LOGLISP: An Alternative to Prolog," *Machine Intelligence*, Vol. 10, 399–419, 1982.

Saitta, L., Botta, M., Ravotto, S., and Sperotto, S. "Improving Learning by Using Deep Models," *Proc. of the First International Workshop on Multistrategy Learning*, 131–143, Harpers Ferry, WV, George Mason University Press, Fairfax, VA, 1991.

Salmon, W. *Four Decades of Scientific Explanation*, University of Minnesota Press, Minneapolis, MN, 1989.

Segre, A.M. "On the Operationality/Generality Trade-off in Explanation-based Learning," *Proc. of the IJCAI-87*, 242–248, AAAI Press, Menlo Park, CA, 1987.

Tecuci, G. "Learning as Understanding the External World," *Proc. of the First International Workshop on Multistrategy Learning*, 49–64, Harpers Ferry, WV, 1991.

Torasso, P., and Console, L. *Diagnostic Problem Solving*, Van Nostrand Reinhold, New York, 1989.

APPENDIX A

For the case study reported in this chapter, the following examples have been used (examples of the same type differ for attribute and relation values):

Unsafe-to-Touch	*Safe-to-Touch*
# 1 Plugged-in electric iron	# 3 Unplugged electric iron
# 2 Plugged-in electric iron	# 5 Unplugged electric iron
# 4 Plugged-in electric iron	# 7 Charcoal iron on a table
# 6 Plugged-in electric iron	# 8 Charcoal iron on a cupboard
# 11 Glass filled with hot tea	# 9 Coca-Cola can
# 12 Cup filled with hot coffee	# 10 Glass
# 13 Bright bulb	# 14 Bulb
# 15 Bright bulb	# 17 Neon-bulb on a table
# 16 Bright neon-bulb	# 20 Pot on a table
# 18 Pot on a fire	# 22 Pan inside a cupboard
# 19 Pot on an electrical plate	# 24 Lid inside a cupboard
# 21 Pan on charcoal	# 26 Knife inside a drawer
# 23 Baking-tin inside oven	# 27 Knife on a table
# 25 Lid on a pot on a fire	# 28 Fork on a table
	# 29 Fork inside a bowl
	# 30 Spoon inside a pot
	# 31 Window-shade handle
	# 32 Window-shade handle

The descriptions of objects #1 and #20 are reported in the following for the sake of exemplification.

1 = Plugged-in electrical iron (object's name = a)

{obj(a), medium(a), new(a), body(b), steel(b), gray(b), convex(b), opaque(b), closed(b), handle(c), large(c), bakelite(c), black(c), arch(c), over(c,b), part-of(b,a), full(b), part-of(c,a), cord(d), long(d), cotton(d), white(d), flexible(d), plug(e), connected-to(e,d), part-of(d,a), water-chamber(f), inside(f,b), resistance(g), inside(g,b), connected-to(d,g), bottom(h), part-of(h,b), flat(h), smooth(h)}

20 = Pot on a table (object's name = a)

{obj(a), medium(a), body(b), pottery(b), brown(b), cylinder(b), opaque(b), open(b), empty(b), handle(c), small(c), pottery(c), brown(c), semicircle(c), handle(d), small(d), pottery(d), brown(d), semicircle(d), different(c,d), part-of(b,a), part-of(c,a), part-of(d,a), connected-to(c,b), connected-to(d,b), opposite(c,d), bottom(e), part-of(e,b), flat(e), smooth(e)}

13

INTROSPECTIVE REASONING USING META-EXPLANATIONS FOR MULTISTRATEGY LEARNING

Ashwin Ram
Michael Cox
*(College of Computing,
Georgia Institute of Technology)*

Abstract

In order to learn effectively, a reasoner must not only possess knowledge about the world and be able to improve that knowledge, but it also must introspectively reason about how it performs a given task and what particular pieces of knowledge it needs to improve its performance at the current task. Introspection requires declarative representations of meta-knowledge of the reasoning performed by the system during the performance task, of the system's knowledge, and of the organization of this knowledge. This chapter presents a taxonomy of possible reasoning failures that can occur during a performance task, declarative representations of these failures, and associations between failures and particular learning strategies. The theory is based on Meta-XPs, which are explanation structures that help the system identify failure types, formulate learning goals, and choose appropriate learning strategies in order to avoid similar mistakes in the future. The theory is implemented in a computer model of an introspective reasoner that performs multistrategy learning during a story understanding task.

13.1 INTRODUCTION

It is generally accepted that learning is central to intelligent reasoning systems that perform realistic reasoning tasks, such as understanding natural language stories or solving non-trivial problems (e.g., Schank, 1983). It is impossible to anticipate all possible situations in advance and to hand-program a machine with exactly the right knowledge to deal with all the situations it might be faced with. Rather, during the performance of any non-trivial reasoning task, whether by humans or by machines, there will always be difficulties and failures. Intelligence lies in the ability to recover from such failures and, more importantly, to learn from them so as not to make the same mistake in future situations. In addition, the reasoner needs to identify what it needs to learn and to focus its learning in order to avoid the combinatorial explosion of inferences and search necessary in complex, unrestricted situations.

A general theory of multistrategy learning must provide a taxonomy of the types of reasoning situations that provide an opportunity to learn, strategies for learning in different situations, and methods for selecting appropriate learning strategies based on what needs to be learned. The central claim of this chapter is that in order to learn effectively, a system must not only possess knowledge about the world and be able to improve that knowledge, but it also must introspectively reason about how it performs a given task and identify what particular pieces of knowledge it needs to improve its performance at the current task. To see why this must be so, consider three fundamental problems in learning.

Although several researchers have attempted to develop algorithms for machine learning that can acquire knowledge through the generalization of input examples or experiences, little effort has been made to formulate a general solution to the problem of identifying what needs to be learned in the first place. When a reasoner encounters a problem, a contradiction, or an unexpected event, it is clear there is a need to learn some piece of knowledge that, had it been present, would have prevented such a problem from occurring, but from where does the problem arise? Perhaps the information the reasoner was provided to base its conclusion on was incomplete, or perhaps its own knowledge used to interpret such information was incomplete. Perhaps the reasoner used an inappropriate piece of knowledge for the current situation. Perhaps the reasoner chose the wrong strategy to, say, verify a hypothesis or looked in the wrong place to gather evidence. Identifying the cause of a reasoning failure (or the cause of an expected success) is known as the *blame (or credit) assignment problem* (e.g., Hammond, 1989; Minsky, 1963; Weintraub, 1991).

Traditional approaches in machine learning have assumed that the knowledge to be learned has already been identified by an external agent. In Winston's (1975) arch learning program, for example, the user decided that the concept of an arch was a useful concept to teach the program. Mitchell, Keller, and Kedar-Cabelli's

(1986) explanation-based generalization algorithm relies on a "target concept" to be learned, which is supplied as input to the algorithm. In some approaches, the learning process has no target or goal at all; the program has no sense of what it is trying to learn or why it is trying to learn it. Recently, some researchers have argued that the identification of what might be called the "learning goals" of the reasoner is an important aspect of the learning problem (e.g., Hunter, 1990; Ram, 1991; Ram and Hunter, 1992; Michalski, 1994, Chapter 1 in this book). This view is consistent with psychological data on goal orientation in learning (e.g., Ng and Bereiter, 1991). In the authors' own research, it is argued that active, goal-based learning is important for both computational reasons and cognitive reasons (Ram, 1991; Ram and Hunter, 1992). Furthermore, it is argued that learning goals should not be thought of as external input to a learning program but rather should be generated by the program itself.

Given that the reasoner knows that an error occurred and what type of error it is the second step following blame assignment is to determine what needs to be learned. This is referred to as the problem of *deciding what to learn* or, equivalently, the problem of formulating learning goals to pursue. For any given failure, there could be a large set of possible lessons to be drawn. Choosing the appropriate one depends not only on the type of the reasoning failure but also on the prior goals and tasks of the reasoner and the current state of its knowledge. Often, a desired piece of knowledge will not be immediately available in the input. In such cases, the reasoner must be able to suspend its learning goals and reactivate them later when an appropriate opportunity arises.

Finally, if the reasoner knows what to learn, it still needs to identify what method is best suited for performing the desired learning. In many cases, a combination of learning strategies is necessary. For example, if the reasoner is presented with a novel explanation for a problem, it needs to be able both to acquire such an explanation in a general way (explanation generalization) and to remember it again in future situations in which it is likely to be applicable (index learning). Furthermore, a single learning strategy may be applicable in a number of different reasoning situations. For example, the reasoner may need to learn a new index to an explanation, both when the explanation is newly acquired and when the explanation is already known but incorrectly indexed in memory. Identifying appropriate learning strategies is called the *strategy selection problem* and is particularly important in multistrategy learning systems (e.g., Cox and Ram, 1992; Reich, 1994, Chapter 14 in this book).

Machine learning research, for the most part, has focused on the development of learning algorithms for different situations. Most systems arising from this research are based on the application of a learning algorithm to a well-defined learning problem in the domain of interest. When one attempts to extend these systems to incorporate multiple learning strategies, one runs into an interesting problem: these systems cannot make decisions concerning which learning strategies to use in different circumstances. These decisions are made ahead of time by the system designer. Furthermore, it is difficult to extend these systems to allow them to make their own decisions about which learning strategies to pursue because the knowledge used to make these decisions is buried in the procedures that make up the system. This further complicates the strategy selection problem.

These issues are addressed using the following approach. First, classes of learning situations are identified based on an analysis of the types of reasoning failures that occur. Next, each type of reasoning failure is characterized by a description of how the conclusions were drawn (a description of a chain of reasoning led up to those conclusions), why these conclusions were drawn (a description of the bases for the processing decisions underlying that chain of reasoning), why the conclusions were faulty (an explanation of why the drawn conclusions were incorrect), what the correct conclusions ought to have been (a description of the desired conclusions), and how the reasoner should have drawn them (a description of a chain of reasoning that would lead to the desired conclusions).[1] Finally, each type of reasoning failure is associated with the learning that needs to occur to avoid such a failure and the strategies that can perform the desired learning.

This information is represented explicitly in the system using a meta-model describing the reasoning process itself. In addition to the world model that describes its domain, the reasoning system has access to meta-models describing its reasoning processes, the knowledge that this reasoning is based on, and the indices used to organize and retrieve this knowledge. A meta-model is used to represent the system's reasoning during a performance task, the decisions it took while performing the reasoning, and the results of the reasoning. If a difficulty or failure is encountered, the system introspectively examines its own reasoning processes to determine where the problem lies and uses this introspective understanding to improve itself using the appropriate learning strategies.

Many research projects in AI have demonstrated the advantages of representing knowledge about the world in a declarative manner. Using such knowledge, a reasoner can create an explicit representation of events in the world. Such data structures can be used to reason about the world in a systematic fashion. Similarly, it is claimed here that declarative knowledge about reasoning can be beneficial in reasoning about one's own thoughts. Just as reasoning involves the processing of explicit structures representing physical events in the world, introspection involves the processing of explicit structures representing mental events in the head.

Introspective reasoning of this type is central to the solution of the credit/blame assignment problem, the problem of deciding what to learn, and the strategy selection problem and, hence, to learning. Furthermore, introspective rea-

---

[1] In general, a complete explanation of a reasoning failure would have all these components. In any given situation, however, the reasoner might only be able to construct a partial explanation, which would then determine what the reasoner can learn from that experience.

soning not only guides learning about the world but can also help the reasoner improve its own reasoning processes. Because the decisions made when choosing reasoning strategies, the results of these decisions, and the trace and final outcome of the reasoning process are all made explicit, the reasoner can learn to make better decisions by analyzing its own behavior and, hence, improve its own reasoning. This allows the reasoner to improve the decisions that underlie reasoning and learning and, thus, provides a method for "learning to learn." As noted by Minsky (1985) and others, such learning is the foundation upon which to develop truly intelligent systems.

13.2 OVERVIEW OF THE APPROACH

This chapter proposes a theory of multistrategy learning in which the reasoner models its own reasoning processes explicitly and analyzes this model after a reasoning experience in order to identify what it needs to learn and to select the appropriate learning strategy from a set of available strategies. The introspective analysis is done using a meta-model of the reasoner's own knowledge and reasoning processes. A theory of content and representation of these meta-models is presented along with a computer model, Meta-AQUA, that implements this theory for a story understanding task.

The theory focuses on failure-driven learning. The term "failure" includes not simply performance errors but also expectation failures (Schank, 1986), anomalous situations that the reasoner failed to predict, and other types of reasoning failures. Unlike successful processing where there may or may not be anything to learn, failure situations are guaranteed to provide a potential for learning; otherwise, the failure would not have occurred (Minsky, 1985).[2] When a reasoning failure occurs, the system posts a *knowledge goal* that drives the reasoner to explain or otherwise resolve the gaps in its knowledge. Knowledge goals, often expressed as questions, represent the reasoner's goals to learn (Ram, 1991; Ram & Hunter, 1992). In order to learn from the failure and to avoid repeating the same mistake in the future, the system needs to identify the cause of the failure and then, depending upon the cause, apply a given learning strategy.

The key representational entity in the theory is a *meta-explanation pattern* (Meta-XP), which is a causal, introspective explanation structure that explains how and why an agent reasons and that helps the system in the learning task. The theory of reasoning and learning is based on these structures. There are two broad classes of Meta-XPs. *Trace Meta-XPs* record a trace of the reasoning performed by a system, along with causal links that explain the decisions taken. *Introspective*

---

[2] In Meta-AQUA, an unexpected success also counts as a reasoning "failure" because the reasoner was unable to correctly predict the outcome of the task.

Meta-XPs are structures used to explain and learn from a reasoning failure. They associate a failure type with a particular set of learning strategies and point to likely sources of the failure within the Trace Meta-XP. Note that Trace Meta-XPs explain how a system draws its conclusions, while Introspective Meta-XPs explain why these conclusions fail in particular situations.

Meta-XPs form the basis for the introspective reasoning necessary for experience-based, goal-directed learning in situations when the reasoner encounters a reasoning failure. Consider the following three types of reasoning failures:

- **Novel situation:** An expectation failure can arise when the reasoner does not have the appropriate knowledge structures to deal with a situation. The situation is said to be anomalous with respect to the current knowledge in the system. In such a situation, the reasoner could use a variety of learning strategies, including explanation-based generalization (DeJong and Mooney, 1986; Mitchell, Keller, and Kedar-Cabelli, 1986), inductive generalization from input examples (Michalski, 1983), and explanation-based refinement (Ram, 1993) coupled with index learning to place the new structures appropriately in memory.

- **Incorrect background knowledge:** Even if the reasoner has knowledge structures that are applicable to the situation, these knowledge structures may be incomplete or incorrect. Learning in such situations is usually incremental and involves strategies such as elaborative question asking (Ram, 1993) applied to the reasoning chain and abstraction, generalization, and specialization techniques in conceptual memory (Michalski, 1994, Chapter 1 in this book).

- **Mis-indexed knowledge structure:** The reasoner may have an applicable knowledge structure, but it may not be indexed in memory such that it can be retrieved using the particular cues provided by the context. In this case, the system must add a new index or generalize an existing index based on the context. If on the other hand, the reasoner retrieves a structure that later proves inappropriate, it must specialize the indices to this structure so the retrieval will not recur in similar situations. Learning the right indices to organize knowledge in memory is known as index learning (e.g., Hammond, 1989; Bhatta and Ram, 1991; Ram, 1993).

To learn from such failures, the reasoning system uses a multistrategy learning approach in which it records and analyzes a declarative trace of its own reasoning process using a Trace Meta-XP. The data structure holds explicit information concerning the manner in which knowledge gaps are identified, the reasons why particular hypotheses are generated, the strategies chosen for verifying candidate hypotheses, and the basis for choosing particular reasoning methods for each of these. If the system encounters a reasoning failure, it then uses Introspective Meta-

XPs to examine the declarative reasoning chain. An Introspective Meta-XP performs three functions: (1) it aids in blame assignment (determining which knowledge structures are missing, incorrect, or inappropriately applied), (2) it aids in the formulation of appropriate knowledge goals to pursue, and (3) it aids in the selection of appropriate learning algorithms to recover and learn from the reasoning error. Such meta-explanations augment a system's ability to introspectively reason about its own knowledge, about gaps within this knowledge, and about the reasoning processes that attempt to fill these gaps. The use of explicit Meta-XP structures allows direct inspection of the reasons by which knowledge goals are posted and processed, thus enabling a system to improve its ability to reason and learn.

13.3 EXAMPLE: THE DRUG BUST

To instantiate and test the theory, an introspective version of the AQUA system (Ram, 1991, 1993) called Meta-AQUA has been implemented. AQUA is a question-driven story understanding system that learns about Middle Eastern terrorist activities. Its performance task is to "understand" the story by building causal explanations that link the individual events in the story into a coherent whole and by building motivational explanations of the actions observed in the story that causally relate the actions to the goals, plans, and beliefs of the actors and planners of the actions. Although AQUA is a general model of case-based learning with multiple learning methods (see Ram, 1993), it falls short of being a general model of multistrategy learning, as defined in this chapter, because the knowledge underlying the selection of appropriate learning methods in different situations is not explicitly represented in the system. The Meta-AQUA system extends AQUA by adding a model of introspective reasoning and multistrategy learning using Meta-XP structures. Unlike AQUA, Meta-AQUA does not actually parse the sentences; because this research does not deal with the natural language understanding problem, it is assumed that input sentences are already represented conceptually. To illustrate the type of introspection Meta-AQUA performs and the type of learning that results, consider the following story:

S1: A police dog sniffed at a passenger's luggage in the Atlanta airport terminal.

S2: The dog suddenly began to bark at the luggage.

S3: The authorities arrested the passenger, charging him with smuggling drugs.

S4: The dog barked because it detected two kilograms of marijuana in the luggage.

Several inferences can be made from this story, many of which may be incorrect, depending on the knowledge of the reader. Meta-AQUA's initial knowledge includes general facts about dogs and sniffing, including the fact that dogs bark when threatened by other animate agents, but it has no knowledge of police drug dogs in particular. It also knows of past terrorist smuggling cases but has never seen a case of drug interdiction. Nonetheless, the program is able to recover and learn from the erroneous inferences this story generates.

The line of reasoning that Meta-AQUA pursues in processing this story is as follows. S1 produces no inferences other than the observation that sniffing is a normal event in the life of a dog. However, S2 produces an anomaly because the system's definition of bark specifies that the object of the bark is animate. In this example, the program (incorrectly) believes that dogs bark only when threatened by animate agents. Because luggage is an inanimate object, there is a contradiction, leading to a reasoning failure. This anomaly causes the understander to ask why the dog barked at an inanimate object. This question may lead the system to learn something useful about dogs at some point in the future. Until this question is answered, however, the system can only assume (again, incorrectly) that the luggage somehow threatened the dog.

S3 asserts an arrest scene that reminds Meta-AQUA of a prior incident of weapons smuggling by terrorists. The system then infers the existence of a smuggling bust that includes detection, confiscation, and arrest scenes. Because baggage searches are the only detection method the system knows, the sniffing event remains unconnected to the rest of the story.

Finally, S4 causes the question generated by S2 "Why did the dog bark?" to be retrieved, and the understanding task is resumed. Instead of revealing the anticipated threatening situation, S4 produces a competing hypothesis. The program prefers the explanation given by S4 over the earlier one because it links more of the story together (e.g., see Thagard, 1989). The system uses the trace of its reasoning process, stored in a Trace Meta-XP, to review the understanding process. It characterizes the reasoning error as one in which there is (1) an expectation failure caused by the incorrect retrieval of a known explanation ("dogs bark when threatened by animate objects," erroneously assumed to be applicable) and (2) a missing explanation ("the dog barked because it detected marijuana," the correct explanation in this case). Using this characterization as an index, the system retrieves the Introspective Meta-XP XP-Novel-Situation-Alternative-Refuted.

This composite Meta-XP characterizes a common class of reasoning errors and consists of three basic Meta-XPs: XP-Novel-Situation, XP-Mis-Indexed-Structure, and XP-Incorrect-Background-Knowledge. XP-Novel-Situation directs an explanation-based generalization algorithm to be applied to the node representing the explanation of the bark. Because the detection scene of the drug-bust case and the node representing the sniffing are unified because of the explanation given in S4, the explanation is generalized to drug busts in general. The general explanation is then indexed in memory using an index learning algorithm. XP-Mis-Indexed-Structure directs the indexing algorithm to the defensive barking explanation. It recommends that the explanation be re-indexed so that it is not retrieved in similar situations in the future. Thus, the index for this XP is specialized so that retrieval occurs only for animate agents, not physical objects in general. Finally, XP-Incorrect-Background-Knowledge directs the system to examine the source of the story's anomaly. The solution is to alter the conceptual memory representation so that the constraint on the object of dog-barking instantiations is abstracted to physical objects, not just animate agents.

Though the program is directly provided with an explanation that links the story together, Meta-AQUA performs more than mere rote learning. It learns to avoid the mistakes made during the processing of the story. The application of Meta-XPs allows the system to use the appropriate learning strategy (or, as in the above example, multiple strategies) to learn exactly that which the system needs to know to process similar situations in the future correctly. This is essentially a case-based or experience-based approach, which relies on the assumption that it is worth learning about one's experiences because one is likely to have similar experiences in the future (see, e.g., Schank, 1982; Kolodner and Simpson, 1984; Hammond, 1989; Ram, 1993).

13.4 THE EXPLANATION-BASED UNDERSTANDING TASK

The central task in Meta-AQUA is to build causal explanations that provide conceptual coherence to the story by linking the pieces of the story together. The approach to explanation construction is case-based and is based on Schank's theory of explanation patterns (XPs) in which explanations are built by applying known XPs to the events in the story (Schank, 1986; Ram, 1990a). Expectation failures arise when the world differs from the system's expectations. For example, the system may be faced with an anomalous situation in which the XP that the system believes to be applicable turns out to be contradicted in the story. When the system encounters an anomalous situation, it tries to retrieve and apply a known explanation to the anomalous concept. The process of explanation generates questions, or knowledge goals, representing what the system needs to know in order to be able to explain similar situations in the future, thus avoiding repeated similar failures (Ram, 1991, 1993).

Explanation patterns are similar to justification trees, linking antecedent conditions to their consequences. An XP is essentially a directed graph of concepts, connected with results, enables, and initiates links. A results link connects a process with a state, while an enables link connects a precondition state to a process. An initiates link connects two states. These three links are sufficient to represent goal-based stories of the type discussed here, although other causal links (e.g., disenables) may be added without invalidating the approach.

The set of sink nodes in the graph is called the PRE-XP-NODES. These nodes represent what must be present in the current situation for the XP to apply.

One distinguished node in this set is called the EXPLAINS node. It is bound to the concept that is being explained. Source nodes are termed XP-ASSERTED-NODES. All other nodes are INTERNAL-XP-NODES. For an XP to apply to a given situation, all PRE-XP-NODES must be in the current set of beliefs. If they are not, then the explanation is not appropriate to the situation. If the structure is not rejected, then all XP-ASSERTED-NODES are checked. For each XP-ASSERTED node verified, all INTERNAL-XP-NODES connected to it are verified. If all XP-ASSERTED-NODES can be verified, then the entire explanation is verified. Gaps in the explanation occur when one or more XP-ASSERTED-NODE remains unverified. Each gap results in a question or knowledge goal, which provides the system with a focus for reasoning and learning.

The background knowledge used in the current implementation consists of a frame-based conceptual hierarchy, a case library of past episodes, and an indexed collection of XPs. For the task of story understanding, Meta-AQUA employs the algorithm outlined in Figure 13.1. First, the outer loop inputs a sentence representation and checks to see if the concept can answer a prior question. If it can, the reasoning associated with the question is resumed. Otherwise, the concept is passed on to the understanding algorithm. The understanding algorithm consists of four phases: (1) question identification, (2) hypothesis generation, (3) verification, and (4) review/learning.

The first phase looks for questions associated with the concept by checking the concept for interesting characteristics. Meta-AQUA considers explanations, violent acts, and anomalies to be interesting.[3] Explanations and violent acts are detected by the concept type of the input. Anomaly detection is performed by comparing the input to the conceptual definitions found in the conceptual hierarchy. If a concept contradicts a constraint, then a constraint anomaly exists, and a question is posed. Such questions represent the knowledge goals of the program. If no anomaly is detected, then the concept is instantiated, and control passes back to the top level.

If a knowledge goal is posted, then the understander attempts to answer the question by generating a hypothesis. The basis of this decision, i.e., what knowledge is relevant in making the determination, is then recorded in the Trace Meta-XP. Strategies for hypothesis generation include application of known explanation patterns (Schank, 1986; Ram, 1990a), case-based reasoning (e.g., Kolodner and Simpson, 1984; Hammond, 1989; Ram, 1993), and analogy (e.g., Falkenhainer, 1990). If none of these applies, then the process is suspended until a later opportunity.

---

[3] A better approach to determining interestingness, based on the goals of the reasoner, is discussed by Ram (1990b).

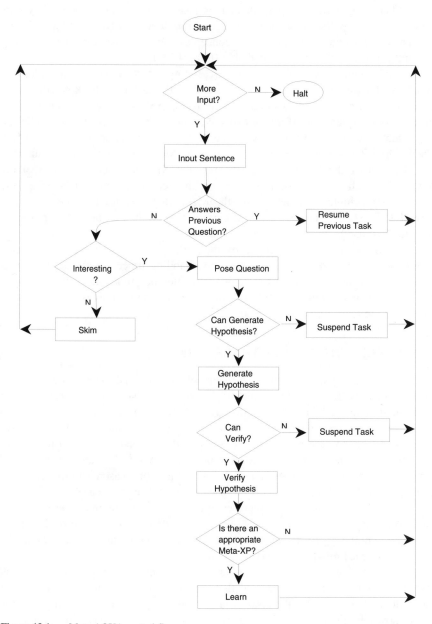

Figure 13.1:   Meta-AQUA control flow

When a hypothesis is generated, it is passed to the verification subsystem. Strategies for hypothesis verification include the devising of a test (currently not implemented), comparison to known concepts, and suspension of the reasoning task until further information is available (Ram, 1991).

The system reviews the chain of reasoning after the verification phase is complete. The review process examines the Trace Meta-XP to check whether there was a reasoning failure. If a failure occurred, the review process searches for an introspective explanation. If an Introspective Meta-XP is retrieved, it is applied to the failure. Meta-XP application is analogous to XP application. Meta-AQUA first checks the PRE-XP-NODES to determine if the Meta-XP is applicable to the failure situation. If the Meta-XP is applicable, the XP-ASSERTED-NODES of the Meta-XP are checked to see if they are in the set of current beliefs. If so, the learning algorithm(s) associated with the Meta-XP is executed. If there are XP-ASSERTED-NODES not in the set of current beliefs, then a question is posed on the Meta-XP itself.

Because learning is moderated by the XP application algorithm, it is necessary to represent the explanation-based understanding process outlined above in a declarative manner. This allows matching and inference functions to be applied to the prior reasoning. Further, it allows the system to pose knowledge goals about aspects of the reasoning process itself.

13.5 REPRESENTATION OF TRACE Meta-XPs

The AQUA system embodies a theory of motivational explanation based on decision models (Ram, 1990a), which represent the decision process that an agent goes through in deciding whether to perform an action. The agent considers its goals, goal priorities, and the expected outcome of performing the action and then decides whether to perform the action. Meta-AQUA extends the model to account for introspective reasoning about knowledge goals. A set of states, priorities, and the expected outcome of a reasoning strategy prompt the reasoner to make a strategy decision. Based on its general knowledge, inferences that can be drawn from this knowledge, and the current representation of the story, the reasoner chooses a particular reasoning strategy. Once executed, a strategy may produce further questions and hypotheses. Each execution node explicitly represents its main result (the structure returned by the function) and its side-effect.

These decide-compute combinations are chained into threads of reasoning such that each one initiates the goal that drives the next. Though the chains can vary widely, the chains for the task of question-driven story understanding take the form shown in Figure 13.2. This reasoning process is recursive in nature. For example, if a hypothesis generates a new question, then the reasoner will spawn a recursive regeneration of the sequence. When insufficient knowledge exists on which to base a decision, a useful strategy is to simply defer making the decision.

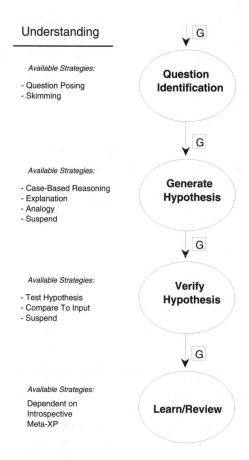

Understanding

Available Strategies:

- Question Posing
- Skimming

Question Identification

Available Strategies:

- Case-Based Reasoning
- Explanation
- Analogy
- Suspend

Generate Hypothesis

Available Strategies:

- Test Hypothesis
- Compare To Input
- Suspend

Verify Hypothesis

Available Strategies:

Dependent on Introspective Meta-XP

Learn/Review

Figure 13.2:   Phases of understanding: Decide-compute chains represented in Trace Meta-XPs

The reasoning task is suspended and later continued if and when the requisite knowledge appears. This is a form of opportunistic reasoning (Birnbaum and Collins, 1984; Hammond, 1988; Ram, 1991).

A Trace Meta-XP, representing the trace of the reasoning process, is a chain of decide-compute nodes (D-C-NODES). These nodes record the processes that formulate the knowledge goals of a system together with the results and reasons for performing such mental actions. As such, the trace of reasoning is similar to a derivational analogy trace as described by Carbonell (1986). Such a Meta-XP is a specific explanation describing the reasoner's choice of a particular reasoning method or strategy and the results of executing that strategy. Like an XP, the Meta-XP can be a general structure applied to a wide range of contexts or a specific instantiation that records a particular thought process. One distinguishing property of Trace Meta-XPs is the fact that a decision at one stage is often based on features in previous stages. For example, the decision of how to verify a hypothesis may be based on knowledge used to initially construct the hypothesis. This property is particularly true of the learning stage, which by definition is based on prior processing.

An understanding system may attempt to retrieve and apply a Meta-XP for reasoning and learning in much the same way that regular XPs are used for explanation. If the antecedent conditions of the Meta-XP exist, then the structure will point to an appropriate learning algorithm without having to analyze all current states in the story representation. This approach provides significant speedup in learning, relying on past successes and failures instead of reasoning from first principles. For example, even though some subquestions on an erroneous hypothesis are verified, Meta-XPs will direct the search for the blame on the basis of the decision to use a given hypothesis generation strategy, not on the basis of the verification strategy.

13.6 REPRESENTATION OF INTROSPECTIVE Meta-XPs

An Introspective Meta-XP is a data structure used to explain why a particular solution or conclusion fails and to learn from a reasoning failure. Thus, an Introspective Meta-XP performs three functions: it aids in (1) assigning blame (determining which knowledge structures are missing, incorrect, or inappropriately applied), (2) determining what knowledge goals the system should formulate, and (3) selecting appropriate learning algorithms to recover and learn from the reasoning error. These functions are accomplished by associating a failure type with likely causes of the reasoning failure and a particular set of learning strategies used to ensure that the failure does not recur. Introspective Meta-XPs have the following components:

- Failure type (one of the types of failures in the taxonomy below).
- Explanation of failure (graph structure of the failure).
- Pointers to locations in the graph likely to be responsible for the failure.
- Specification of knowledge goals to be created (to prevent failure from recurring).
- Temporal information for the explanation (temporal orderings on the nodes and the links in the graph).

The graph structure of the Introspective Meta-XP is similar to that of a justification tree or an explanation pattern (Schank, 1986; Ram, 1990a), linking antecedent (mental) conditions to their (mental) consequences. The major difference between a Meta-XP and an XP is that although both are explanatory causal structures, an XP proposes a causal justification for a physical observation (such as why blowing up a bomb causes objects in its vicinity to be destroyed) or a volitional action (such as why a Lebanese teenager would volunteer for a suicide bombing mission in which he was sure to be killed), whereas a Meta-XP explains how and why an agent reasons in a particular manner. Thus, the representation of a Meta-XP must be able to account for reasoning failures and successes. The three types of reasoning failures discussed in the introduction (novel situations, incorrect or incomplete background knowledge, and mis-indexed knowledge structures) can be represented using the following basic types of successes and failures.

13.6.1 Successful Prediction

The basic types of failures that make up the components of an Introspective Meta-XP graph are expectation failure, retrieval failure, and incorporation failure. A fourth type, successful prediction, does not produce any learning in Meta-AQUA but is represented as a mental event in the same manner as failures. To illustrate the representation, let node A represent an actual occurrence of an event in the world, an explanation, or an arbitrary proposition. Let node E represent the expected occurrence. The node A `mentally-results` from either a mental calculation or an input concept. The expected node E `mentally-results` from some reasoning trace enabled by some goal G. Now if the two propositions are identical so that A = E, or A is a superset of E, then a successful prediction has occurred. If on the other hand, A is a subset of E, then there are more questions remaining on the predicted node E. In such cases, Meta-AQUA waits for more information before it introspects.

13.6.2 Expectation Failure

Failures occur when A ≠ E. This state exists when either A and E are disjoint, or there are conflicting assertions within the two nodes. For example, A and E may represent persons, but E contains an attribute description specifying gender = male, whereas A contains the attribute description gender = female. Inferential expectation failures occur when the reasoner predicts one event or feature, but another occurs instead. The representation of an expectation failure is shown in Figure 13.3. The EXPLAINS node of the Meta-XP (the distinguished node that the Meta-XP explains) is the one marked "Expectation Failure." The system's awareness of the expectation failure is `mentally-initiated` by the not-equals relation between A and E.

13.6.3 Retrieval Failure

Retrieval failure has a similar structure, although the difference here is that instead of an expectation (E) being present, it is instead absent because of the inability of the system to retrieve the knowledge structures that would predict E

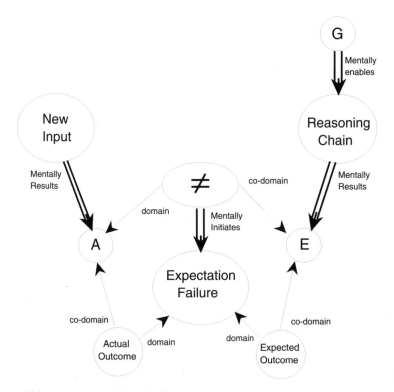

Figure 13.3:   Expectation failure: A ≠ E

(see Figure 13.4). To represent these conditions, Meta-AQUA uses standard non-monotonic logic values of `in` (in the current set of beliefs) and `out` (out of the current set of beliefs) (Doyle, 1979) augmented with `hypothesized-in` (weakly assumed in), `hypothesized-out` (weakly assumed out), and `hypothesized` (unknown). Thus, absolute retrieval failure is represented by A [`truth` = `in`] = E [`truth` = `out`]. The relation that identifies the truth value of E as being `out` of the current set of beliefs `mentally-initiates` the assertion that a retrieval failure exists. Cuts across links in the figure signify causal relations for which the truth slot of the frame is `out`.

13.6.4 Incorporation Failure

An incorporation failure occurs when the reasoner fails to incorporate a fact or assertion in the conceptual representation of the input into its background knowledge. For example, a fact may contradict a belief that the system holds. The difference between an incorporation failure and an expectation failure is that in the latter, the system has an explicit expectation that is violated, whereas in the former,

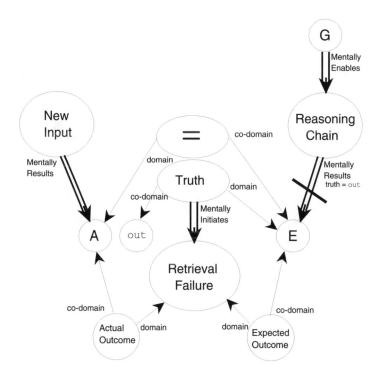

Figure 13.4: Retrieval failure: A [truth = in] = E [truth = out]

the new input is presented before the contradictory belief is explicitly identified by the system.

Incorporation failures represent an important class of anomalies that provide a basis for identifying knowledge goals that drive reasoning and learning. For example, a constraint anomaly occurs when an attribute of the conceptual representation of some proposition conflicts with a constraint defined in the background knowledge. The conflict produces a not-equals relation between the actual occurrence and the conceptual constraint. This relation mentally-initiates the anomaly (see Figure 13.5).

13.7 ASSOCIATING KNOWLEDGE GOALS AND LEARNING STRATEGIES WITH INTROSPECTIVE Meta-XPS

Based on the above representations of basic types of failures, the three types of reasoning failures discussed in Section 13.2 can be represented, along with associated knowledge goals and learning strategies for these situations, using Introspective Meta-XP structures.

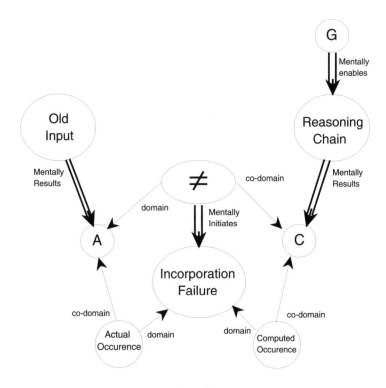

Figure 13.5:   Incorporation failure: Contradiction, constraint conflict, or other anomaly

13.7.1 Mis-Indexed Knowledge Structure

This type of failure occurs when the reasoner's knowledge structures are not indexed in memory in a manner that allows them to be retrieved in appropriate situations using the particular cues provided by the context. There are two variants of this type of failure, represented by the Introspective Meta-XPs XP-Erroneous-Association and XP-Missing-Association. XP-Erroneous-Association is based on an expectation failure structure because this situation arises when an index associates a contextual state with a knowledge structure in the background knowledge that produces incorrect inferences in this context. In such cases, a knowledge goal is spawned to modify the index so that the index will still allow Meta-AQUA to retrieve the knowledge structure when appropriate but not in future instances similar to the current situation in which it was erroneously retrieved. (Because this leads to existing knowledge being reorganized rather than new knowledge being learned, this type of knowledge goal is called a *knowledge organization goal* and the complementary type a *knowledge acquisition goal*.) The learning strategy used for such a goal is to execute a specialization algorithm that produces a more discriminating index. Because the knowledge organization goal has pointers to a declarative representation of the reasoning that produced the goal, the learning strategy has access to the context of the error.

Indexing failures because of missing associations are represented using XP-Missing-Association, which is based on a retrieval failure structure. This situation arises when an appropriate knowledge structure was not retrieved because there was no index to associate the context with that structure. This knowledge structure is represented by a node M in the system's background knowledge that must be in. The knowledge goal associated with the Introspective Meta-XP is to find the node M. If the knowledge goal is achieved, the associated learning strategy directs an indexing algorithm to examine the indices of M, looking for an index compatible with the index calculated for A, the node representing the input assertion currently being processed. If found, this index is generalized so that the current cues provided by the context of A will allow Meta-AQUA to retrieve E. If no such index is found, a new index is created. Furthermore, if an appropriate knowledge structure M cannot be found, a reasoning question is raised concerning the possibility that M exists. The question is represented as a knowledge goal and indexed by the context of A, and the process is suspended until such time as M can be found.

13.7.2 Novel Situation

Novel situations are structurally similar to the missing association variant of the mis-indexed structure situation, except that the node M (and thus its associated index I) has a truth value of out. In other words, a novel situation is one in which there is no knowledge structure in memory that can be retrieved and reasoned with to allow the system to expect a concept that matches A.

Novel situations, represented by XP-Novel-Situation, occur when M is missing (truth-out) and the E node's truth value is either hypothesized-in or out. When a novel situation is identified, Meta-AQUA creates a knowledge acquisition goal to learn a new explanation from the event and a knowledge organization goal to learn an appropriate index for the new explanation. The learning strategy used in this case is to perform explanation-based generalization on the node A to create a knowledge structure that can be applied to a wider set of future situations. The strategy also directs an indexing algorithm to the newly created explanation so that it will be retrieved in similar situations in the future.

13.7.3 Incorrect Background Knowledge

A third class of reasoning failures arises from incorrect background knowledge, which occurs when the system's world model is not accurate or consistent with the real world. In the current implementation, only one situation of type XP-

`Incorrect-Background-Knowledge` is represented. This situation arises when there is an inconsistency with a known fact and a constraint specified in the background knowledge (for example, a constraint in the ISA-hierarchy), leading to an incorporation failure. In this situation, Meta-AQUA spawns a knowledge goal to modify the erroneous constraint in memory. The learning strategy in this case is to check whether the two assertions (the fact and the constraint) are conceptual siblings. If this is true, Meta-AQUA performs abstraction on the constraint, generalizing it to its parent node. The constraint is then marked as being `hypothesized-in` on the basis of induction. The reasoning chain that led to this hypothesis is indexed off the hypothesis so that it can be retrieved when the constraint is invoked in future situations. The hypothesis is verified if the anomalous assertion is re-encountered in later situations.

13.7.4 Combinations and Extensions

An additional class of reasoning failures arises from the inferences used to base a decision on during the hypothesis generation phase. The error is found by searching all hypothesis generation D-C-NODES on the path from the EXPLAINS node of A to the node E, performing elaborative question asking (Ram, 1991, 1993). This case has not yet been represented declaratively. Meta-AQUA reasons about it using a general search heuristic for blame assignment.

Figure 13.6 shows the composite Meta-XP that is used to direct learning in the drug bust example from Section 13.3. The Meta-XP combines an `XP-Novel-Situation`, an `XP-Mis-Indexed-Structure`, and an `XP-Incorrect-Background-Knowledge`. A2, the actual outcome, is bound to the explanation from S4, whereas E, the expected outcome, is bound to the explanation that dogs bark at objects that threaten them. C is bound to the constraint that dogs bark at animate objects. The index in memory, I, is bound to the index used to retrieve the abstract explanation instantiated as E.

In general, Introspective Meta-XPs are built out of reasoning chains involving successful predictions, expectation failures, retrieval failures, and incorporation failures. Table 13.1 illustrates some of the combinations that are representable using this set of building blocks along with the associated learning strategies. Note that the node A is assumed `in` for all entries. In addition, for the two combination Meta-XPs in the table, E′ represents the concept that should have been predicted but was not, and M′ represents the memory item that should have been retrieved but was not.

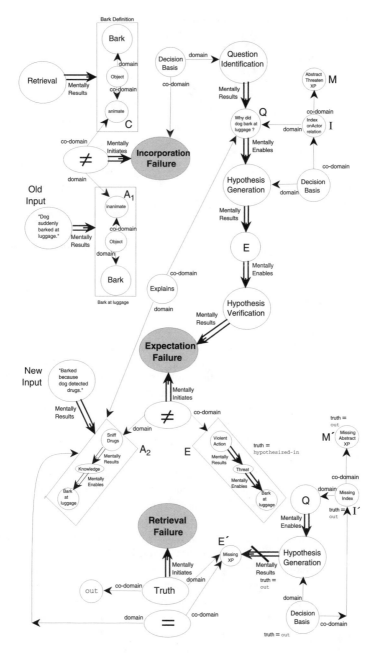

Figure 13.6: XP-Novel-Situation-Alternative-Refuted

Table 13.1: Truth values of nodes in Introspective Meta-XP representations. φ = don't care; hypo-in = hypothesized-in; RC = reasoning chain; SP = successful prediction; EF = expectation failure; RF = retrieval failure.

	E	E'	M	M'	RC	SP	EF	RF	
Successful Prediction	in	φ	in	φ	in	in	out	out	No learning
Novel Situation	out	φ	out	φ	out	out	out	in	EBG on A Index A by context
Retrieval Failure	out	φ	in	φ	out	out	out	in	Generalize index on M
Novel Situation + Expectation Failure	hypo-in	out	in	out	out	out	in	in	EBG on A Index A by context Specialize index on M
Expectation Failure + Retrieval Failure	hypo-in	out	in	in	in	out	in	in	Specialize index on M Generalize index on M'

13.8 RELATED WORK

Several past studies have called for meta-level reasoning (e.g., Davis, 1980; Stefik, 1981; Wilensky, 1981). However, traditional approaches to meta-reasoning stress knowledge about a system's own knowledge and reasoning in the form of rules dealing with belief, preference heuristics for operator selection, or constraints and defaults on the types of values an attribute may assume and do not deal with the process of introspective reasoning itself. Some researchers (e.g., Maes, 1987; Pollock, 1989) distinguish between meta-level knowledge and introspection, that is, between knowledge about one's facts and knowledge about one's motivations and processes. It is argued here that introspective access to explicit representations of knowledge and of reasoning processes is necessary in a learning system that can make sophisticated decisions about what and how to learn and that this ability, in turn, is an essential part of a general theory of multistrategy learning.

Carbonell's (1986) derivational analogy may be viewed as a form of introspective case-based reasoning. However, although his derivational analogy traces are similar to Trace Meta-XPs, there are several differences between the two approaches. The underlying reasoning processes represented in Trace Meta-XPs may be based on a reasoning model other than search-based problem solving. Trace Meta-XPs take into consideration competing reasoning goals and their relative priorities and include a representation of the expected outcome of a processing decision. Finally, Meta-XP theory augments the idea behind derivational traces by adding Introspective Meta-XPs to represent common reasoning situations and reasoning failures along with associated knowledge goals and learning strategies.

The meta-explanations in this approach are also similar to self-explanations (Pirolli and Bielaczyc, 1989; VanLehn, Jones, and Chi, 1992). This research in psychology shows that formulating of self-explanations while understanding input examples significantly improves the subjects' ability to learn from the examples. One difference between the two approaches is that self-explanations are explanations about events and objects in the world, whereas meta-explanations are explanations about events and objects in the reasoner's "mind." Experimental results in the metacognition literature suggest that introspective reasoning of the kind proposed here can facilitate reasoning and learning. For example, Carr (1992) showed that strategic, deliberative control of mental processes facilitated the use of decomposition strategies for a mathematics problem-solving task. The improved performance resulted from meta-knowledge about reasoning strategies and knowledge about when a strategy was appropriate to use.

Outside the introspection paradigm, the work presented here builds on previous research in several areas of machine learning, including case-based reasoning, explanation-based learning, and multistrategy learning. Many multistrategy learning systems are simply integrated systems consisting of a cascade of more than one learning algorithm (e.g., Flann and Dietterich, 1989; Shavlik and Towell, 1989). The control is always the same for every input. Usually an initial learning technique is applied and its output used as the input to the next algorithm. A new generation of systems use more sophisticated schemes, whereby one or many algorithms may apply to different input, depending on the situation. In these paradigms, selection of the learning algorithm becomes computationally important. One of the greatest benefits of using Introspective Meta-XPs in this type of framework is their ability to apply learning tasks that are appropriate to a given situation without having to blindly search all possible learning choices. However, many non-cascaded multistrategy learning systems apply learning algorithms in a predefined order (e.g., Genest, Matwin, and Plante, 1990; Pazzani, 1991). If the first fails, then the next strategy is tried, and so forth. Much effort may be wasted in worst-case scenarios. In the Meta-XP approach, multistrategy learning is viewed as a deliberative, planful process in which the system makes explicit decisions about what to learn and how to learn it. In this sense, the theory is similar to that of Hunter (1990), with the difference that the approach presented here is based on introspective reasoning using explicitly represented meta-explanation structures.

One problem with many of the traditional approaches to machine learning is that they do not address the blame assignment problem and, therefore, the problem of what the reasoner needs to learn. The research presented here is based on the belief that these problems are an integral part of the learning process and, furthermore, that they should be addressed in a unified learning framework based on introspection and Meta-XPs. The approach is to use an analysis of reasoning failures encountered to determine what needs to be learned. In this respect, the approach is similar to that of Birnbaum et al. (1990), Mooney and Ourston's (1994;

Chapter 5 in this book) EITHER system, and Park and Wilkins's (1990) ODYSSEUS and MINERVA systems, but with some important differences. ODYSSEUS only deals with what are called novel situations in Meta-AQUA; when it fails to explain an action, it always assumes that relevant facts or rules are missing from its knowledge base. MINERVA's failure types are closer in spirit to those of Meta-AQUA, but its method relies on an expert to guide the learning process. Furthermore, the types of failures and corresponding learning actions used in EITHER and ODYSSEUS/MINERVA are specific to a particular reasoning paradigm (logic-based deduction and rule-based expert systems, respectively), whereas Meta-AQUA's taxonomy of failure types is not specific to a particular type of reasoning method. Rather than characterize learning actions at the level of "add a new rule" or "generalize the antecedent of an existing rule," Meta-AQUA is based on characterizations of learning strategies such as "generalize a new explanation," which may in turn be implemented in different ways depending on the reasoning paradigm. In addition, none of these approaches deals with the issue of learning indices for knowledge. Birnbaum et al. (1990) focus on the process of blame assignment by backing up through justification structures and not on the declarative representation of types of failures. Furthermore, they do not discuss the use of failure characterizations to select learning strategies in a multistrategy learning system. Finally, none of the above approaches uses declarative characterizations of reasoning failures to formulate explicit learning goals. Despite these differences, it should be emphasized that the above approaches have much in common between them.

From the system design point of view, the use of Meta-XPs in reasoning about knowledge goals during story understanding and problem-solving provides a number of benefits. Because Meta-XPs make the trace of reasoning explicit, an intelligent system can directly inspect the reasons supporting specific conclusions. This avoids hiding knowledge used by the system in procedural code. Instead, there exists an explicit declarative expression of the reasons a given piece of code is executed. With these reasons enumerated, a system can explain how it produced a given failure and can retrieve an introspective explanation of the failure. This approach provides a nice framework for integrated learning approaches in which reasons for processing and learning decisions are made explicitly by the system rather than existing only in the minds of the system's designers.

13.9 DISCUSSION AND FUTURE RESEARCH

The use of introspection by applying Meta-XPs to declarative representations of the reasoning process can aid a reasoner's ability to perform blame assignment and direct the learning algorithms that allow the reasoner to recover from failures and to learn not to repeat the failure. The use of Meta-XP structures aids in the blame assignment problem because all points in the reasoning chain do not have to be inspected. This helps in controlling the search process. Because answers may not be available at the time questions are posed, an opportunistic approach allows the system to improve its knowledge incrementally and to answer its questions at the time the information it needs becomes available. The representation also allows the system to pose questions about its own reasoning.

The approach relies on a declarative representation of meta-models for reasoning and learning. There are several advantages of maintaining such structures in memory. First, because they represent reasoning processes explicitly, the system can directly inspect the reasons underlying a given processing decision it has taken, evaluate the progress toward a goal, and compare its reasoning to past instances of reasoning in similar contexts. Thus, these traces can also be used in credit/blame assignment, the evaluation of how reasoning errors occurred, and the facilitating of learning from these errors. Second, because both the reasoning process and the knowledge base are represented using the same type of declarative representations, processes that identify and correct gaps in a knowledge base can also be applied to the reasoning process itself. In other words, a knowledge goal, or a goal to learn, may be directed at the reasoning process as well as at the knowledge base. If causal representations underlying domain theories and introspective representations underlying reasoning processes are both declarative causal structures, the same types of reasoning and learning algorithms can be applied to both.

A third advantage is the potential for speedup learning that is provided by the declarative trace of past reasoning processes. One does not have to replicate the entire sequence of decisions in solving a current problem. Instead, the system may match a current context to past reasoning experiences to retrieve a "macro reasoning operator" to apply to the situation. In addition, related to the previous two points, the ability of a Meta-XP to provide pointers to applicable learning algorithms to be used in given circumstances provides a basis for multistrategy learning. Because Meta-XPs encapsulate reasoning experiences, they can also help the system select appropriate learning strategies based on an analysis of the difficulties encountered during these reasoning experiences. Finally, from a system design perspective, the Meta-AQUA architecture provides a uniform framework for the integration of multiple learning strategies into an intelligent system.

This chapter focussed on the representation and use of Trace and Introspective Meta-XP structures for multistrategy learning in three types of reasoning failure situations. The class of failures represented by `XP-Incorrect-Background-Knowledge` is still under investigation, including the formulation of a representation for deciding when to use the heuristic search briefly mentioned in Section 13.7.3. Other strategies need to be created as well. The task of knowing when an assertion is incorrect, not just incomplete, is a difficult but interesting research problem.

Additional types of situations that provide the reasoner an opportunity to learn are also being investigated. An important class of failures, for example, is those that occur when the reasoner selects an inappropriate reasoning strategy in a given situation. The Meta-AQUA system is being extended to learn control information by representing Meta-XPs that point to potential problems with the reasoning choices made in each phase. The failure type `Incorrect-Reasoning-Choice` occurs when the reasoner has an appropriate knowledge structure to reason with and index to the structure in memory but incorrectly chooses the wrong knowledge because the reasoning method it decided to use turned out to be inappropriate or inapplicable. An analysis of the choice of reasoning methods will result in learning control strategies designed to modify the heuristics used in this choice.

Many machine learning systems assume noise-free input, and those that deal with noise seldom analyze the source or causes of the noise. A robust story understander should be able to reason about the validity of input concepts, including the possibility of intentional deception by characters in a story. The class of errors arising from input noise needs to be represented and corresponding knowledge goals and learning strategies identified. Another interesting extension of this research currently being pursued is combining story understanding with problem solving. Declarative process representations similar to that of story understanding are being developed. Parallel to story understanding sequences of identify question ⇒ generate hypothesis ⇒ verify ⇒ learn/review, problem-solving sequences would be represented as identify problem ⇒ generate solution ⇒ test ⇒ learn/review. Meta-XPs would then be used to reason about and improve the problem-solving process of the reasoner.

13.10 CONCLUSIONS

Meta-AQUA is a computer model of a reasoner that is active and goal-driven, starting out with an incomplete understanding of a novel domain and learning through experience. Its learning goals are functional to the purpose of the system and are identified during the pursuit of the performance task. The computer program models how an intelligent reasoner reasons about the best way to perform a task; introspectively analyzes its own successes and failures in performing its tasks; reasons about what it needs to learn; selects appropriate learning strategies to acquire that information; and invokes the learning algorithms that then cause the reasoner to acquire new knowledge, modify existing knowledge, or reorganize memory by re-indexing knowledge in memory. The program implements a theory of introspective reasoning using meta-explanations that model typical reasoning situations, types of reasoning failures, and applicable learning strategies. The theory is motivated by cognitive as well as computational considerations and provides a framework for the development of integrated, multistrategy learning systems for real-world tasks.

ACKNOWLEDGMENTS

Research for this article was supported by the National Science Foundation under Grant IRI-9009710 and by the Georgia Institute of Technology.

References

Bhatta, S., and Ram, A. "Learning Indices for Schema Selection," *Proceedings of the Florida Artificial Intelligence Research Symposium*, M.B. Fishman (ed.), pp. 226–231, Florida AI Research Socieiy, Cocoa Beach, FL, 1991.

Birnbaum, L., and Collins, G. "Opportunistic Planning and Freudian Slips," *Proceedings of the Sixth Annual Conference of the Cognitive Science Society*, pp. 124–127, Boulder, CO, Lawrence Erlbaum Assoc., Hillsdale, NJ, 1984.

Birnbaum, L., Collins, G., Freed, M., and Krulwich, B. "Model-based Diagnosis of Planning Failures," *Proceedings of the Eighth National Conference on Artificial Intelligence*, pp. 318–323, AAAI Press, Menlo Park, CA, 1990.

Carbonell, J.G. "Derivational Analogy: A Theory of Reconstructive Problem Solving and Expertise Acquisition," *Machine Learning II: An Artificial Intelligence Approach*, R.S. Michalski, J.G. Carbonell, and T. Mitchell (eds.), pp. 371–392, Morgan Kaufmann Publishers, San Mateo, CA, 1986.

Carr, M. "Metacognitive Knowledge as a Predictor of Decomposition Strategy Use," *Paper Presented at the Southeast Cognitive Science Conference*, Georgia Institute of Technology, Atlanta, Georgia, January 1992.

Cox, M., and Ram, A. "Multistrategy Learning with Introspective Meta-Explanations," *Machine Learning: Proceedings of the Ninth International Conference*, D. Sleeman and P. Edwards (eds.), Morgan Kaufmann, San Mateo, CA, pp. 123–128, 1992.

Davis, R. "Meta-Rules: Reasoning about Control," *Artificial Intelligence*, Vol. 15, No. 3, pp. 179–222, 1980.

DeJong, G.F., and Mooney, R.J. "Explanation-based Learning: An Alternative View," *Machine Learning*, Vol. 1, No. 2, pp. 145–176, 1986.

Doyle, J. "A Truth Maintenance System," *Artificial Intelligence*, Vol. 12, pp. 231–272, 1979.

Falkenhainer, B. "A Unified Approach to Explanation and Theory Formation," *Computational Models of Scientific Discovery and Theory Formation*, J. Shrager and P. Langley (eds.), pp. 157–196, Morgan Kaufmann Publishers, San Mateo, CA, 1990.

Flann, N.S., and Dietterich, T.G. "A Study of Explanation-based Methods for Inductive Learning," *Machine Learning*, Vol. 4, pp. 187–226, 1989.

Genest, J., Matwin, S., and Plante, B. "Explanation-based Learning with Incomplete Theories: A Three-step Approach," *Proceedings of the Seventh International Conference on Machine Learning*, B.W. Porter and R.J. Mooney (eds.), pp. 286–294, Morgan Kaufmann, San Mateo, CA, 1990.

Hammond, K.J. "Opportunistic Memory: Storing and Recalling Suspended Goals," *Proceedings of a Workshop on Case-based Reasoning*, J.L. Kolodner (ed.), pp. 154–168, Morgan Kaufmann, San Mateo, CA, 1988.

———. *Case-based Planning: Viewing Planning as a Memory Task*, Academic Press, San Diego, CA, 1989.

Hunter, L. "Planning to Learn," *Proceedings of the Twelfth Annual Conference of the Cognitive Science Society*, pp. 26–34, Lawrence Erlbaum Associates, Hillsdale, NJ, 1990.

Kolodner, J.L., and Simpson, R.L. "A Case for Case-based Reasoning," *Proceedings of the Sixth Annual Conference of the Cognitive Science Society*, Boulder, CO, Lawrence Erlbaum Associates, Hillsdale, NJ, 1984.

Maes, P. "Introspection in Knowledge Representation," *Advances in Artificial Intelligence II*, B. Du Boulay, D. Hogg, and L. Steels (eds.), Elsevier Science Publishers, New York, 1987.

Michalski, R.S. "Inferential Theory of Learning: Developing Foundations for Multistrategy Learning," *Machine Learning: A Multistrategy Approach, Vol. IV*, R.S. Michalski and G. Tecuci (eds.), Morgan Kaufmann Publishers, San Mateo, CA, 1994.

———. "A Theory and Methodology of Inductive Learning," *Artificial Intelligence*, Vol. 20, pp. 111–161, 1983.

Minsky, M. "Steps towards Artificial Intelligence," *Computers and Thought*, E.A. Feigenbaum and J. Feldman (eds.), pp. 406–450, McGraw-Hill, New York, 1963.

———. *The Society of Mind*, Simon and Schuster, New York, 1985.

Mitchell, T.M., Keller, R., and Kedar-Cabelli, S. "Explanation-based Generalization: A Unifying View," *Machine Learning*, Vol. 1, No. 1, pp. 47–80, 1986.

Mooney, R.J., and Ourston, D. "A Multistrategy Approach to Theory Refinement," *Machine Learning: A Multistrategy Approach, Vol. IV*, R.S. Michalski and G. Tecuci (eds.), Morgan Kaufmann Publishers, San Mateo, CA, 1994.

Ng, E., and Bereiter, C. "Three Levels of Goal Orientation in Learning," *The Journal of the Learning Sciences*, Vol. 1, Nos. 3 & 4, pp. 243–271, 1991.

Park, Y., and Wilkins, D.C. "Establishing the Coherence of an Explanation to Improve Refinement of an Incomplete Knowledge Base," *Proceedings of the Eighth National Conference on Artificial Intelligence*, pp. 511–516, AAAI Press, Menlo Park, CA, 1990.

Pazzani, M.J. "Learning to Predict and Explain: An Integration of Similarity-based, Theory-driven and Explanation-based Learning," *The Journal of the Learning Sciences*, Vol. 1, No. 2, pp. 153–199, 1991.

Pirolli, P., and Bielaczyc, K. "Empirical Analyses of Self-Explanation and Transfer in Learning to Program," *Proceedings of the Eleventh Annual Conference of the Cognitive Science Society*, Lawrence Erlbaum Associates, Hillsdale, NJ, 1989.

Pollock, J.L. "A General Theory of Rationality," *Journal of Theoretical and Experimental Artificial Intelligence*, Vol. 1, pp. 209–226, 1989.

Ram, A. "Decision Models: A Theory of Volitional Explanation," *Proceedings of the Twelfth Annual Conference of the Cognitive Science Society*, pp. 198–205, Lawrence Erlbaum Associates, Hillsdale, NJ, 1990a.

———. "Knowledge Goals: A Theory of Interestingness," *Proceedings of the Twelfth Annual Conference of the Cognitive Science Society*, pp. 206–214, Lawrence Erlbaum Associates, Hillsdale, NJ, 1990b.

———. "A Theory of Questions and Question Asking," *The Journal of the Learning Sciences*, Vol. 1, Nos. 3 & 4, pp. 273–318, 1991.

———. "Indexing, Elaboration and Refinement: Incremental Learning of Explanatory Cases," to appear in *Machine Learning*, Vol. 10, No. 3, pp. 201–248, 1993.

Ram, A., and Hunter, L. "The Use of Explicit Goals for Knowledge to Guide Inference and Learning," to appear in *Applied Intelligence*, Vol. 2, No. 1. pp. 47–73, 1992.

Reich, Y. "Macro and Micro Perspectives of Multistrategy Learning," *Machine Learning: A Multistrategy Approach, Vol. IV*, R.S. Michalski & G. Tecuci (eds.), Morgan Kaufmann Publishers, San Mateo, CA, 1994.

Schank, R.C. *Dynamic Memory: A Theory of Learning in Computers and People*, Cambridge University Press, New York, 1982.

———. "The Current State of AI: One Man's Opinion," *AI Magazine*, Vol. 4, No. 1, pp. 3–8, 1983.

———. *Explanation Patterns: Understanding Mechanically and Creatively*, Lawrence Erlbaum Associates, Hillsdale, NJ, 1986.

Shavlik, J.W., and Towell, G.G. "An Approach to Combining Explanation-based and Neural Learning Algorithms," *Connection Science*, Vol. 1, No. 3, 1989.

Stefik, M.J. "Planning and Meta-planning (MOLGEN: Part 2)," *Artificial Intelligence*, Vol. 16, pp. 141–169, 1981.

Thagard, P. "Explanatory Coherence," *Behavioral and Brain Sciences*, Vol. 12, No. 3, pp. 435–502, 1989.

VanLehn, K.A., Jones, R.M., and Chi, M.T.H. "A Model of the Self-explanation Effect," in *The Journal of the Learning Sciences*, Vol. 2, No. 1, pp. 1–60, 1992.

Weintraub, M.A. "An Explanation-based Approach to Assigning Credit," Ph.D. thesis, Department of Information and Computer Science, The Ohio State University, Columbus, OH, 1991.

Wilensky, R. "Meta-planning: Representing and Using Knowledge about Planning in Problem Solving and Natural Language Understanding," *Cognitive Science*, Vol. 5, pp. 197–233, 1981.

Winston, P.H. "Learning Structural Descriptions from Examples," *The Psychology of Computer Vision*, P.H. Winston (ed.), pp. 157–209 (Chapter 5), McGraw-Hill, New York, 1975.

14

MACRO AND MICRO PERSPECTIVES OF MULTISTRATEGY LEARNING

Yoram Reich
(Carnegie Mellon University)

Abstract

Machine learning techniques are perceived to have a great potential as means for the acquisition of knowledge; nevertheless, their use in complex engineering domains is still rare. Most machine learning techniques have been studied in the context of knowledge acquisition for well defined tasks such as classification. Learning for these tasks can be handled by relatively simple algorithms. Complex domains present difficulties that can be approached by combining the strengths of several complementing learning techniques and overcoming their weaknesses by providing alternative learning strategies. This study presents two perspectives, the *macro* and the *micro*, for viewing the issue of multistrategy learning. The macro perspective deals with the decomposition of an overall complex learning task into relatively well-defined learning tasks, and the micro perspective deals with designing multistrategy learning techniques for supporting the acquisition of knowledge for each task. The two perspectives are discussed in the context of BRIDGER, a system that learns to design bridges.

14.1 INTRODUCTION

Real world engineering problems, in particular, design,[1] are very complex; they involve the execution of many tasks in rich knowledge environments with limited resources. Knowledge-based systems are expected to alleviate the complexity of solving engineering tasks. An effective support for the construction of such systems is crucial to their dissemination in practice. Machine learning has the potential of assisting in this construction.

Several previous attempts at matching learning techniques to the acquisition of design knowledge have failed (Shalin et al., 1988; Witten and MacDonald, 1988), mostly because of the attempt to identify a single technique that will suffice to support knowledge acquisition for design *as a whole*. Design, however, is neither a single process nor a static one. The design of learning techniques for such a complex activity requires its decomposition into simpler tasks and the matching of learning techniques for the acquisition of knowledge for each task. Usually, even this matching is difficult because most machine learning techniques use only one strategy that can partially match the requirements of real learning tasks (Tecuci and Michalski, 1991).

Because single strategy learning approaches are not sufficient for supporting learning in real domains, multistrategy approaches must be employed. Two perspectives of using multistrategy learning techniques emerge: the *macro* and the *micro*, elaborated below.

The macro perspective deals with the design of an architecture that learns and problem-solves in the context of a large engineering task. It assumes that it is not feasible to expect that a single learning program will acquire all knowledge in a real domain. Therefore, an architecture that supports this task must include several learning programs and control mechanisms that direct learning tasks to the appropriate programs. Building such a learning system is a complex design task by itself. Its successful completion depends on following a systematic approach. The approach proposed in this study, called M^2LTD (Matching Machine Learning To Design), is detailed in Section 14.2.1.

Several recent studies incorporated macro-perspective issues in their system implementation. Stirling and Buntine (1988) investigated learning routings of products in a plant. They decomposed the learning task into two subtasks. In the first task, descriptions of routings of products in a mill are used to induce a grammar, which can then be modified by an expert. In the second task, examples are used by ID3 (Quinlan, 1983) to induce routing decisions that are expressed as different branches in the grammar. The rules generated can then be evaluated by an expert.

---

[1]The discussion in this chapter is in the context of design, but it equally applies to other tasks and domains.

The grammar induction was necessary for the execution of the second learning task.

Lu and Chen (1987) described a method for learning evaluations in a manufacturing domain. In the first stage, the behavior of objects is clustered by CLUSTER/2 (Michalski and Stepp, 1983). Then, each class is treated as a concept to be learned by the concept learning program AQ15 (Michalski et al., 1986). The rules generated by AQ15 can assign a new object to the class of behaviors to which it belongs. The two learning programs are both required to perform the overall learning task.

Bergadano, Giordana, and Saitta (1988) described a learning program for noisy domains that uses one module to extract object descriptions from data and makes these description available to a concept learner. Again, the two modules are necessary for performing the learning task.

In all these studies, the macro perspective deals with the use of distinct learning programs, each for a specific aspect of the learning problem. The control of the programs is determined by the problem requirements and is fixed.

The micro perspective deals with the design of specific learning procedures for the acquisition of knowledge for well defined[2] engineering tasks. In real domains, these procedures are bound to employ several learning strategies, operating in an integrated manner. The crucial issue in this perspective is the control of, and cooperation between, the different strategies.

Several recent studies employ multistrategy learning. MTL (Tecuci and Michalski, 1991) dynamically uses deduction, analogy, abduction, and induction to justify an input and potentially learn new knowledge from observations.

AIMS (Lu and Tcheng, 1991) supports the dynamic selection of learning techniques in the recursive-splitting learning paradigm. The system divides the domain based on some criteria, such as information gain, and selects a technique to further learn the subdomain based on the desired accuracy, comprehensibility, and efficiency of the learned knowledge and the characteristics of the available techniques.

Neither the macro nor the micro perspective is sufficient for supporting the knowledge acquisition for real engineering domains; both are equally important. Figure 14.1 illustrates the relationship between the two perspectives. The macro perspective decomposes the problem into simple tasks and identifies machine learning techniques that best—but probably not fully—match the specific engineering tasks. The micro perspective deals with the development of techniques to better suit the well-defined tasks or the adaptation of existing techniques identified by the

---

[2] Note that any engineering task is usually complex. However, at this level of granularity, we make the assumption that the problem can be formulated such that an algorithm can solve it.

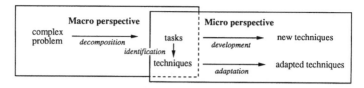

Figure 14.1:   The macro and micro perspectives

macro perspective. Usually, the scope of each technique will be restricted, necessitating the use of several multistrategy programs for supporting a real domain.

Two phases in the development of domain models, an idea similar to the macro and micro perspectives, are discussed by Tecuci (1991): (1) the definition of a suitable framework and (2) the implementation of the model in the framework. These phases correspond to the macro and micro perspectives, respectively.

Plan of the Chapter   The remainder of this chapter is organized as follows. Section 14.2 discusses the macro perspective of multistrategy learning. It reviews M²LTD and illustrates how BRIDGER, a system that assists in the design of cable-stayed bridges, was developed following M²LTD guidelines. Section 14.3 briefly reviews COBWEB and PROTOS. It discusses their shortcomings in relation to engineering domains and outlines some of the extensions that introduce additional learning strategies into these systems. These extensions are implemented in ECOBWEB and EPROTOS, respectively. Section 14.4 provides a common framework for the two perspectives by revisiting the concept of generic-learning tasks and showing that both perspectives operate within the generic task framework but in different grain sizes. Section 14.5 summarizes the chapter and discusses future research directions.

14.2 THE MACRO PERSPECTIVE

This section describes M²LTD, an approach for identifying learning techniques for complex domains, and reviews BRIDGER, the system built following its guidelines.

14.2.1 M²LTD

M²LTD (Matching Machine Learning To Design) is a *manual* approach for designing systems that acquire knowledge in complex domains (Reich, 1991b, 1991c); it reflects the macro perspective of multistrategy learning. As with any design activity, the use of M²LTD does not guarantee the successful development of a learning system; rather, it helps identify *potential* learning techniques that may perform the overall learning task. Feedback from implementation or other concerns

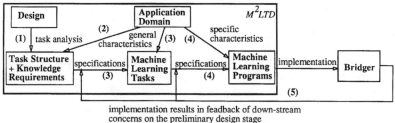

Figure 14.2:   M^{2}LTD: Matching machine learning programs to design tasks

emerging in the integration of the different techniques may dictate the modification of the techniques identified or even their replacements. The collection of experiences using M^{2}LTD is important to its future use. In that sense, the learning in this perspective is done by the developers of large learning systems.

M^{2}LTD is based on four steps (Figure 14.2):

1. Decomposition of the design task into a collection of smaller tasks (e.g., synthesis or analysis).

2. Identification of the representation of design objects used (e.g., lists of attribute-value pairs, trees, or graphs) in each of the tasks described in Step (1) and the strategies each task uses (e.g., top-down refinement).

3. Selection of machine learning paradigms that have the characteristics identified in Step (2) (e.g., inductive generalization or EBL).

4. Use of additional domain characteristics to select particular machine learning programs from the collection available in each paradigm found in Step (3) that can acquire the knowledge in the right representation and support the strategies employed (these well-defined learning techniques are called *generic learning tasks* [Reich and Fenves, 1989; see also Section 14.4]).

Rarely will an existing machine learning program do the task as specified, but a close match eliminates the effort of building a new learning program, leaving the need for modifying an existing one. M^{2}LTD focuses the implementation effort on the important modifications required, which in many cases involve the addition of new learning strategies.

Many concerns enter the decision about the appropriate machine learning task to use for each problem task. Some of the decisions are not conclusive and require revisions when the system is implemented. This is shown as Step (5) in Figure 14.2. Some of the concerns are mentioned in the next section, which discusses BRIDGER, a system that demonstrates the application of M^{2}LTD in the design of a learning system.

14.2.2 BRIDGER

14.2.2.1 Uses of M²LTD

This section describes the design of BRIDGER, a system that assists in the preliminary design of cable-stayed bridges. In Step (1) of M²LTD, preliminary design was decomposed into several tasks executed sequentially: synthesis, analysis, redesign, and evaluation (see Figure 14.3a). In Step (2), the domain of cable-stayed bridge design was analyzed based on the tasks previously identified and resulted in the following observations:

Synthesis.   There is no explicit knowledge about synthesis of cable-stayed bridges. Rather, synthesis uses the collection of previously designed bridges and adapts them to new specifications. Cable-stayed bridges can be described by an elaborate list of property-value pairs. A list sufficient for representing preliminary designs, drawn from existing bridges, contains about 60 properties.

Analysis.   There is extensive knowledge about analysis of bridges that is readily available in programs such as finite-element analysis.

Redesign.   There is a collection of heuristics that can propose design modifications for particular deficiencies in candidate designs. These heuristics were generated from studies of bridge examples. The heuristics are not exact and may conflict; therefore, they can be viewed as weak domain knowledge.

Evaluation.   Subjective judgment is usually used in selecting between candidate designs that satisfy the design requirements and the relevant design codes. In particular, aesthetic criteria have a major impact on evaluation.

The above observations direct the selection of learning tasks (Step (3) in Figure 14.2 and Figure 14.3b) and programs (Step (4) in Figure 14.2 and Figure 14.3c) for the acquisition of knowledge in the domain of cable-stayed bridge design. Both steps are discussed next.

Synthesis is a process that generates a description of an artifact given a list of specifications. In cable-stayed bridge design, both specifications and artifact descriptions can be represented by lists of property-value pairs (Reich, 1991b). A learning process that can capture a relation between two sets of properties is concept formation, which is believed to be fundamental for capturing synthesis knowledge (Reich and Fenves, 1991).

The design domain characteristics determine the use of techniques that do not use knowledge because it does not exist.[3] Step (4) suggests that a program such as

---

[3] Later we show how, in fact, if knowledge exists, it can be used to enhance learning performance.

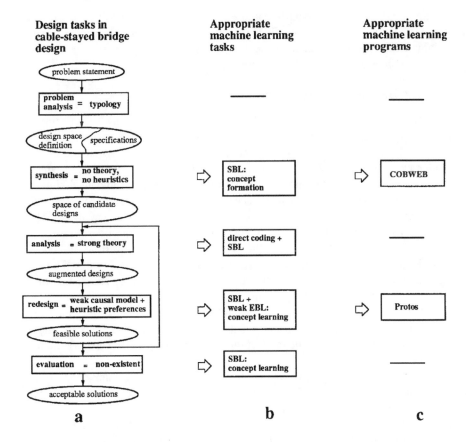

Figure 14.3: Mapping design tasks (a) to machine learning tasks (b), and subsequently to machine learning programs (c).

COBWEB (Fisher, 1987) can perform the learning activity. The reimplementation and testing of COBWEB on several design domains show some deficiencies leading to enhancements that are implemented in ECOBWEB (Enhanced COBWEB; see Section 14.3.1).

Analysis is coded directly; no learning is used in this task. Nevertheless, an experiment was performed to show that ECOBWEB can learn heuristic analysis (Reich and Fenves, 1991).

Redesign is a diagnosis task that can be supported by concept learning. The characteristics of cable-stayed bridge design allow the use of weak domain knowledge. A learning program that supports such learning activity is PROTOS (Bareiss, 1989).

Evaluation is not explicitly captured as knowledge; nevertheless, candidate designs generated by BRIDGER that are chosen by the designer can be used as training examples for enhancing synthesis knowledge. Consequently, the user evaluation becomes an implicit part of synthesis.

14.2.2.2 BRIDGER's Architecture

BRIDGER's architecture is based on the task analysis. BRIDGER contains two main subsystems: synthesis and redesign (see Figure 14.4). The synthesis system is responsible for synthesizing several candidates for a given specification. It is implemented by ECOBWEB (see Section 14.3.1). The redesign system is responsible for the analysis, redesign, and evaluation tasks of design. Candidate designs are analyzed by a finite-element program according to bridge design codes. The analysis results are compared with the code to generate constraint violations. These violations are input to the redesign module that retrieves the best design modification for the particular violations of the bridge. The user can override the redesign modifications and supply explanations that enhance redesign knowledge. The redesign module is implemented in EPROTOS (see Section 14.3.2). The results of the redesign system are acceptable designs.

One of the important issues in multistrategy learning is the interaction between the strategies or programs. In the context of BRIDGER, this question is translated into the nature of the interaction between synthesis (ECOBWEB) and redesign (EPROTOS).

In the macro perspective, the control and, therefore, the interaction are prespecified and limited. The different learning programs interact in the normal course of solving problems in the domain. In BRIDGER, the product of synthesis is delivered to analysis and redesign; therefore, the redesign knowledge acquired will be tuned to the candidates generated by the synthesis module. In addition, candidates modified by redesign may be learned by the synthesis module, therefore enhancing

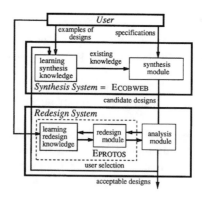

Figure 14.4:   BRIDGER's architecture

its knowledge. As BRIDGER designs more bridges, the candidates generated by synthesis are better and closer to those that redesign can easily correct.

14.2.2.3 Additional Uses of M²LTD

Two other applications of M²LTD for specifying a system that learns to design ships and a system that learns to perform finite element modeling are discussed in Reich (1991b). Because the preliminary design of ships is similar to the preliminary design of bridges, the use of M²LTD in this domain results in a specification of a program that is similar to BRIDGER. Two modifications to BRIDGER's architecture allow the acquisition of analysis and evaluation knowledge of ships. Because of the similarity between the bridge and the ship design domains, the use of M²LTD for the domain of ship design is almost guaranteed to be successful. The third domain, the design of finite-element models, is completely different than the first two domains. The use of M²LTD for this domain results in a rough specification of a learning program. A successful implementation requires the modification of several machine learning programs and substantial testing and further program adaptation.

14.3 THE MICRO PERSPECTIVE

This section discusses the micro perspective of multistrategy learning in the context of the systems implementing the synthesis and redesign modules of BRIDGER: ECOBWEB and EPROTOS. ECOBWEB includes several extensions that make it a multistrategy learning system; ECOBWEB is the major focus of this section. EPROTOS enhances PROTOS, which is already a multistrategy learning system; its operation is only briefly described. Because of space limitation, the description assumes a certain level of familiarity with the original COBWEB and PROTOS.

14.3.1 ECOBWEB

COBWEB is a concept formation program for the creation of hierarchical classification trees (Fisher, 1987). COBWEB evaluates a classification of a set of examples into mutually exclusive classes $C_1, C_2, \cdots, C_n$ by a statistical function called *category utility (CU)*:

$$CU = \frac{\sum_{k=1}^{n} P(C_k) \sum_i \sum_j P(A_i = V_{ij}|C_k)^2 - \sum_i \sum_j P(A_i = V_{ij})^2}{n} \tag{1}$$

where C_k is a class, $A_i = V_{ij}$ is a property-value pair, $P(x)$ is the probability of x, and n is the number of classes.

COBWEB learns by accommodating new examples into an existing hierarchy starting at the root while using one of the following operators (See Fisher, 1987, for a detailed description): (1) expanding the root, if it does not have any sub-classes, by creating a new class and attaching the root and the new example as its sub-classes; (2) adding the new example as a new sub-class of the root; (3) adding the new example to one of the sub-classes of the root; (4) merging the two best sub-classes and putting the new example into the merged sub-class; or (5) splitting the best sub-class and again considering all the alternatives. COBWEB selects the operator that, when applied, maximizes *CU*.

COBWEB predicts using a mechanism similar to the one used for augmenting the hierarchy by new examples but allowing only operator 3 to apply. COBWEB sorts a partial example through the hierarchy to find the best host for the new example. The best host is a leaf node (i.e., one of the training examples) that is used to complete the description of the new example.

COBWEB has a number of drawbacks when used in an engineering design domain.

1. COBWEB can only manipulate nominal properties.[4]
2. COBWEB has a stiff prediction scheme. It only uses an existing leaf node for prediction rather than provide several alternatives.
3. COBWEB uses only the syntactic measure of category utility to guide its learning and prediction. Knowledge is not used, although if available, it could enhance learning substantially.
4. COBWEB's performance depends heavily on the order of example presentation, even though it has two learning operators, split and merge, that are specifically designed to reduce order effects on learning.

Extensions that address each of the deficiencies are described next. They all involve some aspect of using background knowledge or additional learning strategies. Because ECOBWEB prediction is interleaved with its learning, extensions to prediction methods are also important.

14.3.1.1 Extension to Continuous Properties

As a system that learns from bridge examples, ECOBWEB must handle the continuous, ordinal, or nominal property types that appear in bridge descriptions. ECOBWEB implements an extension of *CU* that can handle continuous properties (Reich and Fenves, 1991; Reich, 1991b). In its simplest variant, the term $\sum_j P(A_i = V_{ij} | C_k)^2$ is calculated as

---

[4] A descendant of COBWEB, CLASSIT (Gennari et al., 1989), can handle continuous properties but in a more restricted way than ECOBWEB can (Reich, 1991b).

$$\sum_j P(A_i = V_{ij}|C_k)^2 \Leftrightarrow P(A_i = \overline{V_i}|C_k)^2 \Leftrightarrow \left(\int_{-\frac{d_i}{\sigma_i}}^{+\frac{d_i}{\sigma_i}} p_i(x)dx \right)^2 \tag{2}$$

where $p_i(x)$ is a distribution for the A_i, $2d_i$ is dependent on the range of values of A_i, V_i is the mean of the values of A_i in C_k, and σ_i is the standard deviation of the values of A_i. If no specific knowledge is available about the distribution p_i, the default is the normal distribution. This extension has been tested extensively in several domains and has proven to be effective and relatively insensitive to the choice of d_i (Reich, 1991b).

Knowledge can be used in two ways. The first is the use of domain knowledge about the distribution of continuous properties. The second way is the inspection of *a posteriori* distributions of continuous property values and the revision of their distributions based on this inspection. The first way is fully implemented, and the second can be incorporated in ECOBWEB.

14.3.1.2 Extension of the Prediction Methods

COBWEB's prediction method is too restrictive. Also, it is not clear how an inductive learner of the COBWEB type performs without a rich set of bridge examples. The new prediction methods are designed to operate between a case-based approach when few examples are available to a prototype-based approach when many examples are present.

The basic procedure is similar to COBWEB's prediction: *CU* guides the sorting of a partial example down the hierarchy. The first modification is that at each node, the property values of the example are compared to the characteristic[5] values of the node. A similar value is called a match. When all the property values of the example are matched, the sorting process terminates, potentially at an intermediate node in the hierarchy. To illustrate (see Figure 14.5), assume that the problem is specified by two requirements and that one of the characteristic values of class 1 is the same as one requirement, and one of the characteristics of class 3 equals the other requirement. In this situation, the path from class 1 to class 3 matches the two requirements, and therefore the synthesis process terminates. This behavior generates general solutions to general problems, a good by-product of the design of the new prediction methods.

The second difference between the new and COBWEB's prediction method is the variety of techniques available in the new prediction. ECOBWEB's prediction methods can be described along two dimensions: the refinement (i.e., sorting) pro-

---

[5] Characteristics are property values that satisfy $P(A_i = V_{ij} \mid C_k) \geq$ *threshold* and $P(C_k \mid A_i = V_{ij}) \geq$ *threshold*, where *threshhold* is a pre-determined value. Potentially, this value can be learned for each domain.

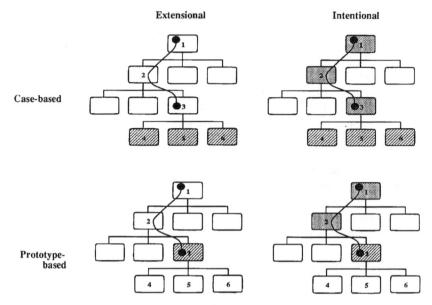

Figure 14.5:   Synthesis methods

cess, which can be *extensional* or *intensional* and the generation process which, can be *case-based* or *prototype-based*. Figure 14.5 illustrates these dimensions. In the extensional approach, refinement classifies a new example with a new subclass, starting from the top node (class 1 in Figure 14.5) until the process terminates (class 3). In this view, a class represents the extension of all its leaves. In the intentional approach, while classifying the new example, characteristic property-values of the classes traversed (classes 1, 2, and 3 in Figure 14.5) are assigned to the new design. In the case-based approach, a set of existing designs are retrieved as candidate designs. For example, designs 4, 5, and 6 are retrieved. In the proto-type-based approach, the last class, i.e., class 3, is used to generate several candidates from the property value data it contains.

14.3.1.3 Use of Knowledge in Concept Formation

Use of Knowledge to Override CU.   An important characteristic of the knowledge generated by ECOBWEB is that it is declarative. This enables an external body of knowledge, domain dependent or independent, to inspect it. This inspection can make inferences that enhance the use of the classification hierarchy in learning and prediction. The ability to benefit from external knowledge relies on the flexible nature of the learning method, which uses weak search methods directed by the category utility function. *CU* can be used as a default mechanism in the absence of

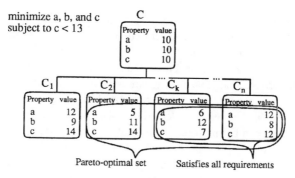

Figure 14.6:   Constrained optimization and exploratory design

knowledge; explicit knowledge, on the other hand, can prefer the execution of a specific operator or other learning strategies and override *CU*.

An example of constraining learning and prediction by Pareto-optimality and hard constraints is given in Figure 14.6. The top level of the classification hierarchy consists of *n* classes. Each class is partially described by three characteristic objectives; all the remaining properties are irrelevant to this discussion. In learning or prediction, instead of trying to find the best host from all the sub-classes, only sub-classes that are Pareto-optimal with respect to the desired objectives $(C_2, \cdots, C_k, \cdots, C_n)$ and that satisfy all the hard constraints $(C_k, \cdots, C_n)$ are considered. Consequently, C_1 is excluded because it is not optimal and violates the constraints, and C_2 is excluded because it violates the constraint. Alternatively, given additional resources, exploratory search might take place by relaxing constraints (permitting the consideration of C_2) or by trading objectives with other considerations (permitting the consideration of C_1).

Use of Knowledge about Modeling.   Another kind of domain knowledge that is investigated is knowledge about modeling. For example, such knowledge can suggest important features of objects. Given an initial description of objects, the knowledge can augment it by additional properties, compress the description of several properties, or erase irrelevant properties.

A simple use of such knowledge is exercised in modifying Equation 1 to account for the *a priori* or *learned* differences in the relative importance of properties. Equation 3 shows how *CU* can accommodate knowledge about the relative importance of properties and the structure of the classification hierarchy:

$$\frac{\sum_{k=1}^{n} P(C_k) \sum_i \sum_j W_i P(A_i = V_{ij}|C_k)^2 - \sum_i \sum_j W_i P(A_i = V_{ij})^2}{n^\alpha} \qquad (3)$$

where W_i is the weight of A_i, and $\alpha \geq 1.0$.

The parameter α makes sure that the classification hierarchy has a reasonable branching factor. For example, a flat hierarchy is computationally inefficient for the retrieval of designs, and a binary hierarchy loses information about similarity between designs. In the cable-stayed bridge design, a flat hierarchy is generated when using the original category utility expression from Equation 1. The variation of the parameter α changes the hierarchy from binary, when α is large, to flat, when α equals 1.0. The value selected for the cable-stayed bridge domain is $\alpha = 1.1$. This value can be modified dynamically by observing the branching factor of the hierarchy. A branching factor of 3 to 4 is experienced to yield good results across domains. The knowledge about the weighting and the α parameter is required if data are sparse and not sufficient to construct a usable hierarchy. The need to use knowledge in empirical learning, when data are limited, is recognized in many learning systems of which EPROTOS, the system used for the acquisition of redesign knowledge, is one example.

Constructive Induction. COBWEB makes use of the original property-value pairs appearing in example descriptions, assuming that the description language is adequate. ECOBWEB has a constructive induction scheme that can generate higher-order features from existing property values (Reich, 1990). The extension to continuous properties can be viewed as grouping values into samples from an assumed distribution. For example, two values V_{11} and V_{12} can be combined into a new feature $G_1 = \{V_{11}, V_{12}\}$. This can be viewed as adding an internal disjunct into the description language. Additional values can be accommodated into, or deleted from, G_1 based on additional information.

The constructive induction capability can be used to handle hierarchical properties. In this case, the only features that will be allowed are those that represent nodes of the hierarchy. For example, $\{circle\}$ and $round = \{circle, ellipse\}$, shown in Figure 14.7, are possible features, whereas $\{square, rectangle\}$ and $\{triangle, circle\}$ are inappropriate features.

Experimentation. Another way of using knowledge is to construct examples that will enhance the performance of the system. This capability is very important because machine learning techniques are sometimes used for extracting knowledge from simulation of behaviors of designs that are examples that are generated on

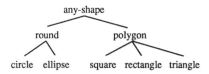

Figure 14.7:   A hierarchical property

demand (Bratko et al., 1989; Reich, 1991b). The availability of good sources of examples is crucial for obtaining a satisfactory learning performance.

For example, in the context of BRIDGER, there are relatively few examples of cable-stayed bridges available, and the generation of new examples is time consuming; it involves the selection of "good" specification and the design of solutions for the specification. It is therefore important to devise a method that will allow the generation of the most useful examples such that the improvement in knowledge because of learning is maximized with minimal training resources.

The problem of selecting good examples is especially dominant when using an incremental learning system (Fisher et al., 1991). In this case, even if all the examples are available, it is useful to impose a good ordering on the training examples (MacGregor, 1988). While using COBWEB in several design domains, it was observed that the order of training examples used to generate synthesis knowledge has a significant effect on the synthesis ability. Deviations of 90% in synthesis performance were observed in statistical experiments with random orderings of training examples.

ECOBWEB's experimentation technique can be performed in two ways. The first method only makes use of the information stored at the root of the hierarchy, namely, the most frequent property-value pairs. The next training example that is selected is one that has property values that are the most distant from the most frequent values observed thus far. The second experimentation method is more complex; it searches for an example that, if learned, will maximize the category utility of the top-level classification. This method is more informative and makes use of ECOBWEB mechanisms. Preliminary experiments in several domains show some improvements, but invariably, the ordering issue remains unsolved (Reich, 1991a).

Hierarchy-correction scheme. Another approach to mitigating the problem of order effects on learning is to use knowledge about properties to reorganize the hierarchical knowledge structure in a process called *hierarchy correction*. This procedure can detect problems in the classification hierarchy that were introduced in spite of the mechanisms that use knowledge to override *CU*, discussed before.

The hierarchy-correction scheme follows three steps. First, properties deemed most critical by domain knowledge are selected as *triggers*. Second, the hierarchy is traversed top-down. Each class with a characteristic value of a trigger property that differs from a characteristic in one of the class' ancestors is removed, along with its subtree, from the hierarchy. Third, the examples at the leaves of all the removed subtrees are re-learned. Because the process is heuristic, learning can reconstruct exactly the same tree after the subtrees are removed; in contrast, the process can iterate several times, each leading to some improvement. The process stops when no change to the hierarchy is obtained or when the limit on the number

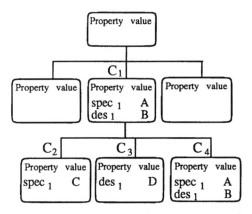

Figure 14.8:   Classification hierarchy with characteristic contradictions

of iterations is reached. The application of this procedure enhances the predictive accuracy of ECOBWEB.

To illustrate, assume that the top classification hierarchy is as appears in Figure 14.8. $spec_1$ is a specification property, and des_1 is a design description property; they are considered triggers by domain knowledge. Only characteristic values are shown in the figure. The hierarchy correction traverses the hierarchy until reaching class C_1. By looking at its sub-classes, C_2, C_3, and C_4, the method detects that the characteristic value of $spec_1$ in class C_2 is different than that in class C_1, the characteristic value of des_1 in class C_3 is different than that in class C_1, and both characteristic values in class C_4 are equal to those in class C_1. The differences suggest that the information stored in C_2 and C_3 contradicts the information stored in the parent class C_1. It is better if this contradiction is removed. Therefore, classes C_2 and C_3 are erased from the hierarchy with all their sons, and the leaf nodes that are training examples are re-learned by ECOBWEB.

User's role.   Besides all the automatic techniques discussed above that make use of some knowledge, there is the most trivial way of using knowledge in learning and prediction: the apprentice mode. In that mode, ECOBWEB allows users to determine the next learning operator or strategy to apply instead of using category utility or one of the additional mechanisms described. Similar ideas to the use of interactive induction, in which users of the learning program observe the results of the program and modify its input, are discussed in Stirling and Buntine (1988). It is expected that in complex domains, a synergistic approach of human-computer induction will be more beneficial than the fully automatic approach (Reich et al., 1991). Future extensions will allow users to incorporate knowledge while they control ECOBWEB's operation.

Summary. This list of implemented and potential uses of knowledge or other learning strategies in the COBWEB framework is not exhaustive. Presently, the user of ECOBWEB determines which learning strategies are used in a specific learning scenario. The automatic control of these strategies is complex and is the subject of future research.

14.3.2 EPROTOS

PROTOS is an exemplar-based learning program that integrates empirical learning with weak domain knowledge in the form of explanation (Bareiss, 1989). The task of PROTOS is heuristic classification: given a new case and knowledge in the form of category structure, find the best category for the new case. This section explains why PROTOS is a multistrategy learning system and how its extension that handles continuous values introduces an additional strategy (for further details, see Reich, 1991b).

PROTOS represents knowledge in categories that contain representative cases called *exemplars*. Exemplars are described by lists of nominal property-value pairs. The exemplars are augmented with domain knowledge that can explain the relationships between categories, exemplars, or other pieces of knowledge.

The first process in PROTOS' algorithm is finding an exemplar that strongly matches the new case. The description of the new case serves as its indexing information, used in the *hypothesis formation* stage of classification. In this process, the properties of a new case remind exemplars that are rated based on their combined remindings' strength. The category that contains the strongest exemplar is selected as the hypothesis of the classification. In the *confirmation* stage, the properties of the old exemplar are matched against the new case. A property that is not matched triggers search through the explanation network to heuristically construct further matchings via the use of explanations. If PROTOS cannot find a suitable explanation between the old exemplar and the new case, it tries to fetch a better exemplar and start the confirmation process again.

PROTOS learns while it interacts with an expert. Difficulties in classification trigger focused queries for the expert. The expert's answers refine PROTOS' domain knowledge; this is PROTOS' first learning strategy. The second learning strategy is learning and strengthening indices after successful hypothesis formation. The third learning strategy involves the learning of an exemplar if it cannot be classified or if there is no good match between it and an existing exemplar. In sum, PROTOS employs several learning strategies tightly integrated with its problem solving.

In BRIDGER, PROTOS is used to acquire redesign knowledge and to redesign objects. In this case, cases contain the description of bridges with some performance values, and a redesign modification contains a list of properties that should be modified to correct the performance. PROTOS has several drawbacks for its use as a redesign system.

1. PROTOS can only manipulate symbolic properties. This problem was discussed before in relation to COBWEB.

2. As a classification program, PROTOS outputs a single class as the confirmed hypothesis. In redesign, it may be necessary to recommend several simultaneous redesign modifications.

3. The explanation language cannot handle exact relationships between terms. For example, it cannot represent an equation.

The first two drawbacks are addressed in extensions implemented in EPROTOS. The second extension is simple; it involves modifying the output function of PROTOS (Reich, 1991b). The first extension is more interesting for multistrategy learning because it involves the use of ECOBWEB as an indexing scheme for the continuous properties, thereby adding one strategy to PROTOS. To elaborate, because a continuous property of a new case is unlikely to be present in memory, ECOBWEB will retrieve the most relevant value from a hierarchy generated from all the values of the existing exemplars. The retrieved value will be used in the normal classification procedure of EPROTOS. In the hypothesis confirmation, a simple modification is made for calculating the strengths of a match between two continuous values (Reich, 1991b).

14.4 GENERIC LEARNING TASKS

Both the macro and the micro perspectives rely on similar principles. In both, it is important to know (1) what is the input and output of a learning program, (2) what is the representation of knowledge used and learned, and (3) how is the program executed. This information is used manually in the macro perspective for identifying learning programs for specific tasks and could be used automatically in the micro perspective for selecting between learning strategies in a multistrategy learning program.

Similar information requirements emerge from the concept of generic tasks as high level building blocks for expert systems (Chandrasekaran, 1986). A generic task is a tuple $G = (I/O, KR, C)$ whose components are

I/O is the Input/Output of the generic task. It represents the task functionality.

KR is the representation of knowledge required to achieve the task functionality.

C is the control structure of the task. It specifies the procedure for achieving the task functionality by operating on the knowledge representation.

This tuple is crafted such that the knowledge representation and control used in the task are directed toward providing the required Input/Output characteristics.

The knowledge representation and control are to be designed such that their syntax matches their semantics. The syntax-semantics correspondence establishes a strong limitation on the task scope but makes it productive for a specific class of problems.

The concept of *generic learning tasks* is the application of the generic task idea to machine learning except that now the task is learning a specific type of knowledge that will be used by some generic task. To illustrate the concept, examples of generic learning tasks from the macro and the micro perspectives are discussed.

Macro generic task. ECOBWEB can be viewed as a generic learning task that acquires knowledge for a class of routine synthesis problems.[6] The information related to the task is

I/O The input to ECOBWEB is examples represented by lists of property-value pairs. The output is a classification hierarchy that can be used for synthesis.

KR Learned knowledge is represented as a probabilistic declarative classification hierarchy. Background knowledge can be represented in a variety of forms.

C ECOBWEB makes use of four learning operators and a heuristic control driven by *CU*. This approximates hill-climbing in the space of classification hierarchies. ECOBWEB exercises fixed control over the learning mechanisms that use domain knowledge. C also includes time and space complexity of all the learning procedures implemented in ECOBWEB.

Micro generic task. The hierarchy-correction procedure can be viewed as a generic learning task that improves the quality of knowledge represented by a classification hierarchy. The information related to this task is

I/O The input to hierarchy-correction is a classification hierarchy and a list of constraints on the hierarchy. The output is a classification hierarchy that heuristically minimizes the constraint violations.

KR This procedure represents the classification hierarchy as a probabilistic declarative structure. The constraints are represented by predicates.

C Hierarchy-correction performs iterative constraint violation detection, forgetting and re-learning the forgotten examples, until the hierarchy is not changed. This constitutes a hill-climbing in the space of classifica-

---

[6] Of course, COBWEB can be viewed as a generic learning task that acquires knowledge for a class of classification problems.

tion hierarchies. The time and space complexity of this procedure is similar to ECOBWEB because it includes the execution of ECOBWEB for relearning the forgotten examples, which is more difficult than detecting the nodes to be erased.

The hierarchy-correction procedure shows how easily complex learning behaviors can be created. Although it is one of ECOBWEB's mechanisms, it can make use of all ECOBWEB's functionality, including itself, for executing one of its sub-processes.

In complex multistrategy learning programs, there will be several generic learning tasks that can provide the same functionality but differ in their accuracy, cost, etc. The control of the multistrategy system will have to consider the overall learning task requirements in determining which learning task will perform each function.

Preliminary experience with developing generic learning tasks and integrating them into larger systems suggests that considerable knowledge about learning techniques is required to successfully employ multistrategy techniques in complex domains. Knowledge is not yet available that would allow the full automation of selecting appropriate learning tasks for specific problems. It is conjectured that a better use of multistrategy learning is facilitated through the use of the generic learning task idea that reflects both the macro and the micro perspectives of multistrategy learning. This idea, in turn, requires the development of a better understanding of existing machine learning techniques. This understanding involves the ability to identify machine learning techniques that can support the knowledge acquisition for a particular domain (i.e., have the right I/O) and support the problem-solving strategies that manipulate knowledge in that domain (i.e., have the right KR). In general, this understanding involves the construction of a mapping as shown in Figure 14.9.[7] A step toward this end is the development of languages to describe the input and output of various learning algorithms (e.g., CKRL, Morik et al., 1991).

14.5 DISCUSSION AND SUMMARY

This chapter discussed two perspectives of viewing multistrategy learning systems: the macro and the micro. The macro perspective deals with the decomposition of large learning problems into manageable pieces and the selection of state-of-the-art learning techniques that can address these simpler learning problems. Because existing techniques rarely satisfy the requirements of real-world learning problems, the specification of new techniques are developed. M^2LTD is a manual

---

[7] Although the surface is shown to be continuous, it is in fact discrete.

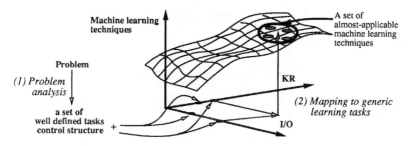

Figure 14.9: Mapping problems into machine learning techniques

procedure that guides the designer of a large learning program in the above decomposition, selection, and specification procedures. One example of the use of M^{2}LTD is the design of BRIDGER, a system that assists in the design of cable-stayed bridges.

The micro perspective deals with the design of multistrategy learning programs that must cope with the simpler learning tasks identified by M^{2}LTD. ECOBWEB and EPROTOS are two multistrategy systems that are incorporated in BRIDGER.

The problem of multistrategy learning is not the building of the mechanisms but their integration and control. The control aspect requires knowledge about the learning strategies: their performance, functionality, representation, accuracy, etc. For multistrategy learning to successfully work, a good understanding of machine learning techniques must be developed.

The automatic use of multiple learning strategies and programs for solving hard learning problems is an important problem that begins to attract new research effort. It is conjectured that the development of a better understanding of generic learning tasks will be beneficial in advancing the use of multistrategy learning.

Future research directions involves the elaboration of the mapping displayed in Figure 14.9. This requires establishing a database whose entries are learning programs described along various practical dimensions. It also involves the creation of integrative frameworks for coordinating the execution of generic learning tasks. These frameworks can range from fixed control to knowledge-based control (e.g., blackboard) to multi-agent cooperative frameworks.

ACKNOWLEDGMENTS

This work was supported in part by the Engineering Design Research Center, a National Science Foundation Engineering Research Center. The comments of the reviewers and especially Ryszard Michalski and Gheorghe Tecuci improved the presentation of this chapter.

References

Bareiss, R., *Exemplar-Based Knowledge Acquisition*, Academic Press, San Diego, CA, 1989.

Bergadano, F., Giordana, A., and Saitta, L., "Automated concept acquisition in noisy environments," *IEEE Transactions on Pattern Analysis and Machine Intelligence*, 10(4): 555–578, 1988.

Bratko, I., Mozetic, I., and Lavrac, N., *KARDIO: A Study in Deep and Qualitative Knowledge for Expert Systems*, MIT Press, Boston, MA, 1989.

Chandrasekaran, B., "Generic tasks in knowledge-based reasoning: High-level building blocks for expert system design," *IEEE Expert*, 1(3): 23–30, 1986.

Fisher, D.H., "Knowledge acquisition via incremental conceptual clustering," *Machine Learning*, 2(7): 139–172, 1987.

Fisher, D., Ling, X., Carnes, R., Reich, Y., Fenves, S., Chen, J., Shiavi, R., Biswas, G., and Weinberg, J., "Selected applications of an AI clustering technique to engineering tasks," Technical Report CS-91-08, Vanderbilt University, Nashville, TN, 1991.

Gennari, J.H., Langley, P., and Fisher, D., "Models of incremental concept formation," *Artificial Intelligence*, 40(1–3): 11–61, 1989.

Lu, S.C.-Y., and Chen, K., "A machine learning approach to the automatic synthesis of mechanistic knowledge for engineering decision-making," *Artificial Intelligence for Engineering Design, Analysis, and Manufacturing*, 1(2): 109–118, 1987.

Lu, S.C.-Y., and Tcheng, D.K., "Building layered models to support engineering decision making: A machine learning approach," *Journal of Engineering for Industry*, 113(1): 1–9, 1991.

MacGregor, J.N., "The effects of order on learning classifications by example: Heuristics for finding the optimal order," *Artificial Intelligence*, 34(3): 361–370, 1988.

Michalski, R.S., and Stepp, R., "Learning from observation: Conceptual clustering," In Michalski, R.S., Carbonell, J.G., and Mitchell, T.M., editors, *Machine Learning: An Artificial Intelligence Approach*, pages 331–363, Palo Alto, CA: Tioga Press, 1983.

Michalski, R.S., Mozetic, I., Hong, J., and Lavrac, N., "The multi-purpose incremental learning system {AQ15} and its testing application to three medical domains," In *Proceedings of AAAI-86*, pages 1041–1045, San Mateo, CA: Morgan Kaufmann, 1986.

Morik, K., Causse, K., and Boswell, R., "A common knowledge representation integrating learning tools," In Michalski, R.S., and Tecuci, G., editors, *Proceedings of the First International Workshop on Multistrategy Learning*, pages 81–96, Fairfax, VA: Center for Artificial Intelligence, George Mason University, 1991.

Quinlan, J.R., "Induction of decision trees," *Machine Learning*, 1(1): 81–106, 1986.

Reich, Y., "Constructive induction by incremental concept formation," In Feldman, Y.A., and Bruckstein, A., editors, *Proceedings of the Seventh Israeli Symposium on Artificial Intelligence and Computer Vision (Ramat-Gan)*, pages 195–208, Amsterdam: Elsevier Science Publishers, 1990.

————, "Automatic selection of examples for training a learning design system," Technical Report 12-42-91, Engineering Design Research Center, Carnegie Mellon University, Pittsburgh, PA, 1991a.

————, *Building and Improving Design Systems: A Machine Learning Approach*. Ph.D. thesis, Department of Civil Engineering, Carnegie Mellon University, Pittsburgh, PA, 1991b. (Available as Technical Report EDRC 02-16-91.)

————, "Design knowledge acquisition: Task analysis and a partial implementation," *Knowledge Acquisition*, 3(3): 237–254, 1991c.

Reich, Y., and Fenves, S.J., "Integration of generic learning tasks," Technical Report EDRC 12-28-89, Engineering Design Research Center, Carnegie Mellon University, Pittsburgh, PA, 1989.

————, The formation and use of abstract concepts in design. In Fisher, D.H.J., Pazzani, M.J., and Langley, P., editors, *Concept Formation: Knowledge and Experience in Unsupervised Learning*, pages 323–353, San Mateo, CA: Morgan Kaufmann, 1991.

Reich, Y., Coyne, R., Modi, A., Steier, D., and Subrahmanian, E., "Learning in design: An EDRC (US) perspective," In Gero, J., editor, *Artificial Intelligence in Design '91, Proceedings of The First International Conference on Artificial Intelligence in Design, Edinburgh, UK*, pages 303–321, Oxford, UK: Butterworths, 1991.

Shalin, V.L., Wisniewski, E.J., Levi, K.R., and Scott, P.D., "A formal analysis of machine learning systems for knowledge acquisition," *International Journal of Man-Machine Studies*, 29(4): 429–446, 1988.

Stirling, D., and Buntine, W., "Process routings in a steel mill: A challenging induction problem," In Gero, J.S., and Stanton, R., editors, *Artificial Intelligence Developments and Applications*, pages 301–313, Amsterdam: North-Holland, 1988.

Tecuci, G., "A multistrategy learning approach to domain modeling and knowledge acquisition," In Kodratoff, Y., editor, *Machine Learning-EWSL91, Proceedings of the European Workshop on Machine Learning*, Berlin: Springer-Verlag, 1991.

Tecuci, G.D., and Michalski, R.S., "A method for multistrategy task-adaptive learning based on plausible justifications," In Birnbaum, L.A., and Collins, G., editors, *Proceedings of the Eighth International Workshop on Machine Learning*, pages 549–553, San Mateo, CA: Morgan Kaufmann, 1991.

Witten, I.H., and MacDonald, B.A., "Using concept learning for knowledge acquisition," *International Journal of Man-Machine Studies*, 29(2): 171–196, 1988.

PART
FOUR

SYMBOLIC AND
SUBSYMBOLIC LEARNING

15

REFINING SYMBOLIC KNOWLEDGE
USING NEURAL NETWORKS

Geoffrey G. Towell
Jude W. Shavlik
(University of Wisconsin—Madison)

Abstract

To use artificial neural networks as part of a multistrategy learning system, there must be a way for neural networks to accept information, often expressed symbolically, from other systems. Moreover, neural networks must be able to transfer the results of their learning. A three-step process for learning using rule-based domain knowledge in combination with neural networks can address this task. Methods for performing the first two steps have previously been described. Hence, this chapter focuses on the final step, extracting symbolic rules from trained neural networks. Proposed and empirically evaluated in this chapter is a new method for rule extraction. The rules extracted by this method closely reproduce the accuracy of the network from which they came, are superior to the rules derived by a learning system that directly refines symbolic rules, and are human comprehensible. Hence, this process allows the use of neural networks as a part of a multistrategy learning system. More generally, this work contributes to the understanding of how symbolic and connectionist approaches to artificial intelligence can profitably be integrated.

15.1 INTRODUCTION

Artificial neural networks (ANNs) have proven to be a powerful and general technique for machine learning (Fisher and McKusick, 1989; Shavlik et al., 1991).

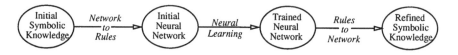

Figure 15.1:   The flow of information through KBANN.

Hence, it is tempting to use ANNs in combination with other, more knowledge intensive, learning strategies. However, ANNs have several well-known shortcomings. Perhaps the most significant of these shortcomings is that it is very difficult to determine why a trained ANN makes a particular decision. However, the extraction of accurate, comprehensible, symbolic knowledge from ANNs is necessary if ANNs are to be useful in a multistrategy framework. In addition, without the ability to explain their decisions, it is hard to be confident in the reliability of networks that solve real-world problems. The extraction of rules directly addresses both of these concerns because rules provide a simple mechanism for explanation and transfer. Therefore, the extraction of comprehensible, symbolic rules from trained networks is desirable. That is the topic of this chapter.

The approach taken to extracting rules from trained ANNs uses KBANN, a tri-algorithmic multistrategy learning system illustrated by Figure 15.1. The first link in the algorithm chain creates a neural network that encodes domain knowledge; the encoded knowledge need be neither complete nor correct (Towell et al., 1990). The second link trains the KBANN-net (i.e., a network created by KBANN) using a set of classified training examples and standard neural learning methods (Rumelhart et al., 1986). The final link extracts rules from trained KBANN-nets.

Rule extraction is an extremely difficult task for arbitrarily configured networks but is somewhat less daunting for KBANN-nets because of their initial comprehensibility. The method described in this chapter takes advantage of their initial comprehensibility to efficiently extract rules from trained KBANN-nets. When evaluated in terms of their ability to correctly classify examples not seen during training, the rules produced by this method are equivalent to the accuracy of the networks from which they came. Moreover, the extracted rules are superior to the rules resulting from methods that act *directly* on the original rules (rather than their re-representation as a neural network). Also, the method is superior to the most widely published algorithm for the extraction of rules from general neural networks.

The next section contains brief reviews of neural networks and the rules-to-network translator of KBANN. Subsequent sections describe two rule extraction methods, one original and one very similar to the best previously reported method. The succeeding section presents empirical tests, using two real-world learning problems taken from molecular biology, that characterize the strengths and weaknesses of both rule-extraction methods. The final sections of this chapter put this work into the context of other approaches to understanding trained neural networks and discuss future research plans.

15.2 REVIEW OF ALGORITHMS

This section briefly reviews learning in neural networks and the KBANN rules-to-network translator. An understanding of both of these topics is required to comprehend the rule-extraction techniques described in the following section.

15.2.1 Neural Learning

Artificial neural networks are a class of learning systems inspired by the architecture of the brain and theories of learning in the brain (McCulloch and Pitts, 1943; Hebb, 1949; Rosenblatt, 1962). They are composed of cell-like entities (referred to as *units*) and connections between the units corresponding to dendrites and axons. (The connections are referred to as *links*.) Links are *weighted*; the weights roughly correspond to the efficacy of synapses in the brain. The effect of the weights is that the signal received by a unit is the product of the link weight and the signal sent across the link. Abandoning the brain metaphor, an ANN is a directed graph with weighted connections.

Units do only one thing—they compute a real-numbered output (known as an *activation*) that is a function of real-numbered inputs. Figure 15.2 shows the behavior of a single unit with N incoming links. The (output) *activation* of the unit is shown to be a function of the sum of the incoming signals and a "bias" term that acts as a threshold for the unit. A typical activation function (the "logistic") is illustrated by Figure 15.3. It shows that the activation of a unit is near zero when the net incoming activation is less than the bias and near one in the opposite case.

Units in neural networks are commonly sorted into three groups: *input, hidden*, and *output*. These groups are shown graphically in Figure 15.4. Input units are so named because they receive signals from the environment. Similarly, output units are so named because their activation is available to the environment. (Generally, the activation of the output units is the answer computed by the network.)

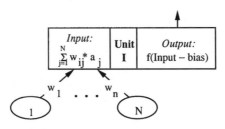

Figure 15.2:   A single unit of an ANN

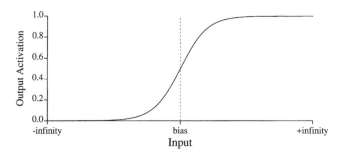

Figure 15.3:   The activation of a unit in an ANN

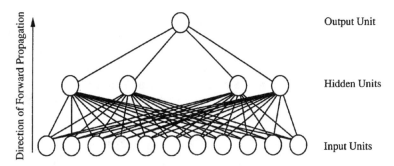

Figure 15.4:   A prototypical artificial neural network

Finally, hidden units are so named because they have no direct interaction with the environment. They are purely internal to the network.

The general process of learning in a neural network, using the standard back-propagation model (Rumelhart et al., 1986), is given by the five-step algorithm in Table 15.1. For the details of the backpropagation algorithm, see Rumelhart et al. (1986) or Hertz et al. (1991).

Table 15.1:   The backpropagation algorithm

---

1. Activations of input units are set by the environment.
2. Activation is propagated forward along the directed connections (links) possibly through hidden units to the output units.
3. Errors are determined as a function of the difference between the computed activation of the output units and the desired activation of the output units.
4. Errors are propagated backward along the same links used to carry activations.
5. Changes are made to link weights to reduce the difference between the actual and desired activations of the output units.

15.2.2 KBANN's Rules-to-Network Translator

KBANN translates symbolic knowledge into neural networks, defining the topology and connection weights of the networks it creates. It uses a knowledge base of domain-specific inference rules, in the form of propositional Horn clauses, to define what is initially known about a topic. Detailed explanations of the procedure used by KBANN to translate rules into a KBANN-net are given by Towell et al. (1990) and Towell (1991); the following is a brief summary.

KBANN translates a collection of rules into a neural network by individually translating each rule into a small subnetwork that accurately reproduces the behavior of the translated rule. These small subnetworks are then assembled to form a single neural network that mimics the behavior of the whole rule. The next paragraphs describe how KBANN creates subnetworks that encode conjuncts and disjuncts. Following that is an example of a full rules-to-network translation.

Conjunctive rules are translated into a neural network by setting weights on all links corresponding to positive (i.e., unnegated) antecedents to ω, weights on all links corresponding to negated antecedents to $-\omega$, and the bias on the unit corresponding to the rule's consequent to $2P-1/2\omega$; P is the number of positive antecedents. KBANN commonly uses a setting of $\omega = 4$, a value empirically found to work well. For example, Figure 15.5 shows the encoding of a conjunctive rule.

To translate a set of rules encoding a disjunct, KBANN sets the weight of each link corresponding to a disjunctive antecedent to ω and the bias on the unit encoding the consequent to $\omega/2$. For example, Figure 15.5 shows the network that encodes a four-rule disjunct.

Intuitively, these strategies for translating conjunctive and disjunctive rules are reasonable. In both cases, the incoming activation overcomes the bias only when the consequent is satisfied.

As an example of the KBANN method, consider the sample knowledge base in Figure 15.6a, which defines membership in category A. Figure 15.6b represents the hierarchical structure of these rules: solid and dotted lines represent necessary and prohibitory dependencies, respectively. Figure 15.6c represents the KBANN-

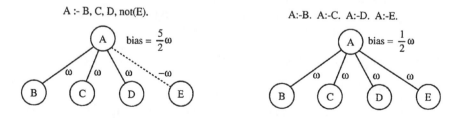

Figure 15.5:   Translation of conjunctive and disjunctive rules into a KBANN-net

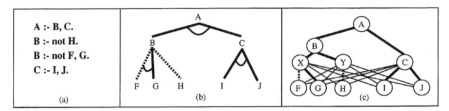

Figure 15.6:   Translation of a knowledge base into a KBANN-net. This figure shows a progression from rules, to a rule structure, to a neural network.

net that results from the translation into a neural network of this knowledge base. Units X and Y in Figure 15.6c are introduced into the KBANN-net to handle the disjunction in the rule set. Otherwise, each unit in the KBANN-net corresponds to a consequent or an antecedent in the knowledge base. The thick lines in Figure 15.6c represent heavily weighted links (i.e., links with weight ω) in the KBANN-net; they correspond to dependencies in the knowledge base. The thin lines represent the links added to the network to allow refinement of the knowledge base.

This example illustrates that the use of KBANN to initialize neural networks has two principal benefits. First, the algorithm indicates the input features that are believed to be important to an example's classification. Second, it specifies important derived features, thereby guiding the choice of the number and connectivity of *hidden units* in the KBANN-net.

15.3 EXTRACTING RULES FROM TRAINED NETWORKS

After KBANN-nets have refined, they can be used as highly accurate classifiers (Towell et al., 1990). However, trained KBANN-nets provide no explanation of how an answer was derived, nor can the results of their learning be shared with humans or transferred to related problems. (The work of Pratt et al. [1991] partially ameliorates this problem.)

The extraction of symbolic rules directly addresses both of these problems. It makes the information learned by the KBANN-net accessible for human review and justification of answers. Moreover, the modified rules can be used as a part of knowledge bases for the solution of related problems.

15.3.1 Underpinnings of Rule Extraction

15.3.1.1 Assumptions

Almost every method of rule extraction makes one assumption about trained networks, specifically that the units in trained nets are always either fully active (≈ 1) or inactive (≈ 0). This assumption is not particularly restrictive; the standard logistic activation function can be modified slightly to ensure that units approximate step functions.

The methods described in this chapter also assume that training does not significantly shift the meaning of units. By making this assumption, the methods are able to attach labels to rules that correspond to terms in the domain knowledge upon which the network is based. These labels enhance the comprehensibility of the rules.

15.3.1.2 Commonalities

The methods for extracting rules from neural networks described below, as well as those in the literature, do so by trying to find combinations of the input values to a unit that result in it having an activation near one. Broadly speaking, if the summed weighted input to a unit exceeds its bias, then its activation will be near one. Otherwise, its activation will be near zero. *Hence, rule extraction methods need only look for ways in which the weighted sum of the inputs exceeds the bias.*

The first of the above assumptions, that all units in trained networks have activations near zero or one, simplifies this task by ensuring that links carry a signal equal to their weight or no signal at all. As a result, rule extractors need only be concerned with the weight of links entering a unit and may ignore the activation of the sending unit.

Rule extraction is further simplified by the fact that in the networks created by KBANN, units always have non-negative activations. Therefore, negatively weighted links can only give rise to negated antecedents, and positively weighted links can only give rise to unnegated antecedents. This considerably reduces the size of the search space (Fu, 1991).

The following subsections present two methods of rule extraction. This first method has previously been described (Saito and Nakano, 1988). It is presented here for purposes of comparison.

15.3.2 The SUBSET Method

Given the above assumptions, the simplest method for extracting rules can be referred to as the SUBSET method. This method operates by exhaustively searching for subsets of the links into a unit such that the sum of the weights of the links in the subset guarantees that the total input to the unit exceeds its bias. In the limit, SUBSET extracts a set of rules that reproduce the behavior of the network. However, the combinatorics of this method render it impossible to execute except on small networks that solve toy problems. Heuristics can be added to reduce the complexity of the search at some cost to the accuracy of the resulting rules. Unfortunately, even using heuristic search, SUBSET tends to produce repetitive rules whose preconditions are difficult to interpret.

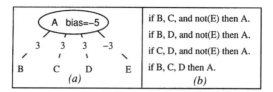

(a)	(b)
A bias=−5 3 3 3 −3 B C D E	if B, C, and not(E) then A. if B, D, and not(E) then A. if C, D, and not(E) then A. if B, C, D then A.

Figure 15.7: Rule extraction using the SUBSET algorithm. This figure shows a small network and the rules extracted from the network by SUBSET.

As a brief example of the SUBSET method, consider the unit in Figure 15.7a. Given that the link weights and the bias are as shown, the four rules listed in Figure 15.7b are extracted by the algorithm. To find these four rules, SUBSET must check all possible rules with 1, 2, 3, or 4 antecedents. (See papers by Saito and Nakano [1988] or Fu [1991] for more detailed explanations of SUBSET.)

15.3.3 The NOFM Method

The second algorithm for rule extraction, referred to as NOFM, explicitly searches for antecedents of the form

```
if (N of these M antecedents are true) then...
```

This approach was taken because the rule sets discovered by the SUBSET method often contain "N-of-M" style concepts. Furthermore, experiments indicate that ANNs are good at learning N-of-M concepts (Fisher and McKusick, 1989) and that searching for N-of-M concepts is a useful inductive bias (Murphy and Pazzani, 1991). Finally, note that purely conjunctive rules result if $N = M$, and a set of disjunctive rules results when $N = 1$; hence, using N-of-M rules does not restrict generality.

The idea underlying NOFM, an abstracted version of which appears in Table 15.2, is that individual antecedents (links) do not have a unique importance. Rather, groups of antecedents form equivalence classes in which each antecedent has the same importance as, and is interchangeable with, other members of the class. This equivalence class idea is the key to the NOFM algorithm; it allows the algorithm to consider groups of links without worrying about the particular links within the group.

The next subsection contains a detailed description of each step of the NOFM algorithm. A detailed example appears in the subsequent subsection.

15.3.3.1 Step-by-Step Description of the NOFM Algorithm

Step 1, Clustering. Backpropagation training tends to group links of KBANN-nets into loose clusters rather than tight equivalence classes as assumed by the NOFM

Table 15.2:   The NOFM approach to rule extraction

---

1. With each hidden and output unit, form groups of similarly weighted links.
2. Set link weights of all group members to the average of the group.
3. Eliminate any groups that do not significantly affect whether the unit will be active or inactive.
4. Holding all link weights constant, optimize biases of all hidden and output units using the backpropagation algorithm.
5. Form a single rule for each hidden and output unit. The rule consists of a threshold given by the bias and weighted antecedents specified by the remaining links.
6. Where possible, simplify rules to eliminate weights and thresholds.

---

algorithm. Hence, the first step of NOFM is to group links into equivalence classes. This grouping can be done in either of two ways.

First, clustering may be done using a standard clustering method such as the *join* algorithm (Hartigan, 1975). This method clusters by joining the two closest clusters, starting with n clusters of size 1. Clustering stops when no pair of clusters is closer than a set distance (KBANN uses 0.25).

An alternative method for clustering links that takes advantage of the constraints on this particular clustering problem is also available. This method is used almost exclusively because its complexity is $O(n \times log(n))$; the complexity of the *join* procedure is $O(n^2)$.

Step 2, Averaging.   After groups are formed, the second step of the algorithm is to set the weight of all links in each group to the average of each group's weight. Thus, the first two steps of the algorithm force links in the network into equivalence classes, as required by the rest of the algorithm.

Step 3, Eliminating.   With equivalence classes in place, the procedure next attempts to identify and eliminate those groups that are unlikely to have any bearing on the calculation of the consequent. Such groups generally have low link weights and few members. Elimination proceeds via two paths: one heuristic and one algorithmic.

The first elimination procedure algorithmically attempts to find clusters of links that cannot have any effect on whether or not the total incoming activation exceeds the bias. This is done by calculating the total possible activation that each cluster can send (taking into account properties of units, e.g., that only one unit related to each nominal input feature may be active at any time). This total possible activation is then compared to the levels of activation that are reachable given link weights in the network. Clusters that cannot change whether the net input exceeds the bias are eliminated.

This procedure is very similar to SUBSET. However, clustering of link weights considerably reduces the combinatorics of the problem. For instance, consider a unit with a bias of −10 and three clusters of links: (A) two links of weight 7, (B) three links of weight 4, and (C) ten links of weight 0.1. In this case, cluster (C) is eliminated. Its total possible activation is 1.0, and the only reachable activations that are less than the bias using the clusters (A) and (B) are 7 and 8. Neither of these activation levels, when combined with the 1.0 total from group C, exceeds 10.0. Hence, the links in cluster (C) can have no effect on the unit into which they feed; so, the cluster is safely eliminated.

The heuristic elimination procedure is based explicitly upon whether the net input received from a cluster ever is necessary for the correct classification of a training example. This procedure operates by presenting a training example to the clustered network and sequentially zeroing the input from each cluster. If doing so results in a change in the activation of the unit receiving activation from the cluster, then the cluster is marked as necessary. After doing this for every example, clusters not marked as necessary are eliminated.

Step 4, Optimizing.   With unimportant groups eliminated, the fourth step of NOFM is to optimize the bias on the unit. This step is necessary because the averaging of the link weights in a cluster and elimination of links can change the times at which a unit is active. As a result, prior to optimization, networks on which the first three steps of the NOFM algorithm have been applied may have error rates that are significantly higher than they were at the end of training.

Optimization can be done by freezing the weights on the links so that the groups stay intact and retraining the biases of the network using backpropagation. To reflect the rule-like nature of the network, the activation function is slightly modified so that it more closely resembles a step function.

Step 5, Extracting.   This step of the NOFM algorithm forms rules that simply re-express the network. That is, rules are created by directly translating the bias and incoming weights to each unit into a rule with weighted antecedents such that the rule is true if the sum of the weighted antecedents exceeds the bias. Note that because of the equivalence classes and elimination of groups, these rules are considerably simpler than the original trained network; they have fewer antecedents, and those antecedents tend to be in a few weight classes. (See the extracted rules presented later in this chapter for examples of unsimplified rules.)

Step 6, Simplifying.   Finally, rules are simplified whenever possible to eliminate the weights and thresholds. Simplification is accomplished by scanning each restated rule to determine the possible combinations of group items that exceed the rule's threshold (i.e., bias). This scan may result in more than one rule. Hence, there is a trade-off in the simplification procedure between complexity of individual rules and complexity resulting from a number of simple rules.

For example, consider the rule[1]

```
A :- 10. 0 < 5.1 x number-true{B, C, D, E} +
              3.5 x number-true{X, Y, Z}
```

The simplification procedure would simplify this rule by rewriting it as the following three rules:

```
A :- 2 of {B, C, D, E}
A :- 1 of {B, C, D, E} and 2 of {X, Y, Z}
A :- X, Y, Z
```

If the elimination of weight and biases requires rewriting a single rule with more than five rules, then the rule is left in its original state.

15.3.3.2 Example of the NOFM Method

As an example of NOFM, consider Figure 15.8. This figure illustrates the process through which a single unit with seven incoming links is transformed by the NOFM procedure into a rule that requires two of three antecedents to be true.

The first two steps of the algorithm (Table 15.2) transform the unit with seven unique input into a unit with two classes of input, one with three links of weight 6.1 and one with four links of weight 1.1. Step 3 of the algorithm eliminates the group with weight 1.1 from consideration because there is no way that these links—either alone or in combination with links in the other group—can affect whether or not the sum of the incoming activation to unit Z exceeds the bias on Z. This step takes advantage of the assumption that units necessarily have activations near zero or one. Figure 15.8 does not illustrate bias optimization (Step 4).

The lower left panel of Figure 15.8 shows the re-expression of the simplified unit as a rule. The sixth and final step of the algorithm is illustrated by the bottom right panel of Figure 15.8, in which the rule with weighted antecedents and a threshold is transformed into a simple N-of-M style rule. (The SUBSET algorithm would find the three rules that are the expansion of the 2-of-3 rule found by NOFM. However, to find these three rules, SUBSET would have had to consider as many as 125 possibilities.)

15.3.3.3 Algorithmic Complexity of NOFM

The complexity of NOFM is difficult to precisely analyze because the bias-optimization phase uses backpropagation. However, the problem addressed in bias optimization is considerably simpler than the initial training of the network. Usually, networks have more than an order of magnitude fewer links during bias optimization than during initial training. This considerably speeds the simulation of

---

[1] The function `number-true` returns the number of antecedents in the following set that are true.

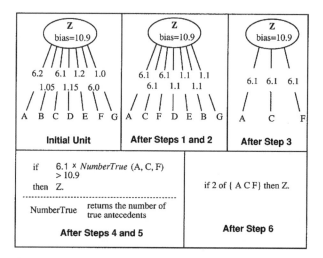

Figure 15.8: An example of rule extraction using NOFM

neural networks on a serial machine. Moreover, only the biases are allowed to change. As a result, this step takes a reasonably short time.[2] Each of the other steps requires $O(m \times n)$ time—m is the number of units, n is the average number of links received by a unit—except for the initial clustering, which requires $O(m \times n \times log(n))$ time, and cluster elimination, which requires $O(x \times m \times n)$ time—x is the number of training examples.

15.3.4 SUBSET and NOFM: Summary

Both of these rule-extraction algorithms have strengths with respect to the other. For example, the individual rules returned by SUBSET are more easily understood than those returned by NOFM. However, because SUBSET can be expected to return many more rules (which are often quite repetitive) than NOFM, the rule sets returned by NOFM are easier to understand than those of SUBSET. More significantly, SUBSET is an exponential algorithm, whereas NOFM is approximately cubic. Finally, results presented in the next section indicate that the rules derived by NOFM are more accurate than the rules derived by SUBSET.

15.4 DATASETS

Before presenting the experiments, this section briefly describes the two real-world datasets from the domain of molecular biology used for testing KBANN.

---

[2] Training neural networks has been proven NP-complete (Blum and Rivest, 1988; Judd, 1988). However, Hinton (1989) suggests that in practice, backpropagation usually runs in $O((m \times n)^3)$ time.

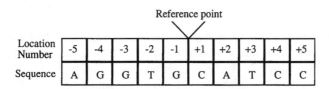

Figure 15.9: The numbering of nucleotide locations in DNA sequences

Both datasets have previously been used to demonstrate the usefulness of the KBANN algorithm (Towell et al., 1990; Noordewier et al., 1991). They are more thoroughly described by Towell (1991).

15.4.1 Background and Notation

The two biological datasets in this chapter are taken from the domain of DNA sequence analysis. DNA, the "blueprint" of almost all living organisms, is a linear sequence from the alphabet {A, G, T, C}. Each of these characters is referred to as a *nucleotide*. Human DNA consists of approximately $3*10^9$ nucleotides. By contrast, the DNA of *E. coli*, a common intestinal bacterium, contains about $5*10^6$ nucleotides.

This chapter uses a special notation for specifying locations in a DNA sequence. The idea is to number locations with respect to a fixed, biologically meaningful reference point. Negative numbers indicate sites preceding the reference point (by biological convention, this appears on the left), and positive numbers indicate sites following the reference point. (Zero is not used.) Figure 15.9 illustrates this numbering scheme. Rules use this referencing scheme by stating a position with respect to the reference location, denoted by @, and giving a subsequence in the positive direction. For example, @-4'GGT' refers to the three nucleotide long sequence in Figure 15.9 that begins at position –4 and ends at position –2.

In addition to this notation for specifying locations in a DNA sequence, Table 15.3 specifies a standard coding scheme for referring to any possible combination of nucleotides using a single letter (IUB Nomenclature Committee, 1985). This scheme is compatible with the codes used by the EMBL, GenBank, and PIR data libraries, three major collections of data for molecular biology.

Table 15.3: Ambiguity codes for DNA nucleotides

Code	Meaning	Code	Meaning	Code	Meaning
M	A or C	R	A or G	W	A or T
S	C or G	Y	C or T	K	G or T
V	A or C or G	H	A or C or T	D	A or G or T
B	C or G or T	X	A or G or C or T		

15.4.2 Promoter Recognition

The first problem is *promoter recognition*. Briefly, promoters are short DNA sequences that precede the beginnings of genes. The input features for promoter recognition are a sequence of 57 DNA nucleotides. Based on biological convention, the reference point for promoter recognition is the site at which gene transcription begins (if the example is a promoter). The reference point is located seven nucleotides from the right. (Thus, positive examples contain the first seven nucleotides of the transcribed gene.)

Table 15.4 contains the initial rule set used in the promoter recognition task. According to these rules, promoters are defined by `contact` and `conformation`. `Contact` requires matching short DNA sequences in two regions, one 35 nucleotides before the reference point and the other ten nucleotides before the reference point.

The training examples include 53 sample promoters and 53 nonpromoter sequences. Prior to training, the rules in Table 15.4 do not classify any of the 106 examples as promoters. Thus, the rules are useless as a classifier. Nevertheless, they do capture a significant amount of information about promoters.

15.4.3 Splice-Junction Determination

The second dataset is for *splice-junction determination*. Splice junctions are points on a DNA sequence at which "superfluous" DNA is removed during the process of protein creation in higher organisms.

In this dataset, there are 1,000 examples, each 60 nucleotides long, divided among three categories. In addition, there is an approximately correct set of 21 rules (not shown) derived from the biological literature (Watson et al., 1987) by Noordewier et al. (1991). This set of rules classifies 61% of the examples correctly.

Table 15.4: The initial rules for promoter recognition

```
promoter   :- contact, conformation.
contact    :- minus-35, minus-10.

minus35 :- @-37 'CTTGAC-'.          minus10 :- @-14 'TATAAT--'.
minus35 :- @-37 '-TTG-CA'.          minus10 :- @-14 '-TA-A-T-'.
minus35 :- @-37 '-TTGACA'.          minus10 :- @-14 '-TATAAT-'.
minus35 :- @-37 '-TTGAC-'.          minus10 :- @-14 '--TA---T'.

conformation :- @-49 '----AA--A'.
conformation :- @-49 '----A---A------------TT---T-AA---T-T---------T'.
conformation :- @-49 'A----T---------------T----A--T-TG-------------A'.
conformation :- @-49 '--CAA-TT-AC---------------G---T-C-------GCGCC-CC'.
```

15.5 EXPERIMENTS IN THE EXTRACTION OF RULES

This section presents a set of experiments designed to determine the relative strengths and weaknesses of the two rule-extraction methods described above. These are evaluated using two measures: *quality*, which is measured both by the accuracy of the rules and their fidelity to the network from which they were extracted, and *comprehensibility*, which is assessed by analyzing individual extracted rules. The part includes a set of the rules extracted from trained KBANN-nets by the NOFM method.

15.5.1 Testing Methodology

Based on the research of Weiss and Kulikowski (1990), networks are trained using repeated 10-fold cross-validation for assessing the quality of learning in both domains. Based on Hinton's (1989) suggestion for improved network interpretability, all weights are subject to gentle "decay" during training.[3] Finally, networks are trained using cross-entropy error function (Hinton, 1989).

15.5.1.1 Accuracy of the Extracted Rules

Figure 15.10 addresses the issue of the accuracy of extracted rules. It plots the percentage of errors on the testing and training sets, averaged over ten repetitions of 10-fold cross-validation, for both the promoter and splice-junction tasks. For comparison, Figure 15.10 includes the accuracy of the trained KBANN-nets prior to rule extraction (the bars labeled "Network"). Also included in Figure 15.10 is the accuracy of the EITHER system, an "all-symbolic" method for the empirical adaptation of rules that has been tested using the promoter dataset (Ourston and Mooney, 1990). The numbers for EITHER are derived from Ourston's thesis (Ourston, 1991); they reflect a slightly different testing method. (EITHER has not been tested on the splice-junction problem.)

Recall the initial rule sets for promoter recognition and splice-junction determination correctly categorized 50% and 61%, respectively, of the examples. Hence, each of the systems plotted in Figure 15.10 improves upon the initial rules. By comparison of only the systems that produce refined rules, the NOFM method is the clear winner. On the training examples, the error rate for rules extracted by NOFM is slightly worse than for EITHER, but superior to the rules extracted using SUBSET. More importantly, on the testing examples, the NOFM rules are much more

---

[3] That is, to the standard weight change function, a term φ is added ($0 < \varphi < 1$). Thus, the weight change formula becomes $(w_{ij}(t) = \varphi * (w_{ij}(t-1) + \Delta_{ij})$, where Δ_{ij} is the standard weight adjustment (Rumelhart et al., 1986). Weights change after each example presentation, so φ is set to a very gentle 0.99999. Weight decay was not used in previously reported experiments simply because it added unnecessary complexity to these experiments. It had little or no measurable effect of the generalization ability of KBANN-nets.

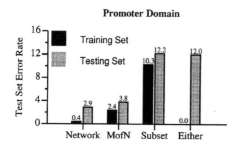
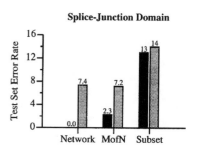

Figure 15.10:   The error rates of extracted rules

accurate than both EITHER and SUBSET. (One-tailed, paired-sample t-tests indicate that for both domains, the NOFM rules are superior to the SUBSET rules with 99.5% confidence. Statistical comparisons to EITHER are not made because of lack of compatible data.)

One of the more interesting results in this chapter is that on the testing examples in the splice-junction domain, the error rate of the NOFM rules is superior to that of the networks from which the rules are extracted. (One-tailed, paired-sample t-tests indicate that the difference is statistically significant with 90% confidence, t=1.6, d.f.=9.) Earlier tests (Towell and Shavlik, 1991) showed the error rate of the extracted rules on the promoter problem was also below that of the networks from which the rules were extracted. However, alterations to the training method (to reduce overfitting) improved the accuracy of the networks without significantly affecting the accuracy of the extracted rules.

Conversely, the error rate of the SUBSET rules on testing examples is statistically worse than the networks in both problem domains. Discussion at the end of this section analyzes reasons why NOFM rules can be superior to the networks from which they are extracted.

15.5.2 Comprehensibility

To be useful, the extracted rules must not only be accurate, they must also be *understandable*. Although understandability is an ill-defined concept, there are several ways in which it might be measured. Several quantitative measures are presented and analyzed by Towell (1991). This section merely presents and discusses the extracted rules.

Table 15.5 presents the rules NOFM extracts from a KBANN-net trained for promoter recognition. Although these rules are somewhat murky, they are vastly more comprehensible than the network of 3,000 links from which they came. Moreover, the rules in this table can be rewritten in a form very similar to one used in the biological community (Stormo, 1990), namely, weight matrices.

Table 15.5: The promoter rules NOFM extracts

```
Promoter :- Minus10, Minus35.

Minus10 :- 10 <    3.8 * nt (@-14 '-TA-A-T-') +
                   3.0 * nt (@-14 '-G--C---') +
                  -3.0 * nt (@-14 '-A--T---').

Minus10 :-         2 of @-14 '--CA---T' and
             not 1 of @-14 '--RB---S') .

Minus10 :- 10 <    3.0 * nt(@-14 '-TAT--T-') +
                   1.8 * nt (@-14 '-----GA--').

Minus10 :- 1 <     3.5 * nt(@-14 'TAWAAY--') +
                  -1.7 * nt(@-14 '-T--TG--') +
                  -2.2 * nt(@-14 'CSSK-A--').

Minus35 :- 10 <    4.0 * nt(@-37 '-TTGAT--') +
                   1.5 * nt(@-37 '---TCC--') +
                  -1.5 * nt(@-37 '-RGAGG--').

Minus35 :- 10 <    5.1 * nt(@-37 '-T-G--A-') +
                   3.1 * nt(@-37 '-GT-----') +
                  -1.9 * nt(@-37 '-CGW----') +
                  -3.1 * nt(@-37 '-A----C-').

Minus35 :-         3 of @-37 'C-TGAC--'.

Minus35 :-              @-37 '-TTG-CA-'.
```

The major pattern in the extracted rules is that KBANN learned to disregard `conformation`. The `conformation` rules are also dropped by EITHER (Ourston, 1990), which suggests that dropping these rules is not an artifact of KBANN but, rather, that DNA bases outside the *minus35* and *minus10* regions are less important than the conformation hypothesis (Koudelka et al., 1987) suggests. Hence, machine learning methods can provide valuable evidence confirming or refuting biological theories.

In general, the rules NOFM extracts confirm the importance of the nucleotides identified in the initial rules. However, whereas the initial rules required matching every base, the extracted rules allow a less than perfect match. In addition, the extracted rules point to places in which changes to the sequence are important. For instance, in the final *minus10* rule, a T in position −12 is a strong indicator that the rule is true. Replacing the T with an A prevents the rule from ever being satisfied.

The rules extracted by NOFM for the splice-junction domain are not shown. They are very similar to those extracted for promoter recognition. The rules extracted by SUBSET are also not shown; they would cover several pages. (See (Towell, 1991) for details.)

15.5.3 Discussion of Rule Extraction

The results presented in this section indicate that the NOFM method is able to extract a good set of rules from trained networks. Specifically, with the NOFM method, not only can comprehensible, symbolic rules be extracted from trained KBANN-nets, the extracted rules can also be superior (at classifying testing examples) to the KBANN-net from which they are extracted. Additionally, the NOFM method produces refined rule sets whose accuracy is substantially better than EITHER, an approach that directly modifies the initial set of rules (Ourston and Mooney, 1990; see Figure 15.10). Although the rule set produced by the NOFM algorithm is slightly larger than that produced by the "all symbolic" approach of EITHER, the sets of rules produced by both of these algorithms are small enough to be easily understood. Hence, although weighing the trade-off between accuracy and understandability is problem and user specific, the NOFM algorithm for network-to-rules translation offers an appealing mixture.

Two hypotheses explain the superiority of NOFM over rule-refinement methods that directly modify rules. First, the re-representation of a rule set as a neural network allows for more fine-grained refinement. When cast as a neural network, rules can be modified in very small steps. Hence, it may be possible to more closely fit a target concept than when taking the large steps required by direct rule-refinement.

Second, the relative success of the rule-extraction method proposed in this chapter might result from its better fitting the nature of the investigated problems.

That is, each problem may have some "natural" language in which it can be most parsimoniously solved. If the language used by the learning system is similar to the "natural" language, then the learning system should be able to effectively learn to solve the problem. If this hypothesis is correct, then successful multistrategy learning may involve searching "language space" as well as the space of solutions possible within a language.

DNA sequence-analysis problems have aspects that can be captured perspicuously by N-of-M style rules. For instance, in the promoter problem, there are several potential sites at which hydrogen bonds can form between DNA and a protein; if enough of these bonds form, promoter activity can occur. Neither EITHER nor the SUBSET method can easily express N-of-M rules. As a result, these algorithms may be at a disadvantage on the molecular biology test domains. Hence, some of the advantage of the NOFM method may result from its output language better fitting that of the "natural" language of DNA sequence-analysis problems.

The observation that NOFM rules can be superior to the networks from which they are extracted cannot be attributed to a language bias because the NOFM rules are only a subset of the languages expressible using neural networks. Instead, the advantage of the NOFM rules most likely occurs because the rule-extraction process reduces overfitting of the training examples. Several pieces of evidence support this hypothesis. First, as noted previously, revising training procedures to reduce overfitting in the promoter domain eliminated the advantage that NOFM rules had over the networks from which they were extracted (Towell and Shavlik, 1991). Second, the difference in ability to correctly categorize testing and training examples is smaller for NOFM rules than for trained KBANN-nets. In other words, the rules that the NOFM method extracts are only slightly better at classifying training examples than at classifying testing examples. (Although the differences between training and testing set performance are smaller, they are statistically significant with 99.5% confidence using a one-tailed, paired-sample t-test.) The rules SUBSET extracts also have this property, but they are worse on the training set than both NOFM rules and trained KBANN-nets on the testing set.

A third piece of evidence in support of the overfitting hypothesis comes from the work on pruning neural networks to eliminate superfluous parts (Mozer and Smolensky, 1988; Le Cun et al., 1989). Note that rule extraction is an extreme form of pruning in which links and units are pruned and actions are taken on the remaining network to transform the network into a set of rules. Pruning efforts have also led to gains in test set performance. Generally, these researchers attribute these gains to reduced overfitting of the training examples.

15.6 RELATED WORK

There are three distinct sets of work that are closely related to the rule-extraction methods presented in this chapter. The first set contains "all symbolic" methods of learning from rules and examples (e.g., Ourston and Mooney, 1990; Thompson et al., 1991). These methods avoid having to extract rules after learning by performing symbolic manipulations directly on the rules. For instance, Ourston and Mooney's EITHER (1990) operates by identifying examples incorrectly classified by the initial rule set and attempting to find a way of altering the rule set so that the previously incorrect example is corrected, without creating new errors among the correct examples. Although these direct symbolic methods are appealing because they do not require a shift between symbolic and neural representations, the results presented in Figure 15.10 indicate that they are not as accurate as the methods presented here.

The second set of ideas related to those in this chapter is made up of methods for understanding neural networks that attempt to prune away unimportant parts of network. In so doing, the complexity of the solution is reduced, thereby making the network more easily understood. For instance, Le Cun et al. (1989) describe a method that eliminates as much as 30% of the free parameters in a network without increasing error. Experiments with Le Cun's method and a related technique described by Weigand, Rumelhart, and Huberman (1990) on the promoter domain indicate that on this problem, a majority of the links can be removed from KBANN-nets without increasing error. Mozer and Smolensky (1988) report a related technique that eliminates whole units rather than just individual free parameters. Although the authors of these papers make claims that their procedures increase the human comprehensibility of networks, no evidence is presented to support the claim. Thus, although the rule-extraction techniques described in this chapter are similar in many ways to these pruning systems, this work differs significantly in its emphasis on comprehensible output.

The third group of work related to this chapter consists of attempts to extract rules from randomly weighted ANNs. Both Saito and Nakano (1988) and Fu (1991) report a method similar to the SUBSET algorithm. Saito and Nakano's method looks at the input/output behavior of trained networks to form rules that map directly from inputs to outputs. To control the combinatorics inherent to algorithms like SUBSET, Saito and Nakano limited rules to four antecedents. However, even with this limitation, they extracted more than 400 rules for just one output unit in an ANN with 23 outputs. Thus, although their method is potentially useful for understanding networks, it may drown users in a sea of rules.

Several groups have reported attempts to extract rules from networks that, like KBANN-nets, have a well-defined architecture. Sestito and Dillon (1990) avoid combinatorial problems in their approach to rule extraction by transforming a network with J inputs and K outputs into a network with $J + K$ inputs. After training, they look for links from the original J inputs that have a similar weight pattern to one of the K additional inputs. When similarities are found, rules are created. The method is able to discover hierarchical rule sets. However, to discover the relationship (robin *isa* bird *isa* animal), the network must have output for robin, bird, and animal. Other methods for the extraction of rules from specially configured networks include McMillan, Mozer, and Smolensky's *connectionist scientist game* (1991) that iteratively learns sets of propositional rules.

15.7 FUTURE WORK

One of the principle areas of future work is in the training of networks to encourage the clustering required by the NOFM method. Doing so could reduce the complexity of the clustering and possibly eliminate the need for optimizing the rule thresholds. One of the methods being investigated is to adapt a training technique described by Nowlan and Hinton (1991). Their method trains networks so that link weights fall into a small number of Gaussian clusters. The network is able to learn the center locations and distributions of these clusters. This idea might be adapted to training KBANN-nets by specifying the starting values of the Gaussians so that they cover the initial link weights. During training, these Gaussians will tend to encourage link weights to stay near their initial values. However, when differentiation among the link weights is required, the Gaussians can adapt to allow it. Networks so trained might be quite amenable to NOFM-style rule extraction.

In addition, an N-of-M style representation appears to be a useful inductive bias for many problems (Murphy and Pazzani, 1991). Hence, it is desirable to enhance the comprehensibility of the rules returned by NOFM. Although the rules extracted from networks by NOFM are much more comprehensible than the networks from which they are extracted, they are often not easily comprehended. The hope is that alternate forms of presentation or some slight modifications to the NOFM algorithm will improve the comprehensibility of the resulting rules.

A final path for future work is the investigation of the training and interpretation of networks that have units not directly specified by the initial rule set (Towell et al., 1991). To this point, efforts have concentrated upon extending networks for the splice-junction problem because the KBANN-net for this problem lacks sufficient freedom to find a highly accurate solution. Unfortunately, expanding networks by the addition of hidden units hampers rule extraction because the hidden units often violate both the assumption that their activations will be near zero or one after training and that they have a meaningful name. Hence, efforts to this time have focused on methods to satisfy these assumptions.

15.8 CONCLUSIONS

Multistrategy learning often requires multiple representations of knowledge. Training examples are often amenable to such representational shifts. However, domain-specific knowledge can be more difficult to shift between representations. The initial paper describing KBANN provided a method for shifting domain-specific knowledge from PROLOG-like rules into neural networks (Towell et al.,

1990). This shift made the knowledge available to neural learning algorithms such as backpropagation (Rumelhart et al., 1986). The result of these initial efforts was classifiers more accurate than those obtainable using only training examples (Towell et al., 1990; Noordewier et al., 1991).

In one sense, these results are a dead end because the refined knowledge in the trained networks is inaccessible for further learning by symbolically oriented methods. Hence, this chapter presents a method for completing the *symbolic* ⇒ *neural* ⇒ *symbolic* circle. By so doing, the dead end is opened, making the highly accurate neural classifiers that result from KBANN accessible to further learning. Access to the results of neural learning is gained by the extraction of rules from trained networks, for which the NOFM algorithm was presented. This technique takes advantage of some of the properties of the KBANN-nets to reduce the problem of the extraction of rules from neural networks to a manageable scale.

Experimental results indicate that concise, comprehensible rules can be extracted by the described NOFM algorithm without a serious loss of accuracy. In fact, the extracted rules can be more accurate at classifying testing examples than the networks from which they are extracted. By comparison, the state-of-the-art technique for rule extraction (i.e., the SUBSET method) is significantly worse than the rules extracted by NOFM and the networks from which the rules were extracted. In addition, these results indicate that the shift between symbolic and connectionist representations improves the accuracy of the resulting rules. Moreover, the extracted rules show the utility of machine learning techniques as a method of validating biological theories. Finally, the extra work required by this three-step system, by comparison to "all symbolic" rule-refinement methods (e.g., Ourston and Mooney, 1990; Thompson et al., 1991), is shown to be worthwhile in that the method provides superior rules with only a small cost to comprehensibility. Hence, this work shows the value of shifting to a fine-grained representation for detailed corrections and back out again for communication of those corrections.

ACKNOWLEDGMENTS

This work is partially supported by Office of Naval Research Grant N00014-90-J-1941, National Science Foundation Grant IRI-9002413, and Department of Energy Grant DE-FG02-91ER61129. We wish to thank Michiel Noordewier for his construction of the two biological rule and data sets and for general comments on this work. Comments by Richard Maclin, Mark Craven, and several anonymous reviewers are also gratefully acknowledged.

Both the promoter recognition and splice-junction determination datasets are a part of the collection of datasets at UC-Irvine available via anonymous ftp from ics.uci.edu in the directory pub/machine-learning-databases.

References

Blum, A., and Rivest, R.L., "Training a 3-node neural network is NP-complete," *Proceedings of the 1988 Workshop on Computational Learning Theory*, pp. 9–18, Cambridge, MA, Morgan Kaufmann, San Mateo, CA, 1988.

Fisher, D.H., and McKusick, K.B., "An empirical comparison of ID3 and back-propagation," *Proceedings of the Eleventh International Joint Conference on Artificial Intelligence*, pp. 788–793, Morgan Kaufmann, San Mateo, CA, 1989.

Fu, L.M., "Rule learning by searching on adapted nets," *Proceedings of the Ninth National Conference on Artificial Intelligence*, pp. 590–595, AAAI Press, Menlo Park, CA, 1991.

Hartigan, J.A., *Clustering Algorithms*, Wiley, New York, 1975.

Hebb, D.O., *The Organization of Behavior*, Wiley, New York, 1949.

Hertz, J., Krogh, A., and Palmer, R.G., *Introduction to the Theory of Neural Computation*, Addison Wesley, Reading, MA, 1991.

Hinton, G.E., "Connectionist learning procedures," *Artificial Intelligence*, Vol. 40, pp. 185–234, 1989.

IUB Nomenclature Committee, "Ambiguity codes," *European Journal of Biochemistry*, Vol. 150, pp. 1–5, 1985.

Judd, S., "On the complexity of loading shallow neural networks," *Journal of Complexity*, Vol. 4, pp. 177–192, 1988.

Koudelka, G.B., Harrison, S.C., and Ptashne, M., "Effect of non-contacted bases on the affinity of 434 operator for 434 repressor and Cro," *Nature*, Vol. 326, pp. 886–888, 1987.

Le Cun, Y., Denker, J.S., and Solla, S.A., "Optimal brain damage," *Advances in Neural Information Processing Systems*, Vol. 2, pp. 598–605, Morgan Kaufmann, San Mateo, CA, 1989.

McCulloch, W.S., and Pitts, W.A., "A logical calculus of ideas immanent in nervous activity," *Bulletin of Mathematical Biophysics*, Vol. 5, pp. 115–133, 1943.

McMillan, C., Mozer, M.C., and Smolensky, P., "The connectionist scientist game: Rule extraction and refinement in a neural network," *Proceedings of the Thirteenth Annual Conference of the Cognitive Science Society*, pp. 424–430. Chicago, IL, Erlbaum, Hillsdale, NJ, 1991.

Mozer, M.C., and Smolensky, P., "Skeletonization: A technique for trimming the fat from a network via relevance assessment," *Advances in Neural Information Processing Systems*, Vol. 1, pp. 107–115, Morgan Kaufmann, San Mateo, CA, 1988.

Murphy, P.M., and Pazzani, M.J., "ID2-of-3: Constructive induction of N-of-M concepts for discriminators in decision trees," *Proceedings of the Eighth International Machine Learning Workshop*, pp. 183–187, Evanston, IL, Morgan Kaufmann, San Mateo, CA, 1991.

Noordewier, M.O., Towell, G.G., and Shavlik, J.W., "Training knowledge-based neural networks to recognize genes in DNA sequences," *Advances in Neural Information Processing Systems*, Vol. 3, Morgan Kaufmann, San Mateo, CA, 1991.

Nowlan, S.J., and Hinton, G.E., "Simplifying neural networks by soft weight-sharing," *Advances in Neural Information Processing Systems*, Vol. 4, Morgan Kaufmann, San Mateo, CA, 1991.

Ourston, D., *Using Explanation-based and Empirical Methods in Theory Revision*, Ph.D. thesis, Department of Computer Sciences, University of Texas, Austin, TX, 1991.

Ourston, D., and Mooney, R.J., "Changing the rules: A comprehensive approach to theory refinement," *Proceedings of the Eighth National Conference on Artificial Intelligence*, pp. 815–820, AAAI Press, Menlo Park, CA, 1990.

Pratt, L.Y., Mostow, J., and Kamm, C.A., "Direct transfer of learned information among neural networks," *Proceedings of the Ninth National Conference on Artificial Intelligence*, pp. 584–589, AAAI Press, Menlo Park, CA, 1991.

Rosenblatt, F., *Principles of Neurodynamics: Perceptrons and the Theory of Brain Mechanisms*, Spartan, New York, 1962.

Rumelhart, D.E., Hinton, G.E., and Williams, R.J., "Learning internal representations by error propagation," *Parallel Distributed Processing: Explorations in the microstructure of cognition, Volume 1: Foundations,* Rumelhart, D.E., and McClelland, J.L., (eds.), pp. 318–363, MIT Press, Cambridge, MA, 1986.

Saito, K., and Nakano, R., "Medical diagnostic expert system based on PDP model," *Proceedings of IEEE International Conference on Neural Networks,* Vol. 1, pp. 255–262, IEEE Computer Society, Washington, DC, 1988.

Sestito, S., and Dillon, T., "Using multi-layered neural networks for learning symbolic knowledge," *Proceedings of the 1990 Australian Artificial Intelligence Conference*, Perth, Australia, 1990.

Shavlik, J.W., Mooney, R.J., and Towell, G.G., "Symbolic and neural net learning algorithms: An empirical comparison," *Machine Learning*, Vol. 6, pp. 111–143, 1991.

Stormo, G.D., "Consensus patterns in DNA", *Methods in Enzymology*, Vol. 183, pp. 211–221, Academic Press, San Diego, CA, 1990.

Thompson, K., Langley, P., and Iba, W., "Using background knowledge in concept formation," *Proceedings of the Eighth International Machine Learning Workshop*, pp. 554–558, Evanston, IL, Morgan Kaufmann, San Mateo, CA, 1991.

Towell, G.G., *Symbolic Knowledge and Neural Networks: Insertion, Refinement, and Extraction*, Ph.D. thesis, Computer Sciences Department, University of Wisconsin, Madison, WI, 1991.

Towell, G.G., and Shavlik, J.W., "Interpretation of artificial neural networks: Mapping knowledge-based neural networks into rules," *Advances in Neural Information Processing Systems*, Vol. 4, Morgan Kaufmann, San Mateo, CA, 1991.

Towell, G.G., Shavlik, J.W., and Craven, M.W., "Constructive induction in knowledge-based neural networks," *Proceedings of the Eighth International Machine Learning Workshop*, pp. 213–217, Evanston, IL, Morgan Kaufmann, San Mateo, CA, 1991.

Towell, G.G., Shavlik, J.W., and Noordewier, M.O., "Refinement of approximately correct domain theories by knowledge-based neural networks," *Proceedings of the Eighth National Conference on Artificial Intelligence*, pp. 861–866, AAAI Press, Menlo Park, CA, 1990.

Watson, J.D., Hopkins, H.H., Roberts, J.W., Steitz, J. A., and Weiner, A.M., *The Molecular Biology of the Gene*, Benjamin-Cummings, Menlo Park, CA, 1987.

Weigand, A.S., Rumelhart, D.E., and Huberman, B.A., "Generalization by weight-elimination with application to forecasting," *Advances in Neural Information Processing Systems*, Vol. 3, pp. 875–882, Morgan Kaufmann, San Mateo, CA, 1990.

Weiss, S.M., and Kulikowski, C.A., *Computer Systems That Learn*, Morgan Kaufmann, San Mateo, CA, 1990.

16

LEARNING GRADED CONCEPT DESCRIPTIONS BY INTEGRATING SYMBOLIC AND SUBSYMBOLIC STRATEGIES

Jianping Zhang
(Utah State University)

Abstract

Concepts involved in real world applications usually possess graded structures. Instead of being equivalent, examples of a concept with a graded structure may be characterized by a degree of typicality in representing the concept. Both pure symbolic and subsymbolic representations are not adequate for describing concepts with graded structures. A pure symbolic representation fails to describe the graded structure of a concept, and a pure subsymbolic representation is unable to capture the central tendency of a concept. This chapter presents an integrated approach that combines a symbolic approach with a subsymbolic one to learn concepts with graded structures. Concepts in this approach are represented by a hybrid representation that is a combination of the symbolic and numeric representations. In the hybrid representation, the symbolic element explicitly captures the central tendency of a concept, and the numeric element implicitly handles the atypical aspect of a concept. A learning algorithm that adjusts both the symbolic and numeric elements of the representation to achieve the best fit between the description and the given concept examples is described. The method has been tested on several problems. The results have shown a statistically meaningful advantage to the proposed method over the other methods on the problems that involved concepts with graded structures.

16.1 INTRODUCTION

Concepts involved in real world applications usually possess graded structure (Barsalou, 1985). Instead of being equivalent, examples of a concept may be characterized by a degree of typicality in representing the concept. The typicality of an example is determined by three factors: (1) the number of the common concept properties shared by the example, (2) the importance of the common concept properties shared by the example, and (3) the closeness by which the example matches the common concept properties. For example, a disease can be predicted by a set of symptoms. Patients of the disease may not possess all symptoms. Patients with more symptoms are more likely to have the disease than patients with fewer symptoms. All symptoms may not be equally important to predict the disease. The patients with important symptoms are more likely to have the disease than the patients with less important symptoms. Some symptoms, such as blood pressure, have a linear domain. The higher (or lower) blood pressure a patient has, the more likely the patient is to have the disease. A concept with a graded structure has a central tendency that is characterized by typical examples.

Pure symbolic representations, e.g., decision trees and rules, are not adequate for describing concepts with graded concepts because they represent a concept as a single symbolic description. In such a pure symbolic description, an example belongs to the concept only if it satisfies all conditions of the concept description. Otherwise, the example does not belong to the concept. Such a yes or no classification makes a pure symbolic representation impossible to capture the "graded" behavior of a concept. On the other hand, subsymbolic representations such as neural networks and Bayesian classifiers do not give explicit descriptions to represent the basic principles underlying a concept, so they fail to represent the central tendency of the concept. This chapter presents an integrated approach that combines a symbolic approach with a subsymbolic one to represent and learn concepts with graded structures.

There have been some efforts in combining these two approaches. Such efforts include the STAGGER system (Schlimmer, 1987), Perceptron trees (Utgoff, 1988), and the NGE approach (Salzberg, 1991). The differences between the approach reported in this chapter and the above approaches were discussed in Zhang and Michalski (1994). Towell and Shavlik (1994, Chapter 15 of this book) described an approach that combined symbolic representation with neural networks.

The approach presented employs a novel hybrid representation to describe concepts. The representation is a simple but powerful form of *two-tiered concept representation* (Michalski, 1987; Bergadano, et al., 1992) and combines symbolic and numeric representations. The symbolic element of the representation explicitly describes the central tendency of a concept, and the numeric element extends the symbolic description to describe the atypical cases of the concept. A learning algorithm presented in this chapter adjusts both the symbolic and numeric elements of the representation to achieve the best fit between the description and the given concept examples.

The method has been implemented in the system FCLS (*F*lexible *C*oncept *L*earning *S*ystem) and tested on several problems. For comparison, other methods, such as the decision tree learning system C4.5 (Quinlan, 1987) and a rule learning system similar to AQ (Michalski and Larson, 1978), were tested on the same problems. The results have shown a statistically meaningful advantage to the proposed method over the other methods both in terms of the classification accuracy and the description simplicity on the problems that involve concepts with graded structure.

16.2 CONCEPT REPRESENTATION

In the proposed method, a concept is represented as a disjunction of Weighted Threshold Disjuncts (WTD), each of which consists of two elements: a symbolic element and a numeric element. A similarity measure unifies these two elements. The symbolic element of a WTD is a base disjunct that explicitly describes a central tendency of the concept. The numeric element consists of a set of weights and a threshold. Each condition of a base disjunct is associated with a weight that reflects the degree of necessity of the condition. The threshold defines the boundary of a WTD.

16.2.1 Weighted Threshold Disjunct (WTD)

A WTD is composed of a base disjunct that is a conjunction of conditions, a set of weights, and a threshold. In the rest of the chapter, we refer to a weighted threshold disjunct as a WTD. Base disjuncts are represented as complexes by the attribute based Logic System VL_1 (Michalski, 1983). A complex in VL_1 is a conjunction of conditions (formally called selectors), each of which is a relational expression

$$[L = R]$$

where L is an attribute, and R, called the *referent*, is a value or a disjunction of values from the domain of L. Such a condition is satisfied by an example if the value of the attribute L in this example is one of the values in R.

Each condition of a base disjunct has a weight that reflects the degree of necessity of the condition. Its value ranges from 0 to $+\infty$. The condition with weight 0 plays no role, while the condition weighted $+\infty$ is necessary. A larger weight means a more important condition.

In addition to weights, each WTD has a threshold that is a real number between 0 and 1. The threshold of a WTD defines the boundary of the WTD. An example is covered by a WTD if its similarity to the WTD is larger than or equal to the threshold of the WTD. The similarity of an example to a WTD is calculated by the similarity measure. Decreasing the threshold relaxes the requirements of the WTD that have to be satisfied to increase the coverage of the WTD.

16.2.2 Similarity Measure

The similarity measure (SM) measures the similarity between an example and a WTD. The SM of an example e and a WTD wtd is defined as the opposite of the distance measure D(e, wtd) normalized by the distance between the farthest example in the example space and wtd. Specifically, it is calculated as

$$SM(e,wtd) = 1 - \frac{D(e,wtd)}{MAX_{i=1..n} \{D(e_i, wtd)\}}$$

where e_1, ..., e_n are all examples in the example space. $D(e, wtd)$ is defined as a weighted sum of the distances between the example e and all conditions of wtd:

$$D(e, wtd) = \sum W_i * CD(e, C_i)$$

where W_i is the weight of the condition C_i. If W_i is $+\infty$, it needs to be specially calculated. $CD(e, C_i)$ is the distance between the example e and the condition C_i. The distance between an example and a condition depends on the type of the attribute involved in the condition. An attribute can be one of two types: nominal and linear. In a nominal condition, the referent is a single value or an internal disjunction of values; e.g., [color = red v blue v green]. The distance is 0 if such a condition is satisfied by an example and 1 otherwise. In a linear condition, the referent is a range of values or an internal disjunction of ranges; e.g., [weight = 1..3 v 6..9]. A satisfied condition returns the value of distance 0. If the condition is not satisfied, the distance between an example and the condition is the difference between the value of the example and the nearest end-point of the interval of the condition normalized by the distance between the farthest value and the condition. For example, if the domain of x is [0 .. 10], the value of x for the event e is 4, and the condition C is [$x = 7$ .. 9], then $CD(e, C) = \frac{7-4}{7-0} = \frac{3}{7}$.

When a condition with $+\infty$ weight is not satisfied, $D(e, wtd)$ is set to $MAX_{i=1..n}\{D(e_i, wtd)\}$ so that

$$SM(e, wtd) = 1 - \frac{(D(e, wtd)}{MAX_{i=1..n}\{D(e_i, wtd)\}} = 0$$

Also, $\infty * CD = 0$ if $CD = 0$.

16.2.3 Examples

To illustrate the idea of the hybrid representation, let us consider a simple example: learning the concept of a labor-management contract (Bergadano et. al, 1988). In this problem, the example space is divided, from the labor point of view, into acceptable and unacceptable contracts. Each contract is described by a set of selected attributes, e.g., general wage increase (gwi), job security (job-sec), extent of pension (p-ext), pension for overtime work, and fringe benefits. Let us assume that the class of acceptable contracts is represented by the following three disjuncts:

(job-sec = yes) & (p-ext = yes) or
(job-sec = yes) & (gwi = medium ∨ large) or
(p-ext = yes) & (gwi = medium ∨ large)

This description says that if a contract satisfies any two of the three conditions (job-sec = yes), (p-ext = yes), and (gwi = medium v large), the contract is acceptable. By using the hybrid representation, these three disjuncts merge into one WTD:

[job-sec = yes : 1] & [p-ext = yes : 1] & [gwi = medium ∨ large : 1]
Threshold = $\frac{2}{3}$ = 0.67

The number following a condition is the weight of the condition. The base disjunct includes three conditions:

[job-sec = yes] & [p-ext = yes] &[gwi = medium v large]

and represents the ideal situation of acceptable contracts. All three conditions are equally important. The description tells that contracts that satisfy all three conditions are ideal contracts, but those that only satisfy two of the three conditions are less ideal.

Now suppose acceptable contracts must have job security. The class of acceptable contracts is defined as the following WTD:

[job-sec = yes : ∞] & [p-ext = yes : 1] & [gwi = medium v large : 1]
Threshold = $\frac{1}{2}$ = 0.5

In this WTD, the condition [job-sec = yes] is necessary and must be satisfied by all acceptable contracts. The other two conditions are not necessary, and one of them must be satisfied.

Suppose that the attribute *gwi* is linear, and the order of its values is small, medium, and large. The WTD representing acceptable contracts becomes

[job-sec = yes : ∞] & [p-ext = yes : 1] & [gwi = large : 1]
Threshold = $\frac{1}{4}$ = 0.25

Under this WTD, the contract whose *gwi* is *large* is better than the contract whose *gwi* is *medium*. For example, let us consider the two contracts C1 (yes yes large) and C2 (yes yes medium). The similarity of C1 and C2 to the WTD is 1 and 3/4, respectively; so, C1 is better than C2.

16.3 CONCEPT RECOGNITION

Concept recognition in traditional concept representations, such as decision trees and rules, is very simple: if an example satisfies all conditions of a concept description, then it belongs to the concept; otherwise, it does not. This simple recognition method is called the strict method. This section describes a flexible classification method that was implemented in FCLS.

In the flexible method, an example is classified to a concept if it is uniquely covered by the concept description. An example is covered by a concept description if its similarity to one of the WTDs of the description is larger than or equal to the threshold of the WTD. The examples covered by no concept description are referred to as no-match examples, and the examples covered by more than one concept description are referred to as multiple match examples. In our method, the classification of no match and multiple match examples is determined by their Relative Similarity (RS) to WTDs. An example is classified as a concept if its RS to one of the WTDs of the concept description is the largest among all concept descriptions. RS between a WTD wtd and an example *e* covered by wtd is defined as follows:

$$RS(e, \text{wtd}) = \frac{SM(e, \text{wtd}) - \text{th}(\text{wtd})}{1 - \text{th}(\text{wtd})}$$

where *th(wtd)* is the threshold of wtd and smaller than 1. If *th(wtd)* = 1, *RS(e, wtd)* = 1. Because e is covered by wtd, *SM(e,wtd)* ≥ *th(wtd)*. Thus, the RS of a multiple match example to a WTD that covers it is between 0 and 1.

The RS between a WTD wtd and an uncovered example *e* is computed as follows:

$$RS(e, \text{wtd}) = \frac{SM(e, \text{wtd}) - \text{th}(\text{wtd})}{\text{th}(\text{wtd})}$$

Because *e* is not covered by wtd, *SM(e, wtd)* < *th(wtd)* and RS of a no match example to a WTD is between 0 and –1. A covered example always has a larger RS than an uncovered example.

For each WTD, all training examples can be divided into three types, according to the way they are covered by the WTD. The examples in different types play different roles during learning.

1. *Strictly covered examples* are strictly covered by the base disjunct of the WTD; namely, they satisfy all conditions of the disjunct.

2. *Flexibly covered examples* are examples covered by the WTD.

3. *Nearly covered examples* are not flexibly covered, but their similarity to the WTD is close to the threshold. For a detailed definition of nearly covered examples, see Zhang (1990).

16.4 The Learning Algorithm

Table 16.1 shows the top-level learning algorithm. The input of the algorithm is a set of concepts with their examples. The output of the algorithm is a disjunction of WTDs for each given concept that covers all positive examples of the concept and no negative examples. This algorithm works in an iterative fashion. In each iteration, the concept description that has the largest error omission is generalized by generating a new WTD. The error omission of a concept description is the percentage of the number of the examples of the concept that are not covered by the description. The new WTD is generated to minimize the error omission.

Each iteration of the algorithm first generates a WTD; then the current concept descriptions are used to classify all examples using the flexible classification method. If all examples are correctly classified, the algorithm terminates and outputs the current descriptions; otherwise, it repeats.

16.4.2 The WTD Generation Algorithm

The WTD generation algorithm generates the "best" WTD for a given concept from a set of positive and negative examples. The process of generating the "best" WTD is divided into two phases. The first phase generates the symbolic

Table 16.1: The top-level learning algorithm

Let DES be empty
Repeat
    Select the concept CNPT that has the largest error omission
    Generalize CNPT by generating a WTD
    Add the new WTD into DES
Until All examples are correctly classified
Return DES

---

description, which is a set of consistent disjuncts. The algorithm of the first phase is called the Base Disjunct Generation Algorithm. The second phase optimizes the symbolic description by creating the numeric description, which contains the weights of all conditions and the threshold. The WTD Optimization Algorithm serves as the algorithm in the second phase.

16.4.2.1 Phase 1: The Base Disjuncts Generation Algorithm

The algorithm generates a set of the most general consistent disjuncts. Table 16.2 gives the disjunct generation algorithm. The algorithm starts with the most general disjunct that strictly covers the whole instance space. In order to find the consistent disjuncts, the covered negative examples must be excluded. The technique used in the algorithm is similar to the *star* algorithm of AQ (Michalski, 1983). During each cycle, the consistency of each disjunct in STAR is tested. If the disjunct is consistent, it is added to the set of CONSISTENT-DNTS and removed from STAR. Otherwise, it is specialized by removing an attribute value from one of its conditions. This specialization is repeated for each condition of the disjunct. The attribute value of a condition is chosen to maximize the number of negative examples and minimize the number of positive examples excluded from the disjunct. This yields several new disjuncts, each of which covers fewer negative examples. The new star is the union of these newly specialized disjuncts. A certain maximum number (MAXSTAR) of these disjuncts are selected for further processing. This set of disjuncts is selected based on their potential quality (Zhang, 1990). When STAR is empty, the algorithm terminates with a set of consistent disjuncts. Figure 16.1(a) shows the most general disjunct that the algorithm starts with, and Figure 16.1(b) shows the set of consistent disjuncts that the algorithm ends up with.

Table 16.2: Phase 1: The disjunct generation algorithm

Let STAR be the set containing the most general disjunct that covers all examples.
Let CONSISTENT-DNTS be empty.
Repeat
    Let NEWSTAR be empty
    For each disjunct DNT in STAR
        For each attribute
            select a value to remove so that a more specific disjunct NEWDNT is generated
            if NEWDNT is consistent,
                then add NEWDNT into CONSISTENT-DNTS
                else add NEWDNT into NEWSTAR
    Let STAR be MAXSTAR disjuncts with the largest potential quality in NEWSTAR.
until STAR is empty
Return CONSISTENT-DNTS

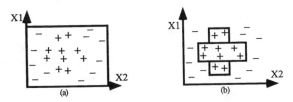

Figure 16.1:   An illustration of the function of the phase 1. (a) The most general disjunct with which the algorithm starts. (b) The set of consistent disjuncts with which the algorithm ends up.

16.4.2.2 Phase 2: The WTD Optimization Algorithm

In a logic type representation, to match a disjunct, an example must satisfy all conditions of the disjunct. In the proposed representation, the conditions of a WTD that need to be satisfied by an example are controlled by the threshold of the WTD. The larger the threshold, the more conditions that need to be satisfied. Decreasing the threshold relaxes the conditions that have to be satisfied. The WTD optimization algorithm tries to increase the coverage of WTDs by decreasing their thresholds. In order to decrease the threshold of a WTD without increasing inconsistency, the similarity of nearly covered negative examples must be reduced so that the threshold can be decreased without covering more negative examples. One way to reduce the similarity of nearly covered negative examples is to specialize the base disjunct of the WTD by removing some values of conditions involved in the base disjunct. The value selected for specialization occurs on many nearly covered negative examples and few nearly covered positive examples. Thus, the process of optimizing a WTD is to further specialize its base disjunct and adjust its threshold.

The WTD optimization algorithm is similar to the base disjunct generation algorithm in that it also performs a general-to-specific beam search. In this algorithm, the threshold is decreased, and the base disjunct is specialized. Thus, a WTD is often generalized although its base disjunct is specialized. Another major difference involves the different negative examples that the two algorithms try to exclude. The base disjunct generalization algorithm reduces the number of strictly covered negative examples, whereas the WTD optimization algorithm reduces the number of nearly covered negative examples. This difference is reflected in the different potential quality evaluation functions and the different ways to select a value of a condition for specialization in the two algorithms. The potential quality of a disjunct is computed solely based on the strictly covered examples, but the potential quality of a WTD is computed based on the flexibly covered examples as well as the nearly covered examples. In the base disjunct generalization algorithm, the value of a condition that occurs most frequently on strictly covered negative examples and least frequently on strictly covered positive examples is selected for specialization, but in the WTD optimization algorithm, the value of a condition that occurs most frequently on nearly covered negative examples and least frequently on nearly covered positive examples is selected for specialization. The quality evaluation functions will be discussed later.

Table 16.3 shows the WTD optimization algorithm. The algorithm first transfers the consistent disjuncts generated in phase 1 to WTDs by computing their weights and thresholds. The weight learning algorithm and the threshold adjustment algorithm will be introduced in the next section. The STAR is initialized as *MAXSTAR* of these WTDs with the highest potential quality. Then the "best" WTD is selected as the initial "best" WTD BEST-WTD. After the algorithm terminates, BEST-WTD is output. The "best" WTD is the WTD with the highest quality.

Like the base disjunct generation algorithm, the algorithm repeats the beam search until the stop condition is satisfied. In each cycle of the loop, a set of new WTDs is generated. Quality and potential quality are computed for each newly generated WTD. The WTD with the highest quality replaces BEST-WTD if its quality is larger than BEST-WTDs. The WTDs that have no value to be improved or cannot be improved are removed from NEWSTAR. Two kinds of WTDs—the most specific WTDs and the WTDs with 0 potential improvement—cannot be improved. The WTDs with very low quality (comparing with BEST-WTD) have no value to be improved. Issues about the potential improvement will be discussed later. The *MAXSTAR* new WTDs with the highest potential quality are selected for further improvement. *MAX-TRIES* is an integer parameter that controls the execution of the loop. If BEST-WTD has not been improved in *MAX-TRIES* steps, the algorithm stops.

Table 16.3: Phase 2: The WTD optimization algorithm

Repeat
    Let NEWSTAR be empty
    For each WTD in STAR
        For each attribute
            select a value to remove
            compute the weights and the threshold to generate a new WTD NEWWTD
            if NEWWTD has equal or higher quality than BEST-WTD
                then replace BEST-WTD by NEWWTD
                    set NO-IMPROVEMENT to 0
                else add 1 to NO-IMPROVEMENT
            add NEWWTD into NEWSTAR
    Remove all WTDs that cannot be improved from NEWSTAR
    Let STAR be *MAXSTAR* WTDs with the largest potential quality in NEWSTAR
until NO-IMPROVEMENT > *MAX-TRIES* or STAR is empty
Return BEST-WTD

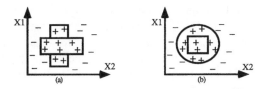

Figure 16.2:   An illustration of the function of the phase 2. (a) Initial WTDs with which the algorithm starts. (b) The WTD with which the algorithm ends up.

Figure 16.2(a) shows the initial WTDs that the algorithm starts with, and Figure 16.2(b) shows the WTD that the algorithm ends up with. In Figure 16.2(b), the circle represents a WTD, and the square inside the circle represents its base disjunct. It can be seen that the disjunct in Figure 16.2(b) is more specific than the two disjuncts in Figure 16.2(a), but the WTD is more general than both of the two disjuncts in Figure 16.2(a).

16.4.3 Weight Learning and Threshold Adjustment

In the hybrid representation, each condition of a WTD is associated with a weight that is the degree of necessity of the condition. A weight is a real value ranging from 0 to $+\infty$. The larger the weight of a condition, the more necessary the condition. Weights are computed during learning. Each time a WTD is generated, its weights are computed. In computing the weight of a condition, the algorithm counts the number of positive and negative examples that do not match the condition

$$w(C) = \frac{p(\text{unmatched} \mid NEG)}{p(\text{unmatched} \mid POS)}$$

where $p(unmatched \mid NEG)$ and $p(unmatched \mid POS)$ are the fraction of negative and positive examples that do not match C. The range for $w(C)$ is from 0 to $+\infty$. When the condition C is satisfied by all positive examples, $p(unmatched \mid POS) = 0$ so that $w(C) = +\infty$, and the condition C is necessary. When the condition C is satisfied by all negative examples, $p(unmatched \mid NEG) = 0$ so that $w(C) = 0$. This case occurs seldom because such a condition is rarely generated by the learning algorithm. The fewer negative examples satisfy the condition C, the larger $p(unmatched \mid NEG)$ and $w(C)$. The more positive examples satisfy the condition C, the smaller $p(unmatched \mid POS)$, therefore the larger $w(C)$. When both $p(unmatched \mid NEG)$ and $p(unmatched \mid POS)$ are equal to 0, $w(C)$ is set to 1.

As described above, in phase 2, each time the base disjunct is specialized, the threshold is decreased to achieve the best fit between the WTD and given concept examples. The decrease in a threshold is divided into a number of steps; the threshold is decreased by a fixed quantity D in each step. After each decrease, the WTD is evaluated to check if the WTD is improved by the decrease in the threshold. If it has not been improved in several steps, say, 3, then the adjustment of the threshold stops, and the threshold on which the WTD achieves the highest quality is the threshold of the WTD. The quantity D decreased in each step for the WTD wtd is determined as follows:

$$\Delta = \frac{1 - \mathrm{MIN}_{i=1...n}\{SM(e_i, \ wtd)\}}{100}$$

where $e_1, ..., e_n$ are all training examples.

16.4.4 Concept Evaluation

Concept learning can be viewed as a search for the "best" solutions (concept descriptions). Because of the complexity of brute force search, all learning systems search the description space heuristically. Therefore, an evaluation function is needed as a heuristic to decide one or more intermediate hypothesis for further improvement. Such intermediate hypotheses should have potential for improvement. Also, an evaluation function is needed to determine the best description that is the final solution of the search when the search algorithm terminates. Most current inductive learning systems use one evaluation function for both purposes. It means that a better description always has greater potential for improvement. Unfortunately, this is not always true. In the following, some examples will be given to show that a good description may not have potential for improvement.

Three different evaluation functions are used in FCLS. The first one, called *Quality Evaluation Function*, evaluates the quality of a WTD; the second one, *Base Disjunct Potential Quality Evaluation Function*, evaluates the potential quality of a disjunct; and the third one, *WTD Potential Quality Evaluation Function*, evaluates the potential quality of a WTD. The WTD with the highest quality is the "best" WTD, but the WTD with the highest potential quality has the "greatest" potential for improvement. In the following subsections, these three evaluation functions are simply described; for further detail, see Zhang (1990).

16.4.4.1 The Quality Evaluation Function

As in most inductive learning systems, the quality of a WTD is evaluated based on its completeness and consistency with regard to the training examples. Generally, one can gain completeness at the expense of consistency, or one can gain consistency by sacrificing completeness. They are two competing criteria. For this reason, quality is evaluated as the product of these two parts: completeness, which is the percentage of positive examples covered, and consistency, which is the

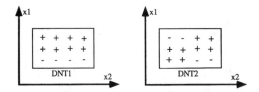

Figure 16.3:   Illustration of the difference between the quality and potential improvement of disjuncts

ratio of the number of negative examples covered and the number of total examples covered.

16.4.4.2 Base Disjunct Potential Quality Evaluation Function

Before describing the details of the base disjunct potential quality evaluation function, let us first discuss some general issues about the potential quality. The potential quality is used to decide whether a WTD or a disjunct is worth being improved, whether a WTD or a disjunct can be improved, and how much a WTD or a disjunct can be improved. Based on the potential quality, both the base disjunct generalization algorithm and the WTD optimization algorithm determine which disjunct or WTD should be selected for further improvement. The potential quality consists of two parts: current quality and potential improvement. Current quality is similar to the quality and is computed based on the completeness and consistency of a WTD or a disjunct, but the concern of potential improvement is how much improvement can be achieved on the basis of current quality. The WTD (disjunct) with low current quality is not worth being improved even it has high potential improvement, but the WTD (disjunct) with low potential improvement has little potential for further improvement.

In evaluating the potential quality of a disjunct, only the examples strictly covered by the disjunct are considered. The current quality of a disjunct is computed based on the number of positive and negative examples strictly covered by the disjunct. The potential improvement of a disjunct is computed based on the distribution of the positive and negative examples inside the disjunct. Some distributions make a disjunct much easier to improve than the others. For example, Figure 16.3 shows two disjuncts DNT1 and DNT2 that cover the same number of positive and negative examples and have the same current quality. However, DNT1 is much easier to improve than DNT2 because the positive examples covered by DNT2 are scattered, but the positive examples covered by DNT1 are very concentrated. A disjunct with dispersed covered positive examples is hard to improve, so it has low potential improvement. A disjunct with concentrated covered positive examples is relatively easier to specialize to a consistent disjunct without losing much coverage of positive examples, so it has high potential improvement.

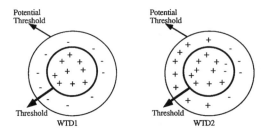

Figure 16.4:   Illustration of the difference between the current quality and potential improvement of
WTDs in phase 2

16.4.4.3 WTD Potential Quality Evaluation Function

The WTD potential quality evaluation function evaluates the potential quality
of a WTD and is used in the WTD optimization algorithm. This algorithm tries to
increase the coverage of positive examples of WTDs by decreasing their thresholds. The nearly covered examples most probably become covered after the threshold decreases. The more nearly covered positive examples a WTD has, the higher
the potential improvement. If all nearly covered examples are negative, the WTD is
surrounded by negative examples, and the decrease of its threshold can only
increase the coverage of negative examples. Such a WTD cannot be improved and
has no potential improvement.

In Figure 16.4, inside circles are thresholds of the two WTDs, and the outside
circles are the potential thresholds of the two WTDs. The potential threshold of a
WTD is used to decide nearly covered examples. The way to decide a potential
threshold was described in Zhang (1990). All examples between a threshold and a
potential threshold are nearly covered examples. The symbols + and – represent
positive and negative examples, respectively. In this figure, WTD1 has higher current quality than WTD2 but has little potential improvement because it is surrounded by negative examples. In contrast, WTD2 has lower current quality but
has larger potential improvement.

The potential improvement and the current quality of a WTD are computed
based on the nearly covered examples and the examples covered by the WTD,
respectively. The more positive nearly covered examples, the higher the potential
improvement. Each of the nearly covered examples is associated with a value that
ranges from 0.5 to 1. This value is used in evaluating the potential improvement.
Examples closer to the threshold get larger value than examples farther from the
threshold because the nearly covered examples closer to the threshold have more
chance to become covered examples than the examples farther from the threshold.
The value of all covered examples can be considered as 1. Thus, most of the nearly
covered examples get a smaller value than covered examples. This is reasonable

Table 16.4: Positive and negative examples of the acceptable labor contracts

#	job-sec	p-ext	gwi	p-ovt	Class
1	yes	yes	large	yes	positive
2	yes	yes	small	no	positive
3	no	yes	medium	no	positive
4	yes	no	large	yes	positive
5	yes	yes	small	yes	positive
6	no	yes	medium	no	positive
7	no	no	small	no	negative
8	yes	no	small	no	negative
9	no	yes	small	yes	negative
10	no	no	large	yes	negative
11	yes	no	small	yes	negative
12	no	yes	small	no	negative

because nearly covered examples only have a chance to become covered, but they are not covered yet.

16.4.5 An Example Illustrating the Learning Algorithm

Let us go back to the labor contract example again. In addition to the three attributes—job-sec, p-ext, and gwi—a less important attribute, p-ovt (pension for overtime work), is added to the problem. Each object in the domain is now described by four attributes. Table 16.4 shows all examples given. The examples 1 to 6 are positive examples, and the examples 7 to 12 are negative examples.

We will ignore the weight learning and set *MAXSTAR* to 1 in the following example. First, the top level algorithm calls the WTD generation algorithm. The base disjunct generation algorithm starts with the most general disjunct:

[job-sec = yes ∨ no][p-ext = yes ∨ no][gwi=large ∨ medium ∨ small][p-ovt
    = yes ∨ no]

For each of the four conditions, the algorithm chooses one value to remove and generates four new, more specific disjuncts. For example, it chooses the value *no* to remove from the first condition because removing the value *no* excludes more negative examples (7, 9, 10, and 12) and fewer positive examples (3 and 6) from the disjunct than removing the value *yes*. This yields the following four new disjuncts:

[job-sec = yes][p-ext = yes ∨ no][gwi = large ∨ medium ∨ small][p-ovt
    = yes ∨ no]
[job-sec = yes ∨ no][p-ext = yes][gwi = large ∨ medium ∨ small][p-ovt
    = yes ∨ no]

[job-sec = yes ∨ no][p-ext = yes ∨ no][gwi = large ∨ medium][p-ovt
        = yes ∨ no]

[job-sec = yes ∨ no][p-ext = yes ∨ no][gwi = large ∨ medium ∨ small][p-ovt
        = yes]

One (because *MAXSTAR* = 1) of the four disjuncts is selected based on their potential quality for further improvement. For simplicity, we will choose the most consistent disjunct:

[job-sec = yes ∨ no][p-ext = yes ∨ no][gwi = large ∨ medium][p-ovt
        = yes ∨ no]

which covers 4 positive examples and one negative example, and has higher consistency than the other three disjuncts, so it is chosen for further improvement. Repeat the same process, and the following four new disjuncts are generated:

[job-sec = yes][p-ext = yes ∨ no][gwi = large ∨ medium][p-ovt = yes ∨ no]

[job-sec = yes ∨ no][p-ext = yes][gwi = large ∨ medium][p-ovt = yes ∨ no]

[job-sec = yes ∨ no][p-ext = yes ∨ no][gwi = medium][p-ovt = yes ∨ no]

[job-sec = yes ∨ no][p-ext = yes ∨ no][gwi = large ∨ medium][p-ovt = no]

All these four disjuncts cover no negative example, but they cover a different number of positive examples. The second disjunct that covers the largest number of positive examples is chosen as the output of the base disjunct generation algorithm. The disjunct

[job-sec = yes ∨ no][p-ext = yes][gwi = large ∨ medium][p-ovt = yes ∨ no]
Threshold = 1

serves as the base disjunct of the initial WTD for the WTD optimization algorithm. Actually, the WTD can be rewritten as

[p-ext = yes][gwi = large ∨ medium]
Threshold = 1

because the conditions [SHAPE = round ∨ square] and [COLOR = white ∨ black] include all values.

In the second phase, this WTD is optimized by specializing its base disjunct and decreasing its threshold. The way to specialize its base disjunct is the same as in phase 1, namely, removing a value from a condition. Because no value can be removed from the condition [p-ext = yes], only three new WTDs are generated. The following WTD is the best one of the three new WTDs:

[job-sec = yes][p-ext = yes][gwi = large ∨ medium][p-ovt = white ∨ black]
Threshold = 2/3

This is same as the WTD

[job-sec = yes][p-ext = yes][gwi = large ∨ medium]
Threshold = 2/3

This WTD covers all six positive examples and none of the negative examples.

16.5 EMPIRICAL EVALUATION

To evaluate the approach described in this chapter, a number of experiments were conducted on various domains with FCLS and C4.5. This section first outlines the experimental methods, then reports the experimental results.

16.5.1 Experimental Design

To thoroughly evaluate the approach, FCLS was tested on eight problems. This chapter will report the results from three problems: M-Of-N concept, congressional voting records, and lymphatic cancer. The results from other problems are reported in Zhang and Michalski (1994).

The learning methods involved in the experiments were a rule learning algorithm, a decision tree learning algorithm, and the algorithm reported in this chapter with and without weight learning. The rule learning algorithm was the base disjunct generation algorithm described; it generated a disjunction of disjuncts as a concept description that was equivalent to the description generated by AQ11 (Michalski and Larson, 1978). It provided the performance baseline for other methods. The decision tree learning algorithm was C4.5 (Quinlan, 1987).

The performance was evaluated on two aspects: classification accuracy and description complexity. Classification accuracy was measured as the percentage of correct classifications made by the concept description on a set of randomly selected test events. Description complexity was measured by the number of WTDs (disjuncts in rule learning) involved in a description. The complexity of decision trees is measured by the number of leaves in a tree.

In all experiments, FCLS ran on randomly generated training sets of various sizes. For each training set size, FCLS was run on four different randomly generated training sets. The final descriptions produced from these four runs were tested for accuracy on a set of test events and were measured for complexity. The results reported are the average of the four runs.

16.5.2 Experimental Results

The experiments described in this section were performed on three problems: M-Of-N concept, congressional voting records, and lymphatic cancer.

The problem of the M-Of-N concept contains two classes (positive and negative) and 10 nominal attributes, each of which has four values (0, 1, 2, and 3). The

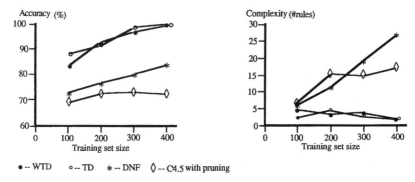

Figure 16.5: Classification accuracy and description complexity on M-Of-N concept

rule for distinguishing positive class from negative has the general form of "at least M of N conditions are satisfied." Specifically, the rule is "if any 5 or more of the first 7 attributes of an event are equal to 0 or 1, then the event belongs to the positive class; otherwise, it belongs to the negative class." The test set included 1,000 randomly selected events and was disjoint with training sets.

Figure 16.5 shows the results of the experiments from M-Of-N concept. In the figure, DNF is the rule learning method that generates DNF expression as a concept description. TD (Threshold Disjunct) represents the method described in the chapter with threshold adjusting but not weight learning. WTD represents the method reported in the chapter with both threshold adjusting and weight learning.

Significant improvements were achieved on both accuracy and complexity by the TD and WTD methods over the DNF method and C4.5 with all training set sizes. The TD and WTD methods have very similar performance. This is because all conditions of the target concept description were equally important, and weights play no role. Actually, the accuracy of the TD method was slightly higher than that of the WTD method, which can be explained as follows. In the WTD method, weights were adjusted based on the training examples during learning. Although all weights learned were close to each other, they were not exactly equal, so that the final description did not exactly describe the target concept that had the same weights for all conditions. The TD method produced the exact target concept descriptions for both the positive and negative classes at three of four training sets of 300 examples and all four training sets of 400 examples. The WTD method generated the target concept with slightly different weights. The significant performance improvement on this problem can be attributed to the clear graded structure that the M-Of-N concept possesses.

The data regarding the U.S. congressional voting records represented the 1981 voting records of 100 selected representatives, each of which was characterized by 19 binary attributes. Each attribute represented a vote and had two values: vote for and vote against. The problem was to learn descriptions discriminating

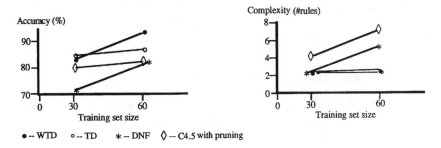

Figure 16.6: Classification accuracy and description complexity on congressional voting records

between the voting records of Democrats and Republicans. The two concepts involved in this problem, voting records of Democrats and voting records of Republicans, had graded structures. For example, Democrats had a tendency to vote for some issues and vote against others. Four training sets for each of two training sizes (30, 60) were formed by randomly drawing examples from the 100 examples; the other 40 examples were used as the testing set. The results are reported in Figure 16.6. The WTD method improved the accuracy over the DNF method and outperformed the TD method at the size of 60. The TD method achieved better results than the DNF method and performed slightly better than the WTD method at the size of 30. At the size of 60, the WTD and TD methods obtained simpler descriptions than the DNF method.

The lymphatic cancer data were characterized by 18 attributes and 4 diagnostic classes. Data of 148 patients were available. Twenty-five, 50, 75, and 100 examples were randomly selected for learning; the remaining 48 examples were used as a testing set. The results are shown in Figure 16.7. Both the WTD and TD methods gave better accuracy, except the size of 25, than the DNT method, but the improvement is not significant. The description generated by the WTD and TD methods was simpler than that given by the other two methods. A striking result was that all

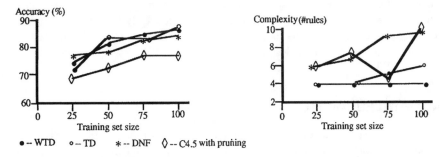

Figure 16.7: Classification accuracy and description complexity on lymphatic cancer

concept descriptions generated by the WTD method consist of only one WTD, with more conditions involved in the base disjunct. It seems that these base disjuncts captured the central tendencies of these four diagnostic classes.

16.6 SUMMARY AND FUTURE WORK

This chapter described a novel integrated approach to learning concepts with graded structures. In this approach, a hybrid representation that combines symbolic and numeric representations was proposed to explicitly describe the central tendency of a concept and implicitly extend the meaning of a concept by a threshold, a set of weights, and a similarity measure to handle the atypical aspect. A two step learning algorithm was designed and implemented to automatically acquire both symbolic and numeric descriptions from given examples. The method was tested in five domains, and the results were very promising and encouraging.

A number of problems need to be addressed in the future. First, the syntactic similarity measure needs to be augmented with a knowledge-based semantic similarity measure. This semantic similarity measure will include a set of inference rules and defines the similarity between an event and a WTD based on the semantics. Another related future research topic is constructive induction. In general, constructive induction produces descriptions that are easier to understand and capture the salient features of concepts. It would be useful to apply constructive induction to generate disjuncts that capture the principles of concepts.

Second, the problem of incremental learning should be addressed. The distribution of knowledge between the symbolic and numeric description may need to be adjusted when a set of new examples becomes available. Thus, incremental learning in the hybrid representation involves not only creating new descriptions but also adjusting the distribution between the symbolic and numeric description.

Finally, the typicality of examples could be very helpful in learning graded concept descriptions. Human experts are often very good at providing such information by telling which examples are typical and which are not. The typicality of examples can be used to reduce the search space and find the optimum distribution of concept meaning between the symbolic description and the numerical one. In the future, we will develop an algorithm to take advantage of typicality of examples in learning concept descriptions. In the algorithm, typical examples will be used first to learn disjuncts, and then less typical examples will be used to extend the disjuncts to WTDs.

ACKNOWLEDGMENTS

This research was done while the author was with the Artificial Intelligence Center of George Mason University. The author thanks R.S. Michalski and G. Tecuci for many discussions on the work reported in this chapter. This research was done in the Artificial Intelligence Center of George Mason University. The research activities of the Center are supported in part by the Office of Naval Research under Grants No. N00014-88-K-0397, No. N00014-88-K-0226, No. N00014-90-J-4059, and No. N00014-91-J-1351; in part by the National Science Foundation under the Grant No. IRI-9020266; and in part by the Defense Advanced Research Projects Agency under the grants administered by the Office of Naval Research, No. N00014-87-K-0874 and No. N00014-91-J-1854. The author was also partially supported by a Utah State University Faculty Grant.

References

Barsalou, L., "Ideals, Central Tendency, and Frequency of Instantiation as Determinants of Graded Structure in Categories," *Journal of Experimental Psychology: Learning, Memory and Cognition*, 11, pp. 629–654, 1985.

Bergadano, F., Matwin, S., Michalski, R.S., and Zhang, J., "Representing and Acquiring Flexible Concepts in Knowledge-based Systems," In *Proceedings of the 3rd International Symposium on Methodologies for Intelligent Systems*, Torino, Itali, October, 1988.

———, "Learning Two-tiered Descriptions of Flexible Concepts," in *Machine Learning*, Vol. 8, No. 1, pp. 5–43, 1992.

Michalski, R.S., "A Theory and Methodology of Inductive Learning," In *Machine Learning: An Artificial Intelligence Approach,* 83–134, Michalski, Carbonell, and Mitchell (eds.), Morgan Kaufmann, San Mateo, CA, 1983.

———, "How to Learn Imprecise Concept: A Method Employing a Two-tiered Representation for Learning," In *Proceedings of the Fourth International Workshop on Machine Learning*, 50–58, (ed.) Pat Langley, Morgan Kaufmann, San Mateo, CA, 1987.

———, "Learning Flexible Concepts: Fundamental Ideas and a Method Bases on Two-tiered Representation," In *Machine Learning: An Artificial Intelligence Approach*, 63–111, Volume III, Kodratoff and Michalski (eds.), Morgan Kaufmann, San Mateo, CA, 1990.

Michalski, R.S. and Larson, J.B., "Selection of Most Representative Training Examples and Incremental Generation of Vl1 Hypotheses: The Underlying Methodology and the Description of Programs ESEL and AQ11," Technical Report 867, Department of Computer Science, University of Illinois, Urbana, IL, 1978.

Quinlan, J.R., "Simplifying Decision Trees," In *International Journal of Man-Machine Studies*, Vol. 27, pp. 221–234, 1987.

Salzberg, S., "A Nearest Hyperrectangle Learning Method," *Machine Learning*, 6, pp. 251–276, 1991.

Schlimmer, J.C., *Concept Acquisition through Representational Adjustment*, Ph.D. thesis, Department of Information and Computer Science, University of California, Irvine, 1987.

Towell J.G, and Shavlik, J.W., "Refining Symbolic Knowledge Using Neural Networks," In *Machine Learning: A Multistrategy Approach*, Vol. IV, R.S Michalski and G. Tecuci (Eds.), Morgan Kaufmann Publishers, San Mateo, CA, 1994.

Utgoff, P.E., "Perceptron Trees: A Case Study in Hybrid Concept Representations," In *Proceedings of the Seventh National Conference on Artificial Intelligence*, pp. 601–606, AAAI Press, Menlo Park, CA, 1988.

Zhang, J., "Learning Flexible Concepts from Examples: Employing the Ideas of Two-Tiered Concept Representation," Ph.D. Thesis, Department of Computer Science, University of Illinois at Urbana-Champaign, 1990.

Zhang, J. and Michalski, R.S., "Combining Symbolic and Numeric Representations in Learning Flexible Concepts: The FCLS System," Submitted to *Machine Learning*, 1994, forthcoming.

17

IMPROVING A RULE INDUCTION SYSTEM USING GENETIC ALGORITHMS

Haleh Vafaie
Kenneth De Jong
(George Mason University)

Abstract

The field of automatic image recognition presents a variety of difficult classification problems involving the identification of important scene components in the presence of noise, changing lighting conditions, and shifting viewpoints. This chapter describes part of a larger effort to apply machine learning techniques to such problems in an attempt to automatically generate and improve the classification rules required for various recognition tasks. The immediate problem attacked is that of texture recognition in the presence of noise and changing lighting conditions. In this context, standard rule induction systems like AQ15 produce sets of classification rules that are not necessarily optimal with respect to (1) the need to minimize the number of features actually used for classification and (2) the need to achieve high recognition rates with noisy data. This chapter describes one of several multistrategy approaches being explored to improve the usefulness of machine learning techniques for such problems. The approach described here involves the use of genetic algorithms as a "front end" to traditional rule induction systems in order to identify and select the best subset of features to be used by the rule induction system. The proposed approach has been implemented and tested on difficult texture classification problems. The results are encouraging and indicate significant improvements can be obtained from a multistrategy approach in this domain.

17.1 INTRODUCTION

In recent years there has been a significant increase in research on automatic image recognition in more realistic contexts involving noise, changing lighting conditions, and shifting viewpoints. The corresponding increase in difficulty in designing effective classification procedures for the important components of these more complex recognition problems has led to an interest in machine techniques as a possible strategy for automatically producing classification rules. This chapter describes part of a larger effort to apply machine learning techniques to such problems in an attempt to generate and improve the classification rules required for various recognition tasks. The immediate problem attacked is that of texture recognition in the context of noise and changing lighting conditions. In this context, standard rule induction systems like AQ15 produce sets of classification rules that are not necessarily optimal in two respects. First, there is a need to minimize the number of features actually used for classification because each feature used adds to the design and manufacturing costs as well as the running time of a recognition system. At the same time, there is a need to achieve high recognition rates in the presence of noise and changing environmental conditions.

This chapter describes one of several multistrategy approaches being explored to improve the usefulness of machine learning techniques for such problems (see, for example, Bala et al., 1994; Chapter 18 of this book). The approach described here involves the use of genetic algorithms as a "front end" to traditional rule induction systems in order to identify and select the best subset of features to be used by the rule induction system. The proposed approach has been implemented and tested on difficult texture classification problems. The results are encouraging and indicate significant advantages to a multistrategy approach in this domain.

17.2 FEATURE SELECTION

Because each feature used as part of a classification procedure can increase the cost and running time of a recognition system, there is strong motivation within the image processing community to design and implement systems with small feature sets. At the same time, there is a potentially opposing need to include a sufficient set of features to achieve high recognition rates under difficult conditions. This has led to the development of a variety of techniques within the image processing community for finding an "optimal" subset of features from a larger set of possible features. These feature selection strategies fall into two main categories.

The first approach selects features independent of their effect on classification performance. This generally involves transforming the original features according to procedures such as those presented by Karhunen-Loeve or Fisher (Tou and Heyden, 1967; Kittler, 1977) to form a new set of features with lower dimensionality than the original one. The difficulty here is in identifying an appropriate set of transformations so that the smaller set of features preserves most of the information provided by the original data and is more reliable because of the removal of redundant and noisy features (Dom, Niblack, and Sheinvald, 1989).

The second approach directly selects a subset d of the available m features in such a way as to not significantly degrade the performance of the classifier system (Ichino and Sklansky, 1984a). Many researchers have adopted this method and have created their own variations on this approach. For example, Blanz, Tou and Heydorn, and Watanabe, after ordering the features, use methods such as simply taking the first d features or a branch and bound technique to select a subset of these features (Dom, Niblack, and Sheinvald, 1989). The main issue for this approach is how to account for dependencies between features when ordering them initially and selecting an effective subset in a later step.

A related strategy involves simply selecting feature subsets and evaluating their effectiveness. This process requires a "criterion function" and a "search procedure" (Foroutan and Sklansky, 1985). The evaluation of feature set effectiveness has been studied by many researchers. Their solutions vary considerably and include using a Bayesian estimate of the probability of error, the Whitney and Stern estimate of probability of error based on a k-nearest neighbor bound Ichino and Sklansky, 1984b), or a measure based on statistical separability (Dom, Niblack, and Sheinvald, 1989).

All of the above mentioned techniques involve the assumption that some *a priori* information (such as a probability density function) about the data set is available, even though in practice such information is generally unavailable (Foroutan and Sklansky, 1985). Also, the search procedures used in these techniques to select a subset of the given features play an important role in the success of the approach. Exhaustively trying all the subsets is computationally prohibitive when there are a large number of features. Non-exhaustive search procedures such as sequential backward elimination and sequential forward selection pose many problems (Kittler, 1978). These search techniques do not allow for backtracking; therefore, after a selection has been made, it is impossible to make any revisions to the search. Also, in order to avoid a combinatorial explosion in search time, these search procedures generally do not take into consideration any interdependencies that may exist between the given features when choosing a subset.

There has been very little research in the machine learning community on optimal feature selection. A literature search revealed only one unpublished report by Forsburg (1976) in which a technique based on an adaptive random search algorithm of Lbov (1965) was implemented for, but not adequately tested on, the problem of feature selection. In the published literature, the machine learning community has only attacked the problem of optimal feature selection indirectly in that the traditional biases for simplicity (Occam's razor) lead to efficient induction procedures that produce individual rules (trees) containing only a few features to be evaluated. However, each rule (tree) can and frequently does use a different set of features, resulting in much larger cumulative features sets than those typically acceptable for image classification problems. This problem is magnified by the tendency of traditional machine learning algorithms to overfit the training data, particularly in the context of noisy data, resulting in the need for a variety of ad hoc truncating (pruning) procedures for simplifying the induced rules (trees).

The conclusion of these observations is that there is a significant opportunity for improving the usefulness of traditional machine learning techniques for automatically generating useful classification procedures for image recognition problems if an effective means were available for finding feature subsets that are "optimal" from the point of view of size and performance. Because genetic algorithms are best known for their ability to efficiently search large spaces about which little is known and because they are relatively insensitive to noise, they seem to be an excellent choice as a feature selection strategy for use with a more traditional rule (tree) induction system. In the following sections, this approach is described in more detail by illustrating the design, implementation, and testing of such a multistrategy system in which AQ15 is used as the rule induction procedure, and the problem setting is that of texture classification.

17.3 A MULTISTRATEGY APPROACH

The overall architecture of the multistrategy system is given in Figure 17.1. It is assumed that an initial set of features will be provided as input as well as a training set in the form of feature vectors extracted from actual images and representing positive and negative examples of the various classes for which rules are to be induced. A genetic algorithm (GA) is used to explore the space of all subsets of the given feature set. Each of the selected feature subsets is evaluated (its fitness measured) by invoking AQ15 with the correspondingly reduced feature space and training set, and measuring the recognition rate of the rules produced. The best feature subset found is then output as the recommended set of features to be used in the actual design of the recognition system. Each of these components is described in more detail in the following sections.

17.3.1 Using Genetic Algorithms as the Search Procedure

Genetic algorithms (GAs) are adaptive search techniques initially introduced by Holland. Genetic algorithms derive their name from the fact that their operations are similar to the mechanics of population genetics models of natural systems.

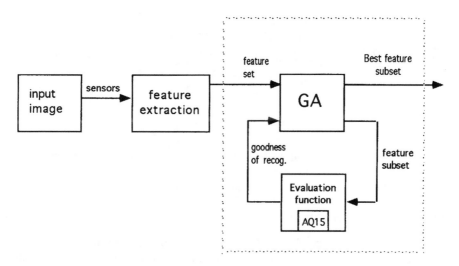

Figure 17.1:   Block diagram of the adaptive feature selection process

Genetic algorithms typically maintain a constant-sized population of individuals that represent samples of the space to be searched. Each individual is evaluated on the basis of its overall fitness with respect to the given application domain. New individuals (samples of the search space) are produced by selecting high performing individuals to produce "offspring" that retain many of the features of their "parents." The result is an evolving population that has improved fitness with respect to the given goal.

New individuals (offspring) for the next generation are formed by using two main genetic operators: crossover and mutation. Crossover operates by randomly selecting a point in the two selected parents' gene structures and exchanging the remaining segments of the parents to create new offspring. Therefore, crossover combines the features of two individuals to create two similar offspring. Mutation operates by randomly changing one or more components of a selected individual. It acts as a population perturbation operator and is a means for inserting new information into the population. This operator prevents any stagnation that might occur during the search process.

Genetic algorithms have demonstrated substantial improvement over a variety of random and local search methods (De Jong, 1975). This is accomplished by their ability to exploit accumulating information about an initially unknown search space in order to bias subsequent search into promising subspaces. Because GAs are basically a domain independent search technique, they are ideal for applications where domain knowledge and theory are difficult or impossible to provide (De Jong, 1988).

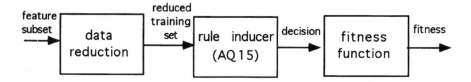

Figure 17.2:   Feature set evaluation procedure

The main issues in applying GAs to any problem are selecting an appropriate representation and an adequate evaluation function. In the following sections, both of these issues are discussed in more detail for the problem of feature selection.

17.3.2 Representation Issues

The first step in applying GAs to the problem of feature selection is to map the search space into a representation suitable for genetic search. Because the main interest is in representing the space of all possible subsets of the given feature set, the simplest form of representation is to consider each feature in the candidate feature set as a binary gene. Then, each individual consists of a fixed-length binary string representing some subset of the given feature set. An individual of length l corresponds to an l-dimensional binary feature vector X, where each bit represents the elimination or inclusion of the associated feature. For example, $x_i = 0$ represents elimination, and $x_i = 1$ indicates inclusion of the ith feature. Hence, a feature set with five features can be represented as $<x_1\ x_2\ x_3\ x_4\ x_5>$. Then, an individual of the form <11111> indicates inclusion of all the features, and <11010> represents the subset where the third and the fifth features are eliminated.

The advantage to this representation is that the classical GA's operators as described before (binary mutation and crossover) can easily be applied to this representation without any modification. This eliminates the need for designing new genetic operators or making any other changes to the standard form of genetic algorithms.

17.3.3 Evaluation Procedures

Choosing an appropriate evaluation procedure is an essential step for successful application of GAs to any problem domain. Evaluation procedures provide GAs with feedback about the fitness of each individual in the population. GAs then use this feedback to bias the search process to provide an improvement in the population's average fitness. For the feature selection problem, the performance of a feature subset is measured by applying the evaluation procedure presented in Figure 17.2.

The evaluation procedure as shown is divided into three main steps. After a feature subset is selected, the initial training data, consisting of the entire set of feature vectors and class assignments corresponding to examples from each of the given classes, are reduced. This is done by removing the values for features that are not in the selected subset of feature vectors. The second step is to apply a rule induction process (AQ15) to the new reduced training data to generate the decision rules for each of the given classes in the training data. The last step is to evaluate the rules produced by the AQ algorithm with respect to their classification performance on the test data. Each of these steps will be discussed in more detail.

17.3.3.1 The AQ Algorithm

The AQ algorithm is a rule induction technique used to produce a complete and consistent description of classes of examples (Michalski and Stepp, 1983; Michalski et al., 1986). A class description is formed by a collection of disjuncts of decision rules describing all the training examples given for that particular class. A decision rule is simply a set of conjuncts of allowable tests of feature values.

For the studies reported here, AQ15 was used as the rule induction component. This system (for more detail, see Michalski et al., 1986) requires a set of parameters, feature descriptions, and a training set as input. It then uses the given parameters to direct the AQ algorithm in its process of searching for a complete and consistent set of class descriptions. The following is a simplified example of decision rules produced by AQ15 for a particular class in which instances were represented by 9 integer-values features:

$< x_1, x_2, \dots, x_9 >$ is a member of the class if
    $[x_1 = 3$ to $7]$ and $[x_4 = 4$ to $9]$ and $[x_8 = 1$ to $10]$ (total:9, unique 6)
    or
    $[x_1 = 6$ to $8]$ and $[x_5 = 4$ or 5 or $9]$ (total:5, unique 3)
    or
    $[x_2 = 4]$ and $[x_3 = 3$ to $9]$ and $[x_7 = 2$ to $6]$ and $[x_9 = 1$ to $8]$
                                        (total:2, unique 1)

This class is described by three decision rules, where each covers a total of 9, 5, and 2 training examples, respectively. The term "unique" refers to the number of positive training examples that were uniquely covered by each rule. Notice that although each individual rule involves the testing of only a few features, the entire rule set involves 8 of the 9 features provided.

17.3.3.2 Fitness Function

In order to use genetic algorithms as the search procedure, it is necessary to define a fitness function that properly assesses the decision rules generated by the AQ algorithm. The fitness function must be able to discriminate between correct and incorrect classification of examples given the AQ-created rules. Finding an appropriate function is not a trivial task because of the noisy nature of most image data. The procedure, as depicted in Figure 17.3, was developed to best achieve this goal.

The fitness function takes as input a set of feature or attribute definitions, a set of decision rules created by the AQ algorithm, and a collection of testing examples defining the feature values for each example. The fitness function then evaluates the AQ-generated rules on the testing examples as follows.

For every testing example, a match score (which will be described in more detail) is evaluated for each of the classification rules generated by the AQ algorithm in order to find the rule(s) with the highest or best match. At the end of this process, if there is more than one rule having the highest match, one rule will be selected based on the chosen conflict resolution process (explained later). This rule then represents the classification for the given testing example. If this is the appropriate classification, then the testing example has been recognized correctly. After all the testing examples have been classified, the overall fitness function is evaluated by adding the weighted sum of the match score of all the correct recognitions and subtracting the weighted sum of the match score of all the incorrect recognitions; more formally,

$$F = \sum_{i=1}^{n} S_i * W_i - \sum_{j=n+1}^{m} S_j * W_j$$

where

S_i is the best match score evaluated for the test example i.

n is the number of testing examples that were classified correctly.

m is the total number of testing examples.

W_i is the weight allocated to the test example i.

The range of the value of F is dependent on the number of testing events and their weights. In order to normalize and scale the fitness function F to a value acceptable for GAs, the following operations were performed:

Fitness = 100 − [(F / TW) *100]

where

TW = total weighted testing examples

$$= \sum_{i=1}^{m} W_i$$

As indicated in the above equations, after the value of F was normalized to the range [−100, 100], the subtraction was performed in order to ensure that the final evaluation is always positive (the most convenient form of fitness for GAs).

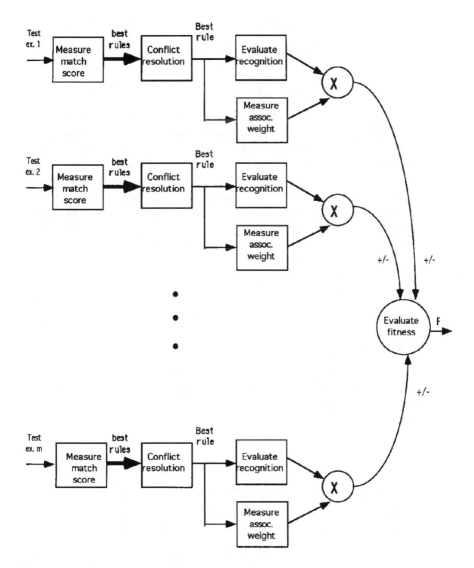

Figure 17.3:   Block diagram for the fitness function **F**

Hence, fitness values for feature subsets fall in the range [0, 200]), with lower values representing better classification performance. For example, a fitness value of zero is achieved when all the testing examples are completely and correctly recognized ($S_i = 1$). Selecting four equally weighted classes, each containing 100 testing examples ($m = 400$, $W_i = 1$ for every i), results in

$$F = \sum_{1}^{400} 1 * 1 = 400$$

and

Fitness = 100 − [(400/400) * 100] = 0

There are two main factors that define how the fitness function evaluates the performance of the decision rules on the testing examples: (1) the method used to calculate the degree to which rules match an example and (2) the procedure for assigning "importance" weights to each correct/incorrect classification.

Match Score (S). The match between a rule and a testing example may be treated as strict or partial. In strict matching, the degree of consonance between a condition and a feature value of a testing example is treated as a Boolean value. That is, it evaluates to zero if the example's feature value is not within the condition's specified range and is one otherwise.

A rule's overall match score is calculated as the minimum of the degree of match for each of the conditions in that rule. Therefore, for each condition in a given rule, if all the conditions match the example value, the match score is 1; otherwise it is 0.

$S_s = \min (S_i)$

With partial matching, the degree of match is expressed as a real number in the range [0, 1] and is computed as follows. For each condition in a given rule, if the feature in that condition has a linear domain, then the following distance measure is used as its match score:

$S = (1 - |a_j - a_k| / n)$

where

a_j is the condition's closest feature value to the testing example's value a_k.

a_k is the testing example's feature value.

n is the total number of values given for the feature.

For non-linear feature value domains, partial matching is defined to be identical to strict matching (i.e., the match score for a given condition is 1 when a match occurs and is 0 otherwise). The total partial match score for a given rule is evaluated by averaging the match scores of all the conditions for the given rule.

$S_p = $ Average (S_i)

To clarify this process, consider the following example of evaluating the match score for a testing example with the given set of rules. The feature set consists of three features, S_1, S_2, and S_3, with the following properties:

Feature	Domain	Total Number of Values
S_1	Linear	10
S_2	Nominal	4
S_3	Linear	3

The rule set to be evaluated consists of

Rule A: $[S_1 = 1 \text{ or } 2 \text{ or } 4]$
Rule B: $[S_1 = 1 \text{ or } 5] \text{ and } [S_2 = 2]$

The testing example to be matched is

S_1 S_2 S_3
 4   1   0

This results in the following strict match scores

Rule A => min(1, 1, 1) = 1
Rule B => min(0, 0, 1) = 0

and the following partial match scores

Rule A => Ave(1, 1, 1) = (1+1+1) / 3 = 1.0
Rule B => Average((1 − | 5 − 4| / 10), 0, 1) = (.9 + 0 + 1) / 3 = 0.633

Conflict Resolution. For any testing example, after the appropriate match score is evaluated for all the rules generated by the AQ algorithm, a single rule representing the highest match score must be selected. However, there may be situations where more than one rule has the highest match score. This is when the conflict resolution process is used to select a single rule. This process is performed by selecting a rule with highest typicality, that is, a rule that covers the most training examples as specified by the total number of examples it covers (see example of Section 3.3.1). However, there may be situations that all the selected rules have the same typicality. In this situation, a rule is randomly selected as the one having the best match score.

In addition to the match score of a given testing example and the conflict resolution process, weights can be associated with the classes to be recognized and can thus play an important role in the evaluation of fitness.

Weight (W). This option is useful when encoding user or expert knowledge into the evaluation function. In the current implementation each class is given a weight according to its importance in the overall recognition process. Therefore, in order to measure the recognition rate accurately, appropriate individual weights need to be allocated to each of the testing examples. The weight of the recognized class is associated with a testing example if the given example is correctly recognized. For situations where an example is incorrectly recognized, the weight is the average of the weight of the correct class and the class that was recognized (incorrect class); hence,

$$
\text{Weight} = \begin{cases} W_c & \text{if } T_i \text{ was correctly recognized} \\ (W_c + W_{in})\,/\,2 & \text{if } T_i \text{ was incorrectly recognized} \end{cases}
$$

where

W_c is the weight associated with the correctly recognized class.

W_{in} is the weight associated with the incorrectly recognized class.

T_i is a testing example.

Consider the following illustrative example, consisting of only two classes (A and B). Suppose the weights assigned to the classes are

Class	Weight
A	1
B	2

and the recognition results are

Example	Correct Class	Recognized Class
1	A	A
2	B	B
3	B	A
4	A	B

Then, the associated weight for each example is

Example	Weight
1	1
2	2
3	1.5
4	1.5

In summary, the "fitness" of a particular subset of features is determined by running AQ on the correspondingly reduced training data sets and then measuring the classification accuracy of the rules produced by AQ on a testing data set using the weighted evaluation function described above. This fitness value is the key element in biasing the GA-based adaptive search of the space of feature subsets toward even more "fit" subsets.

17.4 EXPERIMENTAL RESULTS

The experiments described in this section were performed using two existing systems, GENESIS, a genetic algorithm package (Grefenstette, 1991), and AQ15, an AQ-based rule induction system (Michalski et al., 1986). Because each of these systems has a number of user-controlled parameters, the approach taken was to attempt to identify reasonable settings for these parameters and then hold them fixed for the entire set of experiments.

In the case of GENESIS, the standard parameter settings recommended in De Jong (1975) were used (a population size=50, a mutation rate=0.001, and a crossover rate=0.6) without any further experimentation. Preliminary experiments with AQ15 suggested that there were only a few parameters that significantly affected classification performance. Additional experiments were performed to find reasonable values for these parameters. The resulting settings (Mode=IC, Ambig=NEG, Trim=Spec, and Maxstar=13) were then used throughout all the experiments in conjunction with the standard default setting for the LEF function (which included a preference for small numbers of features).

The proposed multistrategy approach was tested on four texture images randomly selected from Brodatz's (1966) album of textures. These images are depicted in Figure 17.4. Two hundred feature vectors, each containing 18 features, were then randomly extracted from an arbitrary selected area of 30 by 30 pixels from each of the chosen textures. These feature vectors were divided equally between training examples used for the generation of decision rules and testing examples used to

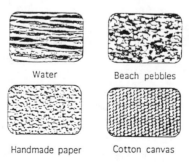

Water   Beach pebbles

Handmade paper   Cotton canvas

Figure 17.4:   The texture images used in the experiments

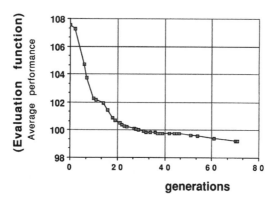

Figure 17.5:   The improvement in feature set fitness over time

measure the performance of the produced rules. In the experiments reported here, equal recognition weights (i.e., $W=1$) were assigned to all the texture classes.

The experimental results are summarized in Figure 17.5 and Table 17.1 and provide rather encouraging support for the adopted multistrategy approach. Figure 17.5 shows the steady improvement in the fitness of the feature subsets being evaluated as a function of the number of generations of the genetic algorithm. This indicates very clearly that the performance of rule induction systems (as measured by recognition rates) can be improved in these domains by appropriate feature subset selection.

Table 17.1 suggests that there are other advantages as well when one compares the results of the multistrategy approach with the best performance obtainable using AQ15 alone. The result of the feature selection process was to reduce the initial feature set consisting of 18 elements to a subset having only 9 elements for the best performing individual. This represented a 50% reduction in the number of features.

Another advantage of using this approach is that choosing the appropriate subset of features reduces the time required to perform rule induction on large data sets (which are typical in the image processing world). This is a direct result of the feature selection process. The time required to generate decision rules grows rather

Table 17.1:   Comparative results of the experiments

	Best Performance [0,200]	Size of Feature Set	Learning Time (sec)	Complexity (# complexes/class)
AQ	111.5	18	5.2	301.5
GA-AQ	95.5	9	3.3	211.5

quickly as a function of the number of features. Attempting rule learning on problems involving more than 50–100 features is generally computationally infeasible. Any significant reduction in the number of features used translates directly into reduced rule learning time, thus extending the applicability of these rule induction techniques to many problems that were previously computationally prohibitive.

Table 17.1 suggests one more benefit of this multistrategy approach. If one measures the complexity of the generated rules in terms of the number of complexes (conditions) per class, the feature selection process also reduces the complexity of generated class descriptions.

17.5 SUMMARY AND CONCLUSIONS

The experimental results obtained indicate the potential power of applying a multistrategy approach to the problem of learning rules for classification of texture images. The reported results indicate that an adaptive feature selection strategy using genetic algorithms can yield a significant reduction in the number of features required for texture classification and simultaneously produce improvements in recognition rates of the rules produced by a rule induction system (AQ15). In addition, the reduction of the number of features improved the execution time required for rule induction substantially. This is an important step toward the application of machine learning techniques for automating the construction of classification systems for difficult image processing problems.

More testing is needed in order to substantiate the results presented here. The robustness and scaling up characteristics of the presented system must be assessed with additional experiments involving more texture classes, larger feature sets, and more testing and training examples.

There are a number of interesting directions one might pursue in extending the ideas presented here. One extension has already been explored and described by Bala, De Jong, and Pachowicz (1994, Chapter 18 of this book), in which further improvements in classification performance can be achieved by using genetic algorithms to refine the AQ generated rules.

Another straightforward direction would be to use GAs with some background knowledge. For example, including user and/or expert provided estimates of the relative importance of various features for texture classification could further improve speed and performance.

A much more provocative but more difficult extension currently under development involves the addition of some form of constructive induction. That is, a more complex set of features could be constructed by including combinations of the given features in the initial set. The feature selection process could then be applied to this set in order to find even more effective feature subsets.

ACKNOWLEDGMENTS

This research was done in the Artificial Intelligence Center of George Mason University. The activities of the Center are supported in part by the Defense Advanced Research Projects Agency under grants administered by the Office of Naval Research, No. N00014-87-K-0874 and No. N00014-91-J-1854; in part by the Office of Naval Research under Grants No. N00014-88-K-0226, No. N00014-88-K-0397, No. N00014-90-J-4059, and No. N00014-91-J-1351; and in part by the National Science Foundation under Grant No. IRI-9020266.

The authors also wish to thank Dr. Pachowicz and Dr. Bala for their informative comments.

References

Bala, J.W., De Jong, K., and Pachowicz, P. "Learning Noise Tolerant Classification Procedures by Integration of Inductive Learning and Genetic Algorithms," *Machine Learning: A Multistrategy Approach*, Vol. IV, R.S. Michalski and G. Tecuci (Eds.), Morgan Kaufmann Publishers, San Mateo, CA, 1994.

Brodatz, P. "A Photographic Album for Arts and Design," Dover Publishing Co., Toronto, Canada, 1966.

De Jong, K. "Analysis of the behavior of a class of genetic adaptive systems," Ph.D. Thesis, Department of Computer and Communications Sciences, University of Michigan, Ann Arbor, MI, 1975.

————. "Learning with Genetic Algorithms: An Overview," *Machine Learning,* Vol. 3, 1988, pp. 121–138.

Dom, B., Niblack, W., and Sheinvald, J. "Feature Selection with Stochastic Complexity," *Proceedings of IEEE Conference on Computer Vision and Pattern Recognition*, IEEE Computer Society Press, Washington, DC, 1989, pp. 241–248.

Forsburg, S. "AQPLUS: An Adaptive Random Search Method for Selecting a Best Set of Attributes from a Large Collection of Candidates," Internal Report, Department of Computer Science, University of Illinios, Urbana-Champaign, 1976.

Foroutan, I., and Sklansky, J. "Feature Selection for Piece Wise Linear Classifiers," *Proceedings of IEEE Conference on Computer Vision and Pattern Recognition*, IEEE Computer Society Press, Washington, DC, 1985, pp. 149–154.

Grefenstette, J.J., David, L., and Cerys, D., *Genesis and OOGA: Two Genetic Algorithms Systems,* TSP: Melrose, MA, 1991.

Holland, J.H. "Adaptation in Natural and Artificial Systems," University of Michigan Press, Ann Arbor, MI, 1975.

Ichino, M., and Sklansky, J. "Optimum Feature Selection by Zero-One Integer Programming," *IEEE Transactions on Systems, Man, and Cybernetics*, Vol. 14, No. 5, 1984a, pp. 737–746.

Ichino, M., and Sklansky, J. "Feature Selection for Linear Classifiers," *Seventh International Conference on Pattern Recognition,* Vol. 1, July 30–Aug. 2, Montreal, Canada, IEEE, New York, 1984b, pp. 124–127.

Kittler, J. "Feature Selection Method Based on the Karhunen-Loeve Expansion," *Pattern Recognition Theory and Application*, Fu, K.S., and Whinston, A.B., Eds., Noordhoff-Leyden, Bondol, France, 1977, pp. 61–74.

———. "Feature set search algorithms," *Pattern Recognition and Signal Processing*, Chen, C.H., Ed., Sijthoff and Noordhoff, The Netherlands, 1978.

Lbov, G.S. "Wybor effektiwnosti sistemy zabisimych priznakow," in a collection of IM SO AN USSR Computer Systems, Nowosibivsk, Vol. 19, 1965.

Michalski, R.S., Mozetic, I., Hong, J.R., and Lavrac, N. "The Multi-purpose Incremental Learning System AQ15 and Its Testing Application to Three Medical Domains, *Proceedings of the Fifth National Conference on Artificial Intelligence,* AAAI, Menlo Park, CA, 1986.

Michalski, R.S., and Stepp, R.E. "Learning from Observation: Conceptual Clustering," *Machine Learning: An Artificial Intelligence Approach,* Michalski, R.S., Carbonell, J.G., and Mitchell, T. M. (Eds.), Tioga, Palo Alto, CA, 1983, pp. 331–363.

Tou, J.T., and Heyden, R.P. " Some Approaches to Optimal Feature Selection," *Computer and Information Sciences-II*, Tou, J.T. (Ed.), New York, Academic Press, 1967, pp. 57–89.

18

MULTISTRATEGY LEARNING FROM ENGINEERING DATA BY INTEGRATING INDUCTIVE GENERALIZATION AND GENETIC ALGORITHMS

Jerzy W. Bala
Kenneth A. De Jong
Peter W. Pachowicz
(George Mason University)

Abstract

The size and complexity of most engineering data and an inherent presence of noise in them pose significant difficulties for traditional concept learning systems. This chapter presents a multistrategy system that addresses these issues. The system integrates two forms of learning—inductive generalization and genetic algorithms—in a closed-loop fashion in order to achieve robust concept learning capabilities for a variety of difficult engineering-oriented classification tasks. The learning process cycles through two phases. In the first phase, initial concept descriptions are acquired by running a noise-tolerant extension of the familiar AQ rule induction system. The resulting concept descriptions are not, however, optimal from a performance point of view because of the strong AQ bias to generate simple, cognitively oriented descriptions. Therefore, in the second phase, the performance of the current set of descriptions is improved using a genetic algorithm. The tuned concept descriptions are then fed back to the inductive learning program for further simplification and refinement. The effectiveness of this multistrategy approach is illustrated on a set of difficult texture recognition problems taken from the field of computer vision.

18.1 INTRODUCTION

Engineering problems encompass a wide variety of tasks, including manufacturing automation, design automation, automated process planning, and vision-based automated manufacturing. Each of these tasks represents a practical application area for machine learning technology. At the same time, these engineering domains present significant challenges to traditional concept learning systems for several important reasons.

The principle source of difficulty lies in the size, complexity, and noise inherent in typical engineering data sets collected for purposes of concept learning. Consider, for example, the process of extracting sets of examples of various texture classes from low level pixel data for the purpose of learning texture classification rules. In real-world situations, noise occurs naturally at the input level because of the discretization of continuous image data and changing environmental conditions as a result of the properties of the camera (lens distortion) and of defective sensing elements. These noise sources are generally very difficult to model *a priori* in that their distributions are usually unknown and can change over time, thus making it difficult to develop noise filters.

Typically, from this already noisy pixel data, exemplar data sets are constructed in the form of vectors of real-valued features, resulting in non-systematic errors in the extracted feature values as well as in the class information of the exemplar data sets. This process tends to produce quite complex and irregular distributions of the extracted feature values and usually requires the construction of fairly large data sets in an attempt to "smooth out" the noise. It is, therefore, essential in such domains to develop approaches to concept learning that are able to work with large, noisy data sets (Quinlan, 1986; Chien et al., 1991; Pachowicz and Bala, 1991; Bergadano et al., 1992).

A second distinguishing feature of these engineering domains is that the learned concepts are used in recognition modules that are just one part of a much larger system. This means that the learned concepts must satisfy a number of important criteria above and beyond the traditional measures of cognitive simplicity and accuracy on a test set. We again take an example from image understanding: a texture recognition module uses the learned concepts to make classification decisions. These classification decisions are then used by other modules to draw borders between textured surfaces of objects. Next, surface areas are grouped into objects (e.g., bushes, roads, sky) and are analyzed at a more global level. To be effective in this context, the learned texture concepts must themselves be able to handle noisy data and must not be the source of additional noise to avoid propagation and amplification of errors to the higher levels.

In many practical applications, a system must also meet additional criteria related to overall recognition effectiveness. Examples of such criteria are recognition stability and full concept recognizability. Recognition stability is typically measured by the deviation of class recognition rates from the average recognition rate and reflects the requirement that there must be similar recognition levels for each class. By requiring high recognition stability of a system, for example, we prefer a situation where class A and class B are both recognizable on the same 80% level and discard a situation where class A is recognizable on 65% and class B on 95% level. A full concept recognizability criterion requires that a system must recognize all classes in the training sets at a high level. Even if a system fails to recognize only one class adequately (e.g., 30%), the criterion of full concept recognizability is not satisfied in spite of the fact that the system recognizes all other classes at a very high level.

In this chapter, a multistrategy system is presented that is designed to address the above issues. The presented system integrates two forms of learning—inductive generalization and genetic algorithms—in a closed-loop fashion in order to achieve robust concept learning capabilities for a variety of difficult engineering-oriented classification tasks. The learning process cycles through two phases. In the first phase, initial concept descriptions are acquired by running a noise-tolerant extension of the familiar AQ rule induction system. The resulting concept descriptions are not, however, optimal from a performance point of view because of the strong AQ bias to generate simple, cognitively oriented descriptions. Therefore, in the second phase, the performance of the current set of descriptions is improved using a genetic algorithm (GA). The tuned concept descriptions are then fed back to the inductive learning program for further simplification and refinement. The effectiveness of the developed multistrategy approach is illustrated on a difficult set of texture recognition problems taken from the field of computer vision.

18.2 INTEGRATING INDUCTIVE GENERALIZATION AND GENETIC ALGORITHMS

The difficulties discussed in the previous section provide the motivation for developing an integrated multistrategy learning system. However, in order for such a system be an improvement over single strategy systems, the incorporated strategies must be both compatible in the sense of being able to share concept descriptions and complementary in the sense that the strengths of one counterbalance some of the weakness of the others. In this section, we discuss the properties of two learning strategies: the traditional inductive generalization approach as typified by AQ-based rule induction systems (Michalski, 1983) and genetic algorithms (De Jong, 1988). We argue that they are well matched for use in a multistrategy system.

Inductive learning algorithms like AQ provide efficient strategies for acquiring simple, cognitively oriented concept descriptions. Typically, their efficiency is achieved via *a priori* models that guide the search toward building plausible concept descriptions and by incorporating a strong bias for simple descriptions. When the (presumably) unknown concepts are well matched to these assumptions, learning is fast and effective.

However, these same features can be a disadvantage in other contexts. The strong biases that produce efficient search can result in descriptions that are only locally optimal. Running the algorithm with reordered learning data or slightly different settings for search control parameters can produce strikingly different concept descriptions. If the learning data are noisy and/or the concepts to be learned are complex, the speed and effectiveness of the algorithm can be affected negatively by the simplicity bias. Similarly, in situations in which there is little or no *a priori* knowledge to guide the search, the speed and effectiveness of learning can fall off quickly.

Finally, inductive learning techniques generally work better on data sets carefully chosen to provide maximum information and no noise because there is usually a strong bias to produce concept descriptions that are complete and consistent with respect to the training set. The presence of noise tends to produce concept descriptions with lots of disjuncts, many of which cover only a few points. Attempting to be complete and consistent with randomly chosen training data leads to overfitting and to poor predictive performance on unseen examples.

Genetic algorithms, on the other hand, are general purpose adaptive search techniques that come with none of the traditional biases for searching the space of concept descriptions. Rather, use performance-oriented feedback to bias the search process in the direction of better performance. This generally results in a more global search procedure than traditional inductive methods but also means that the search time can be considerably longer. Unless explicit biases toward simplicity and consistency are included in the feedback function or in extensions to the algorithm, the concept descriptions produced by GAs will frequently be more complex than those produced by AQ-based systems and less consistent with the training data.

Because GAs maintain a population of samples, they are much less sensitive to noise than other techniques and have been shown to be effective in the presence of high noise levels without assuming any model of noise distribution prior to the learning (Fitzpatrick and Grefenstette, 1988).

This comparison of inductive learning strategies and genetic algorithms suggests that there is an opportunity to combine the two approaches so that the advantages of one learning method can be used to limit disadvantages of the other learn-

Final Concept Descriptions

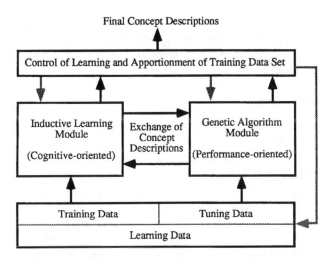

Figure 18.1: An architecture for multistrategy learning from engineering data that integrates inductive learning and genetic algorithms

ing method. The question still remains of how to integrate them in an effective way to achieve cooperative concept learning.

Our answer to this question is presented in Figure 18.1. The learning process cycles between two phases: an inductive learning phase and a genetic algorithm phase. In the inductive learning phase, cognitively oriented concept descriptions are produced in standard disjunctive normal form (DNF). In the GA phase, the performance of these concepts is improved using a set of tuning data. After the concepts are modified, they are refined again by the AQ algorithm, resulting in somewhat simpler descriptions. In this way, the learning loop is closed and two learning modules are able to exchange concept descriptions and improve them according to different criteria.

By combining inductive learning with genetic algorithms, the learned concept descriptions are no longer required to be complete and consistent with respect to the initial training data, which reduces overfitting problems and leads to better predictive performance. Also, the use of GAs reduces the effects of noise on the learned concept descriptions. The fact that the GA starts its search with plausible AQ-generated concept descriptions results in much shorter search times. Also, the performance-oriented GA search provides the ability to escape from some of the local minima traps resulting from AQ biases.

18.3 THE INDUCTIVE LEARNING MODULE

The inductive learning method used to acquire cognitively oriented concept descriptions is executed in two stages: first, inductive generalization and then concept optimization. The AQ learning program (Michalski, 1973, 1983) is used as the inductive generalization strategy. Concept optimization is then applied in an attempt to decrease the influence of noise on the learned concept descriptions (Pachowicz and Bala, 1991).

18.3.1 AQ Algorithm

The AQ algorithm constructs concept descriptions in a top-down fashion (Michalski, 1973, 1983). The system learns classification rules from preclassified sets of examples (events). Examples are observations from the problem domain, where each example is a vector of attribute-value pairs. The examples of a given class for which the algorithm is learning rules are called the positive examples. Other classes represent negative examples with respect to the selected class. AQ begins with the most general description (the empty, all inclusive conjunctive concept) and specializes the concept by adding one or more particular generalized selectors from the seed (a selected positive example) through the process known as *extend against*. The specialized concept covers fewer negative examples than the more general concept. When the concept is consistent (covers no negative events), it is saved in the current concept set by disjoining it with the previous disjuncts. Next, a new seed is selected from the set of positive examples that are not covered by any of the disjuncts in a concept set. The process continues until all positive examples are covered.

The *extend against* process is used to maximally generalize the values in a condition. To extend the seed value for an attribute against the set of values of the negative set for the attribute, the system determines the most general consistent value subrange for the attribute that includes the seed event's value on that attribute but does not intersect the negative set. In effect, each attribute of the seed is compared with the same attribute of a negative event. In case of linear attributes, *extend against* returns a range of values that include the value for the seed and immediately adjacent values not including the negative event's value. The results of extending the seed against each negative event are then combined by intersecting the values for each of the previous tests for each attribute. The system then selects these combined values to get a disjunct that covers the seed but none of the negative events.

The concept descriptions learned by the AQ algorithm are represented in VL_1, which is a simplified version of the Variable-Valued Logic System VL (Michalski, 1973) and are used to represent attributional concept descriptions. A description of a concept is a VL_1 expression in disjunctive normal form, where each disjunct has the form

[L # R]   (1)

where L is called the referee, which is an attribute; R is called the referent, which is a subset of values from the domain of the attribute L; and # is one of the following relational symbols: =, <, >, >=, <=, <>. The following is an example of an AQ disjunct (equality is used as a relational symbol):

$$[x1=1..3] \ [x2=1] \ [x4=0] \ [x6=1..7] \ [x8=1] \qquad\qquad (2)$$

18.3.2 The AQ-NT Learning Method

The AQ-NT learning method is an extension of the AQ algorithm and is intended to deal with some of the effects of noise on the concepts learned by AQ (Pachowicz and Bala, 1991). The objective is to optimize concept descriptions in two ways: (1) to improve the overall recognition effectiveness of learned descriptions and (2) to improve the generality of concepts fragmented by noisy data. The acquisition of concept descriptions (in the form of a set of decision rules) is performed in the following two phases.

Phase 1: Concept-driven Closed-Loop Filtration of the Training Data. This phase consists of a single loop that attempts to remove items from the data set that appear to contain noise. This process is composed of the following stages:

1. Induce an initial set of concept descriptions from the given dataset using the AQ learning program.
2. Truncate the concept descriptions by removing "least significant" disjuncts, that is, disjuncts that cover only a small portion of the training data.
3. Create a new training dataset that includes only training examples covered by the modified concept descriptions.
4. If the size of the dataset falls below an assumed percentage of the training data (that reflects an assumed error rate in the data), then go to Phase 2. Otherwise, return to step 1.

Phase 2: Acquire Concept Descriptions from the Improved Training Dataset Using the AQ Learning Program. A justification for Phase 1 is that the noise in the data is unlikely to constitute any strong patterns in the data and therefore will require separate disjuncts to account for it. Thus, the examples covered by the "light disjuncts" are likely to represent noise and therefore are removed from the dataset. Experiments with the AQ-NT learning approach (incorporating the NEWGEM program [AQ14] [Mozetic, 1985]) applied to computer vision problems involving texture recognition have shown that it systematically produces classification rules that perform better and also are much simpler in the sense that the number of learned disjuncts is significantly decreased.

18.4 THE GENETIC ALGORITHM MODULE

Genetic algorithms typically maintain a constant-sized population of candidate solutions, known as individuals (Holland, 1975; De Jong, 1988). Search proceeded in an efficient manner by exploiting the information contained in the individuals of the current population. An individual is evaluated and recombined with others on the basis of its overall quality or fitness. This process is iterative, and the expected number of times an individual is selected for recombination is proportional to its fitness relative to the rest of population. By allocating more reproductive occurrences to the above average individuals, the overall effect is an increase in the population's average fitness. New individuals are created using two main genetic recombination operators known as *crossover* and *mutation*. *Crossover* operates by selecting a random location in the genetic string of the parents and concatenating the initial segments of one parent with the final segment of the other parent to create a new child. A second child is simultaneously generated using the remaining segments of the two parents. *Mutation* provides for occasional disturbances in the crossover operation to ensure diversity in the genetic strings over long periods of time and to prevent stagnation in the search process. GAs have been shown to be very effective in situations where no *a priori* information is available about the properties of the space to be searched. In addition, they are quite insensitive to noise because they maintain at all times a population of search space samples.

18.4.2 Optimization of the Concept Descriptions Using Genetic Algorithms

GAs traditionally use fixed-length binary strings to representation individuals. However, if the effective cooperative learning between the AQ-NT module and the GA module must be achieved, it makes much more sense to have the GA work directly on the VL_1 expressions produced by AQ-NT. Fortunately, it is rather straightforward to extend the genetic operators to handle this more complex representation language.

The extended mutation operator is designed to introduce small changes to the condition parts of a selected disjunct of a given description. The conditions to be changed are chosen by randomly generating two pointers: the first one points to one of the disjuncts, and the second one points to a condition in this disjunct. Random changes are introduced to the left-most or right-most (this is also chosen randomly) value of this condition. For example, possible mutations of the condition [x1 = 10..23] might generate any of the following conditions: [x1 = 10..20], [x1 = 10..24], [x1 = 12..23] or [x1 = 8..23], as well as others. Such a mutation process samples the space of possible concept description boundaries to improve the performance criteria.

The second operator, crossover, is performed by splitting concept descriptions into two parts: upper disjuncts and lower disjuncts. These parts are exchanged between parent descriptions to produce a new child description. An example of crossover applied to two short, four-disjunct parent descriptions is depicted below:

Parent Description 1:

1   [x1=7..8] & [x2=8..19] & [x3=8..13] & [x5=4..54] & [x6=0..3] or
2   [x1=15..54] & [x3=11..14] & [x4=14..17] & [x6=0..9] & x7=0..11] or
————————————————crossover position ————————————————
3   [x1=9..18] & [x3=16..21] & [x4=9..10] or
4   [x1=10..14] & [x3=13..16] & [x4=14..54] & [x7=4..5]   (3)

Parent Description 2:

1   *[x3=18..54] & [x4=16..54] & [x5=0..6] & [x7=5..12] or*
2   *[x1=8..25] & [x3=8..13] & [x4=9..11] & [x5=0..3] or*
————————————————crossover position ————————————————
3   *[x4=0..22] & [x5=8..9] & [x6=0..7] & [x7=11..48] or*
4 · *[x2=5..8] & [x3=7..8] & [x4=8..11] & [x5=0..3]*   (4)

One of the Two Resulting Child Descriptions:

1   [x1=7..8] & [x2=8..19] & [x3=8..13] & [x5 =4..54] & [x6=0..3] or
2   [x1=15..54] & [x3=11..14] & [x4=14..17] & [x6=0..9] & [x7=0..11] or
3   *[x4=0..22] & [x5=8..9] & [x6=0..7] & [x7=11..48] or*
4   *[x2=5..8] & [x3=7..8] & [x4=8..11] & [x5=0..3]*   (5)

Concept descriptions are evaluated by calculating the degree of match between a given disjunct and an example. Because the degree of match of a given example depends on the degree of match to the "winning" disjunct of that description, the exchange process introduced by crossover enables inheritance of information about strong disjuncts (strongly matching) by the individuals of the next evolved population.

18.4.3 Performance Evaluation

The performance-oriented feedback provided for each concept in the current population is derived from a confusion matrix. The confusion matrix represents information on correct and incorrect classification results. This matrix is obtained by calculating the degree of flexible match between a tuning instance and a given class description. The row entries in the matrix represent a percentage of matched instances from a given class (row index) to all class descriptions (column index). Because some of the testing events can be matched flexibly by more than one class, the sum of the entries in a given row may be larger than 100%. Table 18.1 is an example of the confusion matrix for 12 classes used in our experiments.

Table 18.1: Confusion matrix for 12 classes of texture (average recognition = 74.67%, average mis-classification = 4.83% — from Bala, De Jong, and Pachowicz (1991a). Note: the sum of row entries may be larger than 100% because of multiple matches.

Test Classes	Learned Classes											
	C1	**C2**	**C3**	**C4**	**C5**	**C6**	**C7**	**C8**	**C9**	**C10**	**C11**	**C12**
C1	**45**	5	31	0	0	9	0	28	16	0	6	2
C2	5	**51**	3	12	0	16	1	17	7	0	17	2
C3	31	0	**80**	0	7	1	0	2	10	0	6	5
C4	0	25	0	**72**	0	14	0	12	0	0	1	10
C5	0	0	2	0	**99**	0	0	0	0	0	0	7
C6	8	11	3	25	0	**62**	0	28	0	0	12	1
C7	0	2	0	0	0	0	**98**	0	0	0	0	0
C8	19	14	8	2	1	59	0	**59**	3	0	5	0
C9	16	0	8	0	0	5	0	5	**87**	0	1	2
C10	0	0	1	0	0	0	0	0	2	**95**	0	0
_C11_	_16_	_4_	_32_	_10_	_0_	_4_	_0_	_4_	_2_	_0_	**_44_**	_7_
C12	0	0	0	4	0	0	1	0	0	0	2	**98**

The underlined entries represent the percentage of instances of class C11 (set of tuning instances) matched to learned descriptions of all 12 classes. If class C11 is to be optimized by GAs, we have to evaluate the performance of each individual from the population by calculating its performance to the other classes. Thus, we use the ratio of correct recognition rates to incorrect recognition rates as the performance evaluation measure of each individual of the population, i.e., the CC/MC ratio, where CC is an average recognition for correctly recognized classes (the average of the entries on the diagonal of the confusion matrix), and MC is an average mis-classification (the average of the entries outside the diagonal of the confusion matrix). For the above confusion matrix, CC/MC = 74.67/4.83 = 15.45.

The performance evaluation is based on computing a distance measure between an example (tuning or testing) and a rule. A flexible matching technique is applied to calculate such a distance. This distance measure takes any value in the range from 0 (i.e., does not match) to 1 (i.e., matches). The calculation of this distance measure for a single test instance is executed according to the following schema. For a given condition of a rule $[x_n = val_j]$ and an instance where $x_n = val_k$, the normalized distance measure is

$$1 - (\mid val_j - val_k \mid / \#levels) \tag{6}$$

where #levels is the total number of attribute values. The confidence level of a rule is computed by multiplying evaluation values of each condition of the rule. The total evaluation of class membership of a given test instance is equal to the confidence level of the best matching rule, i.e., the rule of the highest confidence value. For example, the confidence value c for matching the following complex of a rule

$$[x1 = 0] [x7 = 10] [x8 = 10..20] \tag{7}$$

with a given instance x = < 4, 5, 24, 34, 0, 12, 6, 25 > and the number of attribute values #levels=55 is computed as follows:

$$c_{x1} = 1 - (|0 - 4| / 55) = .928 \tag{8}$$
$$c_{x7} = 1 - (|10 - 6| / 55) = .928 \tag{9}$$
$$c_{x8} = 1 - (|20 - 5| / 55) = .91 \tag{10}$$
$$c_{x2}, c_{x3}, c_{x4}, c_{x5}, c_{x6} = 1 \tag{11}$$
$$c = c_{x1} * c_{x2} * c_{x3} * c_{x4} * c_{x5} * c_{x6} * c_{x7} * c_{x8} = 0.78 \tag{12}$$

Once all rule confidence levels have been computed, the recognition process decides class membership on the basis of the highest confidence level among the matched rules.

18.5 OVERALL SYSTEM ARCHITECTURE

The multistrategy system presented in this chapter is a loosely coupled integration of the two learning components discussed above. The overall architecture of the system is presented graphically in Figure 18.2.

The training data are split randomly into two separate datasets of learning examples. The first dataset serves as the training data for the inductive learning module of the system to generate cognitively oriented concept descriptions. The second dataset is used as tuning data by the genetic algorithm module to optimize rules according to the previously described performance criteria.

The cognitively oriented concept descriptions produced by AQ-NT from the initially provided training data are forwarded directly to the GA module, which then proceeds to optimize the concept descriptions according to the given performance criteria. The concept descriptions forwarded to the GA module are tested on the tuning data in order to acquire their performance evaluation. The "weakest" concept description is then identified and is used as input to the concept evolution system. The concept evolution system initializes the population with variations of this "weakest" concept description and uses a GA to find better performing variations of the description. Each candidate is evaluated jointly with rules describing other classes. The descriptions of the other classes are not simultaneously optimized. The best version found is used to replace the current "weakest" description. The effect of this approach is to improve the performance of the weakest concept description without weakening the others.

The modified set of class descriptions is returned back to the inductive learning module for further simplification. This is accomplished by an interface that performs concept-based data filtration. This filtration step uses the modified concept descriptions produced by the GA module to filter the training data that will be used in the next learning loop. In the filtration step, initial training examples are

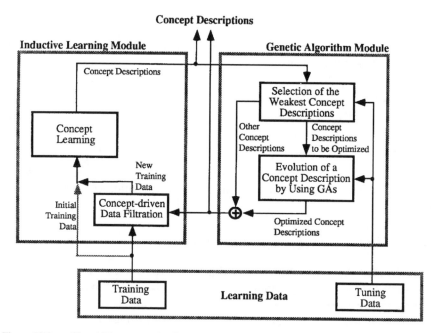

Figure 18.2:   Closed-loop cooperation between inductive learning and genetic algorithm modules

matched with the new set of rules. Examples that are covered by the new ruleset (examples that are consistent and complete with rules) form a new training dataset, which is input again to the AQ program. Examples not matched are discarded. In this way, the training dataset used by AQ-NT is modified over time in such a way that performance-oriented constraints in the training data set are preserved, and training examples that have a negative influence on learning performance-optimal rules are rejected.

The learning loop is repeated again but with the filtered set of training data. The expected overall effect of this multistrategy closed-loop learning approach is (i) a significant increase in the performance of the learned concepts and (ii) a significant decrease in the complexity of the concept descriptions.

18.6 EXPERIMENTAL RESULTS

The experimental validation of the developed multistrategy approach to learning from engineering data and the verification of the expected effects were done using a typical engineering problem involving object recognition (through texture characteristics) for computer vision. The texture data used in our experiments was composed of the 12 texture classes presented in Figure 18.3. Different texture areas

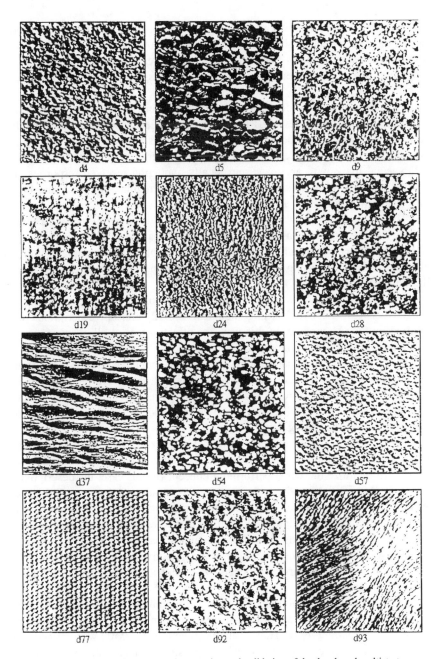

Figure 18.3: Texture images used in the experimental validation of the developed multistrategy learning approach (from Brodatz, 1966)

were provided for the learning and testing phases to secure an independent judgment of the experimental validation. Learning data (both training and tuning examples) were chosen randomly from indicated image areas. Testing examples for the recognition phase were extracted for the same 12 classes but from different image areas.

Examples of a given class were constructed using 8 attributes, and the attribute value extraction process was based on a modified version of Laws' method (Laws, 1980). In this method, texture attributes represent local texture energy at a given position on the image. The value of texture energy is calculated by convolving a special mask with an image and locally averaging received responses. The resulting attribute value is smoothed but still very irregular, complex, and highly noisy (Pachowicz and Bala, 1991).

The learning dataset was composed of 300 examples per class for 12 texture classes. The learning set was divided randomly into a group of training examples (200 examples per class) and a group of tuning examples (100 examples per class). An additional set of testing data of 200 examples per class was extracted from different image areas.

The testing phase was applied whenever (1) concept descriptions were exchanged between the two learning modules, and (2) concept descriptions were modified by the GA module. In this way, the effectiveness of all changes made to the ruleset was monitored continuously.

In the experiments reported here, the loop of inductive learning and genetic algorithms was run twice. The obtained experimental results are presented in Figure 18.4, in which white circles of the diagrams represent characteristics obtained for tuning data used to guide the genetic search, and the black circles represent characteristics for the testing data.

The experiments proceeded as follows. First, texture concepts were acquired by the AQ-NT program from 200 examples per class. Then, the GA module was activated to optimize the worst performing concept (in this case, the description of class d92). After 10 generations, the descriptions of all concepts were fed back to the inductive learning module, and the initial training dataset was filtered by the current set of concept descriptions. Examples that were not matched strictly by the rules were removed from the initial set. Examples that passed the matching criterion were forwarded to the next iteration of the inductive learning. After generating a new set of rules, the learned concepts were sent again to the GA module for further performance improvements.

The correct classification rate for class d92, obtained after two learning loops, was above 60%. That is a significant increase in comparison with 45% obtained from inductive learning only. The evaluation function (CC/MC) was defined to be the ratio of correct classifications to mis-classifications for all twelve texture classes. The CC/MC parameter was monitored for both tuning and testing data. An increase in CC/MC for the tuning data was observed. The CC/MC parameter for

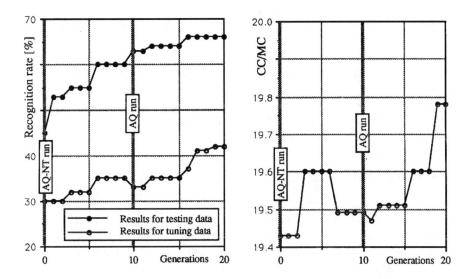

Figure 18.4:   Experimental results for two runs of the learning loop integrating inductive generalization and genetic algorithms

testing data remained at the same level. All three parameters (the recognition rate
of class d92, CC/MC for tuning data, and CC/MC for the testing data) indicate a
significant overall improvement in system performance.

It was also pleasing to note that the number of disjuncts in the optimized class
(d92) was reduced significantly from 36 disjuncts to 27 disjuncts, thus achieving an
improvement in simplicity as well as performance.

The effects on system performance due to running the GA for a larger number
of generations was also investigated. However, it appears that most of the improvement (both the decrease in complexity of the d92 class description and the increase
in performance) is obtained in a very few number of generations.

18.7 CONCLUSIONS

A novel approach to the acquisition of concept descriptions from real-world
engineering data has been presented. The approach is based on the idea of multistrategy learning, and the current system integrates symbolic inductive learning and
genetic algorithms in a loosely coupled closed-loop fashion. The result is a robust
concept learning system capable of learning simple, high performance descriptions
from large, complex datasets with inherent noise.

Although there exist substantial differences between symbolic induction
methods and genetic algorithms (learning algorithm, performance elements, knowl-

edge representation), their integration as presented in this chapter serves as a promising example that a better understanding of abilities of each approach can lead to novel and useful ways of combining them.

There are a number of directions for further research. The methodology must be tested on additional engineering problems presenting similar difficulties. More effective controls must be developed for the closed-loop cycles. The possibility of using constructive induction should be explored.

However, even in its present form the presented system is applicable to a wide range of difficult engineering problems.

ACKNOWLEDGMENT

This research was done in the GMU Center for Artificial Intelligence. Research of the Center is supported in part by the Defense Advanced Research Projects Agency under the grants administered by the Office of Naval Research, No. N00014-87-K-0874 and No. N00014-91-J-1854; in part by the Office of Naval Research under Grants No. N00014-88-K-0397, No. N00014-88-K-0226, and No. N00014-91-J-1351; and in part by the National Science Foundation Grant No. IRI-9020266.

References

Bala, J.W., DeJong, K., and Pachowicz, P.W. "Using Genetic Algorithms to Improve Performance of Classification Rules Produced by Symbolic Inductive Methods," in *Proceedings of the 6th International Symposium on Methodologies for Intelligence Systems,* Charlotte, NC, November, 1991(a).

————. "Learning Noise Tolerant Classification Procedures by Integrating Inductive Learning and Genetic Algorithms," in *Proceedings of the 1st International Workshop on Multistrategy Learning*, Harpers Ferry, WV, pp. 316–323, November 1991(b).

Bergadano, F., Matwin, S., Michalski, R.S., and Zhang, J. "Learning Two-Tiered Descriptions of Flexible Concepts: The POSEIDON System," *Machine Learning,* vol. 8, pp. 5–43, 1992.

Brodatz, P. *Textures: A Photographic Album for Artists and Designers,* Toronto, Dover Publishing, 1966.

Chien, S., Whitehall, B., Dietterich, T., Doyle, R., Falkenhainer, B., Garrett, J., and Lu, S. "Machine Learning in Engineering Automation," in *Proceedings of the 8th International Workshop on Machine Learning*, Evanston, IL, June 1991.

De Jong, K. "Learning with Genetic Algorithms: An Overview," in *Machine Learning,* vol. 3, no. 3, pp. 123–138, 1988.

Fitzpatrick, J.M., and Grefenstette, J. "Genetic Algorithms in Noisy Environments," in *Machine Learning,* vol. 3, pp. 101–12, 1988.

Holland, J. *Adaptation in Natural and Artificial Systems,* The University of Michigan Press, Ann Arbor, MI, 1975.

Laws, K.I. "Textured Image Segmentation," Ph.D. Thesis, Dept. of Electrical Engineering, University of Southern California, Los Angeles, 1980.

Michalski, R.S. "AQVAL/1—Computer Implementation of a Variable-Valued Logic System VL1 and Examples of Its Application to Pattern Recognition," in *Proceedings of the 1st International Joint Conference on Pattern Recognition*, October 30, Washington DC, 1973.

————. "A Theory and Methodology of Inductive Learning," in *Machine Learning: An Artificial Intelligence Approach,* R. Michalski, J. Carbonell, and T. Mitchell (eds.), Tioga Publishing, Palo Alto, CA, pp 83–134, 1983.

Mozetic, I. 1985. "NEWGEM: Program for Learning from Examples. Program Documentation and User's Guide," *Report of the Computer Science Department*, University of Illinois at Urbana-Champaign, UIUCDCS-F-85-040, 1985.

Pachowicz, P.W., and Bala, J. 1991. "Improving Recognition Effectiveness of Noisy Texture Concepts through Optimization of Their Descriptions," in *Proceedings of the 8th International Workshop on Machine Learning*, Evanston, IL, pp. 625–629, June 1991.

———— "Texture Recognition Through Machine Learning and Concept Optimization," *Report of Machine Learning and Inference Laboratory,* George Mason University, MLI91-6, 1991.

Quinlan, J.R. "Induction of Decision Trees," in *Machine Learning* vol. 1, no. 1, Kluwer Academic Publishers, 1986.

19

COMPARING SYMBOLIC AND SUBSYMBOLIC LEARNING:

Three Studies

Janusz Wnek
Ryszard S. Michalski
(George Mason University)

Abstract

This chapter reports on three studies comparing symbolic and subsymbolic methods for concept learning from examples. The first study compared five learning methods, three representing symbolic learning paradigm—decision tree learning (C4.5), rule learning (AQ15), and constructive rule learning (AQ17-HCI)—and the other two representing the subsymbolic paradigm—neural net learning using backpropagation (BpNet) and a classifier system employing genetic algorithm (CFS). All methods have been applied experimentally to learn several different *DNF-type* concepts (i.e., concepts representable by a simple DNF expression). The second study compared performance of a large number of learning programs on learning DNF-type concepts from data with and without noise and a non-DNF-type "m-of-n" concept. The third study compared genetic algorithm based learning (GABIL and Adaptive GABIL) with decision tree learning (C4.5) and decision rule learning (AQ14), on twelve DNF-type concepts. All studies have shown that generally, symbolic methods, in particular those applying constructive induction, outperformed subsymbolic methods in learning DNF-type concepts from data both without and with noise. In case of learning non-DNF-type concepts, symbolic methods without constructive induction performed worse, but those with constructive induction matched the performance of neural network methods.

19.1 INTRODUCTION

In view of a rapidly growing interest in multistrategy learning systems, it is important to develop insights into the performance of diverse learning methods and paradigms and to determine the areas of their most desirable applicability. To this end, this chapter presents various studies of the performance of symbolic and subsymbolic methods as applied to the same learning problems. The first study (Sections 19.2–19.4) involved a comparison of three symbolic and two subsymbolic methods. Symbolic methods were represented by C4.5, a decision tree learning program; AQ15, a decision rule learning program; and AQ17-HCI, a constructive decision rule learning program. Subsymbolic methods were represented by CFS, a genetic algorithm based classifier system, and BpNet, a neural network learning program using backpropagation algorithm. The other two studies (Sections 19.5–19.6) involved the same programs or their different variants.

An important difference between symbolic and subsymbolic learning approaches lies in the cognitive aspects of the employed knowledge representation. Knowledge represented by logic-based rules or decision trees (especially when the latter are small) is relatively easy to comprehend and relate to human knowledge. This is not the case with knowledge represented by classifier systems or neural networks. Although for some applications, it may not be important that the learned concept descriptions are understandable to people, e.g., in an adaptive controller of house temperature, in some other applications, e.g., in expert systems for human disease diagnosis, business or military decision making, this requirement is crucial.

Despite various attempts, there is no established universal measure of cognitive comprehensibility of concept representations (Michalski, 1983). Therefore, we will make a simplifying assumption that the comprehensibility of a concept can be estimated roughly by the number of rules needed to express it or the number of disjuncts in an equivalent DNF expression. In this measure, called the *R-complexity (rule-complexity)* of a concept, elementary conditions in the rules representing a concept (or the components of disjuncts in DNF) are assumed to be simple conditions involving *given* attributes. Based on this definition, one can distinguish between two general classes of concepts:

1. Concepts that can be expressed by a simple DNF expression using given attributes (or described by only few rules): we call them *DNF-type* concepts.
2. Concepts that require a very complex DNF expression: we call them *non-DNF-type*.

It is important to point out that concepts that have a long DNF expression using given attributes may have a short DNF expression if these attributes are replaced by other attributes or are transformed into certain combined attributes through the process of constructive induction (e.g., Wnek and Michalski [1991]). Thus, whether a given concept is DNF-type or not depends on the attributes (generally, descriptors)[1] that are available for constructing a concept representation. In other words, the R-complexity is defined with regard to the assumed concept representation space.

All three studies compared several methods by applying them to learning the same class of DNF-type concepts. We found that concepts generated by human subjects who are asked to create classes of entities and to express them linguistically usually fall into such a category. Given a concept representation, its R-complexity can thus be viewed as an approximate indication of the "cognitive" complexity of the concept. For representations other than rule-based, the R-complexity can be determined by converting them to logically equivalent sets of rules. When the description spaces are not too large, this can be done using the DIAV concept visualization method, outlined in Section 19.3.

Presented studies follow several other efforts to compare different learning methods and paradigms. For example, Fisher and McKusick (1989) compared ID3 and a neural net using a backpropagation (BP) algorithm on the problems of learning diagnostic rules for thyroid diseases, soybean plant diseases, and a few artificial problems. The comparison was based on the performance accuracy of descriptions as applied to testing examples and the training time. Their conclusion was that the neural net gave a better performance but required a significantly longer training time and more training examples than ID3.

Mooney et al. (1989) compared ID3 with perceptron and a backpropagation algorithm using the domain of soybean diseases, chess-end games, audiological disorders, and the Nettalk data set. Their conclusion was that the accuracy of classifying new examples was about the same for all three systems, but the neural net performed better than ID3 when there was noise in the data. Weiss and Kapouleas (1989) compared ID3, predictive value maximization, neural net using BP, and a few statistical methods. They found that the statistical classifiers performed consistently better in terms of accuracy in classifying testing examples.

Dietterich, Hild, and Bakiri (1990) compared ID3 with a neural net using BP on the task of text-to-speech mapping. Their major conclusion was that the neural net consistently outperformed ID3 in terms of the performance accuracy and attributed this result to the capture of better statistical information by the neural net.

Bergadano et al. (1992) compared POSEIDON (an extended version of AQ15 using a *two-tiered* concept representation) with exemplar-based and decision tree learning programs. Their study involved two real-world domains: labor contracts and U.S. congressional voting. In this study, descriptions learned by POSEIDON outperformed those produced by all other methods, both in terms of performance accuracy on new examples and in terms of the description's simplicity.

---

[1] By descriptor is meant an attribute or function whose value characterizes the entity.

The first study presented here differs from the above studies in that it experimentally analyzes five different methods and compares the learned descriptions in terms of their *exact error rate*, rather than a statistical error estimate, and also in terms of their R-complexity. In the study, the target and learned concepts were represented graphically by a novel technique of *diagrammatic visualization* (Wnek and Michalski, 1994). This technique permits one to display an *image* of the target and learned concepts and an *error image* that identifies all errors.

The chapter consists of seven sections. Section 19.2 briefly describes the five learning systems used in the first study. Section 19.3 presents the methodology used to compare the methods and describes training data and the concepts to be learned (five DNF-type concepts created by human subjects). The concepts are illustrated by the diagrammatic visualization technique (DIAV). Section 19.4 describes results of experiments with the methods. Sections 19.5 and 19.6 summarize two related studies done by other research groups. The first one involved three types of problems: learning a DNF-type concept, learning a non-DNF-type concept, and learning a DNF-type concept from noisy data. The results were obtained using a large number of learning programs, which were grouped into four categories according to the representational paradigms used: decision tree, decision rules, neural networks, and inductive logic programming (Thrun et al., 1991). The second study applied a decision tree learning program, a decision rule learning program, and two genetic algorithm-based programs to learn twelve DNF-type concepts (the original study was done by Spears and Gordon [1991]). Section 19.7 summarizes results from the comparison of the systems in learning DNF-type concepts.

19.2 LEARNING SYSTEMS INVOLVED IN THE FIRST STUDY

As mentioned earlier, the symbolic paradigm is represented by a decision tree learning program, C4.5, and two rule learning programs, AQ15 and AQ17-HCI. The subsymbolic paradigm is represented by a backpropagation neural network, BpNet, and a classifier system based on genetic algorithm, CFS. These programs are widely known and well described in machine learning literature. To serve the tutorial purpose of the book, we provide here a brief account of the basic algorithm underlying each program and give references to the literature for readers interested in further details.

19.2.1 Decision Tree Learning Program C4.5

C4.5 learns concepts by building a decision tree that correctly classifies supplied examples of the concepts. Each interior node of the tree is assigned an attribute, and the leaf nodes are assigned concept names. A branch down from an interior node represents a value of the attribute assigned to the node. Any path from the root to a leaf in the tree can be viewed as a decision rule for the class assigned to the leaf.

The input to the algorithm consists of sets of training examples for different concepts (or decision classes). In the first step, the algorithm selects a random subset of training examples from each set (a "window"). Then, for each attribute, the information gain, i.e., the information gained if the attribute were chosen for testing, is computed. The attribute with the highest score is assigned to the root node of the tree. Branches from this node represent different values of this attribute. End-nodes of these branches (current leaves) are assigned subsets of examples in which the attribute takes the value associated with the given branch. If a subset contains examples of only one decision class, then the end-node becomes a leaf of the decision tree. For all other subsets, the algorithm is repeated until all leaves in the tree are assigned single decision classes.

At this point, the created tree correctly classifies all examples in the window. Now the tree is used to classify remaining examples from the training set (outside the "window"). If the tree gives the correct answer for all examples, then the process terminates. If not, misclassified examples are added to the window, and the process continues until the trial decision tree correctly classifies all examples not in the window.

The entire process is repeated by default 10 times, and the best decision tree is selected. Because the examples used in the experiments had no noise, decision trees were not pruned. The C4.5 program (Quinlan, 1993) is a derivative of the ID3 program (Quinlan, 1986). In addition to decision tree generating, C4.5 is able to convert an unpruned decision tree into sets of generalized (pruned) decision rules. A tree is converted to rules by forming a rule corresponding to each path from the root of the tree to each of the leaves. All rules are then examined and some of them are generalized (pruned) by shopping conditions. Next, rules for each class are considered separately and redundant rules are removed. For uncovered examples, a default class is assigned.

We have tested all three representations learned by C4.5 using default parameter setting, i.e., the best tree was selected out of ten generated from the same training set, attributes were selected according to **gainratio** (ratio of information gain and potential information) criterion. As expected, because the training examples did not have noise, on average, unpruned decision trees performed best in terms of predictive accuracy. Pruned decision trees and decision rules were simpler but more erroneous. Thus, here we report the results obtained for unpruned decision trees only.

19.2.2 Rule Learning Program AQ15

The AQ15 program generates concept descriptions from concept examples. The descriptions are in the form of decision rules expressed in an attributional logic calculus, called *variable-valued logic*, VL1 (Michalski, 1973). A distinct feature of this representation is that it employs, in addition to standard logic operators, the *internal disjunction* operator (a disjunction of values of the same attribute), which can significantly simplify rules involving multivalued attributes. The program can optimize the rules according to a user-defined (or default) preference criteria, such as the overall simplicity or the evaluation and/or storage cost of the rules. The main procedure of AQ15 is based on the AQ algorithm that builds a concept description from a set of positive and negative examples (e.g., Michalski [1973]). Below is a simplified version of the AQ algorithm:

1. Randomly select a *seed* example from the set of positive training examples of the concept to be learned.
2. Generate a set of most general rules (a *star*) that cover the seed, and do not cover any negative examples (this operation employs the *extension against* generalization operator (Michalski, 1983).
3. Select the "best rule" from the star (according to the assumed preference criteria), and remove examples covered by this rule from the set of training examples.
4. If the set of training examples does not become empty, return to Step 1. Otherwise, the obtained set of rules constitutes a complete and consistent concept description.

The algorithm is repeated for each concept to be learned. It is biased toward finding a conjunctive description of a concept (a single rule) because if such a description exists for the given set of examples, it will be found in the very first step (the description will be a member of the first star generated). The AQ15 program has various parameters whose default values can be changed by a user according to the requirements of the domain. In all the experiments reported here, the preference criteria were to minimize both the number of rules and the number of conditions in them for each concept learned. Because training examples did not have noise, there was no need for any rule truncation procedure. For further details, see Michalski et al. (1986) and Bergadano et al. (1992).

19.2.3 Constructive Rule Learning Program AQ17-HCI

AQ17-HCI represents a recent major advance in the development of the AQ-based series of inductive learning programs, specifically, the above-described AQ15 system. The main new feature of it is an incorporation of a method for *hypothesis-driven constructive induction* (HCI). Constructive induction, as introduced by Michalski (1978), addresses the problem of changing the representation space so that it is more suitable for the learning problem at hand. This involves creating new attributes (or descriptors) that better characterize the concepts to be learned than the original descriptors. The last few years have witnessed an increasing interest in constructive induction methods because they can produce concept descriptions that are more accurate and/or simpler than the traditional *selective* induction methods (Pagallo and Haussler, 1990; Rendell and Seshu, 1990; Wnek and Michalski, 1991).

The HCI method generates problem-relevant descriptors by analyzing consecutively created inductive hypotheses (Wnek and Michalski, 1991). Below is a brief description of the algorithm used in AQ17-HCI. For the sake of simplicity, it is assumed that the training set consists of subsets of positive examples E^+ and negative examples E^-. If the training set consists of subsets representing different concepts, then E^+ represents the subset of training examples for the concept under consideration, and the union of the remaining subsets plays the role of E^-.

1. Divide randomly each of the training sets, E^+ and E^-, into two subsets: the primary set E_p and the secondary set E_s. $E^+ = E_p^+ \cup E_s^+$. $E^- = E_p^- \cup E_s^-$. (The primary training subset is to be used for rule generation, and the secondary subset is to be used for rule verification).

2. For each concept, induce the most specific (ms) cover of the set E_p^+ against the set E_p^-. (Such a cover is denoted COV_{ms} (E_p^+ / E_p^-) and represents the set of the most specific rules that characterize examples in E_p^+ but no examples in E_p^-).

3. Evaluate the performance of the rules on the secondary training set, E_s. If the performance exceeds a predefined threshold, or all changes in the representation space were exhausted, go to Step 8.

4. Analyze the rules in order to identify possible changes in the representation space.

5. Change the representation space by removing irrelevant attribute values or attributes or by adding new attribute values or attributes.

6. Modify the training set of examples, E, according to the changes in the representation space.

7. Go to Step 2.

8. For each concept, induce a set of the most specific rules from all positive examples against all negative examples, i.e., a cover COV_{ms} (E^+ / E^-), and the most general cover of negative examples against positive examples, COV_{mg} (E^- / E^+).

9. Build final concept descriptions by generalizing the most specific positive rules against the most general negative rules, i.e., COV_{mg} $(COV_{ms}$ $(E^+ / E^-) / COV_{mg}$ $(E^- / E^+))$.

The AQ17-HCI program has two important features that place it within the class of multistrategy learning methods. The first one is an ability to change the representation space using HCI. This means that the method uses additional knowledge transmutations allowing abstraction and concretion, apart from inductive generalization and specialization (Michalski, 1994, Chapter 1 of this book). The second feature is an extended generalization heuristic, employed in steps 8 and 9, that additionally generalizes the most specific generalization of the training set. This extension was proposed by Wnek (1992).

19.2.4 Neural Net Program BpNet

A neural network is defined by a set of processing units. Units can be of three types: input, output, and hidden. The hidden units provide communication links between input and output units in the task of translating the input training/testing example into output classification.

Backpropagation, as originally introduced (Rumelhart, Hinton and Williams, 1986), is a learning algorithm for feed-forward networks (networks in which the interconnections form no feedback loops) based on gradient minimization. We consider a network of units in which a weighted sum of the inputs is performed, the result of this sum (also called the activation level of the unit) being fed through a non-linear element, with a differentiable input-output function, e.g., a sigmoid function.

Learning by backpropagation involves two phases. During the first phase, an example is presented and propagated forward through the network to compute the output values o_n for each unit. These outputs are then compared with the target values t_n, resulting in output errors e_n for each unit. The second phase involves a backward pass through the network (analogous to the initial forward pass) during which the error message is passed to each unit in the network, and the appropriate weight changes are made.

The two phases are repeated until the overall error reaches a predefined level. The output error for a given training example is given by

$$e_n = o_n - t_n$$

Where o_n and t_n are the output and the target values of the output unit n. The total squared error for that input example is

$$E = \sum_{n \in U} e_n^2$$

Where U denotes the set of input units. Thus, learning by backpropagation corresponds to gradient minimization of the average squared error. The average is computed over all examples in a given training set. The BpNet program is an implementation of the backpropagation algorithm (McClelland and Rumelhart, 1988).

19.2.5 Classifier System CFS

A classifier system is a parallel rule-based (production) system that was first introduced by Holland and Reitman (1978). The rules, called classifiers, have the same simple form, so it is easy to determine whether a condition part of a rule is satisfied. Because the rules can be active simultaneously, complex situations are expressed by combinations of rules. The classifiers can be modified by a general-purpose learning system (Holland, 1986; Riolo, 1988).

Classifier system learning and classification are done in cycles. In each cycle, an input example is translated into a message that has the same form as the condition part of the rules. Next, the message is compared with all rules. All matched rules compete with each other in order to become active and to yield new messages. The new messages can either store some intermediate information and then be used in the next cycle or produce a final classification if matched with the system's effectors. During the learning cycles, the final classification is compared with the target class of the example, and payoff is distributed among active rules. Payoff changes the rules' strength and bidding chances in the next cycle. In order to supplement the learning process, some classifier systems utilize genetic algorithms. The genetic operators (e.g., crossover, mutation) provide means for rule evolution.

The shell for the classifier system used in the experiments was developed by Riolo (1988). The CFS package of subroutines and data structures is domain independent and provides routines to perform the major cycle of the classifier system. The CFS system was run in the stimulus-response mode, i.e., without generating internal messages. Training cycles were repeated fifty times for each example. Payoff for correct and incorrect answers was set to 6 and –1, respectively, with a full payoff paid to all active classifiers. Final classification was produced by two effectors. The CFS package uses more then 150 control parameters. The population size of sixty classifiers, the number of training cycles, the payoff, and about 20 other parameters were determined experimentally. The remaining parameters were set to default values.

19.3 METHODOLOGY

The testing domain in this study is the world of robot-like figures in the EMERALD[2] system. For simplicity's sake, the robots are described by just six multivalued attributes (Figure 19.1A). The attributes are Head Shape, Body Shape,

---

[2] EMERALD is a large-scale system integrating several different learning programs for the purpose of education and research in machine learning (Kaufman, Michalski, and Schultz, 1989). It was developed at the Center for Artificial Intelligence at George Mason University. An earlier version, ILLIAN, was developed at the University of Illinois at Urbana-Champaign.

Smiling, Holding, Jacket Color, and Tie and can have 3, 3, 2, 3, 4, and 2 values, respectively. Consequently, the size of event space (the space of all possible robot descriptions) is $3 \times 3 \times 2 \times 3 \times 4 \times 2 = 432$. The space of all possible concepts in this representation space is $2^{432}-1$ ($\approx 10^{143}$). Undergraduate computer science students unfamiliar with machine learning were asked to create five concepts from a predefined set of robots in the EMERALD system (16 examples). Each concept represented a certain class of imaginary robots. Below are descriptions of the concepts ("Target concepts") used in the experiments with the total numbers of positive and negative examples:

C1:	*Head is round and jacket is red*	or	*head is square and is holding a balloon*	(84 positive, 348 negative)
C2:	*Smiling and is holding balloon*	or	*smiling and head is round*	(120 positive, 312 negative)
C3:	*Smiling and not holding sword*			(144 positive, 288 negative)
C4:	*Jacket is red and is wearing no tie*	or	*head is round and is smiling*	(117 positive, 315 negative)
C5:	*Smiling and holding balloon*	or	*holding sword*	(144 positive, 288 negative)

Each such concept represents a partitioning of the event space into robots that belong to the concept (positive examples) and those that do not (negative examples). Based on the concepts C1–C5 the students generated initial sets of training examples used in Experiment 1. Each initial training set consisted of approximately 6% of all positive examples (Pos1) and 3% of all negative examples (Neg1). The remaining sets for Experiments 2–5 were generated by adding to the initial set an appropriate number of randomly generated examples: Pos2 and Neg2 (10% positive and 10% negative), Pos3 and Neg3 (15% positive and 10% negative), Pos4 and Neg4 (25% positive and 10% negative), and Pos5 and Neg5 (100% positive and 10% negative). These additional experiments were performed in order to observe the convergence of the learned concepts to the target concepts.

The concepts C1–C5 are presented graphically in Figures 19.1B and 19.2 using a method for *diagrammatic visualization*. This method employs a *General Logic Diagram* (GLD) that is a planar representation of a multi-dimensional space spanned over multi-valued discrete attributes[3] (Michalski, 1973; Wnek and Michalski, 1993). Each cell in the diagram represents a combination of the attribute val-

---

[3]The system DIAV implementing the visualization method (Wnek and Michalski, 1993) permits one to directly display description spaces with as many as 10^6 cells (e.g., about twenty binary attributes). Larger spaces can also be displayed, but their representations have to be projected to subspaces.

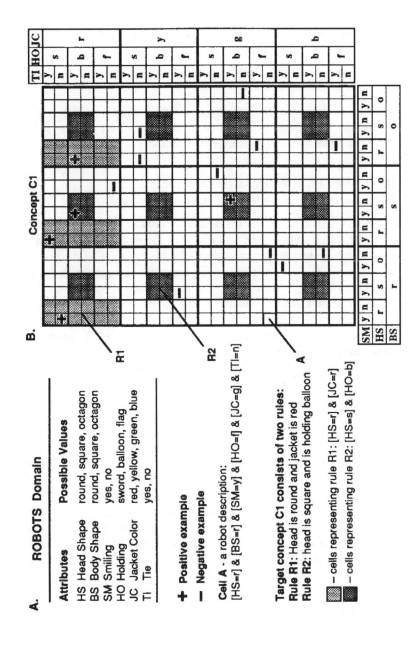

Figure 19.1: (a) Description of the ROBOTS domain; (b) A visualization of the target concept C1 and the initial training examples.

499

ues, e.g., a concept example. For example, the cell A in Figure 19.1B represents the following robot description:

> **H**ead Shape = round, **B**ody Shape = round, **SM**iling = yes, **HO**lding = flag, **J**acket Color = green, **TI**e = no

Positive and negative training examples are marked with + and −, respectively. Concepts are represented as sets of cells. The concept C1 can be viewed as consisting of two rules. They are represented in the diagram by shaded areas marked R1 and R2.

> R1: **H**ead Shape is round *and* **J**acket Color is red.
> R2: **H**ead Shape is square *and* is **HO**lding balloon.

An important advantage of the diagrammatic visualization is that it permits one to display steps in learning processes as well as the errors in concept learning. The set of cells representing the target concept (the concept to be learned) is called *target concept image (T)*. The set of cells representing the learned concept is called *learned concept image (L)*. The areas of the *target concept* not covered by the *learned concept* represent *errors of omission (T \ L)*, and the areas of the learned concept not covered by the target concept represent *errors of commission (L \ T)*. The union of both types of errors represents the *error image*. In the diagrams, errors are marked by slanted lines.

Target and learned concepts are represented in the diagrams by shaded areas. However, if the target and learned concepts are both visualized in the same diagram, then the shaded areas represent learned concept. The location of the target concept is implicitly indicated by correctly learned concept and errors of omission. Because errors of commission are part of a learned concept, corresponding areas on the diagram are both shaded and slanted. Errors of omission are not part of the learned concept: thus, the corresponding slanted areas remain white in the background. The parts of the target concept that were correctly learned are shaded only.

The descriptions learned by the methods were compared in terms of the *exact error rate*, a representation-independent complexity. *Exact error rate* is the ratio between exact error and the size of event space. It is measured as a function of the number of training examples. *Exact error* is defined as the total number of errors of omission and errors of commission or, equivalently, the cardinality of the set-difference between the union and the intersection of the target and learned concepts.

$$Exact\_error\_rate = \frac{Exact\_error}{\#Event\_space}$$

$$Exact\_error = \# \, [(T \setminus L) \cup (L \setminus T)] = \# \, [(T \cup L) \setminus (T \cap L)]$$

There are many ways to define error rates in order to reflect certain inductive capabilities of a learning system. In the definition above, for simplicity, we do not

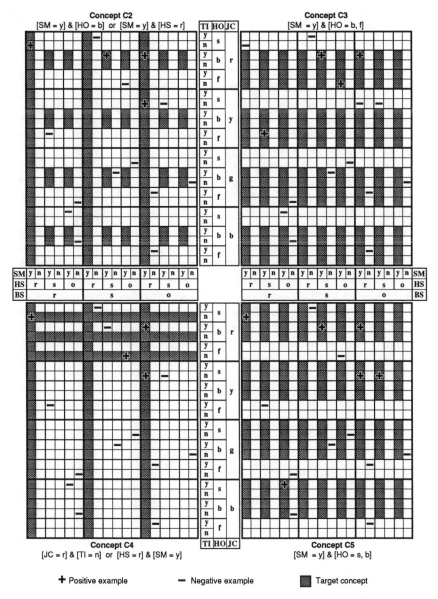

Figure 19.2:   A visualization of the target concepts C2, C3, C4, and C5 and the initial training examples for each concept

make any distinction between errors of omission and errors of commission, which may be important in some real-world domains. Also, the domain is small and well-structured, thus suited to the representation of the specific objects of the domain. Therefore, we can avoid the well-known Hempel's paradox in which confirmation of a concept can be made by the lack of satisfaction of non-examples (Hempel, 1965; Kodratoff, 1994, Chapter 3 of this book).

In order to get complete insight into the performance of the tested methods, we used all examples from the event space to test the performance. Note, however, that training examples are often excluded from the testing phase. The same kind of testing was also used in the remaining two studies.

In addition to the exact error rate, we used a representation-dependent *R-complexity* (rule complexity) measure of a method performance. The *R-complexity* of a concept representation is defined by the number of conjunctive statements (rules) in the minimal DNF expression that is logically equivalent to the given representation. Because finding such a minimal DNF expression for any given representation may be difficult (it is generally an NP-hard task), we use an estimate of the R-complexity. For a method that learns a rule-based representation, the number of rules generated by the method is taken as such an estimate. For example, the R-complexity of the C1–C5 target concepts is 2, 2, 1, 2, and 1, respectively. For a decision tree learning method, the R-complexity is estimated by the number of leaves in the tree (because each leaf corresponds to a rule). For neural nets and classifiers, the R-complexity is estimated by determining the number of conjunctive statements needed to re-express the learned concept as a DNF expression.

19.4 EXPERIMENTS IN THE ROBOTS DOMAIN

19.4.1 Representations Learned

Figure 19.3 presents an example of representations learned by each method. In the figure, the representations were learned in Experiment 1 from 6% positive and 3% negative examples of the target concept C1:

Head is round and jacket is red, or head is square and is holding a balloon.

A Decision Tree Generated by C4.5. Figure 19.3A shows the best, unpruned decision tree selected out of ten different trees generated from the training set. The learned concept is described using two attributes: Jacket Color and Head Shape. The learned concept can be read as follows:

IF Jacket Color is red, and Head Shape is round or
    Jacket Color is red, and Head Shape is square or
    Jacket Color is green, and Head Shape is square
THEN C1

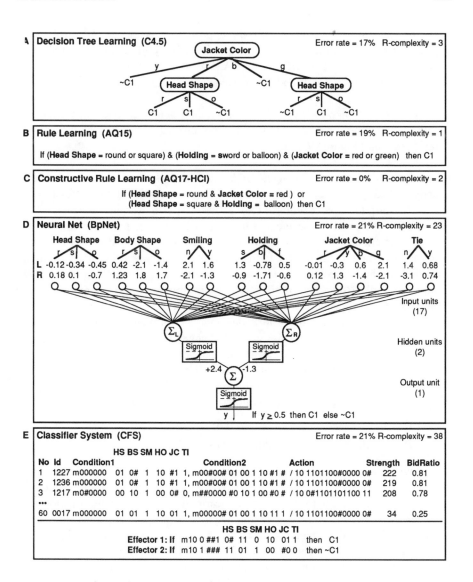

Figure 19.3: Representations of the concept C1 learned by different methods (from the initial set of examples consisting of 6% of positive and 3% of negative examples)

The exact error rate is 16.7% and the R-complexity of this tree is 3. After pruning, the tree is reduced to a root labeled ~C1. Such a tree classifies all examples as not belonging to concept C1 and, thus, produces 84 omission errors (19.4% error rate). The R-complexity of the tree is 1. The third representation learned by

C4.5 are decision rules obtained from the unpruned decision tree. After rule pruning and simplification, the final outcome consists of two rules: (1) If Head Shape is octagonal, THEN ~C1. (2) DEFAULT CLASS is ~C1. These rules are equivalent to the pruned decision tree and produce the same errors. The R-complexity is 2.

A Decision Rule Generated by AQ15. The method generated one rule. It consists of three conditions. Each condition tests one attribute. The internal disjunctions simplify the rule (Figure 19.3B).

A Decision Rule Generated by AQ17-HCI. The rule learned by AQ17-HCI is exactly the target concept (Figure 19.3C). It was generated in a transformed, smaller description space. Figure 19.4 shows steps in learning concept C1 by AQ17-HCI. The input to the method is a set of training examples in the original representation space, as shown in diagram A (the diagram also shows the target concept). The method divides the training set into primary and secondary examples and employs the AQ15 learning algorithm to induce rules from the primary set of training examples (diagram B). Because the performance test on the secondary training set is not satisfactory, the representation space is reduced to contain relevant attributes only, i.e., those attributes that are present or significant in the induced hypothesis. Therefore, the method changes ROBOTS original representation space by removing three irrelevant attributes: Body Shape, SMiling, and TIe (diagram C). In the new representation space, the number of training examples is decreased by 1. It is because two positive examples, E1 and E2, from the original event space have the same description in the new event space.

> **E1:** (**round**, round, yes, **sword**, **red**, no)
> **E2:** (**round**, square, yes, **sword**, **red**, yes)

Although such an abstracted problem is simpler for learning, the resulting hypothesis is still not accurate (diagram D). At this point, the training data set seems to be insufficient to allow proper learning. The lacking information can, however, be induced if both positive and negative hypotheses are considered at the same time. Figure 19.4, diagrams D and E, shows two covers, COV_{ms} (E^+/E^-) and COV_{mg} (E^-/E^+), that were generated using all initial training examples. AQ17-HCI generalized the positive concept description against the negative concept and, by this means, improved the learned concept. The concept C1 was learned precisely as shown in diagram F.

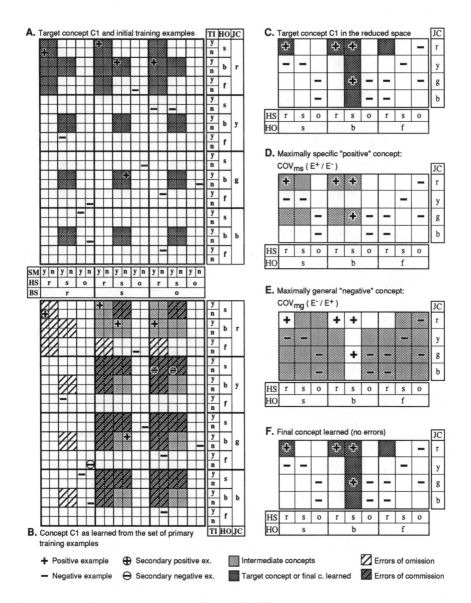

A. Target concept C1 and initial training examples

B. Concept C1 as learned from the set of primary training examples

C. Target concept C1 in the reduced space

D. Maximally specific "positive" concept: $COV_{ms}\,(\,E^+\,/\,E^-\,)$

E. Maximally general "negative" concept: $COV_{mg}\,(\,E^-\,/\,E^+\,)$

F. Final concept learned (no errors)

+ Positive example ⊕ Secondary positive ex. ▨ Intermediate concepts ▨ Errors of omission

− Negative example ⊖ Secondary negative ex. ■ Target concept or final c. learned ▨ Errors of commission

Figure 19.4:   Steps in learning concept C1 by AQ17-HCI

A Neural Net Generated by BpNet. Figure 19.3D shows an architecture of the neural net used in the experiments. There were seventeen input units, all having either value 0 or 1, corresponding to attribute-values. All input units had connections to two hidden units. The number of hidden units was determined experimentally. The two hidden units were connected to one output unit. The network was trained by the BpNet backpropagation algorithm until it reached root mean square error below 0.0007. The final connection weights for the concept C1 are shown in the figure. Because of space limitations, the connections from the input units to the left hidden unit and the right hidden unit are specified in the rows marked L and R, respectively. The weights from the hidden units to the output unit are 2.4 and −1.3. An input example is classified as a C1 class member if it is translated into output value ≥ 0.5.

Classifiers Generated by CFS. Each line in Figure 19.3E represents one classifier in the following format: No, Id, Classifier, Strength, and BidRatio (Riolo, 1988). The total population for representing the concept consists of sixty classifiers. Each of the classifiers (condition-action rules) is in the following form:

   condition1, condition2 / action

Each condition consists of a string of a fixed length (16) built from the tertiary alphabet {0, 1, #}. A condition string with prefix "m" is matched by any message that has 0s and 1s in exactly the same positions as the 0s and 1s in the condition string. The # in the condition is considered a "wildcard" symbol that can match a 0 or a 1. A classifier's condition-part is satisfied when both of its conditions are matched. When the condition-part of a classifier is satisfied, the classifier becomes active; i.e., its action-part produces one output message. The messages generated by active classifiers are compared to effectors in order to produce final classification. In Figure 19.3E, *BidRatio* is a number between one and zero that is a measure of the classifier's specificity, i.e., how many different messages it can match. *Strength* is meant to be a measure of a classifier's "usefulness" to the system. The higher a classifier's strength, the more it bids.

19.4.2 Summary of Results

Figures 19.4 and 19.5 present the results of learning concept C1 by the five learning systems using diagrammatic visualization. In comparison to the representations in Figure 19.3, these diagrams give a uniform image of the learning results. From the diagrams, one can easily determine learning accuracy (correct vs. error areas—black vs. shaded areas) and interpret the errors (why certain areas were covered or not). Most importantly, one can generate rules equivalent to the learned

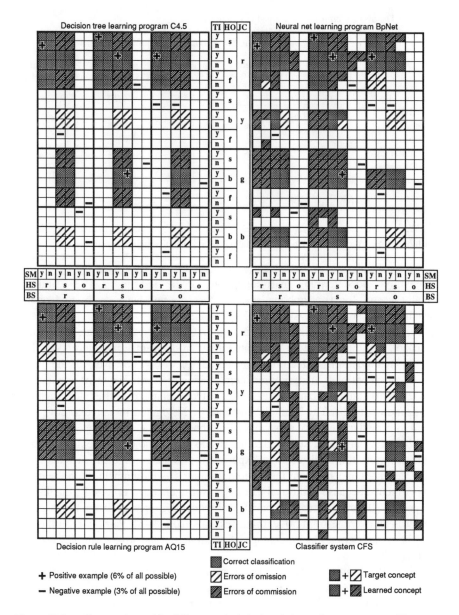

Figure 19.5:   Concepts learned by different methods in the relation to the target concept C1

Table 19.1: The average error rate of learned descriptions

	The Relative Size of the Set of Training Examples in Each Experiment				
	Experiment 1 (6%, 3%)*	Experiment 2 (10%, 10%)*	Experiment 3 (15%, 10%)*	Experiment 4 (25%, 10%)*	Experiment 5 (100%, 10%)*
Genetic Alg. (CFS)	21.3%	20.3%	22.5%	19.7%	16.3%
Neural Nets (BpNet)	9.7%	6.3%	4.7%	7.8%	4.8%
Decision Trees (C4.5)	9.7%	8.3%	1.3%	2.5%	1.6%
Decision Rules (AQ15)	22.8%	5.0%	4.8%	1.2%	0.0%
Decision Rules (AQ17-HCI)	4.8%	1.2%	0.0%	0.0%	0.0%

*In each (x%, y%), x denotes positive training examples and y negative training examples.

representation and determine an R-complexity of the description. This feature is especially useful for subsymbolic systems that do not have easily understood knowledge representation, as shown in Figure 19.3.

The final concept description learned by AQ17-HCI exactly matches the target concept, and thus, there are no slanted areas in diagram F in Figure 19.4. The other four methods did not learn the concept C1 precisely; however, all the methods were consistent with the training examples (Figure 19.5). The error rate level is almost even for all of them (about 20%), but one can note differences in their generalization patterns. The symbolic methods yield regular, rectangular covers as opposed to irregular covers of subsymbolic methods.

Tables 19.1 and 19.2 summarize the results of all the experiments. For each learning program, the final result in Experiment 1 is an average over results from learning the five concepts from their initial training sets (column 1). In the remaining experiments, because additional examples were generated randomly, the testing was repeated 10 times for each concept. Consequently, for each learning program, the result is an average from 50 learning sessions (cols. 2–5). Pairs (a,b) in the top row of the tables denote the percentage of positive and negative examples used in experiments.

Table 19.1 shows the average exact error rate of the descriptions learned in five experiments, and Figure 19.6 presents corresponding learning curves. The error rate of the CFS-generated descriptions was much higher than that of the other descriptions, and what is most surprising, it did not improve much with the growth of the training sets. Differences between decision tree learning (C4.5), neural network (BpNet), and decision rule learning (AQ15) are relatively small, although only AQ15 precisely learned all concepts in Experiment 5. The 4.8% average error

Table 19.2: Numbers of rules representing concepts learned by different methods (R-complexity)

	The Relative Size of the Set of Training Examples in Each Experiment				
	Experiment 1 (6%, 3%)*	Experiment 2 (10%, 10%)*	Experiment 3 (15%, 10%)*	Experiment 4 (25%, 10%)*	Experiment 5 (100%, 10%)*
Genetic Alg. (CFS)	49	45	51	48	41
Neural Nets (BpNet)	35	26	12	22	12
Decision Trees (C4.5)	3.1	2.8	2.5	2.5	2.5
Decision Rules (AQ15)	2.6	2.2	2.0	1.6	1.6
Decision Rules (AQ17-HCI)	2.4	2.0	1.6	1.6	1.6

*In each (x%, y%), x denotes positive training examples and y negative training examples.

rate of the BpNet-generated concepts was primarily because of an inadequate learning of concepts C1 and C4. Also, decision trees generated by C4.5 produced some error even when 100% positive examples were given. This error may be reduced if the function for converting trees into rules is applied (this, however, involves pruning a tree and simplifying rules). For AQ15-generated descriptions, errors in experiments 2–4 were primarily the result of errors in learning concept C1. The results of the constructive rule learning program AQ17-HCI show that all the concepts were precisely learned when the program was given 15% positive and 10% negative examples. Also, it generated the best performing descriptions in the first experiment.

One interesting finding is that increasing the number of training examples in experiments 1 to 5 resulted in only a slight improvement in the performance of the CFS-generated descriptions (from 21.3% to 16.3%). Other interesting findings are that even with 100% positive examples, the neural net, the genetic algorithm, and, to a smaller degree, the decision tree method did not learn the concept precisely. The CFS classifier system does not seem well-suited for classification-type problems. To further test this finding, this chapter reports results involving other genetic algorithm-based systems.

Table 19.2 gives the average R-complexity of the descriptions learned from different training sets. This measure gives a clear division between symbolic and subsymbolic methods. The symbolic methods generate descriptions that are ten times simpler than the subsymbolic methods. The results in this table are correlated with the results in Table 19.1. Methods that better perform in terms of predictive accuracy consistently yield simpler concept descriptions.

As mentioned earlier, target concepts were generated by human subjects, and therefore, the study favored methods that use symbolic representations because

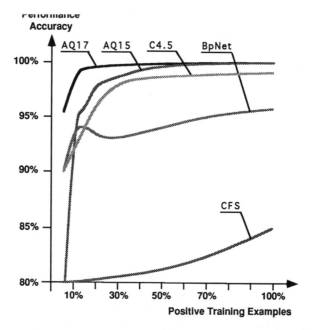

Figure 19.6:   Learning curves for concepts in the ROBOTS domain for the fixed number of 10% negative examples

such representations are more closely related to human representations. Studying how systems learn such human-generated concepts is important for applications where knowledge that needs to be acquired is in such forms and/or applications where the knowledge learned needs to be understood by human experts. There are problem domains in which these factors are not relevant. Next, two studies present a wider range of problems involving both DNF-type and non-DNF-type concepts.

19.5 SECOND STUDY: THE MONK'S PROBLEMS

This study reports results from a performance comparison of different learning algorithms on three problems defined in the ROBOTS domain (Thrun et al., 1991). The so-called MONK's problems address three machine learning problems. Problem 1 is a DNF-type problem. Next is an "m-of-n," non-DNF-type problem. The concept to be learned requires a very complex DNF expression to describe it in terms of the available attributes. Problem 3 is a DNF-type, but the learning data set contains noise.

Problem M1:   *Head shape is the same as the body shape, or color of the jacket is red.* Training set contains 124 randomly selected examples. There is no noise.

Problem M2:   *Exactly two of the six given attributes take their first value.* For example, if attributes Head Shape and Body Shape take value *round*, which is the first value in their value set, then no other attribute may take the first value in its value set. Training set contains 169 randomly selected examples. There is no noise.

Problem M3:   *Jacket is green and holding a sword, or jacket is not blue and body is not octagonal.* Training set contains 122 randomly selected examples. There is 5% noise in the data.

The tested algorithms fall into 4 categories:

- Neural Networks   **Backpropagation** (McClelland and Rumelhart, 1988), **Cascade Correlation** (Fahlman and Lebiere, 1990)
- Decision Trees   **ID3** (Quinlan, 1986), **Assistant Professional** (Cestnik, Kononenko and Brotko, 1987), **ID5R** (Utgoff, 1990), **IDL** (Van de Velde, 1989), **ID5R-hat** (Utgoff, 1990), **TDIDT** (Quinlan, 1986), **PRISM** (Cendrowska, 1988)
- Decision Rules   **AQ14-NT** (Pachowicz and Bala, 1991), **AQR, CN2** (Clark and Niblett, 1989), **AQ15** (Michalski et al., 1986), **AQ15-GA** (Vafaie and DeJong, 1993), **AQ17-DCI** (Bloedorn and Michalski, 1992), **AQ17-FCLS** (Zhang and Michalski, to appear), **AQ17-HCI** (Wnek and Michaleski, 1991), **AQ17** (Bloedorn, Michalski and Wnek, 1993)
- Inductive Logic Programming: mFOIL (Dzeroski, 1991)

Table 19.3 shows all reported results (Thrun et al., 1991). No one classifier based on genetic algorithms was tested as a separate program. In the AQ15-GA program, genetic algorithms are used in conjunction with AQ15. Genetic algorithms are used to explore the space of all subsets of a given attribute set, and AQ15 is used to build concept descriptions. This multistrategy approach improves performance accuracy of the symbolic learning system while the M3 problem is learned.

Problem M1 is of similar complexity to the C1–C5 ROBOTS problems, and it is easily learned by decision rule algorithms, AQ-15 and AQ17-HCI. Backpropagation and ID3 cannot learn concept M1 precisely; however, in both neural nets and decision trees paradigms, one can find programs that correctly learned descriptions (Cascade Correlation, Assistant Professional).

Problems M2 and M3 are difficult for selective decision rule and decision tree algorithms AQ15 and ID3. The learned descriptions have either high R-complexity (problem M2) or contain rules that cover noisy examples (problem M3). These problems were not learned as well by a hybrid of decision rules and decision trees, i.e., decision lists (CN2 algorithm [Clark and Niblett, 1989]). This suggests that techniques other than those implemented in these programs are required to solve this kind of problem.

The hypothesis-driven constructive induction method implemented in AQ17-HCI changes the representation space by narrowing and/or expanding the initial set of attributes. The method analyzes inductive hypothesis generated by a selective program and removes and/or generates new attributes. The new attributes are patterns found either in conditions or in the rules. This is sufficient to solve the M3 problem. Problem M2, however, still remains hard[4]. A solution lies in another type of change in the representation, i.e., attribute generation based on combining initial attributes using logical and/or algebraic operators (Bloedorn and Michalski, 1992). An initial integration of constructive induction methods was done in the AQ17 program. The multistrategy constructive induction program AQ17 learned all three MONK's problems.

19.6 THIRD STUDY: THE nDmC LEARNING PROBLEMS

This study uses another artificial domain to test twelve DNF-type concepts and is based on the experiments conducted by Spears and Gordon (1991). The experiments involved learning concepts in a designed domain defined by 4 nominal attributes, each having 4 distinct values. Therefore, the description space consisted of 256 examples (vectors of attribute values). There were twelve DNF-type target concepts, differing from each other in the number of rules (the number of disjunctions) and in the number of conditions in disjunctions (the conjunctions in the rules). All twelve concepts can be characterized by the formula nDmC, in which n, the number of disjunctions, varied from 1 to 4, and m, the number of conjunctions, varied from 1 to 3.

Spears and Gordon first compare three learning methods. Two symbolic methods represented by C4.5, a decision tree learning program, and AQ14, a deci-

---

[4] Problem M2 was later learned with 100% accuracy by AQ17-HCI as a result of detecting xor-patterns (Wnek, 1993).

Table 19.3: Summary of results for MONK's problems

Paradigm		Program	DNF-type (no noise)	Non-DNF (m-of-n)	DNF-type (noise)
			Prediction Accuracy		
Neural Nets	* (1)	Backpropagation	100%	100%	93%
	(1)	Cascade Correlation	100%	100%	97%
Decision Trees	(2)	Assistant Professional	100%	81%	100%
	* (3)	ID3	99%	68%	94%
	(3)	ID3 (no windowing)	83%	69%	96%
	(3, 4)	ID5R	82%	69%	95%
	(4)	ID5R-hat	90%	66%	—
	(4)	IDL	97%	66%	—
	(4)	TDIDT	76%	67%	—
	(5)	PRISM	86%	73%	90%
Decision Rules	(6)	AQ14-NT	100%	77%	100%
	(3)	AQR	96%	80%	87%
	(3)	CN2	100%	69%	89%
	(6)	AQ15	100%	77%	84%
	(6)	AQ15-GA	100%	87%	100%
	¶ (6)	AQ17-DCI	100%	100%	97%
	(6)	AQ17-FCLS	100%	93%	97%
	*¶ (6)	AQ17-HCI	100%	93%	100%
	¶ (6)	AQ17	**100%**	**100%**	**100%**
Inductive Logic Programming (2)		mFOIL	100%	69%	100%

* Programs compared in the first study. ¶ Constructive induction programs. Experiments were performed at the following laboratories: 1) School of Computer Science, Carnegie Mellon University, Pittsburgh, Pennsylvania, USA; 2) AI Laboratory, Josef Stefan Institute, Ljubljana, Slovenia; 3) Institute for Real-Time Computer Control Systems and Robotics and University of Karlsruhe, Karlsruhe, Germany; 4) Artificial Intelligence Laboratory, Vrije Universiteit Brussel, Brussels, Belgium; 5) AI-Lab, Institute for Informatics, University of Zurich, Switzerland; 6) Center for Artificial Intelligence, George Mason University, Fairfax, Virginia, USA.

sion rule learning program. Subsymbolic methods were represented by GABIL— Genetic Algorithms Batch Incremental Learner. They conclude that AQ14 is the best performer and uses some of AQ's strategies to improve GABIL. The resulting multistrategy system, Adaptive GABIL, is finally evaluated using the same problems.

Tables 19.4 and 19.5 show the results from testing the systems according to the prediction accuracy and the convergence criteria. The prediction accuracy is an

Table 19.4: Prediction accuracy in the four DNF categories

Paradigm (Program)	Prediction Accuracy			
	1DmC	2DmC	3DmC	4DmC
Genetic Alg.				
(GABIL)	96%	93%	90%	89%
(Adaptive GABIL)¶	97%	96%	95%	94%
Decision Trees				
(C4.5) *	98%	95%	89%	84%
Decision Rules				
(AQ14) *	99%	97%	96%	95%

*Programs compared in the first study
¶ Multistrategy learning program

average over all values on a learning curve. The convergence criterion is the number of events seen before a 95% prediction accuracy is maintained (Valiant, 1984). The results in the tables were averaged for each DNF category over three cases (m=1..3).

Problems labeled 1DmC and 2DmC are similar to problems C1–C5 defined in the ROBOTS domain as far as the complexity of descriptions is concerned. In learning such problems, the symbolic learning program AQ14 outperformed the other three programs both in terms of predictive accuracy and convergence to 95%. For the remaining problems, 3DmC and 4DmC, AQ14 maintains the best prediction accuracy. However, the Adaptive GABIL algorithm that combines symbolic

Table 19.5: Convergence to 95% in the four DNF categories

Paradigm (Program)	Convergence (no examples needed to achieve 95% accuracy)			
	1DmC	2DmC	3DmC	4DmC
Genetic Alg.				
(GABIL)	94	169	151	167
(Adaptive GABIL)¶	63	83	84	88
Decision Trees				
(C4.5) *	96	135	209	206
Decision Rules				
(AQ14) *	33	52	102	105

* Programs compared in the first study
¶ Multistrategy learning program

and subsymbolic strategies strongly outperformed the decision tree learning algorithm.

19.7 SUMMARY AND FUTURE WORK

From the multistrategy learning point of view, it is important that capabilities and limitations of different learning strategies and paradigms are well understood. The goal of this study was to make experiments that would help to develop insights into the performance of diverse learning approaches on selected classes of learning problems.

One finding is that symbolic methods outperformed subsymbolic methods in learning DNF-type problems. We found that the performance accuracy of symbolic methods was high, the convergence to the target concept was fast, and the learned descriptions matched or closely matched the target concepts and were easy to understand. In addition, preliminary results show that the symbolic methods performed very well with DNF-type problems with noise, which contradicts a sometimes expressed belief that neural nets are particularly good for such problems, and symbolic methods are not. The most surprising result, however, was that symbolic methods employing constructive induction performed on the par with neural nets on learning non-DNF-type concepts, such as "m-of-n." For such problems, neural nets were supposed to be superior because the problems are easily representable by such nets. Multistrategy induction methods (such as those implemented in the AQ17 family and Adaptive GABIL), although at an early stage of development, have already shown an improved performance over monostrategy methods.

The performance of the programs was analyzed using a *diagrammatic visualization* system, DIAV. This system, working on line with a learning program, turned out to be a very useful tool for visualizing learned and target concepts, comparing the learned concepts, and presenting errors in learning (an "error image"). The method was also exceptionally useful for visualizing concepts learned by subsymbolic methods and comparing them with concepts learned by symbolic methods, such as neural net learning and genetic algorithm learning. Concept images helped comprehending knowledge encoded in a neural network or in a population of classifiers. In addition, the visualization method enabled us to determine the R-complexity of the concepts learned by the subsymbolic methods.

Among important topics for the future is the application of the methods to a wider range of non-DNF-type problems, such as learning a text-to-speech mapping (Sejnowski and Rosenberg, 1987; Dietterich, 1990), and to randomly generated problems in order to evaluate an overall performance of the methods. Future research might also compare the performance of the methods in learning from noisy data and inconsistent examples and in learning imprecisely defined or flexible concepts (Bergadano et al., 1992).

ACKNOWLEDGMENTS

The authors thank Ken Kaufman, Gheorghe Tecuci, and Jianping Zhang for comments on earlier drafts of this chapter. They are grateful to Jayshree Sarma and Ashraf A. Wahab for performing experiments with backpropagation algorithm BpNet and genetic algorithm learning program CFS and to Rick Riolo for providing a copy of his CFS-C software.

This research was done in the Center for Artificial Intelligence at George Mason University. The Center's research is supported in part by the National Science Foundation under Grant No. IRI-9020226, in part by the Defense Advanced Research Projects Agency under the grant administered by the Office of Naval Research No. N00014-91-J-1854, and in part by the Office of Naval Research under Grant No. N00014-91-J-1351.

References

Bergadano, R., Matwin, S., Michalski, R.S. and Zhang, J., "Learning Two-tiered Descriptions of Flexible Concepts: The POSEIDON System," *Machine Learning*, Vol. 8, pp. 5–43, 1992.

Bloedorn, E. and Michalski, R.S., "Data-driven Constructive Induction in AQ17-DCI: A Method and Experiments," *Reports of Machine Learning and Inference Laboratory*, No. MLI-92-03, George Mason University, 1992.

Breiman, L., Freedman, J.H., Olhsen, R.A. and Stone, C.J., *Classification and Regression Trees*, Wadsworth International Group, Belmont, CA, 1984.

Cendvowska, J., "PRISM: An Algorithm for Inducing Modular Rules," in *Knowledge Acquisition for Knowledge-Based Systems*, B.R. Gaines and J.H. Boose (Eds.), Academic Press, New York, pp. 253–274, 1988.

Cestnik, B., Kononenko, I. and Bratko, I., "ASSISTANT 86: A Knowledge-Elicitation Tool for Sophisticated Users," *Progress in Machine Learning*, I. Bratko and N. Lavrec (Eds.), Sigma Press, Wilmslow, 1987.

Clark, P. and Niblett, T., "The CN2 Induction Algorithm," *Machine Learning*, Vol. 3, pp. 261–283, 1989.

Dietterich, T.G., Hild, H. and Bakiri, G., "A Comparative Study of ID3 and Backpropagation for English Text-to-Speech Mapping," *Proceedings of the 7th International Conference on Machine Learning*, Austin, TX, pp. 24–31, Morgan Kaufmann, San Mateo, CA, 1990.

Dzeroski, S., "Handling Noise in Inductive Logic Programming," MS Thesis, Dept. of EE and CS, University of Ljubljana, Slovenia, 1991.

Fahlman, S.E. and Lebiere, C., "The Cascade-Correlation Learning Architecture," in *Advances in Neural Information Processing Systems*, Vol. 2, Morgan Kaufmann, San Mateo, CA, 1990.

Fisher, D.H. and McKusick, K.B., "An Empirical Comparison of ID3 and Back-propagation," *Proceedings of IJCAI-89*, pp. 788–793, AAAI Press, Menlo Park, CA, 1989.

Hempel, C.G., *Aspects of Scientific Explanation*, The Free Press, New York, 1965.

Holland, J.H., "Escaping Brittleness: The Possibilities of General-purpose Learning Algorithms Applied to Parallel Rule-Based Systems," *Machine Learning: An Artificial Intelligence Approach*, Vol. II, R.S. Michalski, J.G. Carbonell, T.M. Mitchell (Eds.), pp. 593–624, Morgan Kaufmann, Los Altos, CA, 1986.

Holland, J.H. and Reitman, J.S., "Cognitive Systems Based on Adaptive Algorithms," *Pattern-directed Inference Systems*, D.A. Waterman and F. Hayes-Roth (Eds.), Academic Press, New York, 1978.

Kaufman, K.A., Michalski, R.S. and Schultz, A.C., "EMERALD 1: An Integrated System of Machine Learning and Discovery Programs for Education and Research," *Reports of Machine Learning and Inference Laboratory*, No. MLI-89-12, George Mason University, 1989.

Kodratoff, Y., "Induction and the Organization of Knowledge," in *Machine Learning: A Multistrategy Approach*, Vol. IV, R.S. Michalski and G. Tecuci (Eds.), Morgan Kaufmann, San Mateo, CA, 1994.

McClelland, J. and Rumelhart, D., *Explorations in Parallel Distributed Processing*, MIT Press, Cambridge, MA, 1988.

Michalski, R.S., "AQVAL/1—Computer Implementation of a Variable-valued Logic System VL1 and Examples of Its Application to Pattern Recognition," *Proceedings of the First International Joint Conference on Pattern Recognition*, pp. 3–17, Washington, DC, October 30-November 1, 1973.

Michalski, R.S., "Pattern Recognition as Knowledge-guided Computer Induction," *Reports of Computer Science Department*, No. 927, University of Illinois, Urbana, 1978.

Michalski, R.S., "A Theory and Methodology of Inductive Learning," *Artificial Intelligence*, Vol. 20, pp. 111–116, 1983.

Michalski, R., Mozetic, I., Hong, J. and Lavrac, N., "The AQ15 Inductive Learning System: An Overview and Experiments," *Reports of Machine Learning and Inference Laboratory*, No. MLI-86-6, George Mason University, 1986.

Mooney, R., Shavlik, J., Towell, G. and Gove, A., "An Experimental Comparison of Symbolic and Connectionist Learning Algorithms," *Proceedings of IJCAI-89*, pp. 775–780, AAAI Press, Menlo Park, CA, 1989.

Pachowicz, P.W. and Bala, J., "Improving Recognition Effectiveness of Noisy Texture Concepts," *Proceedings of the Eight International Workshop on Machine Learning*, pp. 625–629, Morgan Kaufmann, San Mateo, CA, 1991.

Pagallo, G. and Haussler, D., "Boolean Feature Discovery in Empirical Learning," *Machine Learning*, Vol. 5, No. 1, pp. 71–99, 1990.

Quinlan, J.R., "Induction of Decision Trees," *Machine Learning*, Vol. 1, No. 1, pp. 81–106, 1986.

Quinlan, J.R., *C4.5: Programs for Machine Learning*, Morgan Kaufmann, San Mateo, CA, 1993.

Rendell, L.A. and Seshu, R., "Learning Hard Concepts through Constructive Induction: Framework and Rationale," *Computational Intelligence*, Vol. 6, pp. 247–270, 1990.

Riolo, R.L., "CFS-C: A Package of Domain Independent Subroutines for Implementing Classifier Systems in Arbitrary, User-defined Environments," *Technical Report*, Logic of Computers Group, Division of Computer Science and Engineering, University of Michigan, 1988.

Rumelhart, D.E., Hinton, G.E. and Williams, R.J., "Learning Internal Representations by Error Propagation," *Parallel Distributed Processing: Explorations in the Microstructure of Cognition*, D.E. Rumelhart and J.L. McCLelland (Eds.), The MIT Press, Cambridge, MA, 1986.

Sejnowski, T.J. and Rosenberg, C.R., "Parallel Networks That Learn to Pronounce English Text," *Complex Systems*, Vol. 1, pp. 145–168, 1987.

Spears, W.M. and Gordon, D.F., "Adaptive Strategy Selection for Concept Learning," *Proceedings of the First International Workshop on Multistrategy Learning*, Harpers Ferry, WV, pp. 231–246, George Mason University Press, Fairfax, VA, 1991.

Thrun, S.B., Bala, J., Bloedorn, E., Bratko, I., Cestnink, B., Cheng, J., DeJong, K.A., Dzeroski, S., Fahlman, S.E., Hamann, R., Kaufman, K., Keller, S., Kononenko, I., Kreuziger, J., Michalski, R.S., Mitchell, T., Pachowicz, P., Vafaie, H., Van de Velde, W., Wenzel, W., Wnek, J. and Zhang, J., "The MONK's Problems: A Performance Comparison of Different Learning Algorithms," *Technical Report*, Carnegie Mellon University, December 1991.

Utgoff, P.E., "Incremental Learning of Decision Trees," *Machine Learning*, Vol. 4, pp. 161–186, Kluwer Academic, Boston, MA, 1990.

Vafaie, H. and DeJong, K.A., "Improving the Performance of a Rule Induction System Using Genetic Algorithms," in *Machine Learning: A Multistrategy Approach*, Vol. 4, R.S. Michalski and G. Tecuci (Eds.), Morgan Kaufmann, San Mateo, CA, 1994.

Valiant, L.G., "A Theory of the Learnable," *Communications of the ACM*, Vol. 27, pp. 1134–1142, 1984.

Van de Velde, W., "IDL, or Taming the Multiplexer," *Proceedings of the Fourth European Working Session on Learning*, Pitman, London, UK, 1989.

Weiss, S.M. and Kapouleas, I., "An Empirical Comparison of Pattern Recognition of Neural Nets and Machine Learning Classification Methods," *Proceedings of IJCAI-89*, p. 781–787, AAAI Press, Menlo Park, CA, 1989.

Wnek, J. and Michalski, R.S., "Hypothesis-driven Constructive Induction in AQ17: A Method and Experiments," *Proceedings of the IJCAI-91 Workshop on Evaluating and Changing Representations*, K. Morik, F. Bergadano and W. Buntine (Eds.), pp. 13–22, AAAI Press, Menlo Park, CA, 1991.

Wnek, J. and Michalski, R.S., "A Diagrammatic Visualization of Learning Processes," to appear in *Reports of Machine Learning and Inference Laboratory*, George Mason University, 1993.

Wnek, J., "Version Space Transformation with Constructive Induction: The VS* Algorithm," *Reports of Machine Learning and Inference Laboratory*, No. MLI-92-01, George Mason University, 1992.

Wnek, J., "Hypothesis-driven Constructive Induction," *Ph.D. Dissertation*, University Microfilms International, Ann Arbor, MI, 1993.

Zhang, J. and Michalski, R.S., "Combining Symbolic and Numeric Representations in Learning Flexible Concepts: The FCLS Systems," *Machine Learning*, to appear.

PART
FIVE

SPECIAL TOPICS
AND APPLICATIONS

20

CASE-BASED REASONING
IN PRODIGY

Manuela Veloso
Jaime Carbonell
(Carnegie Mellon University)

Abstract

PRODIGY is an integrated intelligent architecture that explores different learning strategies to support efficient general purpose problem solving. This chapter presents the derivational analog reasoner of PRODIGY as a learning method for incorporating and reusing past experience. The analogical reasoner transitions smoothly among case generation, case storage, and case replay. Learning occurs by accumulation of new cases, by tuning the indexing structure of the case library to retrieve progressively more appropriate cases, and by incrementally acquiring more suitable similarity metrics. In this chapter we focus on presenting the mechanisms to generate and retrieve the cases automatically, i.e., the derivational traces of problem-solving episodes. We illustrate our methods with several examples and present empirical results that illustrate the performance of the replay mechanism in two domains using two different similarity metrics. The system is a multistrategy learner in the sense that the retrieval mechanism improves its similarity metric by performing a lazy explanation of the derivational trace, and problem-solving time reduces with accumulated cases. The chapter concludes with a brief discussion of the benefits of a deeper integration of the analogical reasoner with the explanation-based and abstraction modules of PRODIGY.

20.1 INTRODUCTION

PRODIGY is an integrated intelligent architecture that explores different learning strategies to support efficient general purpose problem solving. Robust reasoning in PRODIGY requires learning from problem-solving episodes. Past experience is compiled to guide future problem solving in similar situations and thereby improve performance, reducing search by making progressively fewer incorrect decisions. Significant performance improvements permit scaling up to larger and more complex problems.

This chapter presents the derivational analogy reasoner of PRODIGY as a learning method of incorporating and reusing past experience. Analogical reasoning can be seen as an alternate learning method to the explanation-based learning (EBL) paradigm. EBL uses an example trace of a solved problem and domain axioms to generalize control rules therefrom by proving the correctness of decisions at choice points and synthesizing control rules from these proofs. Instead of investing substantial effort deriving general rules for behavior from each example as EBL does, the analogical reasoner automatically generates and stores annotated traces of solved problems (cases) that are elaborated further when needed to guide similar problems. Compiled experience is then stored with little postprocessing. The explanation effort is done incrementally on an "if needed" basis at storage, retrieval, and adaptation time when new similar situations occur. The immediate support for the utility of this approach over EBL is that, on one hand, some domains may be incompletely specified for which EBL is not able to generate deductive proofs (Duval, 1991). On the other hand, in complex domains EBL can become very inefficient, with long deductive chains producing complex rules for situations that may seldom, if ever, be repeated.

Analogical reasoning in PRODIGY integrates automatic case generation, case retrieval and storage, case replay, and general problem solving, exploiting and modifying past experience when available and resorting to general problem-solving methods when required.

Automatic case generation occurs by extending the general problem solver with the ability to introspect into its internal decision cycle, recording the justifications for each decision during its extensive search process. Examples of these justifications are links between choices capturing the subgoaling structure, records of explored failed alternatives, and pointers to applied control knowledge. A stored problem solving episode consists of the solution trace augmented with these annotations.

Candidate similar past problems match partially a new problem solving situation. To rank these partially similar candidate analogs, the similarity metric explores the relevance of past features by goal regressing in the successful derivational trace. The retrieval module returns to the analogical reasoner a set of past cases that more adequately cover the new situation.

The analogical reasoner's main functionality consists of a sophisticated replay mechanism that is able to reconstruct solutions from the retrieved past cases when only a partial match exists between the new and past situations. The replay mechanism coordinates the set of multiple retrieved cases and uses the annotated justifications to guide the reconstruction of the solution for problem-solving situations where equivalent justifications hold true.

Learning, therefore, occurs by accumulating and reusing cases (problem-solving episodes), especially in situations that required extensive problem solving, and by tuning the indexing structure of the memory model to retrieve progressively more appropriate cases. On one hand, we reduce search at the problem-solving level by replaying past similar cases (derivational traces of problem-solving episodes) (Veloso and Carbonell, 1991a). On the other hand, we learn incrementally better similarity metrics by interpreting the behavior of the problem solver replaying retrieved cases. Furthermore, we explore an efficient way of balancing the costs of retrieval and search (Veloso and Carbonell, 1991b).

In this chapter, we focus on presenting the mechanisms to automatically generate and retrieve the compiled cases. We present empirical results that illustrate the performance of the two domains using two different similarity metrics. Details on the initial one-case replay mechanism can be found in Veloso (1991). The management of the case library exploits the underlying integration of the general problem solver and the analogical reasoner to organize and retrieve the stored cases dynamically. Recent tests with up to 1,000 cases in the library have demonstrated the scaling properties of the memory organization, of the match/retrieval process, and of the reconstruction mechanism replaying multiple cases. Details on the multiple-case replay mechanism and results of these scaling up tests are compiled in Veloso (1992).

This chapter is organized as follows. In Section 20.2, we introduce the automatic case generation as fully annotated derivational traces of problem-solving search episodes. Section 20.3 describes our indexing strategy to organize the library of cases. In Section 20.4, we outline our case retrieval strategy, and we discuss different similarity metrics. The replay strategy is briefly outlined in Section 20.5 and is illustrated with results obtained using the two similarity metrics introduced before. In Section 20.5, we discuss how a deeper integration of EBL and analogy and abstraction and analogy would be useful and is in our future work schedule. Section 20.6 draws conclusions on this work.

20.2 THE DERIVATIONAL TRACE: CASE GENERATION

Derivational analogy is a *reconstructive* method by which *lines of reasoning* are transferred and adapted to the new problem (Carbonell, 1986). The ability to replay previous solutions using the derivational analogy method requires that the problem solver be able to introspect into its internal decision cycle, recording the justifications for each decision during its extensive search process. These justifications augment the solution trace and are used to guide the future reconstruction of the solution for subsequent problem-solving situations where equivalent justifications hold true.

In PRODIGY (Minton et al., 1989), a domain is specified as a set of operators, inference rules, and control rules. Additionally the entities of the domain are organized in a type hierarchy (Veloso, 1989). Each operator (or inference rule) has a precondition expression that must be satisfied before the operator can be applied and an effects-list that describes how the application of the operator changes the world. Search control in PRODIGY allows the problem solver to represent and use control information about the various problem-solving decisions. A problem consists of an initial state and a goal expression. To solve a problem, PRODIGY must find a sequence of operators that, if applied to the initial state, produces a final state satisfying the goal statement. The operator-based problem solver produces a complete search tree, encapsulating all decisions—right ones and wrong ones—as well as the final solution. This information is used by each learning component in different ways: to extract control rules via EBL (Minton, 1988), to build derivational traces (cases) by the derivational analogy engine (Veloso and Carbonell, 1990), to analyze key decisions by a knowledge acquisition interface (Joseph, 1989), or to formulate focused experiments (Carbonell and Gil, 1990). The axiomatized domain knowledge is also used to learn abstraction layers (Knoblock, 1991) and statically generate control rules (Etzioni, 1990).

The derivational analogy work in PRODIGY takes place in the context of PRODIGY's **nonlinear** problem solver (Veloso, 1989). The system is called NoLIMIT, standing for **Nonli**near problem solver using causal com**mit**ment. The basic search procedure is, as in the linear planner (Minton et al., 1989), means-ends analysis (MEA) in backward chaining mode. Basically, given a goal literal not true in the current world, the planner selects one operator that adds (in case of a positive goal) or deletes (in case of a negative goal) that goal to the world. We say that this operator is *relevant* to the given goal. If the preconditions of the chosen operator are true, the operator can be *applied*. If this is not the case, then the preconditions that are not true in the *state* become *subgoals*, i.e., new goals to be achieved. The cycle repeats until all the conjuncts from the goal expression are true in the world. NoLIMIT's nonlinear character stems from working with a **set** of goals in this cycle as opposed to the top goal in a goal stack. Dynamic goal selection enables NoLIMIT to interleave plans, exploiting common subgoals and addressing issues of resource contention.

Automatically generating a case from a problem-solving episode is immediately related to identifying and capturing the reasons for the decisions taken by the problem solver at the different choice points encountered while searching for a solution. In the nonlinear search procedure of NoLIMIT, we identify the following types of choice points (Veloso, 1989):

- What *goal* to choose from the set of pending goals.
- What *operator* to choose in pursuit of the particular goal selected.
- What *bindings* to choose to instantiate the selected operator.
- Whether to *apply* an applicable operator or continue *subgoaling* on a pending goal.
- Whether the search path being explored should be *suspended*, continued, or abandoned.
- Upon failure, which *past choice point* to backtrack to or which *suspended path* to reconsider for further search.

These choice points characterize a nonlinear problem solver that uses causal commitment (Minton, 1988) in its search cycle, i.e., mentally applies operators and considers a set, as opposed to a rigid FILO linear order (a stack), of pending goals (Veloso, 1989).

Justifications at these choice points may point to user-given guidance, to pre-programmed control knowledge, to automatically learned control rules responsible for decisions taken, or to past cases used as guidance (more than one case can be used to solve a complete problem). They also represent links within the different choices and their related generators, in particular capturing the subgoaling structure. At choice points, we also record failed alternatives (explored earlier) and the cause of their failure. Note that "cause of failure" here refers to the reason why the search path starting at that alternative failed. It does not necessarily mean that the failed alternative is directly responsible for the failure of the global search path. It may be an indirect relationship, but this is the best attribution so far. The current reasons for failure in NoLIMIT follow according to PRODIGY's search strategy (Minton et al., 1989):

No Relevant Operators—When NoLIMIT reaches an *unachievable* goal, i.e., a goal that does not have any relevant operator that adds it as one of its effects given the current state and control rules.

State Loop—If the application of an operator leads into a previously visited state, then NoLIMIT abandons this path because a redundant sequence of operators was applied.

Goal Loop—When NoLIMIT encounters an unmatched goal that was previously posted in the search path (i.e., when a pending goal becomes its own subgoal).

NoLIMIT abandons a search path either because of any of these failures or because a situation was heuristically declared not promising (e.g., a search path that is too long).

A step of the search path can only be a goal choice, an instantiated operator choice, or the application of an operator. To generate a case from a search tree episode, we take the successful solution path annotated with justifications for the successful decisions taken and the record of the remaining alternatives that were not explored or that were abandoned and their corresponding reasons. We show below the different justifications annotated at goal, operator, and applied operator decision nodes.

20.2.1 Justification Structures at Decision Nodes

In a casual-commitment search approach, justifications for the decisions made arise in a natural way. Examples of these justifications are links between choices capturing the subgoaling structure, records of explored failed alternatives, and pointers to applied control knowledge.

Figure 20.1 shows the skeleton of the different decision nodes. The different justification slots capture the context in which the decision is taken and the reasons that support the choice.

The *choice* slots show the selection done, namely, the selected goal or operator. The *sibling*-slots enumerate the alternatives to the choice made. At a goal node and applied operator node (see Figure 20.1 (a) and (b)), the goals left in the current set of goals to achieve constitute the sibling-goals annotation. For completeness, the problem solver may postpone applying an operator whose preconditions are satisfied and continue subgoaling on a still unachieved goal. These possible applicable operators are the contents of the alternative sibling-applicable-ops slot. At a chosen operator node, the sibling operators are the possible other different operators that are also relevant to the goal being expanded, i.e., the operators that, if applied, will achieve that goal. NoLimit annotates the reason why these alternatives were not pursued further according to its search experience (either not tried or abandoned due to a described failure reason). The *why*-slots present the reasons (if any) why the particular decision was taken. These reasons range from arbitrary choices to a specific control rule or guiding case that dictated the selection. These reasons are tested at replay time and are interpretable by the analytical problem solver. Finally, the subgoaling structure is captured by the slots *precond-of* at a goal node and the slot *relevant-to* at a chosen operator node. At reconstruction time,

```
Goal Node                   Applied Operator Node      Chosen Operator Node
 :step                        :step                      :step
 :sibling-goals               :sibling-goals             :sibling-relevant-ops
 :sibling-applicable-ops      :sibling-applicable-ops    :why-this-operator
 :why-subgoal                 :why-apply                 :relevant-to
 :why-this-goal               :why-this-operator
 :precond-of
           (a)                          (b)                        (c)
```

Figure 20.1: Justification record structure: (a) at a goal decision node, (b) at an applied operator decision node, (c) at a chosen operator decision node

```
(is-a ROOM TYPE)
(is-a DOOR TYPE)
(is-a OBJECT TYPE)
(is-a BOX OBJECT)
(is-a KEY OBJECT)
(is-a AGENT TYPE)
```

Figure 20.2:   The type hierarchy in the extended-STRIPS domain

these slots play an important role in providing practically matching-costly-free information, on the one hand, on the set of relevant operators for a given goal and, on the other hand, on the set of instantiated preconditions of an operator. The subgoaling structure further allows the replay mechanism to follow only the parts of the case that are relevant to the goals being guided.

The problem and the generated annotated solution become a *case* in memory. The case corresponds to the search tree compacted into the successful path as a sequence of annotated decision nodes, such as the ones presented in Figure 20.1. According to the case utilization method that we briefly present here (and more extensively present in Veloso [1991, 1992]), we note that a case is not used as a simple "macro-operator" (Fikes and Nilsson, 1971; Minton, 1985). A case is selected based on a partial match to a new problem solving situation. Hence, as opposed to a macro-operator, a case *guides* and *does not dictate* the reconstruction process. Intermediate decisions corresponding to choices internal to each case can be bypassed or adapted if their justifications no longer hold.

To illustrate the automatic generator of an annotated case, we now present an example.

20.2.2 An Example in the Extended-STRIPS Domain

We are using an example in the extended-STRIPS domain (Minton, 1988). The world consists of a set of rooms connected by doors. A robot can move around between the rooms carrying or pushing objects along. Doors can be locked or unlocked. Keys to the doors lie in rooms and can be picked up by the robot. The set of operators include going to be next to objects, going through doors, pushing objects to rooms, picking up keys, opening, closing, locking, and unlocking doors. (There are thirteen operators and four inference rules in the version of this domain that we are using.) Variables and instances are organized in a type hierarchy shown in Figure 20.2 where TYPE is the top of the hierarchy.

An example of the operator to push an object through a door is shown in Figure 20.3.[1]

---

[1] The complete set of operators for the nonlinear planner is obtained directly from the set of operators for the linear planner of PRODIGY in Minton (1988) by applying some fixed syntax modifications (Veloso, 1989).

```
(OPERATOR PUSH-THRU-DOOR
 (params
   ((<door> DOOR)
    (<box> BOX)
    (<roomx>
      (and ROOM
           (adjacent-room-p <roomy> <roomx>)))
    (<roomy>
      (and ROOM
           (differentp <roomx> <roomy>)))))
 (preconds
  (and
   (pushable <box>)
   (connects <door> <roomx> <roomy>)
   (dr-open <door>)
   (inroom robot <roomx>)
   (next-to robot <box>)
   (next-to <box> <door>)))
 (effects
  ((del (inroom robot <roomx>))
   (del (inroom <box> <roomx>))
   (add (inroom robot <roomy>))
   (add (inroom <box> <roomy>))
   (if ((<obj> OBJECT))
       (holding <obj>)
       ((del (holding <obj>))
 (add (inroom <obj> <roomx>))
 (add (next-to <obj> <door>)))))))
```

Figure 20.3:   The operator to push an object through a door in the extended-STRIPS domain

Consider Figure 20.4 where in (a) we show the initial state and in (b) the goal statement of an example problem from the extended-STRIPS domain, say, problem *strips2-5.*[2] Rooms are numbered at the corner of their picture, and the number of the boxes can be inferred by the attached description of the initial state. According to the goal statement, it is only important to notice that box3 is the one in room4. The problem solver must find a plan to reach a state where door34, connecting room3 and room4, is closed, and the agent hero is next to box3. The problem is simple, so we can show a full case corresponding to a problem-solving search episode.

Without any analogical guidance (or other form of control knowledge), the problem solver searches for a solution by applying its primitive means-ends analysis procedure. In Figure 20.5, we show a complete successful solution path. (cn0 is a built-in finishing operator whose preconditions are set to the user given goal

---

[2]Problems are named for memory organization purposes (see Section 20.3).

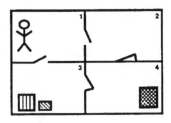

```
(inroom hero room1)    (inroom box1 room3)
(inroom box2 room3)    (inroom box3 room4)
(door-open door12)     (door-open door13)
(door-closed door34)   (door-locked door24)
```

(a) Initial State

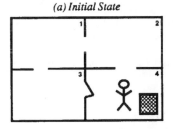

```
(and (door-closed door34)
     (next-to hero box3))
```

(b) Goal Statement

Figure 20.4:   Problem situation in the extended-STRIPS domain (*strips*2-5). The goal statement is a partial specification of the final desired state: the location of other objects and the status of other doors remains unspecified.

statement.) We represent the sequence of decision nodes annotated, for simplicity, only with their subgoaling structure.

NoLimit starts working on the goal (next-to hero box3), node cn1, because door34 is closed in the initial state. The relevant operator for this goal is (goto-box box3), as shown in node cn2. This operator is not applicable because one of its preconditions, namely, that the agent be in the same room as the box, is not true in the state. Therefore, at node cn3, it subgoals on getting hero into room4. Now note that both room2 and room3 are adjacent to room4. By backward chaining, NoLimit finds these two alternatives as relevant operators to the goal (inroom hero room4), namely, the operators (go-thru door34), shown as node cn4, or (go-thru door24). In Figure 20.6, we show the complete annotated decision node cn4 considering that NoLimit searched the alternative (go-thru door24) before pursuing the

Node type and number	:choice	:precond of	:relevant to
goal cn1	(next-to hero box3)	cn0	
chosen-op cn2	(goto-box box3)		cn1
goal cn3	(inroom hero room4)	cn2	
chosen-op cn4	(go-thru dr34)		cn3
goal cn5	(inroom hero room3)	cn4	
chosen-op cn6	(go-thru dr13)		cn5
applied-op cn7	(GO-THRU dr13)		
goal cn8	(door-open dr34)		
chosen-op cn9	(open-door dr34)		cn8
applied-op cn10	(OPEN-DOOR dr34)		
applied-op cn11	(GO-THRU dr34)		
goal cn12	(door-closed dr34)	cn0	
chosen-op cn13	(close-door dr34)		cn12
applied-op cn14	(CLOSE-DOOR dr34)		
applied-op cn15	(GOTO-BOX box3)		

Figure 20.5: A case (simplified) corresponding to the problem in Figure 20.4. A case is an annotated successful problem solving episode.

successful operator (go-thru door34). Note that door24 is locked, and there is no key to it in the initial state. In the search episode, this failure corresponds to a subtree out of the finally successful node cn4. However, the analogical reasoner creates a case by annotating the successful path with its sibling failed alternatives (and other justifications as introduced above). It greedily attributes the reason of a failure to the last failed leaf of the searched subtree.[3]

NoLimit pursues it search as shown in Figure 20.5. It alternates between (1) choosing the relevant operator for each goal and applying it if all its preconditions are true in the state and (2) continuing subgoaling on a goal of the new goal set.

Node cn12 is also worth remarking about, and we show its expansion in Figure 20.7. At that search point, NoLimit has the choice between immediately applying the operator (goto-box box3) as it becomes applicable as soon as hero enters room4 (at node cn11) or subgoaling in the goal (door-closed dr34) that became a goal when door34 was opened at node cn10. Because NoLimit is a nonlinear planner with the ability to fully interleave all the decisions at any search depth (Veloso, 1989; Rosenbloom et al., 1990), it successfully finds the optimal plan to solve this problem. Note that in Figure 20.7, we show the problem-solving search situation where NoLimit explores first the eager choice of applying any

---

[3] In reality, the case generation algorithm stores the conjunction of the pairs roots-failed leaves of the complete failed subtree. However, the important point is that none of the intermediate nodes is stored to keep the size of the case tractable, and no special effort is done in trying to determine the correct or *real* reason of failure.

```
Frame of class chosen-op decision node cn4
 :choice (go-thru dr34)
 :sibling-relevant-ops
   (((go-thru dr24)
       (:no-relevant-ops (is-key dr24 <key>))))
 :why-this-operator nil
 :relevant-to (inroom hero room4)
```

Figure 20.6:   A chosen operator decision node with its justifications: zoom of the decision node cn4 in Figure 20.5

```
Frame of class goal decision node cn12
 :choice (door-closed dr34)
 :sibling-goals nil
 :sibling-applicable-ops
   (((GOTO-BOX box3) (:state-loop)))
 :why-subgoal nil
 :why-this-goal nil
 :precond-of (*finish*)
```

Figure 20.7:   A goal decision node with its justifications: zoom of the decision node cn12 in Figure 20.5

applicable operator, namely, the sibling-applicable-op (GOTO-BOX box3). This choice ordering is however a failure because when returning back to close door34, after achieving (next-to hero box3), NoLIMIT encounters a state loop. It recognizes that it was in the same state before and backtracks to the correct ordering, postponing applying the operator (GOTO-BOX box3) at node cn15 until accomplishing the goal (door-closed dr34).

Without guidance, NoLIMIT explores the space of possible attention foci and orderings of alternatives, and only after backtracking does it find the correct goal interleaving. The idea of compiling problem solving episodes is to learn next time from its earlier exploration and reduce search dramatically by replaying the same reasoning process in similar situations.

The generated case corresponds to the search tree compacted into the successful path annotated with the justifications that resulted in the sequence of correct decisions that led to a solution to the problem. In the next section, we introduce a global view of the organization of the accumulated library of cases.

20.3 ORGANIZATION OF THE CASE LIBRARY—INDEXING

As we have seen above, the goal statement and the initial state of a problem are its immediate indices. The cases are accessed in a three-level access structure.

At the top level of access, a hash table, named *CASE-LIBRARY*, associates each generalized goal literal with the list of problems that has a corresponding instantiated literal as a conjunct in its goal statement.

```
Top *CASE-LIBRARY* hash table
*****************************

Typed-goal: (door-closed DOOR)
  Problems: (strips2-5)

Typed-goal: (next-to AGENT BOX)
  Problems: (strips2-5 strips3-9)

Typed-goal: (inroom BOX ROOM)
  Problems: (strips2-17 strips3-9)

Typed-goal: (door-open DOOR)
  Problems: (strips2-17)

Typed-goal: (holding KEY)
  Problems: (strips3-9)
```

Figure 20.8:   The hash table *CASE-LIBRARY*: the hash key is the generalized literal, and the value is the list of problems that have a corresponding instantiated literal in their goal statement

As an example, consider the problem *strips2-5* shown in Figure 20.4 with goal statement (and (door-closed door34)(next-to hero box3)) and the problem *strips2-17* shown in Figure 20.14 with goal statement (and (inroom box1 room2) (door-open door34)). For the purpose of better illustration, consider the additional problem *strips3-9* with goal statement (and (next-to hero box4) (inroom box4 room1)(holding key13)). In Figure 20.8, we show the relevant entries of the *CASE-LIBRARY* after *strips2-5*, *strips2-17*, and *strips3-9* are stored into memory.

For example, the hash key (inroom BOX ROOM) has as its value the list (strips2-17 strips3-9) because these two problems have an instantiated corresponding literal in their goal statement, respectively, (inroom box1 room2) and (inroom box4 room1).

The pointer to the initial state is stored at a second level of access. For exactly the same goal conjunct, there may be several different problems with different initial states. The initial state is itself stored in a discrimination net that corresponds to the third level of access, as we will describe below.

An association list *STATE-NET-NAMES* stores each conjunctive generalized goal with the name of the discrimination network where the initial state is stored.

Each instance in the goal conjunct is translated into a variable, and the goal conjunct is sorted alphabetically. In Figure 20.9, we show the relevant entries of the *STATE-NET-NAMES* after *strips2-5* and *strips2-17* are stored into memory.

```
Top *STATE-NET-NAMES* assoc table
*********************************

Sorted generalized goal: ((door-closed <door0>)
                          (next-to <agent0> <box0>))
       State-net-name: "state-net-1"

Sorted generalized goal: ((door-open <door0>)
                          (inroom <box0> <room0>))
       State-net-name: "state-net-2"

Sorted generalized goal: ((holding <key0>)
                          (inroom <box0> <room1>)
                          (next-to <agent0> <box0>))
       State-net-name: "state-net-3"
```

Figure 20.9: The association table *STATE-NET-NAMES*: it associates the sorted generalized goal conjunct with the pointer to the discrimination network where the initial state is stored

Finally, the initial state is organized in a discrimination network. Each network has a root frame of class "state-root," as shown in Figure 20.10, that summarizes the contents of the network. The nodes of the network are frames of class "state," also shown in Figure 20.10. Their content is a set of literals in the initial state.

```
(def-frame state-root (:is-a tofu)
   :prob-names nil      ;list of problem names stored
                        ;in the state discrimination net
   :goal nil            ;goal conjunct of state-root
   :case-names nil      ;list of all the cases in net
   :children nil        ;points to a state frame,
     ;though the root of state discrimination net has
     ;only one child node, the slot is named children,
     ;instead of child, to be uniform with the state frame.
   )

(def-frame state (:is-a tofu)
   :content nil         ;list of state-goal literals
   :parent nil          ;state-root frame or state frame
   :children nil        ;list of state frames or nil
   :cases nil           ;list of leaf cases
   :x-pos-par 0         ;just to draw (is not stored)
   :y-pos-par 0         ;just to draw (is not stored)
   :x-pos-child 0       ;just to draw (is not stored)
   :y-pos-child 0       ;just to draw (is not stored)
   )
```

Figure 20.10: The frame structure of the nodes of the discrimination net for the initial state

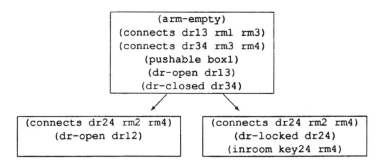

Figure 20.11:   A simple discrimination tree for the initial state

The goal of the dynamic organization of the discrimination state network is to learn what are the levels of relevance of the literals in the initial state as a function of the common goal they address. The structure of the network should be such that the literals closer to the root are more relevant than the ones at the leaves.

Each leaf of the network points to one or more cases (derivational analogy trace) whose relevant initial state is the set of literals in the path from the corresponding leaf up to the root of the network (Kolodner, 1983). It is hard to show here an example because the discrimination network is dynamically maintained. For the sake of illustration, in Figure 20.11 we show the contents of "state-net-2," where two different solutions for problem *strips2-17* (see Figures 20.14, 20.15, and 20.16) are stored. The understanding of the contents of the state nodes requires, however, knowledge of the concept of *foot-printing* the initial state. The reader is advised to look now at this example only from the organizational point of view and, after reading Section 20.4, to return to this example and comprehensively follow its contents.

In the next section, we describe the retrieval algorithm and mention how it makes use of the memory organization. The complete algorithm for the dynamic memory update is still under development; we are still analyzing results of its performance in scaled-up domains.

20.4 RETRIEVING SIMILAR PAST CASES FOR GUIDANCE

Several research projects study the problem of assigning adequate similarity metrics (recent work includes Bareiss and King, 1989; Kolodner, 1989; Porter et al., 1989). Our approach relies on an incremental understanding of an increasingly more appropriate similarity metric. In Veloso and Carbonell (1990), we presented our proposed memory model, SMART (standing for **S**torage in **M**emory and **A**daptive **R**etrieval over **T**ime). NOLIMIT, the nonlinear analogical problem solver, provides SMART with information about the utility of the candidate cases suggested as similar in reaching a solution. This information is used to refine the case library organization and, in particular, the similarity metric. In this section, we analyze two similarity metrics with different degrees of problem-context sensitivity. We first introduce a simple direct similarity metric and proceed to refine it by analyzing the derivational trace produced by the analytical problem solver.

20.4.1 A Direct Similarity Metric

Let S be the initial state and G be the goal statement, both given as conjunctions of literals. A *literal* is an instantiated predicate, i.e., literal = (predicate argument-value*). As an example, (inroom key12 room1) is a literal where inroom is the predicate, and key12 and room1 are its instantiated arguments.

Each past case P in memory is indexed by the corresponding initial state and goal statement, respectively, S^P and G^P. When a new problem P' is given to the system in terms of its $G^{P'}$ and $S^{P'}$, retrieving one (or more) analog consists of finding a *similar* past case by comparing these two input $G^{P'}$ and $S^{P'}$ to the indices of past cases.

*Definition 1. We say that a conjunction of literals $L = l_1,...,l_n$ **directly matches** a conjunction of literals $L' = l'_1,...,l'_m$ under a substitution σ with **match value** δ if there are δ **many** literals in L that directly match some literals in L' under σ. A literal l directly matches a literal l' iff*

- *The predicate of l is the same as the predicate of l'.*
- *Each argument of l is of the same class (type) as its corresponding argument of l'.*

In this case, there is a substitution σ, such that $l = \sigma(l')$.

We first compute a simple partial match value between problems as the sum of the match value of their corresponding initial states and goal statements calculated independently, as presented in definition 2.

*Definition 2. Let P and P' be two particular problems, respectively, with initial states S^P and $S^{P'}$ and goals G^P and $G^{P'}$. Let $\delta_G^{\sigma(P),P'}$ be the match value of G^P and $G^{P'}$ under some substitution σ. Let $\delta_S^{\sigma(P),P'}$ be the match value of S^P and $S^{P'}$ under the substitution σ. Then we say that the two problems P and P' **directly match** with **match value** $\delta^{\sigma(P),P'} = \delta_G^{\sigma(P),P'} + \delta_S^{\sigma(P),P'}$ under substitution σ.*

As an example, the literal (inroom box1 room1) *directly matches* the literal (inroom boxA roomX), where box1 and boxA are both of class BOX, and room1 and roomX are of class ROOM. Under the substitution, σ = (box1/boxA, room1/roomX), (inroom box1 room1) = σ ((inroom boxA roomX)).

Input: List of problems hashed from the *CASE-LIBRARY*, $\mathcal{L} = \mathcal{P}_1, \ldots, \mathcal{P}_p$,
and a new problem $\mathcal{P}'$.
Output: The set of problems from $\mathcal{L}$ most directly similar
to $\mathcal{P}'$.

procedure Retrieve_Most_Similar_Past_Cases($\mathcal{L}$, $\mathcal{P}'$):
1. **current_max_match** $\leftarrow 0$
2. **Most_Similar** $\leftarrow \{\}$
3. **for** $i \leftarrow 1$ **to** p **do**
4.   Compute $\delta_G^{P_i, P'}$ for all the possible goal substitutions.
5.   **If** not (forall substitutions $\delta_G^{P_i, P'} = 0$)
6.   **for** each substitution σ **do**
7.   Apply substitution to the initial state S_i.
8.   Compute $\delta_S^{\sigma(P_i), P'}$.
9. $\delta^{\sigma(P_i), P'} \leftarrow \delta_G^{\sigma(P_i), P'} + \delta_S^{\sigma(P_i), P'}$
10.   **If** $\delta^{\sigma(P_i), P'} >$ **current_max_match**
11.   **current_max_match** $\leftarrow \delta^{\sigma(P_i), P'}$
12.   **Most_Similar** $\leftarrow \{(P_i, \sigma)\}$
13.   **If** $\delta^{\sigma(P_i), P'} =$ **current_max_match**
14.   Add (P_i, σ) to **Most_Similar**.
15. Return **Most_Similar**

Figure 20.12:   Retrieving the most similar past cases

The partial match value of two problems, as expected, is substitution dependent. As an example, consider the goal $G = \{$(inroom key 12 room 1), (inroom box1 room1)$\}$ and the goal $G' = \{$(inroom key13 room4), (inroom key14 room2), (inroom box53 room4)$\}$. Then G directly matches G' *with match value* $\delta = 2$ under the substitution $\sigma = \{$key12/key13, room1/room4, box1/box53$\}$ and *match value* $\delta = 1$ under the substitution $\sigma' = \{$key12/key14, room1/room2$\}$.

In a first experiment, we used this direct similarity metric to evaluate the partial match between problems, not considering therefore any relevant correlations between the initial states and the goal statements. The procedure in Figure 20.12 retrieves the set of *most similar* past cases. Each goal conjunct is generalized to its class arguments. By hashing each goal conjunct in the *CASE-LIBRARY* (see Section 20.3), we retrieve directly all and only the past problems that share at least one goal conjunct with the current new problem. This set of problems is the input for the procedure shown in Figure 20.12.

20.4.1.1 Examples in Process-Job Planning and Extended-STRIPS Domains

We ran NOLIMIT without analogy over a set of problems in the process-job planning and the extended-STRIPS domains.[4] We accumulated a library of cases. In

---

[4]This set is a sampled subset of the original set used by Minton (1988).

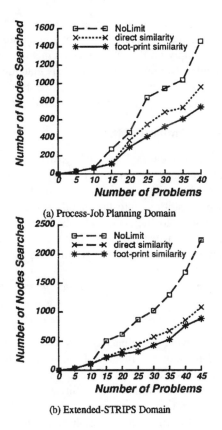

(a) Process-Job Planning Domain

(b) Extended-STRIPS Domain

Figure 20.13:   Comparison in the process-job planning and extended-STRIPS domains

order to factor away other issues in memory organization, the case library was simply organized as a linear list of cases. We then ran a new set of problems using the case library.

The dotted curves in Figures 20.13 (a) and (b) show the results for these two domains. We plotted the average cumulative number of nodes searched. We note from the results that analogy showed an improvement over basic blind search (dashed curves): a factor of 1.5-fold for the process-job planning and scheduling domain and 2.0-fold for the extended-STRIPS domain. (We will see later the meaning of the solid curves.) In general, the direct similarity metric led to acceptable results. However, analyzing the results, we notice that the straightforward similarity metric does not always provide the best guidance when there are several conjuncts in the goal statement.

The problem of matching conjunctive goals turns out to be rather complex. Because conjunctive goals may interact, it is not at all clear to decide that problems are more similar based simply on the *number* of literals that match the initial state and the goal statements. Noticing therefore that matching conjunctive goals involves reasoning over a large lattice of situations, we developed a new similarity metric by refining the indexing based on the derivational trace of a past solution.

20.4.2 The Foot-Print Similarity Metric

The derivational trace identified for each goal the set of *weakest preconditions* necessary to achieve that goal. Then recursively, we create the *foot-print* of a user-given goal conjunct by doing a goal regression of the final plan, i.e., projecting back its weakest preconditions into the literals in the initial state (Waldinger, 1981; Mitchell et al., 1986). The literals in the initial state are therefore *categorized* according to the goal conjunct that employed them in its solution. Goal regression acts are an explanation of the successful path (Cain et al., 1991).

*Definition 3. For a given problem P and corresponding solution, a literal s in the initial state is in the **foot-print** of a goal conjunct g if it is in the set of weakest preconditions of g according to the derivational trace of the solution.*

The purpose of retrieving a similar past case is to provide a problem solving episode to be replayed for the construction of the solution to a new problem. We capture into the similarity metric the role of the initial state in terms of the different goal conjuncts for a particular solution found. Situation details are not similar per se. They are similar as a function of their relevance in the solution encountered.

Consider Figure 20.14 where in (a) we show the initial state and in (b) the goal statement of an example problem from the extended-STRIPS domain, say, problem *strips2-17*.

Assume we solved the problem in Figure 20.14 by pushing box1 from room1 into room2 and then going to room3 back through room1 to open the door dr34. The actual solution searched and found would be the plan shown in Figure 20.15 (a).

In this way of solving the problem, for example, the key24 for the locked door dr24 did not play any role and is therefore not a *relevant* literal in the initial state of this problem if this problem solving episode is to be replayed. In Figure 20.15 (b), we show the actual foot-print of the initial state corresponding to this first solution to the problem. Each literal in the initial state is associated with the list of goals that it contributed to achieve.

However, NoLIMIT could have encountered a different solution to this problem, namely, to push box1 along on its way to door dr34, open it, and push box1 through door dr24 into room2 after unlocking this door. The actual solution searched and found would be the plan shown in Figure 20.16 (a). In this way of

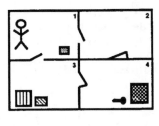

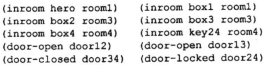

```
(inroom hero room1)        (inroom box1 room1)
(inroom box2 room3)        (inroom box3 room3)
(inroom box4 room4)        (inroom key24 room4)
(door-open door12)         (door-open door13)
(door-closed door34)       (door-locked door24)
```

(a) Initial State

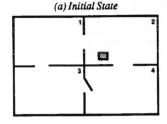

```
(and (inroom box1 room2)
     (door-open door34))
```

(b) Goal Statement

Figure 20.14:   Problem situation in the extended-STRIPS domain (*strips*2-17). The goal statement is a
partial specification of the final desired state: the location of other objects and the status of other doors remained unspecified.

solving the problem, for example, the key24 for the locked door dr24 is a *relevant*
literal in the initial state of this problem if this problem solving episode is to be
replayed. In Figure 20.16 (b), we show the actual foot-print of the initial state for
this solution.

 We formally define the new similarity metric that evaluates the degree (or
value) of match of the initial state as a function of the goal conjuncts that directly
matched. This similarity emphasizes the goal oriented behavior (Kedar-Cabelli,
1985; Hammond, 1989) even more than the one introduced earlier by focusing only
on the goal-relevant portions of the initial state (Hickman and Larkin, 1990;
Pazzani, 1990) as determined by the problem solver for each case in the library.

*Definition 4.   We say that the initial state S **foot-print matches** an initial state S′
under a substitution σ and given matched goals $g_1^m,...,g_k^m$ **with match value** δ if*

```
(GOTO-BOX box1)
(PUSH-THRU-DOOR box1 dr12)
(GO-THRU dr12 room1)
(GOTO-DOOR dr13)
(GO-THRU dr13 room3)
(GOTO-DOOR dr34)
(OPEN-DOOR dr34)
```

(a)

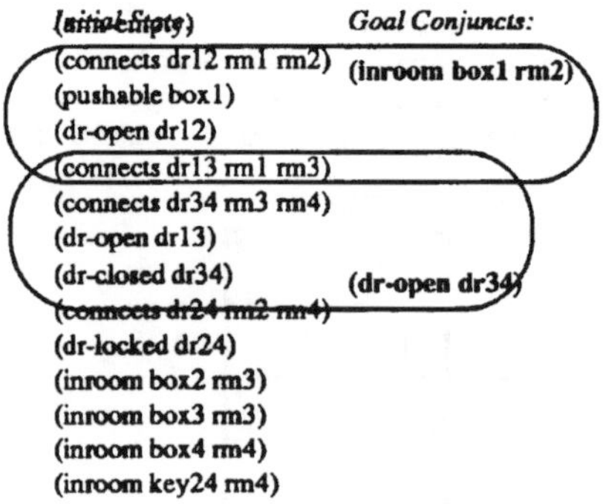

(b)

Figure 20.15:   One solution for problem *strips2*-17: (a) plan, (b) foot-print: The initial state literals
                      are associated with the goal conjunct(s) they contributed to achieve, according to the
                      goal regression of the plan in (a).

there are δ **many** *literals l in S such that (i) l directly matches some literal l' in S'
under* σ *and (ii) l is in the foot-print of some goal* g_i^m *for i = 1,...,m.*

When assigning a match value to two problems, we now consider not only the
number of goals that match but also use the matched goals themselves to determine
the match degree of the initial state.

From the definition 4, we change steps 4 and 8 of the procedure presented in
Figure 20.12 accordingly. Namely in step 4, we computed the match value for the
goal statements but further return which goals matched. In step 8, we use these
goals to compute the match value for the initial states. The rest of the algorithm is
invariant to selection of the similarity metric.

20.4.2.1 Further Search Reduction Examples

We ran new experiments with this foot-print similarity metric in the extended-
STRIPS and process-job planning domains. The solid curves in Figures 20.13 (a) and
(b) show the results for these two domains. We note that the results with the
foot-print similarity metric show an improvement over base search of a factor of

```
(GOTO-BOX box1)
(PUSH-THRU-DOOR box1 dr13)
(PUSH-TO-DOOR box1 dr34)
(OPEN-DOOR dr34)
(PUSH-THRU-DOOR box1 dr34)
(GOTO-KEY key24)
(PICK-UP key24)
(GOTO-DOOR dr24)
(UNLOCK-DOOR dr24)
(OPEN-DOOR dr24)
(GOTO-BOX box1)
(PUT-DOWN key24)
(PUSH-THRU-DOOR box1 dr24)
```

(a)

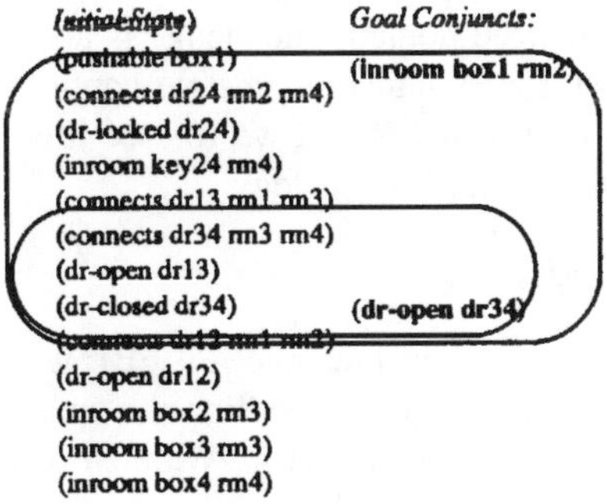

(b)

Figure 20.16: A different solution for problem *strips*2-17: (a) plan, (b) foot-print: The initial state literals are associated with the goal conjunct(s) they contributed to achieve, according to the goal regression of the plan in (a).

2.0-fold for the process-job planning and scheduling domain and 2.6-fold for the extended-STRIPS domain. The curves obtained do not represent the best improvement expected because the set of forty problems used is far from completely covering the full range of problems in either domain. One of the directions of our current research is to develop techniques for learning similarity metrics by further automatically analyzing the analogical replay mechanism.[5]

To scale the system well in both the size and diversity of domains, we have currently a 1,000-case library in a complex logistics transportation domain. In this domain, packages are to be moved among different cities. Packages are carried

---

[5] In fact, we currently have generated a more sophisticated similarity metric also derived from the derivational trace where better improvements are noticed (Veloso, 1992).

within the same city in trucks and across cities in airplanes. Trucks and airplanes may have limited capacity. At each city, there are several locations, e.g., post offices and airports. Although our analysis in this large-scale domain is not complete yet, the results so far show high positive transfer, including total memory retrieval and problem-solving times. We experience that the scale capabilities of our methods have been demonstrated.

20.5 DISCUSSION: EBL AND ANALOGY, ABSTRACTION AND ANALOGY

Previous work in the linear planner of PRODIGY uses explanation-based learning (EBL) techniques (Minton, 1988) to extract from a problem solving trace the explanation chain responsible for a success or failure and to compile search control rules therefrom. The axiomatized domain knowledge is also used to learn abstraction layers (Knoblock, 1991) and statically generate control rules (Etzioni, 1990). In this section, we discuss the benefits that we foresee in a deeper integration of EBL and analogy and in abstraction and analogy.

20.5.1 EBL and Analogy

Although we do not directly yet integrate full EBL with analogy, we believe in the benefits of that integration. We discuss first the simple explanation mechanism we use in the foot-print similarity metric. We then extend our discussion to the deeper integration that we envision.

While performing the goal regression on the derivational trace to determine the foot-print of the initial state, the analogical reasoner performs a lazy explanation of the solution encountered. It is lazy because it goes up the successful path following the subgoaling chain without trying to prove any generalization of the immediate success or recorded failures. However, it turned out quite useful to take into account this explanation although it is simple, as we discussed in Section 20.4.

We plan to pursue a deeper integration with the EBL module in PRODIGY (Minton, 1988; Etzioni, 1990). On one hand, this integration would allow the joint EBL-analytical reasoner to decide whether to invest effort in statically analyzing a domain theory or a trace of a solved problem to generalize control rules therefrom or to store the problem solving episode as a case for eventual future retrieval and replay. On the other hand, the dynamic memory organization in analogy converges to some clustering of problems that are similar to each other. We further envision some explanation-based strategy that would be capable of generalizing the situations captured by the clusters and subsequently generating control rules therefrom.

Analogy would benefit from the integration because some simple cases and simple problem solving situations would be translated into general control rules. On the other hand, EBL would benefit in incomplete domain theories where the proofs cannot be pursued. Additionally, in the nonlinear problem solving context, the number of alternatives explored is very large, and very complex goal interactions can be explored. The joint EBL-analytical reasoner could switch from an eager costly attempt to explain a difficult trace to a lazy attitude of storing it as a case, based on a function that computes the relative cost of the two approaches.

20.5.2 Abstraction and Analogy

A key issue in the process of solving problems by analogy is the identification of what are the *details* and what are the *relevant* features of a particular situation. Because new and past situations are not expected to fully match, knowing the relevance of the information available increases the ability for successful partial matching of different problems. ALPINE (Knoblock, 1991) provides a mechanism that analyzes a particular domain and generates abstraction levels that group together features (literals) in a hierarchical structure, the most crucial, interrelated ones at the top. We plan to explore the use of the abstraction levels generated by ALPINE as a measure of relevance to rank partially matched candidate analogs.

The way the case memory is organized directly relates to the eventual success of the retrieval phase. As we have seen before, a new situation is presented in terms of an initial world state and a goal statement. The initial similarity metric we use requires a total match at the goal predicate level; i.e., situations that refer to different uninstantiated goals are not proposed as candidate analogs. This supports a goal-oriented matching method (Kedar-Cabelli, 1985) that we advocate as the base strategy.

The dynamic organization of memory currently does a simple abstraction by generalizing instances into their type classes. However, we plan to use the abstraction levels to help the dynamic organization of the discrimination network. Namely, we would like to have the most relevant features of the problem being unified with the new problem before the detailed ones, where relevant is both a function of past experience and the level in the abstraction hierarchy.

A second major benefit of the integration of analogy and abstraction is the *generality* of stored plans for later indexing. That is, a solution at an abstract level is much more likely to be an applicable candidate analog than one at the ground level—although it will require refinement by adding in details of the current problem. In general, we propose to use abstract analogs when specific grounded ones are not present to guide search in derivational analogy.

20.6 CONCLUSION

In this chapter, we presented the automatic case generation, storage, and retrieval of cases in the derivational analogy module in the PRODIGY architecture.

We showed how the problem solver introspects into its decision cycle recording the justifications of the decisions taken and automatically generating cases from its problem solving experience. These cases are organized in a case library indexed by their goal and relevant initial state. We illustrated the case generation procedure and the organization of memory with simple examples from the extended-STRIPS domain. We presented results of the performance of the replay mechanism when the retrieval procedure used two different similiarity metrics: the direct and foot-print ones. The direct metric does not consider any correlations between the initial state and the goal conjuncts. The foot-print metric performs a goal regression in the solution path and is able to identify the relevant features of the initial state for each goal conjunct. The system shows better performance when the foot-print similarity metric is used because more similar cases are replayed. Finally, we discussed the benefits we foresee of a deeper integration of the EBL and abstraction modules with the analytical reasoner within PRODIGY.

ACKNOWLEDGMENTS

The authors thank Daniel Borrajo for a major part of NoLIMIT's implementation and Alicia Perez, Craig Knoblock, Oren Etzioni, Yolanda Gil, Robert Joseph, and Steve Minton for many useful discussions and suggestions on both the analogy work and the synergy of the learning modules. The authors thank the whole PRODIGY research group for helpful comments on this chapter. The first author increased her interests on multistrategy learning at the European Working Session on Learning 1991. For this, she thanks the participants of the EWSL '91 who were related to this theme.

This research was sponsored by the Defense Advanced Research Projects Agency (DOD) and monitored by the Avionics Laboratory, Air Force Wright Aeronautical Laboratories, Aeronautical Systems Division (AFSC), Wright-Patterson AFB, OH 45433-6543 under Contract F33615-87-C-1499, ARPA Order No. 4976, Amendment 20. The views and conclusions contained in this chapter are those of the authors and should not be interpreted as representing the official policies, either expressed or implied, of the Defense Advanced Research Projects Agency or of the U.S. Government.

References

Bareiss, R., and King, J.A. Similarity assessment in case-based reasoning. In *Proceedings of the Second Workshop on Case-Based Reasoning*, pages 67–71. Morgan Kaufmann, San Mateo, CA, 1989.

Cain, T., Pazzani, M., and Silverstein, G. Using domain knowledge to influence similarity judgements. In *Proceedings of the 1991 DARPA Workshop on Case-Based Reasoning*. Morgan Kaufmann, San Mateo, CA, 1991.

Carbonell, J.G. Derivational analogy: A theory of reconstructive problem solving and expertise acquisition. In Michalski, R.S., Carbonell, J.G., and Mitchell, T.M., editors, *Machine Learning: An Artificial Intelligence Approach, Volume II*. Morgan Kaufmann, San Mateo, CA, 1986.

Carbonell, J.G., and Gil, Y. Learning by experimentation: The operator refinement method. In Michalski, R.S., and Kodratoff, Y., editors, *Machine Learning: An Artificial Intelligence Approach, Volume III*. Morgan Kaufmann, San Mateo, CA, 1990.

Duval, B. Abduction for explanation-based learning. In *Proceedings of the European Working Session on Learning*. Springer-Verlag, New York, 1991.

Etzioni, O. *A Structural Theory of Explanation-Based Learning*. Ph.D. thesis, School of Computer Science, Carnegie Mellon University, 1990. Available as technical report CMU-CS-90-185.

Fikes, R.E., and Nilsson, N.J. Strips: A new approach to the application of theorem proving to problem solving. *Artificial Intelligence*, 2:189–208, 1971.

Hammond, K. *Case-based Planning: Viewing Planning as a Memory Task*. Academic Press, New York, 1989.

Hickman, A.K., and Larkin, J.H. Internal analogy: A model of transfer within problems. In *The 12th Annual Conference of the Cognitive Science Society*. Lawrence Erlbaum Associates, Hillsdale, NJ, 1990.

Joseph, R.L. Graphical knowledge acquisition. In *Proceedings of the 4th Knowledge Acquisition For Knowledge-Based Systems Workshop*, Banff, Canada, 1989.

Kedar-Cabelli, S. Purpose-directed analog. In *Proceedings of the Seventh Annual Conference of the Cognitive Science Society*, pages 150–159, 1985.

Knoblock, C.A. *Automatically Generating Abstractions for Problem Solving*. Ph.D. thesis, School of Computer Science, Carnegie Mellon University, Pittsburgh, PA, 1991. Forthcoming.

Kolodner, J. Maintaining organization in a dynamic long-term memory. In *Cognitive Science*, volume 7, 1983.

———. Judging which is the "best" case for a case-based reasoner. In *Proceedings of the Second Workshop on Case-Based Reasoning*, pages 77–81. Morgan Kaufmann, San Mateo, CA, 1989.

Minton, S. Selectively generalizing plans for problem solving. In *Proceedings of AAAI-85*, pages 596–599, 1985.

———. *Learning Effective Search Control Knowledge: An Explanation-Based Approach*. Ph.D. thesis, Computer Science Department, Carnegie Mellon University, 1988.

Minton, S., Knoblock, C.A., Kuokka, D.R., Gil, Y., Joseph, R.L., and Carbonell, J.G. PRODIGY 2.0: The manual and tutorial. Technical Report CMU-CS-89-146, School of Computer Science, Carnegie Mellon University, 1989.

Mitchell, T.M., Kellar, R.M., and Kedar-Cabelli, S.T. Explanation-based generalization: A unifying view. *Machine Learning*, 1:47–80, 1986.

Pazzani, M. *Creating a Memory of Causal Relationships: An Integration of Empirical and Explanation-based Learning Methods*. Lawrence Erlbaum Associates, Hillsdale, NJ, 1990.

Porter, B., Bareiss, R., and Holte, R. Knowledge acquisition and heuristic classification in weak-theory domains. Technical Report AI-TR-88-96, Department of Computer Science, University of Texas at Austin, 1989.

Rosenbloom, P.S., Lee, S., and Unruh, A. Responding to impasses in memory-driven behavior: A framework for planning. In *Proceedings of the DARPA Workshop on Innovative Approaches to Planning, Scheduling, and Control*. Morgan Kaufmann, San Mateo, CA, 1990.

Veloso, M.M. *Nonlinear problem solving using intelligent casual-commitment*. Technical Report CMU-CS-89-210, School of Computer Science, Carnegie Mellon University, 1989.

————. Efficient nonlinear planning using casual commitment and analogical reasoning. In *Proceedings of the Thirteenth Annual Conference of the Cognitive Science Society*, pages 938–943. Lawrence Erlbaum Associates, Hillsdale, NJ, 1991.

————. *Learning by Analogical Reasoning in General Problem Solving*, Ph.D. Thesis and Technical Report CMU-CS-92-174, School of Computer Science, Carnegie Mellon University, Pittsburgh, PA, 1992.

Veloso, M.M., and Carbonell, J.G. Integrating analogy into a general problem-solving architecture. In Zemankova, M. and Ras, Z., editors, *Intelligent Systems*, Ellis Horwood Ltd., Chichester, England, 1990.

————. Learning by analogical replay in PRODIGY: First results. In *Proceedings of the European Working Session on Learning*, pages 375–390. Springer-Verlag, New York, 1991.

————. Variable-precision case retrieval in analogical problem solving. In *Proceedings of the 1991 DARPA Workshop on Case-Based Reasoning*, pages 93–106, Morgan Kaufmann, San Mateo, CA, 1991.

Waldinger, R. Achieving several goals simultaneously. In Nilsson, N.J., and Webber, B., editors, *Readings in Artificial Intelligence*, pages 250–271, Tioga, Palo Alto, CA, 1981.

21

GENETIC PROGRAMMING:

Evolutionary Approaches to Multistrategy Learning

Hugo de Garis
(ATR, Kyoto, Japan
George Mason University)

Abstract

This chapter introduces the concept of Genetic Programming (GP) and discusses its relevance to Multistrategy Learning. Genetic Programming is concerned with applying Genetic Algorithms (GAs) to build/evolve complex systems. For the purposes of this chapter, complex systems are defined to be those that have structures and/or dynamics that are too complex to be predictable or even analyzable in practical terms. With the coming of molecular scale technologies, it will be possible to build devices with a huge number of components. The potential complexity of such systems will make traditional approaches to building and teaching them increasingly difficult. An alternative approach is to imitate nature's method of creating (hyper)complex systems, namely, a form of simulated or "applied evolution," which basically is what GP is about. This chapter shows how various learning strategies can be combined (e.g., those from neural networks and GAs or from cellular automata and GAs) to produce systems that are very complex in the above sense yet are capable of performing as desired. By employing these multistrategy (in the above cases, dual-strategy) learning techniques, more complex and interesting systems can be constructed than are possible by using the usual mono-strategy learning approaches, e.g., neural network learning algorithms, such as "back-propagation," or hand coded reproduction rules for cellular automata.

21.1 INTRODUCTION

One of the author's primary research interests concerns the conceptual problems that will arise when molecular scale technologies of the 1990s and beyond will allow devices to be built with a huge number of components. For example, it has been estimated that by the mid 1990s, Wafer Scale Integration (WSI), where one very large electronic circuit is placed over the full surface of a slice or wafer of silicon, will be capable of placing ten million artificial neurons on a single wafer (Rudnick & Hammerstrom, 1989). This is only the beginning however. Molecular Electronic Devices (MED) (which represent an attempt to devise molecules capable of computation (Carter et al., 1988) promises to produce devices with an Avogadro number of components (i.e., of the order of a trillion trillion). Even more interesting is Nanotechnology (Drexler, 1992), which is attempting to build molecular scale machinery.

What all these technologies have in common is that they are capable of producing devices with an order of millions and billions (and upwards) of components. Such large numbers will focus increasing attention upon the problem of complexity. For example, "How complex should one allow these components (modules) to become? How complex should the connections between them be?" The traditional approach to designing and building systems with a large number of components has been to use a rather homogeneous approach, building what the author calls "Homogeneous Machines." A Homogeneous Machine is defined to be one that uses a large number of copies of a small number of simple modular designs, connected in rather simple ways. Typical examples of such homogeneous machines are computer mass memories, von Neumann computers, and the Connection Machine (Hillis, 1985). Homogeneous machines are usually constructed by means of a plan, a blueprint, meaning that human beings conceive solutions to the design of these machines, which means that the design must be simple enough that this can be done with human intellectual capacities. This places upper limits on the complexity levels of such machines. They have to be "humanly blueprintable."

However, the above technologies have the obvious potential of generating systems well beyond what is "humanly blueprintable." Such machines are called "Heterogeneous Machines" by the author. Heterogeneous machines are defined to be machines that are not homogeneous. Heterogeneous machines can be composed of huge numbers of complex modules, which may differ from each other, and be connected together in complex ways, making the ensemble impossible to understand in human terms. Typical examples of heterogeneous systems can be taken from nature, e.g., the human brain and embryos.

It is likely that the initial devices constructed using these molecular scale technologies will of the homogeneous variety, for reasons of human understandability. However, it is also likely that once these technologies become fully operational, pressures will grow to find ways to build heterogeneous machines. After all, the most interesting "machines" that human beings are aware of are heterogeneous, namely, ourselves. It is unlikely that researchers in the fields of Artificial Intelligence and Artificial Life will ever fulfill their respective long term dreams of building artificial intelligences and artificial life forms without solving the problem of building successful heterogeneous machines.

At this point, it is probably useful to make a distinction between being able to build a machine that functions successfully as desired and being able to understand that machine. One of the major ideas of Genetic Programming is that one can have the one without the other; i.e., one may be able to build a machine successfully without knowing in detail how it functions. It is possible that this simple idea may serve as a basis of those 21st century technologies that will be inherently "massively complex." What then is so special about Genetic Programming?

Genetic Programming (GP) is defined to be the art of using Genetic Algorithms (GAs) to build/evolve complex systems. Several examples of GP will be given in this chapter. Traditionally, GAs have been used as optimizers, for example, optimizing multiparameter mathematical functions (De Jong, 1975), but lately, a growing number of people have begun to use GAs more as builders than as optimizers (e.g., de Garis 1990, 1991, 1992, 1993; Koza 1990, 1992; Spofford and Hintz 1991; Louis and Rawlins 1991). Thus, if GAs are considered to be tools, then GP is a particular way of using such tools, namely, to build/evolve complex systems.

The feature that makes a GA so attractive to GP is what the author calls its "complexity independence" (within certain limits), meaning that as long as the population of systems being evolved by a GA continues to return increasing fitness (or system performance quality) values, then the internal complexity (whether structural or dynamic) of those systems is to some extent irrelevant. One finishes with a system that has a high fitness value; i.e., it does what one wants it to do, even though the internal complexity of the system may be too complex to be fully understood. Hence with GP, it is possible to build systems that have a complexity level that is superior to those built using other techniques. Using GP, one can say that one can "extend the barrier of the buildable."

From the point of view of multistrategy learning, one can say equivalently that using GP—i.e., applying GAs to the systems one is evolving (e.g., neural network behaviors or cellular automata "embryos")—allows one to produce a level of behavioral or structural complexity that is superior to using humanly generated algorithms defined explicitly within the mono-strategy framework of those systems (e.g., for neural networks, such algorithms could be backpropagation, Boltzman, Hopfield, etc. For cellular automata however, there may even be no humanly generated rules to generate "embryos" of desired shapes).

Although the ability of GAs to separate "buildability" from "understandability" is one of its most attractive features (from the viewpoint of GP), its usefulness should not be taken too far. As later sections in this chapter will show, human intervention is often required to help steer the evolution in desired directions. Choosing when and how to intervene is part of the art of GP. This human intervention is usually required when a desired evolution fails to occur.

Of course, if one wishes to build/evolve some system, that system must be "evolvable," i.e., be capable of returning increasing fitness values over the generations. This is not always the case. Not all systems have good "evolvabilities." Just why this is so is not well understood at the moment, and a lot more research work needs to be undertaken to generate "Evolvability Criteria." In practice, one often finds that a particular form of evolution does not occur as desired, which usually means that the human Genetic Programmer needs to impose constraints that "push" the evolution in such a way as to achieve a desired result. Several examples of this process will be presented in later sections. In practice then, GP usually consists of a series of intermediate evolutionary steps toward some final evolutionary goal.

The remainder of this chapter is structured as follows. Sections 21.2 and 21.3 present, respectively, two examples of GP techniques in action. Section 21.2 shows how combining GAs and neural nets (a dual-strategy approach) produces a tool that allows the exploration of complex and qualitatively new behaviors in neural nets. It is highly unlikely that these new phenomena would have been discovered with traditional mono-strategy neural net algorithms. The neural net modules thus evolved (GenNets) are so versatile that artificial nervous systems for artificial creatures can be built with them. Section 21.3 shows how combining GAs with reproductive cellular automata allows one to build/evolve colonies of cells having a desired overall shape. It is doubtful whether this could even be done using handcrafted reproduction rules (e.g., Wolfram, 1986). Section 21.4 discusses some ideas for future work in GP, particularly the idea of "growing" electronic circuits in an embryological style at various levels of granularity (e.g., at low level analogue RLC circuit level, higher digital logic level, or even higher artificial neuron and synapse level). The importance of doing this is also discussed. Section 21.5 discusses work that is rather similar to GP. Some conclusions are drawn in Section 21.6.

21.2 GenNets: GAs AND NEURAL NETS

21.2.1 Introduction to GenNets

This section shows how GP techniques can be used to evolve complex behaviors in neural networks. A GenNet is a "Genetically Programmed Neural Net," i.e., a fully connected neural network whose weights are evolved with a GA such that the output of the GenNet control some process in some desired way.

However, before discussing GenNets, a brief introduction to the basic principles of Genetic Algorithms now follows for those who are unfamiliar with them. A Genetic Algorithm is a form of simulated evolution. Coded instructions (usually in

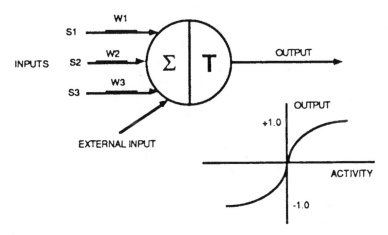

Figure 21.1:   An artificial neuron

binary form) to solve a problem are concatenated onto a string called a "chromo-some." An initial population of such chromosomes (e.g., 50) is usually generated randomly. Each chromosome is decoded and the instructions executed. The quality of the performance (called the fitness) of these instructions is measured. Those chromosomes that have higher fitness values, have more copies made of them-selves, that are then placed in the next generation of chromosomes. Because the population number is fixed (e.g., 50), competition for survival ensures that only the better chromosomes will survive. These chromosome copies are then mutated (e.g., a bit is occasionally flipped) and crossed over (i.e., two chromosomes swap por-tions of themselves). Mutation and crossover are used, respectively, to generate variety in the population and to combine quickly any favorable mutations from two separate parent chromosomes into one offspring chromosome. Over many genera-tions, the average fitness of the population increases. For a clear exposition of the principles of GAs, see Goldberg (1989).

Figure 21.1 shows the type of artificial neuron used in a GenNet. Internal input signals (S_i) are weighted (with weights W_i), summed, and added to an exter-nal input signal. From this sum is usually subtracted a threshold value T. The result (called the Activity, which equals $\Sigma_i S_i W_i + \text{ExtInp} - T$) is then fed through a nonlinear sigmoid function to produce the output value, which is fed back as inter-nal input to every neuron in the GenNet and/or can be tapped as an external output value used to help control some process. Figure 21.2 shows a small fully connected neural network and how the values of its weights are mapped onto a bitstring GA chromosome. Usually the left-hand bit of each weight field is reserved for the sign, and 6–8 bits are used to express each weight (whose absolute value is assumed to be less than 1.0) in binary fraction format. For a GenNet of N neurons, there will be N^2 connections and hence N^2 weights. If p bits are used to express each weight,

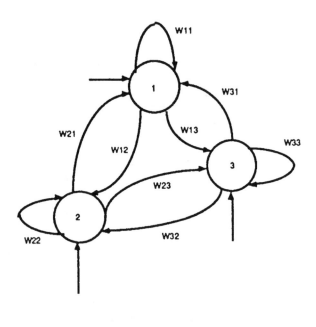

Figure 21.2:   Mapping weights to chromosomes

then the length of the chromosome will be $N^2*(p+1)$ bits. These chromosomes are initialized randomly and used to evolve the weights so that the time dependent output of their corresponding GenNets control some process.

As an example of a controlled process, consider the problem of getting an artificial creature (a quadruped) to move its eight leg components in such a way that it walks straight ahead or turns to the left or right, etc. This would be an extremely difficult problem to solve analytically, but using GP it can be solved without having to worry about how it is done. It is rather a "black box" solution in this sense. The output of the neurons of the GenNet can be interpreted to be the angles of the leg components. If one knows the output values of the GenNet (with one output per degree of freedom of each leg component, i.e., 16 output), then one can determine the positions of all the legs over time. The fitness for a straight ahead walking motion would be simply the distance covered in a given number of cycles. (Note that a GenNet is synchronous or "clocked"; i.e., all neurons calculate their output values from their input values at the same moment). If the desired motion were to make the artificial creature turn clockwise, the fitness definition would be simply the clockwise angle turned by the creature in a given number of cycles.

The GenNets that evolve to generate these desired motions (e.g., walking straight ahead, turning) are essentially black boxes. Their internal (nonlinear) dynamics are very complex, yet the desired result is obtained. This is one of the great advantages of GP. It is also a good example of what can be achieved when one uses a multistrategy approach to learning (in this case combining a GA type approach to learning the weights of a neural net). It is highly doubtful that a traditional (mono-strategy) neural net training algorithm (such as "backprop" (e.g., Rumelhart and McClelland, 1986) could achieve these complex GenNet motions.

21.2.2 GenNet Behaviors

If GP is capable of evolving GenNets that have complex dynamics but that perform as desired, then perhaps the GP approach can be used as a tool to discover and to exploit qualitatively new neural network behaviors. It is widely recognized by neural network researchers that recurrent networks (i.e., those with feedback connections between neurons) are more complex in their dynamics than traditional feed-forward, layered networks. GenNets, which are fully connected and hence recurrent, display all the features of complex nonlinear dynamical systems (i.e., fixed point dynamics, oscillation, limit cycles, and chaos). Prior to the invention of GenNets, neural network researchers had rather inadequate means to teach recurrent networks to behave in desired ways. In practice, the inherent complexity of such networks tended to make them shy away. They prefered to deal with mathematically "tidy" feedforward networks.

However, with GP, one can evolve very complex GenNet behaviors and yet keep a large degree of control over them, provided the behaviors evolved for continue to improve, i.e., that they reasonably high "evolvabilities." With the use of GP techniques, several new forms of neural net (or GenNet) behaviors have been discovered. Two of these new behaviors will be presented here.

21.2.2.1 Shaping

The most important GenNet phenomenon (not only with GenNets but with any GP application) has been called "shaping" by the author. Shaping is a GP term taken from the vernacular of circus animal training, whereby one does not teach an animal a new trick all at once. Instead, one breaks up the trick (i.e., the behavior to be learned) into components, each of which is easier to learn. By assembling the components, one attains the whole trick. In GP terms, shaping usually means that a population of chromosomes is evolved initially to generate a behavior "A." These chromosomes are then used as the initial population in a second phase of evolution to generate the behavior "B." One finds that the resulting behavior "B" contains traces of behavior "A"—a sort of "behavioral inertia." The behavior "A" can be used as a kind of intermediate target behavior, which makes it easier to evolve behavior "B." It is possible that a direct attempt to evolve behavior "B" proves to

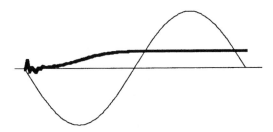

Figure 21.3:   Target and actual full oscillation

be too difficult; i.e., its "evolvability" is too low and so does not evolve much at all, or it evolves in some undesirable way. In practice, it is often necessary to choose intermediate target behaviors to be able to achieve the desired behavior "B" at all.

As an example of the shaping phenomenon, consider trying to evolve a GenNet that outputs a sinusoid of a given amplitude (e.g., 0.5) and period (i.e., number of cycles, e.g., 100). The fitness definition chosen for this case was the inverse of the sum of the squares of the differences between the target (i.e., desired) output values d_i (over each cycle of the period) and the actual values a_i.

$$\text{FITNESS} = \text{Inverse of} \sum_{i=1}^{100} (d_i - a_i)^2$$

The GenNet used here had 15 neurons (a rather arbitrary number), and one neuron (any one) had its output tapped to give the actual output value. All the initial input values were set at 0.0. The external input values were clamped at 0.0 throughout the experiment, except for two (any two) which took the values 0.5 and −0.5, respectively (rather arbitrary values used to generate some initial signals). Six bits were used to express each fractional weight. The population size was 20 chromosomes. The chromosome length was 15*15*(6 + 1) = 1575 bits. The mutation probability was 0.001 per bit. The (uniform) crossover probability was 0.6. Note that each of the figures below shows a result generated by the chromosome with the highest fitness value of the population.

Figure 21.3 shows the desired (i.e., target) output plus the result of an initial attempt to evolve it using the fitness definition above. The number of cycles in the sum amounted to a full oscillation. After several hundred generations and little further fitness improvement, the resulting actual curve was too flat, so it was decided to use shaping techniques. The actual curve would first be forced to evolve over a half oscillation, and if that could successfully be completed, the resulting chromosome population would serve as the initial population for an evolution over a full oscillation. However, a few surprises were in store. Figure 21.4 shows the result of the evolution over a half oscillation (i.e., 50 cycles) using a very similar

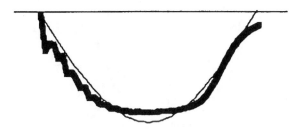

Figure 21.4:   Target and half oscillation

fitness definition. The result seemed quite acceptable at first. However, when a test was made to see what the actual curve would be when using the same chromosome that generated Figure 21.4, the result was Figure 21.5; i.e., the curve did not cross the horizontal axis as it should. To force such a crossing, the chromosome population whose elite chromosome gave Figure 21.5 was used but with the fitness definition modified to be the sum over 65 cycles. This strategy worked, as shown in Figure 21.6. A test was then undertaken to see what kind of actual curve the elite chromosome of Figure 21.6 would produce over 100 cycles. Figure 21.7 shows the results. As can be seen, the actual curve flattens. The chromosomes of Figure 21.6 were then taken as initial chromosomes over 100 cycles for several hundred generations in an attempt to get the actual curve to come down again, but it failed to do so. The fitness definition was changed so that those actual curves that started to bend down slightly were strongly rewarded (i.e., got stronger fitness scores). This was done by weighting the size of the errors in the fitness definition as shown:

$$\text{FITNESS} = \text{Inverse of } \sum_{i=1}^{100} i * (d_i - a_i)^2$$

This strategy worked, as shown in Figure 21.8. With a full oscillation now accomplished, a test was undertaken with the same chromosomes of Figure 21.8 to

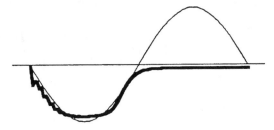

Figure 21.5:   Half oscillation flattens

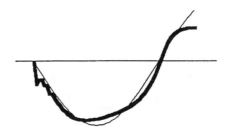

Figure 21.6:   So evolve oscillation over 65 cycles

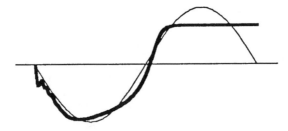

Figure 21.7:   Sixty-five cycle oscillation still flattens

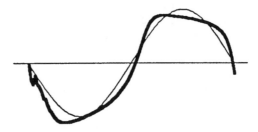

Figure 21.8:   So increase the weighting of later errors

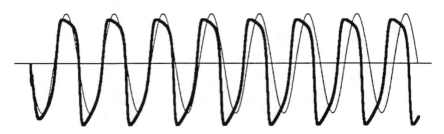

Figure 21.9:   A GenNet oscillation

see whether a run over many hundreds of cycles would give an actual curve that would continue to oscillate. Figure 21.9 shows that it did.

This rather detailed exercise in "shaping" is an example of a typical development sequence that a human Genetic Programmer uses to evolve some desired behavior. Quite often, several intermediate target behaviors are necessary to attain the desired final result. Further examples of this process will be presented in this chapter but in less detail.

21.2.2.2 Behavioral Generalization

The GenNet phenomenon to be described now is a striking example of the power of a dual strategy (NN + GA) approach, as opposed to a mono-strategy neural net algorithm, to generate a complex and interesting behavior. Because GP is capable of evolving complex behaviors, it can be used as a tool to explore complex and qualitatively new phenomena in neural network dynamics. The complexities of such behaviors are probably well beyond the abilities of the traditional mono-strategy techniques to generate.

Such a phenomenon will now be described. It is called "Behavioral Generalization." The idea is to evolve a single GenNet that is capable of generating two distinct behaviors, such as two sinusoidal oscillations of different frequencies, depending only upon the values of clamped external inputs. For example, assume that the GenNet in question is to generate consecutively two oscillations of period 40 and 80 cycles, respectively. All initial internal inputs are set at 0.0, as well as all the external inputs, except for two neurons (any two, so let us say neuron "0" and neuron "1"), which are set (rather arbitrarily) at +0.5 and –0.5, respectively, for the 40-cycle period and +0.5 and +0.5 for the 80-cycle period; i.e., the only difference is the value of the clamped external input on neuron "1."

The interesting possibility then arises that if these two oscillations can be generated, then by clamping an intermediate value at neuron "1," perhaps an oscillation of intermediate period might result. If this occurs, then the GenNet in its evolution to generate the two specified behaviors has learned to generalize or interpolate between them.

The following experiment was undertaken. Benefitting from the above experiment, two slightly more than half oscillations were generated consecutively, i.e., one of 23 cycles (for the 40-cycle period case) and one of 46 cycles (for the 80 cycle period case). The fitness definition was as shown:

$$\text{FITNESS} = \text{Inverse of } (\text{ WF} * \sum_{i=1}^{23} (d_i - a_i)^2 + \sum_{j=1}^{46} (d_j - a_j)^2)$$

where WF is a weighting factor that was used to give the 40-cycle period case a "comparable" influence in the fitness determination. For each chromosome, two runs were undertaken. In the first run, the two external inputs were clamped at +0.5

Figure 21.10: Half period oscillations

and −0.5 for 23 cycles, and in the second run, they were clamped at +0.5 and +0.5 for 46 cycles.

After some experimentation, it was found that a WF of 16 gave good results. Figure 21.10 shows the results of the elite chromosome after 600 generations and little further fitness growth. The parameter settings were similar to those mentioned earlier. The chromosome population generated for the half period oscillations was then used (in typical "shaping" style) as the initial population for the full period oscillations, with a fitness definition using 40 and 80 cycles instead of 23 and 46. Figure 21.11 shows the results after 800 generations. Two more or less "sinusoidal" oscillations were obtained with quite distinct periods depending upon the value of the clamped external input on neuron "1." The fact that a GenNet can be "multi-functional" in this sense is itself rather remarkable.

To see whether these oscillations would continue over a greater number of cycles, two tests were undertaken. The first test had neuron "1" clamped at -0.5 and run for 160 cycles (i.e., 4 small period oscillations), and the second test had neuron "1" clamped at +0.5 and run for 320 cycles (i.e., 4 long period oscillations). Figures 21.12 and 21.13 show the results, which were thought to be reasonably successful.

Now comes the critical question. If neuron "1" is clamped with intermediate values (i.e., between −0.5 and +0.5), will the outputs continue to be oscillations, and if so, will their periods also be intermediate? Figures 21.14 to 21.17 speak for themselves. The neuron "1" settings for these four figures were 0.5, 0.0, −0.3, and

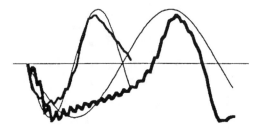

Figure 21.11: Full period oscillations

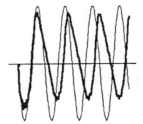

Figure 21.12: Small period oscillations

−0.7 respectively, giving 5.3, 4.3, 4.0, and 2.4 oscillations (corresponding to periods of 46, 57, 61, and 102 cycles) over 246 clock cycles. If one graphs the clamped settings versus the output periods, the curve is roughly linear. From this, one can conclude that the dual period oscillator GenNet is capable of behavioral generalization (or behavioral interpolation). Such a GenNet is effectively functioning as a variable frequency generator.

A related phenomenon, mentioned only briefly here, is that of GenNet frequency detection. A GenNet was evolved that was sent three consecutive sinusoidal inputs (i.e., sent to the external input of one neuron over three separate runs) of periods 8, 12, and 16 cycles. The desired outputs were "static" values (taken from one output neuron) of 0.2, 0.4, and 0.6, respectively. The fitness was defined to be the inverse of the (triple) sum of the squares of the differences between the desired and actual outputs over 48 to 72 cycles.

$$\text{FITNESS} = \text{Inverse of} \left(\sum_{i=48}^{72} (0.2 - a_i)^2 + \sum_{j=48}^{72} (0.4 - b_j)^2 + \sum_{k=48}^{72} (0.6 - c_k)^2 \right)$$

Surprisingly, this GenNet managed to evolve. Furthermore, when oscillations of intermediate periods (i.e., between 8 and 16 cycles) were input to this GenNet, the "static" output were also intermediate. Thus, the GenNet had generalized its behavior by functioning as a frequency detector.

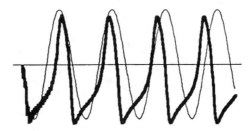

Figure 21.13: Long period oscillations

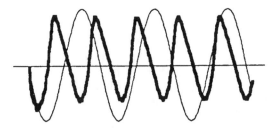

Figure 21.14:   N1=0.5, period=46 cycles

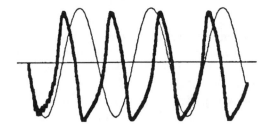

Figure 21.15:   N1=0.0, period=57 cycles

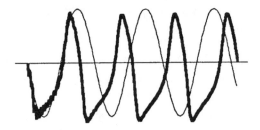

Figure 21.16:   N1=−0.3, period=61 cycles

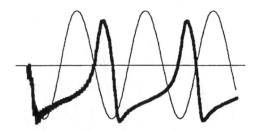

Figure 21.17:   N1=−0.7, period=102 cycles

21.2.3 GenNets and Artificial Creatures (Biots)

The versatility of GenNets makes them good candidates for tools to build "artificial nervous systems" for artificial creatures in the relatively new field of Artificial Life. The author used GenNets to simulate a five behavior "biot" (biological robot). The various GenNets evolved for this biot (called LIZZY, as shown in Figure 21.18) were divided into three main categories: (1) detector GenNets (e.g., for amplitude and frequency detection of sinusoid signals), (2) decision GenNets (e.g., if condition 1 and condition 3 are true, then activate action 4), and (3) motion control GenNets. (Actually, traditional symbolic production rules were used instead of decision GenNets for reasons of simulation speed. Every new GenNet added to the simulation slowed LIZZY's simulated motion).

LIZZY was given 5 motions:

1. Walk straight ahead.
2. Turn to the left (rotate anticlockwise).
3. Turn to the right (rotate clockwise).
4. Peck at food (raise and lower front legs).
5. Mate (raise and lower back legs).

As briefly mentioned in Section 21.2.1, separate GenNets can be evolved for different behaviors. The output of the motion GenNets determine the angles of the leg components, such that LIZZY performs one of the five motions. By switching between these motions (i.e., taking the output values of a GenNet generating an earlier motion and supplying these values to the external input of the GenNet that is to be "switched on"), one obtains a smooth transition (or switching) of behaviors.

There are three kinds of creatures in LIZZY's "environment," namely, prey, mates, and predators. The simulation model was such that a prey emitted a high frequency, a mate a middle frequency, and a predator a low frequency. Each antenna tip was equipped with a signal strength detector. By detecting differences between the signal strengths, LIZZY was able to orientate itself toward or away

Figure 21.18:   LIZZY, a GenNet biot

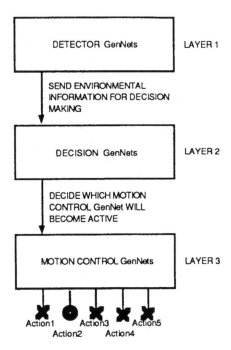

Figure 21.19:   LIZZY's nervous system

from the source of the signal. Symbolic production rules were used to decide how to map incoming detector GenNet information with motion GenNet actions.

If LIZZY detected a prey, it turned toward it, approached until it was close (as detected by a maximum signal strength detector), pecked at the prey, and then walked away. If a mate was detected, instead of pecking, LIZZY mated. If a predator was detected, LIZZY turned away from it and fled. Because there are too many details concerning the implementation of LIZZY to be presented in this short chapter, those readers who would like to know more should see de Garis (1993). A proposal to simulate and build a 100 behavior LIZZY is discussed in Section 21.4 on future work.

21.3 ARTIFICIAL EMBRYOS: GAs AND CELLULAR AUTOMATA

21.3.1 Convex Shapes

As mentioned in the introduction, the author is concerned with the conceptual issues that will arise with molecular scale technologies. At the author's previous lab (Electrotechnical Lab [ETL] in Tsukuba, Japan), there are whole sections of people researching into molecular scale engineering, e.g., how to pick up an atom in one place and to put it in another place to build a molecular scale structure. Molecular scale technologies such as Molecular Electronic Devices (MED) (Carter et al., 1988) (which attempts to construct molecules capable of computation) and Nanotechnology (Drexler, 1992) (which aims to build nanoscale robots that in turn build nanoscale products) will eventually be capable of generating devices with an Avogadro number of components (i.e., of the order of a trillion trillion).

This number ($6*10^{23}$) is so enormous that it will be totally impractical to imagine an Avogadro machine (i.e., one with an Avogadro number of components) being assembled by a single molecular scale robot one atom at a time. If the robot arm moved (let us say) a distance of 100 nanometers (10^{-7}m) per atom, even at the speed of light ($3*10^8$ m/sec), i.e., $3*10^{-16}$ seconds per atom, it would take about $2*10^8$ seconds (i.e., 6 years) to assemble the Avogadro machine.

To be practical, these molecular scale devices will have to be built "in parallel," i.e., many components at a time. Because biological cells and animals are Avogadro machines, perhaps nanotechnologists ought to look at molecular biology to see how nature builds its biological machines. Nature uses "embryogenesis," i.e., a self-assembling, massively parallel, time sequential unfolding of molecular scale instructions that switch on and off in an appropriate sequence, to build local nanoscale components such that a functional macroscale creature emerges. *Embryogenesis is a miracle of nanoscale engineering.* Therefore, if ever molecular scale technologists are to assemble Avogadro machines, it is likely that they will have to develop self-assembling or embryological techniques similar to those already evolved by nature.

Because this kind of self-assembly is inevitable, and nanotechnology research is already heavily funded, it seemed a good idea to the author to start thinking about how to self-assemble structures in an embryological way. Thus the same kind of reasoning that was applied to generating complex behaviors in GenNets, i.e., using a multistrategy approach, was also applied to what the author calls "Artificial Embryology" (de Garis, 1992).

The medium (or vehicle) that the author chose to express these embryological ideas was "cellular automata." Cellular automata, in simple terms, are a grid of cells (e.g., squares in a two-dimensional grid), each of which has a state. The state of a cell at a given moment depends upon the states of its neighboring cells at earlier moments. If the cells are "synchronous," they all update their states at the same tick of a clock. Thus the state of a cell at time "t" depends on the states of its neighboring cells at time "t–1."

It was decided to apply the same kind of GP thinking to evolving artificial shapes (i.e., the final shapes of colonies of reproductive cellular automata) as was used to evolve complex GenNet behaviors. Reproductive cellular automata are capable of placing daughter cells in neighboring vacant slots on the grid. Reproduction rules that specify which cells (i.e., having which states) will reproduce and, if so, in which direction (i.e., east, north, west, or south of the parent cells) they will place their daughter cells, have traditionally been handcrafted (i.e., specified by human beings). Predicting the final shape of such a colony of cells is very difficult. In practice one usually has to write a computer program to simulate the reproductive rules and let the cellular automata run the desired number of iterations or clock ticks.

With handcrafted reproduction rules (e.g., Wolfram, 1986), i.e., with the usual mono-strategic approach, one cannot normally predict the final shape of the colony of cells. However, if one uses GP, i.e. a dual-strategy approach where GAs evolve these cellular automata reproduction rules, then perhaps one can evolve the shapes one wants despite the great complexity of the rules.

Once again, it was thought that the inherent complexity of a system being evolved would not be important, provided that the system's "evolvability" was reasonably high. Thus the internal complexities of both the reproduction rules and the dynamics of their unfolding to build a colony of cells with a final desired shape would be irrelevant to its evolution. One might be able to evolve desired shapes, whether convex or nonconvex in 2-D or 3-D, and thus have the beginnings of an "Artificial Embryology."

As an example of the evolution of reproduction rules for cellular automata, consider the following attempts to grow simple convex shapes such as squares, rectangles, and triangles. One first needs to define the possible states that a cell may have. One simple way of doing this is first to assume that only edge cells can reproduce and that the state of a cell depends upon the configuration of its neighborless sides. Assume that no isolated cells exist (i.e., a cell can have at most 3 neighborless sides). There are therefore 14 such states, as shown in Figure 21.20, where a 0 indicates a neighborless side. Let us assume that for each loop (or iteration) of the algorithm used in the experiment, there is a field of 14 bits in the chromosome, one bit per state, that specifies whether a cell in a given state can reproduce or not in that iteration. Thus if the "i"th bit is set, those cells in the "i"th state can reproduce.

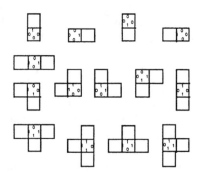

Figure 21.20: The 14 states

NI - NUMBER OF ITERATIONS
REPRO1? - WHICH STATES CAN REPRODUCE IN ITERATION 1
R DIRNS1 - REPRODUCTION DIRECTIONS IN ITERATION 1
REPRO2? - WHICH STATES CAN REPRODUCE IN ITERATION 2
R DIRNS2 - REPRODUCTION DIRECTIONS IN ITERATION 2

Figure 21.21: Chromosome format

A further field of bits is needed to specify the directions in which the daughter cells are to be placed. If a cell has only 1 neighborless side, then no bits are needed to decide where the daughter cell will be placed. If a cell has 2 neighborless sides, 1 bit is needed; there are 6 such states, hence 6 bits are needed. For cells with 3 neighborless sides, 2 bits are needed; there are 4 such states, hence 8 bits are needed, making a total of 14 bits. If a 2-bit decision specifies a neighbored direction, the decision is simply ignored. Thus, for each iteration, 28 bits are needed to specify whether cells in a given state will reproduce or not and in which direction. Because this is a small number of bits, it was decided to evolve these 28 bits for each iteration. The number of iterations is also evolved, according to the binary integer found in the very first field of the bitstring chromosome. Figure 21.21 shows the chromosome format used.

The program then runs the specified number of iterations, which results in a contiguous colony of cells that has some definite shape, as specified by the chromosome. The aim of the exercise then is to evolve the reproduction rules so that the final shape is as close as possible to some desired target shape (e.g., a square, triangle). The fitness of the final shape is determined by the simple formula

Fitness = (#ins − 0.5*#outs)/(#des)

where

#ins = the number of **filled** cells inside the desired shape.
#outs = the number of **filled** cells outside the desired shape.
#des = the number of cells inside the desired shape.

As an example of this type of evolution (for a triangular target shape), see Figure 21.22, which shows the result at each of 4 cycles; i.e., NI evolved to be 4.

In practice, it was found that convex shapes evolved well with the algorithm described above. However it failed badly for nonconvex shapes. After some thought, it was felt that what was needed in order to "grow" more interesting and complex non-convex shapes was to use "differentiable" chromosomes, i.e., chromosomes containing portions of instructions that can switch on and off at appropriate times. How this was done is described in the next subsection.

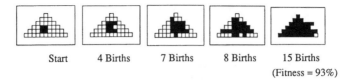

Start   4 Births   7 Births   8 Births   15 Births
                                                            (Fitness = 93%)

Figure 21.22:   Triangular target shape

21.3.2 Nonconvex Shapes

In order to be able to "grow" nonconvex shapes, such as the letter "L," the following basic idea was used. A convex shape would be grown initially using one chromosome (called an "operon") of the form shown in Figure 21.21. Subsequently, a subset of the edge cells of the resulting convex shape would be switched on (and all the other edge cells switched off so that they could no longer reproduce). These switched on cells would then grow to form more complex shapes using a second operon. Figure 21.23 shows the "L" target shape, which consists of two convex shapes, regions A and B. Once region A is grown using operon 1, those edge cells in region R are selected to switch on and to grow to fill region B. The problem then is how to specify the edge cells in region R. This was done by using a simulated concentration gradient of a "chemical" transmitted from parent cell to offspring. Each time a cell reproduced, it transferred 0.95 times the concentration C of a certain chemical it contained to its daughter cell. Thus, the "younger" the cell,

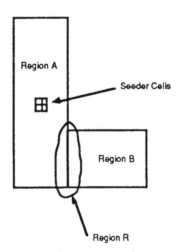

Figure 21.23:   Target shape "L"

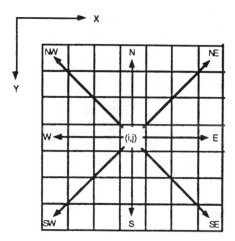

Figure 21.24: Cell neighborhood

the lower its C value. Each edge cell in the colony then calculated the direction (i.e., one of the 8 directions: east, northeast, north, northwest, west, southwest, south, southeast) of the maximum average concentration, as shown in Figure 21.24. In the northwest direction for example, the average concentration (AC) is defined as

$$AC_{nw} = 0.25*[C(i,j) + C(i-1,j-1) + C(i-2,j-2) + C(i-3,j-3)]$$

If a cell is situated at the southeast edge of a colony of cells (as in region R), then its maximum AC will probably point northwest or west. This gives a clue as to how to select those cells in region R. Figure 21.25 shows the format of the chromosome to "grow" the L shape. X and Y are the number of iterations that operons 1 and 2 are to be active. These two operons are simply two concatenated chromosomes of the type shown in Figure 21.21. What is new is the NEWS DIRNS field. This is an 8-bit field, with one bit per neighborhood direction. If the "i"th bit is set in this field, then those edge cells whose maximum average concentration is in the "i"th direction are permitted to switch on their second operon. Figures 21.26 and

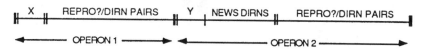

Figure 21.25: Chromosome format for target shape "L"

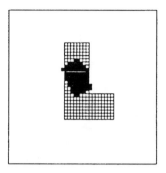

Figure 21.26: After operon 1

21.27 show the results of a colony of cells after operon 1 and operon 2, respectively, have been active. Four seeder cells were placed approximately in the middle of the vertical part of the "L." The evolved values of X and Y for these figures were 10 and 15 respectively. The evolved NEWS DIRNS were [01100011], i.e., northeast, north, south, and southeast, which corresponded to edge cells on the southwest, south, north, and northwest edges of the colony shown in Figure 21.26. The fitness value was 87%, using the same fitness definition as in the previous subsection.

Figure 21.27 shows that a nonconvex shape has been evolved. It is probable that by employing more switchings in a chromosome, i.e., having more operons, it would be possible to grow almost any type of shape, including 3-D embryo shapes. Thus, it has been shown that GP techniques can be used to evolve both the reproduction and switching rules of reproductive cellular automata so that a desired nonconvex shape is formed. These rules are complex and poorly analyzable, but at least in the above case, they are evolvable. Such is the power of GP and hence of multistrategy learning.

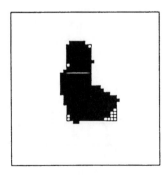

Figure 21.27: After operons 1 and 2

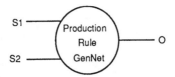

Figure 21.28:   A production rule GenNet

21.4 FUTURE WORK

21.4.1 Production Rule GenNets

This rather brief section suggests ideas for future work, using the GP ideas described in the above sections. Section 21.2 introduced LIZZY the biot and the three categories of GenNets used to implement it. In practice, the middle decision GenNet layer was not evolved, but instead a traditional symbolic production rule approach was used to overcome the slowness of a monoprocessor computer having to process multiple GenNets in series.

Therefore, the challenge of evolving GenNets that are capable of making the kinds of decisions described in Section 21.2 remains open. The author calls such GenNets "logic GenNets." What the author would like to do is to evolve GenNets that behave like production rules. For example, take the GenNet shown in Figure 21.28, which has only two external inputs and one (tapped) output.

Imagine that it is possible to evolve a GenNet that behaves as follows:

IF $(S1 > 0.5)$ & $(S2 < -0.3)$ THEN $(O > 0.5)$ ELSE $(O < 0.0)$

i.e., if the input signal S1 is > 0.5 and the input signal $S2 < -0.3$, then the output signal O should be > 0.5, otherwise < 0.0. If this can be done, perhaps it might be possible to evolve GenNets capable of implementing several such rules (i.e., multi-functional logic GenNets). Perhaps more than two inputs (and corresponding conditions) might be possible. If these logic GenNets can be evolved, then one can imagine evolving a large number of them with many different sets of conditions. The next step might be to combine these logic modules (using GP techniques) to build/evolve quite sophisticated decisional GenNet circuits. If this in turn can be done, then a significant step toward creating a marriage between neural networks and traditional symbolic artificial intelligence may have been made.

21.4.2 A GenNet Biot with 100 Behaviors

Closely linked to the above idea of evolving decisional circuits with GenNet logic modules is the idea of trying to build a 100 behavior GenNet biot. The author's personal experience has shown that the first and third categories of GenNets of the previous section (i.e. detector and motion GenNets) are not too difficult to evolve. What will probably be much harder to evolve, however, are the

GenNet decisional circuits that take the input from the detector GenNets and then decide which motion GenNets to switch on and off. If one is talking about a biot with 100 behaviors with a comparable number of detector GenNets, then the complexity of the decisional layer will probably be considerable. One can imagine using GP techniques to evolve connections between logic GenNets of various kinds to form the decisional interface between detection and motion GenNets. Such a research project remains a major and open challenge.

21.4.3 Embryonics (Embryological Electronics)

The introduction to this chapter discussed the ability of GP to build/evolve complex systems. The author thinks that to build biots of increasing complexity and behavioral sophistication, increasingly complex neural circuitry will need to be constructed. With the future technologies discussed in the introduction, it will be possible to build neural circuits with a huge number of artificial neurons and "synaptic" connections. This raises two problems. One is the need for a type of self-assembly of these neural circuits. They cannot be built mechanically, one component at a time, if the number of components is huge. The other problem is the complexity of the circuitry and the virtual impossibility of predicting its behavior. Even more difficult would be attempting the reverse, i.e., designing a complex neural circuit to perform a given complex behavior. The potential solution to both problems may be to use GP techniques to build these neural circuits in an evolutionary way.

Such reasoning implies that sooner or later, techniques will have to be discovered so that electronic neural circuits can self assemble and then be tested so that GP type evolutionary improvement becomes possible to make the enormous structural and dynamic complexities of such circuits manageable. Thus the idea of using GP to "grow" (i.e., self-assemble), electronic circuits becomes important. The author has coined the term "embryonics" for this new field of "growing" electronic circuits. The structure of these circuits will be specified by coded instructions in GA chromosomes. These chromosomes then "grow" the circuit in a somewhat similar "embryological" way, as described in the previous section. Hence the term "embryonics" (embryological electronics).

Initially, rather simple, low level RLC circuits might be grown. To test each circuit, a simulation program would be needed to see how well the circuit performs according to some fitness definition prespecified by the Genetic Programmer. If the "growth" of simple RLC circuits is successful, one can attempt to "grow" simple digital logic circuits and then more complex higher level, artificial neural circuits, etc. Eventually, it might be possible to "grow" whole artificial nervous systems this way. This is the intention at least and points the way toward the establishment of a major research program.

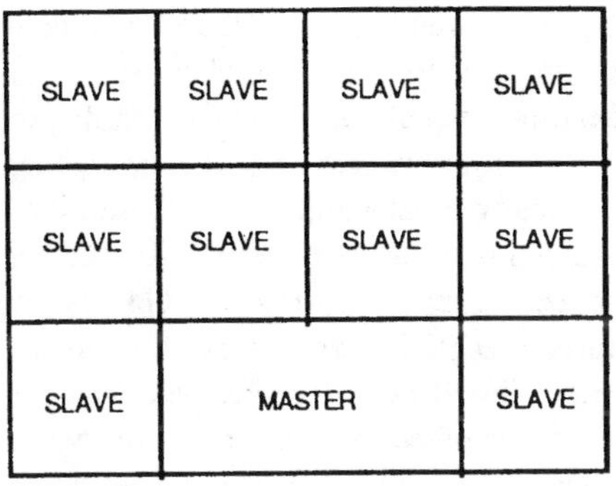

SLAVE	SLAVE	SLAVE	SLAVE
SLAVE	SLAVE	SLAVE	SLAVE
SLAVE	MASTER		SLAVE

Figure 21.29: A Darwin Machine

21.4.4 Darwin Machines

If suitable conceptual (and simulation) techniques can be found to "grow" electronic and possibly neural circuits, then these ideas might be implementable directly in hardware and run in parallel. This leads to the idea of the Darwin Machine. Figure 21.29 shows the basic structure of such a device.

A Darwin Machine is a hardware version of a GA. It contains a single master circuit and a population of slave circuits that function in parallel. The master circuit sends each slave a GA chromosome, the population fitness definition, and initial input values. Each slave takes its chromosome; grows a circuit according to the instructions contained on the chromosome; measures the circuit's fitness according to the fitness definition; and reports this value back to the master, which then calculates the next generation of chromosomes in a GA-like way to complete the cycle.

Over time, the complexity levels of the circuits grown in each slave will probably increase, until one can imagine that whole neural circuits can be grown in this way. Darwin Machines will be needed to self-assemble circuits of great complexity. They will also be needed to accelerate the whole GP process.

21.5 SOME RELATED WORK

21.5.1 Koza's "Genetic Programming"

A growing number of researchers are now using GP techniques to build/evolve increasingly complex and interesting systems, although they may not use the term GP (e.g., de Garis, 1990, 1991, 1992, 1993; Koza, 1990, 1992; Spofford and Hintz, 1991; Louis and Rawlins, 1991). One person who does is John Koza of Stanford University, who started using the term "Genetic Programming" independently of, and more or less simultaneously with, the author. (Actually Koza was in print with the term 6 months later [Koza, 1990] than the author [de Garis, 1990b]).

Koza's definition of GP is the evolution of LISP programs to solve many kinds of problems. His work is interesting and is attracting a growing following (Koza, 1990, 1992). Basically what he does is choose a set of application-dependent LISP function operators and a set of terminals that he feels are sufficient to evolve a program to solve a given problem. His GA chromosomes are LISP programs, i.e., tree-structured recursive lists of these functions and terminals, that can be treated either as data or instructions (one of the advantages of LISP). Crossover in such chromosomes consists of swapping subtrees of two parent trees to form two child trees. To measure the fitness of these chromosome "programs," a set of problem specific test cases are provided, and the (raw) fitness is defined to be the fraction of these test cases for which the chromosome (when treated as instructions by using LISP's EVAL function) gives the correct answer. For details, see Koza's (1992) new book, *Genetic Programming*.

How do the author's and Koza's definitions of GP relate? Because it is likely that the author will also have a book out using the term "Genetic Programming" (de Garis, 1993), it is possible that there will be some confusion amongst readers. This need not be the case if readers of both books realize that it is possible to argue that the author's definition of GP includes Koza's to some extent. What Koza does can be considered in some cases, to be using GAs to build/evolve complex systems (i.e., it satisfies the author's definition). This definition is sufficiently general to include the bitstring chromosomes of the author and the higher level symbolic chromosomes of Koza. Admittedly Koza does not emphasize the complexity building aspect of his work, but other people could. Sometimes the LISP programs he evolves are too complex to be conceivable by human beings, yet they solve the problem. Thus, Koza is doing GP in the author's sense of the term. Hence, there need be no confusion. The two uses of the term are not contradictory. What Koza does is simply an instance of the more general definition given by the author.

21.5.2 Other Work

As mentioned in the above subsection, a growing number of people are starting to do GP. For example, Hintz and his colleagues at George Mason University are using GAs to build/evolve such systems as synchronous and asynchronous 3 bit counters, using artificial neurons with binary output (Spofford and Hintz, 1991). They call the computer program they use for this work "GANNET" (Genetic Algorithm Neural NETwork). Similar work by Louis and Rawlins (1991) at Indiana University uses what they call "designer GAs" to "design structures" such as a 4-bit parity checker and a 2-bit adder. Using "designer GAs" to "design structures" is essentially GP under another name.

21.6 CONCLUSIONS

The essential message of this chapter is that Genetic Programming (GP) is a good example of the benefits that can be derived from a multistrategy (as opposed to a monostrategy) approach to learning. By combining two or more approaches (strategies), the system that is doing the learning can often attain a greater level of performance or complexity in its learned behavior or structure than is possible by using only a single approach. In this chapter, two dual-strategy examples were presented that were instances of a process called Genetic Programming. It is claimed by the author that combining GAs with neural networks or cellular automata (resulting in "GenNets" and "artificial embryos" respectively), has a much greater structural and/or dynamical complexity (yet remains functional) than is possible with (mono-strategy) algorithms that are specific to each domain (e.g., "Backprop" [Rumelhart and McClelland, 1986] to neural nets or humanly specified reproduction rules for reproductive cellular automata [Wolfram, 1986]).

This greater complexity derives from what the author calls the (relative) "complexity independence" of GAs, meaning that as long as the system being built/evolved continues to return increasing fitness values (i.e., that it is "evolvable," a condition not always satisfied by some systems), then the internal complexity of the system is irrelevant (within certain limits; e.g., if the chromosome is very long, the search space becomes enormous and very slow to search). This means that certain complex systems can at least be built, even though they may be too complex for their behaviors or structures to be predictable or even analyzable. Genetic Programming, defined as the art of using GAs to build/evolve complex systems, is thus a technique to "extend the barrier of the buildable." GP mimics nature's approach to building/evolving (hyper)complex systems such as brains and embryos. If this type of "applied evolution" becomes important in the future (perhaps partially as a result of future work on "embryonics" and Darwin Machines), then the importance of multistrategy learning (of which GP is an instance) can only be strengthened.

ACKNOWLEDGMENTS

The author wishes to express his thanks to his colleague Dr. Hitoshi Iba of the Inference Section at ETL for having read an earlier version of this chapter and for giving constructive comments.

This research was partially done in the GMU Center for Artificial Intelligence. The Center is supported in part by the National Science Foundation Grant No. IRI-9020266, in part by the Defense Advanced Research Projects Agency under the grants administered by the Office of Naval Research No. N00014-87-K-0874 and No. N00014-91-J-1854, and in part by the Office of Naval Research under Grants No. N00014-88-K-0397, No. N00014-88-K-0226, and No. N00014-91-J-1351.

References

Carter, F.L., Siatkowski, R.E., and Wohltjen, H. (Eds.), *"Molecular Electronic Devices,"* New York: North Holland, 1988.

de Garis, H., "Genetic Programming: Building Artificial Nervous Systems Using Genetically Programmed Neural Network Modules," *Proceedings of the 7th. Int. Conf. on Machine Learning*, B.W. Porter and R.J. Mooney (Eds.), San Mateo, CA: Morgan Kaufmann, 1990.

————, "Genetic Programming: Modular Evolution for Darwin Machines," *Proceedings of the Int. Joint Conf. on Neural Networks*, M. Caudil (Ed.), Hillsdale, NJ: Lawrence Erlbaum, 1990b.

————, "Genetic Programming," in *Neural and Intelligent Systems Integration*, B. Soucek (Ed.), New York: Wiley, 1991.

————, "Artificial Embryology: The Genetic Programming of an Artificial Embryo," in *Dynamic, Genetic, and Chaotic Programming*, B. Soucek (Ed.), New York: Wiley, 1992.

————, *Genetic Programming: GenNets, Artificial Nervous Systems, Artificial Embryos*, Wiley manuscript, 1993.

De Jong, K.A., *An Analysis of the Behavior of a Class of Genetic Adaptive Systems*, Ph.D. Thesis, University of Michigan, Ann Arbor, 1975.

Drexler, K.E., *Nanosystems: Molecular Machinery, Manufacturing, and Computation*, New York: Wiley, 1992.

Goldberg, D.E., *Genetic Algorithms in Search, Optimization, and Machine Learning*, Reading, MA: Addison-Wesley, 1989.

Hillis, D., *The Connection Machine*, Cambridge, MA: MIT Press, 1985.

Koza, J.R., "Genetic Programming: A Paradigm for Genetically Breeding Populations of Computer Programs to Solve Problems," Stanford Univ. Comp. Sci. Dept. Tech. Rep. STAN-CS-90-1314, June 1990.

————, *Genetic Programming: On the Programming of Computers by Means of Natural Selection*, Cambridge, MA: MIT Press, 1992.

Louis, S.J., and Rawlins, G.J.E., "Designer Genetic Algorithms: Genetic Algorithms in Structure Design," *Proceedings of the 4th Int. Conf. on Genetic Algorithms*, R.K. Belew and L.B. Booker (Eds.), San Mateo, CA: Morgan Kaufmann, 1991.

Rudnick, M., and Hammerstrom, D., "An Interconnect Structure for Wafer Scale Neurocomputers," in *Proceedings of the 1988 Connectionist Models Summer School 1988*, D. Touretzky, G. Hinton, T. Sejnowski, (Eds.), San Mateo, CA: Morgan Kaufmann, 1989.

Rumelhart, D.E., and McClelland, J.L. (Eds.), *Parallel Distributed Processing*, Vols. 1 and 2, Cambridge, MA: MIT Press, 1986.

Spofford, J.J., and Hintz, K.J., "Evolving Sequential Machines in Amorphous Neural Networks, in *Artificial Neural Networks*, T. Kohonen, K. Makisars, O. Simula, and J. Kangas (Eds.), New York: Elsevier, 1991.

Wolfram S. (Ed.), *Theory and Applications of Cellular Automata*, Singapore: World Scientific, 1986.

22

EXPERIENCE-BASED
ADAPTIVE SEARCH

Jeffrey Gould
Robert Levinson
(University of California, Santa Cruz)

Abstract

This chapter describes adaptive predictive search (APS), a learning system framework that, given little initial domain knowledge, increases its predictive abilities in complex problem domains. APS systems are termed experience-based learners because they are given as much responsibility for the learning process as possible. This framework has been applied to a number of complex domains (including chess, othello, pente, and image alignment) where the combinatorics of the state space is large, and the learning process only receives reinforcement at the end of each search. The unique features of the APS framework are its pattern-weight representation of control knowledge and its integration of several learning techniques, including temporal difference learning, simulated annealing, and genetic algorithms. In addition to APS, Morph, an APS chess system, is described in detail. Through training, despite little initial domain knowledge and with only one ply of search, Morph has managed several dozen draws and two wins against a traditional search based chess program stronger than most tournament players.

22.1 INTRODUCTION

This chapter introduces *experience-based learning*. This term refers to that type of unsupervised reinforcement learning in which almost all responsibility for the learning process is given to the system. These responsibilities include state evaluation, operator (move) selection, feature discovery, and feature significance. As a learning framework, experience-based learning can be applied to many problem domains (Levinson et al., 1990).

The types of problem domains considered here are restricted to complex problem domains characterized by three features. First, the problem must have a formulation as a state space search. Further, reinforcement is only provided occasionally and for many problems only at the end of a given search. Finally, the cardinality of the state space must be sufficiently large so that attempting to store all states is impractical.

This chapter describes a learning system architecture called an *adaptive predictive search* (APS) system (Levinson, 1989a; Levinson et al., 1992), which handles experienced-based learning in complex problem domains. The first key aspect of an APS system is the compilation of search knowledge in the form of pattern-weight pairs (pws). Patterns represent features of states, and weights indicate their significance with respect to expected reinforcement. Second, because the APS system resides within the experience-based learning framework, it must possess facilities for creating and removing search knowledge (pws). Knowledge is maintained to maximize the system's performance given space and time constraints. The APS model uses a variety of techniques for inserting and deleting patterns. Finally, a combination of several learning techniques incrementally assign appropriate weights to the patterns in the database. The specific insertion, deletion, and learning techniques will be described in the next section.

Because APS adheres to the experience-based learning framework, it can be applied to new domains without requiring the programmer to be an expert in the domain. In fact, APS has been applied to a variety of domains, including chess, othello, pente, and image alignment (Levinson et al., 1992). The chess implementation, Morph, is also described in this chapter.

Chess satisfies all the above mentioned requirements of the complex problem domains considered in this chapter: The game tree forms the state space, each game representing a search path through the space; reinforcement is only provided at the end of the game; and finally, it has a large cardinality of states (around 10^{40}) (Shannon, 1950). Furthermore, few efforts use previous search experience in this area despite the high costs of search. In order to focus the research on the learning mechanisms, Morph has been constrained to using only one-ply of search. In addition, Morph has been given little initial chess knowledge, thus keeping it within the experienced based learning framework. Despite these constraints, Morph has managed more than three dozen draws and two wins (after several thousand games of training) against Gnuchess, a traditional search-based chess program stronger than most tournament players.

The structure of the rest of the chapter is as follows. The next section discusses the APS system framework in detail. In Section 22.3, the Morph APS implementation is described. Section 22.4 compares APS to other efforts in adaptive search and adaptive game-playing systems. This is followed by performance results in Section 22.5 and, finally, a conclusion in which future research and open questions are discussed.

22.2 THE APS MODEL

As mentioned previously, the APS framework contains three major parts: (1) the pattern-weight formulation of search knowledge, (2) methods for creating and removing pws, and (3) methods for obtaining appropriate weights for the pws with respect to reinforcement values. This section discusses each of these facets in detail, after which it describes how the parts interact and how the system performs as a whole.

22.2.1 Pattern Weight Formulation of Search Knowledge

A pattern represents a Boolean feature of a state in the state space. This feature typically represents a proper subset of all the possible properties of the state. That is, the feature usually does not represent a single state because such patterns would be far too specific (and numerous) to be useful in complex problem domains. Examples of patterns include graphs and sets of attributes. Often the language in which patterns are expressed is akin to the language used to represent the states but with a higher level of abstraction; e.g., see discussion of Morph below.

Each pattern has associated with it a weight that is a real number within the reinforcement value range. The weight denotes an expected value of reinforcement, given that the current state satisfies the pattern. For example, in a game problem domain, a typical set of reinforcement values is $\{0,1\}$ for loss and win, respectively. If we have a pw, $< p_1, .7 >$, this implies that states that have p_1 as a feature are more likely to lead to a win than a loss.

The major reason for using pws over another form of knowledge representation is their uniformity. Pws can simulate other forms of search control, and because of their low level of granularity and uniformity, more power and flexibility is possible (Levinson, 1989b). For example, pws have all the expressive power of macro tables. Additionally, they allow switching over from one macro sequence to another and allow for the combination of two or more macro tables (Levinson, 1989b).

22.2.2 Adding and Removing Patterns

The patterns used to represent search knowledge are stored within a database that is organized as a partial order on the relation "more-general-than." Patterns are created for insertion into this database through the following four methods: (1)

search context rules, (2) generalization and specialization, (3) reverse engineering, and (4) genetic operators.

Search context rules are the only pattern addition scheme that does not rely on patterns already in the database; thus, they are the only way patterns are added to an empty database. A search context rule takes as input a particular state and the sequence of all states in the last search and returns a pattern to be inserted into the database. A search context rule is just a deterministic procedure that builds up a pattern given the previously mentioned input. Examples of search context rules can be found in Section 22.3.3.

In concept induction schemes (Niblett and Shapiro, 1981; Michalski, 1983; Mitchell et al., 1986a), the goal is to find a concept description to correctly classify a set of positive and negative examples. In general, the smaller description that does the job, the better. Sometimes the concept description needs to be made more specific to make a further distinction. At other times, it can be simplified (generalized) without loss of discriminative power.

Generalization patterns are created by extracting similar structures from within two patterns that have similar weights. A pattern is specialized in an APS system if its weight must be updated a large amount (indicating inaccuracy). In a standard concept induction scheme the more specific patterns may be deleted, but the APS system keeps them around because they can lead to further important distinctions. The deletion module may delete them later if they no longer prove useful.

Reverse engineering is a method used to add macro knowledge into an APS system. Macros can be represented as pws by constructing a sequence of them such that each pattern is a precondition of the following one. Successive weights in the macro sequence will gradually approach a favorable reinforcement; thus, the system is then motivated to move in this direction.

Reverse engineering extends a macro sequence by adding a pattern. This extension is similar to Explanation-Based-Generalization (EBG) (Mitchell et al., 1986b) or goal regression. The idea is to take the most important pattern in one state, s_1, and back it up to get its preconditions in the preceding state, s_2. These preconditions then form a new pattern p_2. If pattern p_2 is the most useful pattern in state s_2, it will be backed up as well, creating a third pattern in the sequence, etc. The advantages of this technique are more than just learning "one more macro"; each of the patterns can be used to improve the evaluation of many future positions and/or to enter the macro at any point in the macro sequence.

Genetic algorithms (Holland, 1985) are a means of optimizing global and local search (Glover, 1987). In these algorithms, solutions to a problem are encoded in bit strings that are made to evolve over time into better solutions in a manner analogous to the evolution of species of animals. The bits in the solution representation are analogous to genes and the entire solution to a chromosome. In such systems, there are a fixed number of solutions at any one time (a generation).

Members of each generation interbreed to form the next generation. Each genetic algorithm has a fitness function that rates the quality of the solution in a particular generation. When it is time for a new generation to be created from the current generation, the solutions that are more fit are allowed to be the more active breeders. Breeding usually involves three processes: crossover, inversion, and mutation.

The APS system makes use of genetic operators in order to add additional patterns into the database. Because patterns are not required to be represented as bit strings (in fact in Morph they are graphs), it is up to the individual APS system to tailor the genetic operators to suit the pattern representation. The APS system does not remove all or most of a population of patterns, however, because of the large amount of time necessary in determining appropriate weights for all patterns.

Although a variety of pattern addition schemes are available, because of memory and processing restrictions, the database must be limited in size. As in genetic algorithms, there must be a mechanism for insignificant, incorrect, or redundant patterns to be deleted (forgotten) by the system. A pattern should contribute to making the evaluations of states it is part of more accurate. The utility of a pattern can be measured as a function of many factors, including age, number of updates, uses, size, extremeness, and variance. These attributes will be elaborated upon in the next section. We are exploring a variety of utility functions (Minton, 1984). With such functions, patterns below a certain level of utility can be deleted. Deletion is also necessary for efficiency considerations: the larger the database, the slower the system learns. For example, after 2,000 games of training and with a database grown to 2,500 patterns, the Morph chess system takes twice as long to play and learn (from about 600 games a day on a Sun Sparc II to about 300 games per day).

22.2.3 Modifying the Weights of Patterns

The modification of weights (of patterns) to more appropriate values occurs every time a reinforcement value is received from the environment. The modification process can be broken down into two parts. First, each state in the sequence of states that preceded the reinforcement value is assigned a new value using temporal difference learning. Second, the new value assigned to each state is propagated down to the patterns that matched that state. A pattern in the database matches a given state if the state satisfies the Boolean feature represented by the pattern, and no other pattern more specific than it matches the state.

TD learning determines new values for the states in the game sequence moving from the last state, S_n, to the first state, S_1. Because state S_n was the state at which reinforcement was delivered, its new value is set to the reinforcement value. For all other states, S_i, the new value is set to a linear combination of its old value and the new value of state S_{i+1}. This method differs from supervised learning, where the value of each state S_i is moved toward the reinforcement value. It has been shown that TD learning converges faster than the supervised method for Markov model learning (Sutton, 1988). The success of TD learning stems from the fact that value adjustments are localized. Thus, if the system makes decisions all the way through the search and makes a mistake toward the end, the earlier decisions are not harshly penalized.

Once each state S_i has been assigned its new value, each pattern matching S_i must have its weight moved toward the new value. Each weight is moved an amount relative to the contribution the pw had in determining the old value for the state.

This weight updating procedure differs from those traditionally used with TD learning in two ways. First, TD learning systems typically use a fixed set of features, whereas in an APS system, the feature set changes throughout the learning process. Second, the APS system uses a simulated annealing type scheme to give the weight of each pattern its own learning rate. In this scheme, the more a pattern gets updated, the slower its learning rate becomes. Furthermore, in addition to giving each pattern its own learning rate, the annealing scheme forces the convergence of patterns to reasonable values.

22.2.3.1 Simulated Annealing

Simulated annealing is a learning procedure that has been derived from a practice in statistical mechanics (Davis and Steenstrup, 1987). In this area, it is often desirable to take a system of molecules and reduce it to the lowest possible energy by lowering temperature. Through experience, it has been found that if the temperature is reduced too quickly, the system will have a small probability of being at an optimally low temperature. Metropolis et al. (1953) developed a technique for lowering the temperature gradually to produce (on the average) very low energy systems at the lowest temperature.

Kirkpatrick et al. (1983) adapted annealing to computer science by finding information analogies for their physical counterparts (Davis and Steenstrup, 1987):

- The energy of the system becomes an objective function that describes the quality of the current system configuration.
- Moving a physical system to its lowest energy configuration is then analogous to finding the configuration that optimizes the objective function.
- The configuration of the system is then the different informational parameters that the system can have.
- The temperature is a mechanism for changing the parameters.

In APS, the system's situation is similar to that of the statistical physicist. The database comprises a complex system of many particles (patterns). The goal is to reach an optimal configuration, i.e., one in which each weight has its proper value.

The average error (i.e., the difference between APS's prediction of a state's value and that provided by temporal-difference learning) serves as the objective evaluation function. Intuitively, the average error is an acceptable performance evaluation metric if one accepts the empirical and analytical arguments that TD learning is a convergent process (Sutton, 1988): because TD learning will produce evaluations close to the true ones, the error will be high or low depending on the APS system's degree of accuracy. Indeed, experimentally we have observed a high correlation between TD error and more domain-specific performance metrics.

The configuration of an APS system is made up of its pws. Temperature corresponds to the rate at which each weight moves toward the value recommended by TD learning. In addition to using a global temperature that applies to all weights, each weight has its own local temperature. This is done to give each pw its own learning curve that depends on the number of states it has occurred in. A pw that occurs in many states has its temperature reduced more quickly than a pw that occurs in only a few states because the first pattern has more examples to learn from, and hence, early convergence is appropriate. Each pw's learning rate is affected by its number of updates and the global temperature as follows:

$$Weight_n = \frac{Weight_{n-1} * (n-1) + k * new}{n + k - 1}$$

$Weight_i$ is the weight after the ith update, new is what TD recommends that the weight should be, n is the number of the current update, and k is the global temperature. When $k = 0$, the system only considers previous experience; when $k = 1$, the system averages all experience; and when $k > 1$, the present recommendation is weighted more heavily than previous experience. Thus, raising k creates faster moving patterns. As an example of how global temperature affects the learning rate, if the system doubles the global temperature, a pattern that has 100 updates will be updated like a pattern that has 50 updates the next time its weight is modified.

The above discussion describes how simulated annealing gives each pattern its own learning rate. The figures below, taken from the Morph system, demonstrate the effectiveness simulated annealing has in forcing convergence of the weights in the system. Figure 22.1 and Figure 22.2 show the weight change over time for the material pattern "down one bishop." The first figure comes from a version of Morph that does not use simulated annealing; the weight fluctuates within a certain range. The second figure displays the same pattern from a Morph with simulated annealing. Here, the weight homes in on a specific value.

22.2.4 Integration: The Workings of the Entire System

This subsection describes the workings of a complete APS system by combining the parts described in the previous three subsections. An APS system executes

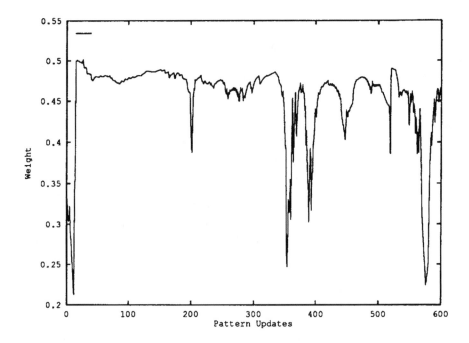

Figure 22.1: This graph depicts the weight change of the material pattern "down 1 bishop" in a system without simulated annealing

by repeatedly cycling through two phases: a search phase and a learning phase (see Figure 22.3). In the search phase, the APS system does not modify its knowledge base but instead performs a search using the current knowledge base. The learning phase then alters the knowledge base by adding and deleting patterns and modifying the weights of patterns.

The search phase traverses a path from the initial state of the problem domain to a reinforcement state. Depth first hill climbing is the search technique used to traverse the search tree. In other words, at each state S_i in the search path, the state moved into next, S_j, is determined by applying an evaluation function to each successor state of S_i and choosing that state with the highest evaluation. Note, however, nothing prevents the database from supporting more sophisticated search strategies.

Although the exact calculations performed by the evaluation function depend on the particular APS system, the function has the following framework. It takes the state to be evaluated and determines the most specific pws in the pw database that match that state. The weights of these most specific pws are then combined by a system dependent rule to determine the final evaluation for that state.

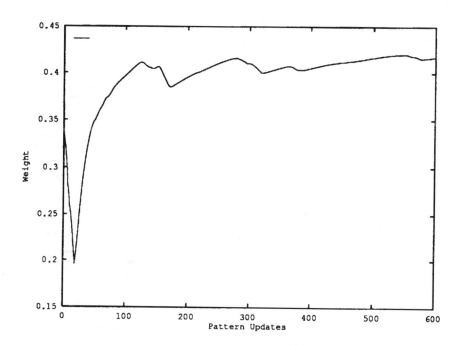

Figure 22.2: This graph depicts the weight change of the same pattern as Figure 22.1 in a system that has simulated annealing added

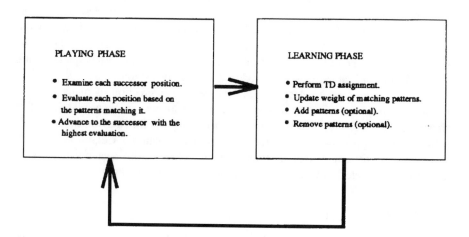

Figure 22.3: The execution cycle of an APS system

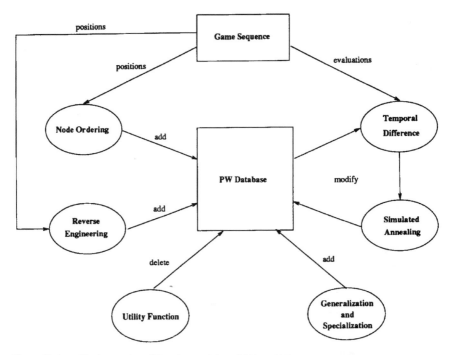

Figure 22.4:   The integration of learning modules within an APS system

The learning phase, the second in the APS cycle of execution, takes as input the sequence of states traversed in the search performed by the first phase. This sequence is used by TD learning and simulated annealing to modify the weights of the patterns in the database. Patterns are then inserted into the database using the four techniques mentioned in Section 22.2.2. Finally, unimportant patterns are removed from the database as described in the same subsection.

The execution of an APS system involves the interaction of many learning techniques. A global view of this interaction is displayed in Figure 22.4. In this figure, the edges are labelled with actions specifying whether a given module adds patterns, deletes patterns, or modifies the weights of patterns. Central to the APS system is the pattern weight database, which holds all the accumulated search knowledge generated and manipulated by the surrounding modules.

22.3 MORPH SYSTEM

The previous section outlined the framework of a generic APS system. This section describes the actual implementation of one. The APS framework only provides general descriptions for several key elements of the system. These elements include the specific pattern representation, the specific evaluation function, and the algorithms used to implement the four pattern addition schemes. This section will describe in detail those decisions that must be made in an actual implementation, in this case, the Morph learning chess program.

Being an APS system, Morph makes a move by generating all legal successors of the current position, evaluating each position using the current pattern database, and choosing the most favorable position. After each game, patterns are created and deleted and weights are changed to make evaluations more accurate (in the system's view) based on the outcome of the game. Patterns are deleted periodically if they are not considered useful. Morph plays against GnuChess Level I, a program that is stronger than most tournament players.

22.3.1 Patterns and Their Representation

To fully exploit previous experience, the method chosen to represent each experience is critical. An ideal representation is one that uses features that are general enough to occur across many experiences (positions, for chess) but are such that their significance is invariant across these experiences. How to construct such a representation for chess is not obvious. The straightforward approach of using a standard chess board representation is not powerful enough because there are over 10^{40} possible chess positions (Shannon, 1950). In fact, after just three moves for each player, there are over 9 million possible positions (Fox and James, 1987). Further, a pattern such as "white bishop can capture black rook" has nearly the same significance regardless of where on the board the white bishop and black rook are located, and one would like to choose a representation that exploits this information.

In Morph, positions are represented as unique directed graphs in which both nodes and edges are labelled (Levinson, 1991). Nodes are created for all pieces that occur in a position and for all squares that are immediately adjacent to the kings. The nodes are labelled with the type and color of the piece (or square) they represent. For kings and pawns (and also pieces that would otherwise be disconnected from the graph), the exact rank and file on the board in which they occur is also stored. The exact squares of kings and pawns allow the system to generate specific endgame patterns and patterns related to pawn structure. Edges represent attack and defend relationships between pieces and pawns: direct attack, indirect attack, or discovered attack (a defense is simply an attack on one's own piece). At most, one directed edge is assigned from one node to another, and the graph is oriented with black to move. Patterns come from subgraphs of position graphs (see Figure 22.5) and, hence, are represented the same way except that they may label any node with an exact or partial square designation. The representation has recently been extended to include other squares as nodes besides those adjacent to kings.

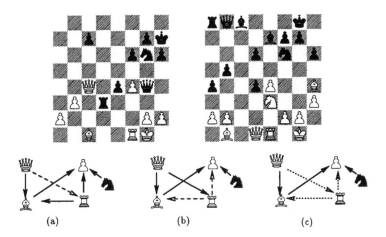

Figure 22.5:   A generalization derived from two different chess positions. Graph (a) is the subgraph
derived from the board on the left, and graph (b) is the subgraph from the board on the
right. The solid edges correspond to direct edges between pieces, and the dashed edges
correspond to indirect edges. Graph (c) is the generalized graph derived from (a) and
(b) in which the dotted edges have been generalized to generic "attacks."

A similar representation scheme has successfully been used to represent chess
generalizations (Zobrist and Carlson, 1973) and to produce a similarity metric for
chess positions (Botvinnik, 1984; Levinson, 1991).

There are actually two types of patterns stored in the Morph system. In addition to the above mentioned graph patterns, Morph stores "material" patterns: vectors that give the relative material difference between the players, e.g., "up 2 pawns
and down 1 rook" and "even material." Material patterns and graph patterns are
processed identically by the system; thus, the pw database contains patterns of
more than one type.

Along with each pattern is stored a weight in [0,1] as an estimate of the
expected true minimax evaluation of states that satisfy the pattern. In order to
determine the utility of a pattern and whether it should be retained, other statistics
about patterns are maintained. These statistics include the number of weight
updates the pattern has had, the number of times the pattern has been referenced
during play, and the degree to which the weight varies over time.

22.3.2 Evaluation Function

The evaluation function takes a set of pws matching the position and returns a
value in [0,1] that represents an estimate of the expected outcome of the game from
that position (0=loss, .5=draw, 1.0=win). It has the following properties, where w_1
and w_2 are the weights of the above-mentioned pws.

$$f(x,y) = \begin{cases} -.5(2-2x)(2-2y)+1 & \text{if } x \geq \dfrac{1}{2} \text{ and } y \geq \dfrac{1}{2} \\[2ex] \dfrac{x-.5+y-.5(2x-1)(2y-1)((2x-1)^2-(2y-1)^2)}{(2x-1)^2(2y-1)^2} & \text{if } x \geq \dfrac{1}{2} \text{ and } y < \dfrac{1}{2} \\[2ex] f(y,x) & \text{if } x < \dfrac{1}{2} \text{ and } y \geq \dfrac{1}{2} \\[1ex] 2xy & \text{otherwise} \end{cases}$$

Figure 22.6:   Move selection evaluation function

1. IF $w_1 > .5$ and $w_2 > .5$, then $f(w_1,w_2) > max(w_1,w_2)$ unless either w_1 or w_2 is 1; then $f = 1$.
2. IF $w_1 = .5$, then $f(w_1,w_2) = w_2$.
3. IF $w_1 = \alpha$ and $w_2 = 1 - \alpha$, then $f = .5$.
4. IF $w_1 < .5$ and $w_2 < .5$, then $f < min(w_1,w_2)$ unless either w_1 or w_2 is 0; then $f = 0$.
5. IF $w_1 > .5$ and $w_2 < .5$, then $w_2 < f < w_1$. f is more toward the most extreme weight.

The entire function is displayed in Figure 22.6. This binary function is applied iteratively to the weights of all matching patterns. Note, however, that this function is not associative; thus, the order of evaluation matters. We are currently working on an associative version of this function.

These mathematical constraints to the evaluation function have a strong intuitive backing. For instance, rule 1 states that if two patterns suggest that a position is good (> .5), the board should then be considered better than either of them alone. The weight that is assigned to a pattern that does not have any positive or negative connotation is .5. Patterns with weight 0 suggest strongly that the current board is a losing position, and patterns with weight 1 suggest that the current board is a winning position. Table 22.1 shows the application of the evaluation function to several sample values.

22.3.3 Pattern Creation in Morph

This section describes the implementation of the pattern addition modules for graph patterns. As will be seen from the following paragraphs, the implementation is heavily dependent on the pattern representation language. All four types of pattern addition procedures, as described in Section 22.2.2, are discussed: search context rules, generalization and specialization, reverse engineering, and genetic operators.

Table 22.1: Results of applying the evaluation function in Morph to various input pairs

Arguments		Result
.5	.5	0.50
.2	.8	0.50
.2	.5	0.20
.8	.5	0.80
.8	.8	0.92
.2	.2	0.08
.1	.8	0.33
.2	.9	0.67
1	.8	1.00
0	.2	0.00

Morph uses two types of search context rules (see Section 22.2.2) to add patterns into the database. The search context rules, called node orderings, produce as output a pattern that is a subgraph of the position (state) that is passed in as input. The output pattern is created by numbering the nodes of the position graph according to a node ordering, choosing a random size n, and returning the induced subgraph formed by the first n nodes in the node ordering (and the edges between them). Morph uses two relatively game-independent node ordering rules: In forward node ordering, nodes are ordered by most recently moved piece while connectivity of the nodes is maintained; see Figure 22.7 for an example. In reverse node ordering, nodes are ordered by which piece is next to move while connectivity of the nodes is maintained. In both schemes, captured pieces and kings in check are placed high in the list, and ties (for squares and unmoved pieces, for instance) are broken randomly. The inclusion of random factors in the above scheme also falls within the genetic algorithm viewpoint, allowing the system to generate and explore a large set of possibilities.

When Morph adds a generalization to the database, it looks for two patterns that have similar weights and then inserts their maximum common subgraph. Specialization occurs when a pattern's weight has a high variance. A new pattern is extracted from the high variance pattern by adding a node and edge to the original graph.

The reverse engineering procedure is performed on each position (state) that occurs in the previous game. For each position, the procedure finds the most extreme pattern p_i that matches it and adds the *precondition pattern* of p_i to the pw database. The precondition pattern pr_i contains all the nodes in p_i; in addition, it may also contain "square nodes," which are nodes that may match any square on the board. To determine the structure of pr_i, the system examines each position, starting from the current position and moving toward the initial position until it finds one in which the structure of the nodes in pr_i differs from that in p_i. pr_i is then extracted from the structure in this earlier position and inserted into the database.

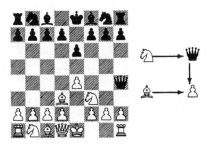

Figure 22.7:   In the position shown on the left, the pieces no longer on their original squares are moved in the order: white pawn, black pawn, white knight, black queen, and white bishop. The subgraph on the right is added when using most recently moved node ordering with a node size of 4. Note that the black pawn is excluded because of node ordering's preference for the connectivity criterion over the most recently moved criterion.

Figure 22.8:   The graph on the left depicts a standard pattern derived from node ordering. By applying reverse engineering to the graph on the left, we get the graph on the right. The node labeled *SQ* matches squares from which the black knight attacks the white queen and white king simultaneously.

An example of a pattern and one of its possible precondition patterns is displayed in Figure 22.8.

Although the genetic operators have not yet been implemented in Morph, mutation and crossover operators are being considered. The mutation operator would be applied each time another addition module was about to insert a pattern. For that pattern, there would then be a small probability per node of either flipping its color or changing its piece designation. Finally, the crossover operator would take two extreme patterns and combine half of the nodes in the first with half of the nodes in the second to form a new hybrid structure.

22.4 RELATIONSHIP TO OTHER APPROACHES

An APS system combines threads of a variety of machine-learning techniques that have been successful in other settings. To produce this combination, design constraints usually associated with these methods have been relaxed.

The integration of these diverse techniques would not be possible without the uniform, syntactic processing provided by the pattern-weight formulation of search knowledge. To appreciate this, it is useful to understand the similarities and differences between APS and other systems for learning control or problem-solving knowledge. For example, consider Minton's explanation-based Prodigy system (Minton, 1984). The use of explanation-based learning is one similarity: APS specifically creates patterns that are "responsible" (as preconditions) for achieving future favorable or unfavorable patterns through reverse engineering (see Section 22.2.2). Also similar is the use of "utility" by the deletion routine to determine if it is worthwhile to continue to store a pattern. The decision is based on the accuracy and significance of the pattern versus matching or retrieval costs. A major difference between the two approaches is the simplicity and uniformity of the APS control structure: no "meta-level control" rules are constructed or used, nor are goals or subgoals explicitly reasoned about. Another difference is that actions are never explicitly mentioned in the system. Yee et al. (1990) have combined explanation-based learning and TD learning in a manner similar to APS. They apply the technique to Tic-Tac-Toe.

It is also interesting to compare APS to other adaptive-game playing systems. Most other systems are given a set of features and asked to determine the weights that go with them. These weights are usually learned through some form of TD learning, with very good success (Samuel, 1959, 1967; Tesauro and Sejnowski, 1989; Tesauro, 1992).

APS extends the TD approaches by exploring and selecting from a very large set of possible features in a manner similar to genetic algorithms. It is also possible to improve on these approaches by using Bayesian learning to determine inter-feature correlation (Lee and Mahajan, 1988).

A small number of AI and machine learning techniques in addition to heuristic search have been applied directly to chess (which, without relying on search, requires much higher precision than backgammon) and then usually to a small sub-domain. The inductive-learning endgame systems (Michei and Bratko, 1987; Muggleton, 1988) have relied on pre-classified sets of examples or examples that are classified by a complete game-tree search from the given position (Thompson and Roycroft, 1983). The symbolic learning work by Flann (Flann and Dietterich, 1989) has occurred on only a very small sub-domain of chess. The concepts capable of being learned by this system are graphs of two or three nodes in Morph. Such concepts are learned naturally by Morph's generalization mechanism.

Tadepalli's work (1989) on hierarchical goal structures for chess is promising. Such high-level strategic understanding may be necessary in the long run to bring Morph beyond an intermediate level (the goal of the current project) to an expert or master level. This brings out both a major weakness and a current topic of research: Morph's current pattern representation scheme is not general and flexible enough for it to create useful plans via EBG. Minton (1984), building on Pitrat's work (1976), applied constraint-based generalization to learning forced mating plans. This method can be viewed as a special case of our pattern creation system. Perhaps the most successful application of AI to chess was Wilkin's Paradise (PAttern Recognition Applied to DIrecting Search) system (Wilkins, 1990), which, also building on Pitrat's work, used pattern knowledge to guide search in tactical situations. Paradise was able to find combinations as deep as 19-ply. It made liberal use of planning knowledge in the form of a rich set of primitives for reasoning and, thus, can be characterized as a "semantic approach." This difference, the use of search to check plans, and the restriction to tactical positions distinguish it from Morph. Also, Paradise is not a learning program: patterns and planning knowledge are supplied by the programmer. Epstein's Hoyle system (Epstein, 1990) also applies a semantic approach but to multiple simultaneous game domains.

Of course, the novel aspects of APS could not have been achieved without the unique combination of learning methods described here.

22.5 PERFORMANCE RESULTS

To date, Morph has defeated GnuChess twice and obtained over 40 draws via stalemate, repetition of position, and the 50-move rule. The versions of Morph that defeated GnuChess had previously played around 3,000 games. However, despite Morph's victory, GnuChess is still much stronger than Morph, which is at best a beginning tournament player. In addition to Morph's limited success against GnuChess, there have been many encouraging signs since Morph was fully implemented in November 1990:

- Even though no information about the relative values of the pieces (or that pieces are valuable) has been supplied to the system, after 30 or more games of training, Morph's material patterns are consistent and credible (Levinson and Snyder, 1991). (See Table 22.2 for a database after 106 games). The weights correspond very well to the traditional values assigned to those patterns. These results reconfirm other efforts with TD learning (Christensen and Korf, 1986) and perhaps go beyond by providing a finer grain size for material.

- After 50 games of training, Morph begins to play reasonable sequences of opening moves and even the beginning of book variations. This is encouraging because no information about development, center control, and king safety has been directly given the system and because neither Morph nor GnuChess uses an opening book. It is not rare for Morph to reach the middlegame or sometimes the endgame with equal chances before making a crucial mistake because of a lack of appropriate knowledge.

Table 22.2: A portion of an actual Morph material database after 106 games. The columns headed by pieces denote relative quantity. The weight column is the learned weight of the pattern in [0,1]. Updates is the number of times that this weight has been changed. Variance is the sum of the weight changes. Age is how many games this pattern has been in the database. Value is the traditional value assigned to this pattern. Note that a weight of 0.5 corresponds to a traditional value of 0. The entire database contained 575 patterns.

Material Pattern					Statistics				Trad. Value
Pawn	Knight	Bishop	Rook	Queen	Weight	Updates	Variance	Age	
0	0	0	0	0	0.455	2485	240.2	106	0
0	0	−1	0	0	0.094	556	7.53	86	−3
0	0	+1	0	0	0.912	653	11.19	88	+3
0	+1	0	0	0	0.910	679	23.59	101	+3
0	−1	0	0	0	0.102	588	17.96	101	−3
0	0	0	−1	0	0.078	667	3.56	103	−5
0	0	0	+1	0	0.916	754	5.74	103	+5
+1	0	0	0	0	0.731	969	22.96	105	+1
−1	0	0	0	0	0.259	861	13.84	105	−1
0	0	0	0	+1	0.903	743	5.68	105	+9
0	0	0	0	−1	0.085	642	3.12	105	−9
0	0	−1	+1	0	0.894	10	0.03	55	+2
0	0	−2	0	0	0.078	146	0.53	71	−6
+1	0	−1	0	0	0.248	26	2.35	73	−2
−1	+1	−1	0	0	0.417	81	4.48	82	0
0	0	−1	0	0	0.081	413	2.14	92	−4
0	−1	+1	0	0	0.478	84	5.72	82	0
+1	0	+1	0	0	0.916	495	3.56	88	+4
0	0	+2	0	0	0.924	168	0.66	91	+6

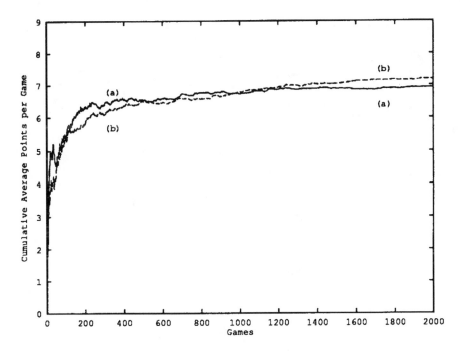

Figure 22.9:   Cumulative average of two versions of Morph. Version (a) is a basic Morph. Version
(b) has the reverse node ordering pattern addition scheme added.

- Morph's database contains many patterns that are recognizable by human players and has given most of these reasonable values. The patterns include mating patterns, mates-in-one, castled king and related defenses and attacks on this position, pawn structures in the center, doubled rooks, developed knights, and attacked and/or defended pieces.

We have discovered that adding patterns too frequently "overloads" Morph so it can't learn proper weights. In the experiment graphed in Figures 22.9 and 22.10, weights are updated after every game, but patterns are added only every 7 games. This allows the system to display a steady learning curve as depicted. Morph's games improve based on other metrics as well, such as average game length and TD error (see Section 22.2.3.1).

22.5.1 Performance Evaluation

To explore new additions to Morph, one implementation is compared with another by using the average number of traditional chess points captured per game as the metric. To be consistent with the experienced-based learning framework, Morph is not made aware of this metric. Each implementation is run until the

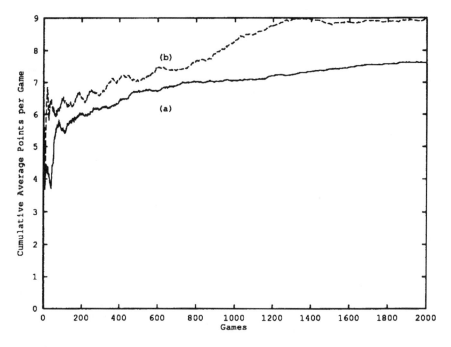

Figure 22.10:   Cumulative average of two versions of Morph. Version (a) improves the evaluation
function from the Morph in Version (b) of Figure 22.9. Version (b) adds annealing on
top of Version (a).

metric is no longer increasing (most Morphs stop learning between 1,500 and 2,000
games of play). The one with the higher rating is considered the better. We have
concluded that only one such comparison is sufficient because the same version of
Morph usually reaches the same average.

22.5.2 Improvement through Adding New Learning Methods

Adding learning strategies is a gradual process. Each method must be added
one at a time to see if it increases performance. If it does, then it is kept. Since
Morph's initial implementation, such additions have produced significant performance increases. The following two graphs show Morph's cumulative average over
time. These graphs compare the performance of four versions of the system. Each
version is an extension of the previous one. Figure 22.9a shows a basic Morph,
Figure 22.9b shows the result of adding reverse node ordering, Figure 22.10a
shows the result of improving the evaluation function, and Figure 22.10b shows the
result of adding simulated annealing.

22.6 CONCLUSIONS AND ONGOING RESEARCH

The development of a computational framework for experience-based learning is a difficult but important challenge. Here, we have argued for the necessity of a multistrategy approach: at the least, an adaptive search system requires mechanisms for credit assignment, feature creation and deletion, weight maintenance, and state evaluation. Further, it has been demonstrated that the TD error measure can provide a mechanism by which the system can monitor its own error rate and steer itself to smooth convergence. The error rate provides a metric more refined but well-correlated with the reinforcement values and more domain-specific metrics. Finally, in a system with many components (pws) to be adjusted, learning rates should be allowed to differ across these components. Simulated annealing provides this capability.

APS has produced encouraging results in a variety of domains studied as classroom projects (Levinson et al., 1992), including Othello, Tetris, 8-puzzle, Tic-Tac-Toe, Pente, image alignment, Missionary and Cannibals, and more. Currently, others are studying the application of the Morph-APS shell[1] to GO, Shogi, and Chinese Chess. Here we have used the Morph project to illustrate the potential for these methods. Clearly, much more distance remains to be covered before Morph or other experience-based systems will learn from experience near the efficiency that humans do. To achieve this, substantial refinement of the learning mechanisms and an enhancement of their mutual cooperation are required. Undoubtedly, advances in pattern-based knowledge representation and associative memory will also be required. This model of experience-based learning has pursued a largely syntactic approach to codifying and exploiting experience. What role can and should semantic knowledge serve?

A limitation of the problem-solving system presented here is the reliance on full-width 1-ply search. This is wasteful: many moves considered may be irrelevant, whereas other moves may require further search to determine their suitability. That is, at times using search may be more economical than developing patterns to make fine distinctions. A selective search more akin to human analysis is desirable for more effective processing. Can such selectivity also be learned from experience? This avenue is currently being pursued.

The key to experience-based learning, beyond recent work in constructive induction (Michalski, 1983; Rendell and Seshu, 1990; Birnbaum and Collins, 1991; Wnek and Michalski, 1991), is that the system is given responsibility for both the structure and significance of learned knowledge. Experience-based learning should have application far beyond chess. Consider a robot (e.g., a Mars rover) that must

---

[1] It is now publicly available via anonymous ftp from ftp.cse.ucsc.edu. The file, morph.tar.Z, is in directory /pub/morph/.

learn to survive and manage effectively in a new environment or a machine tutor that must learn which forms of instruction and examples work better than others. Finally, it may be possible to get organic synthesis systems to improve search time with experience using graph methods similar to Morph (Levinson, 1991).

The following points are worth remembering:

- In combining the many learning methods for experience-based learning, the methods are not taken as they are normally used; their essence is extracted and combined beneficially.
- Guided by appropriate performance measures, modification and testing of the system proceed systematically.
- Interesting ideas arise directly as a result of taking the multistrategy view. The goal is to exploit the strength of individual methods but eliminate their weaknesses. Some examples include

1. *The genetic mutation operator described in Section 22.3.3.*
2. *Higher level concepts via hidden units.* (Once a good set of patterns has been obtained, it may be possible for the system to develop a more sophisticated evaluation function. This function, patterned after neural nets, would have hidden units that correspond to higher level interactions between the patterns. For example, conjunctions and disjunctions may be realized and given weights different from that implied by their components.)
3. *Clarity of system's knowledge.* (The "meaning" of hidden units to which weights are associated in neural nets is usually not clear, whereas in experience-based systems, it is specific structures that are given weights. Indeed, it is the transparency of Morph's knowledge that has allowed its learning mechanisms to be fine tuned; with various system utilities, it is possible to ascertain exactly why Morph is selecting one move over another.)

ACKNOWLEDGMENTS

Thank you to Jeff Keller for constructing the new evaluation function, to Paul Zola and Kamal Mostafa for the initial Morph implementation, and to Richard Sutton for sharing our enthusiasm for reinforcement learning. Finally, we would like to thank Richard Snyder for valuable editing assistance. The research was partially funded by NSF Grant IRI-9112862 and a Faculty Research Grant from the University of California.

References

Birnbaum, A.L., and Collins, G.C., editors. In *Proceedings of the Eighth International Workshop on Machine Learning*. Morgan Kaufmann, San Mateo, CA, pages 117–232, 1991.

Botvinnik, M. *Computers in Chess*. Springer-Verlag, New York, 1984.

Christensen, J., and Korf R. A unified theory of heuristic evaluation. In *Proceedings of AAAI-86*, Morgan Kaufmann, San Mateo, CA, 1986.

Davis, L., and Steenstrup, M. *Genetic Algorithms and Simulated Annealing*, chapter Genetic Algorithms and Simulated Annealing: An Overview. Research Notes in Artificial Intelligence. Morgan Kaufmann, San Mateo, CA, 1987.

Epstein, S.L. Learning plans for competitive domains. In *Proceedings of the Seventh International Conference on Machine Learning*, June 1990.

Flann, N.S., and Dietterich, T.G. A study of explanation-based methods for inductive learning. *Machine Learning*, 4:187–226, 1989.

Fox, M., and James, R. *The Complete Chess Addict*. Faber and Faber, London, 1987.

Glover, D.E. *Genetic Algorithms and Simulated Annealing*, Chapter 1, Solving a Complex Keyboaard Configuation Problem through Generalized Adaptive Search. Research Notes in Artificial Intelligence. Morgan Kaufmann, San Mateo, CA, 1987.

Holland, J.H. *Adaptation in Natural and Artificial Systems*. The University of Michigan Press, Ann Arbor, 1975.

Kirkpatrick, S., Gelatt, C.D., and Vecchi, M.P. Optimization by simulated annealing. *Science*, 220:671–680, 1983.

Lee, K.F., and Mahajan, S. A pattern classification approach to evaluation function learning. *Artificial Intelligence*, 36:1–25, 1988.

Levinson, R. Pattern formation, associative recall and search: A proposal. Technical report, University of California at Santa Cruz, 1989a.

————. A pattern-weight formulation of search knowledge. Technical Report UCSC-CRL-91-15, University of California, Santa Cruz, 1989b. Revision to appear in *Computational Intelligence*.

————. A self-organizing pattern retrieval system and its applications. *International Journal of Intelligent Systems*, 6:717–738, 1991.

Levinson, R., and Snyder, R. Adaptive pattern-oriented chess. In *Proceedings of AAAI-91*, pages 601–605. AAAI Press, Menlo Park, CA, 1991.

Levinson, R., Beach, B., Snyder, R., Dayan, T., and Sohn, K. Adaptive-predictive game-playing programs. *Journal of Experimental and Theoretical AI*, To appear. Also appears as Technical Report UCSC-CRL-90-12, University of California, Santa Cruz, 1992.

Metropolis, N., Rosenbluth, A., Rosenbluth, M., Teller, A., and Teller, E. Equations of state calculations by fast computing machines. *Journal of Chemical Physics*, 21:1087–1091, 1953.

Michalski, R.S. A theory and methodology of inductive learning. In R.S. Michalski, J.G. Carbonell, and T.M. Mitchell, editors, *Machine Learning: An Artificial Intelligence Approach*. Tioga Press, Palo Alto, CA, 1983.

Michie, D., and Bratko, I. Ideas on knowledge synthesis stemming from the KBBKN endgame. *International Computer Chess Association Journal*, 10(1):3–13, 1987.

Minton, S. Constraint based generalization—learning game playing plans from single examples. In *Proceedings of AAAI-84*, pages 251–254, AAAI Press, Menlo Park, CA, 1984.

Mitchell, T.M., Carbonell, J.G., and Michalski, R.S., editors. *Machine Learning: A Guide to Current Research*. Kluwer Academic Publishers, Norwell, MA, 1986.

Mitchell, T.M., Keller, R., and Kedar-Cabelli, S. Explanation based generalization: A unifying view. In *Machine Learning 1*, pages 47–80. Kluwer Academic Publishers, Norwell, MA, 1986.

Muggleton, S.H. Inductive acquisition of chess strategies. In D. Michie, J.E. Hayes, and J. Richards, editors, *Machine Intelligence 11*, pages 375–389. Oxford University Press, Oxford, 1988.

Niblett, T., and Shapiro, A. Automatic induction of classification rules for chess endgames. Technical Report MIP-R-129, Machine Intelligence Research Unit, University of Edinburgh, 1981.

Pitrat, J. A program for learning to play chess. In *Pattern Recognition and Artificial Intelligence*. Academic Press, San Diego, CA, 1976.

Quinlan, J.R. Induction on decision trees. *Machine Learning*, 1:81–106, 1986.

Rendell, L., and Seshu, R. Learning hard concepts through constructive induction: Framework and rationale. *Computational Intelligence*, 6(4):247–270, 1990.

Samuel, A.L. Some studies in machine learning using the game of checkers. *IBM Journal of Research and Development*, 3(3):211–229, 1959.

———. Some studies in machine learning using the game of checkers—ii recent progress. *IBM Journal of Research and Development*, 11(6):601–617, 1967.

Shannon, C.E. Programming a computer for playing chess. *Philosophical Magazine*, 41(7):256–275, 1950.

Sutton, R.S. Learning to predict by the methods of temporal differences. *Machine Learning*, 3(1):9–44, 1988.

Tadepalli, P. Lazy explanation-based learning: A solution to the intractable theory problem. In *Proceedings of the Eleventh International Joint Conference on Artificial Intelligence*, Morgan Kaufmann, San Mateo, CA, 1989.

Tesauro, G. Practical issues in temporal difference learning. *Machine Learning*, Special Issue on Reinforcement Learning, 1992.

Tesauro, G., and Sejnowski, T.J. A parallel network that learns to play backgammon. *Artificial Intelligence*, 39:357–390, 1989.

Thompson, K., and Roycroft, A.J. A prophesy fulfilled. *EndGame*, 5(74):217–220, 1983.

Wilkins, D. Using patterns and plans in chess. *Artificial Intelligence*, 14(2):165–203, 1980.

Wnek, J., and Michalski, R.S., "Hypothesis-driven constructive induction in AQ17: A method and experiments," Presented at the IJCAI-91 Workshop on Evaluating and Changing Representation in Machine Learning, Sydney, Australia, August 1991. (To appear in *Machine Learning*, 1994.)

Yee, R.C., Saxena, S., Utgoff, P.E., and Barto, A.G. Explaining temporal differences to create useful concepts for evaluating states. In *Proceedings of the Eighth National Conference on AI*, AAAI Press, Menlo Park, CA, 1990.

Zobrist, A.L., and Carlson, D.R. An advice-taking chess computer. *Scientific American*, 228:92–105, 1973.

23

CLASSIFYING FOR PREDICTION: A MULTISTRATEGY APPROACH TO PREDICTING PROTEIN STRUCTURE

Lawrence Hunter
(National Library of Medicine)

Abstract

Multistrategy learning is especially important in complex and incompletely understood domains. This chapter explores the application of several machine learning tools in combination with the problem of protein structure prediction. Structure prediction is a fundamental problem in molecular biology, and the current, most effective methods involve the application of neural networks. In this work, Bayesian classification is used to derive a new intermediate level representation for protein structure, and then this induced classification is used as the output representation to train both neural networks and decision tree learners to make structure predictions. This method provides more detailed structure predictions than traditional methods, although they are less accurate. The detail versus accuracy trade-off can be formalized in information theoretic terms, demonstrating that the novel approach provides more information than the traditional one.

23.1 INTRODUCTION

23.1.1 The Importance of Domain Selection

Machine learning (ML) research has a fascination with evaluation. In a lead editorial in the journal of record in the field, Pat Langley claimed, "Therein lies the path to a true science of machine learning" (Langley, 1987). Toward this end, the ML community has developed a repository of standardized datasets to compare algorithms, and most new methods are tested on one or more of these datasets. This approach ensures the comparability of methods. However, the evaluations are only as good as the data.

There is reason to believe, however, that the data used to evaluate learning algorithms do not necessarily provide an ideal empirical testbed. One reason for concern is the fact that nearly all ML programs applied to the standard datasets can, in the limit, perform with nearly perfect accuracy. Most comparisons of learning curves discuss how fast the methods reach 100% correctness, rather than what level of accuracy they can achieve on a more difficult set of problems. Another piece of evidence is the effectiveness of extremely simple learning procedures on these datasets. In a recent survey of dozens of standard machine learning datasets, Holte (1991) found that learning *a single rule that classifies instances on the basis of a single attribute* is only a few percentage points less accurate on most datasets than the majority of results reported in the machine learning literature! A similar finding is reported in a more detailed comparison of several representative learning methods on a variety of datasets in Chapter 6 of Weiss and Kulikowski (1991), which shows that a heuristic search for a *single* good DNF rule is among the best performers.

Another approach to demonstrating the merit of machine learning systems has been to apply a system to an extremely difficult and open-ended task, such as planning (Hammond, 1986) and story understanding (Ram, 1989). Although this method of demonstrating the effectiveness of an ML system can be compelling, these domains make comparing the performance of alternative approaches very difficult.

Finding tasks that occupy a middle ground between problems that are so simple that almost all ML approaches can accomplish them and problems that are AI-complete[1] is a key to developing a method for evaluating ML approaches based on their ability to make meaningful contributions to solving difficult problems. Although there are many goals that ML researchers pursue, ranging from recapitulating historic discoveries and building cognitive models to inducing expert systems and training robots for motion and visual recognition, my research agenda

---

[1] This term, introduced to us by David Kirsch (1986), is a reference to tasks such as general natural language understanding that seem to require an integration of all the cognitive abilities humans possess.

involves building systems that can function as "discovery assistants," programs that can represent, generate, and pursue explicit desires for knowledge (Hunter, 1989a, 1989b, 1990b; Ram and Hunter, 1992). To assess progress toward this goal, it is important to have a good problem: one that is significant, difficult, and (at least in part) doable. In this chapter, I will describe a problem that meets these criteria and describe a multistrategy approach that provides an incremental improvement over other approaches.

23.1.2 Why a Multistrategy Approach?

Applying machine learning techniques to significant, unsolved problems places a great deal of pressure on the methods. The task in this work is the protein structure prediction problem, which I will describe in detail in the next section. Various machine learning approaches to protein structure prediction have been tried in the last three years. In fact, all the currently most accurate prediction methods are based on machine learning techniques, and these approaches are increasingly used in biological research (e.g., for a prediction of the structure of an important HIV protein in Rosa et al. (1990). Nevertheless, the performance of even these methods is far from correct, and it is likely that the problems faced in this domain reflect broader requirements for effective machine learning and discovery.

The general lesson that motivates the work in this chapter is that representation is a central component of learning. It is clear from experience and from formal work (e.g., Rendell and Cho [1990] and Dietterich [1989]) that there is an intimate connection between representations (in effect, biases) used in an ML and its ability to learn. With the right representations, most induction systems can learn a mapping; without a good I/O representation, it can be nearly impossible to learn.

As will become clear in the next section, the output representation traditionally used in this domain problem (i.e., the predicted classes) is not necessarily the best characterization of the high dimensional, continuous solution space. The basic approach was to use an unsupervised learning technique to find a "good" set of categories to describe the solution space and then try to used supervised learning to learn a mapping to the induced categories. Although it is difficult to generalize from this particular problem to statements about the applicability of the approach in other areas, these preliminary results suggest that classification can be used to improve prediction in other applications where a prediction task must be divided into smaller pieces in order to be tractable.

The method involves using Bayesian classification to find an improved output representation and then the application of both backpropagation trained neural networks and information-theoretic decision tree building induction to learn a mapping from input to the induced output representation. Although it is difficult to compare this method to traditional approaches directly, one measure of information content demonstrates a 70% improvement in the information content of these predictions over the best existing method. However, the method is still far short of the desired level of accuracy.

This chapter is divided into four sections. The next section describes the protein structure prediction problem in general, some specific approaches to it, and some of the problems with each approach. I am compelled to describe the protein folding problem in some detail in order to convey what the significance of this machine learning approach has been. The third section describes preliminary results of the application of a multistrategy learning approach to the problem and compares the results of this effort with those of other approaches. The final section speculates about why the approach works and what general lessons might be learned.

23.2 PROTEIN STRUCTURE PREDICTION

Proteins are the building blocks of life. They are large molecules, often containing thousands and even tens of thousands of atoms. Proteins serve many functions, some of them extremely specific. Collagen provides structural support; actin provides the force that underlies muscle contractions; hemoglobin binds oxygen as it is transported around the body and then releases it to individual cells. Protein chemistry depends primarily on the structure of the molecule. That is, the shape of a protein determines its function.

A protein shape (also called *structure, teriary structure, or conformation*) is enumerated by identifying the position in 3-space of each of its thousands of atoms. Even this very complex representation has several shortcomings. First, proteins are not always rigid bodies, and how they move and flex can be very important to their function; none of that is captured in the positions of its atoms. Second, it is very difficult to obtain information about the positions of atoms in a protein. The main method for protein structure determination is crystallography. Crystallography is slow, expensive, and prone to a variety of errors. NMR spectroscopy has the potential to solve protein structures more quickly (and handle some of the motion questions) but is still impractical for large proteins. Third, the functionally important aspects of the structure are only indirectly represented because they depend on the spatial and chemical relationships among many atoms and not directly on their particular positions.

There is another level of description of proteins. Each protein is made up of a linear sequence of amino acids. There are 20 different naturally occurring amino acids, each containing between 10 and 30 atoms. The amino acids in a protein are linked together end to end by peptide bonds (the peptide bond links amino acids by removing two hydrogen atoms and an oxygen atom from the amino acids; hence, amino acids in proteins are often called residues). The ordered list of amino acids is generally called the *primary sequence* or *primary structure* of a protein. Amino acids and peptide bonds are rigid in certain dimensions, dramatically reducing the number of degrees of freedom for the positions of the atoms in a protein. The amino acids are all made from the same core constituents consisting of a central carbon atom (called the alpha-carbon), a carboxyl group (carbon and oxygen), and an amino group (nitrogen). A representative atom from each of these groups (C, Cα, and N) is said to form the backbone of the amino acid. The backbones connect through peptide bonds to form a chain. The atoms that distinguish the amino acids from each other form what is called a side-chain, which is attached to the backbone.

The amino acid sequences that describe proteins have, through the advent of rapid and inexpensive gene sequencing technology, become increasingly available. Acquiring the amino acid sequence of a protein is the easiest method for getting information about the protein. In most cases, the amino acid sequence of a protein completely determines its structure (in certain rare cases, other "helper" molecules or processes are involved).

In principle, it is possible to predict a protein's structure from its sequence. In fact, nature routinely translates the sequence of a protein into its structure. Every time a new protein molecule is synthesized in a living system, it comes off the ribosome as a linear sequence of amino acids and then folds up into its "native" state. This folding process takes on the order of 6 seconds (much longer than a simple chemical reaction) and can easily be replicated in a test tube.

The ability to predict structure from sequence would have a variety of consequences, ranging from facilitating the understanding of basic biology to helping with the design of commercial pharmaceuticals and agricultural products. In practice, however, this task has been quite difficult.

Folding is, in effect, solving an extremely complex many-body physics problem. Each atom can potentially interact with any other atom in the molecule or with the water (or other substances) surrounding the molecule. There are a variety of forces acting on the atoms in the molecule, drawing them together or pushing them apart. The atoms will tend to occupy states that minimize the total free energy of the molecule; that state specifies the positions (and velocities) of the atoms—i.e., the shape of the molecule.

One approach to predicting structure from sequence has been to solve the force equations by simulation. The idea is to begin with the protein in an arbitrary state (usually stretched out linearly) and then calculate the forces acting on the molecule, move all the atoms in the direction indicated by the forces (simulating motion after a very short time step), and iterate. This approach in general is called *molecular dynamics* (Karplus and Petsko, 1990).

The forces acting on the atoms in a protein are completely described by quantum mechanics. Unfortunately, using quantum mechanics to calculate the forces *ab initio* in a molecule with thousands of atoms (surrounded by thousands more molecules of water—proteins do not fold naturally in a vacuum) is computationally intractable. With hundreds of hours of supercomputer time, it is possible to simulate the motion of 6 or even 10 atom systems for a few picoseconds this way. Addressing the protein folding problem this way would require minimally 10^{20} times that computation to solve each protein.

Alternative approaches have been attempted with some success. One important approximation has been to replace the *ab initio* quantum calculations with empirical estimates of the main contributions to the free energy of the molecule. Karplus and Petsko (1990) primarily review these approaches. Although offering a significant improvement in efficiency, a 100 picosecond simulation (10^{-10} seconds) of myoglobin (about 1,500 atoms) takes about six hours of Cray X-MP time. At that rate, a full, 6-second simulation of myoglobin folding would run for about 68 million Cray years, not including analyzing the results! Another step toward applying molecular dynamics to protein folding has been to quantize the space of possible atomic positions and sample the space using Monte Carlo techniques. Although some preliminary results are promising (Skolnick and Kolinski, 1990), difficulties remain.

Simulation approaches appear to face fundamental computational limitations. An alternative method has been to try to find techniques that map directly from sequence to structure, without simulating the folding process. Although the problem is quite large by machine learning standards, it can be stated as a typical supervised learning task.

There are over 60,000 known protein sequences from all species. That number is doubling roughly every two years. Many of these proteins are evolutionarily related to each other (related sequences are called *homologous*), but they represent a fairly broad sampling of the different kinds of proteins in the world. Human beings are made of approximately 300,000 different proteins. Compared to all these sequence data, there are relatively few known protein structures: about 600. The rate of growth of solved protein structures is also much lower than that of sequences, although there has been a recent burst of effort in this area.

As a first pass, it would seem reasonable to build a training set of sequence/structure pairs and try to learn a direct mapping between the sequences and structures. Unfortunately, both the sequences themselves (100+ character strings drawn on a 20 letter alphabet) and structures (real valued 3-D positions of several thousands of atoms) are so large as to make the training tremendously underconstrained with 600 examples—even if it were to be computationally tractable. In order to be addressed by current machine learning methods, the problem must be reduced in size. Fortunately, proteins have many shared segments of highly similar structure.

The fact that there are common substructures among widely varying proteins has been known for some time. Linus Pauling (1960) identified the two most basic protein structural components before the first detailed atomic structure of any protein had been solved. These components, the alpha-helix and the beta-sheet, have been the basis of all previous attempts to use machine learning for protein structure prediction. The composition of a protein in terms of these substructures is called its secondary structure.

Initially, the definition of the secondary structure classes was somewhat ambiguous. A helix was a tightly packed, roughly corkscrew shaped sequence of bonded amino acids. A sheet was an extended (stretched out), nearly linear sequence. However, these definitions were later refined to be based on the hydrogen bonding characteristics of the structures (Kabsch and Sander, 1983), and that definition is now widely accepted. Not all bonds in a protein are between amino acids that are adjacent in the amino acid sequence. Often weak links (called hydrogen bonds) between amino acids that are not adjacent can form. These links play an important role in the overall structure of the protein. In alpha helices, the loops in the corkscrew are about four residues long, and there are hydrogen bonds between the residues in each loop of the helix; that is, there are hydrogen bonds between every fourth residue (see Figure 23.1). The hydrogen bonds that make up beta-sheets are between residues that are even more distant in the primary sequence. Each beta-sheet is made of at least two beta-strands. The residues in the strands form hydrogen bonds with each other. The strands can go in the same direction (parallel) or in opposite directions (anti-parallel). The strands are usually connected to each other by a beta-turn. A strand-turn-strand sequence would form an anti-parallel beta-sheet that looked like the letter "U," with the hydrogen bonds connecting the atoms in the vertical strokes of the "U." Kabsch and Sander (1983) actually defined eight secondary structure classes.

The problem of predicting protein structure from sequence is now generally reduced to the problem of predicting secondary structure from sequence (Qian and Sejnowski, 1988; Holley and Karplus, 1989; Cohen, Presnell, and Cohen, 1990). In fact, all published work to date reduces the problem to the prediction of one of three classes: alpha-helix, beta-strand, and other (usually called random-coil). Each method for identifying secondary structure uses a sliding window of between 7 and 17 amino acids to predict the structure class of the central amino acid. Other methods reported at recent workshops are variants on this basic idea, e.g., taking into account the secondary structure assignments of neighboring residues when making a prediction.

There are a variety of problems with this approach. First, the factors influencing the formation of a particular secondary structure are not always local in nature. That is, a sliding window approach inevitably ignores some of the factors that determine which secondary structure an amino acid will be part of. Second, secondary structure prediction is at best a moderately good proxy for tertiary structure information. Solving the secondary structure problem is only one step toward addressing the real problem of tertiary structure prediction (Cohen and Kuntz, 1989; Holbrook, Muskal, and Kim, 1993). Transforming an even accurate set of secondary structure predictions into an approximately correct tertiary structure is a difficult (potentially insolvable) task. Third, there is relatively little information

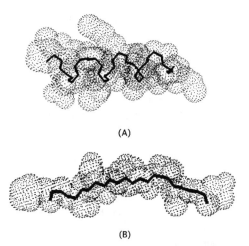

(A)

(B)

Figure 23.1:   Protein secondary structures. The dark lines in each structure represent the bonds
between the C, Cα, and N backbone atoms. The dots indicate the van der Waals surfaces for all the other atoms in the protein fragment. Crystallographers define structural
motifs primarily on the basis of hydrogen bonding patterns: (A) shows an α -helix,
which is a closely packed conformation characterized by hydrogen bonds between
every fourth residue. This helix is thirteen residues long and appears in human hemoglobin (Protein DataBank entry 3HHB, residues 4–17). (B) shows a β-strand, an
extended conformation. A β-strand is part of a larger β-sheet structure, consisting of
several similar strands hydrogen bonded to each other. This strand is seven residues
long and appears in human alpha-1-antitrypsin (PDB entry 9API, residues 139–146).
Note that compared to the helices, the strand extends about twice the linear distance
per residue. These images were generated by the UCSF Midas+ program.

content in helix/sheet/coil predictions on existing datasets. More than half of the
amino acids in proteins of known structure are in helices. A method that always
predicted a helix would have 53% accuracy. Even forcing the prediction method to
guess at the observed frequency of occurrence of the classes, random guessing will
yield an accuracy of over 40% at the helix/sheet/coil prediction task. Compare that
to the 58% accuracy figure of the most widely used statistical method (Chou and
Fasman, 1974) and the reigning champion method's 65% accuracy reported at the
1991 AAAI workshop on AI and molecular biology. Clearly, there is not a great
deal of information in these results (a more formal analysis follows below).

23.3 A MULTISTRATEGY APPROACH

Recall that the prediction of protein secondary structure is a proxy for trying
to predict all of the positions of all the atoms in a protein. Secondary structure
classes are but one way of breaking up the problem of structure prediction into
manageable pieces. The approach taken was to use unsupervised learning to define

a new set of protein substructure classes and then use supervised learning to try to discover a mapping from amino acid sequence to the induced classes. This approach has the potential to both make the path from subsequence prediction to tertiary structure prediction more tractable and increase the information content of the substructure predictions themselves. Although this is still work in progress, there have been some promising indications of the potential of the technique.

23.3.1 Discovery of Substructure Classes

The existing secondary structure classification scheme was generated through the insight and intuition of biochemists. These classifications have proven to be useful and have adequately characterized many of the structures discovered after the classifications were proposed. Nevertheless, it is possible that other classifications could be superior for protein structure prediction or other tasks. The space of possible classifications is so large, however, that the discovery of an optimal classification (and an optimality proof) is highly unlikely. Furthermore, the number of proteins with known structure, although growing rapidly, is quite small compared to the number of proteins in living systems; so, any empirical classification scheme is likely to be incomplete and subject to significant revision.

Bayesian classification was chosen for the unsupervised learning task. There were several reasons for this. Bayesian techniques are well suited to real numbered data with Gaussian distributions, which is a reasonable model for atomic positions in proteins (it is the model used in the molecular dynamics approach). The technique also explicitly balances the ability of the classification to account for the data against the complexity of the classification, yielding an estimate of the most likely number of classes as well as their content. Finally, the technique can also generate classifications that have significantly differing within-class variances. That is, some classes will be defined tightly, and others will be more variable. This is valuable both because the natural classes are likely to differ in this way (e.g., 3_{10} helices are very similar to one another, but beta-sheets exhibit wide variations) and because variance information is useful in trying to fit new data to the model defined by the classification. Other classification systems (e.g., Fisher [1987]) appear to have a strong tendency to minimize differences in variance between classes. The AUTO-CLASS III implementation of Bayesian classification (Cheeseman et al., 1990) was selected, although there are now alternative methods that may be worth exploring (e.g., Neal [1991] or Patrick [1991]).

Bayesian classification, like other unsupervised learning methods, requires a feature vector of fixed size for describing the examples to be classified. This requirement causes at least three problems in the domain of protein substructure: First, natural substructures are likely to vary in length. To use an example from the traditional secondary structure classification, a typical alpha-helix is between 11 and 17 residues in length. Second, substructures appear in various positions and orientations in a protein. In order to be made comparable to one another, they must be rotated and translated to a uniform frame of reference. Third, there are too many atoms in even short stretches of protein to use each as a feature, and their positions are highly correlated with each other. Some sampling criterion is necessary.

The positions of each of the backbone atoms in the amino acids were used as representatives of the positions of the residues.

There are reasonably effective molecular dynamics methods for placing side chains on a protein with a known backbone structure. A canonical coordinate frame was defined by reference to the center of gravity and moment of inertia of each example, and three different fixed fragment sizes (length 5, 6, and 8 residues) were tried with similar results. For more details on the classification, see Hunter and States (1992).

Under a variety of representational selections and parameter choices, a classification containing about 27 classes was found repeatedly (some had 26). For ease of calculation, the classification with the shortest fragment size (5 amino acids long) was chosen for further analysis. The amino acid composition of a protein was then used to try to predict a sequence of substructure classes that describe it.

23.3.2 Prediction of Induced Classes

Although this work is still preliminary, both neural networks (trained with conjugate gradient descent methods) and decision tree learning methods (using C4.5 [Quinlan, 1987, 1991]) have been tried. A novel bitstring representation for amino acids was used for the input (see Hunter [1992]) and 100 bit error correcting output codes (Dietterich and Bakiri, 1991) for the output representation.

The training and test sets come from the June 1991 release of the Brookhaven Protein Databank. Only high resolution protein structures[2] were selected, and they were divided into overlapping fragments of length 5 amino acids, yielding a training set of 9,326 examples and two test sets (of 1,143 and 1,203 examples, respectively) used for cross validation. Relatively little difference between the decision tree learning method and the neural network approach was found in this problem. The neural network gave marginally greater accuracy on the test sets, but the decision tree learner trained thousands of times more quickly (hours instead of weeks), allowing a greater range of experimentation. For example, various input window sizes, various error correcting codes, and alternative representations of amino acids were tried, primarily with the decision tree learner.

---

[2] The IDs of the proteins used are 1ALC 1BP2 1CSE 1CSE 1CTF 1ECD 1GCR 1GD1 1GD1 1GD1 1GD1 1HNE 1LZ1 1MBC 1PAZ 1PCY 1PPT 1PSG 1PSG 1SGT 1SN3 1TON 1TON 1TPP 1UBQ 1UTG 2ACT 2ALP 2APR 2AZA 2AZA 2CCY 2CCY 2CGA 2CGA 2CYP 2FB4 2FB4 2MHR 2OVO 2PRK 2RHE 2SGA 2SNS 3BCL 3BCL 3BCL 3BCL 3CTS 3CTS 3CTS 3CYT 3CYT 3EBX 3EST 3INS 3INS 3INS 3INS 3RNT 3RP2 3RP2 4DFR 4DFR 4FXN 4HHB 4HHB 4HHB 4HHB 4PTI 5CPA 5RXN 6TMN 7RSA 9PAP 9WGA 9WGA.

The best current method results in 35.5% correct predictions on the test sets. This level of accuracy is not as high as that reported in the traditional secondary structure prediction literature (e.g., Holley and Karplus [1989] claim 62.3% correct). On the other hand, the method predicts 35% of 27 possible classes, compared to 62% of 3 possible classes. An information theoretic analysis shows that there is significantly more information being transmitted in the former than the latter.

Consider the sequence of predictions made for a set of N protein fragments as a noisy communication channel, that is, as if a message containing the correct class assignments had been scrambled by random noise. First, consider the capacity of a noiseless channel: The information transmitted by N assignments to i classes (each with frequency f_i) in the absence of noise is

$$-N \bullet \sum_i f_i \bullet \log_2 f_i$$

$$(1)$$

If some fraction E of the N predictions is scrambled, the information transmitted is

$$-N(1-E) \bullet \sum_i f_i \bullet \log_2 f_i$$

$$(2)$$

If E is 0, then $EQ2$ reduces to the channel capacity, as described in eq. 1. If E is 1, then no information is transmitted. When using percentage correct, it is assumed that the incorrect predictions were scrambled and set 1-E equal to the fraction correct. The number of bits per prediction can be calculated, which just removes the factor of N in eq. 2, yielding

$$-C \bullet \sum_i f_i \bullet \log_2 f_i$$

$$(3)$$

Now consider the Holley and Karplus predictions of 63.2% correct on 3 classes:

$$-0.632 \bullet \sum_{i=1}^{3} f_i \bullet \log_2 f_i$$

$$= -0.632 \bullet -1.46 = 0.92 \text{ bits per prediction}$$

Compare to the prediction of 27 classes at 35% accuracy:

$$-0.354 \bullet \sum_{i=1}^{27} f_i \bullet \log_2 f_i$$

$$= -0.354 \bullet -4.62 = 1.63 \text{ bits per prediction}$$

That is, the ability to predict which of 27 substructure classes a given fragment of a protein will fall into based on its amino acid sequence at a level of 35%

correct contains a good deal more information than the ability to predict helix versus sheet versus other at a level of 63% accuracy.

Another way to see this is to consider the chance of predicting correctly by making random guesses. If the guesses must follow the frequency distribution of the actual classes (i.e., one is not allowed to guess the most frequent class all the time), then the expected percentage correct is the sum of the squares of the frequencies. In the traditional three class case (using the frequency statistics from Holley and Karplus [1989]), a random guesser can expect to be correct 39% of the time. For the 27-class induced distribution, the expected accuracy of random guesses is only 4.3% correct. The difference between the random and actual performance is greater in the 27-class case (4.3% versus 35.4%) than in the 3-class case (39.4% versus 63.2%).

23.4 CLASSIFYING FOR PREDICTION

Although there are a variety of additional tests that need to be done to increase confidence in the protein structure prediction work, it is possible to make some tentative generalizations about the usefulness of the multistrategy learning approach used.

All learning methods for complex prediction problems depend crucially on choice of representation and the statement of the problem. Machine learning prediction methods, like their statistical cousins, have been focused on relatively constrained problems, primarily binary or N-way classification tasks. Many realistic problems involve making complex mappings in high dimensional spaces. These problems must be addressed by dividing the domain space into pieces and then developing methods for recognizing and responding to those pieces. In essence, reducing the dimensionality of the problem space is a matter of finding a representation that makes it possible to learn a (relatively) simple map.

At this stage of development in machine learning, it is generally the case that if a researcher can find a good representation of a set of domain concepts, any of several inferential approaches can find an adequate mapping using that representation. However, without an appropriate set of representations, even very powerful learning methods fail in a variety of ways. For example, Almuallim and Dietterich (1991) showed the inability of various widely used learning methods to handle many irrelevant features. Rendell and Cho (1990) demonstrate that a variety of machine learning methods are extremely sensitive to both the character of a concept to be learned and to the representation of the training examples. An important direction for the improvement of machine learning methods is to look for the automatic generation of good representations from data. What counts as a good representation depends on what a learner desires to know, as well as on the structure of the data (Hunter, 1990b).

This research is part of a larger effort (e.g., Hunter [1989b, 1990a]; Ram and Hunter [1991]) to automatically select and combine multiple learning strategies in pursuit of specific goals for knowledge. This work is based on the assumption that there is no general learning method; instead, a general purpose learning system will be able to apply many different methods and will make decisions selecting among and combining those methods based on its goals, knowledge, and abilities. One of the problems that such a general purpose learner will face is generating appropriate representations of "raw" data for use in learning predictive "features." The combination of Bayesian classification and induction (both neural networks and information theoretic decision tree learning) is one such multistrategy approach that a general purpose learner may find useful.

The example presented in this chapter documents an attempt to automatically generate a useful output representation for finding a complex mapping to a very high dimension space. The classification step allowed the transformation of 45 real valued numbers (3 dimensions * 3 backbone atoms * 5 residue long fragments) with roughly 16-bit precision (720 bits) to 27 classes (just under 5 bits) with a minimum loss of information. Even with 10,000 training examples, it is a much easier problem after the transformation than before. This classification is apparently better than the reduction to just three classes because it can lead to more informative predictions.

The ability to automatically design representations that simultaneously meet the requirements of the data, the learning method, and the to be learned concept remains a difficult technical challenge. Nevertheless, this preliminary work indicates that current learning methods can be combined into a system that is able, at least in one case, to generate and use its own representation, resulting in performance that is superior to learning using human generated representations.

ACKNOWLEDGMENTS

Much of the research reported on here would not have been possible without the collaboration of David J. States of the National Center for Biotechnology Information. His knowledge of biology and information theory has been invaluable. Tom Dietterich of Oregon State University generously donated several CPU months and much of his attention to this project. His assistance is also gratefully recognized.

References

Almuallim, H., and Dietterich, T. Learning with Many Irrelevant Features. In *Ninth National Conference on Artificial Intelligence*, pp. 547–552. Menlo Park, CA: AAAI Press, 1991.

Cheeseman, P., Stutz, J., Hanson, R., and Taylor, W. *Autoclass III*, NASA Ames Research Center, Research Institute for Advanced Computer Science, 1990.

Chou, P., and Fasman, G., Prediction of Protein Conformation. *Biochemistry, 13*(2), pp. 222–245, 1974.

Cohen, F.E., and Kuntz, I.D. Tertiary Structure Prediction. In G.D. Fasman (Ed.), *Prediction of Protein Structure and the Principles of Protein Conformation*, pp. 647–705. New York: Plenum Publishing Corporation, 1989.

Cohen, B., Presnell, S., and Cohen, F. Pattern Based Approaches to Protein Structure Prediction. *Methods in Enzymology*, Vol. 202, pp. 252–268, 1990.

Dietterich, T. Limitations on Inductive Learning. In *Sixth International Workshop on Machine Learning*, pp. 125–128. San Mateo, CA: Morgan Kaufmann, 1989.

Dietterich, T.G., and Bakiri, G. Error-Correcting Output Codes: A General Method for Improving Multiclass Inductive Learning Programs. In *Ninth National Conference on Artificial Intelligence*, Menlo Park, CA: AAAI Press, pp. 572–577, 1991.

Fisher, D. Knowledge Acquisition Via Incremental Conceptual Clustering. *Machine Learning, 2*, pp. 139–172, 1987.

Hammond, K. *Case-based Planning: An Integrated Theory of Planning, Learning and Memory*. Ph.D. Thesis, Yale University, 1986.

Holbrook, S., Muskal, S., and Kim, S.-H. Predicting Protein Structural Features with Computational Neural Networks. In L. Hunter (Ed.), *Artificial Intelligence and Molecular Biology*, pp. 161–194, Menlo Park, CA: AAAI Press, 1993.

Holley, L.H., and Karplus, M. Protein Secondary Structure Prediction with a Neural Network, *Proceedings of the National Academy of Sciences USA 86* (January), 152–156, 1989.

Holte, R.C. *Very Simple Classification Rules Perform Well on Most Datasets*. TR-91-16, University of Ottawa, 1991.

Hunter, L. *Knowledge Acquisition Planning: Gaining Expertise through Experience*. Ph.D. Thesis, Yale University, 1989a.

————. Knowledge Acquisition Planning: Results and Prospects. In *The Sixth International Workshop on Machine Learning*, pp. 61–66. San Mateo, CA: Morgan Kaufmann, 1989b.

————. Knowledge Acquisition Planning for Inference from Large Datasets. In *The Twenty Third Annual Hawaii International Conference on System Sciences*, pp. 35–44. Washington, DC: IEEE Press, 1990a.

————. Planning to Learn. In *The Twelfth Annual Conference of the Cognitive Science Society*, pp. 26–34. Hillsdale, NJ: Lawrence Erlbaum Associates, 1990b.

Hunter, L. (Ed.), *Artificial Intelligence and Molecular Biology*. 1993. Technical report available from author.

Hunter, L., and States, D.J. Bayesian Classification of Protein Structure. *IEEE Expert*, 1992.

Kabsch, W., and Sander, C. Dictionary of Protein Secondary Structure: Pattern Recognition of Hydrogen-Bonded and Geometrical Features. *Biopolymers, 22*(12), pp. 2577–2637, 1983.

Karplus, M., and Petsko, G.A. Molecular Dynamics Simulations in Biology. *Nature, 347* (October), pp. 631–639, 1990.

Kirsh, D. Second Generation AI Theories of Learning. *Behavioral and Brain Sciences, 9*(4), pp. 658–659, 1986.

Langley, P. Machine Learning and Concept Formation (editorial). *Machine Learning, 2*(2), 99, 1987.

Neal, R. *Bayesian Mixture Modeling by Monte Carlo Simulation.* Technical Report, #CRG-TR-91–2, Department of Computer Science, University of Toronto, 1991.

Patrick, J.D. *SNOB: A Program for Discriminating between Classes.* Technical Report, #91/151, Department of Computer Science, Monash University (Australia), 1991.

Pauling, L. *The Nature of the Chemical Bond.* Ithaca, NY: Cornell University Press, 1960.

Qian, N., and Sejnowski, T. Predicting the Secondary Structure of Globular Proteins Using Neural Network Models. *Journal of Molecular Biology, 202*, pp. 865–884, 1988.

Quinlan, J.R. Simplifying Decision Trees. *International Journal of Man-Machine Studies, 27*, pp. 221–234, 1987.

———. *C4.5.* Available from the author; quinlan@cs.su.oz.au, 1991.

Ram, A. *Question-driven Understanding: An Integrated Theory of Story Understanding, Memory and Learning.* Ph.D. Thesis, Yale University, 1989.

Ram, A., and Hunter, L. A Goal-based Approach to Intelligent Information Retrieval. In *Proceedings of the Eighth International Workshop on Machine Learning*, pp. 265–269. San Mateo, CA: Morgan Kaufmann, 1991.

———. A Goal-based Approach to Intelligent Information Retrieval. *Applied Intelligence,* Vol. 2, No. 1, pp. 47–73, 1992.

Rendell, L., and Cho, H. Empirical Learning as a Function of Concept Character. *Machine Learning, 5*(3), pp. 267–298, 1990.

Rosa, G.J., Davide, J.P., Weinhold, K., Waterbury, J.A., Profy, A.T., Lewis, J.A., Langlois, A.J., Dreesman, G.R., Boswell, R.N., Shadduck, P., Holley, L.H., Karplus, M., Bolognesi, D., Matthews, T.J., Emini, E.A., and Putney, S.D. Conserved Sequence and Structural Elements in the HIV-1 Principal Neutralizing Determinant. *Science, 249* (August 24), pp. 249–935, 1990.

Skolnick, J., and Kolinski, A. Simulations of the Folding of a Globular Protein. *Science, 250* (November 23), pp. 1121–1125, 1990.

Weiss, S., and Kulikowski, C. *Computer Systems That Learn.* San Mateo, CA: Morgan Kaufmann, 1991.

24

GEST:

A Learning Computer Vision System That Recognizes Hand Gestures

Jakub Segen
(AT&T Bell Laboratories)

Abstract

GEST is a computer vision system that learns to recognize nonrigid 2-D shapes and to compute desired pose parameters. Its learning approach combines six inference methods: constructive induction of relations, vector clustering, graph clustering, stochastic graph inference, learning of attribute lists, and robust inference of numerical parameters.

The recognition in GEST is invariant under planar translation, rotation, and local deformations, and it is not affected by partial occlusion. It has been implemented in real time, with an average throughput rate of 12 video images per second.

The system has been trained to recognize a set of hand gestures, and it is used as a novel form of human-computer interface. Its experimental applications include a graphics editor and a flight simulator, both controlled entirely by hand gestures.

24.1 INTRODUCTION

Few real applications are pure enough to admit a single computational method as a solution. One usually needs to combine different techniques to achieve a desired outcome. Machine learning is not an exception, and there have been attempts to explore the use of multiple learning strategies (e.g. Wilkins et al., 1986; Pazzani, 1988; Tecuci, 1988; Shavlik and Towell, 1989; Whitehall, 1990; Tecuci and Michalski, 1991). Michalski (1990) provides a general framework for methods that select learning strategies according to task.

This chapter describes the use of multiple learning methods in a computer vision system. The system, called GEST, recognizes nonrigid visual shapes such as hand gestures, and computes the numerical parameters describing the transformation and deformation of a viewed object. GEST uses a multistrategy learning approach to infer the models needed for classification and to construct the functions that compute desired numerical parameters. The learning steps in GEST are combined mostly in series or are cascaded; i.e., the results of one learning step are used as input by the succeeding learning steps.

24.2 OVERVIEW

GEST learns and recognizes nonrigid shapes based on their structure. Once it is trained, the system gives a class name of an object placed before a camera. Recognition is insensitive to planar rotation, translation, and local deformations, and it is not affected by objects touching or partial occlusion. In addition to recognizing an object, GEST estimates its position and orientation, as well as parameters describing local deformations. This set of numerical values is later referred to as a *pose*.

In current experiments, GEST recognizes two-dimensional hand gestures and controls real time graphics applications, such as a 3-D graphics editor and a flight simulator. In these applications, the gesture class selects an action, e.g., "move object," "copy," and "change speed." The pose parameters are translated to control values corresponding to the selected action.

GEST consists of three major modules: data collection, learning, and recognition. Data collection is an interactive real-time process that prepares training data for the learning module. In each interactive step, the system prompts the user by drawing a figure on the screen. The user responds by presenting a gesture to a camera, trying to match its location, orientation, and deformations to the parameters of the drawn figure. The information collected by this process is saved and later provided to the learning module.

The learning module is executed off-line. A typical learning run for 300 training instances takes about 40 minutes on a TI Explorer II. All the results of learning are collected in a model file. The recognition module reads the model file and then proceeds in real time, at an average rate of 12 video frames/sec. The recognizer monitors the input from the camera, attempts to classify any object that appears in the image, and computes its pose parameters. The output of the recognizer, consisting of a class symbol and an object's pose, can be sent to an application system.

GEST's ability to recognize nonrigid objects under occlusion results from the expressive power of the representations it employs. GEST uses a hierarchy of representation and models of increasing levels of complexity. They range from lists of complex numbers that describe 2-D curves to stochastic graphs and graph clusters that describe classes of nonrigid shapes in terms of their parts and relations among parts. Recognition of an unknown object involves a costly process of graph matching that finds a mapping between a stochastic graph representing a class and a graph that represents the unknown object. To offset the high cost of graph matching, GEST uses a less powerful but much faster classification method, called a preclassifier, that quickly rates the set of hypotheses and restricts graph matching to a few most likely cases. The preclassifier uses yet another representation: a list of symbols with probability values.

Complexity of the models used by GEST's recognizer makes learning a necessity, not only a convenience. An alternative would be to construct the models by hand, which would take months for a single application.

The shape models constructed by the learning module combine symbolic and numerical elements. The symbols do not have a fixed, predetermined meaning; the system learns a set of symbolic relations from data.

The learning module combines the following inference methods:

1. Vector clustering: Divides a set of n-dimensional vectors into groups.
2. Constructive induction of relations: A data driven method, discovers symbolic relations that are used as the basic primitives in a symbolic description of shape.
3. Inference of an attribute list classifier: Forms a description of a class of relational structures using a list of symbolic attributes and their probabilities.
4. Stochastic graph inference: Builds a probability model that describes a class of graphs.
5. Graph clustering: Divides a set of graphs into groups.
6. Robust parameter inference: Learns numerical parameters from noisy data with outliers, which are values unrelated to the estimated parameter.

24.3 REPRESENTATIONS

GEST uses the following representations. They are further discussed in Section 24.4.

At the input to the recognition and learning programs, shapes are represented numerically by planar curves extracted from an image. A planar **curve** is represented in a discrete parametric form as a list of complex numbers; each complex number describes one point of the curve.

A **local feature** is a point on a curve at a local extremum of curvature, stored together with the local values of curvature and orientation. Local feature describes a singular point in a curve. Local features are often used in computer vision because they provide an adequate description of shape for recognition tasks.

A **structural feature** is defined recursively: It is either a local feature or an object constructed from a pair of structural features.

A **structural pattern** describes a cluster of similar structural features, using mean values and variances of their parameters.

A directed acyclic **graph** with labels attached to its vertices is used as a symbolic representation of shape.

A **graph model** is a stochastic graph that defines a probability distribution on graphs. Each vertex of a graph model contains a probability distribution on vertex labels. When a graph model is matched with a graph describing a shape instance, a vertex of a stochastic graph can match any label with some probability. The product of probabilities of individual vertex matches is included in the overall score of the match. GEST uses a graph model to describe a group of graphs (or shapes represented by graphs).

An **attribute list** is a list of label-probability pairs extracted from vertices of a graph model.

A **pose** of a shape is a set of four numbers. Three numbers describe the position and orientation; the fourth number represents the deformation. The deformation value is related to distances between the local features.

Pose functions are functions that compute the parameters of a pose. The arguments to a pose function are local features.

A **pose model** is a set of pose functions with weights. A weight of a pose function determines its significance. A pose model is associated with a graph model.

24.4 RECOGNITION

The recognition process is described first, before the discussion of learning, to explain the role of induced structures.

To determine the class name of an object presented before a camera, the recognition program searches a library of **graph models**. It finds a model that best corresponds to the presented object, and it returns the class name attached to this model. The recognition program also computes the pose of the object.

The recognition process consists of the following steps:

1. Extraction of local features
2. Identification of relations
3. Preclassification

4. Graph matching
5. Pose estimation

The first step processes the image and extracts curves and their local features, using classical techniques of computer vision (Rosenfeld and Kak, 1976).

The second step is a recursive procedure that identifies symbolic relations over sets of local features. The relations form a hierarchy, and they are organized in layered graph structure.

The third step, a fast preclassifier, selects a number of graph models that are likely to provide good matches. These models are passed to a graph matching program that finds the best match. The last step computes the object pose, using the pose model associated with the best matching graph.

Steps 2–5 use induced structures that had been computed by the learning program. These steps are described below, with a bold face used to highlight the induced structures.

24.4.1 Identification of Relations

To build a structural description of shape, GEST has to identify symbolic relations over local features. In this process, GEST uses an intermediate form—a structural feature. A structural feature is the root of a binary tree. The lower nodes of this tree are also structural features. The leaves of the tree are local features. The binary tree defines the structural feature at its root and determines the order of operations that were used to construct it. The simplest (level 0) structural feature is a local feature. A level 1 structural feature is constructed from a pair of local features. A level 2 structural feature is constructed from a pair of level 1 structural features, etc. A structural feature at level n describes 2^n local features at the leaves of its tree.

A structural feature is characterized by two sets of values. The first set contains values that change under rigid transformations, i.e., three numbers describing the position and orientation of a structural feature. The second set contains values that are invariant under rigid transformations. For a level 0 structural feature, this set contains only one value—the curvature. For a structural feature at level 1 and higher, it consists of five values: the labels of the two children, distance between the children positions, and two angles formed by children orientations and the line joining their positions. Structural features are constructed bottom-up, one level at the time, by an iterative application of two operations: labeling and composition. Labeling assigns a symbolic label to a structural feature by comparing its invariant parameters with a library of **structural patterns**. The symbol associated with the nearest structural pattern becomes the label of the structural feature. The composition takes a pair of labeled structural features at level n and returns a structural feature at level $n + 1$.

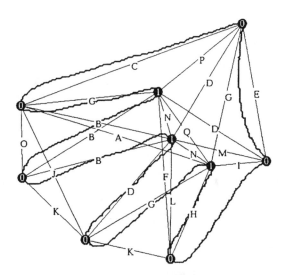

Figure 24.1:   Local features (circles) and binary relations (lines). Numbers and letters represent labels.

The label of a structural feature is an index of a geometric relation. If L is a level 0 structural feature, (local feature) and its label is Q, then $Q(L)$ is a unary relation $|C(L) - M(Q)| <= D(Q)$, which states that the curvature $C(L)$ is within $D(Q)$ from the value $M(Q)$. The values $M(Q)$ and $D(Q)$ are the parameters of the structural pattern associated with the label Q. If L is a level $n > 0$ structural feature, its label P identifies a binary relation $P(C1,C2)$ between its children $C1$ and $C2$ of L. This relation specifies the children labels, the range of values of the distance between the children, and ranges of angles. If the level of L is 2 or higher, then the labels of its children identify binary relations between their children, $C11$, $C12$ and $C21$, $C22$. It means that P also identifies a quaternary relation $Q(C11,C12,C21,C22)$ over four grandchildren of L, and so on, until we reach the local features. In general, the label of a structural feature at level n specifies a 2^n-ary relation over a set of local features. All these geometric relations are invariant under planar translation and rotation.

After the structural features are identified to a preset level, GEST retains only their labels and the parent-child links. The resulting structure is a directed acyclic graph with labeled vertices. The vertices are grouped into layers, according to their depth. Each layer contains relations of the same arity. The leaves of the graph represent local features. Figure 24.1 shows a shape with its local features and binary relations. Figure 24.2 shows a corresponding two layer graph.

The layered graph contains all the information about the shape of an object that GEST uses for its classification.

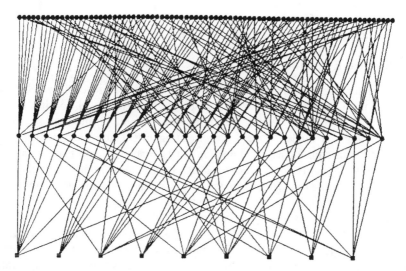

Figure 24.2:   Layered graph representing the shape from Figure 24.1. Vertex labels are not shown.

24.4.2 Classification

To classify an object, GEST compares the graph describing its shape, or object graph, with a library of **graph models** to find the best matching graph model. A match between an object graph and a graph model is a mapping between the vertices of these two graphs. The match is evaluated based on a relative complexity of representation of an object graph with respect to the graph model. One can think of graph matching as a data compression scheme that represents the object graph using the model graph and a mapping of its vertices to the vertices of the object graph. The score of a match is the number of bits saved by such a representation compared to a representation that does not use a graph model.

GEST uses a two-step heuristic (Segen, 1988) to find a match between the object graph and a given graph model. The first step determines an initial mapping by maximizing an approximate score, which it computes from the probability distributions at vertices of the graph model, without considering the full graph structure. The second step iteratively edits the mapping until the true score reaches a maximum.

To avoid matching the object graph with each graph model in the library, GEST uses a fast preclassifier. The preclassifier compares the list of labels extracted from vertices of the object graph with the **attribute list** of each graph model and computes a similarity measure, which is an upper bound of a match score. The graph models to be matched with the object graph are selected in order of decreasing values of this measure. The search process terminates when the similarity measure falls below the score of the best match because it is certain that no better match can be found. In the real-time implementation of this process, the user can set a limit on the number of graph matches.

24.4.3 Pose Estimation

The recognizer computes the object pose for the best matching graph model, using its **pose model** and the vertex mapping. A pose model consists of pose functions and numerical weights. Functions that compute position are attached to leaves of a graph model. Functions computing orientation are associated with leaves and with pairs of leaves. Functions that compute a deformation value are associated with pairs of leaves. Pose functions are applied to the local features of the object, according to the vertex mapping; i.e., a function associated with a leaf is applied to a local feature that had been mapped to this leaf.

The object pose is a weighted average of the values returned by a subset of the pose functions. The overall pose is computed using an iterative elimination algorithm that rejects outliers. In each iteration, this algorithm computes a weighted average from the current set of values; it then eliminates from the set the values that differ from the average by more than a preset amount. It stops when no such values are found.

24.5 LEARNING

The input to the learning module is a training set consisting of shapes, their class names, and pose values. Figure 24.3 shows the structure of the learning module.

The learning process is similar to the recognition program, with the following two distinctions:

1. Each learning step involves generalization, so it processes all training instances before passing to the next step; the recognition program runs each instance through all the steps before passing to the next instance.

2. In places where the recognition program makes use of an induced structure, the learning program creates this structure.

24.5.1 Learning Relations

To learn relations, GEST uses an unsupervised method of *constructive induction* that begins with local features and generates structural patterns. The program iteratively constructs structural features, as described in Section 4.1. Its inductive element is a *vector clustering* program (Segen, 1989c), which is invoked after the composition step that creates a new level of structural features.

Vector clustering is applied to the invariant parts of structural features computed from all training samples. The clusters computed at each level are added to

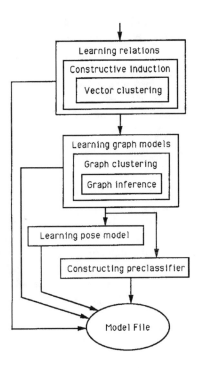

Figure 24.3:   Learning module

the library of structural patterns. They are also used by the labeling step to assign labels to structural features before the program creates the next level features. The set of structural features corresponding to a training instance is represented as a layered graph.

24.5.2 Learning Graph Models

The shape descriptions are formed by a *graph clustering* program that is applied to a set of graphs that represent training instances of the same class. The result is a set of stochastic graphs or graph models, each associated with a name of this class.

The clustering program can generate more than one graph model to represent a single class of shapes. The resulting description of the class has a disjunctive form. Such descriptions are formed for nonhomogeneous classes that cannot be adequately represented by a single graph model.

To construct graph clusters, GEST uses an incremental method called INCLAG (Segen, 1990). It is based on minimal representation criterion (Segen and Sanderson 1979; Segen 1980), also known as a minimal description length (MDL) criterion (Rissanen, 1978). This method uses a classical "leader" approach to grow clusters. A cluster is represented by a graph model. INCLAG takes one graph from the input list at a time and computes the match scores for models of all clusters present. If the best score is positive, then it merges the input graph with the best matching model; otherwise, it starts a new cluster.

The merging operation used in graph clustering is a key element of a supervised technique of *stochastic graph inference* that learns a stochastic graph that best represents a given set of graphs (Segen, 1988). This operation first matches a graph model to an object graph; it then updates the vertex probabilities of the graph model, according to the vertex mapping and the labels of vertices of the object graph.

24.5.3 Constructing a Preclassifier

A preclassifier consists of lists of vertex labels from stochastic graphs ordered by their probability values. All the inductive work reflected in the content of the preclassifier, mainly the computation of label probabilities, is done as a part of graph clustering. Therefore, the construction of a preclassifier involves only extracting and ordering label-probability pairs from the graph models.

24.5.4 Learning Pose Model

A pose model consists of weighted linear functions associated with leaves and pairs of leaves of each graph model. They are computed from the training shapes mapped to a graph model by relating the local features of a shape to the pose, using a robust method of iterative elimination, summarized in Section 24.4.3. The weight of a pose function is the inverse of its average square error from the pose of training instances.

The need for a robust method arises because the graph matching is not perfect. A single vertex mismatch can cause large numerical errors that a nonrobust technique such as regression would not average out.

24.6 IMPLEMENTATION

The learning module is written in Common Lisp and executed on a TI Explorer II. The recognition module is a mixture of Lisp and C programs. The first real time version of the recognizer (Segen and Dana, 1991) was implemented in a highly distributed system. It consisted of an IP-512 image processor, a network of 30 processors (MC68020) that computed structural features and relations, and a TI Explorer II that was used for classification and pose estimation. This system processed images at the rate of four video frames/sec, but the latency was as high as 0.8 sec.

The recognition module has recently been reimplemented, using two SUN4 processors, an Intel i860 accelerator, and a Datacube image card. The recognition module is connected to an AT&T Pixel Machine that renders shaded graphics. The throughput is now 10–20 video frames/sec. The latency is 100–150 ms, which is sufficient for real-time interaction.

24.7 RESULTS AND APPLICATIONS

To judge gesture discrimination, the system is trained to recognize a set of gestures; the results are then evaluated both off-line and on-line. The off-line evaluation is quantitative: the recognizer processes another set of labeled gestures—a test set—and errors are counted. The misclassification errors are counted separately from the less severe rejection errors ("don't know").

In the on-line evaluation, the recognition system runs in real time on the stream of gesture images coming from a camera. When a gesture is recognized, the system places a marker next to an icon representing a gesture class. At this time, we do not have quantifying tools, so the on-line evaluation is only qualitative based on visual judgment of the frequency of errors.

The largest set of gestures consisted of 10 gesture classes. Examples of gestures from these classes are shown in Figure 24.4. The classifier has been trained using 350 gesture examples. An off-line test with a set of 250 samples resulted in only 3 rejection errors. The on-line test showed more errors, judged between 5% and 10% of the cases. Most of these are rejection errors. Some misclassification errors occur during the transitions between gestures and during fast motion. Tests using smaller gesture sets produced similar or better results.

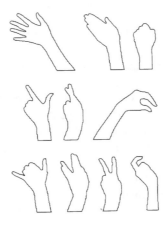

Figure 24.4:   Classifiable gestures

Two experimental applications of GEST have been implemented: a graphics editor and a flight simulator. In these applications, the user interacts in real-time with graphics programs using hand gestures. The editor allows the user to place, move, and copy figures on a screen. The operation is selected by a recognized gesture class. The control parameters of the operation, e.g., location and orientation for figure placement, are computed from the estimated pose.

In the flight simulator, the user controls the flight through a computer generated scene. The images appear on a screen as if seen by a camera, whose position and motion are controlled by gestures. The camera moves in the direction of an extended finger when the user shows a "Move" gesture. Three other gestures are used to control the velocity, elevation angle, and camera height. The fifth gesture is used to bring the camera to a home position.

24.8 EVOLUTION OF MULTISTRATEGY LEARNING IN GEST

GEST was developed over several years, becoming more and more complex with each change. The earliest version of the system (Segen, 1985) used three learning methods: vector clustering; constructive induction; and a classifier, which was based on a set of attributes, similar to the current preclassifier. This version classified nonrigid objects, but it worked only for homogeneous classes; it could not identify local features, and the objects were not allowed to touch or overlap.

In the second version, the attribute set classifier was replaced by a recognition program based on graph matching, and a stochastic graph inference method was used to learn graph models (Segen, 1988, 1989a, 1989b). This change enabled the system to identify local features and allowed objects to overlap. However, the recognition had become much slower, and the shape classes still had to be visually homogeneous.

To make the system work well with nonhomogeneous shape classes, graph clustering (Segen, 1990) was added, so that the system could build multiple graph models for a single class. This increased the size of model libraries, which made recognition even slower. The recognition speed increased several times after the addition of an attribute list preclassifier.

The initial approach to pose estimation from the mapping of local features involved neither learning nor robust inference methods. For each graph model, the leaves to be used in computation and the parameters of pose functions were selected manually. This took time, and the results were not always reliable.

In an attempt to automate the acquisition of pose models, nonrobust methods were tried first, but they did not work well because of significant errors in feature mapping. Therefore, robust techniques for pose learning and estimation were introduced. This not only eliminated the need for manual editing but also improved pose accuracy.

24.9 CONCLUSION

GEST combines six learning methods to construct models for a real-time recognition of visual objects. These models allow the recognition program to classify a nonrigid two-dimensional object independently of its position and orientation, even when the object is partially occluded, to identify an object's parts and to reliably compute its pose. Experimental applications of GEST include the recognition of hand gestures and interactive control of graphics programs through gesturing.

ACKNOWLEDGMENTS

Michael Potmesil loaned his model of a lab scene and a fast rendering program for the flight simulator. Kristin Dana helped to build the distributed version of the recognizer and constructed the graphics editor. David Gibbon and Bob Lyons provided image processing and communication tools for the current recognizer. I gratefully acknowledge these contributions. I also thank Derek Morris and the editors of this volume for their helpful comments.

References

Michalski, R.S., "A methodological framework for multistrategy task-adaptive learning," *Methodologies for Intelligent Systems,* North Holland, New York, pp. 404–411, 1990.

Pazzani, M., "Integrating explanation-based and empirical learning methods in OCCAM," *Proceedings of EWSL-88,* Pitman Publishing, London, pp. 147–165, 1988.

Rissanen, J., "Modeling by shortest data description," *Automatica 14,* pp. 465–471, 1978.

Rosenfeld, A., and Kak, A.C., *Digital Picture Processing,* Academic Press, San Diego, CA, 1976.

Shavlik, J., and Towell, G., "An approach to combining explanation-based and neural learning algorithms," *Connection Science 1(3)*: 231–253, 1989.

Segen, J., and Sanderson, A.C., "A Minimal Representation Criterion for Clustering," *Proceedings of the 12th Annual Symposium on Computer Science and Statistics,* University of Waterloo, Waterloo, Canada, pp. 332–334, May 1979.

Segen, J., *Pattern Directed Signal Analysis*, Ph.D. Dissertation, Carnegie Mellon University, June 1980.

————, "Learning structural descriptions of shape," *Proceedings of the IEEE Conference on Computer Vision and Pattern Recognition, CVPR'85,* IEEE Computer Society, Washington, DC, pp. 96–98, 1985.

————, "Learning graph models of shape," *Proceedings of the 5th International Conference on Machine Learning,* Ann Arbor, MI, Morgan Kaufmann, San Mateo, CA, pp. 29–35, 1988.

————, "Model learning and recognition of nonrigid objects," *Proceedings of Conference on Computer Vision and Pattern Recognition, CVPR'89,* pp. 597–602, San Diego, IEEE Computer Society Press, Washington, DC, June 1989a.

————, "From features to symbols: Learning relational models of shape," *From Pixels to Features,* Simon, J.C. (Ed.), North Holland, New York, pp. 237–248, 1989b.

————, "Incremental clustering by minimizing representation length," *Proceedings of the 6th International Workshop on Machine Learning,* Cornell University, Ithaca, NY, pp. 400–403, Morgan Kaufmann, San Mateo, CA, June 1989c.

————, "Graph clustering and model learning by data compression," *Proceedings of the 7th International Conference on Machine Learning,* Austin, Texas, pp. 93–101, Morgan Kaufmann, San Mateo, CA, 1990.

Segen, J., and Dana, K., "Parallel symbolic recognition of deformable shapes," *From Pixels to Features II,* Burkhardt, H., Neuvo, Y. and Simon, J.C. (Eds.), North-Holland, New York, pp. 387–400, 1991.

Tecuci, G., *DISCIPLE: A theory, methodology and system for learning expert knowledge,* These de Docteur en Science, University of Paris-South, 1988.

Tecuci, G., and Michalski, R.S., "A method for multistrategy task-adaptive learning based on plausible justification," *Proceedings of the 8th International Workshop on Machine Learning,* Evanston, Illinois, pp. 549–553, Morgan Kaufmann, San Mateo, CA, 1991.

Whitehall, B., *Knowledge-based learning: Integration of deductive and inductive learning for knowledge base completion,* Ph.D. Dissertation, University of Illinois at Urbana-Champaign, 1990.

Wilkins, D., Clancey, W., and Buchanan, B., *An overview of the Odysseus learning apprentice,* Kluwer, Norwell, MA, 1986.

25

LEARNING WITH A QUALITATIVE DOMAIN THEORY BY MEANS OF PLAUSIBLE EXPLANATIONS

Gerhard Widmer
*(University of Vienna and
Austrian Research Institute for Artificial Intelligence)*

Abstract

This chapter describes an approach to learning that employs a qualitative domain theory. The theory consists of a mixture of strict rules and general dependency statements. The domain theory supports *plausible explanations* of training instances. These explanations are used to create initial concepts via a kind of "plausible EBG" and also to guide subsequent empirical generalization of learned concepts. The method has been implemented in a system that learns to solve complex problems in the domain of tonal music. This chapter presents the application domain, describes the learning method (with special emphasis on the plausible inference strategies used), presents empirical results, and shows how this approach naturally leads to a framework for multistrategy learning.

25.1 INTRODUCTION

In recent years, there has been a growing awareness among researchers in machine learning that in their pure forms, both inductive learning and explanation-based generalization suffer from severe limitations that restrict their applicability in many domains. The subsequent research has concentrated mainly on combinations of empirical and explanation-based learning (Michalski and Kodratoff, 1990). Newer approaches to this problem now try to flexibly integrate several learning strategies so that a system can dynamically apply these strategies in response to the specific requirements of the learning task (see, e.g., Widmer [1989], Tecuci and Kodratoff [1990], and Tecuci and Michalski [1991]). That also necessitates investigations into the possibilities of guiding or constraining learning by reasoning methods other than pure deductive or inductive inference. This chapter will be devoted to such matters.

There are many motivations for studying these issues. For one thing, psychological evidence suggests that in the absence of precise knowledge, people employ various forms of *plausible reasoning* to arrive at explanations or predictions (Collins and Michalski, 1989) and that such weak forms of inference can considerably constrain the set of hypotheses a person is willing to make. For instance,[1] a person, when asked whether she thinks that Taiwan grows rice, might remember that growing rice has something to do with the amount of water available and, hence, with the amount of rainfall in the area—a very general and abstract piece of knowledge. Now if the person knows that there is a lot of rainfall in China and that China does grow rice and that Taiwan also has high rainfall, then she might conclude that, yes, Taiwan does probably grow rice. (This, incidentally, is an example of *determination-based analogy* [Russell, 1987]). This illustrates how imprecise background knowledge (about the relevance of rainfall to growing rice) can make a similarity-based judgment more plausible. To continue the example, suppose that in addition, the person also knows that the ability of a country to grow rice is roughly *positively proportionally* related to the amount of rainfall in the country; that is, the more rainfall there is, the better the country's chances of growing rice (ignoring other factors). Given this knowledge, the person might be willing to conclude that Taiwan grows rice even in the *absence* of the similar instance China because high rainfall may plausibly be associated with high possibility of growing rice. Both of these examples show how imprecise background knowledge (no knowledge about the exact shape of the function connecting rainfall to growing rice) can be used to produce plausible inferences, given only few examples. The connection to *learning* should be obvious: there, plausible inference can be used in an analogous way to judge the relative plausibility of hypothesized generalizations.

In addition to such psychological considerations, there are also practical reasons for studying learning with qualitative background knowledge and plausible reasoning. In many domains, complete *a priori* knowledge is simply not available, and hence, pure explanation-based learning is out of the question. Even when a lot is known about a domain, the knowledge is often not precise enough to be cast in the form of a strict deductive domain theory. Rather, it may be very abstract knowl-

---

[1] The following example has been adapted from Collins and Michalski (1989).

edge about the structure of the domain and about general dependencies between various parameters. A system wishing to use such knowledge for learning must employ novel reasoning techniques and integrate these into the learning process.

This chapter presents a model of knowledge-intensive learning that was motivated by such considerations. The basis for learning in this model is a qualitative domain theory that consists of a mixture of strict rules and general dependency statements. An implemented system will be presented that realizes the model and learns to solve complex problems (harmonization) in the domain of tonal music. The target concepts are rules specifying conditions for harmonization decisions. The main learning mechanism is a kind of *Plausible Explanation-Based Learning* (DeJong, 1989) where the system tries to construct a plausible explanation of the training instance, using its qualitative domain theory, and then generalizes the explanation to arrive at a general concept. The following sections will describe how this is done and will also show how these plausible explanations can be used to guide subsequent empirical generalization of the learned concepts. The overall effect of the method is that the available background knowledge is maximally exploited to guide the learning process, even though it is incomplete and too abstract for classical explanation-based generalization (EBG) (Mitchell et al., 1986).

Generally, the author's research in knowledge-based learning has been inspired by the idea that for a learner, trying to learn entails trying to relate, by some reasoning mechanisms, the incoming information to the knowledge it already possesses (Michalski, 1994, Chapter 1 of this book; Tecuci, 1994, Chapter 4 of this book). The work presented here shows how methods of plausible inference can be used to verify that the learner's background knowledge at least weakly implies the new information (notwithstanding the abductive element in the reasoning process— see Section 25.3.1.2). In contrast to classical EBG, however, learning is not logically redundant in our model. The model is another instantiation of a framework that was already proposed in Widmer (1989). There, it was argued that the EBG learning model offers a natural basis for many forms of multistrategy learning if we only generalize our notion of what an *explanation* is. If explanations can include non-deductive types of inference and if they can refer to information from outside the current training instance, then multistrategy learning behavior can be achieved naturally within a simple and uniform framework. A similar course of action is being pursued by Tecuci (1994; Chapter 4 of this book).

In the presentation that follows, examples from the particular domain of application will be used to illustrate various features of the learning method. This will also give the reader a feeling for the complexity of the task. Readers not familiar with musical issues should not worry, however. It is not necessary to understand the musical details; it is the structure of the examples and explanations that matters. Also, it should be understood that there is nothing music-specific in the learning method itself; the method is applicable to any domain that can be modelled as a qualitative dependency hierarchy. The author hopes that the generality of the method will become clear throughout the presentation.

25.2 LEARNING PROBLEM AND DOMAIN THEORY

First, a short description of the particular learning task is needed to set the stage for the following presentation. The system is to learn rules for solving a class of problems in tonal music, namely, harmonizing given melodies by attaching harmonies/chord symbols to the notes of a melody in a musically meaningful way. This is the kind of problem a guitar player, say, is confronted with when s/he is asked to accompany a singer and knows only the melody of the song. Examples of harmonized melodies appear later in this chapter.

This domain is a good example of problem areas where there is no precise theory that could be used to prove the correctness of training instances. However, one can easily come up with a lot of general, abstract intuitions that identify potentially relevant domain features and relationships. In the case of harmonization, one possible way to "explain" specific harmonizations is to use general knowledge about how people listen to, and what they expect from, harmonized music. This is the approach that has been chosen for the current project: the *domain theory* is a general *qualitative model* describing in abstract terms how people perceive ("hear") simple tonal music. The model is meant to be a psychologically plausible hypothesis about musical listening; it was conceived independently of the particular learning task. Readers interested in the music-theoretic aspects of the model are referred to Widmer (1992) for a detailed description.

More precisely, the domain theory is an *abstraction hierarchy* that relates certain audible effects of musical situations to more abstract perceivable effects. Its structure resembles that of an EBG-type domain theory. However, it is qualitative in that internal variables in the model can only take qualitative values from the domain {extremely_low ... extremely_high}, and more importantly, most of the relationships between parameters are described in a qualitative way only. Specifically, the domain theory contains statements of the following form:

- *Partial monotonic dependencies:*[2] A statement q+(A,B) means that parameters A and B are positively monotonically related, or in other words, "if A increases or has a high value, B will also, *all other things being equal.*" q+(A,B) does *not* mean that A is the only factor on which B depends, nor does it mean that A must always be present when B is. q– is interpreted analogously for inverse proportionality; for example:

---

[2] The notation "q+" was borrowed from Forbus' qualitative proportionality relations (Forbus, 1984). These relations are also related to Michalski's M-descriptors (Michalski, 1983) and the directed dependencies in Collins and Michalski (1989).

```
q+ ( relative_chord_distance( Chord1, Chord2, D),
     contrast( Chord1, Chord2, C))
```

("Given a sequence of two chords [Chord1, Chord2], the listener may experience a feeling of contrast C between the chords that is positively proportionally related to the harmonic distance D [along the circle of fifths] between the chords.")

- *Additional proportionality relations*: Statements of the form addq+(A,B) and addq-(A,B) are to be interpreted like q+ and q-, respectively, except that they specify only *additional influences*; that is, they are relevant only if there is already some reason to believe that B holds or has a particular value for example:

```
addq+ ( metrical_strength( Chord2, S),
        contrast( Chord1, Chord2, C))
```

("If there is some perceived degree of contrast C, it may be felt the more strongly the stronger Chord2's metrical position S is.")

- The domain theory does also contain some *strict deductive rules* (as in standard EBG domain theories); for example:

```
relative_consonance( Chord, Note, extremely_high) :-
    chord_contains_note( Chord, Note)
```

("The relative consonance between a note and a simultaneously played chord is extremely high if the chord contains the note [in its basic triad].")

In principle, the concept of partial monotonic dependencies is very general; any monotonic function could be hidden behind such an abstract specification of dependency. For instance, for numeric variables X and Y, functions such as $Y = \log(X)$, $Y = \exp(X)$, $Y = 5X^3 + 4X + 17.4$ would all satisfy $q+(X,Y)$. For the current project, however, the dependencies are assumed to describe roughly *linear* relationships. This simplifying assumption seems justified for the types of parameters occurring in the present domain of application. Also, because internal variables in the qualitative model have very restricted discrete domains—they range over only five qualitative values: {extremely_low, low, medium, high, extremely_high}, which are themselves very "fuzzy"—assuming functional dependencies with very complex shapes would seem to be missing the point. The main role of the qualitative dependencies in plausible reasoning is to support a weak notion of relative plausibility of arguments, i.e., to make certain inferences more plausible than others. All this should be kept in mind when the heuristics for finding explanations are discussed in Section 25.3.1.1.

25.3 THE LEARNING METHOD

A teacher is assumed to provide pre-classified training examples, where an example is a specific chord in a harmonized piece along with a particular note in the melody. The *representation* of training instances is just a list of notes and chords along with their basic attributes. The *goal concepts* are good(Chord,Note) and bad(Chord,Note); i.e., the goal is to learn sets of conditions under which a certain chord will be a good or bad harmonization for a given note. The learned concepts are represented in the form of rules, and the terms "concept" and "rule" will be used interchangeably hereafter to refer to the result of learning. The learning scenario is *incremental*, so examples are presented one by one. Two phases can then be distinguished in the process of learning a rule. In phase I, a new, preliminary rule is learned from generalization of a single training instance: the system searches for a plausible explanation of the correctness of the training instance and then compiles the explanation into a general rule. This process could be called "plausible EBG." A rule learned in this way can be generalized incrementally later on when new, similar situations are encountered (phase II). Both the decision whether to generalize an existing rule or create a new one, given a new training instance, and decisions about how to proceed in incremental generalization are based on information provided by the plausible explanation underlying the rule in question. Figure 25.1 gives a sketch of the learning process. This chapter will be more concerned with the "plausible EBG" part. Section 25.3.1 describes how plausible explanations are constructed and how initial concepts are derived from them. Section 25.3.2 then gives a rough account of how incremental empirical generalization can be made more effective by using information from plausible explanations.

25.3.1 Phase I: Single Instance Generalization via "Plausible EBG"

25.3.1.1 Constructing Plausible Explanations

Given a training instance and its classification, the system tries to find an *explanation* of the instance with the help of its domain theory. Such an explanation will be in the form of a justification tree much like in traditional EBG but will have a different semantics. Because the domain theory contains knowledge items of various degrees of strength (strict rules and qualitative dependencies of various sorts), explanation trees will consist of a mixture of explanatory argument types. Stronger arguments are preferred, so features that are defined by strict rules in the domain theory are explained by standard deductive reasoning. When a feature is defined through directed dependencies, however, only a weaker kind of explanation is possible. Given a particular value y of some feature Y to explain and the knowledge that $q+(X,Y)$, one possible way to "explain" why $Y=y$ is to show that X has a value that is roughly proportional (or reasonably close to proportional) to the value

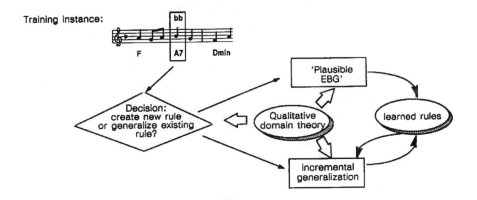

Figure 25.1:   Overall structure of the learning process

y of Y.[3] Such an "explanation" can at best be plausible. Additional problems arise because the domain theory has several layers. This means that an explanation will contain chains of such plausible arguments, where the intermediate features are not observable and can only be hypothesized. It is clear, then, that such plausible explanations are by no means unique and also that they cannot be interpreted as logical proofs in the sense of EBG explanations.

Constructing an explanation is a heuristic search process; the goal is to find the most plausible explanation. Figure 25.2 sketches a typical situation in this search. The explanation that the system is looking for is constrained from two sides: it is constrained from the *top* (in this case, for instance, the goodness of the example is known to be high) and from the *bottom*, by the features of the training instance itself. It is in the middle, so to speak, where decisions have to be made concerning which parameters to pair with which and which arguments to include in the explanation and which ones to omit. For example, for some branch of the explanation, the system might need an explanation for a certain value y of a parameter Y, and there might be a known dependency of type q+ between another parameter x and Y; so, certain values x of x might be used to *explain* parameter Y—at least partially because there may still be other factors that are known to influence Y. The possible domains of x and Y are known (see Figure 25.2); x and y may or may not be known (some values are known by inheritance from above; some are known

---

[3] In a very loose sense, one might say that such dependencies are interpreted as "causal" links. They are assumed to express a directed influence from X to Y but not necessarily the other way round.

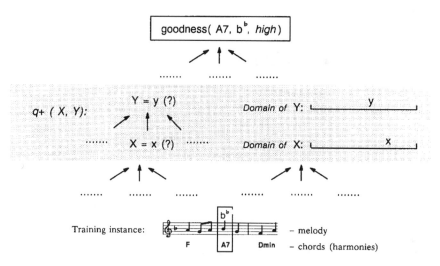

Figure 25.2:   Search for most plausible explanation

by inference from features of the training instance). In such a situation, the following kinds of decisions have to be made:

- If x and/or y are not known, which values should be hypothesized for them?
- If several combinations of x and y are possible, which one is the most plausible by itself and makes the explanation as a whole more plausible?
- Should the explanation "Y=y because X=x" be included at all? Is it consistent with other branches and arguments?

This situation will occur in many places in the process of constructing an explanation. The system makes use of a number of heuristics and constraints in order to make decisions in such a situation:

- *Linearity of qualitative dependencies* (heuristic)
  It is assumed that directed qualitative dependencies describe roughly linear relationships. As a consequence, given two parameters x and y, related via q+(X,Y), an explanation that assigns values to x and y that are roughly in the same range of their respective domains will be more plausible than one that pairs a low value for x with a high value for y, say.

- *Special importance of extremal values* (heuristic)
  The above hypothesis is assumed to be particularly true for *extremal* parameter values. That is, it is assumed to be highly unlikely that a value of, say, extremely_high for some parameter y can be caused by a moderate or low value of another parameter x.

- *Consistency of assignments* (constraint)
  The fact that the qualitative dependencies denote *monotonic* relationships excludes certain combinations of inconsistent parameter mappings. For instance, knowing that $q+(X,Y)$ and that there are no other factors on which Y depends, one cannot use X = moderate to explain Y = extremely_high in one place and X = high to explain Y = high in another. This would conflict with the monotonicity of the relationship between X and Y.

- *Local coherence—agreement of arguments* (constraint)
  Finally, in the case of multiple influences X_i on a parameter Y, only those are included in the explanation of Y that can be made to agree on the value y of Y. The system prefers explanations with many supporting arguments to those with fewer ones.

Underlying these heuristics are two basic assumptions, namely, that multiple influences on a parameter Y are more or less independent in their effect on Y and, what is more, that multiple influences obey a kind of linear additivity; in particular, negative influences may neutralize positive ones. These assumptions may seem rather strong but turned out to be adequate for the current application domain.

The heuristics and the system's preference for multiple support of plausible arguments are combined in an *evaluation function* that rates competing (sub-)explanations. It computes a crude estimate of plausibility that is expressed in qualitative terms (see Figure 25.3). To summarize, the estimated plausibility of an explanation is a function of (1) the degree of "fit," given the known dependencies, between parameters; (2) the number of supporting subexplanations; and (3) the respective plausibilities of these subexplanations.

To find the most plausible explanation of an instance, the system performs a kind of best-first search. The explanation is constructed in a mixed top-down/bottom-up manner: already known instantiations of parameters (e.g., the known value high for goodness in Figure 25.2) are propagated downward through the domain theory, and partial explanations are then constructed bottom-up and combined into explanations of higher-level features. Evaluation of competing partial explanations is based on the above-mentioned evaluation function.

Figure 25.3 presents a major portion of an explanation created by the system. The specific instance explained is the chord-note pair $<A7, b^6>$ (indicated by a box in Figure 25.3). This tree structure explains why it can plausibly be assumed that listeners will hear the A7 chord as a good harmonization for note b^6 (b-flat). The reader is not expected to understand the musical details of the explanation; the figure is just meant to convey a feeling for the structure and complexity of such explanations. Note that each branch of the explanation is labeled according to the type of argument (DEDuctive, based on q+ or q–, etc.). Each argument is also explicitly annotated with the rough degree of plausibility computed during the

Figure 25.3:   Training instance and part of plausible explanation (operational leaves italicized)

search. The annotations are used in the second learning phase—the incremental generalization of learned rules (see Section 25.3.2).

The explanation is then generalized, much like in traditional EBG, by propagating the general goal concept (in this case, good(Chord,Note)) through the explanation tree, and the generalized leaves are conjoined to form a new rule (Figure 25.4). The effect of generalization here is mainly the replacement of specific objects (notes, chords, musical intervals, etc.) by universally quantified variables. Qualitative and quantitative values of domain parameters are generalized only if they are explained by strict rules in the domain theory; arguments based on qualitative dependencies are too uncertain to warrant analytical generalization. They will be generalized incrementally if subsequent examples indicate a need for it (see

Figure 25.4: Rule learned by generalizing and compiling explanation

RULE1: good(Chord,Note) :– chord_root(Chord,Root),
                                chord_mode(Chord,Major),
                                chord_type(Chord,7),
                                global_key(key(KRoot,KMode)),
                                previous_chord(Chord,PrevChord),
                                distance_on_circle_of_fifths(PrevChord,Chord4),
                                chord_type(PrevChord,triad),
                                chord_type(Chord,7),
                                not_chord_contains_note(Chord,Note),
                                chord_scale(Chord,scale(SRoot,SMode)),
                                not_scale_contains_note(scale,(SRoot,SMode),Note),
                                structural_saliance(Note,moderate)
                                metrical_strength(Note,moderate)
                                plausible_local_key(Note,key(LRoot,LMode)),
                                dominant_7_chord(key(LRoot,LMode),Chord).

Section 25.3.2). In this way, the single-instance generalization step serves mainly to select and construct relevant attributes for a first hypothesis and to relate them to the goal concept through a hierarchical explanation structure, which can later provide further guidance in empirical generalization.

25.3.1.2 Plausible Explanation as Constrained Abduction

The notion of "plausible explanation" deserves to be examined in a bit more detail. Although, on the surface, the structure of a plausible explanation very strongly resembles the structure of a "classical" EBG-type explanation, there are important differences.

First, of course, plausible explanations are not logical proofs. Indeed, as DeJong (1989) has already noted, plausible inferences *per se* are weak; that is, evaluation of the theory in a "forward" direction would produce many nonsensical statements that are simply not consistent with the "real world." It is the actual training instances that make certain inferences more plausible than others. To quote DeJong (1989, p.4), "The existence of the training example itself adds credibility to the faithfulness of the plausible explanation and, therefore, to the new generalized concept." Thus, actual observations (instances) play a much more important role in plausible explanation-based learning than in traditional EBG. Rosenbloom and Aasman (1990) also present a lucid discussion on this topic.

Generally, constructing plausible explanations involves non-deductive types of inference. For one thing, because general dependency statements usually allow different combinations of actual parameters, it is a matter of heuristics (see above) to choose between these. Second, constructing a plausible explanation often entails hypothesizing relationships that are not directly observable, and that lends a certain abductive quality to plausible reasoning.

The following example, taken from the current application, illustrates this effect. Among other things, the domain theory contains the following two statements of dependency:

```
q+ ( relative_consonance( Chord, Note, C),
     harmonic_stability( Chord, Note, HS))
```

(The harmonic stability HS of a Chord depends on the relative consonance C between the Chord and the Note that it accompanies.)

```
q+ ( stability_in_local_key( Chord, Note, S),
     harmonic_stability( Chord, Note, HS))
```

(The harmonic stability HS of a Chord also depends on the functional stability S of the Chord in the local key [tonality] that is implied in the current context.)

The abstract features relative_consonance and stability_in_local_key are defined by some strict rules in the domain theory, the relevant ones for the example being

```
relative_consonance( Chord, Note, extremely_low) :-
    dissonant( Chord, Note)
stability_in_local_key( Chord, Note, extremely_high) :-
    local_key( Note, Key),
    tonic_chord( Chord, Key).
stability_in_local_key( Chord, Note, high) :-
    local_key( Note, Key),
    dominant_chord( Chord, Key).
```

Now assume that the example shown in Figure 25.5 has been classified as good by the teacher; the system's goal is to explain good(A7, b^b); that is, the A7 chord is a good harmonization for the note b^b in the melody. In order to explain this, the system must show, among other things, that there is at least a relatively high degree of harmonic stability (HS) in the current situation. Given the two dependencies listed above, this reduces to (1) establishing relative_consonance(A7, b^b, C) and stability_in_local_key(A7, b^b, S) and (2) checking whether the obtained values for C and S do indeed plausibly imply a relatively high value for HS. The relative_consonance(A7, b^b, C) is established with the help of the first of the above rules, with the result C = extremely_low (because A7 and b^b are extremely dissonant). Given the positive proportionality between C and HS that is postulated by the domain theory, this contradicts the assumption that HS is rela-

Figure 25.5:   Training instance to be explained: good(A7,b^b)

tively high (which is the current explanation goal). Thus, the system must at least show that `stability_in_local_key( A7, b`^{b}`, s)` has a high value, which again reduces to (1) finding out what the local key of the musical passage in the vicinity of b^b is and (2) showing that the `A7` chord is either the `tonic_chord` or the `dominant_chord` in this key.

Now, `local_key` is a non-deterministic predicate; there are usually several keys that can plausibly be perceived in a musical situation. Thus, `local_key` returns, upon backtracking, a set of plausible keys, sorted in the order of decreasing plausibility: `Key` ∈ (`F_major`, `B`^{b}`_major`, `E`^{b}`_major`, `G_minor`, `D_minor`). Of these, only `D_minor` would attribute high stability to the `A7` chord (because `A7` is the dominant chord of `D_minor`); so in order to be able to complete its explanation, the system assumes that the `local_key` is `D_minor` and asserts the following explanation branch:

```
harmonic_stability( A7, b , high) because
    stability_in_local_key( A7, b , high) because
        local_key( b , D_minor) and
        dominant_chord( A7, D_minor)
```

The fact `relative_consonance(A7,b`^{b}`,extremely_low)`, contradicting the explanation goal, is excluded from this specific explanation.

To reiterate; given just the knowledge in the domain theory, it would have been more plausible to assume that `local_key` is `F_major` in the example. However, given a specific training instance that is known to be `good` and, by implication, to display relatively high `harmonic_stability`, the system chooses the less plausible (but still possible) assumption that the local key is `D_minor` because that allows it to explain the instance.[4] Many plausible arguments have such a distinctly abductive flavor.

Finally, note that the system also faces the problem of deciding which factors to include in an explanation and which ones to exclude. The present program has a built-in bias in favor of descriptions that include as many influences as possible, as long as they appear consistent with the explanation goal and the instance. In gen-

---

[4] This situation might also be the starting point for a theory revision episode, where the rules for establishing `local_key` might be revised so that in similar situations in the future, `D_minor` would be determined to be the most plausible local key.

eral, whether maximally detailed or maximally simple explanations should be considered more plausible and/or more useful depends very much on the characteristics of the application domain and also on the learning task.

25.3.2 Phase II: Incremental Generalization

As noted above, the domain theory was conceived as a general qualitative theory of musical listening for a restricted type of tonal music. It mentions a multitude of factors that might potentially influence a listener's perception of a musical situation. Also, the system prefers detailed explanations to simpler ones. As a consequence, the explanations and the rules learned by plausible EBG tend to be too detailed and specific. That is where the need for incremental empirical generalization arises: the system should not create a new rule for every new instance that is not covered by an existing rule. Rather, if an existing rule almost matches the new instance, it should be generalized to accommodate the instance.

The straightforward way to do this would be to somehow measure the "distance" between each of the rules and the new instance (by counting matches and mismatches) and generalize a rule if it is "close enough" to warrant generalization. However, a much higher degree of effectiveness and context-sensitivity of the generalization process can be achieved if empirical generalization is based not only on the *rule* to be generalized but also on the *explanation* that led to that rule. The plausible explanation can be used to *bias* empirical generalization. Similar observations were already made by Danyluk (1987; see also Danyluk, 1994, Chapter 7 of this book) but only for strictly deductive explanations. Plausible explanations provide more differentiated information that can be exploited—they rely on a richer set of types of explanatory link, and they include explicit plausibility information (see Figure 25.6).

Let X denote a condition in a rule (which corresponds to a leaf in the explanation underlying the rule) that is not satisfied by the current instance. The following criteria are then used to decide whether (and if so, how) to generalize the rule:

- *Possibility of safe generalization:* If X can be generalized to apply to the new instance in such a way that the argument in the original explanation that depends on X still holds, the generalization will be *safe* (at least with respect to the plausible explanation). This criterion also provides a strong bias on the *type* of generalization in cases where there are multiple ways to generalize X—only those that preserve the validity of the argument that depends on X will be considered.

- *Strength of explanatory link:* The system considers the *type* of explanatory link of X; some types are intrinsically more important than others. For instance, arguments based on `addq+` or `addq−` relationships are by definition less salient than those based on `q+` or `q−` and may thus more safely be dropped.

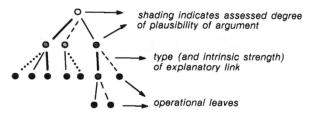

Figure 25.6:   Structure of a plausible explanation

- *Assessed plausibility of argument:* The system looks at the plausibility with which X was thought to hold in the original explanation. An argument that was not very credible to begin with can more safely be dropped or generalized.

- *Strength of remaining arguments:* If X were to be dropped, how strong would the hypothesis depending on X (some ancestor of X in the explanation tree) still be? That is, how many arguments supporting it remain, and how strong are they? Obviously, if there are strong arguments left that support the original hypothesis, the overall integrity of the explanation is not compromised too much by dropping X.

Information from these heuristics is combined to yield one approximate value indicating how "likely" it is that generalization of the explanation (and the rule derived from it) is justified. In summary, the explanations serve a dual purpose: first, they provide a measure of *deep similarity*. Matches and mismatches between instances and rules are rated according to the role they play in an explanation structure; this is a better measure of similarity than just simple counting of syntactic matches. Second, they can provide bias on the type of generalization that seems most plausible. The interested reader can find an example of the heuristics at work in Widmer (1991).

25.4 AN EXPERIMENT

The following experiment was meant to illustrate that this explanation-sensitive approach to incremental generalization can considerably improve the learning performance, both in terms of the number of training instances needed and the generality of the concepts learned. The informed incremental generalization algorithm of Section 25.3.2 (*algorithm 1*) was compared to a simpler incremental generalizer (*algorithm 2*) that did not use the underlying explanations in empirical generalization. Both algorithms used the plausible explanations to derive an initial generalization from the first instance. When considering incremental generalization, however, algorithm 2 based its decisions whether to generalize a particular

Beginning of Sonata # 5 in G major (K.283):

Figure 25.7:   Target problem (piece to be harmonized)

rule on a general threshold (ratio of matching vs. nonmatching conditions in a rule).

The experiment consisted in first selecting a *target problem* (a piece that the system should be able to harmonize after learning) and several *training pieces*, from which training examples (specific pairs of chords and notes) were then presented to the learners until they could solve the target problem. Target problem and training pieces—all of them beginnings of well-known Piano Sonatas by W.A. Mozart —are shown in Figures 25.7 and 25.8.

Figure 25.9 displays the solution to the target problem that was found by both algorithms after the learning session. (Incidentally, this is more or less the harmonization Mozart himself chose.) The main results of the experiment are summarized in Table 25.1. The data indicate that paying attention to the underlying explanations in incremental generalization can considerably improve the learning performance: the set of rules learned by algorithm 1 is both more concise and more general, and what is more, it was learned from a considerably smaller number of training instances.

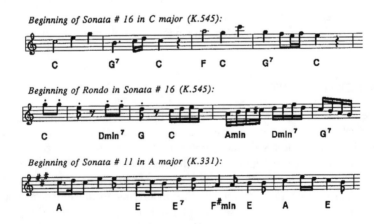

Figure 25.8:   Training pieces from which examples were selected

Figure 25.9:   Solution found after learning

Table 25.1:   Results of comparative learning experiment

	Algorithm 1 (guided by expl.)	Algorithm 2
Complexity of learned rule base:		
# of rules learned	9	12
Total size of rule base (# literals)	103	129
Avg. # literals / rule	11.4	10.8
Cost of learning:		
# of instances required	20	32

25.5 DISCUSSION, RELATED WORK, AND FUTURE DIRECTIONS

To summarize briefly, this chapter has presented a method for learning rules from examples with the help of a qualitative domain theory that consists mainly of qualitative dependency relations. The theory is too weak to permit standard explanation-based learning. Plausible inference strategies are used to guide the learning process, both via a kind of "plausible EBG" and by a biasing of incremental empirical generalization. Section 25.3.1 described the inference techniques used to construct plausible explanations and discussed their non-deductive nature. Section 25.3.2 showed how underlying explanations can be used to guide incremental generalization of learned concepts.

An additional important role of the domain theory that should be pointed out here is the *dynamic construction* of an appropriate hypothesis language depending on the context. The language in which instances are represented and the language for explanations and rules are not the same. In Section 25.3, it was briefly mentioned that training instances are represented simply as lists of notes and chords along with their basic attributes (such as duration, pitch, and chord type). Explanations and rules, on the other hand, refer to higher-level concepts and various relations (see Figures 25.3 and 25.4). These higher-level concepts are introduced by the domain theory and enter into learned concepts because of the particular level of operationality defined in the system. The method thus demonstrates the utilization of a qualitative domain theory for *constructive generalization* (Michalski, 1983).

A general problem with plausible explanations as described here is that they are rather weak, being based as they are on abstract background knowledge and on single examples. This uncertainty effect multiplies if explanations contain chains of plausible arguments. That is why, in the current system, analytical generalization is

applied very cautiously (see Section 25.3.1.1). It is in the incremental generalization phase that the appropriate degree of generality is determined empirically by
analyzing new instances against the background of the explanation of the original
concept. An alternative approach would be to strengthen the explanations by checking the validity of plausible inferences against several examples at once. That
would mean the loss of full incrementality but would produce plausible explanations that have more empirical support. Bergadano and Giordana's (1988) ML-
SMART framework might, in fact, be extended to form the basis for such a "multi-
instance plausible explanation system."

Learning with a qualitative domain theory has also been investigated by
DeJong (1989, 1990). He presented a method for learning in continuous domains,
where the domain is modeled in *Qualitative Process Theory* terms (Forbus, 1984).
The main advances of the method described here over DeJong's approach are (a)
the use of the domain theory for constructive (instead of just selective) generalization; (b) the definition of explicit criteria for assessing the relative plausibility of
competing explanations, which makes possible a heuristic search for the "most
plausible" explanation; and (c) the methods for exploiting plausible explanations to
bias incremental generalization of learned concepts. In case of conflict, DeJong's
system simply discards the old explanation and looks for a more consistent one.
(This is partly because his system generates explanations in a simple-to-complex
order.)

The author's own work on a predecessor of the current system resulted in a
learning algorithm (Widmer, 1989) that flexibly integrated deductive, analogical
(determination-based), and inductive arguments in an explanation-based generalizer
and, thus, exhibited multistrategy learning behavior, depending on the knowledge
available. Tecuci and Michalski (1991; see also Tecuci, 1994, Chapter 4 of this
book) have developed a similar approach based on learning from plausible justifications. They integrate different inference types (deduction, determination-based
analogy, abduction, and empirical generalization) in a plausible explanation system.
The work described in the present chapter adds a new, complex inference type—
hypothesizing consistent explanations on the basis of directed qualitative dependencies—to this collection. On the other hand, empirical generalization is done outside
the explanation process in a separate learning phase. Thus, one immediate goal for
further research is the integration of other types of reasoning (analogy and empirical similarity arguments, various forms of abduction, etc.) directly into the explanation process. That would allow explanations to refer to information outside the
current training instance and would naturally lead to generalization effects during
explanation.

A problem that needs to be addressed is the specialization of overly general
concepts. In the current application, the richness of the domain theory and the fact
that the heuristics for including plausible arguments in an explanation (Section
25.3.1.1) are very much on the permissive side, render specialization virtually

unnecessary: Initial concepts constructed by plausible EBG are very specific, and finding the "correct" degree of generality is then a matter of stepwise (careful) generalization. However, overgeneralization may become a problem in other applications. Investigations are under way to find out whether plausible reasoning can also be used to help in the problem of effectively specializing concepts in the face of conflicting evidence.

The improvement of the qualitative domain theory in response to specific experiences is another interesting topic for further research. Currently, the learning problem is restricted to concept learning, with the underlying domain theory remaining unchanged, being used only to guide the system in acquiring rules. More research is needed both on the automatic *refinement* of the domain theory (i.e., filling in missing details, making abstract relationships more precise) by induction from examples and the *revision* of the theory in response to incorrect generalizations or abductive explanation needs (see, e.g., the `local_key` example in Section 25.3.1.2).

In conclusion, the author hopes that the work presented in this chapter is another step in the direction of flexible multistrategy learning, both from a theoretical and from a practical point of view. The chapter has shown how qualitative background knowledge can support powerful explanation methods and how these methods, when integrated in an EBG-like "Explain, Generalize, and Compile" schema, lead to very effective learning. The idea of extending the notion of "explanation" to include weaker kinds of inference is now gaining more and more popularity. In principle, a wide variety of types of knowledge and an equally wide variety of inference types, including abduction and determination- or similarity-based analogy, can be used in plausible reasoning. If all these can be integrated directly into the plausible explanation process, flexible multistrategy learning behavior will naturally emerge.

On the practical side, it seems worthwhile to emphasize once again the idea of using qualitative models as powerful tools for describing common, abstract domain knowledge. There are many domains where qualitative models are much easier to obtain than precise domain theories. For such domains, the approach outlined here appears very promising. The complexity of the musical application—the entire domain theory comprises about 1,000 lines of PROLOG code—could be taken as an indication that real-world problems are within the reach of this approach.

ACKNOWLEDGMENTS

The author would like to thank Prof. Robert Trappl for his support and Christian Holzbaur, Werner Horn, and Igor Mozetic for helpful comments. Special thanks are owed to the editors of this book for their clarifying and challenging comments. This research was sponsored in part by the Austrian *Fonds zur*

Förderung der wissenschaftlichen Forschung under Grant P8756-TEC. Financial support for the Austrian Research Institute for Artificial Intelligence is provided by the Austrian Federal Ministry for Science and Research.

References

Bergadano, F. and Giordana, A., "A Knowledge Intensive Approach to Concept Induction," in *Proceedings of the Fifth International Conference on Machine Learning*, Ann Arbor, MI, pp. 305–317, Morgan Kaufmann, San Mateo, CA, 1988.

Collins, A. and Michalski, R.S., "The Logic of Plausible Reasoning: A Core Theory," *Cognitive Science*, Vol. 13, No. 1, pp. 1–49, 1989.

Danyluk, A., "The Use of Explanations for Similarity-Based Learning," in *Proceedings of the Tenth International Joint Conference on Artificial Intelligence (IJCAI-87)*, pp. 274–276, Morgan Kaufmann, Los Altos, CA, 1987.

———, "GEMINI: An Integration of Analytical and Empirical Learning," in *Machine Learning: A Multistrategy Approach, Vol. IV*, R.S. Michalski and G. Tecuci (Eds.), Morgan Kaufmann, San Mateo, CA, 1994.

DeJong, G., "Explanation-Based Learning with Plausible Inferencing," in *Proceedings of the 4th European Working Session on Learning (EWSL-89)*, Montpellier, France, pp. 1–10, Pitman, London, 1989.

———, "Explanation-Based Control: An Approach to Reactive Planning in Continuous Domains," in *Proceedings of the DARPA Workshop on Innovative Approaches to Planning, Scheduling, and Control*, San Diego, CA, pp. 325–336, 1990.

Forbus, K.D., "Qualitative Process Theory," *Artificial Intelligence*, Vol. 24, No. 1–3, pp. 85–169, 1984.

Michalski, R.S., "A Theory and Methodology of Inductive Learning," in *Machine Learning: An Artificial Intelligence Approach, Vol. I*, R.S. Michalski, J.G. Carbonell, and T.M. Mitchell (Eds.), Tioga, Palo Alto, CA, pp. 83–129, 1983.

———, "Inferential Learning Theory as a Conceptual Basis for Multistrategy Learning," in *Machine Learning: A Multistrategy Approach, Vol. IV*, R.S. Michalski and G. Tecuci (Eds.), Morgan Kaufmann, San Mateo, CA, 1994.

Michalski, R.S. and Kodratoff, Y., "Research in Machine Learning: Recent Progress, Classification of Methods, and Future Directions," in *Machine Learning: An Artificial Intelligence Approach, Vol. III*, Y. Kodratoff and R.S. Michalski (Eds.), Morgan Kaufmann, San Mateo, CA, pp. 3–30, 1990.

Mitchell, T., Keller, R., and Kedar-Cabelli, S., "Explanation-Based Generalization: A Unifying View," *Machine Learning*, Vol. 1, No. 1, pp. 47–80, 1986.

Rosenbloom, P. and Aasman, J., "Knowledge-Level and Inductive Uses of Chunking (EBL)," in *Proceedings of the 8th National Conference on Artificial Intelligence (AAAI-90)*, pp. 821–827, AAAI Press, Menlo Park, CA, 1990.

Russell, S., *Analogical and Inductive Reasoning*, Ph.D. Thesis, Report STAN-CS-87-1150, Stanford University, Stanford, CA, 1987.

Tecuci, G., "An Inference-based Framework for Multistrategy Learning," in *Machine Learning: A Multistrategy Approach, Vol. IV*, R.S. Michalski and G. Tecuci (Eds.), Morgan Kaufmann, San Mateo, CA, 1994.

Tecuci, G. and Kodratoff, Y., "Apprenticeship Learning in Imperfect Domain Theories," in *Machine Learning: An Artificial Intelligence Approach, Vol. III*, Y. Kodratoff and R.S. Michalski (Eds.), Morgan Kaufmann, San Mateo, CA, pp. 514–551, 1990.

Tecuci, G. and Michalski, R.S., "A Method for Multistrategy Task-adaptive Learning Based on Plausible Justifications," in *Proceedings of the 8th International Workshop on Machine Learning*, Evanston, IL., pp. 549–553, Morgan Kaufmann, San Mateo, CA, 1991.

Widmer, G., "A Tight Integration of Deductive and Inductive Learning," in *Proceedings of the 6th International Workshop on Machine Learning*, Ithaca, NY, pp. 11–13, Morgan Kaufmann, San Mateo, CA, 1989.

―――――, "Using Plausible Explanations to Bias Empirical Generalization in Weak Theory Domains," in *Proceedings of the 5th European Working Session on Learning (EWSL-91)*, Porto, Portugal, pp. 33–43, Springer, Berlin, 1991.

―――――, "Qualitative Perception Modelling and Intelligent Musical Learning," *Computer Music Journal*, Vol. 16, No. 2, pp. 51–68, 1992.

BIBLIOGRAPHY OF MULTISTRATEGY LEARNING RESEARCH

Janusz Wnek
Michael Hieb
(George Mason University)

INTRODUCTION

The purpose of this bibliography is to provide a useful source of reference for researchers, students, and other readers interested in multistrategy learning (MSL). Although this bibliography is primarily concerned with multistrategy learning, it continues in the style of the bibliographies provided in the previous volumes of *Machine Learning*. Volume I (ML1) covered the period from the beginning of the field until 1982 and contained 572 entries. Volume II (ML2) covered the period from 1983 until 1984 and contained 312 entries. Volume III (ML3) covered the period from 1985 until 1989 and contained 1,095 entries.

The present bibliography differs from the above ones in that it focuses on a specific area of machine learning: multistrategy learning. As stated by Michalski (Chapter 1 of this book), multistrategy learning methods combine two or more inference types and/or different computational paradigms. Within this focus, we have attempted to include all relevant works since the inception of the field. The increasing interest in multistrategy learning can be measured by examining the number of papers published in the past few years: In 1986, we counted 10 papers published on this topic; in 1987, eleven papers; in 1988, twenty-one papers; in 1989, forty-four papers; in 1990, thirty-two papers, and in 1991, there were 95 papers (including 33 from The First International Multistrategy Learning Workshop). This sharp increase in the number of multistrategy learning publications reflects the rapid growth of the field.

With the intention of making the bibliography more useful in a general sense, we have included a background material category ("B"). This category contains a representative selection of books and publications that cover the entire field of machine learning and can serve as background information when studying MSL. For each learning strategy and computational paradigm, we have also included a small selection of some of the most relevant papers in that area, even if the papers are not necessarily concerned with multistrategy learning.

For each MSL reference (category "I"), we have listed the learning strategies involved. In addition, we have constructed an index to each significant combination of learning methods (where there are five or more references in that category). This index appears at the end of the "Categories Index."

In selecting the items for the bibliography, we looked for learning methods that were relevant to research in multistrategy learning. To help the reader locate publications of interest, all the entries have been assigned one or more categories from seven categories reflecting the type of article and/or research methodology used. All entries were sorted in lexicographic order, where the key is defined as the concatenation of the last name and initials of the first author, the year of publication and when applicable, and the last names and initials of other authors. The selection of papers is representative rather than exhaustive. We restricted ourselves specifically to publications in English because of their greater availability throughout the world. The bibliography contains approximately 630 entries, including 272 papers on multistrategy learning.

In preparing this bibliography, we used the following sources to provide a basic set of references (we completely searched these publications for relevant research):

- Machine Learning: An Artificial Intelligence Approach, Vols. I & II, R.S. Michalski, J.G. Carbonell, and T.M. Mitchell (Eds.), 1983, 1986; Vol. III, Y. Kodratoff and R.S. Michalski (Eds.), 1990; Vol. IV, R.S. Michalski and G. Tecuci (Eds.), 1994
- Readings in Machine Learning, J.W. Shavlik and T.G. Dietterich (Eds.), 1990
- Machine Learning journal, 1986–1992
- Proceedings of the International Machine Learning Workshops: Skytop, PA, 1985; Irvine, CA, 1987; Ann Arbor, MI, 1988; Ithaca, NY, 1989; Austin, TX, 1990; Chicago, IL, 1991
- Proceedings of the First International Workshop on Multistrategy Learning, Harpers Ferry, WV, 1991
- Proceedings of the Workshop on Combinations of Genetic Algorithms and Neural Networks, Baltimore, MD, 1992
- Proceedings of IJCAI: Los Angeles, 1985; Milan, Italy, 1987; Detroit, 1989; Sydney, Australia, 1991
- Proceedings of IJCAI Workshop on Evaluating and Changing Representations, Sydney, Australia, 1991

- Proceedings of AAAI: Philadelphia, 1986; Seattle, WA, 1987; Saint Paul, MN, 1988; Boston, MA, 1990; Anaheim, CA, 1991
- Proceedings of the International Conference on Genetic Algorithms: Pittsburgh, PA, 1985; Cambridge, MA, 1987; Fairfax, VA, 1989; San Diego, CA, 1991
- Proceedings of the European Conference on Artificial Intelligence (ECAI): Brighton, England, 1986; Munich, Germany, 1988; Stockholm, Sweden, 1990; Vienna, Austria, 1992
- Proceedings of the European Working Session on Learning (EWSL): Bled, Yugoslavia 1987; Glasgow, Scotland, 1988; Montpellier, France, 1989; Porto, Portugal, 1991
- Proceedings of the Annual Workshop on Computational Learning Theory (COLT): Pittsburgh, PA, 1988; Santa Cruz, CA, 1989; Rochester, NY, 1990; Santa Cruz, CA, 1991
- Proceedings of the IEEE International Workshop on Tools for AI: Fairfax, VA, 1989; Los Alamitos, CA, 1990, 1991
- AI Magazine, 1986–1991
- Artificial Intelligence journal, 1970–1991
- Cognitive Science journal, 1977–1991

We also used other relevant periodicals and publications to extend the basic references (we did not completely search these references for multistrategy learning, however):

- Proceedings of International Symposiums on Methodologies for Intelligent Systems, 1986–1991
- Proceedings of the Conferences of the Cognitive Science Society
- Proceedings of the International Conference on Principles of Knowledge Representation and Reasoning: Toronto, Canada, 1989; Cambridge, MA, 1991
- ACM Computing Surveys
- Biological Cybernetics
- Communications of the ACM
- Connection Science
- IBM Journal of Research and Development
- IEEE Transactions on Pattern Analysis and Machine Intelligence, 1980–1988
- IEEE Transactions on Systems, Man, and Cybernetics, 1983–1989
- Information and Control
- Information Processing Letters
- International Journal for Man-Machine Studies

- International Journal of Policy Analysis and Information Systems
- Journal of Complexity
- Journal of Mathematical Psychology
- Journal of the American Society for Information Science
- Journal of the Applied Intelligence, 1992
- Knowledge Acquisition Journal
- Neural Computation
- Neural Networks Journal
- Psychological Review
- Theory Probability and Its Applications

ACKNOWLEDGMENTS

The authors wish to thank Ryszard Michalski for his many suggestions, his council, and the guidance he provided in the development of this bibliography. The authors are also grateful to Haleh Vafaie, Tomasz Dybala, and Ibrahim F. Imam for help in maintaining the bibliography data base and thank the faculty and researchers in the AI Center of George Mason University for generously making available many of their journals and proceedings. Ashwin Ram, Michael Pazzani, Jakub Segen, and Gheorghe Tecuci were especially helpful in providing MSL references.

Despite all the author's efforts, some references may have been overlooked, and the editors apologize in advance to the authors of these works, as well as to the readers, for any omissions or errors.

This research was done in the Center for Artificial Intelligence at George Mason University. The Center's research is supported in part by the Defense Advanced Research Projects Agency under the grant administered by the Office of Naval Research No. N00014–91-J-1854, in part by the Office of Naval Research under Grant No. N00014–91-J-1351, and in part by the National Science Foundation under Grant No. IRI-9020226.

EXPLANATION OF THE CATEGORIES AND STRATEGIES

Following the style used in the previous volumes of Machine Learning, we have categorized publications with respect to the topic of the publication and learning strategies and/or computational paradigms utilized. Each publication is marked with a label, denoting the categories it belongs to. In the case of multistrategy publications, the label also indicates which learning strategies and/or computational paradigms are included. We also provide an index to the categories to enable readers to find publications belonging to a particular category of interest. Below are the labels, names of the associated categories, and a brief explanation.

CATEGORIES

B   Background material, overviews, and conference proceedings

These publications are foundational sources and introductory material to the field of artificial intelligence and machine learning. Also included are proceedings of the major AI-related conferences that contain papers on machine learning.

E   Experimental applications and comparisons

Publications in this category concern applications of learning methods to artificial or real-world problems, as well as experimental comparisons of different learning systems as applied to various testing problems.

I(...)   Multistrategy learning

These publications describe a methodology integrating two or more strategies. In parentheses is a list of symbols indicating integrated strategies or computational paradigms. For example, a publication marked I(s,x) describes a combination of symbolic empirical learning with explanation-based learning. In the categories index, we use the designation I(y...) in order to indicate that a publication integrates a given strategy "y" with some other strategies without identifying them. For example, a publication marked I(c...) deals with a multistrategy method using conceptual clustering as one of the integrated learning strategies.

K   Knowledge acquisition for expert systems and learning apprentice systems

Publications in this category describe methods or systems that acquire and improve knowledge through an interaction with a human expert during the particular problem solving task. Also includes publications on intelligent information retrieval.

M   Cognitive modeling of learning and reasoning

Research in this category is based on investigations of human methods of learning and reasoning. Primary effort is to build computational models of these processes and eventually apply them to some practical tasks.

P   Problem solving and planning with learning capabilities

Publications in this category describe systems for learning domain and control knowledge through observing their own performance on subsequent tasks. Some of these methods are closely related to learning apprentice systems.

T   Theoretical analysis

This category includes research concerned with theoretical analysis of formalized, abstract learning systems.

LEARNING STRATEGIES AND/OR COMPUTATIONAL PARADIGMS

a   Analogy and case-based reasoning

Strategy employs analogy to known problem solutions, concepts, or past cases. It includes the use of determinations or causal relationships.

c   Conceptual clustering

Strategy is concerned with organizing a set of observations into a hierarchy of meaningful categories. Each category is associated with a simple descriptive concept.

d   Quantitative and/or qualitative discovery

Strategy explores a given domain either in passive or active way, trying to develop empirical laws and theories about it. Conceptual clustering can be viewed as one of the forms of discovery, as can be any form of unsupervised learning.

g   Genetic algorithms and classifier systems

This computational paradigm describes methods based on the idea of probabilistic search through large spaces involving states that can be represented as strings in some language.

n   Neural nets and connectionist systems

This computational paradigm describes a broad class of methods using algorithms for training a network from a set of examples by appropriately modifying its connection weights.

r   Prediction and pattern discovery in sequences or processes

This strategy deals with prediction of sequences or time-dependent processes.

s   Symbolic empirical learning from examples

This inductive strategy within a symbolic computational paradigm uses examples in order to induce new concepts or solve problems. It uses symbolic representation, easily comprehensible to humans, such as decision rules, decision trees, frames, scripts, semantic networks, Horn clauses, and general logic expressions.

v   Change of the representation space

This strategy utilizes background knowledge to create knowledge represented at a higher level of abstraction or explanatory knowledge (e.g., causal knowledge) and/or in a different form than the original input information. It includes constructive induction, abduction, and knowledge representation shift.

x   Explanation-based learning and other analytic methods

This strategy relies heavily on background knowledge in order to learn/improve the quality of overall knowledge.

CATEGORIES INDEX

B   Background material and overviews

Davis, 1987, 1990, 1991; Davis and Lenat, 1980; Dean and McKeown, 1991; Dean and Wellman, 1991; Defays, 1989; DeJong, 1975, 1987, 1988, 1990; DeJong and Mooney, 1986; Dietterich, 1986; Dietterich and Michalski, 1981; Dietterich and Michalski, 1983; Dietterich and Swartout, 1990; Dollas et al., 1990; Doyle, 1979, 1980; Duda and Hart, 1973; Ellman, 1989; Feigenbaum, 1961; Fikes et al., 1972; Firebaugh, 1988; Fisher, 1987; Fisher et al., 1991; Flann and Dietterich, 1989; Forbus and Shrobe, 1987; Forsyth and Rada, 1986; Fu, 1986; Fu and Booth, 1986; Fulk and Case, 1990; Gale, 1986; Gardner, 1985; Genesereth and Nilsson, 1987; Gentner, 1989; Georgeff and Lansky, 1987; Giarratano, 1989; Ginsberg, 1987; Glymour, 1987; Gold, 1967; Goldberg, 1983, 1989; Graubard, 1989; Grefenstette, 1985, 1987, 1988a, 1988b; Greiner, 1985; Greiner and Lenat, 1980; Hall, 1988; Halpern, 1986; Hamburger and Wexler, 1975; Hammond, 1989a, 1989b; Haussler, 1988; Haussler and Pitt, 1988; Hayes-Roth, 1983; Hayes-Roth et al., 1981; Hayes-Roth and McDermott, 1978; Hecht-Nielsen, 1989; Helman, 1988; Hinton and Anderson, 1981; Hofstadter, 1985a, 1985b; Holland, 1975, 1987; Holland et al., 1986; Hopfield, 1982, 1984; Horning, 1969; Hunt et al., 1966; Johnson-Laird, 1983; Joshi, 1985; Judd, 1988; Kahneman et al., 1982; Kanal and Lemmer, 1986; Kedar-Cabelli, 1985; Kehler and Rosenschein, 1986; Keller, 1988; Kibler and Aha, 1987; Kibler and Langley, 1988; Klein and Kuppin, 1970; Knobe and Knobe, 1977; Kodratoff, 1988, 1989a, 1989b, 1989c, 1994; Kodratoff and Michalski, 1990; Kohonen, 1982; Kolodner, 1988; Kononenko and Bratko, 1991; Kowalski, 1979; Kowalski and Kuchner, 1971; Kuipers, 1985; Laird, 1988, 1984; Laird, 1988; Laird et al., 1985; Laird et al., 1986; Lang et al., 1990; Langley, 1980; Langley et al., 1983; Langley et al., 1986; Langley et al., 1987a, 1987b; Langley and Carbonell, 1984, 1986, 1987; Larson and Michalski, 1977; Lee et al., 1991; Lenat, 1976, 1977, 1978, 1983, 1989; Lewis, 1991; Lindsay et al., 1980; Ling, 1991; Loveland, 1978; MacGregor, 1987; Marcus, 1989; Maryanski, 1974; Matheus, 1991; Maturane and Varela, 1987; McCarthy, 1958, 1980; McClelland and Rumelhart, 1988; McClelland et al., 1986; McDermott, 1978; McDermott, 1987, 1989; McDermott and Doyle, 1980; Mechelen et al., 1992; Michalski, 1969, 1973a, 1973b, 1974, 1975, 1978, 1979a, 1979b, 1980, 1983a, 1983b, 1985, 1986a, 1986b, 1987a, 1987b, 1988, 1989, 1991, 1992, 1994; Michalski and Chilausky, 1980; Michalski and Kodratoff, 1990; Michalski and Larson, 1978; Michalski and Littman, 1989; Michalski and Stepp, 1983, 1987; Michalski and Tecuci, 1991, 1994; Michalski and Winston, 1986; Michalski et al., 1983, 1986; Michalski et al., 1986; Michalski et al., 1988; Michie, 1988; Minsky, 1968, 1975, 1986; Minsky and Papert, 1969; Minton, 1989, 1990; Mitchell, 1977,

1978, 1980, 1982, 1988; Mitchell et al., 1981; Mitchell et al., 1983; Mitchell et al., 1985, 1986; Mooney et al., 1989; Moore, 1980; Morik, 1989a, 1989b; Mortimer, 1988; Mostow, 1981, 1983; Mylopoulos and Brodie, 1989; Mylopoulos and Reiter, 1991; Natarajan, 1991; Neumann, 1992; Newell and Simon, 1972; Nillson, 1965, 1971, 1980, 1986; Nirenburg et al., 1991; Norvig, 1991; O'Rorke, 1987; Pao, 1969; Parikh, 1990; Parker, 1985; Pawlak, 1984; Pazzani, 1990; Pearl, 1984, 1988; Pearl and Dechter, 1989; Piatetsky-Shapiro and Frawley, 1991; Pinker, 1979; Porter, 1984, 1987; Porter et al., 1990; Porter and Mooney, 1990; Prieditis, 1985, 1988; Quillian, 1968; Quinlan, 1979, 1983, 1986; Ram, 1991; Rawlins, 1991; Reeker, 1976; Reinke and Michalski, 1988; Reisbeck and Schank, 1989; Reiter, 1980; Rendell, 1986; Rich and Knight, 1991; Rissland and Soloway, 1980; Rivest et al., 1989; Robinson, 1965; Robinson and Wos, 1969; Rosenblatt, 1958, 1962; Rosenbloom, 1985; Rumelhart et al., 1986a, 1986b; Rumelhart and Zipser, 1985; Russell, 1989; Sacerdotti, 1974; Samuel, 1959, 1967; Schaffer, 1984, 1989, 1992; Schank, 1986, 1991; Schank and Abelson, 1977; Schank and Kass, 1990; Schwartz, 1990; Segre, 1987, 1988, 1989, 1991; Shafer and Pearl, 1990; Shapiro, 1987; Shavlik, 1990; Shavlik and Dietterich, 1990; Shortliffe, 1976; Shrager and Langley, 1990; Shrobe and AAAI, 1988; Simon, 1969, 1979, 1983; Simon and Lea, 1974; Simpson, 1985; Sleeman, 1983; Sleeman and Brown, 1982; Sleeman and Edwards, 1992; Smith and Mitchell, 1988; Solomonoff, 1964; Soloway, 1978; Sowa, 1984, 1991; Sridharan, 1989; Stefik, 1980; Stepp, 1984; Stillings et al., 1987; Subramanian, 1989; Sussman, 1975; Sutton, 1984; Touretzky, 1989; Tsypkin, 1973; Utgoff, 1986; Valiant, 1984; VanLehn, 1987; Vardi, 1988; Vere, 1978; Vosniadou and Ortony, 1989; Warmuth and Valiant, 1991; Waterman, 1970; Waterman and Hayes-Roth, 1978; Webber and Nilsson, 1981; Wechsler, 1990, 1992a, 1992b; Weinert and Kluwe, 1987; Weiss and Kapouleas, 1989; Weiss and Kulikowski, 1990; Weld and DeKleer, 1990; Werbos, 1984; Whitley, 1992; Wilkins, 1988; Winston, 1970, 1975, 1984; Winston and Brown, 1979; Zadeh, 1979; Zaremba, 1988; Zito-Wolf, 1991; Zytkow and Simon, 1986

E   **Experimental applications and comparisons**

Anderson, 1977; Bala et al., 1994; Baroglio et al., 1994; Belyaev, 1991; Bergadano et al., 1990, 1992; Bradshaw, 1985; Buchanan, 1989; Carpineto, 1988; Chien, 1991; Clark et al., 1991; Dietterich et al., 1990; Ellman, 1989; Friedrich and Nejdl, 1989; Fu, 1986; Gutknecht et al., 1991; Hall, 1988; Holder, 1991; Hunter, 1989, 1991, 1994; Kaufman et al., 1989; Kazman, 1991; Kodratoff, 1989a, 1989b, 1989c; Kodratoff and Tecuci, 1987; Lang et al., 1990; Lebowitz, 1987; Maclin and Shavlik, 1991, 1992; Michalski, 1975, 1985; Michalski and Chilausky, 1980; Miller and Laird, 1991; Minton, 1990; Mooney et al., 1989; Morik et al., 1991; Murphy and Pazzani, 1991; Nirenburg et al., 1991; Porter et al., 1990; Quinlan, 1983; Ram and Hunter, 1992; Reich, 1991a, 1991b, 1994; Reinke and Michalski, 1988; Richards, 1991; Saitta and Botta, 1992; Saitta et al., 1991; Segen, 1985, 1988, 1989a, 1989b, 1991, 1994; Spears and Gordon, 1991; Tecuci, 1988, 1992; Tecuci and Kodratoff, 1990; Tecuci et al., 1987; Thrun et al., 1991; Touretzky and Wheeler, 1990; Weiss and Kapouleas, 1989; Weiss and Kulikowski, 1990; Whitehall and Lu, 1991; Whitehall et al., 1991; Whitehall et al., 1994; Wnek and Michalski, 1991, 1994; Zhou, 1990

K   **Knowledge acquisition for expert systems and learning apprentice systems**

Addis et al., 1991; Barr et al., 1979; Boose, 1989; Buchanan, 1989; De Raedt and Bruynooghe, 1991, 1994; De Raedt et al., 1991; Gutknecht et al., 1991; Henrion, 1991; Hunter, 1989; Kodratoff, 1990; Kodratoff and Tecuci, 1986, 1987a, 1987b; Lavrac and Vassilev, 1989; Lenat, 1983, 1989; Lewis, 1991; Marcus, 1989; Martin, 1991; Michalski and Chilausky, 1980; Michalski and Littman, 1989; Morik, 1991, 1992, 1994; Nedellec, 1991; Pazzani and Brunk, 1991; Ram, 1991; Reich, 1991, 1994; Shen, 1991; Tecuci, 1988, 1991, 1992; Tecuci and Kodratoff, 1990; Tecuci et al., 1987; Wilkins, 1990; Wrobel, 1989; Zhou, 1990

M   **Cognitive modeling of learning and reasoning**

Anderson, 1983, 1989; Bergadano et al., 1992; Bolc, 1987; Collins, 1988; Collins and Michalski, 1989; Cox and Ram, 1992; Gams, 1991; Gardner, 1985; Helman, 1988; Hofstadter, 1985; Hunter, 1990; Johnson-Laird, 1983; Kazman, 1991; Kuipers, 1985; Langley and Allen, 1991; Lebowitz, 1986a, 1986b, 1986c; Levinson and Snyder, 1991a, 1991b; Maturane and Varela, 1987; McClelland et al., 1986; Michalski, 1992; Miller and Laird, 1991; Minsky, 1986; Morik, 1991, 1992, 1994; Pazzani, 1988, 1991; Pazzani et al., 1986, 1987; Ram, 1992; Ram and Hunter, 1992; Rissland and Skalak, 1989; Rumelhart et al., 1986; Simon and Lea, 1974; Sleeman, 1983; Sleeman and Brown, 1982; Stillings et al., 1987; Towell et al., 1991; VanLehn and Jones, 1991; Weinert and Kluwe, 1987; Wisniewski and Medin, 1991a, 1991b, 1994

P　　Problem solving and planning with learning capabilities

Allen et al., 1990, 1991; Amarel, 1968; Anderson, 1977, 1983; Anderson, 1986; Botta et al., 1991; Brazdil et al., 1991; Carbonell, 1983, 1986; Dean and Wellman, 1991; Fawcett, 1991; Fikes et al., 1972; Fu, 1986; Goldberg, 1983; Gordon, 1991; Grefenstette, 1988; Hayes-Roth, 1983; Henrion, 1991; Keller, 1988; Knoblock et al., 1991; Ko, 1988; Kodratoff, 1990; Kodratoff and Tecuci, 1986, 1987a, 1987b; Laird, 1984; Laird et al., 1986, 1985; Langley and Allen, 1991; Levinson and Snyder, 1991a, 1991b; McCluskey, 1989; Michalski, 1969, 1990; Millan and Torras, 1991; Minton, 1990; Mitchell et al., 1983; Porter, 1984; Ram and Hunter, 1992; Sacerdotti, 1974; Samuel, 1959, 1967; Segre, 1987, 1988; Shavlik, 1990; Simon and Lea, 1974; Simpson, 1985; Stefik, 1980; Tecuci, 1988, 1991, 1992; Tecuci and Kodratoff, 1990; Tecuci et al., 1987; VanLehn, 1987; VanLehn and Jones, 1991; Veloso and Carbonell, 1991, 1994; Wilkins, 1990; Wrobel, 1991; Zerr and Ganascia, 1991

T　　Theoretical analysis

Angluin and Smith, 1987; Baum and Haussler, 1989; Bergadano, 1991; Blumer et al., 1987; Buntine, 1988, 1991; Fulk and Case, 1990; Giordana, 1991; Haussler, 1988; Haussler and Pitt, 1988; Judd, 1988; Kononenko and Bratko, 1991; Ling, 1991; Mortimer, 1988; Natarajan, 1991; Pazzani, 1991a, 1991b; Pearl and Dechter, 1989; Rendell, 1986; Rivest et al., 1989; Valiant, 1984; Warmuth and Valiant, 1991

I(a...)　Analogy and case-based reasoning

Anderson, 1989; Botta et al., 1991; Cox and Ram, 1991, 1992; De Raedt and Bruynooghe, 1991, 1994; De Raedt et al., 1991; Duval, 1991; Falkenhainer, 1987; Genest et al., 1990; Helman, 1988; Henrion, 1991; Kass, 1989; Kodratoff, 1990; Kodratoff and Tecuci, 1987a, 1987b; Michalski, 1989, 1990a, 1990b, 1991a, 1991b, 1992, 1994; Pazzani, 1991, 1992, 1994; Prieditis, 1985; Rajamoney and Lee, 1991; Ram, 1992; Ram and Cox, 1994; Ram and Hunter, 1994; Redmond, 1989; Reisbeck and Schank, 1989; Rissland and Skalak, 1989; Russell, 1986, 1987, 1989; Shen, 1990; Skalak and Rissland, 1990; Tausend and Bell, 1991; Tecuci, 1988, 1991a, 1991b, 1992a, 1992b, 1994; Tecuci and Kodratoff, 1989, 1990; Tecuci and Michalski, 1991; Tecuci et al., 1987; Touretzky and Wheeler, 1990; VanLehn and Jones, 1991; Veloso and Carbonell, 1991, 1994; Vosniadou and Ortony, 1989; Vrain and Kodratoff, 1989; Zhou, 1990; Zhou and Grefenstette, 1989

I(c...)   Conceptual clustering

Danyluk, 1991, 1994; Greene, 1988; Hunter, 1991, 1994; Kaufman et al., 1989; Lebowitz, 1986, 1987; Michalski, 1979; Ram, 1992; Reich, 1991, 1994; Segen, 1991, 1994; Tecuci, 1988, 1991; Yoo and Fisher, 1989

I(d...)   Quantitative and/or qualitative discovery

Falkenhainer, 1987, 1990; Falkenhainer and Michalski, 1990; Falkenhainer and Rajamoney, 1988; Greene, 1988; Kaufman et al., 1989; Lenat, 1983; Nordhausen and Langley, 1987, 1989; Shrager and Langley, 1990; Sims, 1987

I(g...)   Genetic algorithms and classifier systems

Ackley, 1987; Bala et al., 1991, 1994; Buntine, 1991; Davis, 1991; De Garis, 1990, 1991, 1994; DeJong, 1990; Eberhart, 1992; Elias, 1992; Goldberg, 1983; Gordon, 1991; Gordon and Grefenstette, 1990; Gould and Levinson, 1991, 1994; Gruau, 1992; Kadaba and Nygard, 1990; Kelly and Davis, 1991a, 1991b; Levinson and Snyder, 1991a, 1991b; Lindgren et al., 1992; Rogers, 1991; Schaffer, 1992; Schizas et al., 1992; Spears, 1990; Spears and Gordon, 1991; Thrun et al., 1991; Vafaie and DeJong, 1991, 1994; Whitley, 1992; Whitley et al., 1991; Wnek and Michalski, 1991, 1994; Zhou and Grefenstette, 1989

I(n...)   Neural nets and connectionist systems

Ackley, 1987; Belyaev, 1991; De Garis, 1990, 1991, 1994; Diederich, 1989; Dietterich et al., 1990; Eberhart, 1992; Elias, 1992; Gruau, 1992; Gutknecht et al., 1991; Hall and Romaniuk, 1990; Henrion, 1991; Hunter, 1991, 1994; Kadaba and Nygard, 1990; Katz, 1989; Levinson and Snyder, 1991a, 1991b; Lindgren et al., 1992; Liu and Cios, 1991; Maclin and Shavlik, 1991, 1992; Millan and Torras, 1991; Mooney et al., 1989; Rumelhart et al., 1986; Schaffer, 1992; Schizas et al., 1992; Shavlik and Towell, 1989a, 1989b; Spears, 1990; Thrun et al., 1991; Touretzky and Wheeler, 1990; Towell and Shavlik, 1991, 1994; Weiss and Kapouleas, 1989; Whitley, 1992; Whitley et al., 1991; Wnek and Michalski, 1991, 1994; Zhang, 1991, 1994

I(r...)   Prediction and pattern discovery in sequences or processes

Dietterich and Michalski, 1986; Greene, 1988; Kaufman et al., 1989; Maclin and Shavlik, 1991, 1992; Michalski et al., 1988; Pazzani, 1991a, 1991b, 1992, 1994

I(s...)   Symbolic empirical learning from examples

Aha, 1991; Ahmad et al., 1991; Anderson, 1989; Bala et al., 1991, 1992, 1994; Barletta and Kerber, 1989; Belyaev, 1991; Bergadano and Giordana, 1988, 1990; Bergadano et al., 1988, 1989, 1990, 1992; Bergadano et al., 1989, 1991; Bergadano and Ponsero, 1989; Carpineto, 1988, 1989, 1991; Danyluk, 1987, 1988, 1989, 1991, 1994; De Raedt, 1991; De Raedt and Bruynooghe, 1991, 1994; Dietterich and Flann, 1988; Dietterich and Michalski, 1986; Dietterich et al., 1990; Drastal et al., 1989a, 1989b; Duval, 1991; Elio and Watanabe, 1991; Flann and Dietterich, 1989; Friedrich and Nejdl, 1989; Gemello, 1991; Giordana et al., 1991; Goldberg, 1983; Granger and Schlimmer, 1985; Gutknecht et al., 1991; Hall and Romaniuk, 1990; Hall, 1988; Hamakawa, 1991; Holder, 1991; Kaufman et al., 1989; Kelly and Davis, 1991; Knight and Gil, 1991; Ko and Michalski, 1988; Kodratoff, 1991, 1992; Kodratoff and Tecuci, 1986, 1987a, 1987b; Lavrac and Vassilev, 1989; Lebowitz, 1986a, 1986b, 1990; Liu and Cios, 1991; Martin, 1991; McCluskey, 1989; Michalski, 1978, 1979, 1983a, 1983b, 1989, 1990a, 1990b, 1991a, 1991b, 1992a, 1992b, 1994; Michalski and Ko, 1988; Michalski and Watanabe, 1988; Michalski et al., 1988; Millan and Torras, 1991; Miller and Laird, 1991; Mitchell et al., 1983; Mooney and Ourston, 1989; Mooney and Ourston, 1991, 1994; Mooney et al., 1989; Morik, 1994; Morik et al., 1991; Murphy and Pazzani, 1991; Nedellec, 1991; Numao and Shimura, 1989; Pazzani, 1988a, 1988b, 1989, 1990, 1991a, 1991b, 1991c; Pazzani and Brunk, 1991; Pazzani and Kibler, 1992; Pazzani et al., 1991; Ragavan, 1991; Rajamoney and Lee, 1991; Redmond, 1989; Reich, 1991; Richards, 1991; Russell, 1986, 1987, 1989; Sarrett and Pazzani, 1989; Segen, 1985, 1988, 1989a, 1989b; Shen, 1991, 1990; Silver et al., 1990; Skalak and Rissland, 1990; Spears and Gordon, 1991; Tausend and Bell, 1991; Tecuci, 1988, 1991a, 1991b, 1992a, 1992b, 1994; Tecuci and Kodratoff, 1989, 1990; Tecuci and Michalski, 1991a, 1991b; Tecuci et al., 1987; Thrun et al., 1991; Towell et al., 1991; Vafaie and DeJong, 1991, 1994; Vilain et al., 1990; Vosniadou and Ortony, 1989; Vrain and Kodratoff, 1989; Weiss and Kapouleas, 1989; Whitehall and Lu, 1991; Whitehall et al., 1991, 1994; Widmer, 1989a, 1989b, 1991a, 1991b, 1994; Wisniewski and Medin, 1991a, 1991b; Wnek, 1992; Wnek and Michalski, 1991, 1994; Wollowski, 1989; Wrobel, 1989; Wu et al., 1990; Yamamura and Kobayashi, 1991; Yoo and Fisher, 1991; Zerr and Ganascia, 1991; Zhang, 1991, 1994

I(v...)   Constructive induction, abduction, or knowledge representation shift

Aha, 1991; Bala et al., 1994; Baroglio et al., 1994; Belyaev, 1991; Bergadano et al., 1991; Cohen, 1990; Davis, 1991; De Raedt, 1991; De Raedt and Bruynooghe, 1991, 1994; De Raedt et al., 1991; Drastal et al., 1989a, 1989b; Elio and Watanabe, 1991; Falkenhainer, 1990; Falkenhainer and Michalski, 1990; Fawcett, 1991; Genest et al., 1990; Giordana, 1991; Granger and Schlimmer, 1985; Kokar and Zadrozny, 1989; Lenat, 1983; Maclin and Shavlik, 1989; Matwin and Plante, 1991, 1994; Michalski, 1978, 1983a, 1983b, 1989, 1990a, 1990b, 1991a, 1991b, 1992, 1994; Michalski and Watanabe, 1988; Mitchell et al., 1983; Mooney, 1991; Mooney and Ourston, 1991, 1994; Murphy and Pazzani, 1991; Nedellec, 1991; Pazzani, 1991, 1992, 1994; Ragavan, 1991; Saitta and Botta, 1992; Saitta et al., 1991; Segen, 1985, 1988, 1989a, 1989b, 1991, 1994; Subramanian and Mooney, 1991; Tausend and Bell, 1991; Tecuci, 1988, 1991a, 1991b, 1992a, 1992b, 1994; Tecuci and Kodratoff, 1990; Tecuci and Michalski, 1991a, 1991b; Towell et al., 1991; Widmer, 1991, 1994; Wisniewski and Medin, 1991, 1991b, 1994; Wnek, 1992; Wnek and Michalski, 1991, 1994; Wrobel, 1989, 1991

I(x...)   Explanation-based learning and other analytic methods

Ahmad et al., 1991; Anderson, 1977, 1989; Barletta and Kerber, 1989; Baroglio et al., 1994; Bergadano et al., 1989, 1991; Bergadano et al., 1988, 1989, 1990, 1992; Bergadano and Giordana, 1988, 1990; Bergadano and Ponsero, 1989; Botta, 1991; Carpineto, 1988, 1989, 1991; Cohen, 1990; Cox and Ram, 1991, 1992; Danyluk, 1987, 1988, 1989, 1991, 1994; Dietterich and Flann, 1988; Duval, 1991; Elio and Watanabe, 1991; Falkenhainer, 1990; Falkenhainer and Michalski, 1990; Falkenhainer and Rajamoney, 1988; Fawcett, 1991; Flann and Dietterich, 1989; Friedrich and Nejdl, 1989; Genest et al., 1990; Giordana et al., 1991; Gordon, 1991; Gordon and Grefenstette, 1990; Gould and Levinson, 1991, 1994; Hall, 1988; Hamakawa, 1991; Hirsh, 1988, 1990; Holder, 1991; Kass, 1989; Knight and Gil, 1991; Knoblock et al., 1991; Ko and Michalski, 1988; Kodratoff, 1990; Kodratoff and Tecuci, 1986, 1987a, 1987b; Lebowitz, 1986, 1990; Levinson and Snyder, 1991a, 1991b; Maclin and Shavlik, 1989; Martin, 1991; Matwin and Plante, 1991, 1994; McCluskey, 1989; Michalski, 1989, 1990a, 1990b, 1991a, 1991b, 1992a, 1992b, 1994; Michalski and Ko, 1988; Michalski and Watanabe, 1988; Mitchell et al., 1983; Mooney, 1991; Mooney and Ourston, 1989, 1991, 1994; Morik, 1994; Numao and Shimura, 1989; Pazzani, 1988a, 1988b, 1988c, 1989,

1990, 1991a, 1991b, 1991c; Pazzani and Brunk, 1991; Pazzani et al., 1987; Pazzani et al., 1991; Pazzani and Kibler, 1992; Ram, 1992; Ram and Cox, 1994; Redmond, 1989; Reich, 1991; Richards, 1991; Saitta and Botta, 1992; Saitta et al., 1991; Sarrett and Pazzani, 1989; Shavlik and Towell, 1989a, 1989b; Shen, 1991; Silver, 1988; Silver et al., 1990; Sims, 1987; Subramanian and Mooney, 1991; Swaminathan, 1988; Tecuci, 1988, 1991a, 1991b, 1992a, 1992b, 1994; Tecuci and Kodratoff, 1989, 1990; Tecuci and Michalski, 1991a, 1991b; Tecuci et al., 1987; Towell and Shavlik, 1991, 1994; VanLehn and Jones, 1991; Veloso and Carbonell, 1991, 1994; Vilain et al., 1990; Whitehall and Lu, 1991; Whitehall et al., 1991, 1994; Widmer, 1989a, 1989b, 1991a, 1991b, 1992; Wisniewski and Medin, 1991a, 1991b, 1994; Wnek, 1992; Wollowski, 1989; Wu et al., 1990; Yamamura and Kobayashi, 1991; Yoo and Fisher, 1989; Yoo and Fisher, 1991; Zerr and Ganascia, 1991

I(av...)

De Raedt and Bruynooghe, 1991, 1992; De Raedt et al., 1991; Genest et al., 1990; Michalski, 1989, 1990a, 1990b, 1991a, 1991b, 1992a, 1992b; Pazzani, 1991, 1992a, 1992b; Tausend and Bell, 1991; Tecuci, 1988, 1991a, 1991b, 1992a, 1992b, 1994; Tecuci and Kodratoff, 1990; Tecuci and Michalski, 1991

I(gn...)

Ackley, 1987; De Garis, 1990, 1991, 1994; Eberhart, 1992; Elias, 1992; Gruau, 1992; Kadaba and Nygard, 1990; Levinson and Snyder, 1991a, 1991b; Lindgren et al., 1992; Schaffer, 1992; Schizas et al., 1992; Spears, 1990; Thrun et al., 1991; Whitley, 1992; Whitley et al., 1991; Wnek and Michalski, 1991, 1994

I(sa...)

Anderson, 1989; De Raedt and Bruynooghe, 1991, 1994; Duval, 1991; Kodratoff and Tecuci, 1987a, 1987b; Michalski, 1989, 1990a, 1990b, 1991a, 1991b, 1992a, 1992b; Rajamoney and Lee, 1991; Redmond, 1989; Russell, 1986, 1987, 1989; Shen, 1990; Skalak and Rissland, 1990; Tausend and Bell, 1991; Tecuci, 1988, 1991a, 1991b, 1992a, 1992b, 1994; Tecuci and Kodratoff, 1989, 1990; Tecuci and Michalski, 1991; Tecuci et al., 1987; Vosniadou and Ortony, 1989; Vrain and Kodratoff, 1989

I(sc...)

Danyluk, 1991, 1994; Kaufman et al., 1989; Lebowitz, 1986; Michalski, 1979; Tecuci, 1988, 1991

I(sg...)

Bala et al., 1991, 1994; Goldberg, 1983; Kelly and Davis, 1991; Spears and Gordon, 1991; Thrun et al., 1991; Vafaie and DeJong, 1991, 1994; Wnek and Michalski, 1991, 1994

I(sn...)

Belyaev, 1991; Dietterich et al., 1990; Gutknecht et al., 1991; Hall and Romaniuk, 1990; Liu and Cios, 1991; Millan and Torras, 1991; Mooney et al., 1989; Thrun et al., 1991; Weiss and Kapouleas, 1989; Wnek and Michalski, 1991, 1994; Zhang, 1991, 1994

I(sx...)

Ahmad et al., 1991; Anderson, 1989; Barletta and Kerber, 1989; Bergadano and Giordana, 1988, 1990; Bergadano and Ponsero, 1989; Bergadano et al., 1988, 1990; Bergadano et al., 1989, 1991; Bergadano et al., 1989, 1992; Carpineto, 1988, 1989, 1991; Danyluk, 1987, 1988, 1989, 1991, 1994; Dietterich and Flann, 1988; Duval, 1991; Elio and Watanabe, 1991; Flann and Dietterich, 1989; Friedrich and Nejdl, 1989; Giordana et al., 1991; Hall, 1988; Hamakawa, 1991; Holder, 1991; Knight and Gil, 1991; Ko and Michalski, 1988; Kodratoff and Tecuci, 1986, 1987a, 1987b; Lebowitz, 1990; Martin, 1991; McCluskey, 1989; Michalski, 1989, 1990a, 1990b, 1991a, 1991b, 1992a, 1992b, 1994; Michalski and Ko, 1988; Michalski and Watanabe, 1988; Mitchell et al., 1983; Mooney and Ourston, 1989, 1991, 1994; Morik, 1994; Numao and Shimura, 1989; Pazzani, 1988a, 1988b, 1989, 1990, 1991a, 1991b, 1991c; Pazzani and Brunk, 1991; Pazzani and Kibler, 1992; Pazzani et al., 1991; Redmond, 1989; Reich, 1991; Richards, 1991; Sarrett and Pazzani, 1989; Shen, 1991; Silver et al., 1990; Tecuci, 1988, 1991a, 1991b, 1992a, 1992b, 1994; Tecuci and Kodratoff, 1989, 1990; Tecuci and Michalski, 1991a, 1991b; Tecuci et al., 1987; Vilain et al., 1990; Whitehall and Lu, 1991; Whitehall et al., 1991, 1994; Widmer, 1989a, 1989b, 1991a, 1991b, 1994; Wisniewski and Medin, 1991; Wnek, 1992; Wollowski, 1989; Wu et al., 1990; Yamamura and Kobayashi, 1991; Yoo and Fisher, 1991; Zerr and Ganascia, 1991

I(sxa...)

Anderson, 1989; Duval, 1991; Kodratoff and Tecuci, 1987a, 1987b; Michalski, 1989, 1990a, 1990b, 1991a, 1991b, 1992, 1994; Redmond, 1989; Tecuci, 1988, 1991a, 1991b, 1992a, 1992b, 1994; Tecuci and Kodratoff, 1989, 1990; Tecuci and Michalski, 1991; Tecuci et al., 1987

I(sxv...)

Bergadano et al., 1991; Elio and Watanabe, 1991; Michalski, 1989, 1990a, 1990b, 1991a, 1991b, 1992a, 1992b; Michalski and Watanabe, 1988; Mitchell et al., 1983; Mooney and Ourston, 1991, 1992; Tecuci, 1988, 1991a, 1991b, 1992a, 1992b, 1992c; Tecuci and Kodratoff, 1990; Tecuci and Michalski, 1991a, 1991b; Widmer, 1991, 1992; Wnek, 1992

I(xa...)

Anderson, 1989; Botta, 1991; Cox and Ram, 1991, 1992; Duval, 1991; Genest et al., 1990; Kass, 1989; Kodratoff, 1990; Kodratoff and Tecuci, 1987a, 1987b; Michalski, 1989, 1990a, 1990b, 1991a, 1991b, 1992, 1994; Ram, 1992; Ram and Cox, 1992; Redmond, 1989; Tecuci, 1988, 1991a, 1991b, 1992a, 1992b, 1994; Tecuci and Kodratoff, 1989, 1990; Tecuci and Michalski, 1991; Tecuci et al., 1987; VanLehn and Jones, 1991; Veloso and Carbonell, 1991, 1994

I(xc...)

Danyluk, 1991, 1994; Ram, 1992; Tecuci, 1988, 1991; Yoo and Fisher, 1989

I(xg...)

Gordon, 1991; Gordon and Grefenstette, 1990; Gould and Levinson, 1991, 1994; Levinson and Snyder, 1991a, 1991b

I(xn...)

Levinson and Snyder, 1991a, 1991b; Shavlik and Towell, 1989a, 1989b; Towell and Shavlik, 1991, 1994

I(xv...)

Baroglio et al., 1994; Bergadano et al., 1991; Cohen, 1990; Elio and Watanabe, 1991; Falkenhainer, 1990; Falkenhainer and Michalski, 1990; Fawcett, 1991; Genest et al., 1990; Maclin and Shavlik, 1989; Matwin and

Plante, 1991, 1994; Michalski, 1989, 1990a, 1990b, 1991a, 1991b, 1992, 1994; Michalski and Watanabe, 1988; Mitchell et al., 1983; Mooney, 1991; Mooney and Ourston, 1991, 1994; Saitta and Botta, 1992; Saitta et al., 1991; Subramanian and Mooney, 1991; Tecuci, 1988, 1991a, 1991b, 1992a, 1992b, 1994; Tecuci and Kodratoff, 1990, 1991a; Tecuci and Michalski, 1991b; Widmer, 1991, 1994; Wisniewski and Medin, 1991, 1994; Wnek, 1992

I(xav...)

Genest et al., 1990; Michalski, 1989, 1990a, 1990b, 1991a, 1991b, 1992, 1994; Tecuci, 1988, 1991a, 1991b, 1992a, 1992b, 1994; Tecuci and Kodratoff, 1990; Tecuci and Michalski, 1991

REFERENCES

B I(g,n)   **Ackley, D.H.,** *A Connectionist Machine for Genetic Hillclimbing-Automating Knowledge Acquisition for Expert Systems,* Kluwer Academic, Boston, MA, 1987.

B K   **Addis, T.R., Kodratoff, Y., Lopez de Mantaras, R., Morik, K. and Plaza, E.,** "Panel: Four Stances on Knowledge Acquisition and Machine Learning," *Proceedings of the European Working Session on Learning,* Y. Kodratoff (Eds.), Porto, Portugal, pp. 514–533, Springer-Verlag, New York, 1991.

I(s,v)   **Aha, D.W.,** "Incremental Constructive Induction: An Instance-Based Approach," *Proceedings of the Eighth International Workshop on Machine Learning,* Evanston, IL., pp. 117–121, Morgan Kaufmann, San Mateo, CA, 1991.

I(s,x)   **Ahmad, A., Matwin, S. and Ould-Brahim, H.,** "Acquiring the Second Tier: An Experiment in Learning Two-Tiered Concepts," *Proceedings of the First International Workshop on Multistrategy Learning,* R.S. Michalski and G. Tecuci (Eds.), Harpers Ferry, WV, pp. 419–426, George Mason Univ. Center for AI, Fairfax, VA, 1991.

B   **Aiello, L.C. (Ed.),** *Proceedings of the 9th European Conference on Artificial Intelligence,* Pitman, London, 1990.

B n   **Aleksander, I. (Ed.),** *Neural Computing Architectures: The Design of Brain-Like Machines,* The MIT Press, Cambridge, MA, 1989.

B   **Ali, M. (Ed.),** *Proceedings of the 2nd International Conference on Industrial and Engineering Applications of Artificial Intelligence and Expert Systems,* The University of Tennessee Space Institute, Tullahoma, TN, 1989.

B   **Ali, M. and Matthews, M.M. (Eds.),** *Proceedings of the 3rd International Conference on Industrial and Engineering Applications of Artificial Intelligence and Expert Systems,* Charleston, SC, ACM, New York, 1990.

B   **Allen, J., Fikes, R. and Sandewall, E. (Eds.),** *Principles of Knowledge Representation and Reasoning: Proceedings of the 2nd International Conference (KR91),* Morgan Kaufmann, San Mateo, CA, 1991.

B P   **Allen, J., Hendler, J. and Tate, A. (Eds.),** *Readings in Planning,* Morgan Kaufmann, Los Altos, CA, 1990.

B P   **Allen, J., Kautz, J.F., Pelavin, R. and Tenenberg, J.,** *Reasoning about Plans,* Morgan Kaufmann, Los Altos, CA, 1991.

B P   **Amarel, S.,** "On Representations of Problems of Reasoning about Actions," in *Machine Intelligence 3,* D. Michie (Ed.), American Elsevier, New York, 1968.

B   **Amarel, S.,** "Expert Behavior and Problem Representation," in *Human and Artificial Intelligence,* A. Elithron and R. Banerji (Eds.), North-Holland, Amsterdam, 1984.

B n   **Amit, D.J.,** *Modeling Brain Function: The World of Attractor Neural Networks,* Cambridge University Press, Cambridge, UK, 1989.

B P n   **Anderson, C.W.,** "Learning and Problem Solving with a Multilayer Connectionist System," *Ph.D. Thesis,* Computer Science Dept., University of Massachusetts, 1986.

B   **Anderson, J.R.,** *Language, Memory, and Thought,* Lawrence Erlbaum Associates, Hillsdale, NJ, 1976.

B E P x **Anderson, J.R.,** "Induction of Augmented Transition Networks," *Cognitive Science,* Vol. 1, pp. 125–157, 1977.

B P   **Anderson, J.R.,** "Acquisition of Proof Skills in Geometry," in *Machine Learning: An Artificial Intelligence Approach,* Vol. I, R.S. Michalski, J.G. Carbonell and T.M. Mitchell (Eds.), Tioga/Morgan Kaufmann, Los Altos, CA, 1983.

B M   **Anderson, J.R.,** *The Architecture of Cognition,* Harvard University Press, Cambridge, MA, 1983.

M I(a,s,x)   **Anderson, J.R.,** "A Theory of the Origins of Human Knowledge," *Artificial Intelligence*, Vol. 40, pp. 313–351, 1989.

B   **Anderson, J.R.,** *The Adaptive Character of Thought*, Lawrence Erlbaum Associates, Hillsdale, NJ, 1990.

B n   **Anderson, J.A. and Rosenfeld, E.,** *Neurocomputing: Foundations of Research*, The MIT Press, Cambridge, MA, 1988.

B   **Anderson, J.R. (Ed.),** *Cognitive Skills and Their Acquisition*, Lawrence Erlbaum Associates, Hillsdale, NJ, 1981.

B T   **Angluin, D. and Smith, C.H.,** "Inductive Inference," in *Encyclopedia of Artificial Intelligence*, S.C. Shapiro (Ed.), John Wiley & Sons, New York, 1987.

I(s,g)   **Bala, J., De Jong, K. and Pachowicz, P.,** "Learning Noise Tolerant Classification Procedures by Integrating Inductive Learning and Genetic Algorithms," *Proceedings of the First International Workshop on Multistrategy Learning*, R.S. Michalski and G. Tecuci (Eds.), Harpers Ferry, WV, pp. 316–323, George Mason Univ. Center for AI, Fairfax, VA, 1991.

I(s,g)   **Bala, J., De Jong, K. and Pachowicz, P.,** "Multistrategy Learning from Engineering Data by Integrating Inductive Generalization and Genetic Algorithms," in *Machine Learning: A Multistrategy Approach*, Vol. IV, R.S. Michalski and G. Tecuci (Eds.), Morgan Kaufmann, San Mateo, CA, 1994.

E I(s,v)   **Bala, J.W., Michalski, R.S. and Wnek, J.,** "The Principal Axes Method for Constructive Induction," *Proceedings of the 9th International Machine Learning Conference*, Aberdeen, Scotland, Morgan Kaufmann, San Mateo, CA, 1992.

I(s,x)   **Barletta, R. and Kerber, R.,** "Improving Explanation-Based Indexing with Empirical Learning," *Proceedings of the 6th International Workshop on Machine Learning*, Ithaca, NY, pp. 84–86, Morgan Kaufmann, San Mateo, CA, 1989.

E I(v,x)   **Baroglio, C., Botta, M. and Saitta, L.,** "WHY: A System That Learns Using Causal Models and Examples," in *Machine Learning: A Multistrategy Approach*, Vol. IV, R.S. Michalski and G. Tecuci (Eds.), Morgan Kaufmann, San Mateo, CA, 1994.

B   **Barr, A. and Feigenbaum, E.A. (Eds.),** *The Handbook of Artificial Intelligence*, Vols. I & II, HeurisTech Press/William Kaufmann, Stanford, CA, 1981.

B K   **Barr, A., Bennet, J. and Clancey, W.,** "Transfer of Expertise: A
                Theme for AI Research," *Heuristic Programming Project*,
                HPP-79–11, Stanford University, 1979.

B n   **Barto, A.B., Sutton, R.S. and Anderson, C.W.,** "Neuronlike
                Adaptive Elements That Can Solve Difficult Learning Control
                Problems," *IEEE Transactions on Systems, Man and Cybernetics*,
                Vol. 13, No. 5, pp. 834–846, 1983.

B T n   **Baum, E.B. and Haussler, D.,** "What Size Net Gives Valid
                Generalization?" *Neural Computation*, Vol. 1, pp. 151–160, 1989.

E I(n,s,v)   **Belyaev, L. and Falcone, L.P.,** "Noise-Resistant Classification,"
                *Proceedings of the Eighth International Workshop on Machine
                Learning*, Evanston, IL, pp. 581–585, Morgan Kaufmann, San
                Mateo, CA, 1991.

B v   **Benjamin, D.P. (Ed.),** *Change of the Representation and
                Inductive Bias*, Kluwer Academic, Boston, MA, 1990.

B T s,x   **Bergadano, F.,** "The Problem of Induction and Machine
                Learning," *Proceedings of IJCAI-91*, pp. 1073–1078, AAAI Press,
                Menlo Park, CA, 1991.

I(s,x)   **Bergadano, F. and Giordana, A.,** "A Knowledge Intensive
                Approach to Concept Induction," *Proceedings of the 5th
                International Conference on Machine Learning*, Ann Arbor, MI,
                pp. 305–317, Morgan Kaufmann, San Mateo, CA, 1988.

I(s,x)   **Bergadano, F. and Giordana, A.,** "Guiding Induction with
                Domain Theories," in *Machine Learning: An Artificial Intelligence
                Approach*, Vol. III, Y. Kodratoff and R.S. Michalski (Eds.),
                Morgan Kaufmann, San Mateo, CA, 1990.

I(s,x)   **Bergadano, F. and Ponsero, S.,** "Integrating Empirical and
                Analytic Learning in Concept Acquisition," *Proceedings of the 4th
                International Symposium on Methodologies for Intelligent
                Systems*, pp. 273–280, Elsevier Science Publishing, New York,
                1989.

B I(s,v,x)   **Bergadano, F., Esposito, F., Rouveirol, C. and Wrobel, S.,**
                "Panel: Evaluating and Changing Representation in Concept
                Acquisition," *Proceedings of the European Working Session on
                Learning*, Y. Kodratoff (Ed.), Porto, Portugal, pp. 89–100,
                Springer-Verlag, New York, 1991.

I(s,x)   **Bergadano, A., Giordana, A. and Ponsero, S.,** "Deduction in Top-Down Inductive Learning," *Proceedings of the 6th International Workshop on Machine Learning*, Ithaca, NY, pp. 23–25, Morgan Kaufmann, San Mateo, CA, 1989.

I(s,x)   **Bergadano, F., Giordana, A. and Saitta, L.,** "Concept Acquisition in an Integrated EBL and SBL Environment," *Proceedings of ECAI-88*, Munich, W. Germany, pp. 363–368, Pitman, London, 1988.

E I(s,x)   **Bergadano, F., Giordana, A., Saitta, L., DeMarchi, D. and Brancadori, F.,** "Integrated Learning in a Real Domain," *Proceedings of the 7th International Conference on Machine Learning*, B.W. Porter and R.J. Mooney (Eds.), Austin, TX, pp. 322–329, Morgan Kaufmann, San Mateo, CA, 1990.

I(s,x)   **Bergadano, F., Matwin, S., Michalski, R.S. and Zhang, J.,** "Learning Flexible Concepts through a Search for Simpler but Still Accurate Descriptions," *Proceedings of the Fourth AAAI-Sponsored Knowledge Acquisition for Knowledge-Based Systems Workshop*, pp. 1–10, AAAI Press, Menlo Park, CA, 1989.

E M I(s,x)   **Bergadano, F., Matwin, S., Michalski, R.S., and Zhang, J.,** "Learning Two-Tiered Descriptions of Flexible Concepts: The POSEIDON System," *Machine Learning*, Vol. 8, pp. 5–43, 1992.

B g   **Bethke, A.D.,** "Genetic Algorithms as Function Optimizers," *Ph.D. Thesis,* University of Michigan, Ann Arbor, MI, 1981.

B x   **Biermann, A.W., Guiho, G. and Kodratoff, Y.,** *Automatic Program Construction Techniques*, Macmillan Publishing Company, New York, 1984.

B   **Birnbaum, L.A. and Collins, G.C. (Eds.),** *Proceedings of the 8th International Conference on Machine Learning*, Morgan Kaufmann, San Mateo, CA, 1991.

B T   **Blumer, A., Ehrenfeucht, A., Haussler, D. and Warmuth, M.,** "Occam's Razor," *Information Processing Letters*, Vol. 24, pp. 377–380, 1987.

B   **Bobrow, D.G. and Collins, A.,** *Representation and Understanding*, Academic Press, San Diego, CA, 1975.

B M s   **Bolc, L.,** *Computational Models of Learning*, Springer-Verlag, Berlin, 1987.

B g   **Booker, L.B.,** "Intelligent Behavior as an Adaptation to the Task Environment," *Ph.D. Thesis,* University of Michigan, Ann Arbor, MI, 1982.

B g   **Booker, L.B.,** "Improving the Performance of Genetic Algorithms in Classifier Systems," *Ph.D. Thesis,* University of Pittsburgh, 1985.

B g   **Booker, L.B., Goldberg, D.E. and Holland, J.H.,** "Classifier Systems and Genetic Algorithms," *Artificial Intelligence*, Vol. 40, pp. 235–282, 1989.

B K   **Boose, J.H. and Gaines, B.R.,** "Knowledge Acquisition for Knowledge-Based Systems: Notes on the State of the Art," *Machine Learning*, Vol. 4, 1989.

P I(a,x)   **Botta, M., Ravotto, S., Saitta, L. and Sperotto, S.B.,** "Improving Learning Using Causality and Abduction," *Proceedings of the Eighth International Workshop on Machine Learning*, Evanston, IL, pp. 480–484, Morgan Kaufmann, San Mateo, CA, 1991.

B   **Bourbakis, N.G. (Ed.),** *Proceedings of the IEEE International Workshop on Tools for Artificial Intelligence*, IEEE Computer Society Press, Washington, DC, 1989.

B   **Brachman, R.J. and Levesque, H.J. (Eds.),** *Readings in Knowledge Representation*, Morgan Kaufmann, Los Altos, CA, 1985.

B   **Brachman, R.J., Levesque, H.J. and Reiter, R. (Eds.),** *Proceedings of the 1st International Conference on Principles of Knowledge Representation and Reasoning (KR89)*, Morgan Kaufmann, San Mateo, CA, 1989.

B E a   **Bradshaw, G.L.,** "Learning to Recognize Speech Sounds: A Theory and Model," *Ph.D. Thesis,* Department of Psychology, Carnegie Mellon University, 1985.

B   **Bratko, I.,** "Machine Learning," in *Prolog Programming for Artificial Intelligence*, I. Bratko (Ed.), Addison-Wesley, Reading, MA, 1989.

B   **Bratko, I. and Lavrac, N. (Eds.),** *Progress in Machine Learning*, Sigma Press, Wilmslow, England, 1987.

B   **Brazdil, P.B. and Konolige, K. (Eds.),** *Machine Learning, Meta-Reasoning and Logics*, Kluwer Academic, Boston, 1989.

B P   **Brazdil, P., Gams, M., Sian, S., Torgo, L. and Van de Velde, W.,** "Panel: Learning in Distributed Systems and Multi-Agent Enviroments," *Proceedings of the European Working Session on Learning*, Y. Kodratoff (Ed.), Porto, Portugal, pp. 412–423, Pitman, London, 1991.

B s   **Breiman, L., Friedman, J.H., Olshen, R.A. and Stone, C.J.,** *Classification and Regression Trees*, Wadsworth, Belmont, CA, 1984.

B   **Brown, F.M.,** *The Frame Problem in Artificial Intelligence: Proceedings of the 1987 Conference*, Morgan Kaufmann, Los Altos, CA, 1987.

B E K   **Buchanan, B.G.,** "Can Machine Learning Offer Anything to Expert Systems?" *Machine Learning*, Vol. 4, pp. 251–254, 1989.

B   **Buchanan, B.G., Mitchell, T.M., Smith, R.G. and Johnson, C.R.J.,** "Models of Learning Systems," in *Encyclopedia of Computer Science and Technology*, Vol. 11, J. Belzer, A.G. Holzman and A. Kent (Eds.), Marcel Dekker, New York, 1977.

B T s   **Buntine, W.,** "Generalized Subsumption and Its Applications to Induction and Redundancy," *Artificial Intelligence*, Vol. 36, pp. 149–176, 1988.

B   **Buntine, W.,** "Myths and Legends in Learning Classification Rules," *Proceedings of AAAI-90*, T. Dietterich and W. Swartout (Eds.), pp. 736–742, AAAI Press, Menlo Park, CA, 1990.

T g   **Buntine, W.,** "Classifiers: A Theoretical and Empirical Study," *Proceedings of IJCAI-91*, pp. 638–644, AAAI Press, Menlo Park, CA, 1991.

B P a   **Carbonell, J.G.,** "Learning by Analogy: Formulating and Generalizing Plans from Past Experience," in *Machine Learning: An Artificial Intelligence Approach*, Vol. I, R.S. Michalski, J.G. Carbonell and T.M. Mitchell (Eds.), Tioga/Morgan Kaufmann, Los Altos, CA, 1983.

B P a   **Carbonell, J.G.,** "Derivational Analogy: A Theory of Reconstructive Problem Solving and Expertise Acquisition," in *Machine Learning: An Artificial Intelligence Approach*, Vol. II, R.S. Michalski, J.G. Carbonell and T.M. Mitchell (Eds.), Morgan Kaufmann, Los Altos, CA, 1986.

B   **Carbonell, J.G.,** "Introduction: Paradigms for Machine Learning," *Artificial Intelligence*, Vol. 40, pp. 1–9, 1989.

B   **Carbonell, J.G.,** *Machine Learning: Paradigms and Methods*, The MIT Press, Cambridge, MA, 1990.

B   **Carbonell, J.G. and Langley, P.W.,** "Machine Learning," in *Encyclopedia of Artificial Intelligence*, S.C. Shapiro (Ed.), John Wiley & Sons, New York, 1987.

B   **Carbonell, J.G., Michalski, R.S. and Mitchell, T.M.,** "An
               Overview of Machine Learning," in *Machine Learning: An
               Artificial Intelligence Approach*, Vol. I, R.S. Michalski, J.G.
               Carbonell and T.M. Mitchell (Eds.), Tioga/Morgan Kaufmann, Los
               Altos, CA, 1983.

B   **Carbonell, J.G., Michalski, R.S. and Mitchell, T.M.,** "Machine
               Learning: A Historical and Methodological Analysis," in *Readings
               from AI Magazine, Vols. 1–5, 1980–1985*, R. Engelmore (Ed.),
               American Association for Artificial Intelligence, Menlo Park, CA,
               1988.

B   **Carnap, R.,** *Logical Foundations of Probability*, University of
               Chicago Press, Chicago, 1950.

E I(s,x)   **Carpineto, C.,** "An Approach Based on Integrated Learning to
               Generating Stories from Stories," *Proceedings of the 5th
               International Conference on Machine Learning*, Ann Arbor, MI,
               pp. 298–304, Morgan Kaufmann, San Mateo, CA, 1988.

I(s,x)   **Carpineto, C.,** "Inductive Refinement of Causal Theories,"
               Reports of Machine Learning and Inference Laboratory, MLI
               89–3, George Mason University, Center for AI, Fairfax, VA, 1989.

I(s,x)   **Carpineto, C.,** "Analytical Negative Generalization and Empirical
               Negative Generalization Are Not Cumulative: A Case Study,"
               Proceedings of the European Working Session on Learning, Y.
               Kodratoff (Ed.), Porto, Portugal, pp. 81–88, Springer-Verlag, New
               York, 1991.

B n   **Charniak, E.,** "Bayesian Networks without Tears," *AI Magazine*,
               Vol. 12, No. 4, pp. 50–63, 1991.

B   **Charniak, E. and McDermott, D.,** *Introduction to Artificial
               Intelligence*, Addison-Wesley, Reading, MA, 1985.

B c   **Cheeseman, P., Kelly, J., Self, M., Stutz, J., Taylor, W. and
               Freeman, D.,** "AutoClass: A Bayesian Classification System,"
               *Proceedings of the 5th International Conference on Machine
               Learning*, Ann Arbor, MI, pp. 54–64, Morgan Kaufmann, San
               Mateo, CA, 1988.

B E   **Chien, S., Whitehall, B., Dietterich, T., Doyle, R.,
               Falkenhainer, B., Garrett, J., and Lu, S.,** "Machine Learning in
               Engineering Automation," *Proceedings of the Eighth International
               Workshop on Machine Learning*, Evanston, IL, pp. 577–580,
               Morgan Kaufmann, San Mateo, CA, 1991.

B   **Chomsky, N.,** *Syntactic Structures*, Mouton, The Hague, 1957.

B   **Chomsky, N.,** *Aspects of the Theory of Syntax*, MIT Press, Cambridge, MA, 1965.

B E   **Clark, P., Cestik, B., Sammut, C. and Stender, J.,** "Panel: Applications of Machine Learning: Notes from the Panel Members," *Proceedings of the European Working Session on Learning*, Y. Kodratoff (Ed.), Porto, Portugal, pp. 457–462, Springer-Verlag, New York, 1991.

B   **Cohen, P.R.,** *Heuristic Reasoning about Uncertainty: An AI Approach*, Pitman, Boston, 1985.

B   **Cohen, P.R.,** "Methodological Problems, a Model-Based Design and Analysis Methodology, and an Example," *Proceedings of the 5th International Symposium on Methodologies for Intelligent Systems*, Z.W. Ras, M. Zemankova and M.L. Emrich (Eds.), Knoxville, TN, pp. 33–50, Elsevier Science Publishing, New York, 1990.

B   **Cohen, P.R. and Feigenbaum, E.A. (Eds.),** *The Handbook of Artificial Intelligence*, Vol. III, HeurisTech Press/William Kaufmann, Stanford, CA, 1981.

I(v,x)   **Cohen, W.W.,** "Learning Approximate Control Rules of High Utility," *Proceedings of the 7th International Conference on Machine Learning*, B.W. Porter and R.J. Mooney (Eds.), Austin, TX, pp. 268–276, Morgan Kaufmann, San Mateo, CA, 1990.

B M   **Collins, A. and Michalski, R.S.,** "The Logic of Plausible Reasoning: A Core Theory," *Cognitive Science*, Vol. 13, pp. 1–51, 1989.

B M   **Collins, A., and Smith, E.E.,** *Readings in Cognitive Science: A Perspective from Psychology and Artificial Intelligence*, Morgan Kaufmann, San Mateo, CA, 1988.

B   **Collins, A.M.,** "Fragments of a Theory of Human Plausible Reasoning," in *Theoretical Issues in Natural Language Processing II*, D. Waltz (Ed.) University of Illinois, Urbana, Illinois, pp. 194–201, 1978.

I(a,x)   **Cox, M. and Ram, A.,** "Using Introspective Reasoning to Select Learning Strategies," *Proceedings of the First International Workshop on Multistrategy Learning*, R.S. Michalski and G. Tecuci (Eds.), Harpers Ferry, WV, pp. 217–230, George Mason Univ., Center for AI, Fairfax, VA, 1991.

I(a,x)M   **Cox, M. and Ram, A.,** "Multistrategy Learning with Introspective Meta-Explanations," *Proceedings of the 9th International Conference on Machine Learning*, Aberdeen, Scotland, Morgan Kaufmann, San Mateo, CA, 1992.

B   **Crowder, R.G.,** *Principles of Learning and Memory*, Lawrence Erlbaum Associates, Hillsdale, NJ, 1976.

I(s,x)   **Danyluk, A.P.,** "The Use of Explanations for Similarity-Based Learning," *Proceedings of IJCAI-87*, pp. 274–276, AAAI Press, Menlo Park, CA, 1987.

I(s,x)   **Danyluk, A.P.,** "Integrated Learning Is a Two-Way Street," *Proceedings of the AAAI 1988 Symposium on Explanation-Based Learning*, Stanford, CA, pp. 36–40, 1988.

I(s,x)   **Danyluk, A.P.,** "Finding New Rules for Incomplete Theories: Explicit Biases for Induction with Contextual Information," *Proceedings of the 6th International Workshop on Machine Learning*, Ithaca, NY, pp. 34–36, Morgan Kaufmann, San Mateo, CA, 1989.

I(s,x,c)   **Danyluk, A.P.,** "Gemini: An Integration of Analytical and Empirical Learning," *Proceedings of the First International Workshop on Multistrategy Learning*, R.S. Michalski and G. Tecuci (Eds.), Harpers Ferry, WV, pp. 191–206, George Mason Univ., Center for AI, Fairfax, VA, 1991.

I(s,x,c)   **Danyluk, A.P.,** "Gemini: An Integration of Analytical and Empirical Learning," in *Machine Learning: A Multistrategy Approach*, Vol. IV, R.S. Michalski and G. Tecuci (Eds.), Morgan Kaufmann, San Mateo, CA, 1994.

B a   **Davies, T.R. and Russell, S.J.,** "A Logical Approach to Reasoning by Analogy," *Proceedings of IJCAI-87*, pp. 264–270, AAAI Press, Menlo Park, CA, 1987.

B g   **Davis, D.,** *Genetic Algorithms and Simulated Annealing*, Pitman Press, Cambridge, MA, 1987.

B   **Davis, E.,** *Representations of Commonsense Knowledge*, Morgan Kaufmann, Los Altos, CA, 1990.

I(g,v)   **Davis, L.,** "Bit-Climbing, Representational Bias, and Test Suite Design," *Proceedings of the 4th International Conference on Genetic Algorithms*, San Diego, CA, pp. 18–23, Morgan Kaufmann, San Mateo, CA, 1991.

B g   **Davis, L. (Ed.),** *Handbook of Genetic Algorithms*, Van Nostrand Reinhold, New York, 1991.

B   **Davis, R. and Lenat, D.B. (Eds.),** *Knowledge-Based Systems in Artificial Intelligence,* McGraw-Hill, New York, 1980.

B P   **Dean, T. and Wellman, M.P.,** *Planning and Control,* Morgan Kaufmann, San Mateo, CA, 1991.

B   **Dean, T.L. and McKeown, K. (Eds.),** *Proceedings of AAAI-91, Ninth National Conference on Artificial Intelligence,* AAAI Press, Menlo Park, CA, 1991.

B   **Defays, D.,** "Statistics and Artificial Intelligence," *Proceedings of the Conference on Data Analysis, Learning Symbolic and Numeric Knowledge,* INRIA, Antibes, pp. 381–388, Nova Science Publishers, Lommack, NY, 1989.

I(g,n)   **DeGaris, H.,** "Genetic Programming," *Proceedings of the 7th International Conference on Machine Learning,* B.W. Porter and R.J. Mooney (Eds.), Austin, TX, pp. 132–139, Morgan Kaufmann, San Mateo, CA, 1990.

I(g,n)   **De Garis, H.,** "Using the Genetic Algorithm to Train Time Dependent Behaviors in Neural Networks," *Proceedings of the First International Workshop on Multistrategy Learning,* R.S. Michalski and G. Tecuci (Eds.), Harpers Ferry, WV, pp. 273–280, George Mason Univ., Center for AI, Fairfax, VA, 1991.

I(g,n)   **De Garis, H.,** "Genetic Programming: Evolutionary Approaches to Multistrategy Learning," in *Machine Learning: A Multistrategy Approach,* Vol. IV, R.S. Michalski and G. Tecuci (Eds.), Morgan Kaufmann, San Mateo, CA, 1994.

B x   **DeJong, G.F. and Mooney, R.,** "Explanation-Based Learning: An Alternative View," *Machine Learning,* Vol. 1, No. 2, pp. 145–176, 1986.

B g   **DeJong, K.A.,** "An Analysis of the Behavior of a Class of Genetic Adaptive Systems," *Ph.D. Thesis,* University of Michigan, 1975.

B g   **DeJong, K.A.,** "On Using Genetic Algorithms to Search Program Spaces," *Proceedings of the 2nd International Conference on Genetic Algorithms,* Cambridge, MA, pp. 210–216, Morgan Kaufmann, San Mateo, CA, 1987.

B g   **DeJong, K.A.,** "Learning with Genetic Algorithms: An Overview," *Machine Learning,* Vol. 3, pp. 121–138, 1988.

B g   **DeJong, K.A.,** "The Genetic Algorithm Approach to Machine Learning," in *Machine Learning: An Artificial Intelligence Approach,* Vol. III, Y. Kodratoff and R.S. Michalski (Eds.), Morgan Kaufmann, San Mateo, CA, 1990.

I(s,v,a) K   **De Raedt, L. and Bruynooghe, M.,** "CLINT: A Multistrategy Interactive Concept Learner and Theory Revision System," *Proceedings of the First International Workshop on Multistrategy Learning*, R.S. Michalski and G. Tecuci (Eds.), Harpers Ferry, WV, pp. 175–190, George Mason Univ., Center for AI, Fairfax, VA, 1991.

I(s,v,a) K   **De Raedt, L. and Bruynooghe, M.,** "Interactive Theory Revision," in *Machine Learning: A Multistrategy Approach*, Vol. IV, R.S. Michalski and G. Tecuci (Eds.), Morgan Kaufmann, San Mateo, CA, 1994.

I(s,v)   **De Raedt, L., Bruynooghe, M., and Martens, B.,** "Integrity Constraints and Interactive Concept-Learning," *Proceedings of the Eighth International Workshop on Machine Learning*, Evanston, IL, pp. 394–398, Morgan Kaufmann, San Mateo, CA, 1991.

I(a,v) K   **De Raedt, L., Feyaerts, J. and Bruynooghe, M.,** "Acquiring Object-Knowledge for Learning Systems," *Proceedings of the European Working Session on Learning*, Y. Kodratoff (Ed.), Porto, Portugal, pp. 245–264, Springer-Verlag, New York, 1991.

I(n,v)   **Diederich, J.,** " 'Learning by Instruction' in Connectionist Systems," *Proceedings of the 6th International Workshop on Machine Learning*, Ithaca, NY, pp. 66–68, Morgan Kaufmann, San Mateo, CA, 1989.

B   **Dietterich, T.G.,** "Learning at the Knowledge Level," *Machine Learning*, Vol. 1, No. 3, pp. 287–316, 1986.

I(s,x)   **Dietterich, T.G. and Flann, N.S.,** "An Inductive Approach to Solving the Imperfect Theory Problem," *Proceedings of the AAAI 1988 Symposium on Explanation-Based Learning*, Stanford University, pp. 42–46, Morgan Kaufmann, San Mateo, CA, 1988.

B E s   **Dietterich, T.G. and Michalski, R.S.,** "Inductive Learning of Structural Descriptions: Evaluation Criteria and Comparative Review of Selected Methods," *Artificial Intelligence*, Vol. 16, pp. 257–294, 1981.

B E s   **Dietterich, T.G. and Michalski, R.S.,** "A Comparative Review of Selected Methods for Learning from Examples," in *Machine Learning: An Artificial Intelligence Approach*, Vol. I, R.S. Michalski, J.G. Carbonell and T.M. Mitchell (Eds.), Tioga/Morgan Kaufmann, Los Altos, CA, 1983.

I(r,s)   **Dietterich, T.G. and Michalski, R.S.,** "Learning to Predict
               Sequences," in *Machine Learning: An Artificial Intelligence
               Approach*, Vol. II, R.S. Michalski, J.G. Carbonell and T.M.
               Mitchell (Eds.), Morgan Kaufmann, Los Altos, CA, 1986.

B   **Dietterich, T.G. and Swartout, W. (Eds.),** *Proceedings of
               AAAI-90, Eighth National Conference on Artificial Intelligence*,
               AAAI Press, Menlo Park, CA, 1990.

E I(s,n)   **Dietterich, T.G., Hild, H. and Bakiri, G.,** "A Comparative Study
               of ID3 and Backpropagation for English Text-to-Speech
               Mapping," *Proceedings of the 7th International Conference on
               Machine Learning*, B.W. Porter and R.J. Mooney (Eds.), Austin,
               TX, pp. 24–31, Morgan Kaufmann, San Mateo, CA, 1990.

B   **Dollas, A., Tsai, W.T. and Bourbakis, N.G. (Eds.),** *Proceedings
               of the 2nd International Conference on Tools for Artificial
               Intelligence*, IEEE Computer Society Press, Los Alamitos, CA,
               1990.

B   **Doyle, J.,** "A Truth Maintenance System," *Artificial Intelligence*,
               Vol. 12, pp. 231–272, 1979.

B   **Doyle, J.,** "A Model for Deliberation, Action, and Introspection,"
               Ph.D. Thesis, MIT, 1980.

I(s,v)   **Drastal, G., Meunier, R. and Raatz, S.,** "Error Correction in
               Constructive Induction," *Proceedings of the 6th International
               Workshop on Machine Learning*, Ithaca, NY, pp. 80–83, Morgan
               Kaufmann, San Mateo, CA, 1989.

B   **Duda, R.O. and Hart, P.E.,** *Pattern Classification and Scene
               Analysis*, Wiley, New York, 1973.

I(a,s,x)   **Duval, B.,** "Abduction and Induction for Explanation-Based
               Learning," *Proceedings of the European Working Session on
               Learning*, Y. Kodratoff (Ed.), Porto, Portugal, pp. 348–360,
               Springer-Verlag, New York, 1991.

I(g,n)   **Eberhart, R.,** "The Role of Genetic Algorithms in Neural
               Network Explanation Facilities and Query-Based Learning,"
               *Proceedings of the Workshop on Combinations of Genetic
               Algorithms and Neural Networks*, Baltimore, MD, 1992.

I(g,n)   **Elias, J.,** "Genetic Generation of Connection Patterns for a
               Dynamic Artificial Neural Network," *Proceedings of the
               Workshop on Combinations of Genetic Algorithms and Neural
               Networks*, Baltimore, MD, 1992.

I(s,v,x)   **Elio, R. and Watanabe, L.,** "An Incremental Deductive Strategy for Controlling Constructive Induction in Learning from Examples," *Machine Learning*, Vol. 7, pp. 7–44, 1991.

B E x   **Ellman, T.,** "Explanation-Based Learning: A Survey of Programs and Perspectives," *ACM Computing Surveys*, Vol. 21, No. 2, pp. 163–222, 1989.

I(a,d)   **Falkenhainer, B.C.,** "Scientific Theory Formation through Analogical Inference," *Proceedings of the 4th International Machine Learning Workshop*, University of California, Irvine, pp. 218–229, Morgan Kaufmann, San Mateo, CA, 1987.

I(d,v,x)   **Falkenhainer, B.C.,** "A Unified Approach to Explanation and Theory Formulation," in *Computational Models of Scientific Discovery and Theory Formation*, J. Shrager and P.W. Langley (Eds.), Morgan Kaufmann, San Mateo, CA, 1990.

I(d,v,x)   **Falkenhainer, B.C. and Michalski, R.S.,** "Integrating Quantitative and Qualitative Discovery in ABACUS," in *Machine Learning: An Artificial Intelligence Approach*, Vol. III, Y. Kodratoff and R.S. Michalski (Eds.), Morgan Kaufmann, San Mateo, CA, 1990.

I(d,x)   **Falkenhainer, B.C. and Rajamoney, S.,** "The Interdependences of Theory Formation, Revision, and Experimentation," *Proceedings of the 5th International Conference on Machine Learning*, Ann Arbor, MI, pp. 353–366, Morgan Kaufmann, San Mateo, CA, 1988.

I(v,x) P   **Fawcett, T.E. and Utgoff, P.E.,** "A Hybrid Method for Feature Generation," *Proceedings of the Eighth International Workshop on Machine Learning*, Evanston, IL, pp. 137–141, Morgan Kaufmann, San Mateo, CA, 1991.

B c   **Feigenbaum, E.A.,** "A Simulation of Verbal Learning," *Proceedings of the Western Joint Computer Conference*, Los Angeles, pp. 121–132, 1961.

B P   **Fikes, R.E., Hart, P.E. and Nilsson, N.J.,** "Learning and Executing Generalized Robot Plans," *Artificial Intelligence*, Vol. 3, pp. 251–288, 1972.

B   **Firebaugh, M.W.,** *Artificial Intelligence: A Knowledge-Based Approach*, Boyd and Fraser, Boston, 1988.

B c   **Fisher, D.H.,** "Knowledge Acquisition Via Incremental Conceptual Clustering," *Machine Learning*, Vol. 2, No. 2, pp. 139–172, 1987.

B   **Fisher, D., Pazzani, M.J. and Langley, P.W. (Eds.),** *Concept Formation: Knowledge and Experience in Unsupervised Learning,* Morgan Kaufmann, San Mateo, CA, 1991.

B I(s,x)   **Flann, N.S. and Dietterich, T.G.,** "A Study of Explanation-Based Methods for Inductive Learning," *Machine Learning,* Vol. 4, No. 2, pp. 187–266, 1989.

B   **Forbus, K. and Shrobe, H. (Eds.),** *Proceedings of AAAI-87, Sixth National Conference on Artificial Intelligence,* AAAI Press, Menlo Park, CA, 1987.

B   **Forsyth, R. and Rada, R.,** *Machine Learning: Applications in Expert Systems and Information Retrieval,* Ellis Horwood Ltd., Chichester, England, 1986.

E I(s,x)   **Friedrich, G. and Nejdl, W.,** "Using Domain Knowledge to Improve Inductive Learning Algorithms for Diagnosis," *Proceedings of the 6th International Workshop on Machine Learning,* Ithaca, NY, pp. 75–77, Morgan Kaufmann, San Mateo, CA, 1989.

B E P   **Fu, K.S.,** "Learning Control Systems—Review and Outlook," *IEEE Transactions on Pattern Analysis and Machine Intelligence,* PAMI-8, No. 3, pp. 327, 1986.

B   **Fu, K.S. and Booth, T.L.,** "Grammatical Inference: Introduction and Survey," *IEEE Transactions on Pattern Analysis and Machine Intelligence,* PAMI-8, No. 3, pp. 343–380, 1986.

B T   **Fulk, M. and Case, J. (Eds.),** *Proceedings of the 3rd Annual Workshop on Computational Learning Theory,* Morgan Kaufmann, San Mateo, CA, 1990.

B   **Gale, W.A.,** *AI and Statistics,* Addison-Wesley, Reading, MA, 1986.

B M   **Gams, M.,** "Human Multistrategy Learning," *Proceedings of the First International Workshop on Multistrategy Learning,* R.S. Michalski and G. Tecuci (Eds.), Harpers Ferry, WV, pp. 355–360, George Mason Univ., Center for AI, Fairfax, VA, 1991.

B M   **Gardner, H.,** *The Mind's New Science: A History of the Cognitive Revolution,* Basic Books, New York, 1985.

I(s,x)   **Gemello, R., Mana, F. and Saitta, L.,** "Rigel: An Inductive Learning System," *Machine Learning,* Vol. 6, pp. 7–35, 1991.

B   **Genesereth, M.R. and Nilsson, N.J.,** *Logical Foundations of Artificial Intelligence,* Morgan Kaufmann, San Mateo, CA, 1987.

I(a,v,x) **Genest, J., Matwin, S. and Plante, B.,** "Explanation-Based Learning with Incomplete Theories: A Three-Step Approach," *Proceedings of the 7th International Conference on Machine Learning*, B.W. Porter and R.J. Mooney (Eds.), Austin, TX, pp. 286–294, Morgan Kaufmann, San Mateo, CA, 1990.

B a **Gentner, D.,** "The Mechanisms of Analogical Learning," in *Similarity and Analogical Reasoning*, S. Vosniadou and A. Ortony (Eds.), Cambridge University Press, London, 1989.

B **Georgeff, M.P. and Lansky, A.L.,** *Reasoning about Actions and Plans: Proceedings of the 1986 Workshop*, Morgan Kaufmann, Los Altos, CA, 1987.

B **Giarratano, J. and Riley, G.,** *Expert Systems: Principles and Programming*, PWS-KENT Publishing Company, Boston, MA, 1989.

B **Ginsberg, M.L. (Ed.),** *Readings in Nonmonotonic Reasoning*, Morgan Kaufmann, Los Altos, CA, 1987.

I(s,x) **Giordana, A., Roverso, D. and Saitta, L.,** "Abstracting Background Knowledge for Concept Learning," *Proceedings of the European Working Session on Learning*, Y. Kodratoff (Ed.), Porto, Portugal, pp. 1–13, Springer-Verlag, New York, 1991.

I(s,v) T **Giordana, A., Saitta, L. and Roverso, D.,** "Abstracting Concepts with Inverse Resolution," *Proceedings of the Eighth International Workshop on Machine Learning*, Evanston, IL, pp. 142–146, Morgan Kaufmann, San Mateo, CA, 1991.

B d **Glymour, C., Scheins, R., Spirites, P. and Kelly, K.,** *Discovering Causal Structure*, Academic Press, San Diego, CA, 1987.

B **Gold, E.,** "Language Identification in the Limit," *Information and Control*, Vol. 16, pp. 447–474, 1967.

B P I(g,s) **Goldberg, D.E.,** "Computer-Aided Gas Pipeline Operation Using Genetic Algorithms and Rule Learning," *Ph.D. Thesis,* University of Michigan, 1983.

B g **Goldberg, D.E.,** *Genetic Algorithms in Search, Optimization, and Machine Learning*, Addison-Wesley, Reading, MA, 1989.

I(g,x) P **Gordon, D.F.,** "An Enhancer for Reactive Plans," *Proceedings of the Eighth International Workshop on Machine Learning*, Evanston, IL, pp. 505–509, Morgan Kaufmann, San Mateo, CA, 1991.

I(g,x)   **Gordon, D.F. and Grefenstette, J.J.,** "Explanations of
                Empirically Derived Reactive Plans," *Proceedings of the 7th
                International Conference on Machine Learning*, B.W. Porter and
                R.J. Mooney (Eds.), Austin, TX, pp. 198–203, Morgan Kaufmann,
                San Mateo, CA, 1990.

I(g,x)   **Gould, J. and Levinson, R.,** "Method Integration for
                Experience-Based Learning," *Proceedings of the First
                International Workshop on Multistrategy Learning*, R.S. Michalski
                and G. Tecuci (Eds.), Harpers Ferry, WV, pp. 378–394, George
                Mason Univ., Center for AI, Fairfax, VA, 1991.

I(g,x)   **Gould, J. and Levinson, R.,** "Experience-Based Adaptive
                Search," in *Machine Learning: A Multistrategy Approach*, Vol. IV,
                R.S. Michalski and G. Tecuci (Eds.), Morgan Kaufmann, San
                Mateo, CA, 1994.

I(s,v)   **Granger, R. and Schlimmer, J.,** "Combining Numeric and
                Symbolic Learning Techniques," *Proceedings of the 3rd
                International Machine Learning Workshop*, Skytop, PA, Morgan
                Kaufmann, San Mateo, CA, 1985.

B   **Graubard, S.R.,** *The Artificial Intelligence Debate: False Starts,
                Real Foundations*, The MIT Press, Cambridge, MA, 1989.

I(c,d,r)   **Greene, G.H.,** "The Abacus 2 System for Quantitative Discovery:
                Using Dependencies to Discover Non-Linear Terms," *Reports of
                Machine Learning and Inference Laboratory*, MLI 88–4, George
                Mason Univ., Center for AI, Fairfax, VA, 1988.

B g   **Grefenstette, J.J. (Ed.),** *Proceedings of the 1st International
                Conference on Genetic Algorithms and Their Applications*,
                University of Pittsburgh, PA, 1985.

B g   **Grefenstette, J.J. (Ed.),** *Proceedings of the 2nd International
                Conference on Genetic Algorithms and Their Applications*,
                Lawrence Erlbaum Associates, Hillsdale, NJ, 1987.

B P g   **Grefenstette, J.J.,** "Credit Assignment in Rule Discovery Systems
                Based on Genetic Algorithms," *Machine Learning*, Vol. 3, pp.
                225–245, 1988.

B g   **Grefenstette, J.J.,** "Genetic Algorithms and Their Applications,"
                in *The Encyclopedia of Computer Science and Technology*, A.
                Kent and J.G. Williams (Eds.), Marcel Dekker, New York, 1988.

B a   **Greiner, R.,** "Learning by Understanding Analogies," *Ph.D.
                Thesis,* Computer Science Dept., Stanford University, 1985.

B   **Greiner, R. and Lenat, D.B.,** "A Representation Language Language," *Proceedings of AAAI-80*, pp. 165–169, AAAI Press, Menlo Park, CA, 1980.

I(g,n)   **Gruau, F.,** "Genetic Synthesis of Boolean Neural Networks with a Cell Rewriting Developmental Process," *Proceedings of the Workshop on Combinations of Genetic Algorithms and Neural Networks*, Baltimore, MD, 1992.

E K I(n,s)   **Gutknecht, M., Pfeifer, R. and Stolze, M.,** "Cooperative Hybrid Systems," *Proceedings of IJCAI-91*, pp. 824–829, AAAI Press, Menlo Park, CA, 1991.

I(n,s)   **Hall, L.O. and Romaniuk, S.G.,** "A Hybrid Connectionist, Symbolic Learning System," *Proceedings of AAAI-90*, T. Dietterich and W. Swartout (Eds.), pp. 783–788, AAAI Press, Menlo Park, CA, 1990.

B E I(s,x)   **Hall, R.J.,** "Learning by Failing to Explain Using Partial Explanations to Learn in Incomplete or Intractable Domains," *Machine Learning*, Vol. 3, No. 1, pp. 45–78, 1988.

B   **Halpern, J.P.,** *Theoretical Aspects of Reasoning about Knowledge: Proceedings of the 1st Conference (TARK 1986)*, Morgan Kaufmann, Los Altos, CA, 1986.

I(s,x)   **Hamakawa, R.,** "Revision Cost for Theory Refinement," *Proceedings of the Eighth International Workshop on Machine Learning*, Evanston, IL, pp. 514–518, Morgan Kaufmann, San Mateo, CA, 1991.

B   **Hamburger, H. and Wexler, K.,** "A Mathematical Theory of Learning Transformational Grammar," *Journal of Mathematical Psychology*, Vol. 12, pp. 137–177, 1975.

B a   **Hammond, K. (Ed.),** *Proceedings of Case-Based Reasoning Workshop*, Pensacola Beach, FL, Morgan Kaufmann, San Mateo, CA, 1989.

B a   **Hammond, K.J.,** "CHEF," in *Inside Case-Based Reasoning*, C.K. Reisbeck and R.C. Schank (Eds.), Lawrence Erlbaum Associates, Hillsdale, NJ, 1989.

B T s   **Haussler, D.,** "Quantifying Inductive Bias: AI Learning Algorithms and Valiant's Learning Framework," *Artificial Intelligence*, Vol. 36, pp. 177–221, 1988.

B T   **Haussler, D. and Pitt, L. (Eds.),** *Proceedings of the 1988 Workshop on Computational Learning Theory*, Morgan Kaufmann, San Mateo, CA, 1988.

B P   **Hayes-Roth, F.,** "Using Proofs and Refutations to Learn from Experience," in *Machine Learning: An Artificial Intelligence Approach*, Vol. I, R.S. Michalski, J.G. Carbonell and T.M. Mitchell (Eds.), Tioga/Morgan Kaufmann, Los Altos, CA, 1983.

B   **Hayes-Roth, F. and McDermott, J.,** "An Interference Matching Technique for Inducing Abstractions," *Communications of the ACM*, Vol. 26, pp. 410–410, 1978.

B   **Hayes-Roth, F., Klahr, P. and Mostow, D.,** "Advice-Taking and Knowledge Refinement: An Iterative View of Skill Acquisition," in *Cognitive Skills and Their Acquisition*, J.R. Anderson (Ed.), Lawrence Erlbaum Associates, Hillsdale, NJ, 1981.

B n   **Hecht-Nielsen, et al. (Eds.),** *Proceedings of the International Joint Conference on Neural Networks*, Vol. I & II, IEEE TAB Neural Network Committee, IEEE Computer Society, Washington, DC, 1989.

B M a   **Helman, D.H. (Ed.),** *Analogical Reasoning*, Kluwer Academic, Boston, 1988.

I(a,n) K P **Henrion, M., Breese and J.S., Horvitz, E.J.,** "Decision Analysis and Expert Systems," *AI Magazine*, Vol. 12, No. 4, pp. 64–91, 1991.

B n   **Hinton, G.E. and Anderson, J.A. (Eds.),** *Parallel Models of Associative Memory*, Lawrence Erlbaum Associates, Hillsdale, NJ, 1981.

B M a   **Hofstadter, D.R.,** *Analogies and Roles in Human and Machine Thinking*, Basic Books, New York, 1985.

B   **Hofstadter, D.R.,** *Metamagical Themas: Questing for the Essence of Mind and Pattern*, Basic Books, New York, 1985.

E I(s,x)   **Holder, L.B.,** "Selection of Learning Methods Using an Adaptive Model of Knowledge Utility," *Proceedings of the First International Workshop on Multistrategy Learning*, R.S. Michalski and G. Tecuci (Eds.), Harpers Ferry, WV, pp. 247–254, George Mason Univ., Center for AI, Fairfax, VA, 1991.

B g   **Holland, J.H.,** *Adaptation in Natural and Artificial Systems*, University of Michigan Press, Ann Arbor, MI, 1975.

B g   **Holland, J.H.,** "Genetic Algorithms and Classifier Systems: Foundations and Future Directions," *Proceedings of the 2nd International Conference on Genetic Algorithms*, Cambridge, MA, pp. 82–89, Morgan Kaufmann, San Mateo, CA, 1987.

B d,g,s   **Holland, J.H., Holyoak, K., Nisbett, R. and Thagard, P.,** *Induction: Processes of Inference, Learning and Discovery*, MIT Press, Cambridge, MA, 1986.

B n   **Hopfield, J.,** "Neural Networks and Physical Systems with Emergent Collective Computational Abilities," *Proceedings of the National Academy of Sciences USA*, Vol. 79, pp. 2554–2558, National Academy of Sciences of the USA, Washington, DC, 1982.

B n   **Hopfield, J.,** "Neurons with Graded Response Have Comparable Properties Like Those of 2-State Neurons," *Proceedings of the National Academy of Sciences USA*, Vol. 81, pp. 3088–3092, National Academy of Sciences of the USA, Washington, DC, 1984.

B   **Horning, J.J.,** "A Study of Grammatical Inference," *Technical Report*, CS-139, Computer Science Dept., Stanford University, 1969.

B   **Hunt, E.B., Marin, J. and Stone, P.J.,** *Experiments in Induction*, Academic Press, San Diego, CA, 1966.

E K   **Hunter, L.E.,** "Knowledge Acquisition Planning: Results and Prospects," *Proceedings of the 6th International Workshop on Machine Learning*, Ithaca, NY, pp. 61–65, Morgan Kaufmann, San Mateo, CA, 1989.

M   **Hunter, L.E.,** "Planning to Learn," *Proceedings of the 12th Annual Conference of the Cognitive Science Society*, Boston, MA, pp. 26–34, Lawrence Erlbaum, Hillsdale, NJ, 1990.

E I(c,n)   **Hunter, L.E.,** "Classifying for Prediction: A Multistrategy Approach to Predicting Protein Structure," *Proceedings of the First International Workshop on Multistrategy Learning*, R.S. Michalski and G. Tecuci (Eds.), Harpers Ferry, WV, pp. 394–402, George Mason Univ., Center for AI, Fairfax, VA, 1991.

E I(c,n)   **Hunter, L.E.,** "Classifying for Prediction: A Multistrategy Approach to Predicting Protein Structure," in *Machine Learning: A Multistrategy Approach*, Vol. IV, R.S. Michalski and G. Tecuci (Eds.), Morgan Kaufmann, San Mateo, CA, 1994.

B M   **Johnson-Laird, P.N.,** *Mental Models: Toward a Cognitive Science of Language, Inference, and Consciousness*, Harvard University Press, Cambridge, MA, 1983.

B   **Joshi, A. (Ed.),** *Proceedings of the 9th International Joint Conference on Artificial Intelligence*, Morgan Kaufmann, San Mateo, CA, 1985.

B T n   **Judd, S.,** "On the Complexity of Loading Shallow Neural Networks," *Journal of Complexity,* Vol. 4, pp. 177–192, 1988.

I(g,n)   **Kadaba, N. and Nygard, K.E.,** "Improving the Performance of Genetic Algorithms in Automated Discovery of Parameters," *Proceedings of the 7th International Conference on Machine Learning,* B.W. Porter and R.J. Mooney (Eds.), Austin, TX, pp. 140–148, Morgan Kaufmann, San Mateo, CA, 1990.

B   **Kahneman, D., Slovic, P. and Tversky, A.,** *Judgement under Uncertainty: Heuristics and Biases,* Cambridge University Press, Cambridge, UK, 1982.

B   **Kanal, L.N. and Lemmer, J. (Eds.),** *Uncertainty in Artificial Intelligence,* North-Holland, Amsterdam, 1986.

I(a,x)   **Kass, A.,** "Adaptation-Based Explanation: Explanations as Cases," *Proceedings of the 6th International Workshop on Machine Learning,* Ithaca, NY, pp. 49–51, Morgan Kaufmann, San Mateo, CA, 1989.

E I(c,d,r,s) **Kaufman, K.A., Michalski, R.S. and Schultz, A.C.,** "EMERALD 1: An Integrated System of Machine Learning and Discovery Programs for Education and Research," User's guide MLI-89–12, George Mason Univ., Center for AI, Fairfax, VA, 1989.

E M   **Kazman, R.,** "Babel: A Psychologically Plausible Cross-Linguistic Model of Lexical and Syntactic Acquisition," *Proceedings of the Eighth International Workshop on Machine Learning,* Evanston, IL, pp. 75–79, Morgan Kaufmann, San Mateo, CA, 1991.

B a   **Kedar-Cabelli, S.T.,** "Toward a Computational Model of Purpose-Directed Analogy," in *Analogica,* A. Prieditis (Ed.), Pitman, London, 1985.

B   **Kehler, T. and Rosenschein, S. (Eds.),** *Proceedings of AAAI-86, Fifth National Conference on Artificial Intelligence,* Morgan Kaufmann, San Mateo, CA, 1986.

B P x   **Keller, R.M.,** "Defining Operationality for Explanation-Based Learning," *Artificial Intelligence,* Vol. 35, pp. 227–241, 1988.

I(g)   **Kelly, J.D. and Davis, L.,** "Hybridizing the Genetic Algorithm and the K Nearest Neighbors Classification Algorithm," *Proceedings of the 4th International Conference on Genetic Algorithms,* San Diego, CA, pp. 377–383, Morgan Kaufmann, San Mateo, CA, 1991.

I(g,s)   **Kelly, J.D.J. and Davis, L.,** "A Hybrid Genetic Algorithm for
            Classification," *Proceedings of IJCAI-91*, pp. 645–650, AAAI
            Press, Menlo Park, CA, 1991.

B s   **Kibler, D. and Aha, D.W.,** "Learning Representative Exemplars
            of Concepts: An Initial Case Study," *Proceedings of the 4th
            International Machine Learning Workshop*, University of
            California, Irvine, CA, pp. 24–30, Morgan Kaufmann, San Mateo,
            CA, 1987.

B   **Kibler, D. and Langley, P.W.,** "Machine Learning as an
            Experimental Science," *Proceedings of EWSL-88*, Glasgow,
            Scotland, pp. 81–92, Pitman, London, 1988.

B   **Klein, S. and Kuppin, M.,** "An Interactive Heuristic Program for
            Learning Transformational Grammars," *Computer Studies in the
            Humanities and Verbal Behavior*, Vol. 3, pp. 144–162, 1970.

I(s,x)   **Knight, K. and Gil, Y.,** "Automated Rationalization,"
            *Proceedings of the First International Workshop on Multistrategy
            Learning*, R.S. Michalski and G. Tecuci (Eds.), Harpers Ferry,
            WV, pp. 281–288, George Mason Univ., Center for AI, Fairfax,
            VA, 1991.

B   **Knobe, B. and Knobe, K.,** "A Method for Inferring Context-Free
            Grammars," *Information and Control*, Vol. 31, pp. 129–146, 1977.

I(s,x) P   **Knoblock, C.A., Minton, S. and Etzioni, O.,** "Integrating
            Abstraction and Explanation-Based Learning in PRODIGY,"
            Proceedings of AAAI-91, pp. 541–546, AAAI Press, Menlo Park,
            CA, 1991.

I(s,x)   **Ko, H. and Michalski, R.S.,** "Types of Explanations and Their
            Role in Constructive Closed-Loop Learning," *Reports of Machine
            Learning and Inference Laboratory*, MLI 88–2, George Mason
            Univ., Center for AI, Fairfax, VA, 1988.

B   **Kodratoff, Y.,** *Introduction to Machine Learning*, Pitman,
            London, 1988.

B E   **Kodratoff, Y.,** "Characterizing Machine Learning Programs: A
            European Compilation," *Reports of the Machine Learning and
            Inference Laboratory*, MLI 89–1, George Mason Univ., Center for
            AI, Fairfax, VA, 1989.

B E   **Kodratoff, Y.,** "Characterizing Machine Learning Programs,"
            Artificial Intelligence: The State-of-the-Art, D. Sleeman (Ed.),
            Pitman, London, 1989.

K I(a,x) P   **Kodratoff, Y.,** "Learning Expert Knowledge by Improving the Explanations Provided by the System," in *Machine Learning: An Artificial Intelligence Approach*, Vol. III, Y. Kodratoff and R.S. Michalski (Eds.), Morgan Kaufmann, San Mateo, CA, 1990.

B   **Kodratoff, Y.,** "Induction and the Organization of Knowledge," *Proceedings of the First International Workshop on Multistrategy Learning*, R.S. Michalski and G. Tecuci (Eds.), Harpers Ferry, WV, pp. 34–48, George Mason Univ., Center for AI, Fairfax, VA, 1991.

B   **Kodratoff, Y.,** "Induction and the Organization of Knowledge," in *Machine Learning: A Multistrategy Approach*, Vol. IV, R.S. Michalski and G. Tecuci (Eds.), Morgan Kaufmann, San Mateo, CA, 1994.

B E   **Kodratoff, Y., and Hutchinson, A.,** *Machine and Human Learning, Advances in European Research*, Kogan Page, London, 1989.

B   **Kodratoff, Y. and Michalski, R.S. (Eds.),** *Machine Learning: An Artificial Intelligence Approach*, Vol. III, Morgan Kaufmann, San Mateo, CA, 1990.

I(s,x) K P   **Kodratoff, Y. and Tecuci, G.,** "Rule Learning in DISCIPLE," *Proceedings of the First European Working Session on Learning*, Orsay, France, 1986.

I(a,s,x) K P **Kodratoff, Y. and Tecuci, G.,** "DISCIPLE1: A Learning Apprentice System for Weak Theory Domains," *Proceedings of the 10th International Joint Conference on Artificial Intelligence*, pp. 271–273, AAAI Press, Menlo Park, CA, 1987.

E I(a,s,x) K P **Kodratoff, Y. and Tecuci, G.,** "Techniques of Design and DISCIPLE Learning Apprentice," *International Journal on Expert Systems: Research and Applications*, Vol. 1, No. 1, pp. 39–66, 1987.

B c   **Kohonen, T.,** "Self-Organized Formation of Topologically Correct Feature Maps," *Biological Cybernetics*, Vol. 43, pp. 59–69, 1982.

I(s,v)   **Kokar, M.M. and Zadrozny, W.,** "A Logic Structure of a Learning Agent," *Proceedings of the 4th International Symposium on Methodologies for Intelligent Systems*, pp. 305–312, 1989.

B a   **Kolodner, J.L. (Ed.),** *Proceedings of the Case-Based Reasoning Workshop*, Clearwater Beach, FL, 1988.

B T s   **Kononenko, I. and Bratko, I.,** "Information-Based Evaluation Criterion for Classifier's Performance," *Machine Learning*, Vol. 6, pp. 67–80, 1991.

B   **Kowalski, R.,** *Logic for Problem Solving*, American Elsevier, New York, 1979.

B   **Kowalski, R. and Kuchner, D.,** "Linear Resolution with Selector Function," *Artificial Intelligence*, Vol. 2, pp. 227–260, 1971.

B M x   **Kuipers, B.,** "Commonsense Reasoning about Causality: Deriving Behavior from Structure," in *Qualitative Reasoning about Physical Systems*, D.G. Bobrow (Ed.), MIT Press, Cambridge, MA, 1985.

B P   **Laird, J.E.,** "Universal Subgoaling," *Ph.D. Thesis,* Carnegie Mellon University, 1984.

B   **Laird, J.E. (Ed.),** *Proceedings of the 5th International Conference on Machine Learning*, Morgan Kaufmann, San Mateo, CA, 1988.

B P   **Laird, J.E., Rosenbloom, P.S. and Newell, A.,** *"Universal Subgoaling and Chunking of Goal Hierarchies,"* Automating Knowledge Acquisition for Expert Systems, Kluwer Academic, Boston, 1985.

B P   **Laird, J.E., Rosenbloom, P.S. and Newell, A.,** "Chunking in SOAR: The Anatomy of a General Learning Mechanism," *Machine Learning*, Vol. 1, No. 1, pp. 11–46, 1986.

B   **Laird, P.D.,** "Learning from Good and Bad Data," *Automating Knowledge Acquisition for Expert Systems*, Kluwer Academic, Boston, 1988.

B E n   **Lang, K.J., Waibel, A.H. and Hinton, G.E.,** "A Time-Delay Neural Network Architecture for Isolated Word Recognition," *Neural Networks*, Vol. 3, pp. 33–43, 1990.

B d   **Langley, P.W.,** "Descriptive Discovery Processes: Experiments in Baconian Science," *Ph.D. Thesis,* Carnegie Mellon University, 1980.

M P   **Langley, P.W. and Allen, J.A.,** "The Acquisition of Human Planning Expertise," *Proceedings of the Eighth International Workshop on Machine Learning*, Evanston, IL, pp. 80–84, Morgan Kaufmann, San Mateo, CA, 1991.

B   **Langley, P.W. and Carbonell, J.G.,** "Approaches to Machine Learning," *Journal of the American Society for Information Science*, Vol. 2, pp. 306–316, 1984.

B   **Langley, P.W. and Carbonell, J.G.,** "Language Acquisition and
               Machine Learning," in *Mechanisms for Language Acquisition*, B.
               MacWhinney (Ed.), Lawrence Erlbaum Associates, Hillsdale, NJ,
               1986.

B   **Langley, P.W. and Carbonell, J.G.,** "Machine Learning:
               Techniques and Foundations," *Technical Report*, University of
               California, Irvine, CA, 1987.

B d   **Langley, P.W., Bradshaw, G.L. and Simon, H.A.,**
               "Rediscovering Chemistry with the BACON System," in *Machine
               Learning: An Artificial Intelligence Approach*, Vol. I, R.S.
               Michalski, J.G. Carbonell and T.M. Mitchell (Eds.), Tioga/Morgan
               Kaufmann, Los Altos, CA, 1983.

B d   **Langley, P.W., Simon, H.A. and Bradshaw, G.L.,** "Heuristics for
               Empirical Discovery," in *Computational Models of Learning*, L.
               Bolc (Ed.), Springer-Verlag, Berlin, 1987.

B d   **Langley, P.W., Simon, H.A., Bradshaw, G.L. and Zytkow, J.M.,**
               *Scientific Discovery: Computational Explorations of the Creative
               Processes*, The MIT Press, Cambridge, MA, 1987.

B d   **Langley, P.W., Zytkow, J.M., Simon, H.A. and Bradshaw, G.L.,**
               "The Search for Regularity: Four Aspects of Scientific
               Discovery," in *Machine Learning: An Artificial Intelligence
               Approach*, Vol. II, R.S. Michalski, J.G. Carbonell and T.M.
               Mitchell (Eds.), Morgan Kaufmann, Los Altos, CA, 1986.

B s   **Larson, J. and Michalski, R.S.,** "Inductive Inference of VL
               Decision Rules," *SIGART Newsletter*, Vol. 63, pp. 38–44, 1977.

I(s,x) M   **Lebowitz, M.,** "Concept Learning in a Rich Input Domain:
               Generalization-Based Memory," in *Machine Learning: An
               Artificial Intelligence Approach*, Vol. II, R.S. Michalski, J.G.
               Carbonell and T.M. Mitchell (Eds.), Morgan Kaufmann, Los
               Altos, CA, 1986.

I(s,x) M   **Lebowitz, M.,** "Integrated Learning: Controlling Explanation,"
               Cognitive Science, Vol. 10, No. 2, pp. 219–240, 1986.

I(c,s) M   **Lebowitz, M.,** "UNIMEM, a General Learning System: An
               Overview," *Proceedings of ECAI-86*, Brighton, England, 1986.

E I(c,s)   **Lebowitz, M.,** "Experiments with Incremental Concept
               Formulation: UNIMEM," *Machine Learning*, Vol. 2, No. 2, pp.
               103–138, 1987.

I(s,x)   **Lebowitz, M.,** "The Utility of Similarity-Based Learning in a
                 World Needing Explanation," in *Machine Learning: An Artificial
                 Intelligence Approach*, Vol. III, Y. Kodratoff and R.S. Michalski
                 (Eds.), Morgan Kaufmann, San Mateo, CA, 1990.

B   **Lee, S., Wah, B., Bourbakis, N.G. and Tsai, W.T. (Eds.),**
                 *Proceedings of the 3rd International Conference on Tools for
                 Artificial Intelligence*, IEEE Computer Society Press, Los
                 Alamitos, CA, 1991.

B   **Lenat, D.B.,** "AM: An Artificial Intelligence Approach to
                 Discovery in Mathematics as Heuristic Search," *Ph.D. Thesis,*
                 Stanford University, 1976. (Reprinted in Davis, R. and Lenat,
                 D.B., 1980.)

B   **Lenat, D.B.,** "On Automated Scientific Theory Formation: A Case
                 Study Using the AM Program," in *Machine Intelligence 9*, J.E.
                 Hayes, D. Michie and L.I. Mikulich (Eds.), Halsted Press, New
                 York, 1977.

B d   **Lenat, D.B.,** "The Ubiquity of Discovery," *Artificial Intelligence*,
                 Vol. 9, pp. 257–285, 1978.

B I(d,v) K   **Lenat, D.B.,** "The Role of Heuristics in Learning by Discovery:
                 Three Case Studies," in *Machine Learning: An Artificial
                 Intelligence Approach*, Vol. I, R.S. Michalski, J.G. Carbonell and
                 T.M. Mitchell (Eds.), Tioga/Morgan Kaufmann, Los Altos, CA,
                 1983.

B K   **Lenat, D.B.,** "When Will Machines Learn?" *Machine Learning*,
                 Vol. 4, No. 3/4, pp. 255–258, 1989.

I(g,n,x) M P **Levinson, R. and Snyder, R.,** "Adaptive Pattern-Oriented Chess,"
                 Proceedings of AAAI-91, pp. 601–606, AAAI Press, Menlo Park,
                 CA, 1991.

I(g,n,x) M P **Levinson, R. and Snyder, R.,** "Adaptive Pattern-Oriented Chess,"
                 *Proceedings of the Eighth International Workshop on Machine
                 Learning*, Evanston, IL, pp. 85–89, Morgan Kaufmann, San
                 Mateo, CA, 1991.

B K   **Lewis, D.D.,** "Learning in Intelligent Information Retrieval,"
                 *Proceedings of the Eighth International Workshop on Machine
                 Learning*, Evanston, IL, pp. 235–239, 1991.

I(g,n)   **Lindgren, K., Nilsson, A., Nordahl, M. and Rade, I.,** "Regular
                 Language Inference Using Evolving Neural Networks,"
                 *Proceedings of the Workshop on Combinations of Genetic
                 Algorithms and Neural Networks*, Baltimore, MD, 1992.

B   **Lindsay, R.K., Buchanan, B.G., Feigenbaum, E.A. and Lederberg, J.,** *Applications of Artificial Intelligence for Organic Chemistry: The DENDRAL Project,* McGraw-Hill, New York, 1980.

B T v   **Ling, X. and Narayan, M.A.,** "Comparison of Methods Based on Inverse Resolution," *Proceedings of the Eighth International Workshop on Machine Learning,* Evanston, IL, pp. 168–172, Morgan Kaufmann, San Mateo, CA, 1991.

I(n,s)   **Liu, N. and Cios, K.J.,** "Sequential Concept Learning: The SCL System," *Proceedings of the First International Workshop on Multistrategy Learning,* R.S. Michalski and G. Tecuci (Eds.), Harpers Ferry, WV, pp. 427–434, George Mason Univ., Center for AI, Fairfax, VA, 1991.

B   **Loveland, D.,** *Automatic Theorem Proving: A Logical Basis,* North-Holland, Amsterdam, 1978.

B n   **MacGregor, R.J.,** *Neural and Brain Modeling,* Academic Press, San Diego, CA, 1987.

I(v,x)   **Maclin, R. and Shavlik, J.W.,** "Enriching Vocabularies by Generalizing Explanation Structures," *Proceedings of the 6th International Workshop on Machine Learning,* Ithaca, NY, pp. 444–446, Morgan Kaufmann, San Mateo, CA, 1989.

E I(n,r)   **Maclin, R. and Shavlik, J.W.,** "Refining Domain Theories Expressed as Finite-State Automata," *Proceedings of the Eighth International Workshop on Machine Learning,* Evanston, IL, pp. 524–528, Morgan Kaufmann, San Mateo, CA, 1991.

E I(n,r)   **Maclin, R. and Shavlik, J.W.,** "Refining Algorithms with Knowledge-Based Neural Networks: Improving the Chou-Fasman Algorithm for Protein Folding," *Machine Learning,* Special Issue on Multistrategy Learning, pp. 195–215, 1993.

B K   **Marcus, S. (Ed.),** *Automating Knowledge Acquisition for Expert Systems,* Kluwer Academic, Boston, 1989.

I(s,x) K   **Martin, M., Sanguesa, R. and Cortes, U.,** "Knowledge Acquisition Combining Analytical and Empirical Techniques," *Proceedings of the Eighth International Workshop on Machine Learning,* Evanston, IL, pp. 657–661, Morgan Kaufmann, San Mateo, CA, 1991.

B   **Maryanski, F.J.,** "Inference of Probabilistic Grammars," *Ph.D. Thesis,* University of Connecticut, 1974.

B v   **Matheus, C.J.,** "The Need for Constructive Induction," *Proceedings of the Eighth International Workshop on Machine Learning*, Evanston, IL, pp. 173–178, Morgan Kaufmann, San Mateo, CA, 1991.

B M   **Maturane, H.R. and Varela, F.J.,** *The Tree of Knowledge: The Biological Roots of Human Understanding*, Shambhala Publications, Boston, 1987.

I(x,v)   **Matwin, S. and Plante, B.,** "A Deductive-Inductive Method for Theory Revision," *Proceedings of the First International Workshop on Multistrategy Learning*, R.S. Michalski and G. Tecuci (Eds.), Harpers Ferry, WV, pp. 160–174, George Mason Univ., Center for AI, Fairfax, VA, 1991.

I(x,v)   **Matwin, S. and Plante, B.,** "Theory Revision by Analyzing Explanations and Prototypes," in *Machine Learning: A Multistrategy Approach*, Vol. IV, R.S. Michalski and G. Tecuci (Eds.), Morgan Kaufmann, San Mateo, CA, 1994.

B   **McCarthy, J.,** "Programs with Common Sense," *Proceedings of the Symposium on the Mechanization of Thought Processes, National Physical Laboratory*, pp. 1, 77–84, H.M. Stationery Off., London, 1958.

B   **McCarthy, J.,** "Circumscription—A Form of Non-Monotonic Reasoning," *Artificial Intelligence*, Vol. 13, pp. 27–39, 1980.

B n   **McClelland, J. and Rumelhart, D.,** *Explorations in Parallel Distributed Processing*, MIT Press, Cambridge, MA, 1988.

B M n   **McClelland, J.L., Rumelhart, D.E. and Group, T.P.R.,** *Parallel Distributed Processing: Psychological and Biological Models*, The MIT Press, Cambridge, MA, 1986.

I(s,x) P   **McCluskey, T.L.,** "Explanation-Based and Similarity-Based Heuristic Acquisition in a General Planner," *Proceedings of EWSL-89*, Montpellier, France, 1989.

B   **McDermott, D.,** "Planning and Acting," *Cognitive Science*, Vol. 2, pp. 71–109, 1978.

B   **McDermott, D. and Doyle, J.,** "Non-Monotonic Logic I," *Artificial Intelligence*, Vol. 13, pp. 41–72, 1980.

B   **McDermott, J.,** "The World Would Be a Better Place If Non-Programmers Could Program," *Machine Learning*, Vol. 4, No. 3/4, pp. 337–338, 1989.

B   McDermott, J. (Ed.), *Proceedings of the 10th International Joint
             Conference on Artificial Intelligence*, Morgan Kaufmann, San
             Mateo, CA, 1987.

B   **Mechelen, I.V., Hampton, J., Michalski, R.S. and Theuns, P.
             (Eds.),** *Categories and Concepts: Theoretical Views and Inductive
             Data Analysis*, Academic Press, San Diego, CA, 1992.

B P s   **Michalski, R.S.,** "On the Quasi-Minimal Solution of the General
             Covering Problem," *Proceedings of the 5th International
             Symposium on Information Processing, FCIP-69*, Bled,
             Yugoslavia, pp. 125–128, 1969.

B s   **Michalski, R.S.,** "AQVAL/1—Computer Implementation of a
             Variable-Valued Logic System VL1 and Examples of Its
             Application to Pattern Recognition," *Proceedings of the First
             International Joint Conference on Pattern Recognition*,
             Washington, D.C., pp. 3–17, Institute of Electrical and Electronics
             Engineers, New York, 1973.

B s   **Michalski, R.S.,** "Discovering Classification Rules Using
             Variable-Valued Logic System VL1," *Proceedings of the Third
             International Joint Conference on Artificial Intelligence*, pp.
             162–172, AAAI Press, Menlo Park, CA, 1973.

B s   **Michalski, R.S.,** "Variable-Valued Logic: System VL1,"
             *Proceedings of the 1974 International Symposium on
             Multiple-Valued Logic*, West Virginia University, Morgantown,
             WV, pp. 323–346, 1974.

B E s   **Michalski, R.S.,** "Variable-Valued Logic and Its Applications to
             Pattern Recognition and Machine Learning," in *Computer Science
             and Multiple-Valued Logic Theory and Applications*, D.C. Rine
             (Ed.), North-Holland, Amsterdam, 1975.

B I(s,v)   **Michalski, R.S.,** "Pattern Recognition as Knowledge-Guided
             Computer Induction," *Technical Report*, 927, Computer Science
             Dept., University of Illinois, Urbana, 1978.

B c   **Michalski, R.S.,** "Conceptual Clustering: A Theoretical
             Foundation and a Method for Partitioning Data into Conjunctive
             Concepts," *Proceedings of the Seminaries IRIA, Classification
             Automatique et Perception par Ordinateur*, INRIA, France, pp.
             253–295, 1979.

B I(c,s)   **Michalski, R.S.,** "Detection of Conceptual Patterns through
                Inductive Inference," *Proceedings of the Seminaries IRIA,
                Classification Automatique et Perception par Ordinateur*, INRIA,
                France, pp. 297–339, 1979.

B s   **Michalski, R.S.,** "Pattern Recognition as Rule-Guided Inductive
                Inference," *IEEE Transactions on Pattern Analysis and Machine
                Intelligence*, Vol. PAMI-2, pp. 349–361, 1980.

B I(s,v)   **Michalski, R.S.,** "A Theory and Methodology of Inductive
                Learning," *Artificial Intelligence*, Vol. 20, pp. 111–116, 1983.

B I(s,v)   **Michalski, R.S.,** "A Theory and Methodology of Inductive
                Learning," in *Machine Learning: An Artificial Intelligence
                Approach*, Vol. I, R.S. Michalski, J.G. Carbonell and T.M.
                Mitchell (Eds.), Tioga/Morgan Kaufmann, Los Altos, CA, 1983.

B E   **Michalski, R.S.,** "Knowledge Repair Mechanisms: Evolution
                versus Revolution," *Proceedings of the 3rd International Machine
                Learning Workshop*, Skytop, PA, pp. 116–119, Morgan Kaufmann,
                San Mateo, CA, 1985.

B   **Michalski, R.S.,** "Emerging Principles in Machine Learning,"
                *Proceedings of the 1st International Symposium on Methodologies
                for Intelligent Systems*, Knoxville, TN, pp. 289, Elsevier Science
                Publishing, New York, 1986.

B   **Michalski, R.S.,** "Understanding the Nature of Learning: Issues
                and Research Directions," in *Machine Learning: An Artificial
                Intelligence Approach*, Vol. II, R.S. Michalski, J.G. Carbonell and
                T.M. Mitchell (Eds.), Morgan Kaufmann, Los Altos, CA, 1986.

B s   **Michalski, R.S.,** "Concept Learning," in *Encyclopedia of
                Artificial Intelligence*, S.C. Shapiro (Ed.), John Wiley & Sons,
                New York, 1987.

B   **Michalski, R.S.,** "Learning Strategies and Automated Knowledge
                Acquisition—An Overview," in *Computational Models of
                Learning*, L. Bolc (Ed.), Springer-Verlag, Berlin, 1987.

B   **Michalski, R.S.,** "On the Nature of Learning: Problems and
                Research Directions," *Informatyka*, No. 2&3, E. Pierzchala and P.
                Zielczynski (trans.), 1988.

I(a,s,v,x)   **Michalski, R.S.,** "Multistrategy Constructive Learning,"
                Proceedings of the ONR Workshop on Knowledge Acquisition,
                Washington, DC, 1989.

B s   **Michalski, R.S.,** "Two-Tiered Concept Meaning, Inferential
                 Matching and Conceptual Cohesiveness," in *Similarity and
                 Analogical Reasoning*, S. Vosniadou and A. Ortony (Eds.),
                 Cambridge University Press, London, 1989.

I(a,s,x,v) P **Michalski, R.S.,** "A Methodological Framework for Multistrategy
                 Task-Adaptive Learning," *Proceedings of the 5th International
                 Symposium on Methodologies for Intelligent Systems*, Z.W. Ras,
                 M. Zemankova and M.L. Emrich (Eds.), Knoxville, TN, pp.
                 404–411, Elsevier Science Publishing, New York, 1990.

I(a,s,v,x)   **Michalski, R.S.,** "Toward a Unified Theory of Learning:
                 Multistrategy Task-Adaptive Learning," *Reports of Machine
                 Learning and Inference Laboratory*, MLI-90–1, George Mason
                 Univ., Center for AI, Fairfax, VA, 1990.

B I(a,s,v,x) **Michalski, R.S.,** "Inferential Learning Theory as a Basis for
                 Multistrategy Task-Adaptive Learning," *Proceedings of the First
                 International Workshop on Multistrategy Learning*, R.S. Michalski
                 and G. Tecuci (Eds.), Harpers Ferry, WV, pp. 3–18, George Mason
                 Univ., Center for AI, Fairfax, VA, 1991.

I(a,s,v,x)   **Michalski, R.S.,** "Toward a Unified Theory of Learning: An
                 Outline of Basic Ideas," *Invited presentation at the First World
                 Conference on the Fundamentals of Artificial Intelligence*, Paris,
                 France, 1991.

I(s,x) M   **Michalski, R.S.,** "Beyond Prototypes and Frames: The
                 Two-Tiered Concept Representation," in *Categories and
                 Concepts: Theoretical Views and Inductive Data Analysis*, I.V.
                 Mechelen, J. Hampton, R.S. Michalski and P. Theuns (Eds.),
                 Academic Press, San Diego, CA, 1992.

B I(a,s,v,x) **Michalski, R.S.,** "Inferential Learning Theory as a Conceptual
                 Basis for Multistrategy Learning," *Machine Learning*, Special
                 Issue on Multistrategy Learning, pp. 111–151, 1993.

B I(a,s,v,x) **Michalski, R.S.,** "Inferential Learning Theory: Developing
                 Foundations for Multistrategy Learning," in *Machine Learning: A
                 Multistrategy Approach*, Vol. IV, R.S. Michalski and G. Tecuci
                 (Eds.), Morgan Kaufmann, San Mateo, CA, 1994.

B E K s   **Michalski, R.S. and Chilausky, R.L.,** "Learning by Being Told
                 and Learning from Examples: An Experimental Comparison of the
                 Two Methods of Knowledge Acquisition in the Context of
                 Developing an Expert System for Soybean Disease Diagnosis,"
                 International Journal of Policy Analysis and Information Systems,
                 Vol. 4, pp. 125–161, 1980.

I(s,x)   **Michalski, R.S. and Ko, H.,** "On the Nature of Explanation or Why Did the Wine Bottle Shatter," *Proceedings of the Spring Symposium Series: Explanation-Based Learning*, pp. 12–21, AAAI Press, Menlo Park, CA, 1988.

B   **Michalski, R.S. and Kodratoff, Y.,** "Research in Machine Learning: Recent Progress, Classification of Methods, and Future Directions," in *Machine Learning: An Artificial Intelligence Approach*, Vol. III, Y. Kodratoff and R.S. Michalski (Eds.), Morgan Kaufmann, San Mateo, CA, 1990.

B s   **Michalski, R.S. and Larson, J.B.,** "Selection of the Most Representative Training Examples and Incremental Generation of VL1 Hypotheses: The Underlying Methodology and the Description of Programs ESEL and AQ11," *Technical Report*, 867, Computer Science Dept., University of Illinois, May 1978.

B K   **Michalski, R.S. and Littman, D.C.,** "Future Directions of AI in a Resource-Limited Environment," *Proceedings of IJCAI-89 Workshop on Knowledge Discovery in Databases*, AAAI Press, Menlo Park, CA, 1989.

B c   **Michalski, R.S. and Stepp, R.E.,** "Learning from Observation: Conceptual Clustering," in *Machine Learning: An Artificial Intelligence Approach*, Vol. I, R.S. Michalski, J.G. Carbonell and T.M. Mitchell (Eds.), Tioga/Morgan Kaufmann, Los Altos, CA, 1983.

B c   **Michalski, R.S. and Stepp, R.E.,** "Clustering," in *Encyclopedia of Artificial Intelligence*, S.C. Shapiro (Ed.), John Wiley & Sons, New York, 1987.

B I(...)   **Michalski, R.S. and Tecuci, G. (Eds.),** *Proceedings of the First International Workshop on Multistrategy Learning*, George Mason Univ., Harpers Ferry, WV, George Mason Univ., Center for AI, Fairfax, VA, 1991.

B I(...)   **Michalski, R.S. and Tecuci, G. (Eds.),** *Machine Learning: A Multistrategy Approach*, Vol. IV, Morgan Kaufmann, San Mateo, CA, 1994.

I(s,v,x)   **Michalski, R.S. and Watanabe, L.M.,** "Constructive Closed-Loop Learning: Fundamental Ideas and Examples," *Reports of Machine Learning and Inference Laboratory*, MLI-88–1, George Mason Univ., Center for AI, Fairfax, VA, 1988.

B   **Michalski, R.S. and Winston, P.H.,** "Variable Precision Logic," *Artificial Intelligence*, Vol. 29, pp. 121–146, 1986.

B   **Michalski, R.S., Carbonell, J.G. and Mitchell, T.M. (Eds.),** *Machine Learning: An Artificial Intelligence Approach*, Vol. I, Tioga/Morgan Kaufmann, Los Altos, CA, 1983.

B   **Michalski, R.S., Carbonell, J.G. and Mitchell, T.M. (Eds.),** *Machine Learning: An Artificial Intelligence Approach*, Vol. II, Morgan Kaufmann, Los Altos, CA, 1986.

I(r,s)   **Michalski, R.S., Ko, H. and Chen, K.,** "Qualitative Prediction: the SPARC/G Methodology for Inductively Describing and Predicting Discrete Processes," in *Current Issues in Expert Systems*, V. Lamsweerde and O. Dufour (Eds.), Academic Press, San Diego, CA, 1988.

B   **Michalski, R.S., Amarel, S., Lenat, D., Michie, D. and Winston, P.H.,** "Machine Learning: Challenges of the Eighties," in *Machine Learning: An Artificial Intelligence Approach*, Vol. II, R.S. Michalski, J.G. Carbonell and T.M. Mitchell (Eds.), Morgan Kaufmann, Los Altos, CA, 1986.

B   **Michie, D.,** "Machine Learning in the Next Five Years," *Proceedings of EWSL-88*, Glasgow, Scotland, pp. 107–122, Pitman, London, 1988.

I(n,s) P   **Millan, J.R. and Torras, C.,** "Learning to Avoid Obstacles through Reinforcement," *Proceedings of the Eighth International Workshop on Machine Learning*, Evanston, IL, pp. 298–302, Morgan Kaufmann, San Mateo, CA, 1991.

B E M s   **Miller, C.S. and Laird, J.E.,** "A Constraint-Motivated Model of Lexical Acquisition," *Proceedings of the Eighth International Workshop on Machine Learning*, Evanston, IL, pp. 95–99, Morgan Kaufmann, San Mateo, CA, 1991.

B   **Minsky, M.L. (Ed.),** *Semantic Information Processing*, MIT Press, Cambridge, MA, 1968.

B   **Minsky, M.L.,** "A Framework for Representing Knowledge," in *The Psychology of Computer Vision*, P.H. Winston (Ed.), McGraw-Hill, New York, 1975.

B M   **Minsky, M.L.,** *The Society of Mind*, Simon and Schuster, New York, 1986.

B n   **Minsky, M.L. and Papert, S.A.,** "Learning," in *Perceptrons: An Introduction to Computational Geometry*, The MIT Press, Cambridge, MA, 1969.

B x   **Minton, S.,** "Learning Search Control Knowledge: An Explanation-Based Approach," *Knowledge Representation, Learning, and Expert Systems,* Kluwer Academic, Boston, 1989.

B E P x   **Minton, S.N.,** "Quantitative Results Concerning the Utility of Explanation-Based Learning," *Artificial Intelligence*, Vol. 42, pp. 363–392, 1990.

B s   **Mitchell, T.M.,** "Version Spaces: A Candidate Elimination Approach to Rule Learning," *Proceedings of IJCAI-77*, pp. 305–310, AAAI Press, Menlo Park, CA, 1977.

B s   **Mitchell, T.M.,** "Version Spaces: An Approach to Concept Learning," *Ph.D. Thesis,* Stanford University, 1978.

B s   **Mitchell, T.M.,** "The Need for Biases in Learning Generalizations," CBM-TR-117, Dept. of Computer Science, Rutgers University, 1980.

B s   **Mitchell, T.M.,** "Generalization as Search," *Artificial Intelligence*, Vol. 18, pp. 203–226, 1982.

B   **Mitchell, T.M.,** "Can We Build Learning Robots?" *Proceedings of the Workshop on Representation and Learning in an Autonomous Agent*, Lagos, Portugal, 1988.

B   **Mitchell, T.M., Carbonell, J.G. and Michalski, R.S. (Eds.),** *Machine Learning: A Guide to Current Research*, Kluwer Academic, Boston, 1985.

B x   **Mitchell, T.M., Keller, R.M. and Kedar-Cabelli, S.T.,** "Explanation-Based Generalization: A Unifying View," *Machine Learning*, Vol. 1, No. 1, pp. 47–80, 1986.

B P I(s,v,x)   **Mitchell, T.M., Utgoff, P.E. and Banerji, R.,** "Learning by Experimentation: Acquiring and Refining Problem-Solving Heuristics," in *Machine Learning: An Artificial Intelligence Approach*, Vol. I, R.S. Michalski, J.G. Carbonell and T.M. Mitchell (Eds.), Tioga/Morgan Kaufmann, Los Altos, CA, 1983.

B   **Mitchell, T.M., Utgoff, P.E., Nudel, B. and Banerji, R.B.,** "Learning Problem-Solving Heuristics through Practice," *Proceedings of IJCAI-81*, pp. 127–134, AAAI Press, Menlo Park, CA, 1981.

I(s,x)   **Mooney, R.J. and Ourston, D.,** "Induction over the Unexplained: Integrated Learning of Concepts with Both Explainable and Conventional Aspects," *Proceedings of the 6th International Workshop on Machine Learning*, Ithaca, NY, pp. 5–7, Morgan Kaufmann, San Mateo, CA, 1989.

I(s,v,x)   **Mooney, R.J. and Ourston, D.,** "A Multistrategy Approach to
                  Theory Refinement," *Proceedings of the First International
                  Workshop on Multistrategy Learning*, R.S. Michalski and G.
                  Tecuci (Eds.), Harpers Ferry, WV, pp. 115–130, George Mason
                  Univ., Center for AI, Fairfax, VA, 1991.

I(v,x)   **Mooney, R.J. and Ourston, D.,** "Constructive Induction in
                  Theory Refinement," *Proceedings of the Eighth International
                  Workshop on Machine Learning*, Evanston, IL, pp. 178–182,
                  Morgan Kaufmann, San Mateo, CA, 1991.

I(s,v,x)   **Mooney, R.J. and Ourston, D.,** "A Multistrategy Approach to
                  Theory Refinement," in *Machine Learning: A Multistrategy
                  Approach*, Vol. IV, R.S. Michalski and G. Tecuci (Eds.), Morgan
                  Kaufmann, San Mateo, CA, 1994.

B E I(n,s)   **Mooney, R.J., Shavlik, J., Towell, G. and Gove, A.,** "An
                  Experimental Comparison of Symbolic and Connectionist
                  Learning Algorithms," *Proceedings of IJCAI-89*, pp. 775–780,
                  AAAI Press, Menlo Park, CA, 1989.

B   **Moore, R.C.,** *Reasoning from Incomplete Knowledge in a
                  Procedural Deduction System*, Garland, New York, 1980.

B   **Morik, K. (Ed.),** *Knowledge Representation and Organization in
                  Machine Learning*, Springer-Verlag, Berlin, 1989.

B   **Morik, K. (Ed.),** *Proceedings of the 4th European Working
                  Session on Learning*, Pitman/Morgan Kaufmann, San Mateo, CA,
                  1989.

I(s,v,x) K M **Morik, K.,** "Balanced Cooperative Modeling," *Proceedings of the
                  First International Workshop on Multistrategy Learning*, R.S.
                  Michalski and G. Tecuci (Eds.), Harpers Ferry, WV, pp. 65–80,
                  George Mason Univ., Center for AI, Fairfax, VA, 1991.

I(s,v,x) K M **Morik, K.,** "Balanced Cooperative Modeling," in *Machine
                  Learning: A Multistrategy Approach*, Vol. IV, R.S. Michalski and
                  G. Tecuci (Eds.), Morgan Kaufmann, San Mateo, CA, 1994.

I(s,v,x) K M **Morik, K.,** "Balanced Cooperative Modeling," *Machine Learning*,
                  Special Issue on Multistrategy Learning, pp. 217–235, 1993.

E I(s,v,x)   **Morik, K., Causse, K. and Boswell, R.,** "A Common Knowledge
                  Representation Integrating Learning Tools," *Proceedings of the
                  First International Workshop on Multistrategy Learning*, R.S.
                  Michalski and G. Tecuci (Eds.), Harpers Ferry, WV, pp. 81–97,
                  George Mason Univ., Center for AI, Fairfax, VA, 1991.

B T   **Mortimer, H.,** *The Logic of Induction*, Ellis Horwood Limited, Chichester, UK, 1988.

B x   **Mostow, D.J.,** "Mechanical Transformation of Task Heuristics into Operational Procedures," *Ph.D. Thesis,* Carnegie Mellon University, 1981.

B x   **Mostow, D.J.,** "Machine Transformation of Advice into a Heuristic Search Procedure," in *Machine Learning: An Artificial Intelligence Approach*, Vol. I, R.S. Michalski, J.G. Carbonell and T.M. Mitchell (Eds.), Tioga/Morgan Kaufmann, Los Altos, CA, 1983.

E I(s,v) **Murphy, P.M. and Pazzani, M.J.,** "ID2-of-3: Constructive Induction of M-of-N Concepts for Discriminators in Decision Trees," *Proceedings of the Eighth International Workshop on Machine Learning*, Evanston, IL, pp. 183–187, Morgan Kaufmann, San Mateo, CA, 1991.

B   **Mylopoulos, J. and Brodie, M.L.,** *Readings in Artificial Intelligence and Databases*, Morgan Kaufmann, San Mateo, CA, 1989.

B   **Mylopoulos, J. and Reiter, R. (Eds.),** *Proceedings of the 12th International Joint Conference on Artificial Intelligence*, Morgan Kaufmann, San Mateo, CA, 1991.

B T   **Natarajan, B.K.,** *Machine Learning: A Theoretical Approach*, Morgan Kaufmann, San Mateo, CA, 1991.

I(s,v) K **Nedellec, C.,** "A Smallest Generalization Step Strategy," *Proceedings of the Eighth International Workshop on Machine Learning*, Evanston, IL, pp. 529–533, Morgan Kaufmann, San Mateo, CA, 1991.

B   **Neumann, B. (Ed.),** *Proceedings of the 10th European Conference on Artificial Intelligence*, Wiley, Vienna, Austria, 1992.

B   **Newell, A. and Simon, H.A.,** *Human Problem Solving*, Prentice Hall, Englewood Cliffs, NJ, 1972.

B   **Nillson, N.J.,** *Learning Machines*, McGraw-Hill, New York, 1965.

B   **Nillson, N.J.,** *Problem Solving Methods in Artificial Intelligence*, McGraw-Hill, New York, 1971.

B   **Nillson, N.J.,** *Principles of Artificial Intelligence*, Tioga, Palo Alto, CA, 1980.

B   **Nilsson, N.J.,** "Probabilistic Logic," *Artificial Intelligence*, Vol. 28, pp. 71–87, 1986.

B E **Nirenburg, S., Carbonell, J.G., Tomita, M. and Goodman, K.,** *Machine Translation: A Knowledge-Based Approach*, Morgan Kaufmann, San Mateo, CA, 1991.

I(d...) **Nordhausen, B. and Langley, P.W.,** "Towards an Integrated Discovery System," *Proceedings of IJCAI-87*, pp. 198–200, AAAI Press, Menlo Park, CA, 1987.

I(...) **Nordhausen, B. and Langley, P.W.,** "An Integrated Approach to Empirical Discovery," *Proceedings of Office of Naval Research Workshop on Knowledge Acquisition*, A.L. Meyrowitz (Ed.), Arlington, VA, 1989.

B **Norvig, P.,** *Paradigms of AI Programming: Case Studies in Common Lisp*, Morgan Kaufmann, San Mateo, CA, 1991.

I(s,x) **Numao, M. and Shimura, M.,** "Explanation-Based Acceleration of Similarity-Based Learning," *Proceedings of the 6th International Workshop on Machine Learning*, Ithaca, NY, pp. 58–60, Morgan Kaufmann, San Mateo, CA, 1989.

B x **O'Rorke, P.V.,** "Explanation-Based Learning via Constraint Posting and Propagation," *Ph.D. Thesis,* Computer Science Dept., University of Illinois at Urbana-Champaign, 1987.

B **Pao, T.W.,** "A Solution of the Syntactical Induction-Inference Problem for a Non-Trivial Subset of Context-Free Languages," *Interim Report*, 69–19, Moore School of Electrical Engineering, University of Pennsylvania, 1969.

B **Parikh, R. (Ed.),** *Proceedings of the 3rd Conference (TARK 1990)*, Morgan Kaufmann, Los Altos, CA, 1990.

B n **Parker, D.,** "Learning-Logic: Casting the Cortex of the Human Brain in Silicon," *Technical Report*, TR-47, Center for Computational Research in Economics and Management Science, MIT, Cambridge, MA, 1985.

B **Pawlak, Z.,** "On Rough Sets," *Bulletin of the European Association for Theoretical Computer Science*, pp. 94–109, 1984.

I(s,x) **Pazzani, M.J.,** "Integrated Learning with Incorrect and Incomplete Theories," *Proceedings of the 5th International Conference on Machine Learning*, Ann Arbor, MI, pp. 291–297, 1988.

I(s,x) **Pazzani, M.J.,** "Integrating Explanation-Based and Empirical Learning Methods in OCCAM," *Proceedings of EWSL-88*, Glasgow, Scotland, pp. 147–166, Morgan Kaufmann, San Mateo, CA, 1988.

I(s,x) M   **Pazzani, M.J.,** "Learning Causal Relationships," *Ph.D. Thesis,* University of California, Los Angeles, Pitman, London, 1988.

I(s,x)   **Pazzani, M.J.,** "Detecting and Correcting Errors of Omission after Explanation-Based Learning," *Proceedings of IJCAI-89,* pp. 713–718, AAAI Press, Menlo Park, CA, 1989.

B I(s,x)   **Pazzani, M.J.,** *Creating a Memory of Causal Relationships: An Integration of Empirical and Explanation-Based Learning Methods,* Lawrence Erlbaum Associates, Hillsdale, NJ, 1990.

I(s,x) T   **Pazzani, M.J.,** "A Computational Theory of Learning Causal Relationships," *Cognitive Science,* Vol. 15, pp. 401–424, George Mason Univ., Center for AI, Fairfax, VA, 1991.

I(s,x) T   **Pazzani, M.J.,** "The Influence of Prior Knowledge on Concept Acquisition: Experimental and Computational Results," *Journal of Experimental Psychology: Learning, Memory and Cognition,* Vol. 17, No. 3, pp. 416–432, 1991.

I(a,r,v)   **Pazzani, M.J.,** "Learning Causal Patterns: Deliberately Overgeneralizing to Facilitate Transfer," *Proceedings of the First International Workshop on Multistrategy Learning,* R.S. Michalski and G. Tecuci (Eds.), Harpers Ferry, WV, pp. 19–33, 1991.

I(r,s,x) M   **Pazzani, M.J.,** "Learning to Predict and Explain: An Integration of Similarity-Based, Theory-Driven and Explanation-Based Learning," *The Journal of the Learning Sciences,* Vol. 1, No. 2, pp. 153–199, 1991.

I(a,r,v)   **Pazzani, M.J.,** "Learning Causal Patterns: Making a Transition from Data-Driven to Theory-Driven Learning," *Machine Learning,* Special Issue on Multistrategy Learning, pp. 173–194, 1993.

I(a,r,v)   **Pazzani, M.J.,** "Learning Causal Patterns: Making a Transition from Data-Driven to Theory-Driven Learning," in *Machine Learning: A Multistrategy Approach,* Vol. IV, R.S. Michalski and G. Tecuci (Eds.), Morgan Kaufmann, San Mateo, CA, 1994.

I(s,x) K   **Pazzani, M.J. and Brunk, C.,** "Detecting and Correcting Errors in Rule-Based Expert Systems: An Integration of Empirical and Explanation-Based Learning," *Knowledge Acquisition,* Vol. 3, pp. 157–173, 1991.

I(s,x)   **Pazzani, M.J. and Kibler, D.,** "The Role of Prior Knowledge in Inductive Learning," *Machine Learning,* Vol. 9, pp. 57–94, 1992.

I(s,x)   **Pazzani, M.J., Brunk, C.A. and Silverstein, G.,** "A
              Knowledge-Intensive Approach to Learning Relational Concepts,"
              *Proceedings of the Eighth International Workshop on Machine
              Learning*, Evanston, IL, pp. 432–436, Morgan Kaufmann, San
              Mateo, CA, 1991.

I(s,x) M   **Pazzani, M.J., Dyer, M. and Flowers, M.,** "The Role of Prior
              Causal Theories in Generalization," *Proceedings of AAAI-86*, pp.
              545–550, AAAI Press, Menlo Park, CA, 1986.

I(s,x) M   **Pazzani, M.J., Dyer, M. and Flowers, M.,** "Using Prior Learning
              to Facilitate the Learning of New Causal Theories," *Proceedings
              of IJCAI-87*, pp. 277–279, AAAI Press, Menlo Park, CA, 1987.

B   **Pearl, J.,** *Heuristics: Intelligent Search Strategies for Computer
              Problem Solving*, Addison-Wesley, Reading, MA, 1984.

B   **Pearl, J.,** *Probabilistic Reasoning in Intelligent Systems:
              Networks of Plausible Inference*, Morgan Kaufmann, San Mateo,
              CA, 1988.

B T   **Pearl, J. and Dechter, R.,** "Learning Structure from Data: A
              Survey," *Proceedings of the 1989 Workshop on Computational
              Learning Theory, COLT'89*, University of California, Santa Cruz,
              pp. 230–244, Morgan Kaufmann, San Mateo, CA, 1989.

B   **Piatetsky-Shapiro, G. and Frawley, W.J. (Eds.),** *Knowledge
              Discovery in Databases*, AAAI Press, Menlo Park, CA, 1991.

B   **Pinker, S.,** "Formal Models of Language Learning," *Cognition*,
              Vol. 7, pp. 217–283, 1979.

B P   **Porter, B.W.,** "Learning Problem Solving," *Ph.D. Thesis,*
              University of California, Irvine, 1984.

B   **Porter, B.W.,** "A Review of the First International Meeting on
              Advances in Learning," *Machine Learning*, Vol. 2, No. 1, pp.
              77–83, 1987.

B   **Porter, B.W. and Mooney, R.J. (Eds.),** *Proceedings of the 7th
              International Conference on Machine Learning*, Morgan
              Kaufmann, San Mateo, CA, 1990.

B E s   **Porter, B.W., Bareiss, R. and Holte, R.C.,** "Concept Learning
              and Heuristic Classification in Weak-Theory Domains," *Artificial
              Intelligence*, Vol. 45, pp. 229–263, 1990.

B a   **Prieditis, A.E. (Ed.),** *Analogica*, Kluwer, Boston, MA, 1988.

B   **Quillian, M.R.,** "Semantic Memory," in *Semantic Information
              Processing*, M.L. Minsky (Ed.), MIT Press, Cambridge, MA, 1968.

B s   **Quinlan, J.R.,** "Induction over Large Data Bases," *Heuristic Programming Project*, HPP-79–14, Computer Science Dept., Stanford University, 1979.

B E s   **Quinlan, J.R.,** "Learning Efficient Classification Procedures and Their Application to Chess End Games," in *Machine Learning: An Artificial Intelligence Approach*, Vol. I, R.S. Michalski, J.G. Carbonell and T.M. Mitchell (Eds.), Tioga/Morgan Kaufmann, Los Altos, CA, 1983.

B s   **Quinlan, J.R.,** "Induction of Decision Trees," *Machine Learning*, Vol. 1, No. 1, pp. 81–106, 1986.

I(s,v)   **Ragavan, H. and Rendell, L.,** "Relations, Knowledge and Empirical Learning," *Proceedings of the Eighth International Workshop on Machine Learning*, Evanston, IL, pp. 188–192, Morgan Kaufmann, San Mateo, CA, 1991.

I(a,s)   **Rajamoney, S.A. and Lee, H.-Y.,** "Prototype-Based Reasoning: An Integrated Approach to Solving Large Novel Problems," *Proceedings of AAAI-91*, pp. 34–39, AAAI Press, Menlo Park, CA, 1991.

I(a,c,x) M   **Ram, A.,** "Indexing, Elaboration and Refinement: Incremental Learning of Explanatory Cases," *Machine Learning*, pp. 201–248, 1993.

I(a,x)   **Ram, A. and Cox, M.,** "Introspective Reasoning Using Meta-Explanations for Multistrategy Learning," in *Machine Learning: A Multistrategy Approach*, Vol. IV, R.S. Michalski and G. Tecuci (Eds.), Morgan Kaufmann, San Mateo, CA, 1994.

B K   **Ram, A. and Hunter, L.,** "A Goal-Based Approach to Intelligent Information Retrieval," *Proceedings of the Eighth International Workshop on Machine Learning*, Evanston, IL, pp. 265–269, Morgan Kaufmann, San Mateo, CA, 1991.

E I(a,x) M P **Ram, A. and Hunter, L.E.,** "The Use of Explicit Goals for Knowledge to Guide Inference and Learning," *Journal of Applied Intelligence*, Vol. 2, No. 1, pp. 47–73, 1992.

B g   **Rawlins, G.J.E. (Ed.),** *Foundations of Genetic Algorithms*, Morgan Kaufmann, San Mateo, CA, 1991.

I(a,s,x)   **Redmond, M.,** "Combining Cased-Based Reasoning, Explanation-Based Learning, and Learning from Instruction," *Proceedings of the 6th International Workshop on Machine Learning*, Ithaca, NY, pp. 20–22, Morgan Kaufmann, San Mateo, CA, 1989.

B   **Reeker, L.H.,** "The Computational Study of Language Acquisition," in *Advances in Computers 15*, M. Rubinoff and M.C. Yovits (Eds.), Academic Press, San Diego, CA, 1976.

E I(s,x)   **Reich, Y.,** "Designing Integrated Learning Systems for Engineering Design," *Proceedings of the Eighth International Workshop on Machine Learning*, Evanston, IL, pp. 635–639, Morgan Kaufmann, San Mateo, CA, 1991.

I(c...) K E   **Reich, Y.,** "Macro and Micro Perspectives of Multistrategy Learning," *Proceedings of the First International Workshop on Multistrategy Learning*, R.S. Michalski and G. Tecuci (Eds.), Harpers Ferry, WV, pp. 97–112, George Mason Univ., Center for AI, Fairfax, VA, 1991.

I(c...) K E   **Reich, Y.,** "Macro and Micro Perspectives of Multistrategy Learning," in *Machine Learning: A Multistrategy Approach*, Vol. IV, R.S. Michalski and G. Tecuci (Eds.), Morgan Kaufmann, San Mateo, CA, 1994.

B E s   **Reinke, R.E. and Michalski, R.S.,** "Incremental Learning of Concept Descriptions: A Method and Experimental Results," in *Machine Intelligence 11*, J.E. Hayes, D. Michie and J. Richards (Eds.), Clarendon Press, Oxford, 1988.

B a   **Reisbeck, C. and Schank, R. (Eds.),** *Inside Case-Based Reasoning*, Lawrence Erlbaum Associates, Hillsdale, NJ, 1989.

B   **Reiter, R.,** "A Logic for Default Reasoning," *Artificial Intelligence*, Vol. 13, pp. 81–132, 1980.

B T s,v   **Rendell, L.,** "A General Framework for Induction and a Study of Selective Induction," *Machine Learning*, Vol. 1, No. 2, pp. 177–226, 1986.

B   **Rich, E. and Knight, K.,** *Artificial Intelligence*, McGraw-Hill, New York, 1991.

E I(s,x)   **Richards, B.L. and Mooney, R.J.,** "First-Order Theory Revision," *Proceedings of the Eighth International Workshop on Machine Learning*, Evanston, IL, pp. 447–451, Morgan Kaufmann, San Mateo, CA, 1991.

I(a,s) M   **Rissland, E.L. and Skalak, D.B.,** "Combining Case-Based and Rule-Based Reasoning: A Heuristic Approach," *Proceedings of IJCAI-89*, pp. 524–530, AAAI Press, Menlo Park, CA, 1989.

B   **Rissland, E.L. and Soloway, E.M.,** "Overview of an Example Generation System," *Proceedings of AAAI-80*, pp. 256–258, AAAI Press, Menlo Park, CA, 1980.

B T   **Rivest, R., Haussler, D. and Warmuth, M.K. (Eds.),** *Proceedings of the 2nd Annual Workshop on Computational Learning Theory*, Morgan Kaufmann, San Mateo, CA, 1989.

B   **Robinson, G.A. and Wos, L.,** "Paramodulation and Theorem-Proving in First Order Theories with Equality," in *Machine Intelligence 4*, D. Michie (Ed.), Edinburgh University Press, Edinburgh, Scotland, 1969.

B   **Robinson, J.A.,** "A Machine-Oriented Logic Based on the Resolution Principle," *Journal of the ACM*, Vol. 12, pp. 227–234, 1965.

I(g…)   **Rogers, D.,** "G/SPLINES: A Hybrid of Friedman's Multivariate Adaptive Regression Splines (MARS) Algorithm with Holland's Genetic Algorithm." *Proceedings of the 4th International Conference on Genetic Algorithms*, San Diego, CA, pp. 3384–3391, Morgan Kaufmann, San Mateo, CA, 1991.

B n   **Rosenblatt, F.,** "The Perceptron: A Probabilistic Model for Information Storage and Organization in the Brain," *Psychological Review*, Vol. 65, pp. 386–408, 1958.

B   **Rosenblatt, F.,** *Principles of Neurodynamics: Perceptrons and the Theory of Brain Mechanisms*, Spartan Books, Washington, DC, 1962.

B   **Rosenbloom, P.S., Laird, J.E., Newell, A., Golding, A., and Unruh,** "Current Research on Learning in SOAR," *Proceedings of the 3rd International Machine Learning Workshop*, Skytop, PA, pp. 163–172, Morgan Kaufmann, San Mateo, CA, 1985.

B n   **Rumelhart, D.E., Hinton, G.E. and Williams, R.J.,** "Learning Internal Representations by Error Propagation," in *Parallel Distributed Processing*, Vol. 1, D.E. Rumelhart and J.L. McClelland (Eds.), The MIT Press, Cambridge, MA, Morgan Kaufmann, San Mateo, CA, 1986.

B M n   **Rumelhart, D.E., McClelland, J.L. et al. (Eds.),** *Parallel Distributed Processing: Foundations*, Vol. I, The MIT Press, Cambridge, MA, 1986.

B n,v   **Rumelhart, D.E. and Zipser, D.,** "Feature Discovery by Competitive Learning," *Cognitive Science*, Vol. 9, pp. 75–112, 1985.

I(a,s)   **Russell, S.J.,** "Analogical and Inductive Reasoning," *Ph.D. Thesis,* Stanford University, 1986.

I(a,s)   **Russell, S.J.,** "Analogy and Single-Instance Generalization,"
                Proceedings of the 4th International Machine Learning Workshop,
                University of California, Irvine, pp. 390–397, Morgan Kaufmann,
                San Mateo, CA, 1987.

B I(a,s)   **Russell, S.J.,** *The Use of Knowledge in Analogy and Induction,*
                Morgan Kaufmann, San Mateo, CA, 1989.

B P   **Sacerdotti, E.D.,** "Planning in a Hierarchy of Abstraction
                Spaces," *Artificial Intelligence,* Vol. 5, pp. 115–135, 1974.

I(v,x) E   **Saitta, L. and Botta, M.,** "Multistrategy Learning and Theory
                Revision," *Machine Learning,* Special Issue on Multistrategy
                Learning, pp. 153–172, 1992.

I(v,x) E   **Saitta, L., Botta, M., Ravotto, S. and Sperotto, S.B.,** "Improving
                Learning by Using Deep Models," *Proceedings of the First
                International Workshop on Multistrategy Learning,* R.S. Michalski
                and G. Tecuci (Eds.), Harpers Ferry, WV, pp. 131–143, George
                Mason Univ., Center for AI, Fairfax, VA, 1991.

B P   **Samuel, A.L.,** "Some Studies in Machine Learning Using the
                Game of Checkers," *IBM Journal of Research and Development,*
                Vol. 3, pp. 211–229, 1959.

B P   **Samuel, A.L.,** "Some Studies in Machine Learning Using the
                Game of Checkers: Part II—Recent Progress," *IBM Journal of
                Research and Development,* Vol. 11, pp. 601–617, 1967.

I(s,x)   **Sarrett, W.E. and Pazzani, M.J.,** "One-Sided Algorithms for
                Integrating Empirical and Explanation-Based Learning,"
                *Proceedings of the 6th International Workshop on Machine
                Learning,* Ithaca, NY, pp. 26–28, Morgan Kaufmann, San Mateo,
                CA, 1989.

B g   **Schaffer, J.D.,** "Some Experiments in Machine Learning Using
                Vector Evaluated Genetic Algorithms," *Ph.D. Thesis,* Vanderbilt
                University, 1984.

B g   **Schaffer, J.D. (Ed.),** *Proceedings of the 3rd International
                Conference on Genetic Algorithms,* Morgan Kaufmann, San
                Mateo, CA, 1989.

B I(g,n)   **Schaffer, J.D.,** "Genetic Algorithms and Neural Networks: The
                State of the Art," *Proceedings of the Workshop on Combinations
                of Genetic Algorithms and Neural Networks,* Baltimore, MD, June
                4–7, 1992.

B   **Schank, R.C.,** *Explanation Patterns: Understanding Mechanically and Creatively,* Lawrence Erlbaum Associates, Hillsdale, NJ, 1986.

B   **Schank, R.C.,** "Where's the AI?" *AI Magazine,* Vol. 12, No. 4, pp. 38–49, 1991.

B   **Schank, R.C. and Abelson, R.P.,** *Scripts, Plans, Goals, and Understanding,* Lawrence Erlbaum Associates, Hillsdale, NJ, 1977.

B   **Schank, R.C. and Kass, A.,** "Explanations, Machine Learning and Creativity," in *Machine Learning: An Artificial Intelligence Approach,* Vol. III, Y. Kodratoff and R.S. Michalski (Eds.), Morgan Kaufmann, San Mateo, CA, 1990.

I(g,n)   **Schizas, C., Pattichis, C., Livesay, R. and Middleton, L.,** "Neural Networks, Genetic Algorithms and K-Means Algorithm," *Proceedings of the Workshop on Combinations of Genetic Algorithms and Neural Networks,* Baltimore, MD, 1992.

B n   **Schwartz, E.L. (Ed.),** *Computational Neuroscience,* The MIT Press, Cambridge, MA, 1990.

E I(s,v)   **Segen, J.,** "Learning Structural Descriptions of Shape," *Proceedings of the IEEE Conference on Computer Vision and Pattern Recognition,* pp. 96–98, IEEE Computer Society, Washington, DC, 1985.

E I(s,v)   **Segen, J.,** "Learning Graph Models of Shape," *Proceedings of the 5th International Conference on Machine Learning,* Ann Arbor, MI, pp. 29–35, Morgan Kaufmann, San Mateo, CA, 1988.

E I(s,v)   **Segen, J.,** "From Features to Symbols: Learning Relational Models of Shape," in *From Pixels to Features,* J.C. Simon (Ed.), North-Holland, Amsterdam, 1989.

E I(s,v)   **Segen, J.,** "Model Learning and Recognition of Nonrigid Shapes," *Proceedings of the Conference on Computer Vision and Pattern Recognition,* San Diego, CA, pp. 597–602, IEEE Computer Society Press, Washington, DC, 1989.

E I(v,c)   **Segen, J.,** "GEST: An Integrated Approach to Learning in Computer Vision," *Proceedings of the First International Workshop on Multistrategy Learning,* R.S. Michalski and G. Tecuci (Eds.), Harpers Ferry, WV, pp. 403–410, George Mason Univ., Center for AI, Fairfax, VA, 1991.

E I(v,c)   **Segen, J.,** "GEST: A Learning Computer Vision System That Recognizes Hand Gestures," in *Machine Learning: A Multistrategy Approach,* Vol. IV, R.S. Michalski and G. Tecuci (Eds.), Morgan Kaufmann, San Mateo, CA, 1994.

B   **Segre, A. (Ed.),** *Proceedings of the 6th International Conference on Machine Learning,* Morgan Kaufmann, San Mateo, CA, 1989.

B x   **Segre, A., Elkan, C. and Russell, A.,** "A Critical Look at Experimental Evaluations of EBL," *Machine Learning,* Vol. 6, pp. 183–195, 1991.

B P x   **Segre, A.M.,** "Explanation-Based Learning of Generalized Robot Assembly Plans," *Ph.D. Thesis,* University of Illinois at Urbana-Champaign, 1987.

B P x   **Segre, A.M.,** *Machine Learning of Robot Assembly Plans,* Knowledge Representation, Learning and Expert Systems, Kluwer Academic, Boston, 1988.

B   **Shafer, G. and Pearl, J. (Eds.),** *Readings in Uncertain Reasoning,* Morgan Kaufmann, Los Altos, CA, 1990.

B   **Shapiro, S.C. (Ed.),** *Encyclopedia of Artificial Intelligence,* Vols. I & II, John Wiley & Sons, New York, 1987.

B P s,x   **Shavlik, J.W.,** "Acquiring Recursive and Iterative Concepts with Explanation-Based Learning," *Machine Learning,* Vol. 5, pp. 39–70, 1990.

B   **Shavlik, J.W. and Dietterich, T.G. (Eds.),** *Readings in Machine Learning,* Morgan Kaufmann, San Mateo, CA, 1990.

I(n,x)   **Shavlik, J.W. and Towell, G.G.,** "An Approach to Combining Explanation-Based and Neural Learning Algorithms," *Connection Science,* Vol. 1, pp. 233–255, 1989.

I(n,x)   **Shavlik, J.W. and Towell, G.G.,** "Combining Explanation-Based Learning and Artificial Neural Networks," *Proceedings of the 6th International Workshop on Machine Learning,* Ithaca, NY, pp. 90–92, Morgan Kaufmann, San Mateo, CA, 1989.

I(a,s)   **Shen, W.M.,** "Complementary Discrimination Learning: A Duality between Generalization and Discrimination," *Proceedings of AAAI-90,* T. Dietterich and W. Swartout (Eds.), pp. 834–839, AAAI Press, Menlo Park, CA, 1990.

I(s,x) K   **Shen, W.M.,** "Discovering Regularities from Large Knowledge Bases," *Proceedings of the Eighth International Workshop on Machine Learning,* Evanston, IL, pp. 539–543, Morgan Kaufmann, San Mateo, CA, 1991.

B   **Shortliffe, E.H.,** *Computer-Based Medical Consultations: MYCIN*, American Elsevier, New York, 1976.

B T d   **Shrager, J. and Langley, P.W. (Eds.),** *Computational Models of Scientific Discovery and Theory Formation*, Morgan Kaufmann, San Mateo, CA, 1990.

B   **Shrobe, H.E. and AAAI (Eds.),** *Exploring Artificial Intelligence: Survey Talks from the National Conferences on Artificial Intelligence*, Morgan Kaufmann, Los Altos, CA, 1988.

I(x...)   **Silver, B.,** "A Hybrid Approach in an Imperfect Domain," *Proceedings of the AAAI 1988 Symposium on Explanation-Based Learning*, Stanford, CA, pp. 52–56, 1988.

I(s,x)   **Silver, B., Frawley, W., Iba, G., Vittal, J. and Bradford, K.,** "ILS: A Framework for Multi-Paradigmatic Learning," *Proceedings of the 7th International Conference on Machine Learning*, B.W. Porter and R.J. Mooney (Eds.), Austin, TX, pp. 348–356, Morgan Kaufmann, San Mateo, CA, 1990.

B   **Simon, H.A.,** *Sciences of the Artificial*, MIT Press, Cambridge, MA, 1969.

B   **Simon, H.A.,** *Models of Thought*, Yale University Press, New Haven, CT, 1979.

B   **Simon, H.A.,** "Why Should Machines Learn?" in *Machine Learning: An Artificial Intelligence Approach*, Vol. I, R.S. Michalski, J.G. Carbonell and T.M. Mitchell (Eds.), Tioga/Morgan Kaufmann, Los Altos, CA, 1983.

B M P   **Simon, H.A. and Lea, G.,** "Problem Solving and Rule Induction: A Unified View," in *Knowledge and Cognition*, L. Gregg (Ed.), Lawrence Erlbaum, Hillsdale, NJ, 1974.

B P a   **Simpson, R.L.,** "A Computer Model of Case-Based Reasoning in Problem Solving: An Investigation in the Domain of Dispute Mediation," *Ph.D. Thesis,* Georgia Institute of Technology, 1985.

I(d,x)   **Sims, M.H.,** "Empirical and Analytic Discovery in IL," *Proceedings of the 4th International Machine Learning Workshop*, University of California, Irvine, pp. 274–280, Morgan Kaufmann, San Mateo, CA, 1987.

I(a,s)   **Skalak, D.B. and Rissland, E.L.,** "Inductive Learning in a Mixed Paradigm Setting," *Proceedings of AAAI-90*, T. Dietterich and W. Swartout (Eds.), pp. 840–847, AAAI Press, Menlo Park, CA, 1990.

B M   **Sleeman, D.H.,** "Inferring Student Models for Intelligent
                Computer-Aided Instruction," in *Machine Learning: An Artificial
                Intelligence Approach*, Vol. I, R.S. Michalski, J.G. Carbonell and
                T.M. Mitchell (Eds.), Tioga/Morgan Kaufmann, Los Altos, CA,
                1983.

B M   **Sleeman, D.H. and Brown, J.S.,** *Intelligent Tutoring Systems*,
                Academic Press, San Diego, CA, 1982.

B   **Sleeman, D.H. and Edwards, P. (Eds.),** *Proceedings of the 9th
                International Conference on Machine Learning*, Morgan
                Kaufmann, San Mateo, CA, 1992.

B   **Smith, R.G. and Mitchell, T.M. (Eds.),** *Proceedings of AAAI-88,
                Seventh National Conference on Artificial Intelligence*, AAAI
                Press, Menlo Park, CA, 1988.

B   **Solomonoff, R.,** "A Formal Theory of Inductive Learning,"
                Information and Control, Vol. 7, pp. 1–22, 224–254, 1964.

B   **Soloway, E.,** "Learning = Interpretation + Generalization: A Case
                Study in Knowlege-Directed Learning," *Ph.D. Thesis,* Computer
                and Information Sciences Dept., University of Massachusetts,
                Amherst, MA, 1978.

B   **Sowa, J.F. (Ed.),** *Principles of Semantic Networks: Explorations
                in the Representation of Knowledge*, Morgan Kaufmann, Los
                Altos, CA, 1991.

B   **Sowa, J.F.,** *Conceptual Structures: Information Processing in
                Mind and Machine*, Addison Wesley, Reading, MA, 1984.

I(g,n)   **Spears, W.,** "Using Neural Networks and Genetic Algorithms as
                Heuristics for NP-Complete Problems," *International Joint
                Conference on Neural Networks*, Washington, DC, 1990.

I(g,s) E   **Spears, W.M. and Gordon, D.F.,** "Adaptive Strategy Selection
                for Concept Learning," *Proceedings of the First International
                Workshop on Multistrategy Learning*, R.S. Michalski and G.
                Tecuci (Eds.), Harpers Ferry, WV, pp. 231–246, George Mason
                Univ., Center for AI, Fairfax, VA, 1991.

B   **Sridharan, N.S. (Ed.),** *Proceedings of the 11th International Joint
                Conference on Artificial Intelligence*, AAAI Press, Menlo Park,
                CA, 1989.

B P   **Stefik, M.J.,** "Planning with Constraints," *Ph.D. Thesis,*
                Computer Science Dept., Stanford University, 1980.

B c   **Stepp, R.E.**, "Conjunctive Conceptual Clustering: A Methodology and Experimentation," *Ph.D. Thesis,* University of Illinois at Urbana-Champaign, 1984.

B M   **Stillings, N.A., Feinstein, M.H., Garfield, J.L., Rissland, E.L., Rosenbaum, D.A., Weisler, S.E. and Baker-Ward, L.,** *Cognitive Science: An Introduction,* The MIT Press, Cambridge, MA, 1987.

B   **Subramanian, D.,** "Representational Issues in Machine Learning," *Proceedings of the 6th International Workshop on Machine Learning,* Ithaca, NY, pp. 426–429, Morgan Kaufmann, San Mateo, CA, 1989.

I(v,x)   **Subramanian, S. and Mooney, R.J.,** "Combining Abduction and Theory Revision," *Proceedings of the First International Workshop on Multistrategy Learning,* R.S. Michalski and G. Tecuci (Eds.), Harpers Ferry, WV, pp. 207–214, George Mason Univ., Center for AI, Fairfax, VA, 1991.

B   **Sussman, G.J.,** *A Computer Model of Skill Acquisition,* American Elsevier, New York, 1975.

B g   **Sutton, R.S.,** "Temporal Credit Assignment in Reinforcement Learning," *Ph.D. Thesis,* University of Massachusetts, 1984.

I(x…)   **Swaminathan, K.,** "Integrated Learning with an Incomplete and Intractable Domain Theory: The Problem of Epidemiological Diagnosis," *Proceedings of the AAAI 1988 Symposium on Explanation-Based Learning,* Stanford, pp. 62–66, 1988.

I(a,s,v)   **Tausend, B. and Bell, S.,** "Analogical Reasoning for Logic Programming," *Proceedings of the European Working Session on Learning,* Y. Kodratoff (Ed.), Porto, Portugal, pp. 391–397, Springer-Verlag, New York, 1991.

E K P   **Tecuci, G.,** "DISCIPLE: A Theory, Methodology and System for
I(a,c,s,v,x) Learning Expert Knowledge," *Ph.D. Thesis,* University of Paris-South, 1988.

K P   **Tecuci, G.,** "A Multistrategy Learning Approach to Domain
I(a,c,s,v,x) Modeling and Knowledge Acquisition,," *Proceedings of the European Working Session on Learning,* Y. Kodratoff (Ed.), Porto, Portugal, pp. 14–32, 1991.

I(a,s,v,x) **Tecuci, G.,** "Learning as Understanding the External World," *Proceedings of the First International Workshop on Multistrategy Learning,* R.S. Michalski and G. Tecuci (Eds.), Harpers Ferry, WV, pp. 49–65, George Mason Univ., Center for AI, Fairfax, VA, 1991.

I(a,s,v,x)   **Tecuci, G.,** "An Inference-Based Framework for Multistrategy Learning," in *Machine Learning: A Multistrategy Approach*, Vol. IV, R.S. Michalski and G. Tecuci (Eds.), Morgan Kaufmann, San Mateo, CA, 1994.

E K P   **Tecuci, G.,** "Automating Knowledge Acquisition as Extending,
I(a,s,v,x)   Updating and Improving a Knowledge Base," *IEEE Transactions on Systems, Man, and Cybernetics*, Vol. 22, No. 4, pp. 1444–1460, 1992.

I(a,s,v,x)   **Tecuci, G.,** "Plausible Justification Trees: A Framework for the Deep and Dynamic Integration of Learning Strategies," *Machine Learning*, Special Issue on Multistrategy Learning, pp. 237–261, 1994.

I(a,s,x)   **Tecuci, G. and Kodratoff, Y.,** "Multistrategy Learning in Non-Homogeneous Domain Theories," *Proceedings of the 6th International Workshop on Machine Learning*, A. Segre (Ed.), Cornell University, Ithaca, NY, pp. 14–16, Morgan Kaufmann, San Mateo, CA, 1989.

E K P   **Tecuci, G. and Kodratoff, Y.,** "Apprenticeship Learning in
I(a,s,v,x)   Imperfect Theory Domains," in *Machine Learning: An Artificial Intelligence Approach*, Vol. III, Y. Kodratoff and R.S. Michalski (Eds.), Morgan Kaufmann, San Mateo, CA, 1990.

I(a,s,v,x)   **Tecuci, G. and Michalski, R.S.,** "A Method for Multistrategy Task-Adaptive Learning Based on Plausible Justifications," *Proceedings of the Eighth International Workshop on Machine Learning*, Evanston, IL, pp. 549–553, Morgan Kaufmann, San Mateo, CA, 1991.

I(a,s,v,x)   **Tecuci, G. and Michalski, R.S.,** "Input 'Understanding' as a Basis for Multistrategy Task-Adaptive Learning," *Proceedings of the International Symposium on Methodologies for Intelligent Systems*, Z. Ras and M. Zemankova (Eds.), Charlotte, NC, Elsevier Science Publishing, New York, 1991.

E K P I(a,s,x) **Tecuci, G., Kodratoff, Y., Bodnaru, Z. and Brunet, T.,** "DISCIPLE: An Expert and Learning System," in *Research and Development in Expert Systems IV*, D.S. Moralee (Ed.), Cambridge University Press, Cambridge, UK, 1987.

E I(g,n,s) **Thrun, S.B., Bala, J.W., Bloedorn, E., Bratko, I., Cestnink, B., Cheng, J., DeJong, K.A., Dzeroski, S., Fahlman, S.E., Hamann, R., Kaufman, K., Keller, S., Kononenko, I., Kreuziger, J., Michalski, R.S., Mitchell, T., Pachowicz, P., Vafaie, H., Van de Velde, W., Wenzel, W., Wnek, J. and Zhang, J.,** "The MONK's Problems: A Performance Comparison of Different Learning Algorithms," *Computer Science Reports, Carnegie Mellon University*, CMU-CS-91–197, Carnegie Mellon University, 1991.

B n **Touretzky, D.S. (Ed.),** *Advances in Neural Information Processing Systems*, Morgan Kaufmann, San Mateo, CA, 1989.

E I(a,n) **Touretzky, D.S. and Wheeler, D.W.,** "Phonology as a Window on Symbol Processing: Theoretical and Computational Paradigms," *Proceedings of the 5th International Symposium on Methodologies for Intelligent Systems*, Z.W. Ras, M. Zemankova and M.L. Emrich (Eds.), Knoxville, TN, pp. 446–455, Elsevier Science Publishing, New York, 1990.

I(n,x) **Towell, G.G. and Shavlik, J.W.,** "Refining Symbolic Knowledge Using Neural Networks," *Proceedings of the First International Workshop on Multistrategy Learning*, R.S. Michalski and G. Tecuci (Eds.), Harpers Ferry, WV, pp. 257–272, 1991.

I(n,x) **Towell, G.G. and Shavlik, J.W.,** "Refining Symbolic Knowledge Using Neural Networks,," in *Machine Learning: A Multistrategy Approach*, Vol. IV, R.S. Michalski and G. Tecuci (Eds.), Morgan Kaufmann, San Mateo, CA, 1994.

I(s,v) M **Towell, G.G., Craven, M.W. and Shavlik, J.W.,** "Constructive Induction in Knowledge-Based Neural Networks," *Proceedings of the Eighth International Workshop on Machine Learning*, Evanston, IL, pp. 213–217, Morgan Kaufmann, San Mateo, CA, 1991.

B **Tsypkin, Y.Z.,** *Foundations of the Theory of Learning Systems*, Academic Press, San Diego, CA, 1973.

B v **Utgoff, P.E.,** *Machine Learning of Inductive Bias*, Kluwer Academic, Boston, 1986.

I(g,s) **Vafaie, H. and DeJong, K.,** "Improving the Performance of a Rule Induction System Using Genetic Algorithms," *Proceedings of the First International Workshop on Multistrategy Learning*, R.S. Michalski and G. Tecuci (Eds.), Harpers Ferry, WV, pp. 305–315, George Mason Univ., Center for AI, Fairfax, VA, 1991.

I(g,s)   **Vafaie, H. and DeJong, K.,** "Improving a Rule Learning System Using Genetic Algorithms," in *Machine Learning: A Multistrategy Approach,* Vol. IV, R.S. Michalski and G. Tecuci (Eds.), Morgan Kaufmann, San Mateo, CA, 1994.

B T   **Valiant, L.G.,** "A Theory of the Learnable," *Communications of the ACM,* Vol. 27, pp. 1134–1142, 1984.

B P s   **VanLehn, K.,** "Learning One Subprocedure per Lesson," *Artificial Intelligence,* Vol. 31, pp. 1–40, Morgan Kaufmann, San Mateo, CA, 1987.

M P I(a,x)   **VanLehn, K. and Jones, R.M.,** "Learning Physics Via Explanation-Based Learning of Correctness and Analogical Search Control," *Proceedings of the Eighth International Workshop on Machine Learning,* Evanston, IL, pp. 110–116, Morgan Kaufmann, San Mateo, CA, 1991.

B   **Vardi, M.Y. (Ed.),** *Proceedings of the 2nd Conference (TARK 1988),* Morgan Kaufmann, Los Altos, CA, 1988.

I(a,x) P   **Veloso, M. and Carbonell, J.G.,** "Automating Case Generation, Storage, and Retrieval in PRODIGY," *Proceedings of the First International Workshop on Multistrategy Learning,* R.S. Michalski and G. Tecuci (Eds.), Harpers Ferry, WV, pp. 363–377, George Mason Univ., Center for AI, Fairfax, VA, 1991.

I(a,x) P   **Veloso, M. and Carbonell, J.G.,** "Automating Case Generation, Storage, and Retrieval in PRODIGY," in *Machine Learning: A Multistrategy Approach,* Vol. IV, R.S. Michalski and G. Tecuci (Eds.), Morgan Kaufmann, San Mateo, CA, 1994.

B s   **Vere, S.A.,** "Inductive Learning of Relational Productions," in *Pattern-Directed Inference Systems,* D.A. Waterman and F. Hayes-Roth (Eds.), Academic Press, San Diego, CA, 1978.

I(s,x)   **Vilain, M., Koton, P. and Chase, M.P.,** "On Analytical and Similarity-Based Classification," *Proceedings of AAAI-90,* T. Dietterich and W. Swartout (Eds.), pp. 867–874, AAAI Press, Menlo Park, CA, 1990.

B I(a,s)   **Vosniadou, S. and Ortony, A. (Eds.),** *Similarity and Analogical Reasoning,* Cambridge University Press, Cambridge, UK, 1989.

I(a,s)   **Vrain, C. and Kodratoff, Y.,** "The Use of Analogy in Incremental SBL," in *Knowledge Representation and Organization in Machine Learning,* K. Morik (Ed.), Springer Verlag, Berlin, 1989.

B T   **Warmuth, M.K. and Valiant, L. (Eds.),** *Proceedings of the 4th Annual Workshop on Computational Learning Theory*, Morgan Kaufmann, San Mateo, CA, 1991.

B   **Waterman, D.A.,** "Generalization Learning Techniques for Automating the Learning of Heuristics," *Artificial Intelligence*, Vol. 1, pp. 121–170, 1970.

B   **Waterman, D.A. and Hayes-Roth, F. (Eds.),** *Pattern-Directed Inference Systems*, Academic Press, San Diego, CA, 1978.

B   **Webber, B.L. and Nilsson, N.J. (Eds.),** *Readings in Artificial Intelligence*, Tioga, Palo Alto, CA, 1981.

B   **Wechsler, H.,** *Computational Vision*, Academic Press, San Diego, CA, 1990.

B n   **Wechsler, H. (Ed.),** *Neural Networks for Perception: Computation, Learning, and Architectures*, Academic Press, San Diego, CA, 1992.

B n   **Wechsler, H. (Ed.),** *Neural Networks for Perception: Human and and Machine Perception*, Academic Press, San Diego, CA, 1992.

B M   **Weinert, F. and Kluwe, R. (Eds.),** *Metacognition, Motivation, and Understanding*, Lawrence Erlbaum Associates, Hillsdale, NJ, 1987.

B E I(n,s)   **Weiss, S.M. and Kapouleas, I.,** "An Empirical Comparison of Pattern Recognition, Neural Nets, and Machine Learning Classification Methods," *Proceedings of IJCAI-89*, pp. 781–787, AAAI Press, Menlo Park, CA, 1989.

B E   **Weiss, S.M. and Kulikowski, C.A.,** *Computer Systems That Learn: Classification and Prediction Methods from Statistics, Neural Nets, Machine Learning and Expert Systems*, Morgan Kaufmann, San Mateo, CA, 1990.

B   **Weld, D.S. and DeKleer, J. (Eds.),** *Readings in Qualitative Reasoning about Physical Systems*, Morgan Kaufmann, Los Altos, CA, 1990.

B n,r   **Werbos, P.,** "Beyond Regression: New Tools for Prediction and Analysis in Behavioral Sciences," *Ph.D. Thesis,* Harvard University, 1984.

I(s,x) E   **Whitehall, B.L. and Lu, S.C.-Y.,** "A Study of How Domain Knowledge Improves Knowledge-Based Learning Systems," *Proceedings of the Eighth International Workshop on Machine Learning*, Evanston, IL, pp. 559–563, Morgan Kaufmann, San Mateo, CA, 1991.

I(s,x) E   **Whitehall, B.L., Lu, S.C.-Y. and Stepp, R.E.,** "Theory
Completion Using Knowledge-Based Learning," *Proceedings of
the First International Workshop on Multistrategy Learning*, R.S.
Michalski and G. Tecuci (Eds.), Harpers Ferry, WV, pp. 144–159,
George Mason Univ., Center for AI, Fairfax, VA, 1991.

I(s,x) E   **Whitehall, B.L., and Lu, S.C.-Y.,** "Theory Completion using
Knowledge-Based Learning,," in *Machine Learning: A
Multistrategy Approach*, Vol. IV, R.S. Michalski and G. Tecuci
(Eds.), Morgan Kaufmann, San Mateo, CA, 1994.

B I(g,n)   **Whitley, D.,** "Genetic Algorithms and Neural Networks:
Challenges and Opportunities," *Proceedings of the Workshop on
Combinations of Genetic Algorithms and Neural Networks*,
Baltimore, MD, 1992.

I(g,n)   **Whitley, D., Dominic, S. and Das, R.,** "Genetic Reinforcement
Learning with Multilayer Neural Networks," *Proceedings of the
4th International Conference on Genetic Algorithms*, San Diego,
CA, pp. 562–570, Morgan Kaufmann, San Mateo, CA, 1991.

I(s,x)   **Widmer, G.,** "An Incremental Version of Bergadano and
Giordana's Integrated Learning Strategy," *Proceedings of
EWSL-89*, Montpellier, France, 1989.

I(s,x)   **Widmer, G.,** "A Tight Integration of Deductive and Inductive
Learning," *Proceedings of the 6th International Workshop on
Machine Learning*, pp. 11–13, Morgan Kaufmann, San Mateo,
CA, 1989.

I(s,v,x)   **Widmer, G.,** "Learning by Plausible Reasoning and Its
Application to a Complex Musical Problem," *Proceedings of the
First International Workshop on Multistrategy Learning*, R.S.
Michalski and G. Tecuci (Eds.), Harpers Ferry, WV, pp. 411–418,
George Mason Univ., Center for AI, Fairfax, VA, 1991.

I(s,x)   **Widmer, G.,** "Using Plausible Explanations to Bias Empirical
Generalizations in Weak Theory Domains," *Proceedings of the
European Working Session on Learning*, Y. Kodratoff (Ed.), Porto,
Portugal, pp. 33–43, Springer-Verlag, New York, 1991.

I(s,v,x)   **Widmer, G.,** "Learning with a Qualitative Domain Theory by
Means of Plausible Explanations," in *Machine Learning: A
Multistrategy Approach*, Vol. IV, R.S. Michalski and G. Tecuci
(Eds.), Morgan Kaufmann, San Mateo, CA, 1994.

B K P   **Wilkins, D.C.,** "Knowledge Base Refinement Using
                 Apprenticeship Learning," in *Machine Learning: An Artificial
                 Intelligence Approach*, Vol. III, Y. Kodratoff and R.S. Michalski
                 (Eds.), Morgan Kaufmann, San Mateo, CA, 1990.

B   **Wilkins, D.E.,** *Practical Planning: Extending the Classical AI
                 Planning Paradigm*, Morgan Kaufmann, Los Altos, CA, 1988.

B s   **Winston, P.H.,** "Learning Structural Descriptions from
                 Examples," *Technical Report*, TR-231, AI Laboratory, MIT,
                 Cambridge, MA, 1970.

B   **Winston, P.H. (Ed.),** *The Psychology of Computer Vision*,
                 McGraw-Hill, New York, 1975.

B   **Winston, P.H.,** *Artificial Intelligence*, Addison-Wesley, Reading,
                 MA, 1984.

B   **Winston, P.H. and Brown, R.H. (Eds.),** *Artificial Intelligence:
                 An MIT Perspective*, MIT Press, Cambridge, MA, 1979.

I(s,v) M   **Wisniewski, E. and Medin, D.,** "Harpoons and Long Sticks: The
                 Interaction of Theory and Similarity in Rule Induction," in
                 *Concept Formation: Knowledge and Experience in Unsupervised
                 Learning*, D. Fisher and M.J. Pazzani (Eds.), Morgan Kaufmann,
                 San Mateo, CA, 1991.

I(v,x) M   **Wisniewski, E.J. and Medin, D.L.,** "Feature Construction in
                 Human and Machine Learning," *Proceedings of the First
                 International Workshop on Multistrategy Learning*, R.S. Michalski
                 and G. Tecuci (Eds.), Harpers Ferry, WV, pp. 343–354, George
                 Mason Univ., Center for AI, Fairfax, VA, 1991.

I(s,x)   **Wisniewski, E.J. and Medin, D.L.,** "Is it a Pocket or a Purse?
                 Tightly Coupled Theory and Data Driven Learning," *Proceedings
                 of the Eighth International Workshop on Machine Learning*,
                 Evanston, IL, pp. 564–568, Morgan Kaufmann, San Mateo, CA,
                 1991.

I(v,x) M   **Wisniewski, E.J. and Medin, D.L.,** "The Fiction and Nonfiction
                 of Features," in *Machine Learning: A Multistrategy Approach*,
                 Vol. IV, R.S. Michalski and G. Tecuci (Eds.), Morgan Kaufmann,
                 San Mateo, CA, 1994.

I(s,v,x)   **Wnek, J.,** "Transformation of Version Space with Constructive
                 Induction: The VS* Algorithm," *Reports of Machine Learning and
                 Inference Laboratory*, MLI-92–01, George Mason Univ., Center
                 for AI, Fairfax, VA, 1992.

I(s,n,g,v) E   **Wnek, J. and Michalski, R.S.,** "An Experimental Comparison of Symbolic and Subsymbolic Learning Paradigms: Phase I—Learning Logic-Style Concepts," *Proceedings of the First International Workshop on Multistrategy Learning*, R.S. Michalski and G. Tecuci (Eds.), Harpers Ferry, WV, pp. 324–339, George Mason Univ., Center for AI, Fairfax, VA, 1991.

I(s,n,g,v) E   **Wnek, J. and Michalski, R.S.,** "Comparing Symbolic and Subsymbolic Learning: Three Studies," in *Machine Learning: A Multistrategy Approach*, Vol. IV, R.S. Michalski and G. Tecuci (Eds.), Morgan Kaufmann, San Mateo, CA, 1994.

I(s,x)   **Wollowski, M.,** "A Schema for an Integrated Learning System," *Proceedings of the 6th International Workshop on Machine Learning*, pp. 87–89, Morgan Kaufmann, San Mateo, CA, 1989.

I(s,v) K   **Wrobel, S.,** "Demand-Driven Concept Formation," in *Knowledge Representation and Organization in Machine Learning*, K. Morik (Ed.), Springer Verlag, Berlin, 1989.

I(s,v) P   **Wrobel, S.,** "Toward a Model of Grounded Concept Formation," *Proceedings of IJCAI-91*, pp. 712–717, AAAI Press, Menlo Park, CA, 1991.

I(s,x)   **Wu, Y., Wang, S. and Zhou, Q.,** "An Integrated Framework of Inducing Rules from Examples," *Proceedings of the 7th International Conference on Machine Learning*, B.W. Porter and R.J. Mooney (Eds.), Austin, TX, pp. 357–367, Morgan Kaufmann, San Mateo, CA, 1990.

I(s,x)   **Yamamura, M. and Kobayashi, S.,** "An Augmented EBL and Its Application to the Utility Problem," *Proceedings of IJCAI-91*, pp. 623–629, AAAI Press, Menlo Park, CA, 1991.

I(s,x)   **Yoo, J. and Fisher, D.H.,** "Identifying Cost Effective Boundaries of Operationality," *Proceedings of the Eighth International Workshop on Machine Learning*, Evanston, IL, pp. 569–576, Morgan Kaufmann, San Mateo, CA, 1991.

I(c,x)   **Yoo, J.P. and Fisher, D.H.,** "Conceptual Clustering of Explanations," *Proceedings of the 6th International Workshop on Machine Learning*, pp. 8–10, 1989.

B   **Zadeh, L.A.,** "Approximate Reasoning Based on Fuzzy Logic," *Proceedings of the 6th International Joint Conference on Artificial Intelligence*, pp. 1004–1010, AAAI Press, Menlo Park, CA, 1979.

B   **Zaremba, J.,** "Overview of Machine Learning," *Bulletin of Polish Academy of Sciences*, 1988.

I(s,x) P   **Zerr, F. and Ganascia, J.G.,** "Integrating an Explanation-Based Learning Mechanism into a General Problem-Solver," *Proceedings of the European Working Session on Learning,* Y. Kodratoff (Eds.), Porto, Portugal, pp. 62–80, Springer-Verlag, Berlin, 1991.

I(n,s)   **Zhang, J.,** "Integrating Symbolic and Subsymbolic Approaches in Learning Flexible Concepts," *Proceedings of the First International Workshop on Multistrategy Learning,* R.S. Michalski and G. Tecuci (Eds.), Harpers Ferry, WV, pp. 289–304, George Mason Univ., Center for AI, Fairfax, VA, 1991.

I(n,s)   **Zhang, J.,** "Learning Graded Concept Descriptions by Integrating Symbolic and Subsymbolic Approaches," in *Machine Learning: A Multistrategy Approach,* Vol. IV, R.S. Michalski and G. Tecuci (Eds.), Morgan Kaufmann, San Mateo, CA, 1994.

B E K   **Zhou, H.H.,** "CSM: A Computational Model of Cumulative Learning," *Machine Learning,* Vol. 5, pp. 383–406, 1990.

I(a,g)   **Zhou, H.H. and Grefenstette, J.J.,** "Learning by Analogy in Genetic Classifier Systems," *Proceedings of the 3rd International Conference on Genetic Algorithms and Their Applications,* Fairfax, VA, pp. 291–297, Morgan Kaufmann, San Mateo, CA, 1989.

B x   **Zito-Wolf, R.J.,** "Learning Search Control Knowledge: An Explanation-Based Approach," *Machine Learning,* Vol. 6, pp. 197–204, 1991.

B d   **Zytkow, J.M. and Simon, H.A.,** "A Theory of Historical Discovery: The Construction of Componential Models," *Machine Learning,* Vol. 1, No. 1, pp. 107–136, 1986.

ABOUT THE AUTHORS

Jerzy W. Bala is a National Science Foundation postdoctoral Research Associate in the Center for Artificial Intelligence at George Mason University. He received his M.S. in Electrical Engineering in 1985 from the University of Mining and Metallurgy, Cracow, Poland, and his Ph.D. in information technology in 1993 from George Mason University. His interests include machine learning, computer vision, and the combining of symbolic and genetic learning. His research concerns the development of computer vision systems with learning capabilities and their application to visual texture and surface recognition. His current address is Center for Artificial Intelligence, School for Information Technology and Engineering, George Mason University, 4400 University Drive, Fairfax, VA 22030.

Cristina Baroglio is a doctoral candidate in the Computer Science Department of the University of Torino. She graduated from the same department in 1991. Her current research is on learning contextually interdependent concepts. She is also collaborating with CSELT (Center for Telecommunication Studies) to conduct research on neural net models and their application to speech recognition. Her current address is Dipartimento di Informatica, Università di Torino, Corso Svizzera 185, 10149, Torino, Italy.

Marco Botta is a doctoral candidate in the Department of Computer Science at the University of Torino, Italy. His research activity is mainly concerned with concept learning applied to the construction and refinement of expert systems knowledge bases. His current address is Dipartimento di Informatica, Università di Torino, Corso Svizzera 185, 10149, Torino, Italy.

Maurice Bruynooghe is Senior Research Associate at the Belgian National Fund for Scientific Research. He obtained the degree of Engineer in Computer Science at the Katholieke Universiteit in Leuven. He received a Ph.D. degree from the same university in 1979; the subject of the thesis was logic programming. He did work on implementation techniques for Prolog, intelligent backtracking, program transformation techniques, abstract interpretation of logic programs, and inductive learning within a logic programming context. He has published many papers and participated in the Programme Committees of several conferences and workshops and is currently Editor-in-Chief of the Journal of Logic Programming. His main research interest is logic programming. His current address is KULeuven, Department of Computer Science, Celestijnenlaan 200A, B-3001 Heverlee, Belgium.

Jaime G. Carbonell is Professor of Computer Science and Director of the Center for Machine Translation at Carnegie Mellon University. He received his B.S. degrees in Physics and in Mathematics from MIT in 1975 and his M.S. and Ph.D. degrees in Computer Science from Yale University in 1976 and 1978, respectively. Dr. Carbonell has authored some 150 technical papers and has edited or co-edited several books, including *Machine Learning: An Artificial Intelligence Approach*, volumes 1 and 2, and *Machine Learning: Paradigms and Methods*. He was executive editor of the international journal *Machine Learning* from 1988 to 1992 and serves on several editorial boards, including those of *Artificial Intelligence* and *Machine Learning*. Dr. Carbonell is a founder and director of Carnegie Group Inc., one of the leading Artificial Intelligence companies. Dr. Carbonell's research interests span several areas of artificial intelligence, including machine learning, natural language processing, planning and problem solving, knowledge-based machine translation, and analogical reasoning. His current address is School of Computer Science, Carnegie Mellon University, Pittsburgh, PA 15213.

Michael T. Cox is a Ph.D. candidate at the Georgia Institute of Technology. He received a B.S. in Information and Computer Science (highest honor) in 1986 from Georgia Tech, graduating second in his class. His interests in artificial intelligence and psychology center on human self-understanding and its relation to learning and awareness. Related interests are in memory and, in particular, forgetting as passive organizer of knowledge. His internet e-mail address is cox@cc.gatech.edu. His current address is College of Computing, Georgia Institute of Technology, Atlanta, GA 30332–0280.

Andrea Pohoreckyj Danyluk is a member of the Technical Staff at NYNEX Science and Technology, Inc. She received her A.B. in Mathematics/Computer Science from Vassar College in 1984 and her M.S., M.Phil., and Ph.D. degrees in Computer Science from Columbia University in 1986, 1989, and 1992, respectively. Her doctoral research concentrated on combining empirical and analytical learning techniques to augment incomplete knowledge bases. Her current research focuses on using empirical techniques to extract diagnostic knowledge from large, noisy databases. Her current address is NYNEX Science and Technology, 500 Westchester Avenue, White Plains, NY 10604.

Kenneth A. De Jong is Associate Professor of Computer Science and a member of the Center for Artificial Intelligence at George Mason University in Fairfax, Virginia. He received his Ph.D. degree in Computer Science from the University of Michigan in 1975. Since then, he has been a faculty member in the Department of Computer Science at the University of Pittsburgh and a visiting scientist at the Navy Center for Applied Research in Artificial Intelligence. Dr. De Jong's research interests include adaptive systems, machine learning, expert systems, and knowledge representation. He is an active member of the Genetic Algorithms research community with a variety of papers, Ph.D. students, and presentations in this area. He is also responsible for many of the workshops and conferences on genetic algorithms. His current interests include the theoretical analysis of genetic algorithms, as well as their use as heuristics for NP-hard problems and as the learning component of systems capable of learning and refining task programs in domains such as robotics, image understanding, navigation, and game playing. Dr. De Jong is also interested in experience-based learning in which systems must improve their performance while they perform the desired tasks in environments not directly under their control or the control of a benevolent teacher. He is currently directing several genetic learning projects in the areas of game playing, diagnosis, and navigation. His current address is Center for Artificial Intelligence, Department of Computer Science, George Mason University, 4400 University Drive, Fairfax, VA 22030.

Hugo De Garis is a Postdoctoral Fellow of the Science and Technology Agency (STA) at the Electrotechnical Laboratory (ETL), Tsukuba Science City, Japan. He is also head of the CADEPS Artificial Intelligence and Artificial Life Research Unit at the University of Brussels, Belgium, and a senior research associate at the Artificial Intelligence Center at George Mason University, VA. He obtained his Ph.D. in January 1992 from the University of Brussels, with a thesis entitled "Genetic Programming: GenNets, Artificial Nervous Systems, Artificial Embryos." His current research interests include "Genetic Programming," i.e., using genetic algorithms to build/evolve complex systems, such as artificial creatures and artificial embryos. Dr. De Garis has published over 25 papers and book chapters in the areas of machine learning, neural networks, genetic algorithms, artificial life, data analysis, etc. His current address is Brain Builder Group, Evolutionary Systems Department, ATR Human Information Processing Research Laboratories, 2-2 Hikaridai, Seika-cho, Soraku-gun, Kansai Science City, Kyoto, 619-02, Japan.

Jeffrey B. Gould is a doctoral candidate at the University of California at Santa Cruz. He received his B.S. (with highest honors) and M.S. degrees in computer science from the University of California at Santa Cruz in 1990 and 1992, respectively. The title of his master's thesis is "The Development and Testing of an Adaptive Pattern-Oriented Chess System." His research interests are in the area of machine learning. His current address is CIS Department, University of California, Santa Cruz, CA 95064.

Michael R. Hieb is a doctoral candidate in the Information Technology and Engineering Program and a Research Assistant in the Center for Artificial Intelligence at George Mason University. He received his BSNE degree from University of California, Santa Barbara, in 1980 and his Master of Engineering Administration degree from George Washington University in 1991. His interests are in multi-strategy learning, plausible reasoning, and knowledge acquisition. He assisted in implementing an AI testbed at the Goddard Space Flight Center and previously worked as a Nuclear Startup Engineer with General Electric. He is a member of IEEE Computer Society, ACM, and AAAI. His current address is Center for Artificial Intelligence, School for Information Technology and Engineering, George Mason University, 4400 University Drive, Fairfax, VA 22030.

Lawrence E. Hunter directs the Machine Learning Project at the National Library of Medicine. He received a B.A. in Psychology from Yale University in 1982 and a Ph.D. in Computer Science from Yale in 1989. His research focuses on how programs can assemble diverse data sources and analytical tools into coherent plans to achieve specific goals for knowledge. He is particularly interested in applying this methodology to problems in biology and medicine. His research interests also include the cognitive processes of scientists and the development of biologically and evolutionarily informed theories of cognition. His current address is Building 38A—Mail Stop 54, National Library of Medicine, Bethesda, MD 20894.

Yves Kodratoff is Director of Research at the *Centre National de la Recherche Scientifique* unit at the University of Paris-South. He has played an important role in the organization of the European machine learning scientific community by being very active in several ESPRIT projects and by organizing new European conferences. His research interests cover all kinds of inductive inference systems, especially those that merge symbolic and numeric learning techniques. He is also interested in industrial applications of inductive techniques, and he participated actively in the creation of a French company devoted to this purpose. His current address is Equipe Inference et Apprentissage, UA 410 of the CNRS, Laboratoire de Recherche en Informatique, Université Paris-Sud, Bldg. 490, F-91405 Orsay, France.

Robert Levinson is Assistant Professor in the Computer Science Department at the University of California at Santa Cruz, where he has been since 1986. He received B. Math and B. Comp.Sci degrees with high distinction from the University of Minnesota in 1981 and a Ph.D. degree in Computer Science from the University of Texas at Austin in 1985. His current interests cross the broad spectrum of topics in artificial intelligence research, specifically in the areas of machine learning, heuristic search, knowledge representation, and associative pattern retrieval. He has published technical articles on these topics in more than ten different journals and books. His major project, unifying his research, has been an adaptive pattern-oriented chess system named "Morph." In August 1991, he chaired a panel discussion on the Role of Chess in Artificial Intelligence Research at the International Joint Conference on Artificial Intelligence in Sydney, Australia. He is Vice Chair for a 1993 AAAI Spring Symposium on AI and Creativity and is a coordinator of an international collaboration to produce the PEIRCE Conceptual Graph Workbench. His current address is CIS Department, University of California, Santa Cruz, CA 95064.

Stephen C-Y. Lu is Associate Professor in the Department of Mechanical and Industrial Engineering and a Research Associate Professor of the Computer Science Department and the Beckman Institute for Advanced Science and Technology at the University of Illinois at Urbana-Champaign. He is also the founding Director of the Knowledge-Based Engineering Systems Research Laboratory. Dr. Lu received his M.S. and Ph.D. degrees from the Department of Mechanical Engineering and the Robotics Institute of Carnegie Mellon University. His research interests are in the development of artificial intelligence based techniques for advanced engineering automation and in the integration of these techniques with traditional engineering methods. He is actively developing knowledge processing technology to support various concurrent engineering and system management tasks. Dr. Lu has published over 100 technical papers, reports, and book chapters in this area and has served as a keynote speaker for several national and international conferences. He is the recipient of several distinguished awards, among them an NSF Presidential Young Investigator Award in 1987, an Outstanding Young Manufacturing Engineer Award from the Society of Manufacturing Engineers in 1988, and an Outstanding Young Man of America Award in 1988. Dr. Lu was elected Corresponding Member of the International Institution for Production Engineering Research (CIRP) in 1991. His current address is Knowledge-Based Engineering Systems Research Laboratory, Department of Mechanical and Industrial Engineering, University of Illinois at Urbana-Champaign, 1206 W. Green, Urbana, IL 61801.

Stan Matwin is Professor of Computer Science at the University of Ottawa, where he and Rob Holte jointly run the Ottawa Machine Learning Group. He received his degrees from the Department of Mathematics, Computer Science, and Mechanics at the University of Warsaw (M.S. in 1972 and Ph.D. in 1977). He was Assistant Professor at the University of Warsaw until 1979 and, after 1979, a faculty member of the University of Guelph, Acadia University, and the University of Ottawa. He also held visiting appointments with George Mason University and NASA Ames Research Center. He is a member of the Editorial Board of *IEEE Expert*. His current research interests include applications of machine learning, constructive induction, inductive logic programming, and text understanding. His current address is Department of Computer Science, University of Ottawa, Ottawa, Ontario K1N 6N5 Canada.

Douglas L. Medin is Professor of Psychology at Northwestern University. He received his Ph.D. from the University of South Dakota (1968). He has held positions at Rockefeller University, the University of Illinois at Champaign-Urbana, and the University of Michigan. He has had a long standing interest in learning in general and concept formation in particular. He is currently editor of the journal *Cognitive Psychology* and the Psychology of Learning and Motivation series. His current address is Psychology Department, Northwestern University, Evanston, IL 60208.

Ryszard S. Michalski is chaired Professor of Computer Science and Systems Engineering and Director of the Center for Artificial Intelligence at George Mason University. He studied at Cracow and Warsaw Polytechnical Universities, received his M.S. degree from St. Petersburg Polytechnical University, and his Ph.D. degree from the University of Silesia. Prior to immigrating to the U.S. in 1970, he was a research scientist at the Polish Academy of Sciences in Warsaw. In 1970, he joined the University of Illinois at Urbana-Champaign, where he became Professor of Computer Science and Medical Information Science and Director of the Artificial Intelligence Laboratory. In 1988, he moved to George Mason University, where he established the Center for Artificial Intelligence. Dr. Michalski is a co-founder of the field of machine learning and is widely known for his contributions to the field. He originated and co-originated several research directions, including the logic-based approach to inductive learning, conceptual clustering, constructive induction, variable-precision logic (with Patrick Winston), and the computational theory of human plausible reasoning (with Alan Collins). With his collaborators, he developed the first agricultural expert system, which learned its decision rules from examples. Dr. Michalski is a co-founder of the *Journal of Machine Learning* and co-organizer of the initial conferences and workshops on machine learning. He authored or co-authored over 250 technical papers and edited or co-edited several books, including *Machine Learning: An Artificial Intelligence Approach* Vol. 1, 2, 3. His current research interests include multistrategy learning, constructive induction, knowledge discovery in databases, knowledge acquisition for expert systems, and human plausible reasoning. His current address is Center for Artificial Intelligence, George Mason University, 4400 University Drive, Fairfax, VA 22030.

Raymond J. Mooney is Assistant Professor in the Department of Computer Sciences at the University of Texas at Austin. He received his B.S. in Computer Engineering (1983) and his M.S. (1985) and Ph.D. (1988) in Computer Science, all from the University of Illinois at Urbana-Champaign. He was co-chair with Bruce Porter of the Seventh International Machine Learning Conference. His research interests include theory refinement, abductive reasoning, the comparing and combining of symbolic and connectionist learning, and natural language acquisition. His current address is Department of Computer Sciences, University of Texas, Austin, TX, 78712.

Katharina J. Morik is Professor in the Computer Science Department at the University of Dortmund. She studied linguistics and computer science at the University of Hamburg and worked on natural language processing and user modeling within the well-known HAM-ANS project. She became the internal leader of the first German research project for machine learning and knowledge acquisition at the Technical University Berlin. She organized an international workshop on knowledge representation and organization for machine learning as well as the fourth European Working Session on Learning. Together with Yves Kodratoff, she organized the First European Summer School of Machine Learning. From Berlin, she moved to the German National Research Center for Computer Science (GMD), where she and her group developed the system MOBAL as a contribution to the European project "Machine Learning Toolbox." Being still affiliated at the GMD, she became full professor at the University of Dortmund. Her current research is focused on logic-based learning; comparisons of human and machine learning; knowledge representation; and the integration of learning techniques into existing systems, such as term-subsumption systems, robot systems, and database systems. Her current address is University of Dortmund, Computer Science Department LS8, P.O. Box 500 500, 4600 Dortmund 50, Germany.

Dirk Ourston is Research Scientist in the British Petroleum Research Laboratory in Warrensville, Ohio. He received a B.S. in Physics in 1964 from California State University at Los Angeles, an M.S. in Engineering in 1968 from the University of California at Los Angeles, and a Ph.D. in Computer Science in 1991 from the University of Texas at Austin. Prior to returning to school to complete the Ph.D., Dr. Ourston spent several years in the aerospace industry, where he was responsible for a variety of software development applications. His research interests include theory refinement, applications of hybrid learning techniques, and the development of multipurpose learning architectures. His current address is BP America, Warrensville Research and Environmental Science Center, 4440 Warrensville Center Road, Cleveland, OH, 44128-2837.

Peter W. Pachowicz is Assistant Professor of Systems Engineering at George Mason University. He received an M.S. in computer and electrical engineering and a Ph.D. in computer science and engineering from the University of Mining and Metallurgy (Crakow, Poland) in 1981 and 1984. He was a faculty member at the Institute of Control Engineering at that university. In 1986, he received the Alexander von Humboldt Research Award to study self-adaptation capabilities of robot vision systems. From 1986 to 1988, he was a visiting assistant professor at the Cognition Systems Group in the Computer Science Department at the University of

Hamburg, Germany. He moved to the U.S. in 1988 and joined George Mason University. His research interests include intelligent autonomous systems, computer vision, evolving self-adaptive systems, applications of machine learning, and engineering-oriented machine learning (noise-tolerant and performance-oriented learning, model and system evolution). A significant part of his research efforts concerns the integration of high-level symbolic learning with computer vision. He was a co-organizer of the first NSF/DARPA Workshop on Machine Learning and Vision in 1992. His current address is Center for Artificial Intelligence, Department of Computer Science, George Mason University, 4400 University Drive, Fairfax, VA 22030.

Michael Pazzani is Associate Professor of Computer Science at the University of California at Irvine. His research has focused on acquiring efficient diagnostic heuristics through failure-driven, explanation-based learning and on integrating empirical and explanation-based learning methods. He is the author of OCCAM, a system that uses empirical methods to acquire the background knowledge needed for explanation-based learning. He received B.S. and M.S. degrees in computer science from the University of Connecticut. In 1988, he received a Ph.D. degree in computer science from the University of California, Los Angeles. Prior to joining the faculty at the University of California, Irvine, Dr. Pazzani was a member of the technical staff at the Aerospace Corporation and a group leader at the Mitre Corporation. His current address is Department of Information and Computer Science, University of California, Irvine, CA 92717.

Boris Plante is an AI programmer and a Physics teacher. He received his B.S. in Physics from Université Laval, a B.S. in Computer Science from Université du Québec à Hull, and an M.S. in Computer Science from the University of Ottawa. His current interests include applications of machine learning in database management, deductive learning methods, and multimedia teaching software. His current address is CSA Recherche Ltée, 801 Chemin St. Louis, Bureau 240, Québec G1S 1C1 Canada.

Luc De Raedt is Senior Research Assistant at the Belgian National Fund for Scientific Research. He received his Ph.D. in Computer Science in 1991 on a thesis entitled "Interactive Concept-Learning" from the Katholieke Universiteit Leuven. Since 1986, he has worked in Leuven; in the summer of 1988, he visited Yves Kodratoff's group (University of Paris-South) and, in the summer of 1989, Katharina Morik's group (German National Research Center for Computer Science). His main research interests are in inductive logic programming, applications of induction to theory revision and databases, and inductive learning within autonomous agents. His current address is KULeuven, Department of Computer Science, Celestijnenlaan 200A, B-3001 Heverlee, Belgium.

Ashwin Ram is Assistant Professor in the College of Computing at the Georgia Institute of Technology and Adjunct Professor in the School of Psychology. He received his B.Tech. in Electrical Engineering from the Indian Institute of Technology, New Delhi, in 1982 and his M.S. in Computer Science from the University of Illinois at Urbana-Champaign in 1984. He received his Ph.D. degree from Yale University for his dissertation entitled "Question-Driven Understanding: An Integrated Theory of Story Understanding, Memory and Learning" in 1989. His research interests lie in the areas of machine learning, natural language understanding, explanation and abduction, and cognitive science, and he has published several articles in these areas. He is on the editorial board of *Applied Intelligence and the Journal of the Learning Sciences* and on the technical program committees of major conferences in Artificial Intelligence and Cognitive Science. He is a member of the American Association for Artificial Intelligence and the Cognitive Science Society. His current address is College of Computing, Georgia Institute of Technology, Atlanta, GA 30332–0280.

Yoram Reich is senior lecturer at the Department of Solid Mechanics, Materials, and Structures, Faculty of Engineering at Tel Aviv University. He received his B.S. and M.S. degrees in mechanical engineering from Tel Aviv University, Israel, in 1980 and 1984, respectively, and his Ph.D. degree in civil engineering from Carnegie Mellon University in 1991. Dr. Reich practiced engineering design for more than seven years in the audio, structures, and ship industries. His current research includes the use of artificial intelligence and, specifically, machine learning techniques for supporting engineering design, philosophy of design, and methodology of design research. Dr. Reich has authored more than 30 research papers on these subjects. He is also a member of the editorial board of the *International Journal for Artificial Intelligence in Engineering*. His current address is Department of Solid Mechanics, Materials, and Structures, Faculty of Engineering, Tel Aviv University, Tel Aviv 69978, Israel; and his e-mail address is yorma@edrc.cmu.edu.

Lorenza Saitta is Professor of Computer Science at the University of Torino. Her research activity started in Decision Theoretic and Syntactic Pattern Recognition, mostly applied to Speech Recognition. Then, she shifted to Knowledge-Based Systems and Evidence Combination problems and, finally, to Machine Learning, which currently constitutes her main interest. In particular, she is involved in using Causal Reasoning and Abstraction mechanisms in automated knowledge acquisition. A related interest is in the cognitive aspects of learning. Her current address is Dipartimento di Informatica, Università di Torino, Corso Svizzera 185, 10149, Torino, Italy.

Jakub Segen is a member of Technical Staff in the Machine Perception Research Department at AT&T Bell Laboratories. He received an M.S. degree in electrical engineering from Technical University of Wroclaw in 1971, studied at Courant

Institute, and received a Ph.D. in electrical and bioengineering from Carnegie Mellon University in 1980. He has conducted research in machine learning, computer vision, pattern recognition, robotics, signal analysis, and image compression. His recent research interest involves trainable human-computer interfaces based on computer vision. His current address is AT&T Bell Laboratories, Rm. 4E-632, Holmdel, NJ 07733–3030.

Jude Shavlik is Assistant Professor in Computer Sciences at the University of Wisconsin—Madison. He received B.S. degrees in electrical engineering and in biology from the Massachusetts Institute of Technology in 1979. In 1980, he received an M.S. in biophysics from Yale University. After working for the Mitre Corporation for several years, he received his Ph.D. in Computer Science from the University of Illinois at Champaign-Urbana in 1988 and has been at Wisconsin since then. His Ph.D. research was in the area of explanation-based learning (under the direction of Gerald DeJong). His current research interests include integrating symbolic and connectionist approaches to AI, using inductive learning to refine existing domain-specific knowledge, and applying machine learning to problems in the Human Genome Project. His current address is Computer Sciences Department, University of Wisconsin, 1210 W. Dayton Street, Madison, WI 53706.

Gheorghe Tecuci is Associate Professor of Computer Science and a member of the Center for Artificial Intelligence at George Mason University. He received the M.S. degree in computer science from the Polytechnic Institute of Bucharest in 1979, graduating first among all the computer science students at the Polytechnic Universities of Romania. He received two Ph.D. degrees in computer science, one from the University of Paris South and the other from the Polytechnic Institute of Bucharest, in 1988. Since 1979, he has been with the Research Institute for Informatics in Bucharest as researcher and project leader. During the summers of 1986–1990, he worked at the Paris-South University on a joint research program on multistrategy learning sponsored by the Romanian Academy and the French National Research Center. In Spring 1990, he was a visiting scientist in the Center for Artificial Intelligence at George Mason University, and in Fall 1990, he joined the faculty of the Computer Science Department. In 1993, Dr. Tecuci was elected Member of the Romanian Academy. Dr. Tecuci has published over 60 scientific papers in the fields of machine learning, artificial intelligence, advanced robotics, graph theory, and compilers. His current research focuses on multistrategy learning, knowledge acquisition, and expert systems with learning capabilities. His current address is Center for Artificial Intelligence, Department of Computer Science, George Mason University, 4400 University Drive, Fairfax, VA 22030.

Geoffrey Towell is Research Scientist at Siemens Corporate Research. He received a B.A. in economics from Hamilton College in 1983 and put that knowledge to use as an economist with the Federal Reserve Bank of New York. In 1986, Geoff entered the graduate program in Computer Sciences at the University of Wisconsin—Madison, receiving a Ph.D. in 1991. His previous research has focused upon the integration of symbolic and subsymbolic learning methods, with a particular focus on the use of existing symbolic knowledge to enhance subsymbolic learning. In addition to a continuing interest in the integration of subsymbolic and symbolic learning, he is involved in the development of models of learning in elementary school children. His current address is Siemens Corporate Research, 755 College Road East, Princeton, NJ 08540.

Haleh Vafaie is a doctoral candidate in the Information Technology and Engineering Program and Research Assistant in the Center for Artificial Intelligence at George Mason University. She received her B.S. (in 1984) and M.S. (in 1986), both in Electrical Engineering, from Carleton University, Ottawa, Canada. Her interests include machine learning and computer vision. Her dissertation explores methods for applying genetic algorithms to the problem of model reduction and constructive induction. Her current address is Center for Artificial Intelligence, Department of Computer Science, George Mason University, 4400 University Drive, Fairfax, VA 22030.

Manuela M. Veloso is Assistant Professor in the School of Computer Science at Carnegie Mellon University. She received her B.S. in Electrical Engineering and her M.S. in Electrical and Computer Engineering from Instituto Superior Tecnico, Technical University of Lisbon, Portugal, in 1980 and 1984, respectively. She received a second M.S. in Computer Science from Boston University in 1986 and her Ph.D. degree in Computer Science from Carnegie Mellon University in 1992. Her research interests include machine learning, analogical reasoning, planning, and the scaling up of artificial intelligence algorithms and systems. Dr. Veloso is a member of AAAI, ACM, and Sigma Xi. Her current address is School of Computer Science, Carnegie Mellon University, Pittsburgh, PA 15213.

Bradley L. Whitehall is Research Scientist in the Artificial Intelligence Group at United Technologies Research Center. He received a B.S. in Computer Science and Mathematics from Northern Illinois University in 1983 and his M.S. and Ph.D. in Computer Science from the University of Illinois in 1987 and 1990, respectively. His interests include machine learning, the application of machine learning to engineering problems, and the use of artificial intelligence to improve design processes. His current address is United Technologies Research Center, East Hartford, CT 06108.

Gerhard Widmer is Lecturer in Artificial Intelligence at the University of Vienna and Research Scientist at the Austrian Research Institute for Artificial Intelligence. He received M.S. degrees in Computer Science from the Technical University of Vienna (1984) and the University of Madison, Wisconsin (1986), where he spent two years as a Fulbright stipendiary. In his dissertation, for which he received his

Doctorate from the Technical University of Vienna in 1989, he developed a model of integrated deductive-inductive learning. His current research interests include learning from qualitative models, learning models from data, and the role of abstraction in learning. Dr. Widmer is also actively involved in research on Artificial Intelligence models of musical phenomena. His current address is Department of Medical Cybernetics and Artificial Intelligence, University of Vienna, Freyung 6/2, A-1010 Vienna, Austria.

Edward Wisniewski is Assistant Professor of Psychology at Northwestern University. He received his M.S. in Computer Science and Ph.D. in Cognitive Science from Brown University (1989). Prior to joining the faculty at Northwestern, he held a postdoctoral position at the University of Michigan. His current research focuses on models of human learning and conceptual combination. His address is Psychology Department, Northwestern University, Evanston, IL 60208.

Janusz Wnek is a National Science Foundation postdoctoral Research Associate in experimental science at the Center for Artificial Intelligence at George Mason University. He received his M.S. in Computer Science in 1983 from Jagiellonian University, Cracow, Poland, and his Ph.D. in information technology in 1993 from George Mason University. His interests include machine learning, integrated learning paradigms, and application of machine learning to engineering and economic problems. His current address is Center for Artificial Intelligence, Department of Computer Science, George Mason University, 4400 University Drive, Fairfax, VA 22030.

Jianping Zhang is Assistant Professor of Computer Science at Utah State University. He received his B.S. in Computer Science from Wuhan University, China, in 1982 and his Ph.D. in Computer Science from the University of Illinois at Urbana-Champaign in 1990. His research concerns Machine Learning, with a focus on learning flexible concepts. His current address is Department of Computer Science, Utah State University, Logan, UT 84322–4205.

AUTHOR INDEX

SUBJECT INDEX